DYNAMICS OF GLOBALIZATION: LOCATION-SPECIFIC ADVANTAGES OR LIABILITIES OF FOREIGNNESS?

ADVANCES IN INTERNATIONAL MANAGEMENT

Series Editors: (Volume 23) Timothy M. Devinney,
Torben Pedersen and Laszlo Tihanyi

Recent Volumes:

ADVANCES IN INTERNATIONAL MANAGEMENT
VOLUME 24

DYNAMICS OF GLOBALIZATION: LOCATION-SPECIFIC ADVANTAGES OR LIABILITIES OF FOREIGNNESS?

EDITED BY

CHRISTIAN GEISLER ASMUSSEN
Copenhagen Business School, Denmark

TORBEN PEDERSEN
Copenhagen Business School, Denmark

TIMOTHY M. DEVINNEY
University of Technology, Sydney, Australia

LASZLO TIHANYI
Texas A&M University, USA

United Kingdom – North America – Japan
India – Malaysia – China

Emerald Group Publishing Limited
Howard House, Wagon Lane, Bingley BD16 1WA, UK

First edition 2011

British Library Cataloguing in Publication Data
A catalogue record for this book is available from the British Library

ISBN: 978-0-85724-991-3
ISSN: 1571-5027 (Series)

Emerald Group Publishing
Limited, Howard House,
Environmental Management
System has been certified by
ISOQAR to ISO 14001:2004
standards

Awarded in recognition of
Emerald's production
department's adherence to
quality systems and processes
when preparing scholarly
journals for print

INVESTOR IN PEOPLE

We have dedicated this volume to the memory of Lacri Nacu who passed away at too young an age

CONTENTS

PART II

LIST OF CONTRIBUTORS

Ruth V. Aguilera	University of Illinois, Urbana-Champaign, IL, USA
Björn Ambos	WU Vienna, Institute for International Business, Vienna, Austria
Christian G. Asmussen	Department of Strategic Management and Globalization, Copenhagen Business School, Denmark
Fiorenza Belussi	Department of Economics and Management, University of Padova, Italy
Gabriel R. G. Benito	Department of Strategy and Logistics, BI Norwegian Business School, Oslo, Norway
Sjoerd Beugelsdijk	Faculty of Economics and Business Administration, University of Groningen, The Netherlands
Weifeng Chen	Brunel University Business School, Middlesex, UK
John Child	University of Birmingham, The Business School, Birmingham, UK
Kim Clark	The University of Texas – San Antonio, San Antonio, TX, USA
Timothy M. Devinney	University of Technology, Sydney, NSW, Australia
Kirandeep Dhillon	Brunel University Business School, Middlesex, UK

Jonathan P. Doh	Villanova School of Business, PA, USA
Gianluca Fiscato	Department of Economics, Business and Statistics, University of Milan, Italy
Nicolai J. Foss	Department of Strategic Management and Globalization, Copenhagen Business School, Denmark and Department of Strategy and Management, Norwegian School of Economics and Business Administration, Bergen, Norway
Jörg Freiling	University of Bremen, Faculty Business Studies & Economics, LEMEX – Chair of Small Business & Entrepreneurship, Germany
Ajai S. Gaur	Rutgers Business School, Newark, NJ, USA
Florian Kaulich	University of Vienna, Austria
Stephen J. Kobrin	The Wharton School, University of Pennsylvania, PA, USA
Vikas Kumar	Discipline of International Business, University of Sydney, Sydney, NSW, Australia
Sven M. Laudien	University of Bremen, Faculty Business Studies & Economics, LEMEX – Chair of Small Business & Entrepreneurship, Germany
Randi Lunnan	Department of Strategy and Logistics, BI Norwegian Business School, Oslo, Norway
Marin Marinov	University of Gloucestershire, The Business School, Cheltenham, UK

Svetla Marinova	Department of Business and Management, University of Aalborg, Denmark
Derrick McIver	The University of Texas – San Antonio, San Antonio, TX, USA
Sara Melén	Department of Marketing and Strategy, Stockholm School of Economics, Sweden
Stewart R. Miller	The University of Texas – San Antonio, San Antonio, TX, USA
Lilach Nachum	Baruch College, City University New York, NY, USA
Phillip C. Nell	Department of Strategic Management and Globalization, Copenhagen Business School, Denmark
Torben Pedersen	Department of Strategic Management and Globalization, Copenhagen Business School, Denmark
Indu Ramachandran	The University of Texas – San Antonio, San Antonio, TX, USA
Tom Ridgman	Institute for Manufacturing, University of Cambridge, UK
Emilia Rovira Nordman	Department of Marketing and Strategy, Stockholm School of Economics, Sweden
José F.P. dos (Joe) Santos	INSEAD, Fontainebleau, France and MIT Sloan School of Management, Cambridge, MA, USA
Ravi Sarathy	Northeastern University, Boston, MA, USA
Bodo B. Schlegelmilch	WU Vienna University of Economics and Business, Vienna, Austria

Silvia R. Sedita	Department of Economics and Management, Padua University, Italy
D. Deo Sharma	Department of Marketing and Strategy, Stockholm School of Economics, Sweden
Yongjiang S. Shi	Institute for Manufacturing, University of Cambridge, UK
Satwinder Singh	Brunel University Business School, Middlesex, UK
Christine Soo	UWA Business School, University of Western Australia, Nedlands, Australia
Laszlo Tihanyi	Mays Business School, Texas A&M University, College Station, TX, USA
Daniel Tolstoy	Department of Marketing and Strategy, Stockholm School of Economics, Sweden
Sverre Tomassen	Department of Strategy and Logistics, BI Norwegian Business School, Oslo, Norway
Nigel L. Williams	Business Systems Department, The Business School, University of Bedfordshire, UK

EDITORS' BIOGRAPHY

Christian Geisler Asmussen is an assistant professor of strategic management and international business at the Department of Strategic Management and Globalization, Copenhagen Business School. His research revolves around globalization and the international expansion trajectories of multinational corporations (MNCs). Drawing on a background in formal economics but applying a multi-disciplinary approach to his research, he has focused in particular on the interaction between competitive advantage and geographic scope. His work has appeared in the *Journal of International Business Studies, Management International Review* and *International Business Review*. He also serves as an ad-hoc reviewer on numerous international journals including the *Strategic Management Journal, Strategic Entrepreneurship Journal* and *Journal of Management Studies*, and on the editorial review boards of *Management International Review* and *Multinational Business Review*. Christian received his PhD from Copenhagen Business School in 2007. In relation to his dissertation, he has been awarded the Barry M. Richman best dissertation award from the Academy of Management, the Haynes Prize for most promising scholar from the Academy of International Business, as well as several prestigious prizes from the Danish research community. He has been a visiting scholar at Indiana University, University of Victoria, Duke University and Temple University.

Torben Pedersen is a professor of international business at the Copenhagen Business School's Department of Strategic Management and Globalization. He has published over 100 articles and books concerning the managerial and strategic aspects of globalization. His research has appeared in prominent journals such as *Academy of Management Journal, Strategic Management Journal, Organization Science, Journal of International Business Studies, Journal of Management Studies* and *Journal of Corporate Finance*. His research interests are located at the interface between strategy, institutional economics and international business and with a strong interest in areas like knowledge management, offshoring/outsourcing and reconfiguration of the value chain, subsidiary entrepreneurship and management of the differentiated MNC. He is co-editor of *Global Strategy Journal* and serves on numerous editorial boards.

Timothy M. Devinney is a professor of strategy at the University of Technology, Sydney. He has published seven books and more than 80 articles in leading journals. In 2008, he was the first recipient in management of an Alexander von Humboldt Research Award and was Rockefeller Foundation Bellagio Fellow. He is a fellow of the Academy of International Business, an International Fellow under the auspices of the AIM Initiative in the UK and a fellow of ANZAM (Australia New Zealand Academy of Management). He served as chair of the International Management Division of the Academy of Management. He is associate editor and incoming co-editor of *Academy of Management Perspectives* and the head of the International Business & Management Network of SSRN. He is on the editorial board of more than 10 of the leading international journals.

Laszlo Tihanyi is the B. Marie Oth associate professor in business administration in the Mays Business School at Texas A&M University, USA. He received a PhD in strategic management from Indiana University and a doctorate in business economics from Corvinus University of Budapest in his native Hungary. He is also a honorary professor at Corvinus University. His main research areas are internationalization, corporate governance in multinational firms and organizational adaptation in emerging economies. His current research interests include the involvement of board of directors in foreign direct investment, the institutional environment of internationalization decisions and the effects of social movements on multinational firms. His papers have been published or are in press in the *Academy of Management Journal, Academy of Management Review, Strategic Management Journal, Organization Science, Journal of International Business Studies* and others.

EDITORS' INTRODUCTION

This is the second volume of *Advances in International Management* under the new editorial team plus Christian Geisler Asmussen (Copenhagen Business School) who has been added as a special co-editor on this particular volume. When the new team took over in 2009, we believed that it was important that our first volume (Volume 23) be 'exploratory' – covering a broad swathe of International Management (IM) research. Beginning with this volume, our intent is to move onto specific areas of research that the first volume's output indicated were particularly salient to our discipline. As always, our intention is not to just have a collection of papers as normally seen in a journal but a cohesive set of papers that not only informs a debate but also provides scholars with a forum within which to push the envelope.

The main body of this volume focuses on the role of 'location' in IM and scrutinizes the paradoxical effect of both Location-Specific Advantages and Liability of Foreignness. The criticality and salience of this issue was revealed to us by the fact that 5 of 21 chapters in Volume 23 (Smith, 2010; Ramachandran & Pant, 2010; Mezias & Mezias, 2010; Bell, Filatotchev, & Rasheed, 2010; Bae & Salomon, 2010)[1] spoke on this issue. In the chapters here, we see a wide spectrum of informed opinion ranging from the 'flat earthers' – those arguing that the 'world is becoming flat' or flatter – to the 'mountaineers' – those claiming that the 'world is becoming more spiky'.

OVERVIEW OF VOLUME 24

The first part of Volume 24 contains our annual feature from a leading scholar. Professor Stephen Kobrin was the recipient of the 2010 Booz & Co./strategy + business Eminent Scholar in International Management Award, given by the International Management Division of the Academy of Management, and in his acceptance speech gives us his view on the evolution of the nation state and global governance. This is a particularly salient introduction to this volume as Professor Kobrin's work very neatly addresses the question of what is the role of location when political power is now spanning traditional locational boundaries. Jonathan Doh and Ruth

Aguilera provide commentaries that integrate Kobrin's work with that of stakeholder theory and transnational governance.

The second part of Volume 24 focuses on the theme of the volume – *Dynamics of Globalization: Location-Specific Advantages or Liabilities of Foreignness?* The process at arriving to this final volume of *Advances in International Management* has been long and bumpy with two to three rounds of reviewing and revision of each chapter. The process has also included a workshop for all authors involved in this volume that was held in Copenhagen, 17–18 January 2011. As illustrated in all the chapters presented here research on the location factor is very vibrant, fuelled by the many changes taking place globally that have, most particularly, added emerging markets into location decisions. New developments have raised many new questions; for example, on the interaction between the location and the multinational firm, and how location-specific factors and liabilities of foreignness can be endogenized in our models. In this volume, we have created a platform for ongoing discussion of these issues.

In closing, we would like to thank Hedorfs fond for their support of the workshop in Copenhagen as well as Mary Miskin and all the Emerald editorial team for their patience and support. In addition, Lacri Nacu provided critical editorial and administrative assistance in completing the volume on time. Without this support the volume would still be in process!

NOTE

1. All these five chapters are featured in *Advances in International Management*, Vol. 23: The Past, Present & Future of International Business & Management. Emerald, 2010.

Timothy M. Devinney, Sydney
Torben Pedersen, Copenhagen
Laszlo Tihanyi, College Station
Series Editors

PART I

INTRODUCTION TO PART I: BOOZ & CO./STRATEGY + BUSINESS EMINENT SCHOLAR IN INTERNATIONAL MANAGEMENT 2010

Timothy M. Devinney

The Booz & Co./strategy + business Eminent Scholar in International Management is an annual award given by the International Management Division of the Academy of Management and sponsored by Booz & Co./ strategy + business.

The 2010 awardee was Professor Stephen Kobrin, the William H. Wurster Professor of Multinational Management at the Wharton School at the University of Pennsylvania. Professor Kobrin was recognized for his contribution to the field of international business and management based upon his long-standing and well-respected work addressing the roll of politics and policy in international business and the influence of business and technology of politics and policy.

Professor Kobrin received his PhD from the University of Michigan in 1975 after a six-year post-MBA stint at Procter & Gamble. While spending the dominant proportion of his career at the Wharton he has also been on the faculties of New York University and Massachusetts Institute of Technology. Since that time he has authored dozens of books and hundreds of

Dynamics of Globalization: Location-Specific Advantages or Liabilities of Foreignness?
Advances in International Management, Volume 24, 3–4
Copyright © 2011 by Emerald Group Publishing Limited
All rights of reproduction in any form reserved
ISSN: 1571-5027/doi:10.1108/S1571-5027(2011)0000024005

articles and stands as one of the most cited scholars in the field of cross-cultural psychology. His work stands at the base of much of the work linking political science and international management, particularly that examining governance and political risk.

He is a fellow of the Academy of International Business and the World Economic Forum. He has also served as both a vice-president and president of the Academy of International Business. He has published more than 100 scholarly articles and is perhaps best known for his work on political risk, including the classic work, *Managing Political Risk Assessment*. Long before it was popular to do so, he was discussing the role of globalization and social change as evidenced by his 1977 book, *Foreign Direct Investment, Industrialization, and Social Change*. In the chapter that follows Professor Kobrin outlines his thinking on the evolution of the economic and political nexus. It is a powerful logic that not only helps us understand the role that technology plays in economics and politics but also how these three forces interact.

Two commentaries follow Professor Kobrin's chapter. Jonathan Doh provides an overview of Professor Kobrin's work from his early days to the present and also gives us a personal glimpse of the man and how he has served as a mentor. Ruth Aguilera focuses more tightly on the chapter in this volume and shows how Professor Kobrin's thinking serves as a nexus where thinking in international business, law and political science meets. The breadth of both these commentaries highlights the importance not only of Professor Kobrin's discussion in the chapter but also on his large volume of work going back three decades.

THE TRANSNATIONAL
TRANSITION AND THE
MULTINATIONAL FIRM

Stephen J. Kobrin[1]

ABSTRACT

Virtually all of the literature of the MNC assumes that the modern or Westphalian international order of geographically defined sovereign states is the context in which international business takes place. I argue that we are in the midst of a deep-seated systemic transformation to a transnational or post-Westphalian world order characterized by a redefinition of space and geography, the fragmentation of political authority and a more diffuse distinction between public and private spheres. The emergence of a transnational order will have significant implications for the multinational firm in terms of the depth of its involvement in politics and how it formulates strategy. MNCs will both be subject to and a participant in governance, the latter in terms of hybrid public–private regimes. Strategy will have to be reformulated to incorporate a non-territorial context where firms function as actors in the international political process.

Dynamics of Globalization: Location-Specific Advantages or Liabilities of Foreignness?
Advances in International Management, Volume 24, 5–23
ISSN: 1571-5027/doi:10.1108/S1571-5027(2011)0000024006

INTRODUCTION

The modern international order is organized through the division of the earth's surface into mutually exclusive territorial jurisdictions enclosed by discrete and meaningful borders. That implies a spatial symmetry among politics, economics and social relations: that the geographic territory contained within a state's borders has meaning as a political-economic construct (Held, 2006). The system is state centric in that states are the only actors in international politics and the only subjects of international law. An international economy is thus an aggregation of territorially defined and delineated national markets where international transactions take the form of discrete cross-border flows: it is a 'space of places' (Castells, 1996).

The multinational firm inhabits, and is defined by, this world of spaces and places, comprised of mutually exclusive territoriality and significant and meaningful borders. Legally, and to some extent politically, the multinational corporation (MNC) exists only as an ' apparition', it is comprised of a collection of national firms each subject to the laws of the state in which it was incorporated (Johns, 1994; Vagts, 1970).

Virtually all of the extensive literature of the MNC assumes that the modern or Westphalian international order of geographically defined sovereign states is the context in which international business takes place. In what may be the earliest use of the term, Lilienthal (1960) defined MNCs as firms based in one country which operate under the laws of multiple countries. In a widely cited article, Perlmutter (1969) explained the evolution of the MNC in terms of attitudes towards home and host countries arguing that the 'ultimate goal of geocentrism' involves a 'collaborative effort between subsidiaries and headquarters to establish universal standards and permissible local variations' (1969, p. 13). The title of Vernon's seminal book on the MNC is *Sovereignty at Bay* (Vernon, 1971).

It follows that most analyses of the strategic and organizational problems of the MNC assume that international business takes place within this geographically defined international world order. Thus, Fayerweather (1982) formulated the fundamental strategic problem of the multinational firm as a trade-off between exploiting the advantages of global integration on the one hand and the need to respond to political, social and cultural differences among national markets on the other: a tension between pressures for unification and fragmentation of strategy. Bartlett and Ghoshal (1989) further developed and expanded the concept, categorizing MNCs as nationally responsive, globally integrated or transnational, the last facing pressures to respond simultaneously to the need for local adaptation through national responsiveness and efficiency through global integration.

Conceptualizing the MNC's strategic problem in terms of integration and fragmentation reflects a world where politics, economics and society are organized in terms of national borders and mutually exclusive territoriality. It forces managers to think about the relative importance of economic, social, political, legal and regulatory differences among territorially defined states versus the benefits of *cross-border* integration. It assumes that geography is the fundamental principle underlying the organization of politics and economics and that the world economy is comprised of territorially defined national markets.

Much of my work over the last decade and a half[2] has argued that we are in the midst of a deep-seated systemic transformation in the organization of international economics and politics: a transition to a transnational or post-Westphalian world order that may be analogous in scope and impact to that from the medieval to the modern mode of organization in the 16th and 17th centuries. I have argued that the state-centric and geographically rooted Westphalian order is but one possible mode of organization of politics (and economics) and that it may reflect conditions specific to a given historical era. The transnational transformation would entail significant changes in the meaning and import of space and geography, the rise of multiple actors with significant authority in international politics and a blurring of the liberal distinction between the public and private spheres, between the state and the market.

THE TRANSNATIONAL TRANSFORMATION

A transition to a transnational order will have significant implications for multinational firms: in fact the term itself may become anachronistic as territoriality and borders become compromised as a basis for economic organization. Indeed, Perlmutter (1969) (perhaps presciently) defined the multinational firm as 'a new type of industrial social architecture particularly suitable for the last third of the twentieth century' (p. 10). As borders become less meaningful and space relational rather than geographic, network forms of organization will take on increased importance. The MNC's external environment will become more complex as it is forced to deal with multiple actors such as NGOs and international organizations in addition to states, and participate in hybrid public–private partnerships. As the line between the public and private spheres blurs, some MNCs will find that the assumption of private political authority entails reciprocal obligations and duties that extend well beyond that traditionally expected of a 'private' profit-focused firm. All of these changes, and others to be discussed, will dramatically complicate the strategic problem facing the MNC.

The Neo-Medieval Analogy

In 'Back to the Future: Neomedievalsim and the Postmodern Digital Economy' (Kobrin, 1998), I argued that the geographic structure of the modern international system may be an historical anomaly, that mutually exclusive territoriality may not be a privileged transhistorical principle of political organization. There have been other modes of non-geographic organization in the past and there may well be in the future. The medieval to modern transition, which is marked conventionally by the Peace of Westphalia in 1648, entailed the territorialization of politics (Anderson, 1986): the replacement of interlaced and overlapping systems of authority with states whose sovereignty is defined in terms of borders and geography.

As noted above, the transnational transformation may well mark a transition comparable to that which took place as the modern world order replaced the medieval mode of organization in Europe. If we are again at a point of transition, and particularly if the modern era is an anomaly, looking back to medieval Europe may help us understand possibilities for the emerging post-modern future. Three aspects of political organization discussed in 'Back to the future ... ' are relevant here: the conceptualization of space, geography and borders; political authority and loyalty; and the separation of the public and private spheres.

Medieval borders were diffuse, shifting and permeable; the idea of discrete borders and mutually exclusive territoriality was not even conceptually possible before the revival of Ptolemaic geography and the development of modern maps. Given the complex, overlapping systems of authority and the absence of fixed boundaries, the distinction between domestic and foreign affairs – and the idea of independence – had little meaning.

In the 21st century, both discrete borders and mutually exclusive territoriality may become once again problematic. The construction of markets as electronic networks renders space as symbolic and distance as relational rather than geographic: in Castells' (1996) words, the digital revolution has replaced a 'space of places' with a 'space of flows'. Economic globalization, complex interdependence (Keohane & Nye, 1977), and particularly the deep integration associated with foreign direct investment, make the once clear distinction between domestic and international affairs or transactions questionable. The complex – and largely unanticipated – international impact of the Sarbanes–Oxley legislation in the United States provides an excellent example. The legislation, which was intended to protect American investors, affected all firms – regardless of nationality – listed on U.S. exchanges, particularly German firms as it directly contradicted some aspects of that country's law.

Medieval political organization was characterized by multiple, overlapping and often competing political authorities enveloped in a heteronomous, 'lattice-like network of authority relations' (Ruggie, 1983, p. 274). Popes and emperors as well as kings and local lords all commanded interwoven political authority. Similarly, political loyalty was ambiguous and non-territorial, with individuals enmeshed in complex networks of reciprocal relationships with conflicting duties and obligations. The state-centric system, with its unambiguous territorially defined political authority and loyalty, emerged only with the Westphalian transition to the modern international world order.

Authority is fragmenting once again with the emergence of non-territorial actors in international politics such as NGOs, international institutions and multinational firms. While states are certainly still the most powerful actors, they are no longer the sole source of political authority or the only subjects of international law. Private, that is non-state based, political authority has become a reality (Hall & Biersteker, 2002). Ruggie's (1983) characterization of medieval political organization equally describes a transnational world order as a relational, networked space of flows.

The clear distinction between the public and private spheres, of private property and the idea of collective or public ownership, arose with the modern era and the modern state (North, 1981). In medieval Europe, there were multiple rights to land rather than land ownership and any distinction between public and private interests was diffuse to say the least. Indeed, the sharp liberal distinction between the public sphere as government and the private sphere as a self-regulating market was a product of the 19th century.

The line between the public and private is once again becoming blurred with the proliferation of sovereign wealth funds and the increased importance of state-owned enterprises. The diffusion of public authority to 'private' actors and the corresponding imposition of 'public' duties on multinational firms also blur the line between the public and private spheres. MNCs are increasingly seen as providers of public goods taking on roles that were the province of the state until relatively recently.

While I would emphasize the metaphorical nature of the neo-medieval analogy, it is reasonable to think of the international to transnational transition as marking the end of an exceptional historical era: when borders, territory and Euclidian geography were singularly important as the basis of political and economic organization; when there was a clear distinction between international and foreign affairs and the international economy was comprised of discrete cross-border transactions; and when the only actors in 'international' politics and the only subjects of international law were sovereign states. The reconceptualization of space, fragmentation of political authority and the intermingling of the public and private spheres define the transnational transition. I now turn to a more extended discussion of each of them.

SPACE AND GEOGRAPHY

Modern communications and the digital revolution have undermined the Westphalian conception of both place and space as political-economic constructs, raising questions about the viability of borders, the meaning of location and the relevance of geographic proximity. In fact, Giddens (1990) argues that modernity has separated 'place' (the physical setting of social activity) and 'space', that social systems are disembedded or lifted out of local contexts and restructured 'across indefinite spans of time-space'. Both local and 'distanciated' relations define any give locale.

Proximity can now be defined relationally rather than geographically: for example, given the internet and digital imaging, a CAT scan or MRI taken in an emergency room can be read as quickly and as easily in Bangalore, India, as in the hospital's radiology department in Baltimore. In either case, the radiologist is 'near' the patient: it is the meaning of 'near' that has changed. While markets have typically been defined geographically, by providing simultaneity in time without regard for distance, digital communications allow the construction of markets in terms of relational networks rather than a 'string of places' (Amin, 2002).

Changes in the political-economic meaning of space and geography are a function of changes in the nature of the structure of the MNC itself, and more generally, in the structure of international production. During the last two decades, digitalization, container shipping and the combination of the increased complexity of technology with the geographic dispersion of capabilities have led to the disaggregation of the value chain into 'specialized slivers of economic activity', which has been called 'trade in tasks' (Buckley & Ghauri, 2004; Grossman & Rossi-Hansberg, 2006). In a number of industries, this has led to the disintegration of vertically integrated 'Fordist' firms and the restructuring of international production in terms of global production networks, as opposed to markets or hierarchy (Dicken, 2007; Gereffi, 2005).

As I discuss in more detail elsewhere (Kobrin, 2010), to the extent global production networks represent a change in the underlying mode of organization of international production from markets (trade) and hierarchy (MNCs) to relational networks, the Westphalian principle of mutually exclusive territoriality may be compromised. In a network space, distance and position are relational. As a result, the meaning of 'place' as a political-economic construct becomes ambiguous referring to both the physical location of any given node and its position within the network structure.

As noted above, operations of the traditional multinational firm are perfectly consistent with Westphalian organization in terms of geographic sovereignty: it requires access to territory to function. The MNC internalizes international transactions. In doing so, it mediates separate local and global geographies or scales, linking its diverse units through its hierarchical managerial structure. This separation of geographic scales is perfectly consistent with the structure of the international system in terms of mutually exclusive territorial jurisdiction and a clear demarcation between domestic and international transactions.

Hymer (1979) suggested a correspondence principle which imposes the hierarchical structure of the firm on the international economy as corporations create a world order in their own image. He envisioned a hierarchical division of labour between geographic regions corresponding to the vertical division of labour within the multinational firm: headquarters cities where wealth and resources are concentrated, regional 'sub-capitals' where lower levels of management are located; and 'branch plant' countries relegated to lower levels of activity and income.

Hymer's correspondence principle is consistent with the spatial construction of the modern international economy: local, national and global scales of production are geographically separate and distinct. Cross-border linkages among subunits of the traditional multinational firm take place through the firm's organizational structure. The distinct scales are nested in the sense that transactions move from local to national to global geographies through the mediation of the MNCs hierarchy.

It is of interest here that Hymer foresaw the possibility of the emergence of a relationally structured world economy made possible by developments in communications. 'Communications linkages could be arranged in the form of a grid in which each point was directly connected to many other points, permitting lateral as well as vertical communication. This system would be polycentric since messages from one point to another would go directly rather than through the center; each point would become a center on its own ... ' (Hymer, 1979, p. 395). In fact, as Hymer forecast, there has been a dispersal of authority within organizational structure of the MNC and the corresponding emergence of the networked view of the multinational firm (Ghoshal & Bartlett, 1990).

The digital revolution and the emergence of networks as a mode of organization of the world economy have rendered the distinction between local and global as separate geographies or scalar fields problematic. Processes and transactions no longer move through a set of nested scales from the local to the national to the international, rather entities interact directly both locally and across borders (Sassen, 2008). Local operations (or nodes of a network) become multiscalar, with each unit existing simultaneously in both the national and global geographies.

The transnational transition entails significant change in the underlying structure of the Westphalian international system in terms of mutually exclusive territoriality, geographic sovereignty and the state's borders as bounding or containing a distinct polity, economy and society. The implications that might have for the management of the multinational firm are discussed below.

THE FRAGMENTATION OF POLITICAL AUTHORITY

The transnational transition entails the fragmentation of political authority, the emergence of non-state actors with significant political power. The modern, international system is state-centric: states are, at least in theory, the only actors in international politics; the primary subjects of international law; and the only sources of international political authority. While states may still 'sit at the head of the table', we are in the midst of an evolution from a state-centric to a multi-actor system.

Private or non-governmental entities now have political authority: they can exert decision making power which is regarded as *legitimate* in a given issue area (Cutler, Haufler, & Porter, 1999). Examples are civil society organizations such as NGOs, international organizations and MNCs. These non-state actors' authority is non-territorial; in fact they are geographically multiscalar as they link organizations and individuals in multiple jurisdictions directly without the mediation of hierarchy. They are transnational actors in the most basic sense of that term (Nye & Keohane, 1971).

An example from my own work is the coalition of NGOs that forced Talisman Energy to withdraw from its successful venture in Sudan in 2003 (Kobrin, 2004). Despite explicit concerns on the part of both the Canadian and American governments regarding Talisman's investment in Sudan, neither was able to either prevent entry or force divestment. The decision to withdraw reflected an exercise of what can only be seen as power in international politics by non-governmental actors, the coalition of NGOs that brought pressure on Talisman's institutional investors.

Institutions not associated with government can become authoritative – that is being seen to exercise power legitimately – because of perceived expertise, access to resources, historical practice or an explicit or implicit grant of power by states. While business firms have always exerted influence in both national and international politics, MNCs are now 'increasingly engaged in authoritative decision making that was previously the prerogative of sovereign states' (Cutler et al., 1999). The acquisition of political authority by non-governmental actors is relatively new, a function of the more general fragmentation of authority in international politics associated with the transnational transition. The consequences of that phenomenon will be explored below.

STATES AND MARKETS

As noted above, the emergence of the modern or Westphalian international order resulted in the gradual separation of the private and public arenas. This, to a large extent, culminated in the 19th century with the emergence of the liberal ideal of the separation of the public sphere of government and politics from the private arena of economics and markets – the emergence of the idea of a self-regulating market. While there has always been considerable variation in the form of relationships between the state and the market – in the institutional framework of capitalism (Hall & Soskice, 2001) – a line of varying clarity separating the state and the market, has been characteristic of the Westphalian international system. However, both the emergence of private political authority and the rise of state-based/ authoritarian capitalism have blurred that line considerably.

Authority implies responsibilities and power duties. Thus, the MNC's cloak of private political authority may encompass reciprocal duties, which entails assuming what were heretofore seen as 'public' responsibilities for the supply of public goods. Ruggie (2004, p. 502) characterizes this as 'the apparent assumption by TNCs and global business associations of roles traditionally associated with public authorities, sometimes in conjunction with CSO [Civil Society Organizations], but more widely on their own'.

In a recent chapter dealing with multinational firms and human rights (Kobrin, 2009), I noted that MNCs have become actors with significant power and authority in the international political system: they can set standards, supply public goods and participate in negotiations. Given that power and authority implies responsibilities and duties, I argued that MNCs should be held directly liable for human rights violations. As Muchlinski (2001, p. 31) observes, the 'traditional notion that only states and sate agents can be held responsible for human rights violations is being challenged as the economic and social power of MNE's appears to rise ... '

More generally, Valente and Crane (2010, p. 53) argue that firms are now placed in 'quasi-governmental roles where major decisions about public welfare and social provision have to be made'. These activities extend beyond what is normally encompassed under the rubric of philanthropy or corporate social responsibility. They include the provision of public services such as physical infrastructure, hospitals or even government capacity building in some circumstances. This assumption of new responsibilities results from societal pressure and it may or may not contribute positively to the firm's bottom line, even in the long run.

At least one CEO agrees, promising that 'government leaders will find in business willing partners to reform health care and education ... train and enable the displaced and dispossessed, grapple with environmental problems and infectious diseases, tackle the myriad other challenges that globalization raises' (Palmisano, 2006, p. 135).

While MNEs are taking on responsibilities previously confined to the public sector, public sector entities are increasingly engaged in commercial activity. Sovereign wealth funds from countries such as Abu Dhabi, China and Kuwait have invested in private enterprises in the United States. For example, the Abu Dhabi Investment Authority invested in Citigroup and the China Investment Corporation in Morgan Stanley (both were more than welcome at the time). Are these arms of government investing for political purposes or commercial enterprises chasing potential profits? Furthermore, is the distinction still relevant? Similarly, are the Chinese national oil company's (and other state-owned enterprises) investments abroad an effort to secure natural resources as a public policy objective or attempts to find potentially profitable petroleum deposits? Again, is the question still relevant?

While one can debate the specifics in each case, I believe that one cannot do so productively if the framework for doing so is the modern or Westphalian international system. The evolution to a transnational order entails a blurring of the once clear line between politics and markets – between the public and private spheres – making unambiguous answers to these questions difficult. In summary, the transnational transition is defined by changes in the meaning of space, geography and borders; the fragmentation of political authority; and the blurring of the distinction between politics and markets. I now turn to the implications for multinational firms. Any suggestions must, perforce, be speculative.

IMPLICATIONS FOR THE FIRM

We are still in the very early stages of the transnational transition, the endpoint is not yet clear and the implications for the multinational firm are complex and uncertain. That said, I will focus on three interrelated potential impacts on the MNC: the idea of the corporation and its meaning for managers; the firm as a 'subject' rather than an 'object' – the MNC's direct involvement in international politics; and some thoughts about strategy.

While it is accepted at this point that corporations have responsibilities to stakeholders over and above those to their owners or shareholders, few authors dealing with corporate social responsibility argue that the corporation has a responsibility to undertake activities that bear no relation to profitability (Vogel, 2005). That argument assumes, however, that there is a clear distinction between the public and private spheres, and between politics and markets. As that line becomes diffuse, as MNCs assume the duties and responsibilities associated with private political authority, the basic idea of the corporation as an entirely private actor may become problematic. Put differently, the stakeholders to whom the firm is directly responsible may expand beyond that consistent with the traditional notion of a private sector firm.

The MNC may become, in some respects, a quasi-public entity whose duties are assumed rather than imposed by the state (this *assumption* of public responsibilities contrasts with the early forms of the corporation which were *chartered* by the state for public purposes). That would raise more general questions about the nature of the corporation and the responsibilities of managers which I will not explore further here.

The Firm as a Subject

Traditionally, the multinational firm – or any firm, for that matter – has been seen as an object rather than a subject of international law. Every subsidiary of an MNC is incorporated in a given national jurisdiction, and its rights as well as its duties are specified by national law. The MNC and all of its subsidiaries are *objects* of international law in that any obligations it imposes are indirect or mediated by the state.

John Ruggie's work as special representative to the Secretary General on human rights and transnational firms provides an example. His policy framework, which has been endorsed by the United Nations Human Rights Council, has three pillars: the state's duty to *protect* against human rights abuses by third parties; the firm's responsibility to *respect* human rights; and greater access by victims to effective remedy (Ruggie, 2010). States, as subjects of international law, have a duty to prevent human rights violations within their territory which occur either as a result of their own actions or those of others within their jurisdiction: they have a clear duty to prevent abuses of human rights by third parties such as business firms.

Ruggie makes the distinction between the state and the firm quite clear: the 'term "responsibility" to respect rather than "duty" is meant to indicate that respecting rights is not an obligation current international law generally imposes directly on companies … ' (Ruggie, 2010, p. 2). Although companies are asked to exercise due diligence to ensure that they respect human rights, it is the duty of the state to ensure that they do so. Thus, the MNC's obligations are indirect, mediated by states and national law. Put differently, it is currently not possible to hold MNCs responsible directly for violations of international human rights law.

This distinction between subject and object may not be consistent with the fragmentation of political authority and the emergence of significant non-state transnational actors. Rosenau (1990, pp. 249, 252) describes our current situation in terms of the coexistence of state-centric and multi-centric worlds where 'both sovereignty-bound and sovereignty-free actors have come to define themselves the subjects of world politics, while viewing the other as objects'. As the transnational system evolves, MNCs will find themselves to be both governed and governor, both objects and actors (subjects) in international politics.

As Scherer and Palazzo (2009) have observed, in a post-Westphalian order nation states and international organizations alone may not be able to regulate the global economy or provide for public goods. They suggest that a multilateral process involving governments, business firms, international organizations and civil society groups will now be necessary for governance to be effective.

As the transition from an international to a transnational system results in increased reliance on multi-actor governance processes, MNCs are increasingly likely to find themselves part of hybrid or public–private regimes which provide 'soft-law' solutions to problems by developing standards or norms, providing public goods and implementing international agreements (Benner, Reinicke, & Witte, 2004). Current examples of public–private partnerships include the Forest Stewardship Council (2009) and the natural resource industries' Voluntary Principles on Security and Human Rights (2006).

While regime theory was developed originally to explain the persistence of informal arrangements in international politics (Krasner, 1982), the concept has been extended to include 'an integrated complex of formal and informal institutions that is a source of governance for an economic area as a whole' (Cutler, 1999, p. 13). International regimes could take the form of hybrid public–private governance mechanisms involving firms, NGOs, states and, perhaps, international organizations.

These public–private partnerships constitute 'a hybrid type of governance, in which nonstate actors co-govern along with state actors for the provision of collective goods and adopt governance functions that have formerly been the sole authority of sovereign nation-states' (Schaferhoff & Kaan, 2009, p. 451). While it is difficult to specify the mechanism at this point, I have argued elsewhere (Kobrin, 2009) that a transnational equivalent of hard international law may evolve over time with multiple actors, both state and non-state, involved in both legislation and enforcement.

It is important to note that MNCs will function as both subject and object in a transnational system. They will both participate in and be subject to governance. The idea of strict territoriality was always compromised in the Westphalian system by inter-jurisdictional conflict: attempts to enforce American boycotts and sanctions in third countries and anti-trust legislation provide the best examples (Kobrin, 1989). However, extraterritoriality was limited, it was the exception rather than the rule. If a transnational world order evolves and overlapping and interwoven systems of authority become the norm, both territorial and non-territorial systems of regulation will coexist and certainly be in conflict with one another at times. MNCs will have to learn to function in a complex environment where they are both object and subject and are enmeshed in overlapping and fundamentally different systems of order.

While multinational firms have always been concerned with the policy-making process, their involvement in the past entailed attempts at influence rather than direct participation. That will change as multi-actor attempts at solutions to problems become more common and that, in turn, will directly affect the nature of the corporation, the roles of managers and what needs to be taken into account in the development and implementation of strategy.

Transnational Strategy

As noted above, Giddens (1990) makes a distinction between 'space' and 'place'. As space becomes relational and proximity a non-geographic construct, defining both politics and markets in terms of discrete borders and mutually exclusive territoriality will be increasingly problematic. That does not mean, however, that borders and territoriality have become irrelevant for the MNC. In fact, Ghemawat (2007) argues that to the contrary, we live in an age of semi-globalization that is still dominated by national cultural, administrative, geographic and economic differences.

The world in which the 21st century MNC will be enmeshed will be multidimensional and complex comprised of territorial and non-territorial realities that are interwoven and overlap. As Ruggie has noted, the non-territorial region in the world economy – the space of flows – exists along side of the national economies where economic relations are mediated by the state. In the non-territorial global economy, 'the conventional distinctions between internal and external are once again problematic ... ' (Ruggie, 1993, p. 172).

The multinational firm will have to function simultaneously in both the territorial and non-territorial regions of the world economy. Bartlett and Ghoshal's (1987) categorization of multinational firms responding primarily to local differences, global firms responding to pressures to integrate across borders and transnationals which have to deal with pressures for efficiency through global integration, local responsiveness and knowledge transfer simultaneously is still very relevant (the appropriate strategy for the MNC is seen, to a large extent, as a function of industry structure). Relevance, however, does not imply sufficiency under changed conditions.

While the idea of non-market strategies is not new (e.g. Boddewyn & Brewer, 1994), the discussion to date assumes a world of sovereign states, borders and territoriality. Non-market strategies deal with interactions with states in the context of an international system. Over a decade ago, Susan Strange (1996) argued that while the state as an institution was not about to disappear, the 'metamorphosis' brought on by the structural change in the world economy limits the state's claim to unique or exceptional status as it becomes one of a number of sources of political authority. As we enter the second decade of the 21st century, the MNC must deal with this duality. It is caught in the midst of a transition from international to transnational modes of organization and both are relevant. I would agree with Ghemawat's (2007) concept of 'semi-globalization' if that construct were considered to be dynamic rather than static.

National differences in the structure of the economy, society and polity are still important, and the MNC must continue to deal with simultaneous pressures to integrate across borders and respond to local conditions if it is to optimize at the level of the global organization. That said, economic, political and social space may no longer correspond with national borders: the idea of the state as a 'container' is problematic given the digital revolution.

MNCs now need strategies to function in a transnational or non-territorial context where firms are actors with political authority and have corresponding duties and obligations to supply public services and public goods. There are three issues that need to be considered: dealing with a complex, non-territorial regulatory environment; participating as an actor in the governance process; and the provision of public services and public goods.

The idea of an MNC comprised of headquarters and subsidiaries with each unit a 'domestic' firm whose duties are a function of territorial incorporation may be increasingly irrelevant in a transnational order organized in terms of networks. Avi-Yonah (2005) argues that the corporation can be seen as an artificial entity created by the state, an aggregate of its members or shareholders, or a real entity controlled by its managers. He believes that it is the last, the real entity interpretation that prevails and he ties that argument explicitly to the MNC.

The entity view of the corporation is consistent with both networks and a transnational order. With the erosion of territoriality and borders, it will become increasingly difficult for any given unit of an MNC to disclaim responsibility for the actions of others, for example, the violation of human rights by a subsidiary – whether wholly or jointly owned – or even a sub-contractor (Kobrin, 2009). Hedlund's (1986) idea of a heterarchy as a hologram where 'information about the whole is contained in each part' is relevant here.

I would suggest the idea of a transnational strategy as a fruitful area for further research. One question of interest is the relationship between firm and industry characteristics and the need for a transnational strategy. As noted above, the distinction between multinational, global and transna-tional firms (in Bartlett and Ghoshal's terms) while dynamic is largely a function of industry characteristics. To some extent, industry characteristics should determine which firms are likely to function as actors in world politics or assume public responsibilities.

As I have noted elsewhere (Kobrin, 2008), some firms or industries are likely to be unaffected by governance pressures: they will remain private market-based actors which are objects rather than subjects. Others will find that they exercise political authority, have explicit duties as well as rights and are part of the governance structure. They will become hybrid entities with a presence in both the public and private spheres.

Whether an industry is politically salient (e.g. oil, minerals or power generation), the degree of oligopoly and whether or not the product is essential (e.g. pharmaceuticals) are all likely to influence whether or not the firm is likely to find itself functioning as a public–private hybrid. So may region of origin as firms based in democratic societies may be more subject to pressure to assume public responsibilities in issue areas like human or worker rights and the environment.

The Fig. 1 contains a rough first past at a categorization of this added dimension. The two-by-two matrix is delineated by firms operating in a traditional geography of spaces and those which operate in the 'non-territorial' region of the world economy on the horizontal axis, and firms which remain private actors and those which become part of hybrid private–pubic entities on the vertical. Traditional multinational firms are found in the

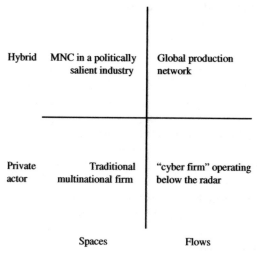

Fig. 1. Transnational Transition and Multinational Strategy.

lower left quadrant, private firms operating in a world of borders and territoriality. The lower right quadrant encompasses firms which remain private, but are, to a large extent, non-territorial. MNCs dealing with services or products which are primarily digital and which have not experienced pressures to either exert political authority or assume public responsibilities fall here. The upper right quadrant contains hybrid firms which are still bound by Westphalian geography: resource-based firms and oil and mining and pharmaceuticals may fit here. Last, the upper right quadrant contains hybrid entities operating in the non-territorial 'space of flows'. Global production networks such as those in the electronics industry are possible examples.

The multinational firm as we know it, and its core strategic problem, both reflect its origins in the international or Westphalian political-economic order. To the extent I am correct and we are in the midst of a systemic transformation from an international to a transnational mode of political-economic organization, we should expect to see significant changes in the nature of the multinational firm and the strategic problems it faces in the future.

NOTES

1. Booz & Co./Strategy + Business Eminent Scholar in International Management Award Panel Academy of Management Annual Meeting, Montreal (August 9, 2010).
2. Parts of this chapter are drawn from Kobrin (1998, 2008, 2009, 2010).

REFERENCES

Amin, A. (2002). Spatialities of globalization. *Environment and Planning A, 34*, 385–399.

Anderson, J. (1986). The modernity of states. In: J. Anderson (Ed.), *The rise of the modern state*. Atlantic Highlands, NJ: Humanities Press International, Inc.

Avi-Yonah, R. S. (2005). The cyclical transformations of the corporate form: A historical perspective on corporate social responsibility. *Delaware Journal of Corporate Law, 30*(3), 767–818.

Bartlett, C. A., & Ghoshal, S. (1987). Managing across borders: New strategic requirements. *Sloan Management Review, 28*(4), 7–17.

Bartlett, C. A., & Ghoshal, S. (1989). *Managing across borders: The transnational solution*. Boston: Harvard Business School Press.

Benner, T., Reinicke, W., & Witte, J. M. (2004). Multisectoral networks in global governance: Towards a pluralistic system of accountability. *Government and Opposition, 39*(2), 191–210.

Boddewyn, J., & Brewer, T. (1994). International-business political behavior: New theoretical directions. *Academy of Management Review, 19*(1), 119–143.

Buckley, P. J., & Ghauri, P. N. (2004). Globalisation, economic geography and the strategy of multinational enterprises. *Journal of International Business Studies, 35*(2), 81–98.

Castells, M. (1996). *The rise of the network society.* Cambridge, MA: Blackwell Publishers.

Cutler, A. C. (1999). Locating "authority" in the global political economy. *International Studies Quarterly, 43*(1), 59–81.

Cutler, A. C., Haufler, V., & Porter, T. (1999). Private authority and international affairs. In: A. C. Cutler, V. Haufler & T. Porter (Eds), *Private authority and international affairs* (pp. 3–30). Albany, NY: State University of New York Press.

Dicken, P. (2007). *Global shift: Mapping the changing contours of the world economy* (5th ed.). London: Sage.

Fayerweather, J. (1982). *International business strategy and administration* (2nd ed.). Cambridge: Ballinger Publishing Company.

Forest Stewardship Council. (2009). FSC-US Standards Revision Process. Available at http:// www.fscus.org/standards_criteria/standards_revision_process.php

Gereffi, G. (2005). The new offshoring of jobs and global developement, *ILO Social Policy Lectures,* International Institute for Labor Studies, Jamaica.

Ghemawat, P. (2007). *Redefining global strategy: Cross borders.* Boston: Harvard Business School Press.

Ghoshal, S., & Bartlett, C. A. (1990). The multinational corporation as an interorganzational network. *Academy of Management Review, 15*(4), 603–625.

Giddens, A. (1990). *The consequences of modernity.* Stanford: Stanford University Press.

Grossman, G. M., & Rossi-Hansberg, E. (2006). *The rise of offshoring: It's not wine for cloth anymore.* Princeton, NJ: Princeton University.

Hall, P., & Soskice, D. (2001). *Varieties of capitalism.* Oxford: Oxford University Press.

Hall, R. B., & Biersteker, T. J. (2002). The emergence of private authority in the international system. In: R. B. Hall & T. J. Biersteker (Eds), *The emergence of private authority in global governance* (pp. 3–22). Cambridge: Cambridge University Press.

Hedlund, G. (1986). The hypermodern MNC – A heterarchy? *Human Resource Management, 25*(1), 9–35.

Held, D. (2006). *Models of democracy* (3rd ed.). Stanford: Stanford University Press.

Hymer, S. (1979). The multinational corporation and the law of uneven development. In: G. Modelski (Ed.), *Transnational corporations and world order.* San Francisco: W.H. Freeman and Company.

Johns, F. (1994). The invisibility of the transnational corporation: An analysis of international law and theory. *Melbourne University Law Review, 19,* 893–923.

Keohane, R. O., & Nye, J. S. (1977). *Power and interdependence: World politics in transition.* Boston: Little Brown.

Kobrin, S. J. (1989). Enforcing export embargoes through multinational corporations: Why it does'nt work anymore. *Business in the Contemporary World, 1*(2), 31–42.

Kobrin, S. J. (1998). Back to the future: Neomedievalism and the postmodern digital world economy. *Journal of International Affairs, 51*(2), 361–386.

Kobrin, S. J. (2004). Oil and politics: Talisman energy in Sudan. *New York University Journal of International Law and Politics, 36*(2–3), 425–456.

Kobrin, S. J. (2008). Globalization, transnational corporations and the future of global governance. In: A. G. Scherer & G. Palazzo (Eds), *Handbook of research on corporate citizenship* (pp. 249–272). Cheltenham: Edward Elgar.

Kobrin, S. J. (2009). Private political authority and public responsibility: Transnational politics, transnational firms and human rights. *Business Ethics Quarterly, 19*(3), 349–374.

Kobrin, S. J. (2010). *Economic governance in a networked world economy: Global production networks, territoriality and political authority.* Philadelphia: The Wharton School, University of Pennsylvania.

Krasner, S. (1982). Structural causes and regime consequences: Regimes as intervening variables. *International Organization, 36*(2), 185–205.

Lilienthal, D. (1960). The multinational corporation. In: M. Ashen & G. I. Bach (Eds), *Management and corporations (1985).* New York: McGraw Hill.

Muchlinski, P. T. (2001). Human rights and multinationals: Is there a problem? *International Affairs, 77*(1), 31–47.

North, D. C. (1981). *Structure and change in economic history.* New York: W.W. Norton & Company.

Nye, J. S., Jr., & Keohane, R. O. (1971). Transnational relations and world politics: An introduction. In: R. O. Kephane & J. S. Nye, Jr. (Eds), *Transnational relations and world politics.* Cambridge: Harvard University Press.

Palmisano, S. (2006). The globally integrated enterprise. *Foreign Affairs, 85*(3), 127–136.

Perlmutter, H. V. (1969). The tortuous evolution of the multinational corporation. *Columbia Journal of World Business, 4,* 9–18.

Rosenau, J. (1990). *Turbulence in world politics.* Princeton, NJ: Princeton University Press.

Ruggie, J. G. (1983). Continuity and transformation in world politics: Toward a neorealist synthesis. *World Politics, 35*(2), 261–285.

Ruggie, J. G. (1993). Territoriality and beyond: Problematizing modernity in international relations. *International Organization, 47*(1), 139–174.

Ruggie, J. G. (2004). Reconstituting the global public domain: Issues, actors and practices. *European Journal of International Relations, 10*(4), 499–531.

Ruggie, J. G. (2010). The protect, respect and remedy framework: Implications for the ILO. *International Labour Conference,* Geneva.

Sassen, S. (2008). *Territory, authority, rights: From medieval to global assemblages.* Princeton, NJ: Princeton University Press.

Schaferhoff, S. C., & Kaan, C. (2009). Transnational public-private partnerships in international relations: Making sense of concepts, research frameworks, and results. *International Studies Review, 11*(3), 451–474.

Scherer, A.G., & Palazzo, G. (2009). The new political role of business in a globalized world: A review of the paradigm shift in CSR and its implications for the firm, governance and democracy. AIB Frontiers Conference, Charleston, SC.

Strange, S. (1996). *The retreat of the state: The diffusion of power in the world economy.* Cambridge: Cambridge University Press.

Vagts, D. F. (1970). The multinational enterprise: A new challenge for transnational law. *Harvard Law Review, 83*(4), 739–792.

Valente, M., & Crane, A. (2010). Public responsibility and private enterprise in developing countircs. *California Management Review, 52*(3), 52–80.

Vernon, R. (1971). *Sovereignty at bay.* New York: Basic Books.

Vogel, D. (2005). *The market for virtue.* Washington, DC: Brookings Insitute Press.

Voluntary Principles on Security and Human Rights. (2006). Voluntary Principles on Security and Human Rights.

CONNECTING THE PLOTS: THE CONTRIBUTIONS OF STEPHEN J. KOBRIN TO INTERNATIONAL MANAGEMENT RESEARCH

Jonathan P. Doh

ABSTRACT

Stephen Kobrin's contributions to international management scholarship are highly influential to the field as it has evolved over the past four decades. They include important insights into political risk, business–government relations, FDI theory and corporate social responsibility. His most recent work has leveraged historical perspectives to inform the emerging nature of the global business environment, with particular attention to the emergence of a globally networked economy and its implications for the range of stakeholders – business, government, non-governmental organizations and citizens. In this chapter, I reflect on Kobrin's contributions from the past to the present, summarizing some of the most important and substantial contributions and offering personal reflections on how those insights have affected the field and leading scholars within it.

Dynamics of Globalization: Location-Specific Advantages or Liabilities of Foreignness?
Advances in International Management, Volume 24, 25–31
Copyright © 2011 by Emerald Group Publishing Limited
All rights of reproduction in any form reserved
ISSN: 1571-5027/doi:10.1108/S1571-5027(2011)0000024007

INTRODUCTION

Stephen Kobrin has made impressive and long-lasting contributions to scholarly research in international management. These contributions have transcended and cut across a number of streams within international business and international management, including political risk, FDI theory, corporate responsibility and global networks. They have revealed important – but not always obvious – connections among phenomena, levels and theories. In this chapter, I summarize some of what I view as the most important and substantial contributions and offer some personal reflections on how those insights have affected the field and leading scholars within it. This is obviously a personal and biased account, reflecting only a slice of Steve's impact on the field.

This chapter is divided into three parts. First, I share a few thoughts about Steve's contribution to our understanding of the concept of political risk and the broader dynamics associated with multinational–host government bargaining. Second, I comment on Steve's insights in the area of globalization and global governance, and his consideration of the historical context to inform current events and future perspectives, something that was evident in his presentation this afternoon. Finally, I offer a few words about Steve's influence as a scholar and teacher and his role as a mentor to many of us who have been inspired by his work and life. I close with a brief mention of three indelible qualities that I associate with Steve's scholarly legacy.

POLITICAL RISK AND MNC–HOST GOVERNMENT BARGAINING

Steve Kobrin provided greater clarity, focus and specificity as to what is political (vs. other types of) risk and how uncertainty and risk relate to each other. At the same time, he also drew attention to the shortcomings of the predictive nature of risk and the difficulty in operationalizing it in a useful way. In two highly influential papers published in 1978 and 1979, Steve Kobrin laid the foundation for our understanding of political risk over the past three and half decades.

In his 1978 paper, Kobrin (1978, p. 113) notes that 'in one increasingly important area of international business – assessing and evaluating the impact of the political environment – major decisions are often made on the basis of superficial and subjective impressions'. Echoing this judgment, in his 1979 JIBS paper he states, 'One of the conclusions of this paper is that most managers' understanding of the concept of political risk, their assessment and evaluation of politics, and the manner in which they integrate political information into decision making are all rather general, subjective, and superficial' (Kobrin, 1979, p. 68).

In these papers, and another published in 1980 (Kobrin, Basek, Blank, & La Palombara, 1980), Kobrin distinguishes between risk and uncertainty by identifying uncertainty as being either objective or subjective in relation to the associated risk. He states that 'if uncertainty is objective, the contribution of political events to business risk is a function only of the events themselves', whereas 'if uncertainty is subjective, the contribution to business risk is a function of both the events themselves and the decision makers' perceptions' (1979, p. 71). Continuing with this perspective, he states: 'The emphasis on the negative consequences of government intervention entails an implicitly normative assumption that may not be universally valid' (1979, p. 69).

Regarding the impact of uncertainty on risk and the challenge of using risk to predict specific, discrete events, Kobrin notes, 'While most authors reviewed agree that political instability and political risk are distinct phenomena, the fact of the matter is that enough is not known about how the former affects the latter to construct reasonable predictive models' (1979, p. 76).

Writing more than two decades after Kobrin, Oetzel, Bettis, and Zenner (2001) found that the range of country risk services can be relied upon to predict risk during periods of relative stability, but that these measures fail to predict any of the periods of discontinuity, a finding consistent with Kobrin's writing two decades earlier.

As scholars have become interested in the broader institutional environment of international business (Henisz & Zelner, 2005), other forms of risk such as that emanating from terrorism or natural disaster, Kobrin's foundational work has helped shape this entire realm of research. Throughout his career, Steve Kobrin has underscored the importance of governmental actors and the various roles they play in facilitating and constraining IB activity. He has also recognized and argued for the emergence of alternate locuses of power to states in the form of non-state actors such as multinational enterprises (MNEs) and non-governmental organizations (NGOs).

Here, Kobrin has a number of co-conspirators, some of whom preceded him and others who were contemporaries or successors. I am thinking, of course, of Hymer, Kindelberger, Vernon, Wells and others; but he has added to, and in some cases, overturned conventional thinking and wisdom.

Specifically, Kobrin has built on, and extended, Vernon's obsolescing bargaining model by noting that the degree to which the MNC's position obsolesces is dependent on – and varies in relation to – a number of factors, including the particular industry and its internal or external orientation. Specifically, Kobrin found that in manufacturing industries, these bargains are less likely to be obsolescent because MNE investments are smaller, more mobile and leverage knowledge-based advantages that are more difficult to replicate.

GLOBALIZATION AND GLOBAL GOVERNANCE

More broadly, Steve Kobrin has made a major contribution in helping to understand the forces of globalization and the role of government, non-governmental actors and MNEs in managing global governance.

Steve has taken on the sensitive issue of MNEs' roles and responsibilities in the area of human rights on other related social issues. Indeed, he has argued that MNEs should be held directly liable for complicity in human rights violations that may involve complicity by governments and other actors and has proposed a public–private regime that relies on non-hierarchical compliance mechanisms to address this issue. He explored the case of Talisman Energy in Sudan to underscore and support his arguments (Kobrin, 2004a). And his recent research on private political authority poses some fascinating but troubling questions about the emergent global governance regimes that appear to be taking shape (Kobrin, 2009).

One of the most significant legacies of Steve's research and teaching is the role of history and context in the international business environment. Personally, I have had the fortune of observing Steve in some of his executive teaching. Steve is always challenging his students – as well as his fellow scholars – to be cautious about assuming a linear view of history. For example, I once saw him point out to a group of students who were mostly in their 30s that the current extent of global economic integration is not unprecedented. On the contrary, by some measures the global economy was more internationally integrated in the inter-war period, peaking in the late 1920s at a level that has not been replicated in the more recent globalization wage.

Yet, Steve is not backward looking – his research and teaching are highly contemporary, even forward looking. He has used network concepts and data and facts regarding offshoring of IT and health care to reinforce points about the changing nature of the global economy. One comment he made to a group that I recall (and repeat) goes something like this: 'The global economy is transitioning from one in which geographic proximity and distance are the main determinants of global integration and economic flows to one in which relational proximity is the relevant and most powerful defining principle'.

SCHOLARLY IMPACT AND PERSONAL REFLECTIONS

The extent to which Steve Kobrin's research has influenced the work of many others is without dispute. We can see his influence especially in the North and Wiliamson-inspired international business and international management scholars. Here I am thinking about the work of Henisz, Zelner and Holburn (Henisz & Zelner, 2005; Holburn & Zelner, 2010), among others. Although not directly connected, the foundation for the renewed interest in the role of context and the broader institutional environment on international management can also be traced to Kobrin's work (Zaheer, 1995).

His work has been a real inspiration to me and many colleagues who have sought to bring in additional actors into the MNE–host government bargaining dynamic – notably civil society actors such as NGOs. Here, in addition to my own work, Teegen, Doh, and Vachani (2004), and many others have gained motivation from Steve's seminal work. This work – building on that of Kobrin and others – has expanded the scope of what are considered relevant stakeholders in the business–government interface and in so doing, presented a more complete picture of the global business environment.

On a personal level, Steve is a gracious and generous senior scholar. I first met Steve about 7 or 8 years ago. I was a very junior faculty member and nervous about meeting one of my idols; Steve was, of course, extremely accessible, humble and supportive. Since that time, we have developed a cordial relationship, one which I value greatly.

CLOSING COMMENTS

I'd like to close with a brief comment about three ways in which I believe Steve Kobrin's scholarship is especially impactful, all of which are in evidence in his perspective in this volume (Kobrin, 2011). First, it is relevant that it deals with real-world issues and problems that have meaning and import for international business and international management scholars and practitioners. I think, for example, of his *Foreign Policy* article 'The Multilateral Agreement on Investment', which detailed the emergence and subsequent breakdown of the first effort and concluding a truly global agreement providing rules concerning government policies towards FDI (Kobrin, 1998). Second, it is interdisciplinary, something that in many scholar's view is necessary in order that it be relevant. Business phenomenon – including international management – inherently cuts across disciplines. It strikes me as odd – even hypocritical – that as we lecture our students about how business problems are increasingly multidimensional, our own in business and allied fields is increasingly narrow, overly specialized, and therefore lacks obvious relevance. Kobrin's research has consistently resisted this trend, drawing on law, economics and even medicine in his research. For example, his *NYU Journal of Law and Politics* article on Talisman energy (Kobrin, 2004a) and his piece in *Review of International Studies* on the transatlantic data privacy dispute (Kobrin, 2004b) explore important contemporary issues that draw from the disciplinary lenses of law, political science and business. Finally, and in keeping with the theme of the 2010 Academy of Management Conference, Steve's research has both 'passion' and 'compassion'. I want to be clear that in no way do these qualities imply a lack of rigor; quite the contrary. I believe scholars must be passionate about what they do in order to be rigorous and compassionate in the way they approach their subjects in order to reveal fundamental truths. It is these final qualities that I think of most when I consider his legacy.

REFERENCES

Henisz, W. J., & Zelner, B. A. (2005). Legitimacy, interest group pressures and change in emergent institutions: The case of foreign investors and host country governments. *Academy of Management Review, 30*(2), 361–382.

Holburn, G. L. F., & Zelner, B. A. (2010). Political capabilities, policy risk, and international investment strategy: Evidence from the global electric power generation industry. *Strategic Management Journal, 31*(12), 1290–1315.

Kobrin, S. J. (1978). When does political instability result in increased investment risk? *The Columbia Journal of World Business, 13*(3), 113–122.

Kobrin, S. J. (1979). Political risk: A review and reconsideration. *Journal of International Business Studies, 10*(1), 67–80.

Kobrin, S. J. (1998). The MAI and the clash of globalizations. *Foreign Policy, Fall*, 97–109.

Kobrin, S. J. (2004a). Safe harbours are hard to find: The trans-Atlantic data privacy dispute, territorial jurisdiction and global governance. *Review of International Studies, 30*(1), 111–131.

Kobrin, S. J. (2004b). Oil and politics: Talisman energy and Sudan. *NYU Journal of Law and Politics, 36*(2-3), 425–456.

Kobrin, S. J. (2009). Private political authority and public responsibility: Transnational politics, transnational firms and human rights. *Business Ethics Quarterly, 19*(3), 349–374.

Kobrin, S. J. (2011). The transnational transition and the multinational firm. In: C. G. Asmussen, T. Pedersen, T. M. Devinney & L. Tihanyi (Eds), *Dynamics of globalization: Location-specific advantages or liabilities of foreignness?* Bingley, UK: Emerald.

Kobrin, S. J., Basek, J., Blank, S., & La Palombara, J. L. (1980). The assessment and evaluation of non-economic environments by American firms: A preliminary report. *Journal of International Business Studies, 11*(1), 32–47.

Oetzel, J. M., Bettis, R. A., & Zenner, M. (2001). *Journal of World Business, 36*(2), 128–145.

Teegen, H., Doh, J. P., & Vachani, S. (2004). The importance of nongovernmental organizations (NGOs) in global governance and value creation: An international business research agenda. *Journal of International Business Studies, 35*(6), 463–483.

Zaheer, S. (1995). Overcoming the liability of foreignness. *Academy of Management Journal, 38*(2), 341–363.

GOVERNANCE IN A TRANSNATIONAL ERA: STEPHEN J. KOBRIN AND THE POST-WESTPHALIAN REALITY

Ruth V. Aguilera

ABSTRACT

This chapter is a commentary on Kobrin's essay on the current transition to the transnational era where there is a shift in the balance of power from sovereign states to non-state stakeholders and what role the multinational corporation (MNC) plays in this transition. It celebrates Kobrin's long-established scholarship and discusses his recent thinking regarding the new reconceptualization of space, the fragmentation of political authority and the intermingling of public and private spheres, in the context of transnational governance. In his essay, Kobrin raises many interesting questions and opens new avenues for inter-disciplinary research on the MNC in the up-and-coming transnational era.

Dynamics of Globalization: Location-Specific Advantages or Liabilities of Foreignness?
Advances in International Management, Volume 24, 33–42
Copyright © 2011 by Emerald Group Publishing Limited
ISSN: 1571-5027/doi:10.1108/S1571-5027(2011)0000024008

INTRODUCTION

Professor Kobrin's work on global governance and country political risk lies at the intersection of international business, law and international relations. His research is deeply concerned with the institutional and political pressures that multinational managers perceive and deal with as they invest in different foreign countries (Kobrin, 1982). In this regard, Kobrin has done a great service to the international business and global strategy fields by effectively co-opting the political science literature on political risk and governance and applying it to managerial perceptions of risk in multinational firms. Kobrin's (1979) essay on political risk assessment in foreign direct investment and organizational responses to environmental change is a classic in the international business research. His thinking about the tensions between global integration and cultural differences among markets offers an excellent road map to conceptualize multinational corporations (MNCs)' strategic dilemmas of integration and fragmentation of the global value chain (Kobrin, 1991). In the remainder of this commentary, I first summarize Kobrin's essay in this volume entitled 'The Transnational Transition and the Multinational Firm'. Then, I discuss two of his arguments that I believe are provocative and engage with broader debates regarding the role of MNCs in the twenty-first century: transnational governance and the global space.

Kobrin's essay on this issue takes yet another step in his well-established scholarship towards understanding the interplay of the local and the global in the context of the post-Westphalian world where there is no longer 'a fundamental distinction between domestic political spheres characterized by institutional density, hierarchical relationships, shared interests, and strong collective identities' (March & Olsen, 1998, p. 944), but a transition towards a new transnational political era. Kobrin identifies three key transformations in this emerging transnational era: (1) a reconceptualization of geographic space; (2) the emergence of new political actors in international politics, diluting conventional political authority and (3) the co-evolution and blurred boundaries between public and private spheres. These three factors shape the international to transnational transition according to Kobrin. This is an emerging space where MNCs are expected to navigate convoluted waters dealing with geographic territories that go beyond national countries such as global production networks, cooperate with multiple actors such as NGOs and civic groups and engage in public–private partnerships such as transnational unions or standard-setting agencies.

THE GLOBAL SPACE

An interesting point raised in Kobrin's essay is that distance and position in the structure of the international production function can no longer be defined merely in geographical terms but must also be understood in the context of global production networks that are increasingly fluid thanks to digitalization and technological advances. In this network space, the organization and distance of the different units in the MNC need to be examined in the context of their position in the global network which is consistent with important recent research pushing the idea of cross-national distance beyond geographical distance. For example, Ghemawat (2001) proposes four dimensions of distance in his CAGE model, *c*ultural distance, *a*dministrative distance, *g*eographic distance and *e*conomic distance, which fits very well in a network MNC mindset.

At a more dynamic level, Berry, Guillen, and Zhou (2010) have constructed a data set that includes cross-national and longitudinal data for nine distance dimensions (including economic, financial, political, administrative, cultural, demographic, knowledge, global connectedness and geographic distance). Their multidimensional notion of distance and Kobrin's discussion on global production networks complement each other nicely. Future research should incorporate both of these constructs as independent variables or controlling factors. A main challenge in examining cross-national distance is that it tends to neglect the interdependent position of the multiple MNC subsidiaries or the position of the different units of the production value chain in the global network. In this regard, Nachum and Song (2011) conceptualize the MNC as a portfolio of interdependent subunits and examine the subsidiary location moves relative to the overall global MNC network. This study nicely details the perhaps overlooked dimensions of path dependency noted by Kobrin – even though firms have choices on where to locate, this decision will be contingent on existing MNC subsidiary locations.

In discussing the reconceptualization of the global space, Kobrin touches briefly on the much debated topic of semi-globalization – or regionalization, where trade and investments occur mostly among a few regions. He links semi-globalization to his continuous emphasis that we are in the 'very early stages of the transnational transition'. I suspect because he recognizes that the world is far from flat. Semi-globalization is an increasingly discussed topic, particularly as countries become regionally integrated and the division between developed and developing countries grows sharper.

Research on the internationalization of MNCs has focused on firm-level characteristics and country-level subsidiary effects (Flores & Aguilera, 2007; Rugman & Verbeke, 2001). Recent research demonstrates that MNCs make international strategic choices contingent on regional affiliation (Arregle, Beamish, & Hebert, 2009) and coordinate their investments in a region as they need to expand across a region to maintain local responsiveness and exploit region-bound firm-specific advantages (Rugman & Verbeke, 2004). The semi-globalization approach highlights the geopolitical importance of regions in MNCs' international strategy due to their incomplete cross-border integration at different levels creating neither extreme geographical fragmentation nor a single homogenous market place (Ghemawat, 2003). Thus, future MNC research will have to pay closer attention not only to host countries but also to the overlapping regions (cultural, trade, socio-political etc.) in which these countries are integrated into (see Aguilera, Flores, & Vaaler, 2007; Vaaler, Aguilera, & Flores, 2007, for a discussion of regional groupings).

TRANSNATIONAL GOVERNANCE AND NEW GOVERNANCE REGULATION

Two of the tenants of Kobrin's transnational transition, 'the emergence of non-state actors with significant political power' and the 'blurring of public and private spheres', speak directly to extant research on transnational governance and new regulation. It is important to note that he does not refer to globalization (which has a larger connotation of harmonization across boundaries), but rather suggests that nation-states continue to be present, yet they need to be considered as one type of political actor amongst others (Cerny, 2006; Katzenstein, Keohane, & Krasner, 1999). I discuss each of these in turn.

With the waning of the United States as a political authority, MNCs are exposed to a more fragmented regulatory environment. International economists (Kindleberger, 1973) and social scientists (Gilpin, 1981) attribute the occurrence of cooperation and integration between countries in the world economy to the presence of a *hegemon*. Cooperation in the international sphere has resulted in the willingness of a powerful sovereign state to maintain, monitor and enforce rules governing interstate cooperation either through the use of coercion or by assuming some of the costs of leadership. The cases of pre-World War I and Bretton Woods constitute two instances of interstate cooperation based on the presence of a hegemonic power (Kindleberger, 1987). Therefore, the relative economic decline of the United States (at least in terms of foreign direct investment), and the emergence of new centres of power often based around non-state actors, has been interpreted as a negative development bringing about the demise of integration and cooperation at the international level (Grieco, Powell, & Snidal, 1993).

The insights of the works of Kobrin on transnational governance highlight how cooperation and integration can take place in the international economy despite the absence of a hegemon – and the rise of many loci of authority and power. International institutions of transnational governance can act as an inducement for integration and cooperation since they decrease transaction costs and reduce uncertainties, thereby limiting the negative consequences of asymmetrical information (Keohane, 2005; Ruggie, 1982). Cooperation in a context of diffused power can take place not because of the constraining nature of international institutions as they are often informal and/or place significant amounts of discretion in the hands of individual actors, but because they internalize the motivation. In addition, current international cooperation does not require altruism, harmony of interests or changes in values of participants. International institutions, whether formal or informal, serve as focal points that release information about the behavior of participants – thereby contributing to the reduction of uncertainty and the promotion of credibility of commitments (Keohane & Martin, 1995; Krasner, 1982). The relative economic decline of the United States does not entail the demise of cooperation and integration; institutional arrangements of transnational governance enable participants to adjust and interact in a power-diffused context characterized by the presence of multiple centres of authority.

Djelic and Sahlin-Andersson (2006) offer a terrific discussion of the complex and dynamic topography of transnational governance in the making. They define transnational governance as 'a complex compound of activities bridging the global and the local and taking place at the same time within, between and across national boundaries' (Djelic & Sahlin-Andersson, 2006, p. 3). In some global industries such as forestry, MNCs are the instigators of regulation (Cashore, Auld, & Newsom, 2004; Cutler, Haufler, & Porter, 1999), while in other cases such as social movements or NGOs private standard-setting initiatives are the ones putting pressure on MNCs to adopt certain practices (Brunsson & Jacobsson, 2000; Schneiberg & Bartley, 2008; Tamm Hallström & Boström, 2010). The key is that transnational governance involves a wide range of actors that redefine the modes of coordination, rule-making and rule-monitoring in a patchy and fragmented fashion because of the coexisting and often overlapping principles, codes and legal rules (Djelic & Quack, 2010). The main challenges in transnational governance as identified by Djelic and Quack (2010) are 'the competition between the different rule-systems or schemes' and the weakness of enforcement and sanctioning mechanisms.

Transnational governance triggers the coexistence of multiple actors and policy spaces, and inevitably a fragmentation in the global space, setting off institutional arbitrage and granting national institutional advantages of some countries over others. As argued by Scott (2010), the interdependence of individuals, firms, countries and transnational organizations – for instance, with the 2008 financial crises or the threat of climate change – presents supranational collective action problems which lead to an increased emphasis on global regulation. It is critical to further understand how this global regulation is developed, monitored and enforced. Typically, on the one hand, we would assume that there are norms and rules that get diffused from the national level to supranational organizations or intergovernmental organizations such as the European Commission. On the other hand, there are societal-based initiatives from NGOs, private firms and so on defining the regulatory space through non-governmental mechanisms such as standard setting or codes of conduct. Scott (2010), like Kobrin, maintains that the cleavage between intergovernmental and non-governmental regulation is becoming increasingly blurred and unimportant for three reasons: lack of coherence across countries in the adoption of global regulation, weaknesses in enforcement and concerns regarding normative effectiveness of non-governmental regimes and finally differential legitimation degrees of private and hybrid regimes vis-á-vis supranational governmental regimes. An important point of consensus in this debate is that sovereign national states no longer have exclusive rights over governance (Cerny, 2006).

In the transition to a transnational era, in addition to the political shift where state actors with centralized, top-down authority share their political space with non-state actors, these political actors are also crafting new forms of regulation, beyond traditional law – referred to as new regulation. There is a school of new regulation in legal studies examining this phenomenon in many different industrial sectors (Black, 2002, 2008; Haufler, 2001; Shamir, 2010). The shift to transnational governance at the national and international level has led to an explosion of rule setting and rule-monitoring activities (Djelic & Sahlin-Andersson, 2006; Levi-Faur, 2005). This new governance framework (formerly coined 'governance without government' because it replaced the government from the centre-state) refers to the fact that not only sovereign national states but also private actors and public–private stakeholders can set standards and policy initiatives in various industries. These then become expected and/or taken for granted. As stated by socio-legal scholar Shamir (2010), the mechanisms to regulate and ensure compliance with legal or quasi-legal arrangements switch from 'formal rules and stipulations, adversarial methods, enforceable means of dispute resolution, and command-and-control regulatory mechanisms' to 'nonadversarial dialogue and organizational learning, presumably leading to the development of principles, guidelines, best-performance standards and various soft law instruments' (p. 3). New governance regulation is a facet of the transnational era and directly engages MNCs in these stakeholder-oriented governance. For example, Koenig-Archibugi (2004) claims that the power and importance of MNCs have increased the process of economic integration and globalization and argues that the most effective mechanism to make MNCs accountable is through voluntary means that link the interests of the principals (i.e. shareholders) with those of the greater public. Rupp, Williams, and Aguilera (2011) develop a similar argument regarding the motivations of individuals and corporations to internalize different rules from a psychological lens and in the context of CSR. In sum, there is a turn towards a coexistence of formal means of authority or hard law (law, rules and regulations) with informal legitimate regulation (e.g. guidelines, principles, codes of conduct and standards) illustrating the transformative capacity of global capitalism.

CONCLUSION

Kobrin has put forth a great example of how to continually push the MNC agenda further by engaging in cross-disciplinary research and by asking relevant questions. First, it is critical that the different fields within international business engage in deeper across-field conversations (Aguilera, 2011; Cheng, Henisz, Roth, & Swaminathan, 2009). For instance, Reuer, Klijn, Van den Bosch, and Volberda (2011) discuss how research in international joint ventures (IJVs) has examined the advantages of alliance design type and modes (equity versus non-equity and type of contracts), yet has fallen short in incorporating the insights from comparative corporate governance in looking at, for instance, the structure of boards in IJVs or principal-agent problems in these cross-national inter-corporate relations. At a more inter-disciplinary level, we have much to learn from the rich literature in regulation studies (Levi-Faur & Jordana, 2005), socio-legal research (Braithwaite & Drahos, 2000; Shamir, 2010), political science, sociology, geography etc.

Kobrin's transnational transition as well as his work on understanding political risk assessment is well suited to address calls for relevant research in the field of international business because it encompasses a wide range of phenomena-driven questions. For example, Kobrin's inquiry into the role of the MNC in a public–private global network intertwined with transnational political actors can tackle important issues. One of the questions that his arguments are well equipped to assess is what the role of MNC should be in the 2011 socioeconomic environment dynamics where the G20 finance ministers are planning to design and implement transnational polices seeking to mitigate the almost 1 billion of chronically hungry people triggered by rising agricultural commodity prices in poor countries. 'Multinational firms are the key players in the global food chain and global food security is at the core of France's G20 presidency' (*Financial Times*, 'Chronic hunger to affect 1bn people', Joe Leahy, 16 February 2011, p. 2). The debate is not only about issues at the bottom of the pyramid but also about how MNCs and nations will compete and cooperate in the emerging transnational order.

ACKNOWLEDGEMENTS

I would like to thank Timothy Devinney, Ricardo Flores and Michel Goyer for their comments on this chapter as well as the participants of the 2010 Booz & Co./Strategy + Business Eminent Scholar in International Management Award Panel at the Academy of Management Annual Meeting.

REFERENCES

Aguilera, R. V. (2011). Inter-organizational governance and global strategy. *Global Strategy Journal*, *1*(1).

Aguilera, R. V., Flores, R., & Vaaler, P. (2007). Is it all a matter of grouping? Examining the regional effect in international business and global strategy research. In: S. Tallman (Ed.), *International strategic management: A new generation* (pp. 209–228). Northampton, MA: Edward Elgar Publishing, Inc.

Arregle, J. L., Beamish, P. W., & Hebert, L. (2009). The regional dimension of MNEs' foreign subsidiary localization. *Journal of International Business Studies*, *40*(1), 86–107.

Berry, H., Guillen, M. F., & Zhou, N. (2010). An institutional approach to cross-national distance. *Journal of International Business Studies*, *41*(9), 1460–1480.

Black, J. (2002). Regulatory conversations. *Journal of Law and Society, 29*(1), 163–196.

Black, J. (2008). Constructing and contesting legitimacy and accountability in polycentric regulatory regimes. *Regulation & Governance, 2*(2), 137–164.

Braithwaite, J., & Drahos, P. (2000). *Global business regulation.* Cambridge: Cambridge University Press.

Brunsson, N., & Jacobsson, B. (2000). *A world of standards.* Oxford: Oxford University Press.

Cashore, B. W., Auld, G., & Newsom, D. (2004). *Governing through markets: Forest certification and the emergence of non-state authority.* New Haven, CT: Yale University Press.

Cerny, P. G. (2006). Restructuring the state in a globalizing world: Capital accumulation, tangled hierarchies and the search for a new spatio-temporal fix. *Review of International Political Economy, 13*(4), 679–695.

Cheng, J., Henisz, W., Roth, K., & Swaminathan, A. (2009). Advancing interdisciplinary research in the field of international business: Prospects, issues, and challenges. *Journal of International Business Studies, 40*(7), 1070–1074.

Cutler, A. C., Haufler, V., & Porter, T. (1999). *Private authority and international affairs.* Albany, NY: State University of New York Press.

Djelic, M.-L., & Quack, S. (2010). *Transnational communities: Shaping global economic governance.* Cambridge: Cambridge University Press.

Djelic, M.-L., & Sahlin-Andersson, K. (2006). *Transnational governance: Institutional dynamics of regulation.* Cambridge: Cambridge University Press.

Flores, R. G., & Aguilera, R. V. (2007). Globalization and location choice: An analysis of US multinational firms in 1980 and 2000. *Journal of International Business Studies, 38*(7), 1187–1210.

Ghemawat, P. (2001). Distance still matters: The hard reality of global expansion. *Harvard Business Review, 79*(8), 137–147.

Ghemawat, P. (2003). Semiglobalization and international business strategy. *Journal of International Business Studies, 34*(2), 138–152.

Gilpin, R. (1981). *War and change in world politics.* Cambridge: Cambridge University Press.

Grieco, J., Powell, R., & Snidal, D. (1993). The relative-gains problem for international-cooperation. *American Political Science Review, 87*(3), 729–743.

Haufler, V. (2001). *A public role for the private sector: Industry self-regulation in a global economy.* Washington, DC: Carnegie Endowment for International Peace.

Katzenstein, P. J., Keohane, R. O., & Krasner, S. D. (1999). *Exploration and contestation in the study of world politics.* Cambridge, MA: MIT Press.

Keohane, R. O. (2005). *After hegemony: Cooperation and discord in the world political economy* (1st Princeton classic ed.). Princeton, NJ: Princeton University Press.

Keohane, R. O., & Martin, L. L. (1995). The promise of institutionalist theory. *International Security, 20*(1), 39–51.

Kindleberger, C. P. (1973). *The world in depression, 1929–1939.* London: Allen Lane.

Kindleberger, C. P. (1987). *Marshall plan days.* Boston: Allen & Unwin.

Kobrin, S. J. (1979). Political risk-review and reconsideration. *Journal of International Business Studies, 10*(1), 67–80.

Kobrin, S. J. (1982). *Managing political risk assessment: Strategic response to environmental change.* Berkeley, CA: University of California Press.

Kobrin, S. J. (1991). An empirical-analysis of the determinants of global integration. *Strategic Management Journal, 12*(Special issue), 17–31.

Koenig-Archibugi, M. (2004). Transnational corporations and public accountability. *Government and Opposition, 39*(2), 234–259.

Krasner, S. D. (1982). Structural causes and regime consequences: Regimes as intervening variables. *International Organization, 36*(2), 185–205.

Levi-Faur, D. (2005). The political economy of legal globalization: Juridification, adversarial legalism, and responsive regulation. A comment. *International Organization, 59*(2), 451–462.

Levi-Faur, D., & Jordana, J. (2005). The rise of regulatory capitalism: The global diffusion of a new order. *Annals of the American Academy of Political and Social Science, 598*(1), 200–217.

March, J. G., & Olsen, J. P. (1998). The institutional dynamics of international political orders. *International Organization, 52*(4), 943–969.

Nachum, L., & Song, S. (2011). The MNE as a portfolio: Interdependencies in MNE growth trajectory. *Journal of International Business Studies, 42*, 381–405.

Reuer, J. J., Klijn, E., Van den Bosch, F. A. J., & Volberda, H. W. (2011). Bringing corporate governance to international joint ventures. *Global Strategy Journal, 1*(1).

Ruggie, J. G. (1982). International regimes, transactions, and change: Embedded liberalism in the postwar economic order. *International Organization, 36*(2), 379–415.

Rugman, A. M., & Verbeke, A. (2001). Subsidiary-specific advantages in multinational enterprises. *Strategic Management Journal, 22*(3), 237–250.

Rugman, A. M., & Verbeke, A. (2004). A perspective on regional and global strategies of multinational enterprises. *Journal of International Business Studies, 35*(1), 3–18.

Rupp, D. E., Williams, C., & Aguilera, R. (2011). Increasing corporate social responsibility through stakeholder value internalization (and the catalyzing effect of new governance): An application of organizational justice, self-determination, and social influence theories. In: M. Schminke (Ed.), *Managerial Ethics: Managing the Psychology of Morality*. New York: Routledge/Psychology Press.

Schneiberg, M., & Bartley, T. (2008). Organizations, regulation, and economic behavior: Regulatory dynamics and forms from the nineteenth to twenty-first century. *Annual Review of Law and Social Science, 4*, 31–61.

Scott, C. (2010). *Regulating in global regimes.* UCD Working Papers in Law, Criminology and Socio-Legal Studies. Research Paper no. 25/2010. University College Dublin, Dublin.

Shamir, A. (2010). Capitalism, governance, and authority: The case of corporate social responsibility. *Annual Review of Law and Social Science, 6*, 531–553.

Tamm Hallström, K., & Boström, M. (2010). *Transnational multi-stakeholder standardization: Organizing fragile non-state authority.* Northampton, MA: Edward Elgar Publishing, Inc.

Vaaler, P., Aguilera, R. V., & Flores, R. G. (2007). Simulated annealing and the impact of country regional groupings on US multinational corporate investment decisions. In: D. J. Ketchen & D. D. Bergh (Eds), *Research methodology in strategy and management* (pp. 161–190). Amsterdam: Elsevier (JAI).

PART II

INTRODUCTION TO PART II: DYNAMICS OF GLOBALIZATION: LOCATION-SPECIFIC ADVANTAGES OR LIABILITIES OF FOREIGNNESS?

Christian G. Asmussen, Torben Pedersen, Timothy M. Devinney and Laszlo Tihanyi

The *location* factor has long been neglected in International Management (IM) studies, traditionally relegated to an exogenous role and ascribed a somewhat trivial impact (Dunning, 1998). One major source of this neglect is in our conceptualization of firms' location-specific advantages (LSAs) as completely distinct from firm-specific advantages – i.e. a factor that only explains the choice of location for different activities but not the variation in firm-specific advantages (FSAs). However, increased globalization has, in many ways, put the location factor back onto the map of international business and management scholarship once again. As we will argue in this introductory chapter, and as the contributions in the 2011 volume of *Advances in International Management* bear out, old questions have been revitalized in a new context and new and challenging questions have been raised pertaining to the importance of location in international business and management.

Dynamics of Globalization: Location-Specific Advantages or Liabilities of Foreignness?
Advances in International Management, Volume 24, 45–53
ISSN: 1571-5027/doi:10.1108/S1571-5027(2011)0000024009

Cross-border flows of goods, services, capital, knowledge and ideas have substantially increased over the past decades. These developments have increased the interdependencies among previously separated economies and given rise to arguments regarding the flattening of the world. Consequently and co-deterministically we have also seen a disappearing sense of nationality (Kobrin, this volume: 'The Transnational Transition and the Multinational Firm'). It has been suggested that firms may exploit these new conditions to internationalize into far-flung locations – where local governments, workers and consumers welcome foreign investments, new knowledge and opportunities for developing closer links into the global economic system. In turn, foreign firms are, themselves, tapping into localized knowledge clusters to augment their competitive advantage.

At the same time, the complexities of operating across borders have never been higher. Firms investing overseas continue to experience substantial liabilities of foreignness (LOF). The risks and uncertainty of global network coordination has been exacerbated by global concerns of security, sustainability and accountability. In addition, the range of participants in international competition has widened – in terms of both the number of countries involved and the types of firms competing – to encompass developed market firms expanding beyond industrialized countries, and emerging market firms joining global competition. These developments broaden the range of consequences of foreignness well beyond those recognized by existing theories.

This paradoxical development is also reflected, practically, in firm strategies and, scholarly, in research on location issues. Traditional strategic approaches, where companies expand abroad to tap into the munificence of the foreign host countries, are based on the factors influencing the competitiveness of locations, like local resources, education base and institutions. In contract, recent strategic thinking suggests that firms look for location advantages that are complementary to their firm-specific advantages (possibly augmenting them). The importance of location has evolved from being purely associated with resources, idiosyncratic to the specific location, to their unique interaction with the firm-specific advantage. In other words, the global competitive advantage of firms can be enhanced by local learning and mutual interactions with local actors.

Avoiding the hazards and exploiting the benefits of differences between locations is the essence of global strategy. Within this context, the well-known paradox of distance has found a fertile ground: although the technological advances in transportation and communication technologies have led observers to bombastically celebrate the death of distance in an increasingly flat world (Friedman, 2005), there is another side to the debate, one that emphasizes a renewed significance of local clusters, agglomeration and advantages that locations may offer to firms.

We are in many ways witnessing a contradictory development that entails increased importance of LSAs that interact with FSAs in new ways. Many firms will be forced to reconsider their configuration of their global value chain activities to be present in the right locations with the right activities for efficiency as well as for knowledge augmenting (e.g. Pyndt & Pedersen, 2006). This enlarged significance of location-specific advantages goes hand-in-hand with the liability of foreignness that will not only persist but become even more essential both to research and practice.

This development is raising more questions than it answers on the importance of location, and many of these questions center around the three concepts of LSA, FSA, and LOF (Rugman & Verbeke, 1992; Zaheer, 1995), the interdependence of which will be scrutinized further in the following discussion and specific chapters of this volume. Although most IM research treats these parameters as exogenous, emerging studies argue that they are really endogenous, affecting one another in a complex feedback cycle and influencing one another via a complex interaction of factors on multiple levels. In the following, we provide a first attempt at formalizing this idea and at the same time provide an overview of how the chapters in this volume collectively contribute to it.

AN ORGANIZING MODEL OF INTERNATIONAL COMPETITION

We can formalize the point of departure for this year's volume by asking a very simple question: what are the determinants of the competiveness (denoted C) of individual MNEs (subscripted M) and local firms (subscripted L) in a host market? The 'classical' view of international competition implies the following relationships:

$$C_L = \text{FSA}_L + \text{LSA}$$
$$C_M = \text{FSA}_M + \text{LSA} - \text{LOF} \tag{1}$$

These equations capture the key assumptions that: (a) local firms and MNEs have equal access to local resources, (b) that they have differential proprietary resources (e.g., intangible assets) and (c) that the MNE suffers an additional penalty to its competitiveness due to the LOF. In order for the

MNE to have a competitive advantage against the local incumbents, a necessary and sufficient condition is that:

$$C_M > C_L \Leftrightarrow \text{FSA}_M - \text{FSA}_L > \text{LOF} \tag{2}$$

In other words, the important question becomes whether the relative advantage of the MNE is strong enough to outweigh the costs of doing business abroad. This horserace was first described by Hymer (1976) and has become the dominant paradigm for how international competition is understood in international business and management research. Thus, Eqs. (1) and (2) will serve as the 'benchmark case' with which we can evaluate the far-reaching implications of the endogenization of these variables. A brief account of the chapters in this volume, and some highly stylized examples of how we might challenge the exogeneity assumption, is given below.

Endogenous LSA

As the chapters in this volume emphasize, the access to local resources in a given host country is not a free-for-all. Although the LOF has traditionally been understood as a phenomenon related to firms' performance in local markets, implicitly evoking a market-seeking motivation for entry, it applies equally well to strategic asset seeking (Dunning, 1993). Hence, foreign firms might suffer from discrimination and uncertainty relative to incumbent firms *also* in their attempts to get access to local resources such as labor and knowledge. The first chapter in this second section, by Nachum ('Home-based Advantages and a Hierarchy of Location Resources: Foreign and Local Firms Dependency on Location Resources'), demonstrates these points and estimates a hierarchy of resources that differ in their degree of accessibility to foreign firms and fungibility within internal MNE networks. If the LOF thus inhibits MNEs' attempts to use LSA as a source of local competitiveness, we might assume a relationship of the form $\text{LSA}_M = \text{LSA}_0(1 - e\,\text{LOF})$, where $e \geq 0$ captures, for lack of a better term, the local 'resource embeddedness', i.e. the extent to which local incumbents have an unfair advantage in sourcing LSA. These local firms, in contrast, do not suffer a penalty like the MNEs do and can freely access the local resources, so that $\text{LSA}_L = \text{LSA}_0$.

Endogenous LOF

At the same time, as argued by several chapters in this volume, the LOF is not a universal constant that can be expected to apply equally to all MNEs.

Firms can organize themselves for better control of LOF – and thus better exploitation of LSA – for example by using regional headquarters (Nell, Ambos and Schlegelmilch, 'The Benefits of Hierarchy? Effects of Regional Headquarters in Multinational Corporations'; Laudien and Freiling, 'Overcoming Liabilities of Foreignness by Modes of Structural Coordination: Regional Headquarters Activities and Their Role in TNCS'), by strategically locating their divisional headquarters (Lunnan, Benito and Tomassen, 'Moving Abroad: Factors that Motivate Foreign Location of Headquarter Activities') or by careful alliance partner selection (Ramachandran, Clark, McIver and Miller, 'Selecting State or Private Joint Venture Partners in Emerging Markets: Impact of Liability of Foreignness and Rule of Law'). The chapter by Beugelsdijk ('Liability of Foreignness and Location-Specific Advantages: Time, Space and Relative Advantage') challenges the notion of LOF itself and argues that there may even be advantages of foreignness in the eyes of consumers. Gaur, Kumar and Sarathy ('Liability of Foreignness and Internationalization of Emerging Market Firms') point out that there is a complex interaction between MNEs' proprietary capabilities, as determined by their home country institutions, and the LOF, leading firms from different backgrounds to experience foreignness differentially. A crude way to capture that interaction would be with an inverse relationship between FSAs and LOF, so that $LOF = LOF_0 - f\,FSA_M$, where $f \geq 0$ is the FSA's fungibility, defined as its ability to suppress the LOF.

Endogenous FSA

A third group of chapters in this volume endogenizes the MNE's resources and capabilities. Several of the chapters look specifically at the way in which home-based locational resources influence MNE's FSA configuration (e.g. Marinova, Child and Marinov, 'Evolution of Firm and Country-Specific Advantages and Disadvantages in the Process of Chinese Firm Internationalization'; Williams, Ridgman and Shi, 'From Stages to Phases, A Theory of Small Developing Country Internationalization' and Sedita, Belussi and Fiscato, 'What Lies Beneath the Internationalization of Firms in a Regional Innovation System?'). Others explore the role of the MNE as an integrator of resources (Singh, Dhillon, Kaulich and Chen, 'Location Determinants of FDI in Sub-Saharan Africa: An Empirical Analysis'). Melén, Nordman, Tolstoy and Sharma ('International Entrepreneurship at the Foreign Market Level: Towards a Network Perspective') argue that network perspectives enable us to analyzse how international entrepreneurs identify and build links between home and host country resources (the former being reflected in the FSA and the latter in the LSA). Extending the view of the 'learning MNE' (Doz, Santos, & Williamson, 2001), Pedersen, Soo and Devinney ('The Importance of Internal and External Knowledge Sourcing and Firm Performance: A Latent Class Estimation') show that MNEs need both internal and external knowledge to compete, and Foss and Santos ('A Knowledge System Approach to the Multinational Company: Conceptual Grounding and Implications for Research') conceptualize the MNE as an efficient governance form linking geographically dispersed complementary resources. Hence, it seems that when the MNE enters a host country, the complementarity of its proprietary assets with local resources would be an important factor. Denoting this complementarity by c, this could be expressed as $FSA_M = FSA_{M0} + c\,LSA_M$. A positive complementarity would imply that the MNE's resources and the local resources are complements (as highlighted by Foss and Santos). On the contrary, if the local resources and the firm's resources are substitutes, it is possible that some of the existing FSA that the firm brings with it into the local market would be redundant. This would lead the 'effective' FSA of the MNE to be lower when it enters the foreign country and sources local resources, suggesting a negative value of c.

REDUCED-FORM SOLUTION[1]

Although a better understanding of these individual determinants of and causal links between LOF, LSA and FSA is important and relevant in itself, they have more significant ramifications in the aggregate. To see this, we can derive the reduced-form solution for FSA based on the earlier assumptions

$$FSA_M = u\,FSA_{M0} + cu(1 - e\,LOF_0)LSA_0 \qquad (3)$$

where $u \equiv 1/(1 - cef\,LSA_0)$. The first term shows how the foreign firm's resource effectiveness is determined by the exogenous part of its FSA (e.g. the resources that it possessed before its entry), but in a scaled form depending on u. If the fit of the MNEs resources with local resources is positive $(c > 0)$, u will be larger than 1, and it will act as a *multiplier* that increases the impact of the ex ante FSA (similar to the fiscal multiplier effect known from macro-economics). This means that a given increase in the MNE's pre-entry FSA results in a much larger increase in the MNE's post-entry FSA. This is because the higher initial FSA enables the firm to better handle the LOF, which in turn improves its ability to utilize LSA, which, in turn, enables it to combine this LSA with its own resources and enhance its FSA. This full-circle feedback loop can be considered a type of indirect absorptive capacity effect for MNE entrants. On the contrary, if the MNE's resources are substitutes for local resources ($c < 0$), u will be smaller than one and the MNE will be relatively weaker after entry. The second term in Eq. (3) demonstrates how the LOF and LSA affect FSA. If local resources are complementary with the firm's proprietary assets, the feedback effect will add something to the FSA, the addition being proportional to the LSA after a correction for the LOF in accessing local resources.

Similar causal patterns can be identified for the LOF and the LSA. Deriving these expressions and substituting these into the relative competitiveness inequality results in

$$\overbrace{FSA_{M0} + c(1 - e\,LOF_0)LSA_0 - FSA_L/u}^{\text{MNE's Relative FSA}} - \overbrace{e(LOF_0 - (FSA_{M0} + cLSA_0)f)LSA_0}^{\text{MNE's Relative LSA}}$$
$$> \underbrace{LOF_0 - f(FSA_{M0} + c\,LSA_0)}_{\text{LOF}} \qquad (4)$$

It is instructive to compare this result with the prediction of the 'classical theory', which was given in Eq. (2). The latter is a special case of the former with $c = e = f = 0$, the difference between the two models resulting exclusively from the endogenization of LOF, LSA, and FSA. The structure of the arguments is also similar: in both cases, we are comparing the FSA-based competitive difference between the MNE and the local firm on one side of the inequality with the LOF on the other. The most important difference is that LSA, which disappeared in the classical model (because both firms had equal access to it) now appears as a potential wedge between the two types of firms. Because local incumbents have an unfair advantage in assessing and exploiting local resources, the MNE may suffer an LSA-related penalty that increases in the degree of resource embeddedness and the LOF, but decreases in the fungibility and strength of the MNE's own FSAs. In any case, it seems that the classical model would lead us to underestimate the importance of the LSAs – a fact that may go some way towards explaining why, as pointed out by Dunning (1998), location has been a 'neglected factor' in IM research.

THE EMERGENCE OF (PRE- AND POST-) EMERGING MARKETS

A sub-theme that underpins many of the contributions in this volume is the potential distinctiveness and importance of emerging markets and the notion that these markets matter to the interaction between LSA, LOF, and FSA described earlier. Emerging markets have LSAs that are inherently different from those of developed markets – in particular, they can offer highly qualified human resources at lower cost, whereas developed markets offer relatively advanced infrastructure, technological knowledge and purchasing power. In a 'flat' world where firms originating from different contexts may source LSAs freely in global markets, this would have little impact on firms FSA configurations – indeed, both emerging and developed market firms should distribute their value chain activities globally to exploit differences in comparative and competitive advantages (Kogut, 1985). However, the LOF may give firms advantages in sourcing the resources in their own 'back yard' (Nachum), implying that emerging market firms should be inherently different from developed market firms in terms of their FSAs (Marinova, Child and Marinov). This has implications, in turn, for the LOF faced by emerging and developed market firms and, hence for the differential internationalization patterns of these firms (Ramachandran, Clark, McIver and Miller). Similar arguments can be made in relation to other locational distinctions, such as small countries (Williams, Ridgman and Shi) and 'pre-emerging' markets with high political risk and limited infrastructure (Singh, Dhillon, Kaulich and Chen). All these studies add to the debate about the relative strengths of the home and host country effects in MNE's resource configurations – a debate which is becoming increasingly important and which perhaps is best illustrated by juxtaposing the two opposite views of Porter (1990) and Doz et al. (2001).

CONCLUSION

If nothing else, this introductory chapter has highlighted the importance of further studying the mechanisms by which LOF, LSA, and FSA are determined and by which they influence one another. In the following pages, the individual chapters take an early but important step in that direction. It is our hope that future work will follow the path set out by this year's volume of *Advances in International Management* and further enlighten us on the paradoxes presented by location in IM research.

NOTE

1. To solve the model, we normalize the incumbent firm's fit with LSA to 0 without loss of generality. Hence, c captures the MNE's fit with local resources, *relative* to that of the incumbent firm. Also, in order for the feedback loop to be stable, we have to impose the restriction that $c\,e\,f < 1/LSA_0$; otherwise we get the unrealistic result that our three endogenous variables will reinforce one another *ad infinitum*.

REFERENCES

Doz, Y., Santos, J., & Williamson, P. (2001). *From global to metanational: How companies win in the knowledge economy*. Boston, MA: Harvard Business School Press.

Dunning, J. H. (1993). *Multinational enterprises and the global economy*. Reading, MA: Addison Wesley.

Dunning, J. H. (1998). Location and the multinational enterprise: A neglected factor? *Journal of International Business Studies*, 29(1), 45–66.

Friedman, T. (2005). *The world is flat: A brief history of the twenty-first century*. New York: Farrar, Straus and Giroux.

Hymer, S. H. (1976). *The international operations of national firms: A study of foreign direct investment*. Cambridge, MA: MIT Press.

Kogut, B. (1985). Designing global strategies: Comparative and competitive value-added chains. *Sloan Management Review*, 27(summer), 15–28.

Porter, M. E. (1990). *The competitive advantage of nations*. New York: Free Press.

Pyndt, J., & Pedersen, T. (2006). *Managing global offshoring strategies. A case approach*. Frederiksberg, Denmark: Copenhagen Business School Press.

Rugman, A. M., & Verbeke, A. (1992). A note on the transnational solution and the transaction cost theory of multinational strategic management. *Journal of International Business Studies*, 23(4), 761–771.

Zaheer, S. (1995). Overcoming the liability of foreignness. *Academy of Management Journal, 38*, 341–363.

THE HOME-BASED ADVANTAGES AND A HIERARCHY OF LOCATION RESOURCES: FOREIGN AND LOCAL FIRMS DEPENDENCY ON LOCATION RESOURCES

Lilach Nachum

ABSTRACT

This chapter seeks to explain cases whereby locationally advantageous countries do not give rise to internationally competitive national firms, as theory suggests. Rather, foreign firms enjoy equal access to the country resources and build strong competitive position based on them. It suggests that location resources vary in terms of the extent to which foreign firms experience liabilities in accessing them, and in the ability of MNE internal networks to provide substitute for them. It introduces a hierarchy of location resources along these two dimensions and suggests that the position of resources in the hierarchy determines variations between foreign and national firms in terms of their ability to access location resources. When critical advantages are based on location resources that are high on the hierarchy, that is, are exclusive to national firms, the latter are likely to take the lead in an industry, establishing strong competitive position based on these superior resources. In contrast, when critical

Dynamics of Globalization: Location-Specific Advantages or Liabilities of Foreignness?
Advances in International Management, Volume 24, 55–83
Copyright © 2011 by Emerald Group Publishing Limited
All rights of reproduction in any form reserved
ISSN: 1571-5027/doi:10.1108/S1571-5027(2011)0000024010

*advantages are based on location resources which foreign firms can access
on similar terms to those of national firms, or else can rely on the MNE
network for their provision, the leading firms in an industry are likely to
originate in multiple countries and no apparent home country effect will
be observed. This chapter outlines the implications of the findings for
MNE location strategies and for policy makers.*

INTRODUCTION

A fundamental assumption that has been driving the theory of MNE
competitive advantages is that these advantages are, in some sense, shaped
by the immediate environment in which MNEs operate (Rosenzweig &
Singh, 1991), and that the home environment is the foremost among them.
Porter (1990) argued that the home environment is critical in shaping the
nature and type of the competitive advantages of firms. This explains why
the leading firms in many industries emerge from one or a few countries.
Chandler (1990) assigned the different organizational forms, structures and
practices embraced by firms to the historical developments of the legal,
social and political characteristics of their home environments. Empirical
studies have illustrated that the strategic behaviour and competitive
advantages of firms reflect specific characteristics of their home countries
(e.g. Hitt, Dacin, Tyler, & Park, 1997; Gedajlovic & Shapiro, 1998; Thomas &
Waring, 1999; Wan & Hoskisson, 2003; Makino, Isobe, & Chan, 2004;
Gugler & Guillen, 2010).

Underlying this association between the competitive advantages of firms
and their home country characteristics is the assumption that national firms
enjoy favourable access to the resources of their home countries, which is
denied of foreign firms investing there (Hymer, 1960). A number of studies
have shown that the ability of firms to tap into foreign country resources is
inferior to that of national firms (Solvell, Zander, & Porter, 1991; Thomas &
Waring, 1999; Nachum, 2000). Hu (1992) argued that if a resource could be
accessed via investment in a country, it would not form a basis for an
exclusive advantage to national firms because the possibility of accessing it
would be equally available to all firms.

Casual observations, however, are not always consistent with these theoretical arguments and empirical findings. In some cases, the characteristics of
firms bear no relation to the characteristics of their home countries. Firms
originating in countries that do not have favourable characteristics, what Doz,

Santos, and Williamson (2001) named 'companies born in the wrong place' (p. 53), sometimes emerge as highly competitive international players, a position they develop based on resources and knowledge available elsewhere. For example, since their origin at the turn of the 20th century, the world's largest privately owned oil companies developed by exploiting oil fields overseas, not in their home countries (Chandler, 1990). In other cases, countries with favourable economic and institutional environment attract foreign investors, who become the main beneficiaries of these advantages, rather than facilitate the development of competitive national firms. The British and the United States car industries suggest an example of such developments (Whisler, 1999). In yet other cases, firms develop without favourable home conditions, based on their ability to draw on sources of learning and demand elsewhere. The Indian software industry is a case in point (Arora & Gambardella, 2005).

Such examples suggest that under certain circumstances, the competitive advantages of firms are dissociated from the characteristics of their home country. They also imply that there are limits to the exclusive access of firms to their home country resources, which underlies the link that has been assumed to exist between the characteristics of firms and those of their home countries.

These cases have received limited research attention. Doz et al. (2001) is perhaps the most elaborated treatment of such dissociations between the characteristics of firms and those of their home countries, but they sought to provide normative prescriptions on how to 'break free of geography' (p. 29) and become meta-nationals, rather than a theoretical understanding of the causes of such outcomes. As a result, we know little on the interaction of firms with their home environments and we are unable to explain the varying outcomes in relation to the impact of home countries on the competitive advantages of firms and the resulting country patterns in international competition. In this study I seek to start filling this gap by introducing a hierarchy of location resources that vary in terms of their importance for firms' advantages, as well as in terms of the access that foreign firms have to these resources.

Building on resource dependency theory (Pfeffer & Salancik, 1978), and extending it to the context of the MNE, I suggest that there is an inherent variation in foreign firms' ability to access different local resources in foreign countries and to employ them as the basis for their firm-specific advantages. I attribute this variation to differences in the strength of the liabilities of foreignness (Zaheer, 1995) and the provision of the MNE internal networks (Nohria & Ghoshal, 1997), and suggest that these are experienced to varying degrees in relation to different location resources.

I empirically test these ideas with reference to the wholesale insurance industry in London. London's local resources for insurance activities – its pool of employees, support services and the cluster of local knowledge and expertise – are widely regarded superior to those elsewhere (Carter & Falush, 1998; Heracleous & Barrett, 2001; IFSL, 2004), and access to these resources is recognized as critical for success (London Business School, 1995). Indeed, London is the leading market for internationally traded insurance and reinsurance services, accounting for more than two-thirds of the world's total turnover (Sigma, 2002). This position, however, is based on foreign ownership, with more than three quarters of the companies operating in London foreign-owned (IFSL, 2004). London's superior location resources do not provide basis for British companies in London and elsewhere, where firms originating from other countries (e.g. Switzerland and Germany) maintain the lead.[1] In the late 1990s, British companies accounted for only 6 and 8 of the world's top 100 insurance and reinsurance companies respectively (Sigma, 2002).

With reference to this research setting, I address the questions why, given the favourable economic and institutional conditions of London for insurance activities, British firms are not the first ones to benefit from them? What is the basis for the superior performance of foreign insurance firms in London and elsewhere? Comparative analyses of foreign and local firms are employed to examine differences associated with nationality across varying location resources, using local firms as a means of isolating those attributes that apply to all firms from those that are distinctive to foreign firms. Based on the findings I introduce a hierarchy of location resources that vary in terms of their importance as bases for home-based advantages. I argue that the position of a resource in this hierarchy determines whether national or foreign firms would maintain the lead in an industry. From this analysis I draw some general lessons regarding the circumstances that support a home-based advantage and those that fail to do so.

Gaining a better understanding of the association (or lack thereof) between the resources of firms and those of their home countries has important implications for theory and practice. Such an understanding would contribute to the debate regarding the role of home countries in shaping the advantages of MNEs and their strategic choices (Hitt et al., 1997; Thomas & Waring, 1999; Doz et al., 2001; Makino et al., 2004). Underlying this debate is a fundamental question regarding the sources of MNE advantages, whether in product-market attributes and global competition or in the characteristics of their home countries (Johns, 2006; Adegbesan, 2009). The study contributes also to the understanding of the role of location resources in shaping firm resources, an understanding that is of particular importance in relation to MNEs, because the multiple environments in which they operate assign this issue additional complexity and increase its importance as a source of competitive advantage.

For MNEs, the possibility to tap into foreign country resources and develop capabilities based on them widens the scope for foreign investment. It also provides a rationale for transferring high value-added activities overseas, those on which the core advantages of firms may depend, including R&D functions (Bas & Sierra, 2002) and the headquarters themselves (Forsgren, Holm, & Johanson, 1995; Birkinshaw, Braunerhjelm, Holm, & Terjesen, 2006). At the same time, if firms do not always have privileged access to their home country resources, there are limits to the exclusive advantages that these resources provide them, a lesson that should be explicitly incorporated in firms' strategies.

RESOURCE DEPENDENCY THEORY AND THE MNE: THE IMPACT OF FOREIGNNESS AND THE MNE INTERNAL NETWORK

The essence of resource dependency theory is that organizations are not self-sufficient and hence depend on their environments for the acquisition of necessary resources (Pfeffer & Salancik, 1978). This dependency implies that the context in which organizations are embedded determines their strategic behaviour and performance outcome.

I build on this notion of dependency and extend it to the context of the MNE, in two directions. First, I acknowledge variation in firms' dependency on their environment that is associated with nationality. Pfeffer and Salancik (1978) have recognized the role of strategic choices in the relationships between organizations and their environment that in turn leads to variation across organizations in terms of their dependency on the environment. I extend this idea, and argue that nationality of ownership affects this variation, and hence foreign and local firms differ in terms of their dependency on the environment. These differences originate in two distinctive attributes of MNEs. One is the liability of foreignness (LOF) (Zaheer, 1995) that inhibits the ability of foreign affiliates to draw on resources in foreign environments; the other is the MNE internal network (Nohria & Ghoshal, 1997) that diminishes their need for some external resources by providing alternative sources for their acquisition. Hence, the same environmental resources would differentially affect foreign and local firms.

The ability to establish effective mechanisms for the acquisition of resources is a major factor that determines the dependency of organizations on their environments (Pfeffer & Salancik, 1978). This requires organizations to identify important resource providers in the environment and to manage their relationships with them. The difficulties experienced by foreign affiliates in developing relationships with other organizations in foreign environments have been acknowledged already by Hymer (1960). Recent research has illustrated greater difficulties of foreign affiliates in accessing local customers and suppliers, the labour market and the local information network, compared with those confronted by local firms (Zaheer, 1995; Zaheer & Mosakowski, 1997; Mezias, 2002; Miller & Parkhe 2002; Hau, 2002). Foreign ownership also raises specific challenges in establishing legitimacy. The MNE legitimacy theory (Kostova & Zaheer, 1999) is explicit regarding the difficulties that foreign affiliates confront being accepted by other organizations as legitimate. As a result, foreign affiliates are likely to be less able to draw on the resources in foreign environments than local firms in the same environment and be less dependent on it for resource acquisition.

The second distinctive attribute of foreign affiliates that affects their dependency on the environment originates in them being part of an international network (Nohria & Ghoshal, 1997). The availability of alternative sources from which a needed resource can be obtained are major determinants of organizations' self-sufficiency and their dependency on their environment (Pfeffer & Salancik, 1978). Compared with local firms, foreign affiliates have alternative sources of resources, via the MNE internal network (Rosenzweig & Singh, 1991), and hence are more self-sufficient. This is consistent with current thinking in international management that conceptualizes the MNE as a network of capital, product and knowledge transactions among sub-units located in different countries (Gupta & Govindarajan, 2000).

It should be noted that the two distinctive attributes of the MNE that affect their resource dependency – the LOF and the MNE internal network – differentially distinguish them from local firms. The LOF originates in nationality itself and is by definition an attribute that MNEs have in relation to all local firms. The internal network of the organization of which they are part is an attribute that distinguishes them only from single unit local firms. Other local firms might be part of a multi-unit organization that is entirely domestic, such as chains and some domestic business groups. Others may themselves be MNEs. The ability to draw on the internal network as an alternative source of resources is shared with these local firms.

These two distinctive attributes of MNEs – the constraining effect of the LOF and the substituting effect of the MNE internal networks – imply that foreign and local firms operating in the same environment would differ in terms of their dependency on that environment. The same set of environmental resources would have different values for them.

The second extension I introduce to the resource dependency theory is the explicit recognition of varying levels of dependency on different environmental resources. Building on Pfeffer and Salancik's (1978) conceptualization of the multi-dimensional nature of the environment, I conceptualize the environment as composed of a complex combination of resources, including the labour market, governmental authorities, suppliers and customers. I suggest that foreign affiliates are dependent on these resources to varying degrees because the constraining impact of the LOF and the substituting effect of the MNE network vary across them.

A major force driving the LOF is the inferior ability of foreign affiliates to grasp local norms of behaviour, rooted in culture and tradition whose understanding requires deep understanding of the local environment. Resources vary in their cultural and local contents and the need for local knowledge to access them. For example, foreign firms often stand at a considerable disadvantage in accessing local information and knowledge (Zaheer, 1995; Zaheer & Mosakowski, 1997), since this requires deep levels of local embeddedness and understanding, developed over long time, and may never be fully understood by foreigners. In contrast, foreign firms are on a more equal footing with local firms in accessing general services provided on the market, as this usually does not require deep familiarity with the locality as a condition of participation. Government policies, while denying foreign firms access to certain resources, treat them equally to local firms with respect to others, introducing additional variation across resources in the strength of the LOF.

Resources vary also in terms of their location specificity and mobility within the MNE, representing variations of transferring these assets across cultural and institutional contexts, which constrain the potential advantages they hold in settings different from those in which they were developed (Rugman & Verbeke, 2001). Such variation may also arise as a result of resource fungibility and the inability to split them geographically without them losing their value (Teece, 1998). These difficulties introduce variation across resources in the extent to which the MNE internal network serves as an alternative source for them. Location-specific resources often lose their value outside a particular context, so the MNE internal network becomes a weak, if any, alternative for their acquisition (Hu, 1992). Further, the MNE network is an alternative source only to the extent that the resource in question is mobile and can be transferred to another location. For example, the MNE internal network might be used as (partially at least) source of employees, by employing expatriates (Gong, 2003). Likewise, foreign affiliates often use the MNE network as a source of capital (Lessard, 1979). However, the MNE internal network usually cannot provide an alternative to local customers. It may also be of limited value as a substitute for the local network of information. Certain resources are subject to government regulations and cannot be transferred freely across borders, whereas others are free from such constraints.

Thus, I expect the dependency of foreign affiliates on local resources to vary, reflecting variation in the strength of the LOF and the substituting effect of the MNE internal network. Foreign affiliates will display greater similarity to local firms in their dependency on local resources where the LOF is weak and where the MNE internal network does not provide an effective alternative source. In the following sections, I seek to verify these predictions with reference to foreign and local firms in the London insurance market.

The selection of specific environmental resources is based on a definition of the portion of this universe that is relevant for the analysis of the dependency of organizations on their environments (Castrogiovanni, 1991). I consider the immediate environment as the relevant one because it exercises important influences on the organizational characteristics and strategic behaviour that are of interest here. The environment to be studied thus includes the set of individuals and organizations with whom an organization directly interacts.[2] I add to this space-less definition a geographic aspect, and confine the study environment to London.

The specific location resources for the analyses were selected based on two criteria. One, that they are likely to affect the strategic behaviour and competitive performance of insurance firms. Second, active action is required to turn the location resources into firm-specific resources. Location resources that cannot be manipulated by strategic actions of firms (e.g. the regulatory system, certain types of infrastructure) were excluded because they cannot provide basis for firm-specific resources. The actual selection was derived from an intensive study of the insurance industry and the London insurance market, which included extensive consultation with industry analysts and representatives of the leading institutions in this market, supplemented by a comprehensive study of a variety of secondary sources. I focus the analysis on labour, services, capital, consumers and knowledge which I regard as representing the major location resources appropriate for the purpose of this study.

METHODOLOGY

The Data

The study's population was drawn from the FAME-DVD database and was defined based on a combination of geographic and industrial criteria, to include all firms whose main activities are in wholesale insurance and are located in what is known as 'the London insurance market' (Carter & Falush, 1998), the area corresponding to the EC postal code area of Central London, which is part of the City of London. The FAME-DVD database lists 1.8 million public and private UK firms registered in the United Kingdom and is recognized as a most comprehensive listing of UK firms. The 472 firms met these criteria and form the study's population. The narrow geographic scope controls for differences between foreign and local firms that may arise as a result of different location preferences.

The sample population was approached by means of mailed questionnaire, in which I inquired about the utilization of local resources and their perceived value as bases of a firm's resources. The questionnaire also included a set of questions directed to foreign affiliates in which they were asked about the nature and magnitude of the resources transferred between the London office and the headquarters. Before mailing the questionnaire, it was piloted on a large number of industry analysts including representatives of all the major organizations in the London insurance market and firms. This extensive piloting led to a number of major revisions until the final version was reached. The questionnaire was addressed to the top management as the people with the ultimate responsibility for aspects of strategic behaviour that are of interest here.

To partially address the common method variance problem (Avolio, Yammarino & Bass, 1991), I asked that questions related to the dependent and independent variables will be answered by different people within the organization. In addition, I tested whether the relationships among the variables of interest exist after the common method variance has been statistically controlled. Following Podsakoff and Organ (1986), I conducted factor analysis on all the variables in the study. If the common method variance were a problem, a single factor would emerge with most of the covariance in the independent and dependent variables. This analysis yielded five factors with eigenvalues greater than one, with the first one explaining only 21.8% of the variance, suggesting that the common method variance is not a problem in the dataset. These results are consistent with expectations, because the type of data employed, which although collected directly from firms is based mostly on hard data, is less sensitive to the common method variance problem. Respondents' opinions – the type of data that is particularly sensitive to this problem – are used to operationalize only a few of the constructs tested, all of whom are independent variables.

After a number of follow-ups, by mail and telephone (Roscoe, Lang, & Sheth, 1975; Heberlein & Baumgartner, 1978; Cycyota & Harrison, 2002), 163 firms returned complete, useable questionnaires (a 34.5% response rate). Tests of difference between respondents and non-respondents in terms of a number of characteristics for which data are available from secondary sources, and were considered to be of relevance for this research, show no significant differences at the 0.05 level or higher. To examine possible differences between respondents to successive waves of mailings (Armstrong & Overton, 1977), I split the sample into three categories according to the number of follow-ups from the initial mailing until the receipt of the returned questionnaire. ANOVA test indicated no statistically significant differences ($p < .05$ or higher) in the mean responses for all the included variables. The sample contains 89 foreign affiliates and 74 British-owned firms. This breakdown does not mirror the population, probably because establishments that are part of larger corporations tend to have lower response rates (Tomaskovic-Devey & Leiter, 1994).

The data collection took place during 2000–2001. To examine the strategic stability of the industry during the period studied (Fiegenbaum & Thomas, 1990), I tested the movement of sales, capital intensity, debt and market value over a period of three years prior and after the data collection. None of these tests showed that the period in which the data were collected was statistically different, removing a concern that it represents an unusual period in the life of the industry.

The Models

To examine the differences between foreign and local firms in terms of their resource dependency, and to test for dependency variation across resources, I construct two models that link performance as the dependent variable with dependency on London's resources as the independent variables. The link with performance is based on the assumption that the contribution of a resource in question to competitive performance is indicative of a firm's dependency. This link with performance is consistent with Pfeffer and Salancik's notion of the criticality of a resource for an organization as a major factor determining their dependency on resources. The two models correspond to the testing of the impact of foreignness and multi-nationality, respectively. The models are of the following form:

(1) Foreignness model: $Y_i = \beta_0 + \beta_1 F_i + \beta_2 LR_i + (\beta_3 F_i * LR_i) + \lambda_i + \varepsilon_i$
(2) Multi-nationality model: $Y_i = \beta_0 + \beta_1 M_i + \beta_2 LR_i + (\beta_3 M_i * LR_i) + \lambda_i + \varepsilon_i$

where Y_i stands for performance of firm i; LR_i a vector of local location resources used by firm i; F_i and M_i represent, respectively the foreignness dummy and the measures of MNE internal transfer in models 1 and 2; λ_i a vector of control variables; ε_i a firm-specific random disturbance that is attributable to errors associated with distortions resulting from an elimination of some important resources, and firm-specific idiosyncrasies. The errors are assumed to follow the standard normal distribution.

The Dependent Variable: Performance

The combined ratio, the most commonly used indicator of performance of insurance firms by both practitioners and academics (Fiegenbaum & Thomas, 1990; Sigma, 2001) is used to measure performance. It is defined as

$$\frac{\text{Incurred losses} + \text{loss adjustment expenses} + \text{underwriting expenses} + \text{dividend}}{\text{Net premium written}}$$

This performance measure is particularly suitable for a comparison of foreign and local firms because it is free of potential biases caused by profit transfer within MNEs. The Kolmogorov–Smirnov test with a Lilliefors significance test for normality shows that the dependent variable is not normally distributed; hence I take the natural logarithm.

The Independent Variables

Dependency on Local Resources. Pfeffer and Salancik (1978) suggest that dependency can be measured by assessing the proportion of the resource in question in the total inputs accounted for by a particular exchange. This is a well-established indicator of dependency in empirical testing of the resource dependency theory (Salancik, 1979; Pfeffer & Davis-Blake, 1987). I follow this approach and operationalize the dependency of firms on local resources by measuring the shares of resources employed locally. For some resources, however, such an operation is not appropriate, and I adopt other measures, as explained below.

Employees – The share of employees recruited locally may not be meaningful for the purpose of the comparison of foreign and local firms, because local firms rely mostly on the local labour market. Instead, I use pay levels as they reflect variations in employees' knowledge and education, arguably most important determinants of the resources employees bring to organizations (Pfeffer & Davis-Blake, 1987).

Services – The share of services purchased locally, also including claims, premiums and reinsurance processed in London ($\alpha = .822$).

Customers – The share of revenues generated locally.

Capital – The share of capital raised in the United Kingdom in total capital employed, measured separately for debt and equity ($\alpha = .794$).

Knowledge – measured in two ways:

(1) The intensity of linkages with other firms in the London market, distinguishing between own industry and related industries, measured by the frequency of the interaction on a scale from 1 (minimal) to 5 (high) ($\alpha = .738$). The ability to establish local links and become an insider to the local information network in London has been recognized as crucially important in generating and maintaining business (Thrift, 1994; Heracleous & Barrett, 2001). This measure is indicative of local embeddedness, a condition for becoming part of the local network of information which provides access to local knowledge.

(2) The share of partners based in London sharing a slip. The common practice for insurance and re-insurance firms is to place risks with two or more insurers or re-insurers who subscribe to a 'slip'. The leading underwriter indicates on the slip the premium, the policy terms, and the share of the risk she will accept. Each following underwriter in turn notes his share on the slip (Carter & Falush, 1998). I combined these values into a single index as the sum of shares weighted by the number of partners.

I create a single measure of local knowledge as the average of the standardized values of the two measures.

Nationality Variables

1. Foreignness – a dummy variable that gets the value 1 if the firm in question is foreign; 0 if it is local.

2. MNE internal network. This measure is based on responses to two questions in relation to each of the resources included:
   (a) To what extent do you regard the MNE internal network as an alternative to local resources (1 – not at all; 5 – complete substitute)
   (b) Please assess the intensity of resource transfer from the parent company and other sub-units of your organization to your London affiliate (1 – none; 5 – high).

The two measures were combined for each resource, with α Cronbach exceeding the recommended .70 cut-off point in all cases.

Control Variables

1. Size, as substantial research shows that it affects the performance of insurance firms (Fiegenbaum & Thomas, 1990; Cummins & Santomero, 1999; Kielholz, 2000). Number of employees in the London office is used to measure size. Employees are the major source of value creation of insurance firms and their numbers is thus a proper indicator of the magnitude of their activity.
2. Industrial affiliation. Dummy variables for different insurance activities: insurance and reinsurance companies, brokers, underwriters, others. These variables control for possible industrial variation in terms of the value of specific location resources for performance and the strategic options available for firms in different insurance activities to utilize them (Webb & Pettigrew, 1999). They also partially account for unobserved heterogeneity, arising as a result of differences in omitted variables that might affect both independent and dependent variables. These industry dummies were not significant in the statistical analyses and their inclusion did not change the results, so they are not reported in the analyses that follow. I do not explicitly correct for endogeniety or self-selection bias, because nationality is pre-determined, diminishing the possibility of self-selection.

Table 1 summarizes the variables included in the analysis, descriptive statistics and correlation coefficients. The latter are usually low (for the most part well below .5), enabling one not to be concerned about correlation in the dataset. Since low correlations do not exclude the possibility of multi-collinearity, I also calculated the VIFs and found that with the exception of interaction terms and their components, which do not raise a concern, the VIFs are below the suggested cut-off point of 10.

Table 1. The Explanatory Variables Included in the Model, Descriptive Statistics and Correlation Coefficients.

Constructs	Descriptive Statistics		Correlation Coefficients (Pearson Correlations)										
	Mean	Standard Deviation	1	2	3	4	5	6	7	8	9	10	11
Local resources													
1. Employees	47,997	28,461	1										
2. Services	93.513	14.026	.264 / .076	1									
3. Clients	69.403	35.132	-.050 / .698	-.028 / .783	1								
4. Capital	36.872	84.258	-.100 / .467	-.041 / .715	.027 / .782	1							
5. Knowledge	.275	.141	.358** / .008	.137 / .218	.113 / .246	.060 / .554	1						
Nationality variables: foreignness; MNE internal network[a]													
6. Foreignness	1.565	.497	.214 / .090	.059 / .565	.096 / .277	.115 / .224	-.002 / .980	1					
7. Employees	1.980	1.593	.439** / .060	.059 / .689	.033 / .814	-.216 / .154	.029 / .857	-.171 / .212	1				
8. Services	2.050	2.257	-.323 / .177	.058 / .694	.133 / .334	-.221 / .145	-.003 / .987	-.177 / .195	.421** / .000	1			
9. Clients	3.250	1.756	-.291 / .227	.113 / .446	.165 / .228	-.221 / .144	-.068 / .667	-.176 / .198	.356* / .015	.436** / .015	1		
10. Capital	3.750	2.171	-.325 / .175	.005 / .973	.139 / .310	-.221 / .144	-.005 / .974	-.174 / .205	.411* / .080	.376* / .023	.529** / .000	1	
11. Knowledge	3.517	4.593	.365 / .108	.168 / .350	.371 / .227	.067 / .695	-.449* / .089	.412* / .026	.441** / .009	.319 / .136	.314 / .126	.133 / .431	1
Control variables[b]													
12. Size	137.038	253.068	-.269* / .031	.199* / .050	.074 / .405	.067 / .480	.077 / .431	-.007 / .937	.212 / .121	.111 / .419	.021 / .877	.068 / .620	.066 / .698

**Correlation is significant at the 0.01 level (2-tailed).
*Correlation is significant at the 0.05 level (2-tailed).
[a]Foreign sample only.
[b]Industry dummy variables are not reported.

STATISTICAL ANALYSIS

The testing of the impact of foreignness and multi-nationality I based on the models constructed above. To test the impact of foreignness on resource dependency and its variation across different resources, I use the entire sample, combining both British and foreign firms, and add the foreignness interaction variables (Table 2). The test of the moderating effect of MNE internal transfers is based only on the foreign sample, with the interaction variables measuring the impact of the MNE network (Table 3). Significant signs of the interaction variables imply that foreignness and MNE transfers affect the link between performance and dependency on the local resource in question (Aiken & West, 1991). Moderated multiple regression, a common

Table 2. Moderated Regression Analyses Connecting Performance and Resource Dependency: The Impact of Foriegness.

(Standardized Coefficients) DV: Performance Whole Sample (Foreign and British Firms)			
Constructs	Model I	Model II	Model III
Local resources			
Employees	$.36(2.55)^{**}$	$.19(1.77)^{*}$	$.30(.62)$
Services	$.35(1.49)^{\dagger}$	$.14(1.34)$	$.19(.47)$
Clients	$.403(2.03)^{*}$	$-.127(-1.28)$	$-.14(-.28)$
Capital	$.409(2.21)^{**}$	$.438(2.11)^{*}$	$.12(.11)$
Knowledge	$.679(3.74)^{***}$	$.595(3.33)^{**}$	$.41(2.53)^{**}$
Foreignness	–	$.395(2.93)^{**}$	$.24(1.43)$
Employees × foreignness	–	–	$-.53(-2.06)^{**}$
Services × foreignness	–	–	$-.08(-.15)$
Clients × foreignness	–	–	$.37(2.25)^{*}$
Capital × foreignness	–	–	$-.44(-2.50)^{**}$
Knowledge × foreignness	–	–	$.25(1.84)^{\dagger}$
Control variables[a]			
Size	$.59(4.64)^{***}$	$.59(4.66)^{***}$	$.599(3.99)^{***}$
Constant	$-87.19(-.47)$	$-141.69(-.72)$	$-345.66(-.44)$
Adjusted R^2	$.70$	$.73$	$.80$
ΔR^2		$.03$	$.06^{**}$
F statistics	16.36^{***}	14.08^{***}	18.40^{***}

$^{***} p<.001;\ ^{**}p<.01;\ ^{*}p<.05;\ ^{\dagger}p<.10$

$N=163.$

[a]Industry dummies were insignificant and their inclusion did not change the results. Hence they were excluded from the analyses.

Table 3. Moderated Regression Analyses Connecting Performance and Resource Dependency: The Impact of the MNE Network.

(Standardized Coefficients) DV: Performance Foreign Sample			
Constructs	Model I	Model II	Model III
Local resources			
Employees	.28(2.16)*	.26(1.85)*	.26(1.64)[†]
Services	.03(.31)	.04(.36)	.03(.19)
Clients	−.06(−.50)	−.07(−.58)	−.03(−.19)
Capital	−.06(−.56)	−.06(−.49)	−.08(.76)
Knowledge	.58(2.50)**	.37(1.57)†	−.22(1.09)
Resources obtained via the MNE network			
Employees	–	.25(.82)	.27(.83)
Services	–	−.15(−.35)	−.19(−.35)
Clients	–	−.26(−.66)	−.18(−.36)
Capital	–	.19(.85)	.18(.75)
Knowledge	–	.22(1.87)†	.14(.80)
Interaction variables			
Employees × MNE network employees	–	–	.42(2.16)**
Services × MNE network services	–	–	.04(.14)
Clients × MNE network clients (i.e. referrals)	–	–	−.08(−.27)
Capital × MNE network capital	–	–	.36(2.45)**
Knowledge × MNE network knowledge	–	–	.50(2.85)**
Control variables[a]			
Size	.47(2.76)**	.44(3.31)**	.43(3.06)**
Constant	443.67(2.40)**	290.42(1.19)	295.60(.87)
Adjusted R^2	.35	.39	.49
ΔR^2		.04*	.10**
F statistics	5.95*	6.01*	7.16**

***$p<.001$; **$p<.01$; *$p<.05$; †$p<.10$
$N=89$.
[a]Industry dummies were insignificant and their inclusion did not change the results. Hence they were excluded from the analyses.

statistical technique for estimating interaction effects, is used for this analysis.

The analyses show that foreign and local firms exhibit different levels of dependency on the same location resources. They also substantiate the variation anticipated across resources, in a manner that reflects the strength of the LOF and the effect of the MNE network. It is possible to distinguish between four types of resources based on these results. The first are those where the interaction terms with foreignness and MNE network (Tables 2 and 3 respectively) are not significant in any of the analyses, implying no differences between foreign and local firms in terms of the value of the resource in question for performance. Local services represent this type of resources.

I interpret these findings as indicating that foreign firms do not experience LOF in accessing these resources locally, and depend on them just as local firms do. Insurance firms are typically organized in a vertically disinte-grated structure and rely on external providers for the provision of insurance related services such as actuarial, underwriting, claims handling and the like (Cummins & Santomero, 1999). Hence, their ability to access service providers of high quality is an important advantage. These relationships are often market-based and as such do not usually require deep local embeddedness and familiarity where foreign affiliates are likely to experience difficulties. Further, London's providers are known for the quality of their services (IFSL, 2003), reducing the incentive to rely on the MNE network for the provision of such services.

The second group represents resources that are significant in both analyses, i.e., the interaction terms of local resources with foreignness and MNE resources are significant (Tables 2 and 3). These results indicate that foreignness introduces difficulties in accessing these resources, such that they differ in terms of their value for the performance of foreign and local firms. Affiliates appear to turn to the MNE network to mitigate their inferior access to these local resources. Employees and capital belong to this category.

The significant negative sign of the interaction variable for employees in the analyses of the whole sample (Table 2) implies that local firms are dependent on the local labour market to a greater degree than foreign firms do, suggesting that foreign affiliates experience liabilities in accessing the local labour pool. Indeed, in the London insurance market, professionals are often recruited through personal networks, school and family ties, what is known as 'the British old boy network' (McDowell, 1997). As an IT director interviewed for the Heracleous and Barrett (2001) study of London's insurance firms put it: 'It's a club, their whole way of doing business is all about contacts, trust and relationships' (p. 763). It has been extremely difficult for foreigners to enter into these cycles and be able to attract employees of significant quality (Thrift, 1994). Another source of difficulties confronted by foreign affiliates is that employees, particularly those sought for top positions, often prefer HQs employment, which puts them at the centre of decision-making and provides a career path open to the highest levels of the company (Jones & Galvez-Munoz, 2002).

The significant sign of the interaction term of the MNE network (Table 3) indicates that foreign affiliates rely on labour transferred internally within the MNE, perhaps as a way to compensate for their liabilities in accessing the local labour market. This is consistent with previous research that has shown that employment of expatriates is a major means of overcoming difficulties in accessing labour locally (Gong, 2003).

Capital is the second resource that is highly significant in both analyses, in interaction with the foreignness dummy and the MNE network variable, suggesting that London's affiliates experience liabilities in raising capital locally and rely on the MNE network for the provision of this resource. Already Hymer (1960) noted that the capital market discriminates among borrowers of equal worth according to their nationality. Researchers in finance have recognized the existence of the 'home bias' phenomenon, that is, the tendency of investors to under-invest in foreign firms, and the subsequent difficulties of firms to raise capital in foreign countries (Bradshaw, Bushee, & Miller, 2004). The negative sign of the interaction term in the analysis of the whole sample (Table 2), which indicates that local firms are dependent on capital raised locally to a greater degree than foreign affiliates, is indicative of the prevalence of this phenomenon in London. Consistent with the conceptualization of the MNE as a network of capital, foreign affiliates rely on the MNE as a source of capital (Lessard, 1979), as the results in Table 3 suggest. These highly significant findings are interesting in that they suggest that capital is an important resource that links sub-units of MNEs and that these internal transfers are critical determinants of affiliates' performance. The neglect of capital in recent discussions of internal MNE interactions, which focus on knowledge transfers, may overlook an important aspect of these interactions.

The third type of resources are those that show only the foreignness effect, to which clients is an example (although the results are not statistically strong) (Table 2). The significant result of the interaction term of clients with the foreignness dummy suggests significant differences between local and foreign firms in terms of the performance implications of dependency on local clients. The negative sign is indicative of LOF in accessing local customers. An important source of the LOF, which was highlighted by Hymer (1960) and in many discussions since then (Zaheer, 1995), is the preference of local customers for local firms, with whom they have long established relationships and who are usually perceived as having more stable links to their home country. Hence, local firms are likely to have a larger local customer base than foreign firms in the same location (Zaheer, 1995). This preference might be particularly apparent in the high-risk insurance industry, where local embeddedness is often perceived as a guarantee for the payment of claims (Zaheer & Venkatraman, 1995).

Knowledge represents a fourth type of resource, whereby only the effect of the MNE network is significant (Table 3). The interaction term for local knowledge is hardly significant in the analysis of the whole sample (Table 2), suggesting small differences between foreign and local firms in terms of their dependency on local knowledge. These findings are at variance with discussions that emphasize the liabilities of foreign affiliates in accessing local knowledge (Zaheer, 1995; Zaheer & Mosakowski, 1997). This can probably be reconciled by acknowledging the type of knowledge that is of value in the setting studied here, which is mostly knowledge of global markets. The transfer of knowledge within MNEs is well recognized as a major means of linking geographically dispersed sub-units and facilitating the transmission of firm-specific, tacit sources of knowledge worldwide (Gupta & Govindarajan, 2000). The findings perhaps suggest that in the globally integrated environment of the London insurance market, the MNE internal network can provide the requisite knowledge because what counts is knowledge of global markets. These findings should be evaluated in light of the recognition of the importance of advanced knowledge base for insurance firms (Cummins & Santomero, 1999; Webb & Pettigrew, 1999). The acquisition and development of knowledge resources is critical for the survival and competitive success of these firms (Thrift, 1994).

Robustness Tests

I conducted several tests to validate the findings (the complete results are available upon request). First, I employ different measures of performance. In insurance, there is always a time-lag between the payment of premiums and the settlement of claims, leaving insurance companies with funds for investment (Fiegenbaum & Thomas, 1990). The income of these investments forms an important part of firms' overall financial performance, and was estimated to account for 15–20% of the total income of insurance firms in the G7 countries (Sigma, 2001). Since this income does not capture the operating performance that is of interest here, it was judged to be a less appropriate indicator of performance than the one used in the main analyses. To examine whether the exclusion of this component affects the results, I conduct the analyses with marginal profitability as the dependent variable. Foreign affiliates were asked to report their operating profits before any transfers to the parent company or other sub-units of their

organization. Although there are differences in the results, the overall
conclusions did not change with this performance measure.

The performance measure used in the previous analyses could convey an
inaccurate picture also due to difficulties in isolating the performance of
foreign affiliates from that of the rest of the MNE (Dess & Robinson, 1984).
To examine this possible effect, I validate the findings based on a self-reported
measure of performance. Respondents were asked to evaluate the performance of their firm relative to other firms in the London market on a five-
point scale from 5 (like the top 20%) to 1 (like the lowest 20%). The general
conclusions continue to hold with this subjective measure of performance.

DISCUSSION AND EXTENSION

In Fig. 1, I suggest how the four types of location resources identified in the
previous analyses affect the extent and nature of the differences between

		(1)	(2)
	High	*Strong home-based advantage –* National firms maintain the lead in an industry; limited investment flowing to the country [Employees, Capital]	*Moderate home-based advantage –* Leadership likely distributed across MNEs of several nationalities; large differences between foreign/local firms [Clients]
	Low	(3) *No (weak) home-based advantage –* Local and foreign firms share the lead; similarity between local/foreign firms [Services]	(4) *No (weak) home-based advantage-* foreign firms take the lead; weak local firms [Knowledge]
		Low	**High**
		Internal MNE transferability	

Impact of foreignness (vertical axis label)

Fig. 1. Resource Hierarchy and Variation of the Home-Based Advantages [Type of Resources as Base of Advantages].

foreign and local firms and subsequently the strength of the home-based advantages.

Box 1 describes situations whereby foreignness limits access to the location resources that are critical for performance, and the possibility to draw on internal MNE transfers is limited. This box corresponds to situations whereby the advantages of resources of group 2 identified above, for which employees and capital are examples, are important base of competitive advantage. In such situations, national firms are likely to become the dominant global leaders in an industry.

Box 2 corresponds to situations where although the LOF is strong, MNEs can rely on internal MNE transfer as the basis for their competitive position. This is the case when the resources corresponding to group 3, for which clients are an example, are critical for competitive advantage. It is likely that in such cases the dominant MNEs in an industry will emerge from a number of countries and there will be moderate country patterns in international competition. Foreign and local firms operating in the same environment will exhibit considerable differences, as they develop their competitive advantages based on different resources. The advantages of local firms are likely to reflect their home-country resources, to which they enjoy exclusive access, whereas foreign affiliates will base their advantages on resources transferred internally within the MNE.

Boxes 3 and 4 describe situations where there will be weak or no home-based advantages, since the low LOF enables firms of different nationalities to access the resource in question (Hu, 1992). In Box 3, internal MNE transfers are limited, implying that foreign and local firms operating in the same environment are likely to develop similar attributes, based on the resources in this environment. They are likely to share the lead in an industry, with no distinctive differences associated with nationality. Such situations are likely when group 1 resources are the dominant basis for competitive advantage. In Box 4, foreign firms are likely to lead, drawing on their access to MNE internal resources, and local firms are likely to be weak. In such situations are likely when advantages are based on knowledge.

In introducing this distinction between location resources in terms of their importance as bases for firm-specific resources, and identifying the factors affecting this variation, I establish a hierarchy of location resources that differ in terms of their importance as bases for competitiveness and competitive advantage. Seen in this manner, the situation in the London insurance market, which appeared to signify a departure from theory, is no longer puzzling. It corresponds to the situation described in Box 4, where the LOF in relation to the critical resources in insurance is weak and British firms do not benefit from exclusive access to them. It is also possible to substitute for some local resources by internal MNE transfer, which explains the superior position of foreign firms in this setting.

These expectations have specific implications for the persistence or otherwise of home-based advantages. When foreign affiliates experience LOF in relation to important location resources driving their investment, local firms are likely to develop strong competitive position, based on their exclusive access to home country resources. When the important location resources are such that foreignness does not raise concerns in accessing them, national firms will not enjoy home-based advantages and there will be no national patterns in an industry. If the MNE internal network is a viable alternative for local resources, foreign firms may compete successfully, but they will likely develop their advantages based on different resources, and will differ considerably from local firms in terms of their competitive advantages and strategic behaviour. When the transfer of critical resources is low, there will probably be limited foreign investment, and national firms will be likely to have a lead in an industry.

CONCLUSION

In this study I sought a rationale for an apparent dissociation between the competitive advantages of firms and their home country resources that is at variance with the theory of the MNE (Hymer, 1960). In this, I contribute to the debate on the home country effect on firms' advantages by accounting for situations whereby the characteristics of firms are dissociated from those of their home countries (Doz et al., 2001). This approach suggests a shift in the debate about the impact of home country characteristics on firms, from questioning its existence (Thomas & Waring, 1999; Thomas, 2004; Makino et al., 2004), to a search for the circumstances that determine its strength and persistence. The interaction between the characteristics of firms and countries is a defining characteristic of international strategy. Deepening the understanding of this issue and its implications for firms is thus of considerable importance for the further development of this research area.

By explicitly acknowledging variations across location resources in terms of their impact on firms, the study contributes to theories of the relationships between firms and their environments that may go beyond the specific context of the MNEs. In these theories, the environment is typically viewed as a unified whole, imposing undifferentiated impact on firms (Castrogiovanni, 1991). The focus is typically comparative across different environments (e.g. Wan & Hoskisson, 2003), or the same environment over time (e.g. Wezel & Lomi, 2003). This approach provides important insights into the ways by which different environments affect firms, but leaves a gap in understanding how different resources in the same environment affect firms, which was the focus of the analysis here. The findings illustrate the merit of this approach in enhancing the understanding of how firms gain competitive advantage through different resources within a single environment. Study at the level of individual resources also provides more immediate implications for firms' strategy and yields analysis that is of greater practical relevance.

The multi-dimensional view of the environment also introduces a more nuanced view of the LOF and MNE internal transfers, by explicitly recognizing variations across different resources in terms of the liabilities of foreign affiliates in accessing them and their transferability within the MNE networks. This contribution is in line with recent developments in the resource-based view that suggests that firms' internal resource development is conditioned by their environment (Aragon-Correa & Sharma, 2004). It implies that the interaction between firms and environmental resources is the determinant of outcome, and calls for an examination of firm resources in the context of their environment (Wan & Hoskisson, 2003), as well as for the acknowledgement that the resources that firms draw from the same environment may not necessarily be identical. The study also suggests an extension of the resource dependency theory, by extending it to the international context. This theory, while providing extensive discussions of organization environment, has not paid attention to national boundaries.

Yet another important contribution of the study lies in deepening the understanding of the ways in which insurance firms generate their competitive advantages. This is an important contribution at a time when occupations with risk and risk management has grown considerably. The range of risks insured has also expended substantially, to include weather risk, political risk, to mention just a few of the new ones (The Economist, 2004), along with the recognition of a growing disconnect between risk and the means available to mitigate it (World Economic Forum, 2007). As the insurance industry transforms itself to meet these new challenges, deepening the understanding of the dynamics of operation in the industry is of considerable importance.

The study also contributes to the broader understanding of the generation of competitive advantages by knowledge-intensive service firms. As Bowen and Ford (2002) noted, although service and product firms share some competitive similarities, there are significant differences in their strategic management, and the production and consumption of their offerings. The prevalence of research on product-based firms often raises a generalizability concern when applying the results to services firms.

Future Research

This study opens up a large area for future research. For one, the static nature of the study may limit generalizations, and the validity of the findings to different time periods should be examined by future research. This is a limitation in all industries but might be particularly severe in insurance, due to the inherently cyclical nature of this industry, what is known as 'the insurance cycle' (Webb & Pettigrew, 1999).[3] It might be that some of the relationships found here are sensitive to the stage in the cycle. Both the nature of the external environment and the type of firms operating tend to vary in different periods of the insurance cycle (Sigma, 2001).

There is also a need to further deepen the understanding of the relationships between MNE internal transfers and dependency on local resources. For example, knowledge transferred within MNEs perhaps differs from the type of local knowledge obtained via the local information network. If this is the case, there is a need to better understand the extent to which the former can substitute for dependency on the later. Another important task for future research is to test the framework introduced here on a large scale, to identify industrial and geographical patterns in the relationships between firm and location resources, and to draw out their consequences for the home-based advantages. In a one-country, one-industry study like the present one such issues naturally cannot be addressed, but future research may fill in this gap.

The focus here was the strategic implications of the relationships between country resources and firms, but this issue also has important policy implications, which might be addressed by future research, especially as they affect MNEs. Policy makers have the ultimate power to shape the environmental attributes of the geographic areas under their jurisdiction, and often exercise direct control over who might benefit from them. A possible dissociation of the characteristics of firms from their home resources requires a shift in policies from the improvement of specific location resources to a direct reference to the firms themselves. Further, if under certain circumstances foreign and national firms do not differ in terms of their ability to access local resources, specific actions are required if policy makers wish to confine certain benefits to national firms.

NOTES

1. Furthermore, these leading firms themselves appear to regard their national origin as a source of advantage and an indication of the quality of their services. This perhaps explains the tendency to select names that stress their national origin – Munich Re, Swiss Re, Cologne Re, Zurich Re, Hanover Re, among others.

2. This definition is in affinity with the conceptualization of the 'task environment' as consisting of all those organizations with which a focal organization must interact to grow and survive (Dess & Beard, 1984).

3. The need to take into account this cyclical nature is well recognized in the industry. For example, Lloyd operates a three-year accounting system, intended to account for this inherent volatility.

ACKNOWLEDGMENTS

I thank Mr. Chris Aujard, Head of Development Projects, Lloyd's; Ms. Marie-Louis Rossi, Chief Executive International Underwriting Association; Mr. Jim Bannister, a reporter on the London insurance market; Mr. P. Falush, London insurance market Consultant; Mr. R. Cook, Head of International Affairs, Association of British Insurers (ABI); as well as various representatives of the British Insurance Brokers' Association (BIBA) for generously sharing with me their knowledge of the London Insurance Market. My thanks also go to the large number of chief executives and senior managers of insurance firms, who took time out of very busy schedules to fill in my questionnaire. Without their willingness to introduce me to the working of their organizations this research would have not been possible. I also acknowledge the comments of Shyam Kumar and the participants in a department seminar at Baruch College on earlier drafts.

REFERENCES

Adegbesan, J. A. (2009). On the origins of competitive advantage: Strategic factor markets and heterogeneous resource complementarity. *Academy of Management Review, 34*(3), 463–475.

Aiken, L. S., & West, S. G. (1991). *Multiple regression: Testing and interpreting interactions.* London: Sage Publications.

Aragon-Correa, A. J., & Sharma, S. (2004). A contingency resource-based view of proactive corporate environmental studies. *Academy of Management Review, 28*(1), 71–88.

Armstrong, J. S., & Overton, T. S. (1977). Estimating nonresponse bias in mail surveys. *Journal of Marketing Research, 14*, 396–402.

Arora, A., & Gambardella, A. (2005). *The rise and growth of the software industry in some emerging economies.* Oxford: Oxford University Press.

Avolio, B. J., Yammarino, F. J., & Bass, B. M. (1991). Identifying common methods variance with data collected from a single source: An unresolved sticky issue. *Journal of Management, 17*(3), 571–587.

Bas, C. L., & Sierra, C. (2002). Location versus home country advantages in R&D activities: Some further results on multinationals' locational strategies. *Research Policy, 31*(4), 589–609.

Birkinshaw, J., Braunerhjelm, P., Holm, U., & Terjesen, S. (2006). Why do multinational corporations relocate their corporate headquarters overseas? *Strategic Management Journal, 27*(7), 681–700.

Bowen, J., & Ford, R. C. (2002). Managing service organizations: Does having a 'thing' make a difference? *Journal of Management, 28*(3), 447–469.

Bradshaw, M. T., Bushee, B., & Miller, G. S. (2004). Accounting choice, home bias and US investment in non-US firms. *Journal of Accounting Research, 42*(5), 795–841.

Carter, R. L., & Falush, P. (1998). The London Insurance Market. A report prepared for the London Insurance Market Strategy Committee, London.

Castrogiovanni, G. J. (1991). Environmental munificence: A theoretical assessment. *Academy of Management Review, 16*(3), 542–565.

Chandler, A. D. (1990). *Scale and scope: The dynamics of industrial capitalism.* Cambridge, MA: Harvard University Press.

Cummins, J. D., & Santomero, A. M. (1999). *Changes in the life insurance industry: Efficiency, technology and risk management.* Boston: Kluwer Academic Publishers.

Cycyota, C. S., & Harrison, D. A. (2002). Enhancing survey response rates at the executive level: Are employee- or consumer-level techniques effective? *Journal of Management, 28*(2), 151–176.

Dess, G. G., & Beard, D. W. (1984). Dimensions of organizational task environments. *Administrative Science Quarterly, 29*(1), 52–73.

Dess, G. G., & Robinson, R. B. (1984). Measuring organizational performance in the absence of objective measures: The case of the privately held firm and conglomerate business unit. *Strategic Management Journal, 5*(3), 265–273.

Doz, Y., Santos, J., & Williamson, P. (2001). *From global to metanational: How companies win in the knowledge economy.* Boston, MA: Harvard University Press.

The Economist. (2004). Living dangerously: A survey of risk. *The Economist*, January 24, Survey.

Fiegenbaum, A., & Thomas, H. (1990). Strategic groups and performance: The US insurance industry, 1970–84. *Strategic Management Journal, 11*(3), 197–215.

Forsgren, M., Holm, U., & Johanson, J. (1995). Division headquarters go abroad – A step in the internationalization of the Multinational Corporation. *Journal of Management Studies, 32*(4), 475–491.

Gedajlovic, E. R., & Shapiro, D. M. (1998). Management and ownership effects: Evidence from five countries. *Strategic Management Journal, 19*(6), 533–553.

Gong, Y. (2003). Subsidiary staffing in multinational enterprises: Agency, resources and performance. *Academy of Management Journal, 46*(6), 728–739.

Gugler, I., & Guillen, M. F. (2010). Home country networks and foreign expansion: Evidence from the venture capital industry. *Academy of Management Journal, 53*(2), 390–410.

Gupta, A. K., & Govindarajan, V. (2000). Knowledge flows within multinational corporations. *Strategic Management Journal, 21*(4), 473–496.

Hau, H. (2002). Location matters: An examination of trading profits. *Journal of Finance, 56*(5), 1959–1983.

Heberlein, T. A., & Baumgartner, R. (1978). Factors affecting response rates to mailed questionnaires: A qualitative analysis of the published literature. *American Sociology Review, 43*(4), 447–462.

Heracleous, L., & Barrett, M. (2001). Organizational change as discourse: Communicative actions and deep structures in the context of information technology implementation. *Academy of Management Journal, 44*(4), 755–778.

Hitt, M. A., Dacin, M. T., Tyler, B. B., & Park, D. (1997). Understanding the differences in Korean and US executives' strategic orientations. *Strategic Management Journal, 18*(2), 159–167.

Hu, Y. S. (1992). Global or stateless corporations are national firms with international operations. *California Management Review, 34*(2), 107–126.

Hymer, S. (1960). *The international operations of national firms: A study of direct foreign investment.* Cambridge, MA: MIT Press.

IFSL (International Financial Services, London). (2003). *International financial markets in the U.K.* London: IFSL.

IFSL (International Financial Services, London). (2004). *Insurance. Business city series.* London: IFSL.

Johns, G. (2006). The essential impact of context on organizational behavior. *Academy of Management Review, 31*(2), 386–408.

Jones, G., & Galvez-Munoz, L. (2002). *Foreign multinationals in the United States: Management and performance.* London: Routledge.

Kielholz, W. (2000). The cost of capital for insurance companies. *The Geneva Papers on Risk and Insurance, 25*(1), 4–24.

Kostova, T., & Zaheer, S. (1999). Organizational legitimacy under conditions of complexity: The case of the multinational enterprise. *Academy of Management Review, 24*(1), 64–81.

Lessard, D. R. (1979). Transfer prices, taxes, and financial markets: Implications of internal financial transfers within the multinational corporation. In: R. G. Hawkins (Ed.), *Research in international business and finance* (Vol. 1, pp. 101–135). JAI Press.

London Business School. (1995). The Competitive Position of London's Financial Services: Final Report. A report prepared for the Corporation of London, London.

Makino, S., Isobe, T., & Chan, C. M. (2004). Does country matter? *Strategic Management Journal, 25*(10), 1027–1043.

McDowell, L. (1997). A tale of two cities? Embedded organizations and embodied workers in the City of London. In: R. Lee & J. Wills (Eds), *Geographies of economics* (pp. 118–129). London: Arnold.

Mezias, J. M. (2002). Identifying liabilities of foreignness and strategies to minimize their effects: The case of labor lawsuit judgments in the United States. *Strategic Management Journal, 23*(3), 229–244.

Miller, S., & Parkhe, A. (2002). Is there a liability of foreignness in global banking? An empirical test of banks' x-efficiency. *Strategic Management Journal, 23*, 55–75.

Nachum, L. (2000). FDI, the location advantages of home countries and the competitiveness of TNCs: US FDI in professional service industries. In: Y. Aharoni & L. Nachum (Eds),

The globalization of services: Some implications for theory and practice (pp. 75–92). London: Routledge.

Nohria, N., & Ghoshal, S. (1997). *The differentiated network: Organizing multinational corporations for value creation.* San Francisco: Jossey-Bass Publishers.

Pfeffer, J., & Davis-Blake, A. (1987). Understanding organizational wage structures: A resource dependence approach. *Academy of Management Journal, 30*(3), 437–455.

Pfeffer, J., & Salancik, G. R. (1978). *The external control of organizations: A resource dependence perspective.* New York: Harper & Row.

Podsakoff, P. M., & Organ, D. W. (1986). Self-reports in organizational research: Problems and prospects. *Journal of Management, 12*(4), 531–544.

Porter, M. (1990). *The competitive advantage of nations.* New York: Macmillan.

Roscoe, M. A., Lang, D., & Sheth, J. N. (1975). Follow-up methods, questionnaire length, and market differences in mail surveys. *Journal of Marketing, 39*(2), 20–27.

Rosenzweig, P. M., & Singh, J. V. (1991). Organizational environments and the multinational enterprise. *Academy of Management Review, 16*(2), 340–361.

Rugman, A. M., & Verbeke, A. (2001). Subsidiary-specific advantages in multinational enterprises. *Strategic Management Journal, 22*(3), 237–250.

Salancik, G. R. (1979). Interorganizational dependence and responsiveness to affirmative action: The case of women and defence contractors. *Academy of Management Journal, 22*, 375–394.

Sigma. (2001). Profitability of the non-life insurance industry: It's back-to-basics time. Sigma papers 2001/5, Swiss Re, Zurich.

Sigma. (2002). The London market in the throes of change. Sigma papers 3/2002, Swiss Re, Zurich.

Solvell, O., Zander, I., & Porter, M. (1991). *Advantage Sweden.* Stockholm: Norstedts.

Teece, D. J. (1998). Capturing value from knowledge assets: The new economy, markets for know-how and intangible assets. *California Management Review, 40*(3), 55–79.

Thomas, L. G. (2004). Are we all global now? Local vs. foreign sources of corporate competence: The case of the Japanese pharmaceutical industry. *Strategic Management Journal, 25*(Special issue), 865–886.

Thomas, L. G., & Waring, G. (1999). Competing capitalisms: Capital investment in American, German and Japanese firms. *Strategic Management Journal, 20*(8), 729–748.

Thrift, N. (1994). On the social and cultural determinants of international financial centers: The case of the City of London. In: S. Corbridge, N. Thrift & R. Martin (Eds), *Money, power and space* (pp. 327–355). Oxford, UK: Blackwell.

Tomaskovic-Devey, D., & Leiter, J. (1994). Organizational survey nonresponse. *Administrative Science Quarterly, 39*(3), 439–457.

Wan, W. P., & Hoskisson, R. E. (2003). Home country environments, corporate diversification strategies, and firm performance. *Academy of Management Journal, 46*(1), 27–45.

Webb, D., & Pettigrew, A. (1999). The temporal development of strategy: Patterns in the UK insurance industry. *Organization Science, 10*(5), 601–621.

Wezel, F. C., & Lomi, A. (2003). The organizational advantage of nations: An ecological perspective on the evolution of the motorcycle industry in Belgium, Italy and Japan, 1898–1993. In: J. C. Baum & O. Sorenson (Eds), *Geography and strategy, advances in strategic management Volume 20* (pp. 377–409). Amsterdam: JAI.

Whisler, T. R. (1999). *The British motor industry 1945–1994: A case study of industrial decline.* Oxford: Oxford University Press.

World Economic Forum. (2007). Global risks report 2007. World Economic Forum, Davos.
Zaheer, S. (1995). Overcoming the liability of foreignness. *Academy of Management Journal,* *38*(2), 341–363.
Zaheer, S., & Mosakowski, E. (1997). The dynamics of the liability of foreignness: A global study of survival in financial services. *Strategic Management Journal, 18*(6), 439–464.
Zaheer, A., & Venkatraman, N. (1995). Relational governance as an interorganizational strategy: An empirical test of the role of trust in economic exchange. *Strategic Management Journal, 16,* 373–392.

THE BENEFITS OF HIERARCHY? – EXPLORING THE EFFECTS OF REGIONAL HEADQUARTERS IN MULTINATIONAL CORPORATIONS

Phillip C. Nell, Björn Ambos and
Bodo B. Schlegelmilch

ABSTRACT

This chapter investigates the role Regional Headquarters (RHQs) play in large multinationals and probes to what degree the establishment of RHQs provides hierarchy benefits according to the M-form principles. Nine large multinational corporations (MNCs) provided the empirical setting for 55 in-depth interviews with decision-makers at corporate, regional and local levels. Case reports were developed for each MNC and the industries they operated in. Observations, company documents, detailed workshops with managers and a follow-up survey within one of the MNCs complemented the data. We find evidence for benefits of hierarchy when RHQs are introduced very much along the lines of the classic M-form organisation with product divisions. However, M-form principles are taken ad absurdum by the fact that there seems to be constant reorganisation regarding the mandates and the geographic scope of the regions. The practical implications of the chapter show that MNCs need to be aware that RHQs

Dynamics of Globalization: Location-Specific Advantages or Liabilities of Foreignness?
Advances in International Management, Volume 24, 85–106
ISSN: 1571-5027/doi:10.1108/S1571-5027(2011)0000024011

and the regional divisions they manage seem to be more difficult to manage in a stable way than product divisions. A clear rationale needs to underlie regional groupings to minimise instability, dissatisfaction among subsidiaries and, hence, ruptures of the M-form principles. Further research is needed to compare the stability of product versus regional divisionalisation. Future research on organisational structures should focus on firm-specific definitions of regional scope.

INTRODUCTION

Despite research suggesting a relative superiority of network-like organisations in today's turbulent environments (Hedlund, 1986; Bartlett & Ghoshal, 1989; Prahalad & Doz, 1987), a growing body of scholars have started to re-stress the important roles of hierarchy and organisational architecture within large diversified firms (e.g. Egelhoff, 2010; Gulati, Puranam, & Tushman, 2009). A key line of argument in these studies and calls for papers is that hierarchical structures with centralised decision authority and fiat help the organisation to manage complexity (Goold & Campbell, 2002), speed up knowledge flows along vertical lines (Egelhoff, 2010; Tran, Mahnke, & Ambos, 2010; Tallman & Chacar, 2011), ensure strategic consistency (Ambos & Schlegelmilch, 2007) and promote strategic initiatives (Ambos & Andersson, 2010; Ciabuschi, Martin, & Stahl, 2010). Hence, it has been concluded that network mechanisms cannot completely substitute hierarchical elements within large organisations (Egelhoff, 2010; Verbeke & Kenworthy, 2008).

The theoretical pleas for a reassessment of the benefits of hierarchy have been echoed by recent empirical findings. Ambos and Schlegelmilch (2010), for example, show that the number of European Regional Headquarters (RHQ), that is, organisational units with a formal mandate to manage a region within the multinational corporations (MNCs) global structure, increased by 76% over the past decade alone. Similarly, research by Enright (2005a, 2005b) identifies more than 1,100 RHQs in the Asia-Pacific region. Both studies suggest a trend within large diversified MNCs to (re-)build hierarchical structures in addition and beyond the well-accepted focus on product divisions and network elements. Results of these studies also coincide with Rugman's (2005) thesis, suggesting that only few firms operate with global strategies but rather limit their international scope to the home region or one additional host region (Rugman, 2005; Asmussen, 2009).

Despite this evidence, we still know little about regional management and how it complements other organisational mechanisms in managing and coordinating dispersed activities (Yeung, Poon, & Perry, 2001; Rugman, 2005; Piekkari, Nell, & Ghauri, 2010). The dominance of the global–local dichotomy stressed in the prominent integration responsiveness (e.g. Prahalad & Doz, 1987) framework has led to a conceptual lacuna for intermediate geographic levels between global (headquarters) and local (subsidiaries) (Siddiqi, 2000; Enright, 2005b; Ambos & Schlegelmilch, 2010). The dominance of this thinking is evident even in some of the more recent writings on the topic. Verbeke and Kenworthy (2008), for example, discuss the M-form organisation and compare it to the meta-national network organisation (Doz, Santos, & Williamson, 2001) neglecting to some extent intermediate geographic levels. Furthermore, the few publications on regional strategies and structures at the macro level of the organisation ('area divisions') only vaguely explicate the role RHQs play (Egelhoff, 1988; Stopford & Wells, 1972; Wolf & Egelhoff, 2002). Other studies have focused on individual regional management centres (e.g. Daniels, 1987; Lasserre, 1996; Schütte, 1996) but often without a clear focus, offering lists of advantages and disadvantages instead of detailed functioning. Piekkari et al.'s (2010) review concludes that this 'stream [of literature] is rather managerial and descriptive in its approach' (p. 514). They also observe a general lack of in-depth case studies that look at RHQ activity over time so that it can tease out mechanisms and problem areas.

In light of these shortcomings, the purpose of this chapter is to investigate the role RHQs play in large multinationals. We apply an exploratory multimethod approach based on case-based qualitative data of nine MNCs from different industries. Utilising this data, we probe to what degree the establishment of RHQs alters interdependencies and coordination within and subsequently across geographic markets. Along the lines of recent work (Egelhoff, 2010; Verbeke & Kenworthy, 2008), we suggest that if RHQs are indeed a rather hierarchical form of management, they should benefit the organisation in a similar way product divisions do in the M-form organisation, that is, a clear separation between centralised decision-making (the role of the corporate HQ and the RHQ) and local decision-making (the role of the subsidiary), restrained direct intervention of corporate headquarters in regional matters, largely vertical information flows that support the decision-making as it helps aggregating information, and selectivity in inter-regional interactions (for a good summary of the M-form principles, see Verbeke & Kenworthy, 2008; Egelhoff, 2010).

We investigate these principles in the context of regional divisionalisation and thus contribute to the scarce knowledge on regional structures, their application and benefits. On the basis of the discussion earlier, special focus will be put on the intra-regional versus the inter-regional perspective very much alike the focus on intra-divisional versus inter-divisional issues emphasised in work on the M-form organisation (Chandler, 1991; Eisenmann & Bower, 2000; Williamson, 1996). The intra-regional perspective focuses on interdependencies and interaction between the RHQ and its subsidiaries in the region. The inter-regional perspective deals with interdependence and interaction between the region and other MNC units outside the region (e.g. between the RHQ and the HQ).

We find that the RHQs help managing interdependencies *within* the region that is between the RHQ and the various subsidiaries under its responsibility, no matter which other structural elements are in place (e.g. product divisions). Furthermore, the introduction of RHQs increases the risk that interdependencies *across* the regions are not well managed even if they are present: RHQs cut off interdependencies between regions managed on the subsidiary level. The responsibility of managing cross-regional interdependencies shifts to the regional level, but also here, we observed that RHQs focus a lot on their regions and neglect cross-regional interdependencies. Although this seems perfectly in line with the above-mentioned M-form principles, we found important challenges for a well-functioning hierarchy effect. Our case firms have severe difficulties in allocating decision-making authority across the levels and to group countries optimally into regions. They frequently regroup countries and reallocate decision rights, which leads to substantial frictions and inefficiencies. We conclude that the introduction of RHQs is an act of emphasising hierarchy within the MNC organisation, but that the clearly outlined M-form-type benefits of such divisionalisation are seldom achieved. With our work, we attempt to contribute to the wider debate on regionalisation of MNC activity (e.g. Rugman, 2005). We confirm the idea that regional structural elements might be increasingly needed in large and complex MNCs. However, the observed difficulties of regional groupings and the identification and management of crucial interdependencies means that more research is needed that bridges the gap between Rugman's triad-based evidence (e.g. Rugman, 2005; Rugman & Verbeke, 2004) and the more firm-specific situations, which need a balance between within-regional and across-regional effects often on a sub-triad level. We propose that future research should investigate why many firms apparently lack this scaling capability, which allows them to build efficient and effective regional divisions. This involves the investigation of antecedents and consequences of regional grouping.

LITERATURE REVIEW

The question how to best structure large firms has spurred academic work for many years. Early work analysed multiproduct firms (diversified firms) and their challenges to align environmental conditions with firm strategy and organisation (e.g. Chandler, 1991; Argyres, 1996). They documented the emerging multidivisional or M-form organisation and described precisely why such organisations are effective and efficient, for example, by outlining the differentiation of tasks and decision-making authority between corporate headquarters and the individual divisions. Later, scholarly work added a further, highly complex dimension to the analysis of large firms. In addition to product diversification, geographic diversification was integrated in holistic analyses (Vernon, 1966; Stopford & Wells, 1972; Egelhoff, 1991). It was recognised that the geographic dispersion of firm activities matters as it creates new challenges, such as liability of foreignness (Zaheer, 1995) and the coordination over geographic and cultural distance. In case of strong pressures to pursue global strategies, it was found that the multinational firm can cope with a traditional M-structure, whereas industries with strong local responsiveness pressures more frequently require the usage of area instead of product divisions or simply a set of very independent local units also called multidomestic organisations. Nowadays, it is suggested that most industries suffer from the dual pressure of global integration and local responsiveness, complicating a firm's quest for efficient and effective organisational structures that are able to cope with such environments (Nohria & Ghoshal, 1997).

Central to the discussion on hierarchical versus network-like structures is the management of interdependencies. Simon (1962) defined hierarchies as systems that are composed of interrelated subsystems. In hierarchic systems, 'we can distinguish between the interactions *among* subsystems on the one hand, and the interactions *within* subsystems – i.e., among the parts of those subsystems – on the other' (Simon, 1962, p. 473). The efficiency of the M-form organisation is based on the insight that interdependencies between divisions can be rare (selectivity principle) and that corporate HQs intervene in divisional business only to a limited extent. The divisions act as 'quasi-firms' that are essentially self-contained. Cross-divisional interaction as well as HQ-divisional interaction is limited to cases when synergy potential has been identified or when general, firm-level strategic issues are concerned (Williamson, 1971).

Although these issues remain valid for multinationals, the geographic dispersion adds a fundamental source of complexity to the operations and the management of the firm (Egelhoff, 1991). Similar to inter-dependencies (synergies) between divisions, there are potential benefits from integrating foreign markets. Complex interdependencies between international markets have been growing in the past decades (Porter, 1986; Prahalad & Doz, 1987). Subsidiaries might be able to learn from each other, products invented in one market can add value to another market, successful competitors' attacks in one location can be analysed and subsequently blocked in the home market, and the most efficient way of structuring the value chain might mean that design, manufacturing of input products and assembly are carried out at three different international subsidiaries and so on. Consequently, it has been suggested that avoiding (or reducing) interdependence has a devastating effect on performance for the multinational firm (Nohria & Ghoshal, 1997) and that managing it through different means of coordination is, therefore, crucial (O'Donnell, 2000).

Contrary to the large body of work on the M-form, however, the corresponding work on regional/area divisions that operate usually with RHQs (Egelhoff, 1991) is surprisingly small and much less prominently discussed. Instead, the field of international management focused much more on the multinational *network* organisations during the past two decades disregarding or disqualifying to a large extent hierarchical governance principles (Bartlett & Ghoshal, 1989). Network-based models of the MNC have been developed with the tenor that MNCs should develop a web of semi-autonomous, differentiated units (Hedlund, 1986; Prahalad & Doz, 1987; Bartlett & Ghoshal, 1989). These units are first and foremost governed through socialisation (e.g. Gates & Egelhoff, 1986; Ghoshal & Nohria, 1989), flexible 'integration mechanisms' (O'Donnell, 2000) and a high degree of self-coordination (Gencturk & Aulakh, 1995; Bartlett & Ghoshal, 1989). Hierarchical control (centralisation) is largely supposed to be ineligible (Astley & Sachdeva, 1984; Bartlett & Ghoshal, 1989).

Only recently, critique of such extreme network organisations is gaining ground again. For example, Egelhoff (2010, p. 428) concludes that large firms such as multinationals are 'likely to remain a mixture of hierarchy and networks'. Similarly, Verbeke and Kenworthy (2008) doubt that network-like governance mechanisms substitute conventional governance principles. Furthermore, empirically, the existence of many network organisations have not been confirmed (e.g. Wolf, 1997), and recent studies found that high levels of interdependence do lead to a higher degree of centralisation (Sullivan, 1992; Ambos & Schlegelmilch, 2007) giving credit to the idea that hierarchical governance still produces benefits.

Yet, in all these discussions – with a few exceptions (Piekkari et al., 2010; Ambos & Schlegelmilch, 2010) – intermediate geographic levels such as regions and RHQs are not emphasised. Instead, global networks are often compared to global hierarchical organisations (e.g. Egelhoff, 2010; Verbeke & Kenworthy, 2008). The scarce work that focused specifically on regional management centres or RHQs investigated specific aspects of RHQs such as their staffing (Sing, 2000), their location choice (Yeung et al., 2001; Holt, Purcell, Gray, & Pedersen, 2008) and their mandates and functional coverage (Lasserre, 1996; Erramilli, 2003; Enright, 2005a, 2005b; Paik & Sohn, 2004) without discussing it in the wider context of hierarchical versus network governance mechanisms.

METHODOLOGY

To investigate the issues outlined earlier, we apply a multiple case design. Following Yin (1994), this inductive approach is an appropriate research strategy that helps to understand the phenomenon of RHQs and its effect on managing interdependence because the phenomenon is highly context related and it allows for collecting and analysing rich data. To achieve variance in our data, we chose to analyse nine MNCs originating from different home countries in lead countries of the triad markets (US, Germany and Japan). The MNCs are all large, that is, operating in more than 40 countries with a considerable number of subsidiaries, and were selected because they are operating or planning to operate with regional structures. The MNCs employ on average 70,000 employees and are managing roughly 42 billion USD of revenues per year.

We focus on RHQs located in Europe and define them as an organisational unit concerned with and involved in the integration and coordination of activities that provide the link between the region and the HQ (cf. Schütte, 1996; Enright, 2005a, 2005b). This definition has the advantage that it excludes pure financial or representative offices (e.g. in Brussels) that are not involved in management activities. Of course, the mandates of such RHQs can still differ substantially (cf. Lasserre, 1996; Enright, 2005a). To focus our research further, we only considered RHQs that operate with a wide range of responsibilities in both integrative and entrepreneurial areas (cf. Chandler, 1991) often having profit and loss responsibility for the region.

Three manufacturing industries were selected, from which we recruited the participating case study firms. The selected industries are the sports industry (shoes and apparel), the pharmaceutical industry and the automobile industry. In each of the MNCs, we conducted interviews on three organisational levels: the corporate, regional and local subsidiary level to enhance unit triangulation of data (Marschan-Piekkari, Welch, Pentti-nen, & Tahvanainen, 2004). Interview partners were mainly senior executives in the functions general management or marketing, and they were chosen on the basis that they all were involved in some kind of cross-border interaction (e.g. between RHQ and subsidiary) and had hence insight into existing interdependencies and governance mechanisms. In total, the case data consists of 55 interviews that lasted on average roughly one hour (see Table 1).

In addition to the interview data, we collected information to complement the interviews including observations and company documentations. The process of data gathering and analysis was intertwined. To enhance reliability and validity of the case data, all interviews were recorded and transcribed. The transcriptions were interpreted and discussed by the members of the research group. The interview language was English or German depending on the interview partners' choice, and transcriptions stuck to the interview language as all researchers are fluent in both languages. The interview data was coded and classified, thereby discussing and adapting the meaning of emerging codes regularly within the group to ensure inter-rater reliability. Finally, a case report was produced for each case company and industry to create a base, which maintains a chain of evidence (Yin, 1994).

In addition to the qualitative interview data, we were invited by one pharmaceutical company in our sample to conduct workshops with general managers and marketing executives within a European region covering 28 countries. Six focus-group-type workshops were held within two different business units. The groups were mixed in terms of functions (marketing and general management) and levels (regional and local subsidiaries). The firm

Table 1.   Interviews per Respondent Level.

Level of Interview Partners	No. of Interviews
Global/corporate	9
Regional	22
Local	24
Total	55

allowed us to complement our qualitative data with a short survey covering both divisions and 21 country units. We used the survey to further probe some of the conclusions from the interview data and to complement our analysis.

FINDINGS

Although not originally primed to distinguish between intra- and inter-regional issues and challenges, virtually all of our interview partners raised these topics. In the following, we structure our report according to these two dimensions as shown in Fig. 1 along the lines of Simon's (1962) definition of systems and their subsystems.

Intra-Regional Perspective

Across all our cases, the introduction of RHQs had the effect of closing information asymmetries between the HQ and the subsidiaries in the regions. Regional managers stressed that they have to cope only with a limited number of subsidiaries and that they share certain characteristics, which makes it easier to understand the context at the level of the RHQ. One RHQ manager from a pharmaceutical firm illustrated this with the following words:

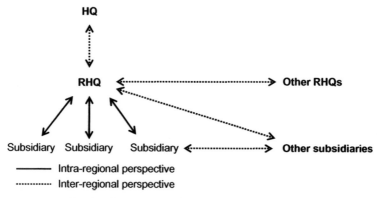

Fig. 1. Intra- versus Inter-Regional Perspective.

We have people here [in the RHQ] who know what's going on in the countries, and if the marketing head or country head changes, we still know what's going on in the markets. We can support that through that period of time. It's not going to collapse. Basically you build know-how that is consistent.

A sports industry manager on the subsidiary level concluded that 'my colleagues in the RHQ know much more about the market in Eastern Europe than my colleagues in the HQ. Most of the guys of the HQ have never been here before. And if you talk to these people about something it could be not so easy'.

Furthermore, across all case study MNCs, the RHQs were very involved in pursuing normative integration or integrative mechanisms (O'Donnell, 2000) giving credence to the idea that corporate HQs need support in establishing a strong corporate culture. Our RHQs used a wide set of socialisation mechanisms and increased face-to-face interaction, for example, workshops in the regions, intra-regional teams, regional tasks for subsidiary managers and intra-regional personnel development. For example, a pharmaceutical manager at the regional level described that 'we are now organizing a project team consisting of senior management people from each country. And those senior managers work together and discuss what kind of corporate culture or what kind of message should be easily shared and understood by our employees'.

An equivalent manager in a competitor firm revealed that 'we would issue the corporate culture handbook. And then we will start a training program in order to share our corporate culture in the European region'.

Furthermore, our research showed that RHQs often engage in organising regional meetings to discuss business processes and procedures and to formalise these where possible. Their improved understanding of local idiosyncrasies enhanced the ability to formalise and standardise processes and procedures where possible. Hence, in addition to implementing globally standardised processes, RHQs developed formalised regional processes and procedures. A regional general manager said, 'Now we try to streamline, so that everybody has to adhere to a couple of standard processes'.

Our RHQs were perceived as being effective in implementing higher levels of formalisation. Some subsidiary managers were highlighting the increasing professionalism. On the contrary, subsidiaries were complaining about the bureaucratic overload. Interestingly, among these subsidiaries were two subsidiaries from the pharmaceutical MNC for which we have conducted focus group discussion. Those two subsidiaries had just recently switched from HQ to RHQ responsibility. These subsidiary managers explained,

> There has been a lot of change. One thing is that before we were the daughter of X and we had a lot of freedom (...). That means that now, we have a lot more communication and directives from the parent which we have to coordinate in Austria [the location of the RHQ] first. For us that means 20%–30% more coordination effort.

Another subsidiary manager described the consequences with 'a lot of paperwork coming' from the RHQ level, which did not exist before and which is a burden to especially small subsidiaries.

With regard to the controversially discussed issue of centralisation, we found that, from a national subsidiary perspective, RHQs represented a move towards centralised decision-making. This is in contrast to the literature that interprets a decrease of decision-making authority at corporate headquarters as an act of decentralisation (Egelhoff, 1991). Indeed, the decision-making power of the RHQs came usually from both sides, the corporate level and the subsidiary level, and, therefore, subsidiary managers felt a general increase of centralised control (Yeung et al., 2001). One manager explained that 'there are nearly no decisions that I can take alone'. A RHQ manager from the automotive industry explained with regard to their decision-making rights that 'it's not autarky, but it [the region] is effectively an autonomous business entity'.

On the basis of the above-mentioned discussion, we propose that the establishment of RHQs is an act of strengthening hierarchical control within the region through means of centralised decision-making, vertical information processing and formalisation. Network-type governance mechanisms such as flexible coordination processes and socialisation mechanisms are also strengthened within the region.

Inter-Regional Perspective

Our results have shown that RHQs focus strongly on the region, try to understand local and regional contexts and increase the coordination intensity within the region. Yet, according to the M-form logic, we expected a different picture when it comes to inter-regional interaction. Note that we define inter-regional issues as existing either between the corporate HQ and the RHQ or between the RHQ and all other subunits outside the regions. A true network organisation would rely often on self-governed coordinative interaction between subsidiaries across regions whenever important cross-regional synergies such as learning opportunities are identified. An M-form-type organisation with regional divisions would limit the interaction between divisions to a very limited extent – the RHQ itself would be the prime coordination point between corporate headquarters and other units outside the region.

One important result of our investigation of inter-regional management was that, indeed, many subsidiary managers reported to be bound by the region regarding their patterns of interaction. In practice, RHQs seem to imply that inter-regional links between subsidiaries become less frequent on the subsidiary level. That was particularly mentioned from subsidiaries that existed before the RHQ had been established or that had been switched from HQ to RHQ responsibility. For example, asked to what extent the subsidiary has contact with subsidiaries outside the region, one sports industry subsidiary manager answered, 'Not a lot, that's a clear disadvantage. (...) we have only a few interfaces to other regions; basically we don't have contacts'. The interviewing researcher probed if there are not cross-regional meetings such as a pan-European Marketing Meeting. The subsidiary manager answered, 'Yes, that exist, but the participant is only one regional representative, one from Sales, Marketing and one from Finance. However, it is only this person that has contact – not the markets'.

A pharmaceutical manager explained, '[Inter-regional contact], that's rather by coincidence. There is not really something that we compare ourselves with the Americans, let's see what they do, what we do, let's talk about best practices. That's something I haven't experienced yet'. A representative from another case firm said 'There is [inter-regional] cooperation on higher levels – above our level. We, as national units, have that now to a lesser extent'.

Thus, instead of direct interaction and coordination between subsidiaries, interdependencies between the subsidiaries in the region and other units in the MNC are mainly managed through increased interaction on the regional level:

> There are several relationships. Let me start from the marketing. Right now we sell several global products and those products should be controlled under a unified brand concept and brand image, because our marketers are regularly participating in global medical conference. And we are organizing kind of a joint team between the US, Japan and Europe for having one global [...] symposium or exhibition, etc. At that time, product's global brand concept should be unified. Therefore we are regularly contacting each other in order to avoid any serious discrepancy on the product brand image or the marketing concept in particular.

As this example shows, the RHQ levels serve as a bridging point towards the rest of the MNC, that is, all the units outside the region itself. A country manager explains, 'Mr. X is responsible for our region. We have telephone conferences very regularly and exchange information. And it's from him where we get input regarding what is happening in the Nordic European Region or in the big direct countries [outside the region]'.

Direct inter-regional management of interdependence at the subsidiary level occurred in combination with an explicit mentioning of informal relationships between the subsidiary managers, as the following example (from the sports industry) shows,

Interviewer: Do you also have contact with subsidiaries outside your region?

Subsidiary Manager: Yes from time to time, if I need something. I know General Managers from other subsidiaries, if I need something I'm asking for help or support, or they are asking me about something. For [...] last year we had the case that they pushed us very hard to give them much higher discounts. What I did: I talked to my colleague in France [...] to give me the information how it works in France. He gave me all portfolios. When I got all the information-the guys stopped to play with me.

In sum, RHQs seem to imply that coordination of interdependence across regional frontiers is harmed. Unless the subsidiary has informal relationships established to units outside the region, the subsidiary suffers from such regional limitation. Regional meetings and exchanges seem to crowd out inter-regional interaction. Therefore, we conclude that the establishment of RHQs shifts inter-regional coordination away from the subsidiary level to regional and corporate levels where this is pursued selectively. From the RHQ, independent inter-regional coordination is only pursued when informal ties and relationships facilitate the interaction.

To this end, the effect of RHQs, that is, the effect of regional divisionalisation, is very much aligned with the divisionalisation effect in the M-form organisation. There is a certain specialisation of decision-making that can be observed and that differentiates the corporate HQ from the RHQ and the subsidiary. The corporate HQ only selectively intervenes in regional matters, and the regions are very independent quasi-firms. Inter-regional coordination is reduced substantially – the locus of interaction moves upwards from the subsidiary to the regional and the corporate levels. The whole setup is supported through standardised monitoring and formalisation (Verbeke & Kenworthy, 2008), which facilitates vertical information processing (Egelhoff, 2010).

However, our data also revealed that RHQs did vary substantially from the clear M-from principles/benefits.

First, the specialisation in decision-making, that is, the specific allocation of rights between corporate, regional and local levels, was in nearly all cases contested and constantly challenged. Even if RHQs disposed of a formally defined level of decision authority, this did not necessarily lead to a situation in which the RHQ was de facto the deciding authority. Very revealing were the efforts of RHQ managers to increase their centrality in the network by restricting direct contact between their subsidiaries and other units outside the region. Subsidiary managers as well as corporate HQs had the tendency to bypass the RHQ. This behaviour has been noted also in other studies (e.g. Piekkari et al., 2010). The relationship to corporate HQs was frequently described as mediocre. For example, one regional manager explained,

> The relationship, also the emotional relationship between the Head Office and the Regional Office is, indeed, very often quite strained.

A regional manager at a Japanese Pharmaceutical formulated it in the following way:

> In our case where the role of the European Headquarter is not made clear for ourselves but also not for the countries, it is very sensitive sometimes and especially in the executional role that both myself and Mr. X sit in and not being 100% backed by Japanese Top managers.

A third RHQ even released a formal code of conduct agreed upon with HQ and the subsidiaries. The agreement centred on the exclusivity of the RHQ being the bridging role to the rest of the MNC, which can be seen as an attempt to secure the decision-making rights and a clear specialisation in decision-making between the three different levels. The regional head explained,

> And if we are responsible for the performance of the countries, then it is fully clear to us that it is not possible that the HQ directly communicates with our countries. So we tried to synthesize that on a sheet of paper and now the challenge is to implement that in the heads of the HQ managers (...). But that is not something you write down and then it is lived, every day – every day, we have to fight for that at countless foresides.

Second, the regional grouping or clustering was criticised heavily within the firms and we observed also constant reorganisations. That is, our case firms reallocated subsidiaries from one region to another or moved them from direct HQ responsibility to the region or back. One manager was sighing when questioned regarding the optimal regional clustering, stating with some resignation that there is 'a lot of tinkering around' with regard to the regional scope. As mentioned earlier, in one of the case firms, two subsidiaries were taken away from the RHQ for Central and Eastern Europe (CEE) and allocated to corporate HQs just to take this decision back a few years later. A sports' firm emerged with a CEE RHQ, which developed such strong capabilities in building up and managing fast-growing, emerging markets that soon, similar markets outside the region, even outside Europe, were allocated to the RHQ's portfolio of operations. The 'bridging' country of Austria was frequently a topic in reorganisations as some organisational solutions tended to integrate Austria with CEE, whereas others built a German-speaking region just to switch again a few years later.

It was obvious that, frequently, critical synergies between country operations were actually cut off by a certain regional divisionalisation approaches – synergies that could be reaped before the changes. One subsidiary manager stated,

For a country like Poland it would be more interesting to get more info on how things work e.g. in the UK [outside the region] … Slovakia, Ukraine are much smaller countries

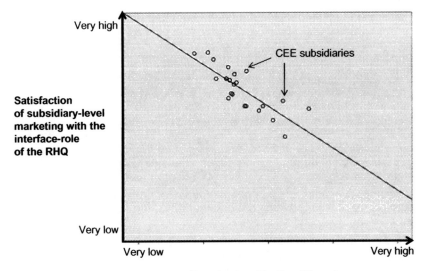

Fig. 2. The Relationship between Perceived Ambiguities of the RHQ Role and the Subsidiary's Satisfaction. *Note*: Ambiguity was captured with a 3-item construct, which asked subsidiary respondents to assess the extent to which the different roles (corporate HQ, RHQ and subsidiary) where unclear, reporting lines were complex and specific RHQ responsibilities were ambiguous. Satisfaction with RHQ interface activities was captured based on questions to what extent the RHQ was linking the subsidiaries to other regions as well as the corporate HQ.

and some are not in the EU, so we are trying to reach the bigger countries rather than regional countries. So that should be improved by the RHQ, that's a key issue for me. I think we had better access to this kind of information when we were under the HQ. Now we only have the comparison from the region, but we would need better examples.

A pharmaceutical manager explained,

We had big synergies between Austria, Switzerland, and Germany – these will be gone now. [...] Synergies will be lost. Since there were no language barriers we had a lot more information exchange, the General Practitioner cultures are also not very different. [...] We now have completely different colleagues – if, for example, they arrange a meeting, then Austria and Switzerland are now together with all the CEE countries. They are very unhappy about that.

The resulting substantial 'groping' was perceived very negatively at both the regional and even more so at the subsidiary level. Regional managers complained about their need to fight constantly for their mandate, whereas subsidiary manager responses to our survey within one of the firms suggested a clear link between the perceived ambiguity of the RHQ's role and the subsidiary's satisfaction with the RHQ's way of linking their business to the rest of the corporation (Fig. 2).

DISCUSSION AND CONCLUSION

Overall, our findings indicate that RHQs are a rather hierarchical means of coordination with very similar effects as described for the M-form. Structural divisionalisation (here: regionalisation) leads to a situation in which interaction increasingly takes place within the division, which might cut off interdependencies between the divisions (Argyres, 1996). This is to some extent mirrored in the existing literature. It is acknowledged that RHQs allow for more face-to-face contact due to a limited number of subsidiaries and limited time spent for travelling and closer time zones (Daniels, 1987). Authors suggest that RHQs improve the internal communication, and they add largely vertical information-processing capacities (Egelhoff, 1991; Piekkari et al., 2010; Daniels, 1987), and they act as a fundamental driver of socialisation mechanisms as they engage in organising regional meetings, workshops and task forces within the region (Schütte, 1996; Sing, 2000). Furthermore, authors emphasise RHQ's ability to re-establish control, because they are closing some of the information asymmetries that can arise between local and global levels of the organisation (Yamin & Forsgren, 2006; Argyres, 1996). Argyres (1996) argues, in general, that the threat of hierarchical fiat is more credible when reaching a solution may require punishing only a limited number of units, which is given when operations are allocated to RHQs. In sum, RHQs are in a very good position to manage economies of scale and scope within the region through means of centralisation, formalisation and socialisation. Simultaneously, the inter-regional activities are limited and 're-located'. Interaction between regions is increasingly difficult for subsidiaries to achieve. Such interaction, discussion and decision-making about inter-regional economies of scale and scope is moved to the regional and the corporate levels. We find network-type governance only within regions (strong socialisation) and to a limited extent across regions when individual managers profit from their interpersonal connections that transcend regional boundaries (cf. Piekkari et al., 2010, for similar findings).

In sum, we contend that studies of regional structures need to focus on intra- versus inter-regional interaction and coordination. This is in contrast to much work on individual regional management centres, which to some extent disregard these issues and focus solely on identifiable functions and activities (e.g. Enright, 2005a, 2005b). We also suggest treating RHQ organisations as being different from the network organisation, as it emphasises rather hierarchical governance, that is, MNCs benefit from this increase in 'hierarchy'. The introduction of a RHQ results in a first-order and second-order structure very much alike Simon's (1962) system and sub-system concept. The first-order structure is given by the regional units and their interactions. The second-order structure cuts across regions, that is, shapes the interaction between RHQs and between the RHQs and the corporate HQ.

Notwithstanding this general effect, however, the challenges and issues associated with RHQs and their introduction are, in our mind, a strong disqualification of the M-form benefits. The above describes the regional divisionalisation as having an effect similar to the product divisionalisation in the M-form organisation. Yet, our case examples make clear that M-form principles of hierarchical governance (cf. Verbeke & Kenworthy, 2008) are not fully met.

- Principle 1: A clear specialisation in decision-making between corporate HQs, RHQs and subsidiaries is often not achieved. There is substantial ambiguity of the roles of the individual levels and this results, in turn, in frequent and substantial reorganisations. This has negative consequences for employee motivation and satisfaction.
- Principle 2: Corporate HQs does not seem very willing, in general, to limit interventions in regional divisions. The interference seems quite

substantial and RHQs report nearly unanimously that they are 'squeezed' between expanding corporate HQs as well as expanding subsidiary mandates. This is also mirrored in some previous work on RHQs (e.g. Daniels, 1987; Schütte, 1996).

• Principle 3: Selectivity in inter-regional interactions is given but taken ad absurdum because – apparently – most of the MNCs do have difficulties in finding a relatively stable scope of the region, which makes selective inter-regional coordination somehow random.

In view of the broader literature on regionalisation, we contribute to a number of discussions with our findings.

First, Rugman's (2005) compelling data is based on defining the region 'externally' as comprising the triad regions. In our case firms, while most of the firms do operate with some kind of Europe or EMEA (Europe Middle East Africa) HQ, which is not reorganised that frequently, the interesting questions are managed on lower levels of regional integration. That is, most of our case firms integrate bundles of country operations on a level below the triad markets and that is where synergies and learning opportunities between country markets are an issue. Thus, from a structural perspective, the triad markets are less relevant. Hence, there is still a large gap between Rugman's seminal work on MNC strategy and structural issues. Future research on organisational structures should focus on a more firm-specific definition of regional scope. Contrary to the work of Rugman (2005), it might be more productive to study regional organisations from a firm perspective, independently of externally defined geographic clusterings. This could help identifying how firms actually shape interdependencies and interaction within and between the region, which might not necessarily be congruent with the triad or any other external definition of the region (cf. Ghemawat, 2003).

Second, the RHQ solution does not seem to be as clear to MNCs, because many MNCs are struggling with the implementation. While other organisational parameters, such as the top-level product divisions, remain relatively stable, MNCs seem to constantly increase and decrease the power of their RHQs, reallocate individual markets from HQ to RHQ responsibility and back again, regroup countries to form regional entities, establish sub-regional offices and dissolve them again (e.g. Piekkari et al., 2010). This observed behaviour has two implications.

On the one hand, it calls into question if MNCs have 'scaling-capabilities', the ability to cluster operations into stable regions so that M-form principles are met to fully benefit from the hierarchical effect.

Traditional organisational theory seem to indicate that firms first analyse interdependencies (potential for economies of scope and scale) between markets and product groups and, in a second step, to shape the divisions so that efficiency and effectiveness is given. Constant post-divisionalisation restructuring indicates that this rational process is severely undermined by bounded rationality issues/a lack of capabilities and that hidden costs occur that have not been foreseen by the management (cf. the recent work on offshoring, which has focused strongly on hidden costs and their effects). Furthermore, besides some notable exceptions (Ambos & Schlegelmilch, 2010), there is – to our knowledge – no work investigating the specific antecedents as well as consequences of regional clustering decisions. The data suggests that firms struggle fundamentally with defining the extent to which certain firm-specific advantages are location-bound or non-location-bound (Rugman, 2005) and how to allocate them and the resulting activities to the different organisational levels on the local–global continuum.

On the other hand, this calls for more research investigating the extent to which firms are more successful in managing the classic M-form decisions, that is, product divisionalisation issues such as the question where to draw the boundary between divisions and how to shape inter-divisional interaction and interdependence. We have not focused on comparing product versus regional divisionalisation in our study, which is a clear limitation of our study. Overall, we have the impression that product divisionalisation is more established and stable within the firms that we studied and that, frequently, the product divisions are dominating the regional divisions. This is along the lines of Piekkari et al.'s (2010) findings. However, the perception of more stability among and dominance of the product divisions has to be verified – our analysis is just a first step into this direction. If our impression is valid, it would mirror the status quo in academia where strong evidence has produced a consistent and clear picture of the M-form benefits, whereas regional structures have been neglected to some extent. This imbalance has presumably found its way into our teaching programs, but it represents an interesting avenue for future research.

ACKNOWLEDGMENT

We are indebted to the Austrian National Bank (OeNB) for supporting this project.

REFERENCES

Ambos, T., & Andersson, U. (2010). What are the consequences of initiative-taking in multinational subsidiaries. *Journal of International Business Studies, 41*(7), 1099–1118.

Ambos, B., & Schlegelmilch, B. B. (2007). Innovation and control in the multinational firm: A comparison of political and contingency approaches. *Strategic Management Journal, 28*(5), 473–486.

Ambos, B., & Schlegelmilch, B. B. (2010). *The new role of regional management*. Basingstoke, UK: Palgrave Macmillan.

Argyres, N. (1996). Capabilities, technological diversification and divisionalization. *Strategic Management Journal, 17*(5), 395–410.

Asmussen, C. G. (2009). Local, regional, or global: Quantifying MNE geographic scope. *Journal of International Business Studies, 40*(7), 1192–1205.

Astley, G. W., & Sachdeva, S. P. (1984). Structural sources of intraorganizational power: A theoretical synthesis. *Academy of Management Review, 9*(1), 104–113.

Bartlett, C., & Ghoshal, S. (1989). *Managing across borders: The transnational solution*. Boston: Harvard Business School Press.

Chandler, A. D. (1991). The functions of the HQ unit in the multibusiness firm. *Strategic Management Journal, 12*(1), 31–50.

Ciabuschi, F., Martin, O., & Stahl, B. (2010). Headquarters' influence on knowledge transfer performance. *Management International Review, 50*(4), 471–491.

Daniels, J. D. (1987). Bridging national and global marketing strategies through regional operations. *International Marketing Review, 4*(3), 29–44.

Doz, Y., Santos, J. F. P., & Williamson, P. J. (2001). *From global to metanational*. Boston: Harvard Business School Press.

Egelhoff, W. G. (1988). Strategy and structure in multinational corporations: A revision of the stopford and wells model. *Strategic Management Journal, 9*(1), 1–14.

Egelhoff, W. G. (1991). Information-processing theory and the multinational enterprise. *Journal of International Business Studies, 22*(3), 341–368.

Egelhoff, W. G. (2010). How the parent HQ adds value to an MNC. *Management International Review, 50*(4), 413–432.

Eisenmann, T. R., & Bower, J. L. (2000). The entrepreneurial M-form: Strategic integration in global media firms. *Organization Science, 11*(3), 348–355.

Enright, M. J. (2005a). Regional management centers in the Asia-Pacific. *Management International Review, 45*(1), 59.

Enright, M. J. (2005b). The roles of regional management centers. *Management International Review, 45*(1), 83.

Erramilli, M. K. (2003). Regionalization of multinationals: Implications for research in international marketing. In: S. C. Jain (Ed.), *Handbook of research in international marketing*. Cheltenham, UK; Northampton, MA: Edward Elgar.

Gates, S. R., & Egelhoff, W. G. (1986). Centralization in HQ-subsidiary relationships. *Journal of International Business Studies, 17*(2), 71–92.

Gencturk, E. F., & Aulakh, P. S. (1995). The use of process and output controls in foreign markets. *Journal of International Business Studies, 26*(4), 755–786.

Ghemawat, P. (2003). Semiglobalization and international business strategy. *Journal of International Business Studies, 34*(2), 138–152.

Ghoshal, S., & Nohria, N. (1989). Internal differentiation within multinational corporations. *Strategic Management Journal, 10*(4), 323–337.

Goold, M., & Campbell, A. (2002). Parenting in complex structures. *Long Range Planning, 35*(3), 219–243.

Gulati, R., Puranam, P., & Tushman, M. (2009). Strategy and the design of organizational architecture. *Strategic Management Journal, 16*(Special issue), 7–20.

Hedlund, G. (1986). The hypermodern MNC: A heterarchy? *Human Resource Management, 25*(1), 9–36.

Holt, J., Purcell, W. R., Gray, S. J., & Pedersen, T. (2008). Decision factors influencing MNEs regional headquarters location selection strategies. In: A. Y. Lewin, S. T. Cavusgil, G. T. M. Hult & D. A. Griffith (Eds), *Thought leadership in advancing international business research*. New York: Palgrave Macmillan.

Lasserre, P. (1996). Regional headquarters: The spearhead for Asia Pacific markets. *Long Range Planning, 29*(1), 30.

Marschan-Piekkari, R., Welch, C., Penttinen, H., & Tahvanainen, M. (2004). Interviewing in the multinational corporation: Challenges of the organisational context. In: R. Marschan-Piekkari & C. Welch (Eds), *Handbook of qualitative research methods for international business* (pp. 244–263). Cheltenham, UK: Edward Elgar.

Nohria, N., & Ghoshal, S. (1997). *The differentiated network: Organizing multinationals for value creation*. San Francisco: Jossey-Bass.

O'Donnell, S. W. (2000). Managing foreign subsidiaries: Agents of headquarters, or an interdependent network? *Strategic Management Journal, 21*(5), 525–548.

Paik, Y., & Sohn, J. H. D. (2004). Striking a balance between global integration and local responsiveness: The case of Toshiba Corporation in redefining regional headquarters' role. *Organizational Analysis, 12*(4), 347–359.

Piekkari, R., Nell, P. C., & Ghauri, P. (2010). Regional management as a system: A longitudinal study. *Management International Review, 50*(4), 513–532.

Porter, M. E. (1986). Changing patterns of international competition. *California Management Review, 28*(2), 13–14.

Prahalad, C. K., & Doz, Y. (1987). *The multinational mission: Balancing local demands and global vision*. New York: The Free Press.

Rugman, A. M. (2005). *The regional multinationals*. Cambridge: Cambridge University Press.

Rugman, A. M., & Verbeke, A. (2004). A perspective on regional and global strategies of multinational enterprises. *Journal of International Business Studies, 35*(1), 3–18.

Schütte, H. (1996). *Regional headquarters of multinational corporations*. Ph.D. Dissertation, Universität St. Gallen.

Siddiqi, S. (2000). Customizing core competencies: The regional challenge. *International Journal of Commerce & Management, 10*(1), 91–104.

Simon, H. A. (1962). The architecture of complexity. *Proceedings of the American Philosophical Society, 106*(6), 467–482.

Sing, R. (2000). *Management teams at Asia Pacific regional headquarters*. Ph.D. Dissertation, Universität St. Gallen.

Stopford, J., & Wells, L. T. (1972). *Managing the multinational enterprise*. New York: Basic Books.

Sullivan, D. (1992). Organization in American MNCs: The perspective of the European regional headquarters. *Management International Review, 32*(3), 237–250.

Tallman, S., & Chacar, A. S. (2011). Knowledge accumulation and dissemination in MNEs: A practice-based framework. *Journal of Management Studies, 48*(2), 278–304.

Tran, Y., Mahnke, V., & Ambos, B. (2010). The effect of quantity, quality, and timing of headquarters-initiated knowledge flows on subsidiary performance. *Management International Review, 50*(4), 493–511.

Verbeke, A., & Kenworthy, T. P. (2008). Multidivisional vs metanational governance of the multinational enterprise. *Journal of International Business Studies, 39*(6), 940–956.

Vernon, R. (1966). International investment and international trade in the product cycle. *Quarterly Journal of Economics, 80*(2), 190–207.

Williamson, O. E. (1971). Managerial discretion, organization form, and the multi-division hypothesis. In: R. Marris & A. Wood (Eds), *The corporate economy, growth, competition and innovative potential* (pp. 343–386). London: Macmillan.

Williamson, O. E. (1996). *The mechanisms of governance.* Oxford: Oxford University Press.

Wolf, J. (1997). From "Starworks" to networks and heterachies? Theoretical rationale and empirical evidence of HRM organization in MNC. *Management International Review, 37*(1), 145–169.

Wolf, J., & Egelhoff, W. G. (2002). A re-examination and extension of international strategy-structure theory. *Strategic Management Journal, 23*(2), 181–189.

Yamin, M., & Forsgren, M. (2006). Hymer's analysis of the multinational organization: Power retention and the demise of the federative MNE. *International Business Review, 15*(2), 166–179.

Yeung, H. W.-C., Poon, J., & Perry, M. (2001). Towards a regional strategy: The role of regional headquarters of foreign firms in Singapore. *Urban Studies, 38*(1), 157–183.

Yin, R. (1994). *Case study research design and methods* (2nd ed.). Thousand Oaks, CA: Sage.

Zaheer, S. (1995). Overcoming the liability of foreignness. *The Academy of Management Journal, 38*(2), 341–363.

OVERCOMING LIABILITIES OF FOREIGNNESS BY MODES OF STRUCTURAL COORDINATION: REGIONAL HEADQUARTERS AND THEIR ROLE IN TNCs

Sven M. Laudien and Jörg Freiling

ABSTRACT

In our chapter, we show how internationalisation-based performance outcomes can be amended by using a Regional Headquarters (RHQ) structure. We assume that 'transnational corporations' (TNCs) act restrained by a so-called GLOCAL dilemma caused by a coeval need for realising standardisation advantages and 'location-specific advantages' (LSA). Thereby, we believe that these opportunities are not necessarily linked to the same level of geographical aggregation. We further take into account that emerging 'liabilities of foreignness' (LOF) exert influence on the performance effect of cross-border transactions and highlight the important role information quality plays in this context. To back our general line of reasoning, we employ the information cost approach (Casson, 1998, 1999) as theoretical frame of our chapter. This approach enhances the common one-dimensional view on transactions costs (e.g. Williamson, 1985) by understanding these costs as two-dimensional

Dynamics of Globalization: Location-Specific Advantages or Liabilities of Foreignness?
Advances in International Management, Volume 24, 107–125
ISSN: 1571-5027/doi:10.1108/S1571-5027(2011)0000024012

*phenomenon made up of 'observation costs' and 'communication costs'.
Additionally, the approach explicitly considers information quality, which
is useful to our analysis. Against this background, we discuss how
performance effects triggered by a use of RHQ evolve subject to basic
types of organisational structures used by TNCs. We contribute to
business research by providing a theoretically founded and widely new
performance-based angle on the RHQ phenomenon. It combines different
research streams that focus influences on cross-border business activities
by relying on either the idea of LOF or the idea of LSA.*

INTRODUCTION

Benefits of a *division of labour* are well known for more than a century (see, e.g.,
the seminal work of Smith, 1904 or Ricardo, 1817). Nevertheless, spreading
value chain activities (Porter, 1986) across borders requires considerable intra-
firm coordination to the end of an adequate *integration of labour* (Babbage,
1832). Otherwise, ongoing specialisation and differentiation could lead to
fragmentation that may constrain a smooth run of operational sequences.
Although this is beyond dispute in general, to date, little has been said on how
an adequate integration of labour could be achieved.

Against this general background, we shed light on how RHQ as structural
coordination mode can help TNCs (Bartlett & Ghoshal, 1989) solving the
coordinative requirements of a 'glocalised' world. Pursuing this aim, we need
to discuss drivers of these coordination requirements before focusing in detail
on the coordinative impact of RHQ.

In particular, two conflictive aspects cause complex problems of coordination. First, TNCs are committed to – at least to a certain extent – standardise
their worldwide business activities to realise economies of scale and scope
(Kogut, 1990). However, too much standardisation may be problematic as
well for it could lead to a non-awareness of important peculiarities of local
markets (Schütte, 1996; Porter, 1986; Chakravarthy & Perlmutter, 1985;
Cray, 1984; Heenan & Perlmutter, 1979). Furthermore, ex ante unrealised
foreign market entry barriers caused by cultural, political and economic
differences (Zaheer, 1995) may jeopardise the success of the chosen
standardisation strategy. Context-specific LOF (Asmussen, 2009; Nachum,
2003; Petersen & Pedersen, 2002; Zaheer & Mosakowski, 1997; Hymer, 1976)
as catalysts of these obstacles play a major role in this context. However, the
effect of these market entry barriers is not coercively negative as their

occurrence could also comprise prospects of standardisation – which are to a certain extent consequence of arising LSA – on a level lower than the global one (van Houten, 1989). Thus, the TNC ability to collect market-related information comes to an issue as the strategic decision about implementing a suitable degree of standardisation and differentiation of cross-border business activities is linked to the availability of detailed information as basis for decision-making. Given that TNCs are in most cases forced to follow a hybrid strategy to go along with the market development (Bartlett & Ghoshal, 1989), specific structural needs come to an issue (Porter, 1986). In particular, the necessity to secure a constant, cost-efficient and qualitatively adequate flow of information on global as well as local market conditions influences the structural configuration of the TNC.

Responding to standardisation, a centralistic structure seems to be the best choice for TNCs (Pugh, Hickson, Hinings, & Turner, 1968). Such structure allows a considerable reduction of fixed operation costs as a consequence of economising administrative units that operate on a regional level. However, due to geographic distance, it is more and more difficult and costly to collect information on local market characteristics. As for differentiation, a decentralised organisational structure would be a better choice (Rugman & Verbeke, 2007). Here, so-called *RHQs* (Enright, 2005; Yeung, Poon, & Perry, 2001; Schütte, 1996) that operate on a regional or even local level come into play. By implementing these units, fixed operation costs rise – but costs caused by collecting local market information may decline as the RHQ are located closer to the respective markets than the headquarters (HQ). In addition, a better quality of information may be achieved in this case due to RHQ's closeness to the market.

Against this background, we employ the information cost approach (Casson, 1998, 1999) to explain coordinative benefits of using RHQs. We believe that RHQs can serve as facilitator between the HQ and local subsidiaries as they exert considerable influence on the information flow between TNC local subsidiaries and the HQ. Due to closeness to regional and/or local markets, using a RHQ structure influences the quality of information available within the TNC. More than that, related to the information cost approach, the run of information costs, consisting of observation costs (related to 'collecting information') and communication costs (related to 'transferring information'), follows a non-linear U-shaped cost function (Casson, 1999). Despite of the costs triggered by implementing RHQ, it is possible that TNC's overall costs of operation decline if the costs of implementing and running RHQ do not exceed the economisation of information costs that can coevally be achieved by implementing a RHQ structure. As we acknowledge the important influence of basic types of organisational structures on the coordination effect of RHQ, we discuss in a second step the effectiveness of this structural coordination mode related to different types of basic TNC structures and try to highlight patterns of RHQ effectiveness. We close by discussing our findings and pointing to consequences for further research.

Our chapter contributes to business research in the following ways: We employ a widely new coordination-based perspective on the RHQ phenomenon and show a structural solution to the GLOCAL dilemma. So doing, we bring together different research streams that focus on the consequences of transnational business activities and either highlight the relevance of LOF or LSA. Furthermore, we provide a theory-based groundwork for future empirical research on the RHQ phenomenon.

TERMINOLOGY AND THEORETICAL BACKGROUND

Entering this emerging field of research requires some terminological groundwork for the purpose of clarification. Hence, we start with briefly discussing the term *transnational corporation* before we introduce *RHQs* as coordination mode.

Transnational Corporation

According to Bartlett and Ghoshal (1989), TNCs are *footloose companies* with a very low commitment to the country of origin. They easily transcend national economic boundaries by integrating global value-added processes into heterarchical structures. Different from multinational firms as rather decentralised federations and centralised global enterprises, TNCs respond to the need of *glocalisation* by some kind of 'hybrid' governance. As outlined in more detail later, hierarchical elements are connected with some market-like mechanisms. Compared to multinational enterprises, TNCs are typically not hub-focused but more or less 'hub-less' firms with a high number of linkages among their local and, in particular, regional units. Thus, their organisational structure and the mode of control employed are – at least in its archetype – unique and differ considerably from other types of firms that carry out cross-border transactions.

Against this particular background, economic governance comes to an issue as it prevents TNCs from only striving for an exploitation of local advantages. Inverse, economic governance reminds TNCs to respect their duties of corporate citizenship when taking chances on a global scale. Moreover, in a context of considerable uncertainty in transnational transactions, TNCs need to reduce this uncertainty in the absence of reliable supra-national legal structures of the nation state(s). Thus, they find themselves confronted with a need to develop modes of control for cross-border transactions on their own for the sake of protection against the negative impact of uncertainty.

Therefore, it is not surprising that TNCs tend to respond to a declining level of legal certainty by escaping from market transactions and transforming them into several different types of hierarchical structures to defend from opportunistic behaviour in cross-border transactions. The notion of the *varieties of hierarchy* best describes the different types of internal coordination relevant to TNCs. These varieties can be structured by two dimensions: the mode of control (formal or informal) and the sphere of influence (internal or external). In this chapter, we address RHQ as element of the formal internal organisational TNC structure. Therefore, our chapter contributes to a deeper understanding of *formal governance* in an *internal context*.

The Nature of Regional Headquarters

In general, RHQ are administrative units hierarchically located between the HQ and the local subsidiaries. RHQs are governed by the firm's HQ. However, there is considerable discretion in handling this governance role by the HQ so that the both active and more passive roles of the HQ are possible. Notwithstanding, the core function of the RHQ is to coordinate the subsidiaries in a region in a more specific manner that the corporate HQ is able to. RHQ align activities of local subsidiaries on a regional, function-oriented, product-oriented or customer-oriented basis.

Enright (2005) distinguishes between regional management centers, RHQ, regional offices and local offices. He uses the term *regional management centre* as generic term for all kinds of administrative units acting region-oriented. RHQ possess in his understanding more *autonomy* than regional offices. Local offices are integrated into the organisational structure on a lower hierarchical level than regional offices and take managerial responsibility for, for example, only one overseas branch.

Schütte (1996) stresses that RHQ conduct a strategic assignment and find themselves in conflict between global integration and local responsibility. He specifies his definition insofar as RHQ are in his view the *main tie between foreign subsidiaries and HQ*. Their major task is to ensure the integration and coordination of TNC activities within a specific geographic region. Formation, legal status and positioning of RHQ are not important in this context. The RHQ definition suggested by Schütte (1996) is broad and covers a variety of organisational units. Although this may be helpful to understand the phenomenon in general, it complicates a precise analysis of RHQ. Nevertheless, he focuses on the aspect of management responsibility and excludes administrative units solely founded for tax reasons from his understanding of RHQs.

According to Lasserre (1996), RHQ are *specific, region-oriented organisational units* that take responsibility for the activities of a TNC within a certain region and are, in addition to that, located in this region. Although he discusses the location aspect in a traceable manner, he misses to expose which specific activities are carried out by RHQs.

Yeung et al. (2001) define RHQ as organisational units that are responsible for business operations of one or several local subsidiaries within a specific geographic region. Administrative units without any *managerial discretion* are in their opinion no RHQs. Thus, they also stress the way of decision-making and autonomy issues. However, they do not make a statement on the preferable geographic position of RHQ.

The understandings outlined above shed some light on the nature of RHQ and help to develop a basic definition. In this sense, we understand *RHQ as organisational units that are hierarchically situated between the HQ and local subsidiaries. Endowed with managerial discretion and responsibility* confined to a certain region, they execute a managerial function towards the hierarchically subordinated local subsidiaries. The primary purpose of RHQ consists in carrying out a *coordinative* and an *administrative* function; aside, they can also fulfil a market function.

Information Cost Approach

The information cost approach employed here traces back to an idea mainly popularised by Casson (1999, 1998). On the basis of the insight that companies always have a certain amount of information on their disposal, this approach stresses that companies have to handle these information properly to be able to ensure a goal-oriented coordination of their activities. Provisioning and (internal) propagation of information is not free of costs for companies as, for example, geographical distances gain importance in this context. This holds particularly true for TNCs that are forced to manage a continuous and extensive flow of information within a geographically widespread structural network.

Basically enrooted in Williamsonian transaction cost economics (TCE) (Williamson, 1985), the information cost approach extends the one-dimensional TCE view by understanding transaction costs (i.e. information costs in this context) as a two-dimensional phenomenon and splitting them up into *observation costs* and *communication costs*. Furthermore, this approach explicitly highlights importance and relevance of information quality (Casson, 1998). Thus, we consider the information cost approach useful to serve as theoretical background for our chapter as it builds a strong framework for analysing the coordinative impact of RHQ structures and covers the aspects to be discussed in this context.

We think that the availability of information on both the internal situation of the TNC and external factors influencing TNC options for action is a major prerequisite for a high performance. As the relevant sources of information – like TNC value-added activities – are normally geographically widespread, it is essential for TNCs to employ an organisational structure that is suitable to optimise quantity and quality of required information considering the costs of information search, the costs of ensuring information quality and the consequential costs caused by incorrect or missing information (Casson, 1999). Thus, the relation between observation costs and communication costs and following its configurative implication is of particular importance.

Observation costs cover all costs emerging from the information search of the observer. *Communication costs* include all costs caused by the information transfer between the observer and the decision-maker responsible for the final (strategic) decision within the TNC. The closer the observer is located to the information source, the lower the observation costs are. Inversely, with growing distance between observer and decision-maker, communication costs rise (Casson, 1999) (Fig. 1).

When we apply this more general insight to our specific research topic, it is evident that RHQ adopt the observer role: RHQ monitor market developments that evolve for each market in their area of responsibility. Following this, a complex multilevel process is triggered off: RHQ have to record the information on changes, to evaluate the importance of each particular observation, to bring together these individual observations on a regional level and to transfer the result of this process to the HQ as decision-maker with responsibility for the final decision. In other words, the main duties of RHQ are collecting information, conditioning information,

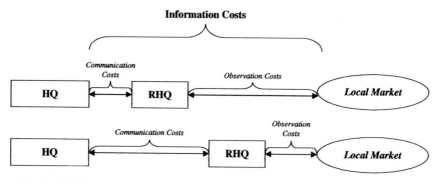

Fig. 1. RHQ/HQ Relationship in the View of the Information Cost Approach.

harmonising information and transmitting information (Casson, 1998; Aoki & Tachiki, 1992).

When estimating the overall information costs, we need to consider a non-linear alteration of observation costs and communication costs depending on the geographical distances of both HQ and RHQ (communication costs) as well as RHQ local market (observation costs). Thus, the aspect of how to locate the RHQ comes to an issue, in particular, in the face of (negative) effects due to LOF and (positive) effects of realising LSA. As for this decision process, we first need to consider issues of coding and decoding information because a transfer – and connected to that a transformation – of 'implicit information', that is information embedded in tacit knowledge structures, is necessary. Second, cultural and value-based differences between transmitter and receiver influence the interpretation of received information. If not adequately managed, both aspects might cause disproportional increases of information costs. Furthermore, the varying costs of the information transfer that depend on the chosen medium influence the information costs (Casson, 1999). Therefore, TNCs have to design and implement modes of governance to resolve the trade-off between information costs and information quality. Enhanced information quality typically goes hand in hand with increasing information costs. Thus, TNCs aspire to implement an efficient organisational structure ensuring a sound relation of information costs and information quality. In this respect, effective coordination can lead to higher information quality and, at the same time, decreasing information costs.

The information cost function LC_0EC_1 in Fig. 2 is the curve that describes the run of the minimal information costs depending on the degree of coordination. By means of using an organisational structure as well as other coordination

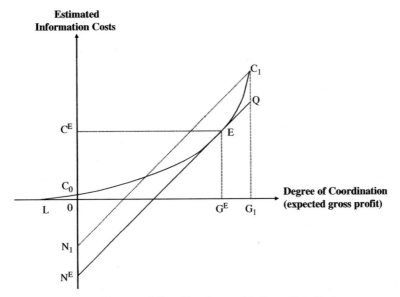

Fig. 2. Degree of Coordination and Information Costs.

methods providing in interaction best possible information supply, C_1 could be reached. L is the situation with no information collection at all, which causes an expected gross loss. Hence, TNCs need coordination modes to reach information costs of at least C_0 to attain the break-even point. Assuming a maximal degree of coordination (C_1), a gross profit of $0G_1$ can be reached. When subtracting the accumulating information costs, a net profit of $0N_1$ remains. Presuming suboptimal coordination, only a gross profit of $0G^E$ but a higher net profit of $0N^E$ could be achieved. Reason for this development is a – compared to the implemented degree of coordination – disproportionate reduction of information costs. According to Casson (1998), E describes the point where TNCs are able to maximise their net profit due to information costs and coordinative efforts.

Therefore, TNCs have to (re-)design their organisational structure to resolve the trade-off between information costs and information quality. Corresponding to the information cost approach, neither an entirely centralised organisational structure nor a completely decentralised organisational structure appears to be advantageous for TNCs when simultaneously taking into account information costs and information quality. This gives rise to the impression of the superiority of 'hybrid' structures, such as RHQ bridging global and local needs within TNC structures.

According to the information cost approach, the exact RHQ location determines the performance-related benefit that can be achieved by employing such structural coordination instruments. The reason for this is that TNC make their decision about locating their RHQ structures based on information costs and the necessary information quality. From a cost perspective, the location of the RHQs, which is initially influenced by the necessary information quality, defines the costs stemming from collecting and transmitting information. Assuming that RHQs possess considerable managerial discretion, a reduction of communication and information costs can be achieved by implementing a RHQ structure due to the fact that the transfer of information from RHQ to the HQ considerably decreases in intensity (Laudien & Freiling, 2010). Furthermore, TNCs could enhance their reaction time related to environmental influences by using RHQ (Casson, 1999, 1998). As communication costs are due to modern information and communication technology not that important for TNCs any more, it is from a cost-oriented as well as an information quality-oriented perspective advisable to locate RHQ preferably close to their area(s) of responsibility (Casson, 1999) to ensure high information quality. This is momentous as exact information fosters effective coordination of TNC activities and therefore reduces coordination effort and coordination costs in general.

Besides that, establishing or using RHQ causes costs itself and normally goes along with growing organisational complexity triggered by a growing number of units involved in the production of goods and services (Root, 1994). This complexity rests to a large extent on a growing number of organisational interdependencies (Thompson, 1967). The handling of these ties causes costs as well. Thus, when using RHQ, TNCs have to ensure that the structure-based increase of costs does not exceed the earnings achieved by following a coeval intraregional standardisation and interregional differentiation strategy (Schütte, 1996).

A STRUCTURAL APPROACH TO SOLVE THE 'GLOCAL' DILEMMA

Against the chosen theoretical framework, we now concentrate on analysing the consequences of implementing a RHQ structure. Particularly, we focus on the influence of this structural change on LOF as well as LSAs. Subsequently, we proceed in two steps: We start with identifying general pros and cons of using a RHQ structure. Next, we look at RHQ from a more organisational viewpoint and show (organisational) prerequisites for implementing such a type of structure.

General Prerequisites for Implementing RHQ

The performance of TNCs is to a large extent influenced by the availability of information on both the internal situation of the TNC and the external factors that influence the TNC scope of action. However, gaining necessary information is difficult for TNCs because their value-added activities and the relevant sources of information are typically geographically widely spread. Nevertheless, it is necessary for TNCs to gather relevant and detailed information not only on a global but also on a local scale as they have to identify local prospects and local risks to ensure or improve their performance and to make sure their long-term survival. Therefore, it deems essential for TNCs to implement a coordination mode like RHQ, which can be used to ensure the availability of a sufficient quantity and quality of required information considering the costs of information search, the costs of ensuring information quality and the consequential costs caused by incorrect or missing information (Casson, 1999; Morrison, Ricks, & Roth, 1991).

However, using RHQ structures is sometimes difficult and goes along with a need to integrate specific foreign markets into (more) homogeneous, non-overlapping regional markets to be able to strive for a realisation of standardisation advantages (Laudien & Freiling, 2010; Yeung et al., 2001; Sullivan, 1992). In this context, aspects like the geographical position of the markets (Schuh, 2000; Davidson & McFetridge, 1985; Fayerweather, 1978), the future market-specific development of demand (Enright & Scott, 2000) as well as cultural and political market characteristics (Schlie & Yip, 2000; Erramilli & Rao, 1993; Kuin, 1972) matter. Furthermore, TNCs have to define regional markets thoroughly to ensure a critical mass as a prerequisite for realising standardisation advantages (Bélis-Bergouignan, Bordenave, & Lung, 2000). Besides that, by defining these internally homogeneous regional markets, TNCs have to assure an external heterogeneity to capitalise on LSAs by considering local peculiarities (Singh, 2000).

As for the uncertainty in international coordination, the geographical and cultural distances challenge TNCs often considerably. In this context, the TNC structure allows for a better control of uncertain coordination by replacing markets by hierarchy. Thus, a RHQ structure may provide a safer governance framework for carrying out international business activities from a TNC point of view for they could carry out an observer function related to the foreign (local) markets subsidiaries as well as a – normally bilateral – transmitter function between the HQ and the foreign subsidiaries they are responsible for.

However, RHQ need certain capabilities to carry out their role in an adequate way. In this context, the construct of *absorptive capacity* (Minbaeva, Pedersen, Björkman, Fey, & Park, 2003; Lane & Lubatkin, 1998; Cohen & Levinthal, 1990) comes into play. The absorptive capacity describes a firm's ability to recognise, assimilate and exploit external information. The construct seems to be of particular importance for TNCs when using RHQ. It reveals that acquiring information is not enough. Aiming at value creation, TNCs are forced to combine externally absorbed knowledge with internally acquired knowledge (Kogut & Zander, 1992). Schumpeter (1934) was the first to point out that such *combinative capability* is crucial for firm development in general. Having a look at RHQ, *combinative capability* seems to be important for moving knowledge within the TNC and integrating knowledge from different sources (Phene & Almeida, 2008; Schmid & Schurig, 2003).

As RHQ act as facilitator between HQ and subsidiaries, they also need a great deal of diplomatic aptitude as well as substantial persuasive power and not at least experience to carry out their role professionally. This is especially important because RHQ, apart from expert power, do not have much other sources of power to enforce their opinion against the HQ simply because of the fact that they are hierarchically subordinated under the HQ. Focusing on the relationship between RHQ and foreign subsidiaries, the RHQ could use power to extrude decisions but that would not be effective for such a proceeding may destroy trust and therefore have a negative impact on future communication and collaboration between the RHQ and the subsidiaries the RHQ is responsible for (Leonard-Barton, 1995). Thus, the course of action (and also the success) of the RHQ seem to be very much influenced by the RHQ's reliability in transactions with the subordinated subsidiaries and the HQ as well.

Organisational Prerequisites for Implementing Regional Headquarters

The effect of using RHQ is not universal but to a large extent influenced by the type of organisational structure used by the TNC (Laudien & Freiling, 2010). Therefore, we take a look at relevant organisational structures (Carper & Snizek, 1980; Davis, 1979; Clee & Sachtjen, 1964). Two criteria are relevant to identify adequate types of organisational structures – the organisational involvement of national and international activities and the form of specialisation employed.

As to the organisational involvement, differentiation and integration of national and international activities are the typical options to deal with this challenge. As differentiated structures are often only used by companies when international activities are of minor interest, such types of structures can be excluded analysing a use of RHQ in a TNC context. Focusing on specialisation, we can differ among one-dimensional structural types (functional structure, product-oriented structure, regional structure and customer-oriented structure) and the multidimensional ones (matrix structure and tensor structure).

As for multidimensional organisational structures, RHQ cannot be expediently implemented in such structures due to the hierarchical multi-subordination, which is quintessential for these types of structure. This leads to the conclusion that RHQ can only be valuable in distinct one-dimensional organisational structures that may be worth discussing related to the increasing use of network structures (Yang, Ziang, & Ya, 2010).

Analysing one-dimensional organisational structures in detail, an implementation of RHQ could be possible in general. But employing the same specialisation criterion (function, product, region and customers) on different hierarchical levels seems to be problematic at first glance while it may be impossible to distinguish subcategories in each case. Related to the criterion 'region', this aspect is not of importance as subregions can be defined easily. To some extent, the same holds true for the criteria 'function' and 'product'. But with regard to the criterion 'customers', it would be difficult to reason a further distinction as customers cannot be arbitrarily parted. On the basis of this, we assume that only in case of using the criterion 'region' on different hierarchical levels, the achievable cost benefit, which is mostly based on coeval cultural intraregional standardisation and interregional differentiation, will be big enough to compensate the complexity-based negative cost effect.

In general, the obtainable cost benefit of using RHQ in a one-dimensional organisational structure is related to the extent foreign subsidiaries can be clearly assigned to RHQ. This is not astonishing because the increase of organisational complexity triggered by a use of RHQ is directly linked to the number of existing organisational interdependencies. Following this train of thought, a distinction of two cases seems to be helpful to analyse the cost-oriented benefit that can be generated by establishing RHQ. *Case 1* is characterised by a clear attribution of foreign subsidiaries to (only) one certain RHQ. In contrast, *case 2* is about foreign subsidiaries subordinated under more than one RHQ. Ceteris paribus, the attainable benefit (loss) of using a RHQ structure is always at least marginally greater (lesser) related to the presence of *case 1* than of *case 2*. Two directly opposed effects account for this outcome: a positive standardisation/differentiation effect and a negative complexity effect. Although the function-, product-, region- or customer-related positive standardisation/differentiation effect – an effect that allows for overcoming LOF and coevally realising LSAs – stays constant for both cases, the complexity effect that originates from an increasing number of inter-organisational interdependencies differs considerably related to the employed organisational specialisation criterion. This holds generally true except for using region as specialisation criterion while a clear subordination of foreign subsidiaries under only one RHQ seems to be guaranteed using this criterion.

On the basis of this insight, it transpires that the impact of implementing RHQ is always twofold and the overall benefit is considerably determined by the type of organisational structure that is basically used by the TNC. First, using RHQ could contribute to the realisation of LSAs by offering an organisational way to consider peculiarities of certain demarcated, internally homogeneous but externally heterogeneous regions. Second, within these regions, standardisation effects can be realised by TNCs that constrain LOF. Notwithstanding that, the overall effect of implementing a combined standardisation/differentiation strategy stays prima facie undetermined for specific organisational characteristics come into play and hamper the exploitation of the chosen strategy to a certain extent. Anyhow, from a governance perspective, employing a RHQ structure seems an interesting mode for TNCs to reduce uncertainty and to expand the predictability of transnational business activities.

Evidence on the RHQ Phenomenon

First insights from the automotive industry give evidence for our thoughts presented here. On the basis of telephone interviews with middle managers and backed up by an analysis of the latest annual reports of the General Motors Corporation, the Daimler AG and the Toyota Motor Corporation, we found evidence that these firms employ RHQ in coordinative function – but also have to admit that the use of RHQ is quite limited within these companies.

GM employs RHQ in a functional (divisional) type of organisational structure to control activities in very complex regions such as North America or Asia-Pacific. This supports our educated guess that ensuring information quality and reducing complexity are two major reasons for a use of RHQ. As a clear subordination of subsidiaries under a certain RHQ can be detected, it gives also backup for our presumption that the benefit of employing RHQ is to a large extent influenced by the degree of the complexity effect triggered by implementing RHQ.

Daimler uses a product-oriented structure and employs RHQ especially in the area *Financial Services*. As local law and provisions are of major relevance in this context, the aspect of ensuring a certain information quality seems to be relevant for structuring this area following a geographic (but very general and mostly US-focused) segmentation. A deeper look at the organisation structure of Daimler reveals that certain units combining a functional and geographic scope are also employed within the product divisions. These units are not RHQ in a classical understanding but are nevertheless a first hint for the relevance of RHQ.

Toyota is the only company that explicitly mentions RHQ and uses them inter-divisionally in a basic functional (divisional) structure. These RHQ take responsibility for certain geographic areas. Their main duties are to coordinate the Toyota activities within the region, to support national Toyota subsidiaries, to collect information on local trends and to announce these trends to the HQ. Furthermore, these RHQ are responsible for (regional) public relations. This substantially supports our view on RHQ functions, their tasks and their embeddedness in organisational structures of TNCs.

To sum up the evidence on RHQ we collected, only Toyota seems to be really aware of the benefits that can be achieved by using RHQ and consequently admits that certain administrative units carry out a – quite clearly described – RHQ function. The other two companies also use organisational units in a RHQ function but do not point that out directly. This may be a question of strategy but could also relate to missing awareness. Future research will show the reason for that.

SUMMARY AND LIMITATIONS

In this chapter we show how TNCs can resolve the 'GLOCAL' dilemma by implementing RHQ and generating a cost-oriented benefit from coevally paying attention to LSA and LOF and give some very first evidence. Our reasoning is based on the information cost approach. In detail, we point out how a use of RHQ can stabilise internal transactions and contribute to a realisation standardisation and differentiation advantages at the same time. We thereby explicitly consider the influences of LSAs and LOF. Furthermore, we combine the ideas of LSAs and LOF and try to integrate them into one way of thinking, an approach that is up to now widely new for business research. By focusing on structural coordination of transnational business activities, we draw on an aspect whose importance is currently mostly ignored by researchers as informal coordination normally takes the front seat in latest research (Cantwell, Dunning, & Lundan, 2010).

In detail, we show prerequisites for implementing RHQ as structural governance mechanism and demonstrate that the cost-oriented impact of using RHQ is always twofold: On the one hand, a positive standardisation/ differentiation benefit can be realised; on the other hand, a negative complexity effect occurs out of this structuring procedure. Thereby, the overall effect stays prima facie undetermined and is largely influenced by the type of organisational structure implemented. We further presume that a superior cost-oriented benefit can be raised within a regional structure, whereas a customer-oriented structure comprises only little possibilities to gain a cost advance by using RHQ. The cost benefits that can be generated by using RHQ within a product-oriented or a functional structure are limited by these two extreme examples.

Our chapter contributes to business research by highlighting how TNCs can coevally benefit from standardisation and differentiation effects by employing RHQ structures. Thereby, our reasoning integrates widely conflictive research streams that identify the existence of either LOF or LSA as a consequence of transnational business activities. Furthermore, we present a widely new access to the RHQ phenomenon and prepare the field for further (empirical) research. Finally, we emphasise the relevance of self-created organisational structures in governing TNC activities.

Newness and complexity of our research topic animated us to employ a mainly conceptual, but theoretically well-founded approach. We are aware of the possibilities and the shortcomings of this procedure. Useful for the purpose of clarification and the development of first causalities, mainly conceptual papers do normally not aim at verifying/falsifying the conclusions they give. The same holds true for our paper. The empirical test, insofar, is still open. Other shortcomings are highlighted in literature (e.g. Punch, 2005). All in all, we are persuaded of the necessity of carrying out conceptual work when entering a new field of research to provide a sustainable basis for further (empirical) research and hope that our study contributes to an understanding how TNCs can consider the coeval existence of LSAs and LOF and overcome negative effects emerging from this initial situation by a use of RHQ. Furthermore, newness, complexity and strategic relevance of the RHQ phenomenon complicate at least meaningful quantitative empirical research on this topic. Thus, qualitative empirical research (e.g. case studies) on this topic seems to be a promising first step to confront the findings with reality.

In addition to that, by employing the information cost approach, we chose a quite simple theoretical approach to display the effectiveness of RHQs. The approach is static and deterministic. Nevertheless, we made this choice intentionally for the reason that a simple theoretical background enables us to focus our analysis on clear and essential impact of RHQs on meaningful performance measure. Future studies may show if relying on a more complex background will expand the knowledge on RHQ.

To date, only little is known about assets and drawbacks of RHQ structures in terms of transnational governance. We hope that this chapter contributes to call attention to this phenomenon, which is presumably of considerable practical relevance.

REFERENCES

Aoki, A., & Tachiki, D. S. (1992). Overseas Japanese business operations: The emerging role of regional headquarters. *Pacific Business and Industries, 1*(3), 29–39.

Asmussen, C. G. (2009). Local, regional, or global? Quantifying MNE geographic scope. *Journal of International Business Studies, 40*(9), 1192–1205.

Babbage, C. (1832). *On the economy of machinery and manufacturers.* London: Charles Knight Pall Mall East.

Bartlett, C. A., & Ghoshal, S. (1989). *Managing across borders: The transnational solution.* Boston, MA: McGraw-Hill.

Bélis-Bergouignan, M.-C., Bordenave, G., & Lung, Y. (2000). Global strategies in the automobile industry. *Regional Studies, 34*(1), 41–53.

Cantwell, J., Dunning, J. H., & Lundan, S. (2010). An evolutionary approach to understanding international business activity: The co-evolution of MNEs and the institutional environment. *Journal of International Business Studies, 41*(3), 567–586.

Carper, W. B., & Snizek, W. E. (1980). The nature and types of organizational taxonomies: An overview. *Academy of Management Review, 5*(1), 65–75.

Casson, M. (1998). Information costs and the organisational structure of the multinational enterprise. In: N. J. Foss & B. J. Loasby (Eds), *Economic organization, capabilities, and co-ordination* (pp. 204–221). New York, NY: Routledge.

Casson, M. (1999). The organisation and evolution of the multinational enterprise: An information cost approach. *Management International Review, 39*(1), 77–121.

Chakravarthy, B., & Perlmutter, H. V. (1985). Strategic planning for a global business. *Columbia Journal of World Business, 20*(2), 3–10.

Clee, G. H., & Sachtjen, W. M. (1964). Organizing a worldwide business. *Harvard Business Review, 42*(6), 55–67.

Cohen, W., & Levinthal, D. (1990). Absorptive capacity: A new perspective on learning and innovation. *Administrative Science Quarterly, 35*(1), 128–152.

Cray, D. (1984). Control and coordination in multinational corporations. *Journal of International Business Studies, 15*(2), 85–89.

Davidson, W. H., & McFetridge, D. G. (1985). Key characteristics in the choice of international technology transfer mode. *Journal of International Business Studies, 16*(2), 5–21.

Davis, S. (1979). Basic structures of multinational corporations. In: S. Davis (Ed.), *Managing and organizing the multinational corporation* (pp. 193–211). New York: Pergamon Press.

Enright, M. J. (2005). The roles of regional management centers. *Management International Review, 45*(1), 83–102.

Enright, M. J., & Scott, E. (2000). The RHQ question. *Business Asia, 32*(1), 1–4.

Erramilli, K., & Rao, C. (1993). Service firms' international entry mode choice: A modified transaction cost analysis approach. *Journal of Marketing, 57*(3), 19–38.

Fayerweather, J. (1978). *International business strategy and administration.* Cambridge, MA: Bullinger.

Heenan, D. A., & Perlmutter, H. V. (1979). *Multinational organization development.* Reading, MA: Addison Wesley Publishing.

Hymer, S. H. (1976). *The international operations of national firms: A study of direct investment.* Cambridge, MA: MIT Press.

Kogut, B. (1990). International sequential advantages and network flexibility. In: A. Bartlett, Y. Doz & G. Hedlund (Eds), *Managing the global firm* (pp. 47–68). London: Routledge.

Kogut, B., & Zander, U. (1992). Knowledge of the firm, combinative capabilities and the replication of technology. *Organisation Science, 3*(3), 383–396.

Kuin, P. (1972). The magic of multinational management. *Harvard Business Review, 50*(6), 89–97.

Lane, P., & Lubatkin, M. (1998). Relative absorptive capacity and interorganizational learning. *Strategic Management Journal, 19*(5), 461–477.

Lasserre, P. (1996). Regional headquarters: The spearhead for Asia Pacific markets. *Long Range Planning, 29*(1), 30–37.

Laudien, S. M., & Freiling, J. (2010). *Reasoning a use of regional headquarters in TNCs as structural instrument of coordination.* SSRN Working Paper, September. Available at http://ssrn.com/abstract=1674389.

Leonard-Barton, D. (1995). *Wellsprings of knowledge: Building and sustaining the sources of innovation.* Boston, MA: Harvard Business School Press.

Minbaeva, B., Pedersen, T., Björkman, I., Fey, C., & Park, H. (2003). MNC knowledge transfer, subsidiary absorptive capacity, and HRM. *Journal of International Business Studies, 34*(6), 586–599.

Morrison, A. J., Ricks, D. A., & Roth, K. (1991). Globalization vs. regionalization: Which way for the multinational? *Organizational Dynamics, 19*(3), 17–29.

Nachum, L. (2003). Liability of foreignness in global competition? Financial service affiliates in the city of London. *Strategic Management Journal, 24*(12), 1187–1208.

Petersen, B., & Pedersen, T. (2002). Coping with liability of foreignness: Different learning engagements of entrant firms. *Journal of International Management, 8*(3), 339–350.

Phene, A., & Almeida, P. (2008). Innovation in multinational subsidiaries: The role of knowledge assimilation and subsidiary capabilities. *Journal of International Business, 39*(4), 901–919.

Porter, M. E. (1986). Competition in global industries: A conceptual framework. In: M. E. Porter (Ed.), *Competition in global industries* (pp. 15–60). Boston, MA: Harvard Business School Press.

Pugh, D. S., Hickson, D. J., Hinings, C. R., & Turner, C. (1968). Dimensions of organization structure. *Administrative Science Quarterly, 13*(1), 65–105.

Punch, K. F. (2005). *Introduction to social research: Quantitative & qualitative approaches*. London: Sage.

Ricardo, D. (1817). *On the principles of political economy and taxation*. London: John Murray.

Root, F. R. (1994). *Entry strategies for international markets* (2nd ed.). San Franciso, CA: Jossey-Bass.

Rugman, A. M., & Verbeke, A. (2007). Liabilities of regional foreignness and the use of firm-level versus country-level data: A response to Dunning et al. (2007). *Journal of International Business Studies, 38*(1), 200–205.

Schlie, E. H., & Yip, G. S. (2000). Regional follows global: Strategy mixes in the automotive industry. *European Management Journal, 18*(4), 343–354.

Schmid, S., & Schurig, A. (2003). The development of critical capabilities in foreign subsidiaries: Disentangling the role of the subsidiary's business network. *International Business Review, 12*(6), 755–782.

Schuh, A. (2000). Global standardization as a success formula for marketing in central and Eastern Europe? *Journal of World Business, 35*(2), 133–148.

Schumpeter, J. (1934). *The theory of economic development*. Cambridge, MA: Harvard University Press.

Schütte, H. (1996). *Regional headquarters of multinational corporations*. St. Gallen, Switzerland: St. Gallen University Press.

Singh, R. (2000). *Management teams at Asia pacific regional headquarters. Composition, determinants, and effects*. St. Gallen, Switzerland: St. Gallen University Press.

Smith, A. (1904). *An inquiry into the wealth of nations*. London: Methuen & Co. Ltd.

Sullivan, D. (1992). Organization in American MNCs: The perspective of European regional headquarters. *Management International Review, 32*(2), 237–250.

Thompson, J. D. (1967). *Organizations in action*. New York, NY: McGraw-Hill.

van Houten, G. (1989). The implications of globalism: New management realities at Philips. In: P. Evans, Y. Doz & A. Laurent (Eds), *Human resource management in international firms* (pp. 101–112). New York, NY: St. Martin's Press.

Williamson, O. E. (1985). *The economic institutions of capitalism: Firms markets, relational contracting*. New York; London: Free Press.

Yang, H., Ziang, L., & Ya, L. (2010). A multilevel framework of firm boundaries: Firm characteristics, dyadic differences and network attributes. *Strategic Management Journal, 31*(2), 237–261.

Yeung, H. W., Poon, J., & Perry, M. (2001). Towards a regional strategy: The role of regional headquarters of foreign firms in Singapore. *Urban Studies, 38*(1), 157–183.

Zaheer, S. (1995). Overcoming the liability of foreignness. *Academy of Management Journal, 38*(2), 341–363.

Zaheer, S., & Mosakowski, E. (1997). The dynamics of the liability of foreignness: A global study of survival in financial services. *Strategic Management Journal, 18*(6), 439–463.

MOVING ABROAD: FACTORS THAT MOTIVATE FOREIGN LOCATION OF HEADQUARTER ACTIVITIES

Randi Lunnan, Gabriel R. G. Benito and Sverre Tomassen

ABSTRACT

To what extent, why and where do multinational companies locate divisional headquarters (DHQs) abroad? This study of 30 of the largest listed companies in Norway over the 2000–2006 period shows that foreign-located DHQs have become relatively commonplace. A majority of DHQs located abroad are outcomes of foreign acquisitions, which suggests that obtaining legitimacy from local stakeholders such as customers, employees and investors is an important motivation. We also find that Norwegian companies emphasize efficiency and value creation in their location choices, as they tend to prefer other advanced and competitive countries as hosts for their DHQs. Distance from Norway is not significant. The off-shoring of strategic units such as DHQs is a phenomenon that occurs in advanced phases of companies' internationalization, beyond the point when familiarity and proximity still are key decision-making factors.

Dynamics of Globalization: Location-Specific Advantages or Liabilities of Foreignness?
Advances in International Management, Volume 24, 127–151
ISSN: 1571-5027/doi:10.1108/S1571-5027(2011)0000024013

INTRODUCTION

A prominent feature of globalization is an increased internationalization of operational as well as strategic activities in multinational companies (MNCs). Forsgren, Holm, and Johanson (1992) describe this process as internationalization of the first and second degree. Companies typically start their internationalization by exporting and then producing outside their home countries. Then at a second stage, foreign subsidiaries take on strategic roles such as world mandates or centres of excellence (Holm & Pedersen, 2000). More recently, we have started to identify 'internationalization of the third degree' (Birkinshaw, Braunerhjelm, Holm, & Terjesen, 2006), which occurs as companies locate their headquarters to foreign locations.

How widespread is foreign headquarters location? Normally, corporate headquarters are located in the country of origin, and relocations are rare, even within one country. Anecdotal evidence and a handful of studies (Barner-Rasmussen, Piekkari, & Björkman, 2007; Benito, Lunnan, & Tomassen, 2011; Birkinshaw et al., 2006; Forsgren, Holm, & Johanson, 1995) suggest that headquarter functions recently have become increasingly internationalized. Although the growth in foreign-located regional headquarter functions has been addressed in former studies (Enright, 2005a, 2005b; Lasserre, 1996; Piekkari, Nell, & Ghauri, 2010; Ambos & Schlegelmilch, 2010), the role of MNC headquarters as well as their location and relocation have received relatively limited scholarly attention (Birkinshaw et al., 2006; Baaij, Van den Bosch, & Volberda, 2004; Collis, Young, & Goold, 2007). Our understanding of the location choices of multinational headquarter activities is therefore rather limited and deserves more attention.

During the 20th century, most large Western companies became multi-business corporations characterized by a corporate office and more or less autonomous divisions (Collis et al., 2007). Divisionalization is a way to handle increasing size, operational diversity and geographic dispersion (Westney & Zaheer, 2001). Divisions are based on product or geographic markets. Corporate headquarters take responsibility for overall strategy whereas divisional headquarters (DHQ) coordinate activities within a given product or geographic scope, consequently we include the term regional headquarters within our DHQ concept. The managers of DHQs play a vital linking role, cooperating closely with operational subsidiary managers parallel to providing information to corporate headquarters (Forsgren et al., 1995). Whereas corporate relocations are rare, foreign location of DHQs are more frequent.

In this study we focus on DHQs foreign location. We use panel data on a sample of Norwegian MNCs over a period of seven years (2000–2006) to investigate the location dynamics of DHQs. Previously we have shown a massive movement of DHQs between 2000 and 2006 (Benito et al., 2011). That study exposed in particular how company and ownership factors influence the decision of whether or not DHQs are located abroad. Here we take the obvious next step and look more closely into companies' choice of location. Our analysis suggests that DHQs foreign locations are driven by multiple forces, some location bound, others less so. We integrate these factors in a framework conceptualizing factors that drive locations of DHQs abroad.

FIVE PREDICTIONS OF HEADQUARTERS LOCATION CHOICES

The academic literature on headquarters location and relocation is relatively scarce, and most studies are from the Nordic region (Barner-Rasmussen et al., 2007; Benito et al., 2011; Birkinshaw et al., 2006; Forsgren et al., 1995). This is not surprising as any relocation in a small economy is likely to be international, and therefore, this phenomenon is first observed here. There is also a growing body of literature on regional headquarters and their location (Ambos & Schlegelmilch, 2010; Enright, 2005a, 2005b; Lasserre, 1996; Piekkari et al., 2010; Schutte, 1997), regional HQ movements (Holloway & Wheeler, 1991; Baaij et al., 2004), as well as location factors attracting headquarters (Bel & Fageda, 2008). Furthermore, we draw on theories of internationalization to inform a study of motivations of DHQ location choices (Forsgren et al., 1992; Johanson & Vahlne, 1977). From these literatures we can develop at least five overall predictions guiding location choices of DHQs covering location characteristics, value creation, efficiency, legitimacy and control.

The first prediction suggests that DHQs will tend to be located in mature, safe and knowledge-rich locations. Dunning's eclectic framework (2000) maintains that the MNC will locate activities where these demonstrate competitiveness and furthermore benefit from local characteristics such as low cost, access to resources and technologies. Headquarters manage other subsidiaries and need safe and reliable access to these; thus, a factor such as availability of direct intercontinental flights has proved an important location indicator (Bel & Fageda, 2008). Consequently, transportation and

Internet connections as well as political stability are all important factors. In addition, companies value access to a highly qualified workforce as well as interactions with the headquarters of other MNCs (Lovely, Rosenthal, & Sharma, 2005). Birkinshaw et al. (2006) found that two of the important motivational factors of DHQs relocation were attractiveness in terms of competitive positioning, and the quality of suppliers and customers. Headquarter activities represent high-value activities and should therefore be drawn to mature, advanced and knowledge-intensive locations (Mudambi, 2008).

The second prediction states that DHQs will be located where they can be most effective in terms of value creation. One important role of headquarters is strategy development (Chandler, 1991). Headquarters provide corporate governance through parenting of subsidiaries, and the value of this parenting depends on headquarters' understanding of subsidiary resources as well as external challenges (Ambos & Mahnke, 2010; Campbell, Goold, & Alexander, 1995). Egelhoff (2010, p. 428) argues that the advantage of a hierarchy is its ability to gather and centralize at a single point, information from disparate parts of an organization so that it can be comprehensively evaluated and understood. We support this notion and suggest that headquarters must collect and understand not only internal information but also information from customers, suppliers and competitors to provide good parenting through the development of common strategies across subsidiaries. Porter (1998, p. 343) argues that every business division must have a healthy 'home base' that assembles the resources, skills, technologies and information that are most essential for competitive advantage. This base should preferentially be located at home, but if the home location deteriorates and upgrading is unsuccessful, DHQs should be moved to more vibrant locations enjoying stronger cluster conditions. Doz, Santos, and Williamson (2001) argue that to succeed, the meta-national must have units that sense, mobilize and integrate knowledge across activities, locations and subsidiaries, implying a more flexible and active role for headquarters based on closeness to critical new innovations.

There has been a stream of research arguing that regions differ (Asmussen, 2009; Ghemawat, 2001; Rugman & Verbeke, 2004). If a distant location is very different from the home market, the global headquarters will have a lower understanding of challenges facing local subsidiaries (Lasserre, 1996), and it will be more difficult for them to discover strategic opportunities that cut across individual subsidiaries and day-to-day activities (Foss, 1997). If we see a headquarters unit as an orchestrator of a network (Dhanaraj & Parkhe, 2006), the innovation in such a network is greater if hub firms (headquarters) can enhance a common network identity as well as encourage socialization (Brown & Duguid, 2001; Dyer & Nobeoka, 2000). Placing DHQs in resource-rich locations allows an MNC to capture the cross market differences of customers and employees (Schutte, 1998), decreasing the 'liability of foreignness' (Hymer, 1976) and protecting special subsidiary competencies and initiatives from a narrow 'headquarters mentality' (Lehrer & Asakawa, 1999). A DHQ location close to core customers, resources or technologies may therefore enhance the understanding and knowledge of DHQ managers, which in turn would improve their ability to create value for subsidiaries.

The third prediction suggests that DHQs will be located where they can operate most efficiently. The agency problem arises due to information asymmetry and goal incongruence between two entities (Hennart, 1991). Information asymmetry increases with cultural and geographic distance, thereby allowing subsidiaries to act independently (Hitt, Hoskisson, & Ireland, 1994). When involvement of headquarters is limited, it is more difficult to unveil shirking (Foss, 1997). Locating headquarter activities close to the centre of gravity eases communication and facilitates more efficient headquarters–subsidiary relations (Birkinshaw et al., 2006; Forsgren et al., 1995), avoids problems of time–zone differences (Elango, 2004), and facilitates communication and information exchange due to lower 'psychic distance' (Johanson & Vahlne, 1977). Location of headquarters abroad also enhances uses of socialization mechanisms that may reduce agency costs (Eisenhardt, 1989). In summary, the third prediction assumes that an MNC will locate DHQs to improve efficiency through improved control and coordination of local subsidiaries.

The fourth prediction argues that MNCs will locate DHQs abroad to increase their legitimacy. Legitimacy is defined as acceptance and approval of organizational actions by external constituents (Kostova, Roth, & Dacin, 2008, p. 1000). MNCs must establish and maintain legitimacy in multiple environments (Kostova & Zaheer, 1999). Establishing an alliance, like a joint venture may give legitimacy through a local partner (Ang & Michailova, 2008), whereas full acquisitions or greenfields as an entry mode requires legitimacy to be established. This perspective is based on an institutional logic, where the MNC must develop practices that are acceptable and considered purposeful by external stakeholders (Chung & Luo, 2008). Stakeholders may be owners, potential investors, customers, suppliers, governments etc. Stakeholders influence management decisions by withholding or threatening to withhold resources or supplying resources with strings attached (Frooman, 1999). Barner-Rasmussen et al. (2007) report that among the key factors related to headquarter relocation are owners and other stakeholders. They argue that headquarter relocations carry substantial symbolic weight, and pressure from owners and institutions significantly influence location decisions. Benito et al. (2011) add to this line of reasoning with their finding that state ownership prevents relocation of headquarter activities. Birkinshaw et al. (2006) found that dominance of foreign owners as well as listings on foreign stock exchanges enhance corporate headquarters relocation.

The institutional argument is particularly relevant in the case of acquisitions. Acquisitions is the dominant form of foreign direct investments, representing as much as 70% of cross-border investments (Peng, 2008). The relatively high failure rate of acquisitions is often attributed to cultural differences between the acquirer and the target (Brannen & Peterson, 2009; Uhlenbruck, 2004). Cultural differences manifest themselves through managers from the acquirer who are unfamiliar with local management and control systems (Barkema, Bell, & Pennings, 1996) leading to implementation inefficiencies, labour conflicts and law suits (Brannen & Peterson, 2009). An acquisition is often resented by host country stakeholders who fear foreign raiders and depletion of local resources. Keeping the acquired unit autonomous and self-sustained may lower the fear of foreign corporate raids and limit hostile reactions from local stakeholders. Sometimes a headquarters responsibility is included in a takeover deal. We propose that awarding the acquired unit a DHQs status enhances symbolic value signalling importance and long-term commitment to the acquired unit and that this action, rational or not, may increase legitimacy for the foreign MNC.

The fifth prediction suggests that the location choice of foreign DHQs is determined by a need for corporate headquarters control. DHQs occupy a middle position between global headquarters and local subsidiaries. The managers of DHQs play a vital linking role, cooperating closely with operational managers as well as corporate managers at global headquarters. The dual nature of DHQs poses a management dilemma: a location close to a subsidiary facilitates local coordination, whereas a location close to global headquarters eases access to central strategic insights. Forsgren et al. (1995) argue that even if subsidiaries are located abroad, DHQs may be located at home to secure headquarters reliable and 'unbiased' information about markets and products. DHQs may also benefit from closeness to global headquarters to influence resource allocation. Managerial attention in the MNC is a scarce resource (Bouquet & Birkinshaw, 2008), which is further impeded by distance (Mudambi & Navarra, 2004). We argue that global managers are more confident if their DHQs are located close to home to reduce geographical and psychic distance (Johanson & Vahlne, 1977) and ensure rich, quick and unbiased communication.

RESEARCH DESIGN, CONTEXT AND DATA

This study is part of a longitudinal research project covering a sample of 30 companies from the largest, non-financial Norwegian companies listed on the Oslo Stock Exchange in 2006.[1] Norway is an advanced, but small and high-cost economy on the northern periphery of Europe. Its oil, gas and maritime companies are among the global leaders, but the country is otherwise considered to be a relatively disadvantageous location for MNC headquarters functions. Yet, Norway has a very open economy with a substantial presence of foreign ownership, and these aspects make Norway a well-suited context for studying headquarters.

We compiled information on each company spanning a period of seven years from 2000 to 2006. From earlier studies we knew that the number of DHQs located abroad were negligible in the early 1990s, but increased over the next decade (Benito, Larimo, Narula, & Pedersen, 2002). We obtained data from information resources such as Factiva and Kompass, from company annual reports, websites, and if information was still insufficient, we contacted the companies themselves. The companies in the dataset are quite large with an average of 9,600 employees and 26 billion NOK (4 billion USD) in sales (2006). The average foreign sales ratio was 72%. For the purpose of this study, we collected additional data on the location of division headquarters abroad, the establishment mode of the unit (acquisition versus greenfield), and key characteristics of the chosen host country such as their size (measured by GDP), income level (GDP/cap), political conditions (PolconIII),[2] competitiveness of their economies (Global Competitiveness Index), and distance to Norway (flight distance capital to capital).

To be included, the companies needed a divisional structure at some point during the period covered by the study. Because companies structure themselves in rather different ways, deciding what is and what is not a divisionalized structure – and furthermore, figuring out the actual types of divisionalization in the various cases – can be a challenging task. For example, terminologies differ, with some companies referring to product and business areas, while other companies explicitly use the term division. To ensure consistency across cases, divisions were measured at the organizational level directly below corporate headquarters. However, the number of divisions as well as the size and scope of the units vary: some companies have numerous (ten or more), others few (two or three); and some units have world-wide responsibility for a core business, whereas other units have more limited area responsibilities such as a regional hub.

RESULTS

Eighteen of the 30 companies had foreign-located DHQs in at least one of the years between 2000 and 2006. Table 1 provides company and industry information. Five companies are in the oil and natural gas sector, four are manufacturers of transport equipment or machinery, whereas the other companies belong to various industries including construction, fishing, consultancy (oil and gas related) and wholesale. Corporate headquarters were in Norway, except for one company that had – and still has – its global headquarters in London. Three companies moved their corporate head-quarters in our observation period, but these moves took place within Norway.

Table 1. Norwegian Companies with DHQs Abroad: Company Characteristics.

Company Name	Location of Corporate HQ	Main Industry (2-Digit NACE Codes)
Aker	Oslo	35 – manufacturer of transport equipment
Aker Yards	Oslo	35 – manufacturer of transport equipment
DNO International	Oslo	11 – oil and natural gas
Ekornes	Ikornnes	36 – manufacturer of furniture
Ementor	Oslo	51 – wholesale
Farstad Shipping	Ålesund	11 – oil and natural gas
Marine Harvest Group	Ålesund → Stavanger → Oslo	05 – fishing
Norske Skog	Lysaker	21 – manufacturer of paper products
Ocean Rig	Oslo → Stavanger	11 – oil and natural gas
Petroleum Geo-Services	Lysaker/Houston → Lysaker	11 – oil and natural gas
Prosafe	Tananger	11 – oil and natural gas
Schibsted	Oslo	22 – publishing and media
Stolt-Nielsen	London	61 – water transport
TGS-Nopec Geophysical Company	Nærsnes	74 – consultancy
Tomra Systems	Asker	29 – manufacturer of machinery/equipment
TTS Marine	Bergen	29 – manufacturer of machinery/equipment
Veidekke	Oslo	45 – construction
Yara International	Oslo	24 – manufacturer of chemicals

Within the whole sample of 30 companies (Table 2), a comparison of the MNCs with foreign DHQs to those without shows that the number of employees is significantly lower, the share of their equity held by foreigners is higher, ownership concentration is lower and so are also state ownership interests.

Table 2. Comparison of 30 Largest Listed Norwegian MNCs with and without Foreign-Located DHQs. Pooled Data (2000–2006), $n = 210$.

Variable	Mean Values		T-Test
	With foreign-located DHQs	Without foreign-located DHQs	
Number of employees	4454	12296	5.682***
Foreign sales ratio	0.71	0.66	−1.217
Percent foreign held equity	20.0	14.2	−2.351**
Percent state ownership	5.0	27.8	7.132***
Ownership concentration	50.2	60.0	3.665***

Note: ** and *** denote significance at 0.5 and 0.01 levels, respectively.

Table 3. Characteristics of Foreign-Located DHQs.

	Number of Cases
Mode of establishment	
Greenfield	21
Acquisition	49
Operative in year	
2000	32
2001	33
2002	37
2003	43
2004	44
2005	52
2006	57
Location	
Nordic countries	15
Europe	23
North-America	14
South-America	4
Asia and Australia	10
Africa and Middle-East	4

Table 3 shows that around 70% of the DHQs abroad were acquired, which correspond well to previous numbers on cross border investment activities (Peng, 2008). Table 3 also gives the geographic location for the foreign DHQs: about 21% are located in the Nordic countries, 33% in Europe, 20% in North America, 6% in South America, 14% in Asia and Australia and 6% in Africa and the Middle East.

As shown in Table 4, the Nordic region, Germany, France, United Kingdom and North America, as well as the three countries Brazil, Singapore and Australia have been present through the entire observation period, whereas European countries such as Poland, Russia, Spain, Belgium and Austria, as well as locations in the middle and far East and Africa (Iraq, Yemen, Angola, Japan, Mozambique) enter the sample towards the end of the

Table 4. Host Countries for Foreign-Located DHQs.

Country	Number of DHQs						
	2000	2001	2002	2003	2004	2005	2006
Sweden	1	2	2	3	3	4	6
Denmark	3	3	2	3	4	4	3
Finland	2	2	2	3	3	2	3
Estonia	1	1	1	1	1	1	0
Germany	1	1	1	1	1	3	3
Faeroe Islands	1	1	1	1	1	1	1
Poland	0	0	0	0	1	1	1
Belgium	0	0	0	0	0	1	2
UK	7	7	9	9	7	7	9
France	1	1	1	1	1	1	1
Austria	0	0	0	0	0	1	1
Russia	0	0	0	0	0	0	1
Spain	0	0	0	0	1	1	1
Iraq	0	0	0	0	0	0	1
Canada	2	1	1	1	1	1	1
Yemen	0	0	0	0	1	1	1
USA	8	8	11	12	10	11	11
Angola	0	0	0	1	1	1	1
Japan	0	0	0	0	1	1	2
Mozambique	0	0	0	0	0	1	1
Brazil	2	3	3	3	3	2	2
Singapore	1	1	1	1	1	4	3
Australia	2	2	2	3	3	3	2

Note: Countries listed in increasing flight distance from Norway (capital-to-capital).

Table 5. Mode of Establishment of Foreign-Located DHQs.

Country	Number of Cases	
	Greenfield	Acquisition
Sweden	1	5
Denmark	1	4
Finland	1	3
Estonia	0	1
Germany	2	1
Faeroe Islands	0	1
Poland	1	0
Belgium	0	2
UK	3	8
France	1	0
Austria	0	1
Russia	0	1
Spain	1	0
Iraq	0	1
Canada	0	2
Yemen	0	1
USA	4	8
Angola	0	1
Japan	2	0
Mozambique	0	1
Brazil	1	3
Singapore	2	3
Australia	1	2

Note: Countries listed in increasing flight distance from Norway (capital-to-capital).

period. The number of locations for DHQs has over the time period increased from 13 to 23, demonstrating broader and more varied local contexts.

Table 5 exhibits how the headquarter units were established in various countries. There is no apparent association between choice of entry mode and geographical distance, that is there is no systematic connection between distance from headquarters and the DHQs establishment as either acquisitions or greenfields.

ANALYSIS

In our earlier discussion we proposed five factors as key drivers of the decision to locate DHQs abroad:

1) Characteristics of the location
2) Value creation
3) Efficiency
4) Legitimacy
5) Control

In this section, we draw on examples from the companies and the previous tables and discuss the extent to which our data can support these predictions.

Prediction 1. Characteristics of the location influence DHQ foreign location

The pattern displayed in Tables 4 and 5 strongly suggests that country characteristics play an important role in DHQ location choice. Our case companies have selected locations such as Scandinavia, Western Europe, North America, Singapore and Australia. These locations offer politically stable environments, reliable communication and transportation and access to a highly educated workforce, which seems to be important to Norwegian MNCs particularly in their early phases of foreign headquarters location. It is interesting to note, however, that as companies gather experience, they expand headquarter locations; in our sample new locations include Eastern Europe, Latin America, Africa and the Middle East. Companies such as Tomra (Recycling) and TGS-Nopec have increased their foreign location of division headquarters in this period, typically focusing on locations in the USA (Connecticut, Houston), United Kingdom (Bedford), Australia (Perth) and Europe (Vienna, Dusseldorf). These locations are all resource rich, with highly qualified labour as well as easy access to intercontinental flights.

To probe more systematically into whether location choices for DHQs reflect certain country characteristics, we run regression models where the dependent variable is the number of DHQs established in a given country. Specifically, we examine whether location choices are associated with countries' economic size and affluence, their competitiveness and political stability, and their distance from Norway. First, we run an ordinary least squares (OLS) regression with the cases pooled over the entire period. The estimation (model I) indicates that Norwegian MNCs are likely to establish more headquarter functions the higher the GDP and the GDP/capita ratio, the higher competitiveness and the fewer political constraints, whereas distance from Norway is insignificant (Table 6). However, since the Durbin–Watson statistic of 0.5 reveals that the OLS regression performs poorly due to the longitudinal nature of our data, and because of the count nature of

Table 6. Regression Models (Dependent Variable: Number of DHQs Located in Foreign Countries).

Variables	Model I OLS regression, pooled data Coefficient (std. error)	Model II Negative binomial regression, panel random effects Coefficient (std. error)	Model III Negative binomial regression (without Ekornes), panel random effects Coefficient (std. error)
Intercept	0.197	15.81	13.754
	−0.46	−786.623	−420.552
GDP (in billion USD)	0.001	0.00008	0.0001
	(0.000)***	(0.00005)	(0.00006)
GDP per capita	0.00003	0.00003	0.00002
	(0.000)**	(0.00001)**	(0.00001)**
Political constraints index	−2.902	−0.6023	0.114
	(0.970)**	(1.068)	(1.141)
Global competitiveness index	0.325	0.3011	0.264
	(0.146)**	(0.142)**	(0.151)*
Flight distance between capitals	−0.0033	0.00004	0.00006
	(0.000)	(0.00004)	(0.00004)
Model statistics			
Durbin–Watson	0.501		
F	38.255***		
Adjusted R^2	0.538		
Log-likelihood χ^2		−209.685	−176.066
Likelihood test vs. pooled χ^2		76.65***	58.55***
n	161	161	140

Notes: *, **, and *** denote significance at 0.10, 0.05, and 0.01 levels, respectively.

the dependent variable (number of DHQs in a country), we chose to run a more suitable negative binomial regression panel regression (model II). The results do not change dramatically, but only the GNP per capita and Global Competitiveness Index variables turn out significant in the regression. To check the robustness of the results, we also run the model without one company (Ekornes) with a relatively large number of sales-oriented regional hubs (model III). Again, it turns out that the results do not change in any substantial way.

Overall the results from our regressions suggest that the Norwegian companies in our sample tend to prefer developed locations for their DHQs irrespective of distance to home.

Prediction 2. Benefits of being an insider to increase value influence foreign DHQ location

The analysis of our case firms reveals that at least three factors seem important for the choice of DHQ location:

1) Closeness to large and important markets
2) Presence in resource rich areas
3) Presence in locations with advanced technologies

We argue that when these characteristics are present, the DHQ increases value creation through foreign location. By being located close to core resources, the MNC becomes an insider receiving more accurate and timely information as well as accumulating local knowledge. With this knowledge the MNC can improve its understanding and provide better parenting through creating more valuable strategies for subsidiaries within the division.

Closeness to Large and Important Markets

Several companies in our dataset have located DHQs in markets that are large and important. TGS-Nopec Geophysical Company is a geo-science, software and service provider, offering consulting advice to clients in different oil- and gas-related locations. In 2006, the company had eight of nine DHQs abroad, and the main locations were USA, United Kingdom, Australia and Russia. The main idea of the company is to provide locally embedded advice to important customers and therefore the emphasis is on local management teams. Managing these companies from Norway would be less valuable as headquarters need to understand local customers' needs. Tomra, a recycling company, has 7 of its 10 DHQs abroad located in Japan, United Kingdom, USA, Sweden, Belgium, Austria and Germany. Each country has separate rules and subsidies regarding recycling, and Tomra needs strong local presence to be able to capture these nuances and make the necessary adaptations for local companies.

Presence in Resource-Rich Areas

DHQs are also located close to important resources. One such resource is oil, and the company DNO moves its activities to where this resource is available. The company has focused on developing smaller and mature oil fields, and in 2000 its main activities were in United Kingdom and Norway. Throughout the period, the company started to seek oil fields in other areas and acquired licenses in Iraq, Yemen and Mozambique. In each of these locations the company has set up offices to manage local activities. These locations are undoubtedly very different from Norway, and providing good parenting to subsidiaries in the region depends on knowledge of the local resource. Another resource is fish, and Marine Harvest, a fish farming company, has DHQs in locations along the Atlantic brim. Each location will differ regarding type of fish, temperatures and geography, and the company therefore has established DHQs abroad to manage these.

Presence in Locations with Advanced Technologies

Some MNCs operate within technology-rich clusters. Petroleum Geo Services (PGS) is providing geological services. One of their DHQs is located in Houston, USA. This unit consists of seismic operations on land and very shallow water. Houston is a hub for onshore activities, and accessing specific knowledge and resources is important for the development of this division of PGS. It seems reasonable to manage this activity from Houston to provide better and more informed parenting for onshore subsidiaries. The drilling company Prosafe has located its DHQs in Aberdeen and Singapore, both well-known maritime clusters, and Aker yards has located its cruise and ferry division to Finland, a traditional strong maritime construction hub.

Prediction 3. Benefits of efficiency influence foreign DHQ location

Whereas value creation considerations concern access to external resources, efficiency represents internal coordination and control. This argument suggests that MNCs improve control and coordination if headquarter activities are located close to subsidiaries, consequently this argument concerns regional more than DHQ units. Ekornes is a furniture manufacturer with a very high foreign sales ratio (on average 80% in the years covered by this study). They organize sales activities out of regional hubs. Important locations for Ekornes in 2006 were Singapore, Brazil, Japan, Spain, Poland,

Denmark, USA, United Kingdom, Finland, France and Germany. Local sales and marketing of Ekornes' premium priced recliners, and ensuring quality in all offers, demand strong local sales coordination and management organized through foreign headquarters. Other MNCs that have a regional structure organizing their activities include Norske Skog and Veidekke. Norske Skog, a paper producer, organized their global activities from regional centres in Hamburg, Sao Paulo, London and Singapore, whereas Veidekke, a Nordic construction company, has division headquarters in Denmark and Sweden. Locating headquarters activities close to subsidiaries increases control, communication and coordination.

Prediction 4. Benefits of legitimacy influence foreign DHQ location

From Table 3 we note that 49 of 70 foreign-located DHQs had been acquired, which means that most of the increase in foreign headquarters abroad is explained by growth rather than relocation of existing activities. Generally this has been a period of rapid foreign expansion for Norwegian companies, but they have not, however, established DHQs in all foreign locations. Aker Yards has, for example, in this period acquired shipyards in Romania, Brazil, Ukraine, Finland and Norway. They have, however, only established a foreign DHQ, in Finland. This DHQ manages the Cruise and Ferries business area in Aker Yards, a distinct product area within the company. Finland has a strong shipbuilding history and high competence, and maintaining good relations to local authorities, customers and suppliers seems to be important to Aker. Romania, Brazil and Ukraine are still emerging economies mainly providing cost efficient solutions.

Another example is Ementor (now Atea), the leading Norwegian IT company. Ementor had small units in Denmark and Sweden prior to the merger with Topnordic A/S (Denmark) and the acquisition of Atea AB (Sweden) in 2006. The Danish and the Swedish companies were both considerable market actors in their home countries, and Ementor had to get approval from competition authorities in the three countries before the company extensions were acceptable to home authorities. During early phases of the integration, the company announced on its website that each company would use its original brand and focus on localizing customer offerings. An interview with the Swedish CEO Lars Bolin (http://www.idg.se) immediately following the acquisition announcement suggests that the three companies Ementor, Topnordic and Atea were considered equal partners in the new venture and that top positions were distributed in a good (we interpret this a *fair*) manner. Fourteen of 16 consultants at the Helsingborg office of Atea, however, decided to leave the company as a result of the acquisition announcement, indicating some internal resistance to the acquisition (http://www.dn.no.30/06-06). This was a strong signal to Ementor that the existing employees in Sweden were not entirely positive to the acquisition. For an IT company consultants represent core technological and market knowledge as well as experience and are as such important stakeholders. In 2008, Ementor changed its brand name to Atea, the name of the Swedish target signalling the market recognition of this brand, particularly in large and important markets such as Sweden and Finland. This expansion from a Norwegian company to the Nordic region takes place in an industry where Norway is not known to be particularly strong (IT) and the acquired/merged targets have substantial positions within their local markets. Awarding the acquired units a DHQ status shows that Ementor was prepared to delegate strategic control to new units to retain local expertise by pleasing local stakeholders.

Yet another example is found in the company TTS Marine. This company develops and supplies marine equipment. Within its segments it is the second largest supplier in the world. The company has subsidiaries in Norway, Sweden, Finland, Germany, China, Korea and USA. In 2000 the company had two divisions: Marine Cranes and Material Handling, both managed from Norway. In 2001, the company acquired HamworthyKSE AB Cargo division that provided the company with a worldwide network of sales agents and service stations. The acquisition became a separate division in the company, managed from Sweden. The company made two additional acquisitions in 2005: Navcic engineering in Gothenburg and Kocks GmbH in Bremen, Germany. Both acquisitions represented new divisions managed out of Sweden and Germany. In 2006, the company therefore had four divisions, where two were managed from Sweden, one from Germany. The German target was considered innovative having developed a new, slim crane that had awarded it several new projects by ship owners in Hamburg. In a company statement following the acquisition announcement Thomas Krabiell, Head of Sales in Germany expressed that: 'With the merger of both companies, TTS Marine ASA has created a big step ahead as one of the world leaders in ship equipment. The crane program offered by (German target) has a solid reputation in the fields of shipyards, shipowners and consultants, including the after sales service. The German shipowning community has been the traditional market for many years. The (German target) is known for quality, service and its creativity in developing and implementing a distinctive pioneering spirit. A key element for the future business is the existing agent network, purchase resources and a high flexibility of the people'. This statement shows by the use of the term 'merger' instead of acquisition and pointing out the benefits to the acquirer rather than the target that the acquired unit is firmly based within a strong competitive region has a long history of being a trustworthy and innovative supplier to German shipbuilders, and possesses distinct competences that can result in innovations. Both Bremen and Gothenburg represent renowned maritime clusters, and the acquisition targets of TTS Marine came with competencies that were unique in the TTS system. Making sure external, local stakeholders are happy with the acquisition and stay on are therefore concerns that seem prevalent and result in new divisions managed out of their acquired locations.

Other examples include the road construction company Veidekke that has acquired large players in Denmark and Sweden and established DHQs to manage their activities locally. Marine Harvest group, a seafood company, has acquired a series of fish farming companies along the Atlantic and Pacific Oceans. Over the period of our study, the company has awarded division management to units in Faroe Islands, Scotland, Ireland, USA, Canada and Chile. These are all fish farming centres representing high symbolic value to their local communities. The shipping company Farstad Shipping has five of six DHQs abroad, and some of these are related to acquisitions (Melbourne, Australia, and Petroserve, Brazil). The business idea of Farstad is to cooperate with local actors to crew, operate and market Farstad Vessels. This requires close local cooperation and management, and the company has therefore chosen to locate DHQs to acquired divisions in these markets.

Prediction 5. Distance to global HQs influence foreign DHQ location

The data in Table 5 do not lend support to our control prediction as the MNCs in our sample do not generally tend to establish DHQs close to home. About a fifth of our DHQs are, however, located in the Nordic region. Some of our cases also indicate that there are certain advantages of managing foreign divisions from the home location. The media company Schibsted awarded DHQ status to its acquisition in Latvia to control and coordinate Baltic activities from Riga. Over time, however, they reorganized and decided to manage all international activities from Oslo. Latvia therefore lost their DHQ status. When Norske Skog entered into financial difficulties, they decided to move all their foreign DHQs back to Norway, to improve control and coordination with their total global activities. These examples suggest that especially in times of financial constraints, there is a value in locating all headquarter activities close to home to improve overall global control and coordination.

DISCUSSION

Our analysis so far has examined the role of five factors as predictors of headquarter location. In this section we discuss their type and possible interrelations.

As shown in Fig. 1, we propose that three of the aforementioned factors are main drivers of DHQ location: legitimacy, efficiency and value creation. As value creation, location characteristics and distance from HQs all contain aspects of a location, we combine these into one variable that we call location characteristics. This variable describes the foreign location abroad through its resources and its distance to global HQs. We see location characteristics as both a driver and a moderator variable. In addition, we consider entry mode a moderator between legitimacy and DHQ location.

Legitimacy, efficiency and location characteristics are likely to be among the primary motives of DHQ foreign location. That is, companies place DHQs in locations where there are central stakeholders from whom gaining legitimacy is important, and/or they locate DHQs in locations that are abundant in resources needed in the pursuit of global sustainable competitive advantages, and/or they locate DHQs abroad to improve efficiencies in the headquarter–subsidiary relationship. In our proposed framework these

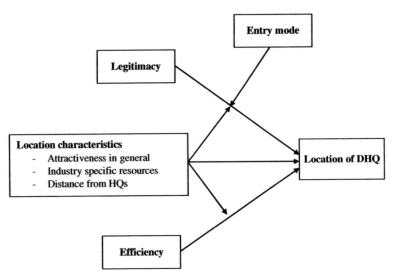

Fig. 1. A Framework for Choice of Location for DHQs.

three factors are separate drivers that may trigger the establishment of a DHQ in a foreign location.

Some factors may, however, moderate these relations. We suggest that when a firm enters a foreign market through acquisitions, legitimacy will be a stronger motivator for foreign-located DHQs. As headquarter functions carry substantial symbolic importance (Barner-Rasmussen et al., 2007), awarding headquarter status to a new division is a way to signal importance and commitment to local stakeholders, including employees, investors and government, and ensure that the new unit will stay locally focused. Foreign acquisitions typically create insecurity with local stakeholders like employees and governments, which increase the need for legitimacy. The effect entry mode has on the relation will most likely be short term, as over time the need to please local stakeholders is reduced.

Our cases offer some support to this notion. The fish farming company Marine Harvest had eight divisions in the year 2000, six of which were located abroad: Scotland, Canada, The Faroe Islands, Ireland, USA and Chile. All were results of acquisitions. Giving DHQ status to each of these locations could be a way to achieve legitimacy as a foreign acquirer. In 2006, the company restructured its divisions, cutting their number to six in total, of which five were abroad. Four of them were located close to important resources: Chile, Canada, the Faroe Islands and Scotland. The units in Chile and USA were combined, so were the units in Ireland and Scotland. The company also established a new division, located in Belgium, with responsibility for marketing and sales to their markets within the EU. This development shows that whereas DHQ status was originally connected to acquisitions, the company over time restructured to keep DHQs that still needed to be close to important resources, and added new DHQs to manage other resources. In their case the other resource was an important consumer market. Consequently, the 'pleasing' of each individual target had given way to an overall leaner structure for the MNC.

We also suggest a possible link between legitimacy and location characteristics as the drive for legitimacy seems to be higher in advanced locations. It is more important to keep strong clients and investors in developed clusters than gain legitimacy with stakeholders in weak locations. Aker, for example, chose to establish their DHQ only in Finland, although they undertook acquisitions also in many other locations. Finland had a strong cluster within the business of Aker, whereas other targets represented weaker, emerging locations.

The motivation to increase efficiency may also be moderated by location characteristics. We have argued that improved efficiency through reduced agency costs is mainly an intra-organizational issue, and as such the DHQs unit could be located several places within a region. We propose that the specific choice of location is influenced by characteristics of the location itself. Our data show that MNCs will tend to choose mature economies, characterized by rich access to financial resources, highly developed human capital and low political risk. Several of our companies have for example chosen Singapore as a location for their DHQs. Among locations in Asia, Singapore is commonly regarded as the most stable, resource rich and advanced. Houston, London and Stockholm are other favoured spots; all established and well developed cities. Efficiency may also be motivated by distance to headquarters. When there is a need for close coordination with global headquarters, as in the case of Norske Skog undergoing strong financial constraints, there is a trade-off between benefits of location in a region close to subsidiaries or advantages by being at home close to headquarters.

This study shows that factors driving location choices of DHQs vary in the extent that they are tied to a specific location. Legitimacy is location specific as it aims at being 'on the inside' with important stakeholders in a specific location. The entry mode could be considered as 'location neutral' since greenfields and acquisitions can in principle be located any place. Conversely, location characteristics are naturally location specific as they describe close access to markets, resources or technologies within a specific location. Efficiency, on the contrary, is less so as it is regional more than local. Closeness to subsidiaries is important, but the specific choice of location may vary. As such our framework suggests that the choice of locations for foreign DHQs is influenced by a set of interrelated location-specific and location independent factors.

CONCLUSION

In a commentary, Devinney (2009, p. 151) raises the question: 'As MNCs expand, do they continue abroad with what they do well at home, or do they change to adapt to changing conditions in foreign markets?' Our study suggests that MNCs from a peripheral economy increasingly adapt to foreign markets, not only operationally, but also by offshoring headquarter functions. Destinations for foreign headquarters are motivated by a range of factors, some of which are location specific. As entry often is done by acquisitions, ensuring legitimacy from local stakeholders is a core motivator, especially in the short run. Over time gaining an insider view from resource rich locations (important markets, input resources and technologies) facilitate insights for improved parenting, whereas closeness to subsidiaries within a region reduces agency costs. Initially, MNCs are drawn to resource rich, well developed locations, but over time they become bolder and accept more emergent locations for their DHQs.

NOTES

1. The selected companies are: Aker, Aker-Kværner, Aker Yards, Cermaq, DNO International, EDB Business Partner, Ekornes, Ementor, Farstad Shipping, Kongsberg Gruppen, Lerøy Seafood Group, Marine Harvest Group, Norsk Hydro, Norske Skogindustrier, Ocean Rig, Odfjell, Orkla, Petroleum Geo-Services, Prosafe, Rieber & Søn, Schibsted, Scana Industrier, Statoil, Stolt-Nielsen, Telenor, TGS-NOPEC Geophysical Company, Tomra Systems, TTS Marine, Veidekke, Yara International.

2. The PolconIII (political constraints) measure was taken from the POLCON database (see Henisz, 2002). The data base is a comprehensive register of national political conditions in basically the entire world over the past two centuries and was set up and is regularly updated by Witold Henisz at the Wharton School, University of Pennsylvania. The database is publicly available at http://www.management.wharton.upenn.edu/henisz.

ACKNOWLEDGMENTS

We are grateful for the helpful comments and suggestions provided by Editors Christian Geisler Asmussen and Torben Pedersen and by Sara McGaughey and Ram Mudambi. We gratefully acknowledge the research assistance of Adina Braha-Honciuc, as well as the financial support offered by BI Norwegian School of Management. Earlier versions of this chapter have been presented in a seminar at Temple University and at the Dynamics of Globalization conference organized by Copenhagen Business School in January 2011.

REFERENCES

Ambos, B., & Mahnke, V. (2010). How do MNC headquarters add value? *Management International Review*, 50(4), 403–412.
Ambos, B., & Schlegelmilch, B. (2010). *The new role of regional management*. New York: Palgrave MacMillan.

Ang, S. H., & Michailova, S. (2008). Institutional explanations of cross border alliance modes: The case of emerging economies firms. *Management International Review, 48*(5), 551–576.

Asmussen, C. G. (2009). Local, regional or global? Quantifying MNE geographic scope. *Journal of International Business Studies, 40*(7), 1192–1205.

Baaij, M., Van den Bosch, F., & Volberda, H. (2004). The international relocation of corporate centres: Are corporate centres sticky? *European Management Journal, 22*(2), 141–149.

Barkema, H. G., Bell, H. J., & Pennings, J. L. (1996). Foreign entry, cultural barriers, and learning. *Strategic Management Journal, 17*(2), 151–166.

Barner-Rasmussen, W., Piekkari, R., & Björkman, I. (2007). Mobility of headquarters in multinational corporations. *European Journal of International Management, 1*(3), 260–274.

Bel, G., & Fageda, X. (2008). Getting there fast: Globalization, intercontinental flights and location of headquarters. *Journal of Economic Geography, 8*(4), 471–495.

Benito, G. R. G., Larimo, J., Narula, R., & Pedersen, T. (2002). Multinational enterprises from small economies: Internationalization patterns of large companies from Denmark, Finland and Norway. *International Studies of Management and Organization, 32*(11), 57–78.

Benito, G. R. G., Lunnan, R., & Tomassen, S. (2011). Distant encounters of the third kind: Multinational companies locating divisional headquarters abroad. *Journal of Management Studies, 48*(2), 373–394.

Birkinshaw, J. M., Braunerhjelm, P., Holm, U., & Terjesen, S. (2006). Why do some multinational corporations relocate their headquarters overseas? *Strategic Management Journal, 27*(7), 681–700.

Bouquet, C., & Birkinshaw, J. M. (2008). Weight versus voice, how foreign subsidiaries gain attention from corporate headquarters. *Academy of Management Journal, 51*(1), 577–601.

Brannen, M. Y., & Peterson, M. F. (2009). Merging without alienating: Interventions promoting cross-cultural organizational integration and their limitations. *Journal of International Business Studies, 40*(3), 468–489.

Brown, J. S., & Duguid, P. (2001). Knowledge and organization: A social-practice perspective. *Organization Science, 12*(2), 198–213.

Campbell, A., Goold, M., & Alexander, M. (1995). Corporate strategy: The quest for parenting advantage. *Harvard Business Review, 92*, 120–132.

Chandler, A. D. (1991). The functions of the HQ unit in the multibusiness firm. *Strategic Management Journal, 12*, 31–50.

Chung, C.-N., & Luo, X. (2008). Institutional logics or agency costs: The influence of corporate governance models on business group restructuring in emergent economies. *Organization Science, 19*(5), 766–784.

Collis, D. J., Young, D., & Goold, M. (2007). The size, structure, and performance of corporate headquarters. *Strategic Management Journal, 28*(4), 383–405.

Devinney, T. M. (2009). Commentary: The liability of foreignness, capabilities, knowledge, and the performance of the subsidiary. In: J. L. C. Cheng, E. Maitland & S. Nicholas (Eds), *Advances in International Management* (Vol. 22, pp. 151–161). Bingley, UK: Emerald.

Dhanaraj, C., & Parkhe, A. (2006). Orchestrating innovation networks. *Academy of Management Review, 31*(3), 659–669.

Doz, Y., Santos, J., & Williamson, P. (2001). *From global to metanational: How companies win in the knowledge economy.* Boston, MA: Harvard Business School Press.

Dunning, J. H. (2000). The eclectic paradigm as an envelope for economic and business theories of MNE activity. *International Business Review, 9*(2), 163–190.

Dyer, J. H., & Nobeoka, K. (2000). Creating and managing a high performance knowledge sharing network: The Toyota case. *Strategic Management Journal, 21*(3), 345–368.

Egelhoff, W. G. (2010). How the parent headquarters adds value to an MNC. *Management International Review, 50*(4), 413–431.

Eisenhardt, K. (1989). Agency theory: An assessment and review. *Academy of Management Review, 14*(1), 57–74.

Elango, B. (2004). Geographic scope of operations by multinational companies: An exploratory study of regional and global strategies. *European Management Journal, 22*(4), 431–441.

Enright, M. J. (2005a). Regional management centers in the Asia-Pacific. *Management International Review, 45*(Special Issue), 59–82.

Enright, M. J. (2005b). The roles of regional management centers. *Management International Review, 45*(Special Issue), 83–102.

Forsgren, M., Holm, U., & Johanson, J. (1992). Internationalization of the second degree: The emergence of European based centres in Swedish firms. In: S. Young & J. Hamill (Eds), *Europe and the multinationals* (pp. 57–75). Worcester, UK: Billing & Sons.

Forsgren, M., Holm, U., & Johanson, J. (1995). Division headquarters go abroad: A step in the internationalization of the multinational corporation. *Journal of Management Studies, 32*(4), 475–491.

Foss, N. (1997). On the rationales of corporate headquarters. *Industrial and Corporate Change, 6*(2), 313–338.

Frooman, J. (1999). Stakeholder influence strategies. *Academy of Management Review, 24*(2), 191–205.

Ghemawat, P. (2001). Distance still matters: The hard reality of global expansion. *Harvard Business Review, 798*, 137–147.

Henisz, W. J. (2002). The institutional environment for infrastructure investment. *Industrial and Corporate Change, 11*(2), 355–389.

Hennart, J. F. (1991). Control in multinational firms: The role of price and hierarchy. *Management International Review, 31*(Special Issue), 71–96.

Hitt, M. A., Hoskisson, R. E., & Ireland, R. D. (1994). A mid-range theory of the interactive effects of international and product diversification on innovation and performance. *Journal of Management, 20*(2), 297–326.

Holloway, S. R., & Wheeler, J. O. (1991). Corporate headquarters relocation and changes in metropolitan corporate dominance, 1980–1987. *Economic Geography, 67*(1), 54–74.

Holm, U., & Pedersen, T. (2000). *The emergence and impact of MNC centres of excellence.* London: Macmillan.

Hymer, S. H. (1976). *The international operations of national firms: A study of direct foreign investment.* Cambridge, MA: MIT Press.

Johanson, J., & Vahlne, J. E. (1977). The internationalization process of the firm: A model of market knowledge and increasing foreign market commitments. *Journal of International Business Studies, 8*(1), 23–32.

Kostova, T., Roth, K., & Dacin, M. T. (2008). Institutional theory in the study of multinational corporations: A critique and new directions. *Academy of Management Review, 33*(4), 994–1006.

Kostova, T., & Zaheer, A. (1999). Organizational legitimacy under conditions of complexity: The case of the multinational enterprise. *Academy of Management Review, 24*(1), 64–81.

Lasserre, P. (1996). Regional headquarters: The spearhead for Asia Pacific markets. *Long Range Planning, 29*(1), 30–37.

Lehrer, M., & Asakawa, K. (1999). Unbundling European operations: Regional management and corporate flexibility in American and Japanese MNCs. *Journal of World Business, 34*(3), 267–286.

Lovely, M. E., Rosenthal, S. S., & Sharma, S. (2005). Information, agglomeration and the headquarters of U.S exporters. *Regional Science and Urban Economics, 35*(2), 167–191.

Mudambi, R. (2008). Location, control and innovation in knowledge-intensive industries. *Journal of Economic Geography, 8*(5), 699–725.

Mudambi, R., & Navarra, P. (2004). Knowledge flows, subsidiary power and rent-seeking. *Journal of International Business Studies, 35*(5), 385–406.

Peng, M. W. (2008). *Global business*. Mason, OH: South Western.

Piekkari, R., Nell, P. C., & Ghauri, P. (2010). Regional management as a system: A longitudinal case study. *Management International Review, 50*(4), 513–523.

Porter, M. E. (1998). Competing across locations: Enhancing competitive advantage through a global strategy. In: M. E. Porter (Ed.), *On competition* (pp. 309–349). Boston, MA: Harvard Business Review.

Rugman, A. M., & Verbeke, A. (2004). A perspective on regional and global strategies of multinational enterprises. *Journal of International Business Studies, 35*, 3–18.

Schutte, H. (1997). Strategy and organization: Challenges for European MNCs in Asia. *European Management Journal, 15*(4), 436–445.

Schutte, H. (1998). Between headquarters and subsidiaries: The RHQ solution. In: J. M. Birkinshaw & N. Hood (Eds), *Multinational corporate evolution and subsidiary development* (pp. 102–136). Basingstoke, UK: Palgrave Macmillan.

Uhlenbruck, K. (2004). Developing acquired foreign subsidiaries: The experience of MNEs in transition economies. *Journal of International Business Studies, 35*(2), 109–123.

Westney, E. D., & Zaheer, S. (2001). The multinational enterprise as an organization. In: A. M. Rugman & T. L. Brewer (Eds), *The Oxford handbook of international business* (pp. 349–379). Oxford: Oxford University Press.

SELECTING STATE OR PRIVATE JOINT VENTURE PARTNERS IN EMERGING MARKETS: IMPACT OF LIABILITY OF FOREIGNNESS AND RULE OF LAW

Indu Ramachandran, Kim Clark, Derrick McIver and Stewart R. Miller

ABSTRACT

The present study develops an international joint venture (IJV) partner selection framework to explain the choice between state-owned or privately owned local partners in the context of emerging economies. We suggest that once an IJV is selected as the mode of entry, a multinational enterprise's strategic motivations – that is, efficiency seeking, market seeking and knowledge seeking – will influence its choice of IJV partner type: state-owned enterprise or privately owned firm. We argue that liability of foreignness and rule of law moderate the multinational enterprise's selection of IJV partner type.

Dynamics of Globalization: Location-Specific Advantages or Liabilities of Foreignness?
Advances in International Management, Volume 24, 153–179
ISSN: 1571-5027/doi:10.1108/S1571-5027(2011)0000024014

INTRODUCTION

Multinational enterprises (MNEs) entering a foreign market have to contend with 'liability of foreignness' (LOF), which leads to additional costs and disadvantages in doing business abroad for MNE business units (Zaheer, 1995). LOF usually arises from differences between home and host country environments that create several challenges for MNEs as they attempt to balance conforming to local environments with global integration initiatives within the MNE network (Kostova & Zaheer, 1999; Rosenzweig & Singh, 1991). Related to LOF, MNEs face dual pressures to achieve organizational legitimacy in the host country and to differentiate themselves from local domestic firms (Kostova & Zaheer, 1999; Miller & Eden, 2006).

Some scholars have examined the role of entry mode choice as a method for MNEs to overcome LOF. International joint ventures (IJVs), in particular, have been discussed as an important mode of entry that helps reduce LOF under various circumstances (Eden & Miller, 2004). The choice of using an IJV as an entry mode has gained traction within the international strategy literature (e.g., Lane & Beamish, 1990; Kale, Singh, & Perlmutter, 2000). IJVs offer many potential benefits such as the development of economies of scale and/or scope advantages, a means of quickly expanding into new markets, and a mechanism for acquiring and internalizing knowledge or technology that, in turn, can help a firm gain competitive advantage (Hitt, Dacin, Levitas, Arregle, & Borza, 2000). IJVs have been shown to benefit both foreign and local partners primarily because of potential pooled synergies and growth opportunities (Miller, Li, Eden, & Hitt, 2008). In addition, MNEs face an important strategic choice of selecting appropriate partners (Hitt, Tyler, Hardee, & Park, 1995; Ireland, Hitt, & Vaidyanath, 2002; Li & Ferreira, 2008). Recently, Roy and Oliver (2009) emphasized the importance of selecting appropriate partners for an IJV and examined the role of host country legal environment (control for corruption and rule of law) on this decision. The influence of the host country environment on partner selection for IJV is crucial, especially when entering an emerging economy, and therefore, there is a need to better understand how these joint venture strategic choices are linked.

Although scholars have examined the role of strategic motivations (Kogut, 1988; Glaister & Buckley, 1996) and the critical decision of partner selection criteria (Geringer, 1988; Hitt et al., 2000; Hitt, Ahlstrom, Dacin, Levitas, & Svobodina, 2004), these strategic issues have been dealt with independently in the literature (see for an exception Dong & Glaister, 2006), rather than linked systematically to understand the association between the two. IJV studies have overlooked issues related to ownership structure (whether the local partner is state-owned) and strategic motivations. Moreover, the literature has yet to explain how LOF and host-country rule of law affect the IJV partner selection decisions between state-owned enterprises (SOEs) and privately owned enterprises (POEs). Most of the research on IJVs has focused on POEs as partners (Miller et al., 2008); however, in this chapter we suggest that in certain cases, it may be useful to consider SOEs as IJV partners. Specifically we suggest that an unanswered question in IJV research is: How does ownership structure in emerging economies influence IJV partner selection?

We attempt to address these understudied areas within the IJV literature by developing a framework to explain strategic motivations and the selection of a preferred ownership structure for an IJV partner. Our partner selection framework also proposes that LOF and rule of law influence MNEs' partner selection decisions. We draw on prior joint venture research that has examined strategic motivations (Kogut, 1988) and partner selection criteria (Dong & Glaister, 2006) to determine IJV partner-type selection. Then we integrate the LOF and rule of law literatures to explain its role in IJV partner ownership preferences.

Our framework is both timely and relevant because emerging markets and ownership structure (SOE vs. POE) have been understudied in the field of management and international business. First, LOF has been studied with respect to foreign affiliate performance (Miller & Parkhe, 2002; Nachum, 2003; Zaheer & Mosakowski, 1997), learning (Pedersen & Petersen, 2004; Petersen & Pedersen, 2002), lawsuits (Mezias, 2002), and mode of entry decisions (Eden & Miller, 2004). However, it represents a theoretically potent, driver of partner selection choices. Second, rule of law varies across emerging markets (La Porta, Lopez-de-Silanes, Shleifer, & Vishny, 1997), and therefore, it has become a crucial factor in IJV partner selection research (Roy & Oliver, 2009).

Second, although business opportunities in emerging markets are abundant, MNEs are more likely to face higher entry barriers and elevated uncertainty (Child, 1994; Luo, 1997). This is predominantly because environments with incumbent SOEs present unique conditions, with which the MNEs may be unfamiliar. For example, despite obvious privileges afforded to some SOEs (such as government financial subsidies and preferential lending rates), they often have ambiguous goals that shift with changing political agendas and operating inefficiencies relative to privately owned firms (Vernon, 1981).

Third, as emerging markets become increasingly important in the global community and the presence of SOEs become more significant, MNEs are increasingly faced with the difficult decision of selecting potential partners for international cooperative ventures (*McKinsey Quarterly*, 2008). The partner selection decision is especially relevant given that state ownership of local firms in emerging markets may have implications for value creation associated with an IJV (Miller et al., 2008). Moreover, despite the high dissolution rate of international strategic alliances, partner selection remains an understudied topic (Hennart, Kim, & Zeng, 1998), especially as it relates to LOF (Eden & Miller, 2004) and rule of law (Roy & Oliver, 2009).

By developing our IJV partner selection framework, we extend the work of Dong and Glaister (2006), Hitt et al. (2000), Hitt et al. (2004) and Roy and Oliver (2009). Our chapter augments the LOF literature by theorizing that LOF can affect an MNE's strategic decisions, in particular, its choice of IJV partner in a particular host country. This new perspective on the role of LOF extends Eden and Miller (2004), Pedersen and Petersen (2004), Petersen and Pedersen (2002) and Zaheer (1995). Furthermore, we underscore the importance of considering the host country's rule of law in such decisions.

CONCEPTUAL BACKGROUND

Before developing our framework, we review prior research on LOF, rule of law, emerging markets and SOEs, IJVs and partner selection.

Liability of Foreignness

MNEs that seek to operate in foreign environments face certain costs in doing business abroad (CDBA), which results in certain competitive disadvantages for the MNE's subunit (Hymer, 1976; Kindleberger, 1969; Zaheer, 1995). These costs generally arise from differences in cultural, political and economic factors, as well as geographic distance, between the MNE's home country and the host country. LOF refers to the additional costs incurred by a foreign affiliate operating in a host country that are not incurred by the local firms (Zaheer, 1995).

Zaheer stressed the importance of considering 'a foreign firm's network position in the host country and its linkages to important actors' (2002,

p. 351) leading to structural/relational and institutional costs of doing business abroad as primary components of LOF. The key driver behind LOF is the institutional distance (cognitive, normative and regulatory) between the home country environment and host country environment (Eden & Miller, 2004; Zaheer, 2002). These LOF costs reflect how well a foreign firm interacts within a host country environment suggesting that LOF encompasses social costs related to access and acceptance (Zaheer, 2002). This is especially relevant when MNEs are in a host country where there are strong relational ties between suppliers, customers, government, etc., and when MNE subunits are faced with strong pressures to conform to local practices (Eden & Miller, 2004; Ghoshal & Bartlett, 1990). MNEs that can successfully achieve local isomorphism are rewarded with the receipt and access to resources, increased legitimacy, and capabilities required for surviving in the host country environment (Eden & Miller, 2004; Kostova & Zaheer, 1999). However, there could be certain intangible aspects of LOF, such as certain tacit cultural factors that exist in the host country that may lead to LOF (Calhoun, 2002). Accordingly, studies have emphasized the importance of other host country characteristics with regard to LOF, including the degree of competition in the host country, where it is suggested that LOF occurs more in highly competitive host countries than in less competitive host countries (Miller & Parkhe, 2002; Zaheer, 2002).

The effect of LOF changes over time and may even disappear, especially when a foreign affiliate becomes more of an insider in a host country (Zaheer & Mosakowski, 1997). Prior research has identified several factors influencing LOF and its dynamic nature. For example, Petersen and Pedersen (2002) provided empirical evidence that managerial discretion is directly related to unfamiliarity hazards associated with LOF. That is, MNEs with a global integration strategy that discourages local learning and adaptation remain unfamiliar with the local environment years after entry (Doz, Bartlett, & Prahalad, 1981). Nachum (2003) showed that firm-specific advantages and multinationality enable foreign firms to outperform local firms in the London financial services industry. Eden and Miller (2004) contended that selecting a local joint venture partner reduces unfamiliarity costs and discriminatory treatment by the local government.

Most of the aforementioned studies have discussed how MNEs seek to reduce LOF by becoming 'insiders' in the host country; however, MNEs need to consider how to mitigate the effects of LOF upon entering a foreign country. As mentioned earlier, Eden and Miller (2004) asserted that IJVs may help to overcome some LOF issues.

Rule of Law

Institutional theory has emphasized the role of institutions in determining what is socially or legally appropriate, especially because these institutions include regulatory structures, governmental agencies, laws, courts, etc. (Meyer & Rowan, 1977; Roy & Oliver, 2009; Scott, 2001). Rule of law is suggested to be a crucial element of such institutions, especially in effecting decisions and behaviours of MNEs (Roy & Oliver, 2009). Rule of law is 'the extent to which agents have confidence in and abide by the rules of society, and in particular the quality of contract enforcement, the police, and the courts, as well as the likelihood of crime and violence' (Kaufmann, Kraay, & Mastruzzi, 2006, p. 4). Research has demonstrated that MNEs (in particular, American MNEs) are wary about entering countries with weak rule of law (Globerman & Shapiro, 2003; Tse, Pan, & Au, 1997). This is primarily due to the possibility of insufficient legal protection and recourse during instances of opportunistic conduct, which in turn increases uncertainty with respect to property rights and legitimate returns (Delios & Henisz, 2000; Roy & Oliver, 2009).

The development of strong regulatory institutions has lagged behind growth in many emerging markets (Meyer, 2001), resulting in weak rule of law with respect to rules of exchange (Williamson, 1991). Weak rule of law is linked to high levels of corruption as firms and individuals tend to engage in more opportunistic and illegal behaviour when the legal and regulatory institution is weak and fail to enforce the law (Miller et al., 2008). This pervasive corruption may impede high levels of transparency, which is an important principle for corporate governance (Millar, Eldomiaty, Choi, & Hilton, 2005). Weak institutions in emerging markets adversely affect the development of financial, organizational and technological resources that local firms need to compete internationally (Hitt et al., 2000). Enforcement of intellectual property rights depends on the abilities of the judicial system. Even if rules are in place, a foreign firm's ability to use its intellectual property in an IJV can be compromised if judicial systems are corrupt and laws are unenforced. The weaker the rule of law in the local firm's emerging market, the greater the likelihood for opportunistic behaviour by the local partner. This includes possible abuse of proprietary knowledge (Teece, 1986) or free riding on the reputation and brand equity of the foreign partner. In host countries with weak rule of law, MNEs enter into an IJV with local partners to mitigate the above mentioned threats (Yiu & Makino, 2002).

Emerging Markets and State-Owned Enterprises

Emerging markets have been defined as 'low income, rapid growth countries using economic liberalization as their engine of growth' (Hoskisson, Eden, Lau, & Wright, 2000; p. 249). Although the terms *emerging* economies and *transition* economies are often used without distinction, according to the World Bank (2002), transition economies, which are a *subset* of emerging economies, are formerly socialist countries in East Asia, Central and Eastern Europe, and the newly independent states of the former Soviet Union. Emerging economies include not only transition economies but also economies in Latin America, the Middle East, Southeast Asia and Africa. Some major factors of transition economies are the emergence of new institutions, the change of coordination mechanisms (from hierarchy to market), privatization, corporate governance issues and the growth of entrepreneurial start-ups (Meyer & Estrin, 2001). Some countries like Poland and Russia proceeded with this transition by choosing to 'drop' central planning, while others like China and Vietnam have proceeded by progressively 'growing out of' central planning through gradualist policies (Peng, 2003). Despite large scale of privatization in transition economies, 11% of enterprises in Russia are state-owned (OECD, 2008). In China, 25% of large and medium sized enterprises are state-owned, comprising 58% of the total assets, and 48% of the total profit (China Statistical Yearbook, 2005). That said, Thomsen and Pedersen (2000) noted that state-ownership is prevalent in many developed markets such as Austria (34%), Finland (28%), France (36%), Italy (38%), Norway (39%) and Spain (27% of the largest 100 companies).

State ownership has been a divisive subject of inquiry within the economics literature (e.g., Hart, Shleifer, & Vishny, 1997; Shleifer, 1998). Following World War II, state ownership played a major role in many economies throughout the world. According to Shleifer (1998), state ownership was limited in some developed markets and prevalent in others. State ownership as a form of ownership structure has been shown to have certain disadvantages that would reduce the attractiveness of SOEs as potential JV partners. Most notably, SOEs tend to suffer from ambiguous goals and production inefficiencies. Even if SOEs have clearly defined goals, such as providing health care to the public, this tends to cause confusion because many different political forces have different socio-political agendas regarding the purposes of the SOEs. This suggests that SOEs goals can also shift with the changing political agenda of a new government regime (Vernon, 1981). Additionally, goals of SOEs may be diverted to social political goals following the completion of its primary purpose such as technological development (Noreng, 1981). Although government-granted privileges accord SOEs an advantage in a competitive market, they are also disadvantaged due to these endowments. With SOEs, the traditional link between ownership and management is problematic (Hanke, 1987) because the state tends not to sell its ownership stake – even with publicly traded firms. Therefore, taxpayers do not have the option of withdrawing themselves from ownership even if they disapprove of the agents' performance and the only way the principals can protest the actions of the managers is through indirect means such as political representatives or re-election (Ramamurti, 2000). When the markets are unable to monitor effectively, large shareholders tend to take over this responsibility, and this situation can result in opportunistic behaviour by the largest shareholder at the expense of minority shareholders.

International Joint Ventures

'Narrowly defined a joint venture occurs when two or more firms pool a portion of their resources within a common legal organization' (Kogut, 1988, p. 319). Traditionally, IJVs were used by MNEs as a vehicle to enter the markets of developing countries that enforce restrictive foreign investment (Glaister & Buckley, 1996). Various theories have been used to identify, often the same, strategic motives for forming a joint venture. Dong and Glaister (2006) showed that strategic motivations such as spreading investment costs, enabling diversification, accessing partner knowledge, establishing presence in markets, sharing R&D costs, accommodating host government policy, reducing costs or generating rents, among other motivations influences IJV partner selection.

Kogut (1988) discussed three theoretical perspectives that lead to differing reasons for alliance formation: economic motivation (transaction cost approach), strategic motivation and organizational learning motivation. He suggested that the use of IJVs could be explained from theories of how firms organize boundaries, how strategic behaviour influences competitive positioning of the firm, and/or how firms developed or acquired capabilities (Glaister & Buckley, 1996). A transaction cost explanation for joint ventures explains how a firm should organize its boundary activities with other firms based on the cost of doing business across firm boundaries versus within firm boundaries. A strategic perspective points to how a firm makes decisions to improve its competitive position relative to rivals. Finally, the organizational learning perspective views IJVs as a vehicle through which firms seek, acquire, and/or learn capabilities (Kogut, 1988).

International Joint Venture Partner Selection

There have been a number of joint venture failures due, in large part, to poor partner selection (Hamel, 1991; Lambe & Spekman, 1997; Shah & Swaminathan, 2008). The search for suitable joint venture partners is enhanced by the complementarity of resources that can be leveraged to create synergy (Hitt et al., 2000). Shah and Swaminathan emphasized partner attractiveness, which is defined as 'the degree to which the initiating firm in a particular alliance project sees a partner as desirable, favorable, appealing, and valuable' (2008, p. 473). They concluded that trust, commitment, complementarity and value or financial payoffs play a vital role in alliance partner selection. Hitt et al. (2000) studied a number of different motivations with regard to partner selection in emerging market firms versus developed market firms and concluded that in most cases, different factors are emphasized from both types of markets. In choosing alliance partners, developed market firms tended to place more emphasis on access to local market knowledge and unique competencies than emerging market firms; however, firms from both types of markets equally emphasize complimentary capabilities, as well as managerial capabilities in the selection of IJVs partners (Hitt et al., 2000).

Prior studies have focused on the analysis of partners' compatible and complementary skills, resources, procedures and policies (Hitt et al., 2000; Lane & Beamish, 1990; Li & Ferreira, 2008). For example, Brouthers, Brouthers, and Wilkinson (1995) presented a '4Cs' framework to analyse the likely success of joint ventures based on partner attributes. They suggested that joint ventures offer a promising strategic alternative when: the partners offer complementary skills, cooperative cultures exist between the firms, the firms have compatible goals, and commensurate levels of risk are involved. Partner attributes have also been broadly classified as task and partner-related criteria (Dong & Glaister, 2006). For example, task-related criteria refers to such attributes as low cost sourcing and raw material access, low cost labour, as well as, value chain access (i.e., distribution channels, links to buyers and suppliers and government and administrative institutions), knowledge of the partner's culture, local market knowledge and to product-specific knowledge (Dong & Glaister, 2006). Similarly, partner-related criteria involve such characteristics as trust, financial stability, reputation and business relatedness.

Therefore, it is evident that motivations to form IJVs may depend on several criteria, and it may be difficult to classify them into specific categories. However, to maintain parsimony, we parallel Kogut's (1988) logic and use the terms efficiency seeking, market seeking and knowledge seeking respectively to discuss IJV strategic motivations. These three categories are discussed below. Table 1 summarizes each IJV motivation and preferences for partner type. The following sections attempt to link these literatures to examine the critical decision and preferences for selecting or not selecting a SOE for a partner in an emerging market.

Efficiency Seeking

Global efficiency is key to achieving worldwide low cost competitive advantage (Ghoshal & Bartlett, 1990). To achieve this objective, many firms have sought to form IJVs to spread investment costs and risk, transfer production to low cost markets and increase economies of scale (Contractor & Lorange, 1988; Glaister & Buckley, 1996; Mariti & Smiley, 1983). This perspective focuses on creating efficiency by reducing costs through the utilization of a partner's capabilities or access to low cost inputs, and through realizing scale economies of large-scale production (Glaister & Buckley, 1996). Similarly, sharing R&D costs, enabling faster payback, and lowering costs due to joint operations are important economic motives for the formations of IJVs based on efficiency motives (Glaister & Buckley, 1996).

Table 1. Alliance Motivation and Partner Selection.

Alliance Motivation	Strategic Objectives	Desired Partner Attributes
Efficiency seeking	Low-cost global competitive advantage by achieving scale	Realizing scale economies Low-cost sourcing Access to raw materials
Market seeking	Enter new markets to expand operations and establish presence	Links to buyers and suppliers Business relatedness Product-specific knowledge
Knowledge seeking	Acquire knowledge and develop capabilities	Partner's culture Local market knowledge

Market Seeking

Market seeking motivations refer to the MNE's decision to enter a new market through IJV primarily to expand its operations and establish a presence in the foreign market (Luo & Park, 2001). Market seeking motivations arise when MNEs realize the possible growth opportunities that exist in foreign markets. IJVs have been associated with the speed of market entry to gain market share (Gannon, 1993; Glaister & Buckley, 1996). Market seeking motivations are emphasized when an MNE serves local markets in a foreign country by local distribution, marketing and/or production (Nachum & Zaheer, 2005). IJVs have played a pivotal role in facilitating entry into a foreign market and establishing a presence or competitive market position (Glaister & Buckley, 1996).

Knowledge Seeking

Finally, knowledge seeking – motivations incorporates firms forming IJVs to acquire knowledge (Hamel, Doz, & Prahalad, 1989; Lyles & Salk, 1996), learn from partners (Dussauge, Garrette, & Mitchell, 2000; Khanna, Gulati, & Nohria, 1998), transfer technology, and learn managerial skills (Beamish, 1987; Datta, 1988). There is a growing body of literature on knowledge seeking motivations with respect to IJVs because IJVs provide access to new forms of knowledge and skills (Contractor & Lorange, 1988; Dunning & Gugler, 1993; Hamel, 1991; Hitt et al., 2004; Inkpen, 1998; Kim & Inkpen, 2005). This growing emphasis on learning has led researchers to focus on the acquisition and exploitation of knowledge developed by partners, thereby speeding capability development (Grant & Baden-Fuller, 1995; Lane & Lubatkin, 1998).

While, gaining access to technological capabilities and managerial skills are important motivations to form learning alliances (Dong & Glaister, 2006; Hitt et al., 2000), MNEs also seek knowledge of local business practices, customers, local and national government actors, and other institutional infrastructures (Dong & Glaister, 2006; Yan & Gray, 1994). Local market knowledge will enable MNEs to build relationships that facilitate access to markets and unique competencies that complement existing resources of the MNEs (Hitt et al., 2000; Khanna et al., 1998).

LOF AND PARTNER SELECTION

We are interested in the strategic motivation of the MNE forming an IJV, how this influences their partner choice in an emerging market, as well as,

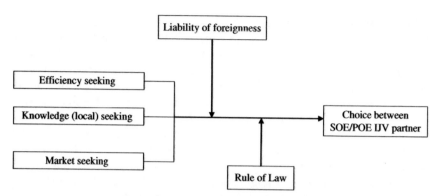

Fig. 1. IJV Partner Selection Framework.

the influence of LOF and rule of law on these decisions. An important mechanism that can impact the preferences and decisions of partners is the relative foreignness of MNEs in emerging economies. A fundamental assumption is that IJV strategic motivations – efficiency seeking, market seeking and knowledge seeking – shape the desired attributes of an IJV partner type, and the presence of these attributes are more (or less) prevalent in a certain type of partner – state-owned or privately owned – thus affecting its attractiveness as an IJV partner. Another key assumption is that firm-specific advantages influence the strategic motivation and entry mode decision, which in our case, has already been made. We present the proposed framework in Fig. 1.

Efficiency Seeking Motivation and Choice of Partner

An MNE with an efficiency seeking strategic motive focuses on creating efficiency, for example, by reducing costs through the utilization of a partner's capabilities or low cost inputs, and through realizing scale economies of large-scale production (Glaister & Buckley, 1996). Higher IJV management costs due to possible increased monitoring may be associated with SOE governance issues. These could arise from lack of market-driven incentives by managers to pursue organizational goals, possibility of outside political actors' influencing decisions, less transparency arising from inadequate disclosure requirements, as well as insufficient tools to provide incentives and discipline to managers (Wang & Xu, 2004). Also, efficiency seeking MNEs may find the SOE less attractive as a potential local partner because of its propensity to emphasize social-economic objectives such as increased hiring to reduce unemployment which inflates costs and makes the ISA less competitive.

If a market structure is developed, then the principal–agent relationship in IJVs with POEs is less uncertain. Shareholders have access to information to monitor agents and sanction their actions (Jensen & Meckling, 1976). Shareholders of POEs induce efficiency through managerial controls and incentives, with the constant threat of market failure or takeover in instances of poor or inefficient performance. Also, shareholders can express their dissatisfaction through withdrawal of the ownership (Ramamurti, 2000). As such, we contend that an MNE with efficiency seeking strategic motivations will perceive partner selection criteria of POEs as more attractive compared with SOEs because of the potential for increased operating and monitoring costs. Therefore:

Proposition 1a. The greater the efficiency motivations for an emerging market IJV, the *more* likely that the MNE will select a POE as a partner.

An MNE establishing an IJV for efficiency seeking reasons may be concerned less with establishing long-term relationships with customers and their network position in the host country. They will seek to reduce their LOF by linking (forming IJVs) with local firms that will be able to gain access to necessary resources. Although LOF alludes to the social costs pertaining to gaining acceptance and access to local information and resources, in these situations MNEs may enter foreign markets with the intention of achieving economies of scale and lowering costs due to the joint operations of the alliance.

An MNE facing a high LOF is likely to face greater efficiency challenges than an MNE with low LOF (Miller & Parkhe, 2002). State ownership of a firm raises corporate governance concerns in emerging economies (Miller et al., 2008; Wang & Xu, 2004). Short-term-oriented state social objectives such as employment creation and socioeconomy policies may promote divergence in the strategic goals of a SOE and an MNE. As a result, valuable resources may be used ineffectively, thereby undermining the primary IJV motivations of the MNE. As such, a state-owned partner becomes even less attractive as a partner to the MNE with a relative high degree of LOF. In contrast, a POE is likely to use resources more efficiently because it does not have unlimited financial resources like the government. In turn, a POE is likely to produce less conflict regarding the use of IJV resources, making it a more attractive partner to an MNE with efficiency seeking motivations in the presence of high LOF.

Regarding host country factors, several emerging economies have been characterized with the possibility of having relatively weak legal and regulatory systems. In these environments, enforcement costs will be high (La Porta et al., 1997). SOEs in a country with weak legal and regulatory systems may be plagued with governance and corruption problems as well as issues inherent to SOEs such as a monopoly on the establishment and enforcement of law (Sundaram & Black, 1992). The state is unlikely to investigate itself for wrongdoings. MNEs may encounter problems ranging from inherent managerial complacency to opportunistic behaviours including bribery, corruption, abuse of power, etc., resulting from lack of reliable control system and legal enforcement. These types of opportunistic behaviour might continue without appropriate sanctions due to the agency issues associated with SOEs. Additionally, in the cases of a breach of contract, legal authority is not independent of the government so that it is less likely for an IJV with an SOE partner to resolve disputes in an impartial judicial system, making an SOE even less attractive as an IJV partner.

In addition, MNEs have varying costs of coordination when they enter into IJVs. These costs of coordination could arise from logistics of coordinated activities as well as interdependence between the partners (Gulati & Singh, 1998; Roy & Oliver, 2009; Pfeffer & Salancik, 1978). Weak rule of law may increase these coordination costs for MNEs due, in part, to institutions that are ambiguous, contested and laden with loopholes (Roy & Oliver, 2009). This is further accentuated by having to deal with governmental organizations, which gives rise to issues such as determining who has authority in a given matter (Peng & Heath, 1996; Roy & Oliver, 2009). In these instances it is possible to get overridden by governmental forces, due to inadequate legal recourse, again making an SOE less attractive as a partner. Therefore:

Proposition 1b. With high LOF, MNEs with efficiency seeking motivations are more likely to select a POE as a partner in an emerging market, ceteris paribus.

Proposition 1c. With weak rule of law, MNEs with efficiency seeking motivations are more likely to select a POE as a partner in an emerging market, ceteris paribus.

Market Seeking Motivation and Choice of Partner

Market seeking alliance motivations refer to the MNE's decision to enter a new market through IJV primarily to expand its operations and to establish a presence or competitive position in a foreign market (Luo & Park, 2001). In the light of the potential for public expropriation hazards by an SOE, an MNE seeking to form an IJV in the local market may reap some benefits from an SOE's discriminatory treatment against other foreign entrants. For example, in some emerging economies, the attractiveness of an SOE as an IJV partner will be further enhanced by privileged access to the state's distribution channels and the receipt of credit guarantees with preferential rates of borrowing. In these situations, MNEs may favourably view the SOE's access to resources in achieving its goals. Also, in certain emerging economies, an SOE will seem more attractive as an IJV partner because a greater likelihood of receiving direct financial subsidies and indirect privileged treatment could exist (Hoskisson et al., 2000). These exclusive privileges of an SOE may allow added security to a strategic alliance in increasingly competitive markets.

MNEs may be more likely to choose SOEs as IJV partners because of other benefits accrued due to SOE characteristics. Foreign firms often lack a track record of reliability and reputation on which to ensure trust-based transactions in the host country. The state, with its monopoly on law, can grant permits and licenses to conduct business in the local market. That is, the state is an institutional "gatekeeper" in that it controls critical resources directly, by awarding contracts, licenses and permits, as well as indirectly, by establishing and enforcing rules and regulations (Hybels, 1995), thus enhancing their attractiveness to market seeking MNEs. In a sense the state can accord market legitimacy to a foreign firm if the foreign firm complies with the necessary government regulations, thus assuring potential customers about the authenticity and long-term viability of their operations.

Having a state-owned local partner may expedite authorization of operating permits, thus enabling the possibility of rapid market entry. Moreover, an SOE can improve access to regulatory mechanisms and the foreign partner's ability to preempt competition (Rondinelli & Black, 2000), making it more attractive to an MNE. In addition to exclusive access to certain resources, SOEs may have immunity from poor decisions that lead to bankruptcy, liquidation, sale, or threat of takeovers, unlike their POE counterparts. Therefore:

Proposition 2a. The greater the market seeking motivations for an emerging market IJV, the *more* likely that the MNE will select a SOE as a partner.

In the event a strategic alliance is based on market seeking motivations, MNEs enter these foreign countries with the intention of establishing a presence and will need to be aware of actual and potential customers' tastes and needs (Nachum & Zaheer, 2005). A market seeking perspective of IJV partner choice implies that the selection of partners is made in the context of competitive positioning vis-à-vis other rivals, and marketing/distributional capabilities (Kogut, 1988). In these situations, LOF arises primarily from discriminatory attitudes towards foreign firms by local employees and customers (Kostova & Zaheer, 1999; Nachum, 2010; Zaheer, 1995). Also, as mentioned earlier, in emerging countries, SOEs goals may be diverted to social political goals especially with changes in the political agenda of a new government regime (Noreng, 1981). Unfamiliarity with the foreign countries institutional laws and regulations will add to the costs of the MNEs as they will have to reorient themselves to the new "rules of the game" (North, 1990, p. 1). It has also been suggested that MNEs sometimes focus on the size of the market and the growth opportunities, without realizing the intricacies necessary for efficient operations (Zaheer, 2002).

When an MNE's motivation is market expansion, it is critical to gain access to the market by establishing the 'rights and qualification to conduct business' in that particular market by quickly establishing local legitimacy (Dacin, Oliver, & Roy, 2007). An MNE needs to gain acceptance from the local government, suppliers or other stakeholders such as employees and customers to gain access to the market. The extent of difficulty of gaining market legitimacy will depend on its LOF, which is based on unfamiliarity, discriminatory and other relational hazards (Eden & Miller, 2004). High LOF accentuates the challenges involved in gaining endorsement from relevant stakeholders. When a foreign firm faces high LOF, a state-owned partner is able to help the foreign partner achieve market legitimacy, enhancing its attractiveness as an ISA partner. As such, the SOE becomes a more attractive partner to the MNE.

The market seeking MNE facing weak rule of law may be more vulnerable to public expropriation hazards (Delios & Henisz, 2003; Rodriguez, Uhlenbruck, & Eden, 2005). An SOE may seek to hold an MNE hostage, and demand additional rents or concessions in order for the MNE to achieve and maintain market legitimacy, thus making an SOE partner less attractive. Although POEs in a weak legal environment may face similar problems with respect to weak corporate governance and corruption, we suggest that POEs have incentives to remedy these problems. A POE partner, confronted with weak rule of law, can distinguish itself and afford more protection to its investors by adopting good corporate governance practices, such as increased transparency (Klapper & Love, 2004). Another means of alleviating concerns is to 'bond' with stronger regulations (such as those in the United States), which is feasible by issuing equity in that country (Coffee, 1999). A high level of transparency will help temper managers' opportunistic behaviour. As POEs have more incentive to implement good corporate governance practices, they will become more attractive in IJV partner selection when rule of law is weak in the environment. Therefore:

Proposition 2b. With high LOF, MNEs with market seeking motivations are more likely to select an SOE as a partner in an emerging market, ceteris paribus.

Proposition 2c. With weak rule of law, MNEs with market seeking motivations are less likely to select an SOE as a partner in an emerging market, ceteris paribus.

Knowledge Seeking Motivation and Choice of Partner

MNEs forming IJVs with knowledge seeking motivations seek to learn from partners (Dussauge et al., 2000; Khanna et al., 1998), transfer technology, and learn managerial skills and/or local market knowledge (Beamish, 1987; Hamel et al., 1989; Lyles & Salk, 1996). Learning in IJVs will be influenced by the partner's ability and willingness to transfer knowledge (Nielsen & Nielsen, 2009), which influences its partner attractiveness. Both POEs and SOEs in emerging markets will seek managerial and technical knowledge from MNEs (Hitt et al., 2000). Trust has been denoted to be a key ingredient in facilitating successful learning and development of new knowledge due to its enabling more propensities to share knowledge (Johanson & Vahlne, 2009; Nielsen & Nielsen, 2009). However, a POE may be cautious about the knowledge it shares with an MNE so as to avoid compromising its competitiveness. A foreign partner that accumulates local market knowledge may undermine the competitive advantages of the POE and thus adversely affect its financial performance. Concerns about competitiveness make a POE partner more protective of its local market knowledge (Nielsen & Nielsen, 2009). Since trust and commitment are vital, and may be more difficult to achieve with a POE partner in emerging markets, POEs may not be suitably attractive as IJV partners in this regard.

In these situations, SOEs may be more suitable primarily because they generally exist for many purposes. For example, SOEs exist to ensure that affordable services are available to low income families, they may exist to create jobs, promote industrialization, advance technology, defend national interest and save declining industries (Vernon, 1984). These state goals are often described as 'public interest' or 'national interest' (Ramamurti, 1987). SOEs are more likely to adopt a holistic perspective in that their focus is on the overall economy and social welfare of the country (Rondinelli & Black, 2000), rather than on an individual firm. Thus they would be more willing to share knowledge and technical know-how to create jobs or improve the competitiveness or attractiveness of the country as a whole. Therefore:

Proposition 3a. The greater the knowledge seeking motivations for an emerging market IJV, the *more* likely that the MNE will select a SOE as a partner.

In the presence of low LOF, an MNE is less likely to require general host country knowledge, but instead, may seek knowledge pertaining to the nuances of the local industry and idiosyncratic customer needs. Thus, decisions and preferences for partner types made by knowledge seekers are likely to be impacted by the level of foreignness. We contend that this form of local market knowledge can be shared by a privately owned local partner, making them more attractive when LOF is low. However, when LOF is high, the need to share local market knowledge and knowledge on institutional differences and operating standards also becomes important. Thus, in circumstances of high LOF, an SOE may be less apprehensive about sharing its general host-country knowledge with a foreign partner, regardless of the extent of 'foreignness' experienced by the MNE. Thus, a state-owned partner may be more attractive to a knowledge seeking MNE in the presence of high LOF.

Again, we contend that rule of law needs to be considered because a government with weak enforcement of regulation and laws is unlikely to track and control unlawful actions of an SOE. As rule of law weakens, state ownership in emerging markets may also increase the likelihood of public appropriation hazards (e.g., due to lack of appropriate patent control structures) to extract added rents from a foreign partner (Delios & Henisz, 2003; Gulati & Singh, 1998; Rodriguez et al., 2005). These factors can discourage foreign partners from sharing and transferring technical knowledge and managerial capabilities to a potential SOE partner and, in turn, the SOE is likely to react by sharing less than the full extent of its local market knowledge with the foreign partner, reducing the SOE's attractiveness to a foreign partner. Therefore:

Proposition 3b. With high LOF, MNEs with knowledge seeking motivations are more likely to select a SOE as a partner in an emerging market, ceteris paribus.

Proposition 3c. With weak rule of law, MNEs with knowledge seeking motivations are less likely to select a SOE as a partner in an emerging market, ceteris paribus.

DISCUSSION AND CONCLUSION

The work of Zaheer and her associates has provided a solid foundation for LOF research (Zaheer, 1995, 2002; Zaheer & Mosakowski, 1997; Kostova & Zaheer, 1999). As we noted earlier, more recent work in this area has emphasized foreign affiliate performance (Miller & Parkhe, 2002; Nachum, 2003), learning (Pedersen & Petersen, 2004; Petersen & Pedersen, 2002), lawsuits (Mezias, 2002), and even mode of entry decisions (Eden & Miller, 2004). The present study takes a first step toward understanding the role of LOF in the IJV partner selection process, given the importance of ownership structure. Specifically, it seeks to develop a partner selection framework and explain how LOF (and rule of law) affect the choice between SOEs and privately owned firms for MNEs forming IJVs in emerging markets.

Our study contributes to the international strategy literature, in general, and the IJV literature, in particular, by providing much needed clarity on partner selection choices as they relate to POEs and SOEs. We drew on the alliance motivation and partner selection literatures to explain why an MNE is more or less likely to choose a POE or SOE as an IJV partner. In doing so, we build on the work of Dong and Glaister (2006), Hitt et al. (2000, 2004) and Roy and Oliver (2009). A key aspect of our framework is the integration of LOF – which had been examined with respect to foreign affiliate performance, entry mode decisions and law suits – and rule of law. Our study introduces fresh opportunities to examine the role of state-ownership, which has been given limited attention in the international strategy literature.

Our study sought to take a first step toward understanding IJV partner selection with respect to decisions regarding ownership structure. In doing so, it offers several points of discussion and opportunities for future research. In emerging markets, it is not uncommon for the state to have an equity stake in publicly traded firms. Therefore, we also need to consider the implications for partner choice when local firms have varying levels of state ownership. Prior research has argued that state ownership of publicly traded firms may produce advantages such as monopoly- or oligopoly-like conditions within the industry (Boardman & Vining, 1989). The level of state ownership of a firm may indicate a close relationship between a local firm and its government that, in turn, can facilitate effective utilization of its resources by the local partner (Miller et al., 2008). A firm with strong government ties generally has stronger bargaining power in negotiations. Firms with strong government ties may gain preferential treatment from their governments in areas such as acquiring permits and accessing distribution channels. These advantages strengthen the bargaining power of a local firm with a high level of state ownership and better access to additional resources.

Related to this point is evidence of less efficient financial markets, due to which, monitoring of managers tends to be done by the largest shareholder, rather than investors. A potential concern is that the largest shareholder may become opportunistic at the expense of smaller shareholders. What is beyond the scope of the present study is the extent of government involvement when the state retains a very low level of ownership. It is reasonable to assume that in these instances, a firm might behave more like a privately owned firm where the state may intervene less, but still provide some of the relational benefits. Accordingly, as the level of state ownership increases, the state is likely to become more opportunistic and the firm might behave more and more like a SOE. Likewise, at moderate levels of state ownership, benefits may outweigh costs that, in turn, affect the likelihood of choosing a partially state-owned firm rather than a POE or SOE. Similarly, understanding the influence of the overall level of state ownership in the industry relative to private ownership, and the relative level of state ownership to private ownership in the country would be important extensions of the theoretical framework presented here. Moreover, understanding the consumer sentiment towards government ownership, both within the country and for specific industries in the host country, would also provide an interesting avenue for future research.

Another issue stemming from our partner selection framework entails methodology and outcomes. One means of testing the value creation associated with partner selection decisions is using an event study methodology (Miller et al., 2008), which may provide an ex ante assessment of investors' perceptions. Another way in which to assess performance is using a survey of IJV managers. However, assessments of performance should include actual financial performance and perceived performance (using several long-term and short-performance criteria). Obtaining both short-term and long-term measures is critical given that the state tends to have a short-term perspective. That said, empirical analysis will need to take into consideration endogeneity, which would naturally arise in testing our framework.

Despite economic growth, many emerging markets are characterized with weak rule of law regarding the rules of exchange (Meyer, 2001), resulting from weak or lack of institutional systems to establish and enforce the exchange. Consequently, MNEs, especially ones from strong legal environments, contemplating partnerships with firms in a country with weak rule of law, have to cope with unique challenges, and this may impact their IJV partner selection. Supporting this view, research indicates that the institutional gap between developed markets and emerging markets affects the degree of uncertainty and ambiguity related to resource sharing decisions between strategic alliance partners (Hitt et al., 2000).

It is important to note that the framework assumed that firm-specific advantages shaped the mode of entry decision and the IJV motivation. But on further examination of LOF and rule of law further, we postulate that IJV motivation may involve a three-way interaction with both LOF and rule of law. We contend that the three-way interactions are more likely to materialize when an IJV partner choice entail a state owned partner because of the state's ability to influence law and enforcement. One such opportunity addresses a self-imposed constraint in that our framework focused on IJVs with only one partner. Admittedly, a situation involving high LOF and weak rule of law may involve ownership structure decisions beyond the scope of the present study – for example, multiple partners (using SOE and POE partners or perhaps an influential non-local partner such as the European Bank for Reconstruction and Development). One may question the need to have more than one state-owned partner since the marginal benefit is likely to decline dramatically while the marginal costs (e.g., bureaucratic costs from engaging different parts of the government) may escalate. That said, scholars may need to examine conditions under which a multinational firm considers a privately owned and state-owned partners, or multiple privately owned partners (Li, Eden, Hitt, & Ireland, forthcoming). Our framework, therefore, can be extended to multiple partners and to a related issue – decisions on IJV equity ownership and management control. We leave these extensions to future research.

A related potential extension involves considering the level of equity of the MNE and its partner(s). As part of this line of inquiry, scholars may gather insights regarding the ownership strategies of MNEs that engage a privately owned versus state-owned partner adoption. To add a layer of complexity, another extension involves predicting ownership strategies in the presence of both privately owned and state-owned partners, as opposed to multiple privately owned partners, and the extent to which publicly traded firms with varying levels of state ownership alter the multination enterprise's ownership decisions.

In sum, we sought to develop a framework that explains IJV partner selection as it relates to the choice of state-owned or privately owned partners. We provided a new lens through which to examine the influence of LOF and rule of law. We hope that this chapter stimulates further research and debate regarding partner selection, SOEs, LOF and rule of law in the global economy.

ACKNOWLEDGMENTS

This chapter was presented first at the 2010 Academy of International Business in Brazil and subsequently at the 2011 AIM CBS workshop (Copenhagen). The authors are grateful for thoughtful comments and suggestions by conference/workshop participants, especially Christian Asmussen, Tim Divinney, Torben Pedersen, Alan Rugman, Rob Weiner and Sri Zaheer.

REFERENCES

Beamish, P. (1987). Joint ventures in LDCs: Partner selection and performance. *Management International Review*, 27(1), 23–37.

Boardman, A., & Vining, A. (1989). Ownership and performance in competitive environments: A comparison of the performance of private, mixed, and state-owned enterprises. *Journal of Law and Economics*, 32(1), 1–33.

Brouthers, K., Brouthers, L., & Wilkinson, T. (1995). Strategic alliances: Choose your partners. *Long Range Planning*, 28(3), 18–25.

Calhoun, M. (2002). Unpacking liability of foreignness: Identifying culturally driven external and internal sources of liability for the foreign subsidiary. *Journal of International Management*, 8(3), 301–322.

Child, J. (1994). *Management in China during the age of reform.* Cambridge: Cambridge University Press.

China Statistical Yearbook. (2005). *China statistical yearbook.* Beijing: China Statistical Press.

Coffee, J. (1999). The future as history: The prospects for global convergence in corporate governance and its implications. *Northwestern University Law Review, 93*(3), 641–708.

Contractor, F., & Lorange, P. (1988). Why should firms cooperate? In: F. Contractor & P. Lorange (Eds), *Cooperative strategies in international business.* Lexington, MA: Lexington Books.

Dacin, M. T., Oliver, C., & Roy, J.-P. (2007). The legitimacy of strategic alliances: An institutional perspective. *Strategic Management Journal, 28*(2), 169–187.

Datta, D. (1988). International joint ventures: A framework for analysis. *Journal of General Management, 14*(2), 78–91.

Delios, A., & Henisz, W. (2000). Japanese firms' investment strategies in emerging economies. *Academy of Management Journal, 43*(3), 305–323.

Delios, A., & Henisz, W. (2003). Political hazards, experience, and sequential entry strategies: The international expansion of Japanese firms, 1980–1998. *Strategic Management Journal, 24*(11), 1153–1164.

Dong, L., & Glaister, K. (2006). Motives and partner selection criteria in international strategic alliances: Perspectives of Chinese firms. *International Business Review, 15*(6), 577–600.

Doz, Y., Bartlett, C., & Prahalad, C. K. (1981). Global competitive pressures and host country demands. *California Management Review, 23*(3), 63–74.

Dunning, J., & Gugler, P. (1993). Technology-based cross-border alliances. In: J. Dunning (Ed.), *The globalization of business.* London: Routledge.

Dussauge, P., Garrette, B., & Mitchell, W. (2000). Learning from competing partners: Outcomes and duration of scale and link alliances in Europe, North America and Asia. *Strategic Management Journal, 21*(2), 99–126.

Eden, L., & Miller, S. R. (2004). Distance matters: Liability of foreignness, institutional distance, and ownership strategy. In: M. A. Hitt & J. L. C. Cheng (Eds), *The evolving theory of the multinational firm. Advances in international management* (Vol. 16). Amsterdam, The Netherlands: Elsevier.

Gannon, M. (1993). Towards a composite theory of foreign entry mode choice: The role of marketing strategy variables. *Journal of Strategic Marketing, 1*(1), 41–54.

Geringer, J. M. (1988). *Joint venture partner selection: Strategies for developed countries.* Westport, CT: Quorum Books.

Ghoshal, S., & Bartlett, C. (1990). The multinational corporation as an interorganizational network. *Academy of Management Review, 15*(4), 603–625.

Glaister, K., & Buckley, P. (1996). Strategic motives for international alliance formation. *Journal of Management Studies, 33*(3), 301–332.

Globerman, S., & Shapiro, D. M. (2003). Governance infrastructure and US foreign direct investment. *Journal of International Business Studies, 34*(1), 19–39.

Grant, R., & Baden-Fuller, C. (1995). A knowledge-based theory of inter-firm collaboration. *Academy of Management Best Papers Proceedings* (pp. 17–21).

Gulati, R., & Singh, H. (1998). The architecture of cooperation: Managing coordination costs and appropriation concerns in strategic alliances. *Administrative Science Quarterly, 43*(4), 781–814.

Hamel, G. (1991). Competition for competence and interpartner learning within international strategic alliances. *Strategic Management Journal, 12*(S1), 83–103.

Hamel, G., Doz, Y., & Prahalad, C. K. (1989). Collaborate with your competitors and win. *Harvard Business Review*, *67*(1), 133–139.

Hanke, S. (1987). The necessity of property rights. In: S. Hanke (Ed.), *Privatization and development*. San Francisco: ICS Press.

Hart, O., Shleifer, A., & Vishny, R. (1997). The proper scope of government: Theory and an application to prisons. *Quarterly Journal of Economics*, *112*(4), 1127–1161.

Hennart, J.-F., Kim, D. J., & Zeng, M. (1998). The impact of joint venture status on the longevity of Japanese stakes in U.S. manufacturing affiliates. *Organization Science*, *9*(3), 382–395.

Hitt, M., Ahlstrom, D., Dacin, T., Levitas, E., & Svobodina, L. (2004). The institutional effects on strategic alliance partner selection in transition economies: China versus Russia. *Organization Science*, *15*(2), 173–185.

Hitt, M., Dacin, M. T., Levitas, E., Arregle, J.-L., & Borza, A. (2000). Partner selection in emerging and developed market contexts: Resource-based and organizational learning perspectives. *Academy of Management Journal*, *43*(3), 449–467.

Hitt, M., Tyler, B., Hardee, C., & Park, D. (1995). Understanding strategic intent in the global marketplace. *Academy of Management Executive*, *9*(2), 12–19.

Hoskisson, R., Eden, L., Lau, C., & Wright, M. (2000). Strategy in emerging economies. *Academy of Management Journal*, *43*(3), 249–267.

Hybels, R. (1995). On legitimacy, legitimation, and organizations: A critical review and integrative theoretical model. *Academy of Management Proceedings Best Papers Procedures*, pp. 241–245.

Hymer, S. (1976). *The international operations of national firms: A study of direct foreign investment*. Cambridge, MA: MIT Press.

Inkpen, A. C. (1998). Learning and knowledge acquisition through international strategic alliances. *Academy of Management Executive*, *12*(4), 69–80.

Ireland, R. D., Hitt, M., & Vaidyanath, D. (2002). Alliance management as a source of competitive advantage. *Journal of Management*, *28*(3), 413–446.

Jensen, M., & Meckling, W. (1976). Theory of the firm: Managerial behavior, agency costs and ownership structure. *Journal of Financial Economics*, *3*(4), 305–360.

Johanson, J., & Vahlne, J.-E. (2009). The Uppsala internationalization process model revisited: From liability of foreignness to liability of outsidership. *Journal of International Business Studies*, *40*(9), 1411–1431.

Kale, P., Singh, H., & Perlmutter, H. (2000). Learning and protection of proprietary assets in strategic alliances: Building relational capital. *Strategic Management Journal*, *21*(3), 217–237.

Kaufmann, D., Kraay, A., & Mastruzzi, M. (2006). *Governance matters V: Aggregate and individual governance indicators for 1996–2005*. World Bank Policy Research Working Paper No. 4012, World Bank, Washington, DC.

Khanna, T., Gulati, R., & Nohria, N. (1998). The dynamics of learning alliances: Competition, cooperation, and relative scope. *Strategic Management Journal*, *19*(3), 193–210.

Kim, C.-S., & Inkpen, A. (2005). Cross-border R&D alliances, absorptive capacity and technology learning. *Journal of International Management*, *11*(3), 313–329.

Kindleberger, C. P. (1969). American business abroad. *The International Executive*, *11*(2), 11–12.

Klapper, L., & Love, I. (2004). Corporate governance, investor protection, and performance in emerging markets. *Journal of Corporate Finance*, *10*(5), 703–728.

Kogut, B. (1988). Joint ventures: Theoretical and empirical perspectives. *Strategic Management Journal*, 9(4), 319–332.

Kostova, T., & Zaheer, S. (1999). Organizational legitimacy under conditions of complexity: The case of the multinational enterprise. *Academy of Management Review*, 24(1), 64–81.

La Porta, R., Lopez-de-Silanes, F., Shleifer, A., & Vishny, R. (1997). Legal determinants of external finance. *Journal of Finance*, 52(3), 1131–1150.

Lambe, C., & Spekman, R. (1997). Alliances, external technology acquisition, and discontinuous technological change. *Journal of Product Innovation Management*, 14(2), 102–116.

Lane, H., & Beamish, P. (1990). Cross-cultural cooperative behavior in joint ventures in LDCs. *Management International Review*, 30(Special issue), 87–102.

Lane, P., & Lubatkin, M. (1998). Relative absorptive capacity and interorganizational learning. *Strategic Management Journal*, 19(5), 461–477.

Li, D., Eden, L., Hitt, M. A., & Ireland, D. (forthcoming). Governance in multilateral R&D alliances. *Organization Science*.

Li, D., & Ferreira, M. (2008). Partner selection for international strategic alliances in emerging economies. *Scandinavian Journal of Management*, 24(4), 308–319.

Luo, Y. (1997). Partner selection and venturing success: The case of joint ventures with firms in the People's Republic of China. *Organization Science*, 8(6), 648–662.

Luo, Y., & Park, S. (2001). Strategic alignment and performance of market-seeking MNCs in China. *Strategic Management Journal*, 22(2), 141–155.

Lyles, M., & Salk, J. (1996). Knowledge acquisition from foreign parents in international joint ventures: An empirical examination in the Hungarian context. *Journal of International Business Studies*, 29(2), 154–174.

Mariti, P., & Smiley, R. (1983). Co-operative agreements and the organization of industry. *Journal of Industrial Economics*, 31(4), 437–451.

McKinsey Quarterly. (2008). *Reassessing China's state-owned enterprises.* Available at http://mkqpreview2.qdweb.net/Public_Sector/Management/Reassessing_Chinas_state-owned_enterprises_2149.

Meyer, K. (2001). Institutions, transaction costs, and entry mode choice in Eastern Europe. *Journal of International Business Studies*, 32(2), 357–367.

Meyer, K., & Estrin, S. (2001). Brownfield entry in emerging markets. *Journal of International Business Studies*, 32(3), 575–585.

Meyer, J. W., & Rowan, B. (1977). Institutionalized organizations: Formal structure as myth and ceremony. *American Journal of Sociology*, 83(2), 340–363.

Mezias, J. (2002). Identifying liabilities of foreignness and strategies to minimize their effects: The case of labor lawsuit judgments in the United States. *Strategic Management Journal*, 23(3), 229–244.

Millar, C., Eldomiaty, T., Choi, C., & Hilton, B. (2005). Corporate governance and institutional transparency in emerging markets. *Journal of Business Ethics*, 59(1–2), 163–174.

Miller, S. R., & Eden, L. (2006). Local density and foreign subsidiary performance. *Academy of Management Journal*, 49(2), 341–355.

Miller, S. R., Li, D., Eden, L., & Hitt, M. (2008). Insider trading and the valuation of international strategic alliances in emerging stock markets. *Journal of International Business Studies*, 39(1), 102–117.

Miller, S. R., & Parkhe, A. (2002). Is there a liability of foreignness in global banking? An empirical test of banks' X-efficiency. *Strategic Management Journal, 23*(1), 55–75.

Nachum, L. (2003). Liability of foreignness in global competition? Financial service affiliates in the city of London. *Strategic Management Journal, 24*(12), 1187–1208.

Nachum, L. (2010). When is foreignness an asset or a liability? Explaining the performance differential between foreign and local firms. *Journal of Management, 36*(3), 713–749.

Nachum, L., & Zaheer, S. (2005). The persistence of distance? The impact of technology on MNE motivations for foreign investment. *Strategic Management Journal, 26*(8), 747–767.

Nielsen, B., & Nielsen, S. (2009). Learning and innovation in international strategic alliances: An empirical test of the role of trust and tacitness. *Journal of Management Studies, 46*(6), 1031–1056.

Noreng, O. (1981). State-owned oil companies: Western Europe. In: R. Vernon & Y. Aharoni (Eds), *State-owned enterprise in the Western Economies*. New York: St. Martin's.

North, D. (1990). *Institutions, institutional change and economic performance*. Cambridge, England: Cambridge University Press.

OECD. (2008). State-owned enterprises in Russia. Presentation at the OECD Roundtable on Corporate Governance of SOEs Moscow, October 27, 2008. Available at http://www.oecd.org/dataoecd/23/31/42576825.pdf

Pedersen, T., & Petersen, B. (2004). Learning about foreign markets: Are entrant firms exposed to a "shock effect"?. *Journal of International Marketing, 12*(1), 103–123.

Peng, M. (2003). Institutional transitions and strategic choices. *Academy of Management Review, 28*(2), 275–296.

Peng, M., & Heath, P. (1996). The growth of the firm in planned economies in transition: Institutions, organizations, and strategic choice. *Academy of Management Review, 21*(2), 492–528.

Petersen, B., & Pedersen, T. (2002). Coping with liability of foreignness: Different learning engagements of entrant firms. *Journal of International Management, 8*(3), 339–350.

Pfeffer, J., & Salancik, G. (1978). *The external control of organizations*. New York: Harper & Row.

Ramamurti, R. (1987). Performance evaluation of state-owned enterprises in theory and practice. *Management Science, 33*(7), 876–893.

Ramamurti, R. (2000). A multilevel model of privatization in emerging economies. *Academy of Management Review, 25*(3), 525–550.

Rodriguez, P., Uhlenbruck, K., & Eden, L. (2005). Government corruption and the entry strategies of multinationals. *Academy of Management Review, 30*(2), 383–396.

Rondinelli, D., & Black, S. (2000). Multinational strategic alliances and acquisitions in Central and Eastern Europe: Partnerships in privatization. *Academy of Management Executive, 14*(4), 85–98.

Rosenzweig, P., & Singh, J. (1991). Organizational environments and the multinational enterprise. *Academy of Management Review, 16*(2), 340–361.

Roy, J.-P., & Oliver, C. (2009). International joint venture partner selection: The role of host country legal environment. *Journal of International Business Studies, 40*(5), 779–801.

Scott, W. R. (2001). *Institutions and organizations*. Thousand Oaks, CA: Sage.

Shah, R., & Swaminathan, V. (2008). Factors influencing partner selection in strategic alliances: The moderating role of alliance context. *Strategic Management Journal, 29*(5), 471–494.

Shleifer, A. (1998). State versus private ownership. *The Journal of Economic Perspectives, 12*(4), 133–150.

Sundaram, A., & Black, J. (1992). The environment and internal organization of multinational enterprises. *Academy of Management Review, 17*(4), 729–757.

Teece, D. (1986). Transactions cost economics and the multinational enterprise. *Journal of Economic Behavior and Organization, 7*(1), 21–45.

Thomsen, S., & Pedersen, T. (2000). Ownership structure and economic performance in the largest European companies. *Strategic Management Journal, 21*, 689–705.

Tse, D. K., Pan, Y., & Au, K. (1997). How MNCs choose entry modes and form alliances: The China experience. *Journal of International Business Studies, 28*(4), 779–805.

Vernon, R. (1981). Sovereignty at bay ten years after. *International Organization, 35*(3), 517–529.

Vernon, R. (1984). Linking managers with ministers: Dilemmas of the state owned enterprise. *Journal of Policy Analysis and Management, 4*(1), 39–55.

Wang, F., & Xu, Y. (2004). What determines Chinese stock returns? *Financial Analysts Journal, 60*(6), 65–77.

Williamson, O. E. (1991). Strategizing, economizing, and economic organization. *Strategic Management Journal, 12*(8), 75–94.

World Bank. (2002). Available at http://www.worldbank.org/depweb/english/beyond/global/glossary.html

Yan, A., & Gray, B. (1994). Bargaining power, management control, and performance in United States-China joint ventures: A comparative case study. *Academy of Management Journal, 37*(6), 1478–1517.

Yiu, D., & Makino, S. (2002). The choice between joint venture and wholly owned subsidiary: An institutional perspective. *Organization Science, 13*(6), 667–683.

Zaheer, S. (1995). Overcoming the liability of foreignness. *Academy of Management Journal, 38*(2), 341–363.

Zaheer, S. (2002). The liability of foreignness, Redux: A Commentary. *Journal of International Management, 8*(3), 351–358.

Zaheer, S., & Mosakowski, E. (1997). The dynamics of the liability of foreignness: A global study of survival in financial services. *Strategic Management Journal, 18*(6), 439–464.

LIABILITY OF FOREIGNNESS AND LOCATION-SPECIFIC ADVANTAGES: TIME, SPACE AND RELATIVE ADVANTAGE

Sjoerd Beugelsdijk

ABSTRACT

Location-specific advantages (LSA) and the liability of foreignness (LOF) are key concepts in international business and management research. To combine these concepts in a systematic framework, I develop a two-by-two matrix focusing on the nature of International Business (IB) research using four key terms: firm, context, comparative and interactive. This framework serves as a heuristic device in describing three main challenges IB scholars face when advancing the role of LOF and LSAs. These challenges relate to our understanding of the nature of relative advantage, to the development of a dynamic (so-called non-ergodic) world view and to the inclusion of the relevant spatial heterogeneity.

Dynamics of Globalization: Location-Specific Advantages or Liabilities of Foreignness?
Advances in International Management, Volume 24, 181–210
Copyright © 2011 by Emerald Group Publishing Limited
All rights of reproduction in any form reserved
ISSN: 1571-5027/doi:10.1108/S1571-5027(2011)0000024015

INTRODUCTION

This issue of *Advances in International Management* aims to 'further our knowledge of how the characteristics of foreign locations interact with entrant firm characteristics in shaping the costs and benefits that multinationals firms experience abroad'. More specifically, the goal is to understand the 'dynamics of globalization by exploring the role of location specific advantages (LSAs), and the liability of foreignness (LOF)'. This touches upon the core of international business and management research. To understand the interaction between the characteristics of foreign locations with entrant firm characteristics, both LOF and LSAs are key concepts. In line with the call for papers, the goal of this chapter is to enrich the different strands of literature associated with both concepts by describing three key challenges associated with IB research and LOF and LSA in specific.

In describing these three challenges, I take a structured approach by starting from a general framework on the nature of IB research. To develop this framework, I go back to the origins of IB research. From my succinct discussion of the definitions of the field, it becomes clear that over time, IB has been concerned with the firm in its international context. To understand this firm level and contextual variation, IB scholars tend to follow either a comparative approach or an interactive approach. These four key terms (firm versus context and comparative versus interactive) capture the nature of IB research. I put them in a two-by-two matrix and discuss each of the cells. This framework provides a heuristic device to discuss the concepts of LOF and LSA and allows me to describe three future challenges in this area related to time, space and the nature of relative advantage.

The contribution I make in this chapter is twofold. My newly developed two-by-two matrix on the nature of IB research allows me to clearly position the dominant role of LSAs and LOF. On the basis of the two-by-two matrix, I describe four 'pure' or unadulterated types of research. Because it is not based on an all encompassing observations of actual research currently done, but derived from key definitions of the field, this two-by-two matrix shows the overall 'research space' in IB. Second, I present three challenges, of which I think they should be dealt with in future research because they enrich our current understanding of LSAs and LOF. These three challenges pertain to the need to understand the nature of relative advantage by advancing our understanding of the role of the home country. Parallel to that, we need to move from a static understanding of firm behaviour to a dynamic approach including the path dependency of investment decisions. Finally, we need to incorporate the relevant levels of spatial variation triggering questions on the fundamental difference between the multinational and the multilocational firm. By relating the three challenges to the two-by-two matrix, I describe how the overall research frontier can be pushed.

DEFINING CHARACTERISTICS OF IB RESEARCH

International business is about profit-maximising activities ('business') that cross national boundaries (Seno-Alday, 2010, p. 19). IB is a field that does not constitute a separate discipline (Cantwell & Brannen, 2011). Instead, it combines and builds upon insights from economics, strategic management and comparative business systems (Negandhi, 1983). In defining the field, Caves (1998) clearly sees IB as a field that slices across the grain of areas of study in business administration. According to Caves (1998, p. 5), 'strategy, finance, marketing, organizational behavior, human-resource management each has its domain of decision making within the firm and its stock of models, frameworks, and research problems for addressing them. International business designates not a class of decisions, but a group of firms that face decision-making problems beyond those that confront single-nation business, or they encounter the same problems transformed by their international context'. For many economics-oriented scholars in IB, the field originated out of the study of foreign direct investment (FDI), but differentiated from economic approaches by a more empirical approach and one in which the multinational firm was not a black box but specifically included. The works by Raymond Vernon, Steven Hymer, Charles Kindleberger and Richard Caves are recognised as important scholarly contributions in IB and in international economics (IE) (Dunning & Lundan, 2008; Rugman & Verbeke, 2008). Both groups of scholars (i.e. the more economics-oriented IB scholars and the more strategy-oriented IB scholars) share their common interest in the international or comparative context. IB has a comparative aspect, because it concerns the comparison of the different ways value added is created by firms in different contexts. IB also has an interactive aspect, because it concerns firms (and employees) of internationalising firms of one country, which are confronted with firms (and employees) of another country, for example, when engaging in an international joint venture.

In 1970 – the year the first issue of the *Journal of International Business Studies* (*JIBS*) was published – Nehrt, Truitt, and Wright (1970) defined IB according to the following criteria (see also Ricks, 1985):

1. It is concerned with firm-level business activity that crosses national boundaries.
2. It is concerned with the interrelationship between the operations of the business firm and the international or foreign environments in which the firm operates.
3. It does not include studies devoted to economic development, development planning, foreign trade and the international monetary system, which belong to development and IE. Excluded also are studies of foreign legal, political, economic and social environments. These belong to the fields of law, political science, economics and behavioural science unless the study itself relates the environment directly to the organisational, operational or decision-making problems of international business.
4. It does not include studies of business activities in given foreign countries. A study of marketing channels in Turkey is still a study about domestic business in Turkey.
5. As an exception to point 4, however, comparative business studies are included within this definition. For example, a study of pharmaceutical marketing channels in Germany, Italy, Brazil and Japan, which makes comparisons and analyses the causes and effects of similarities and differences, would be considered IB research.

Almost 40 years later, similar remarks can be found in one of the editorial letters in the *JIBS* titled 'What makes a study sufficiently international?' (Tung & Van Witteloostuijn, 2008). It is clear that since its official birth, IB scholars deal with the challenges firms and managers are faced with when crossing borders and becoming operationally active in a host country context that differs from their home country. Although the change in context might in principle also relate to intra-country variation (Beugelsdijk & Maseland, 2011; Tung & Verbeke, 2010; Lenartowicz & Roth, 2001; Lenartowicz, Johnson, & White, 2003), most IB research is concerned with firms crossing *national* borders and the development of economic activities in other *nations*. To explore and exploit the LSAs abroad, firms (and managers) have to overcome the distance between the home and the host country.

The distance firms have to overcome does not just relate to geographic distance and the associated transport costs but includes cultural, economic and institutional (legal) differences (Ghemawat, 2001; Slangen & Beugelsdijk, 2010). These contextual differences, driven by the geographic, cultural, institutional and economic differences, are associated with a LOF (Hymer, 1976; Zaheer, 1995). This means that internationalising firms incur costs that domestic firms do not have. Internationalising firms will have to overcome this LOF and exploit their firm-specific advantages (FSAs) abroad to be successful.[1] In general, the assumption in IB research is that the larger the distance that has to be overcome, the more difficult it will be to be successful abroad because the larger the LOF.[2]

Zaheer (1995, p. 343) identified four sources of this LOF as being of prime importance; '(i) costs directly associated with spatial distance, such as the costs of travel, transportation, and coordination over distance and across time zones, (ii) firm specific costs based on a particular company's unfamiliarity with and lack of roots in a local environment, (iii) costs resulting from the host country environment, such as the lack of legitimacy of foreign firms and economic nationalism, and (iv) costs from the home country environment, such as restrictions in high technology sales to certain countries imposed on U.S. owned MNEs'. The first is related to geographic distance and the second and third to cultural distance. The fourth relates to formal institutions, both in the home and in the host country. Whereas certain parts in Zaheer's definition are country-specific, like the institutional restrictions, others are clearly firm-specific concepts, for example, the company's unfamiliarity with the host country environment. This most cited definition of LOF positions the concept both at the firm level and at the country level.[3]

The reason why LOF takes such a prominent position in IB research is in a way because of the existence of LSAs. Dunning and Lundan (2008) distinguish between different types of LSAs. They mention a wide variety of potential LSAs, ranging from natural and created resource endowments, investment (dis-)incentives, economies of agglomeration and spillovers, and the economic and institutional system to mention a few. Whereas LOF is both a country-level construct and firm-level construct, LSAs are often interpreted as (host) country-level constructs (Rugman, 2010, p. 2).

Hence, LOF and LSAs are key constructs in IB research. As such, they also appear in Dunning's Ownership (O) - Location (L) - Internalisation (I) (OLI) framework (Dunning & Lundan, 2008). LOF can be directly related to the O (ownership) dimension. The O dimension captures the notion that firms have FSAs (be it an ownership advantage or a core competency in general) that help them overcome the costs of doing business in a foreign country. As argued before, the notion of LSAs is derived from the L dimension of the OLI paradigm. 'The precise form and pattern of the resulting international production will then be a function of the configuration of the O-specific assets of firms and the L-specific assets of countries, and the extent to which firms perceive that they (rather than markets) can better organize and coordinate these O and L assets' (Dunning & Lundan, 2008, p. 99).[4]

FIRM VERSUS CONTEXT AND COMPARATIVE VERSUS INTERACTIVE: A TWO BY TWO MATRIX

Caves' definition, Nehrt's bullet point description of IB and Dunning's definition of the interaction between O and L focus on the role of firms and the context in which they operate. The difference in context results as a consequence of the distance between home and host country. IB is concerned with the interaction between firms and the new environment in which these firms operate and the comparative analyses of the way firms organise their business activities in different contexts. Irrespective of the specific definition of IB that is chosen, four keywords emerge when discussing the phenomenon of firms crossing borders to become operationally active abroad. These are firm, context, comparative and interactive. On the basis of these four keywords, I develop a two-by-two matrix, which serves as a heuristic device to show the main sources of variation IB scholars are interested in (Beugelsdijk, 2010).

The two-by-two matrix is not meant to categorise and classify existing IB research but serves to show the different sources of variation in a way that is as 'pure' or 'clean' as possible. Although my two-by-two matrix is derived from existing definitions of the field, and not from an assessment of existing research, it is possible to classify existing IB research in the four different cells (more on that later). Depending on the specific combination of either firm or context and a comparative or interactive approach, LOF and LSAs play different roles. Analysing the potential variation at a conceptual level in this two-by-two matrix helps me to specify the gaps in existing research and to develop a future research agenda. Exactly because the matrix is not derived from a classification of approaches currently taken, but from a theoretical delineation based on key definitions, it provides an overview of the sources of variation in a way that is as 'pure' as possible, unadulterated thus.

For each of the four cells of the matrix, I include the key question that is typically asked, the main source of variation and examples of existing IB research that fit the specific approach. Because it is virtually impossible to classify all existing research published in IB, I have delineated my search by selecting *JIBS* decade award-winning papers. These papers are considered the most influential papers published in the *JIBS* one decade prior. One measure of influence is the degree to which candidates' articles have been cited in the 10 years following their publication (a paper must belong to the five most cited articles published in the *JIBS* volume that year). Given the start of *JIBS* in 1970, we have 30 years of decade award winners (1970–2000). An overview of those decade award winners is taken from the website from *JIBS* and included in the appendix of this chapter. Because two papers were selected in 1988, there are 32 *JIBS* decade award-winning articles[5] (Table 1).

The above two-by-two matrix is related to Rugman's classic matrix on FSAs and country-specific advantages (CSAs) (Rugman, 1981). In chapter 8 of his international business textbook, he describes the foundations of the (by now classic) FSA/CSA framework consisting of weak or strong FSAs on the one hand and weak or strong CSAs on the other hand. His two-by-two matrix and mine are complementary. Rugman's focus is on a further theoretical explanation of the 'variables' firm and context in my matrix. The goal of my matrix is to sketch the nature of IB research and not to provide a new theoretical framework.

Type 1: Comparative Analysis of Firms, Contextual Variation is Constant

The first type of research concerns a comparative analysis of firms, in which there is no variation in host or home country contexts. Fig. 1 is a graphical representation of such research. No contextual differences exist as all home country firms are confronted with a similar host country environment. The variation IB scholars are interested in can be found between firms, and as a consequence, this type of IB research is heavily influenced by the resource-based view of the firm (Barney, 1991). Firms should be able to exploit their FSAs in their home country, transfer their FSAs abroad and link them to the LSAs (Rugman & Verbeke, 1990; Verbeke, 2009). Research along these lines tries to open the black box of internationalising firms. At a more practical level, the goal is to find best practices that hold for all firms when entering a certain country: what should firms do when they want to start a venture in China? The question if this is similar for firms entering India is not answered, because the contextual variation is limited to one host country.

In such research, the role of LSAs is limited. Assuming that there are no intra-country differences (excluding the 'Porterian' role of the home country),[6] and ignoring dynamic variation (more on that later), there is no variation in LSAs. The role that LSAs play in such research is limited to a generic effect on all firms. The question is much more if and under what

Table 1.   Sources of Variation and Approaches Taken in IB.

	Source of Variation	
	Main focus on firm	Main focus on context
Comparative approach	Type 1 *Key question:* How do firms from a similar context organise their economic activities in one specific other context? *Main sources of variation:* Firm-specific resources of home (or host) country firms *JIBS decade award winners:* Dyer and Chu (2000) Oviatt and McDougal (1994) Agarwal and Ramaswami (1992) Geringer and Hebert (1989) Reid (1981) Bilkey (1978) Johanson and Vahlne (1977) Rugman (1976) Simpson, Jr. (1974)	Type 2 *Key question:* How do contextual differences affect 'identical' firms? *Main sources of variation:* Home or host country variation *JIBS decade award winners:* Ralston et al. (1997) Gomes-Casseres (1990) Kogut and Singh (1988) Davidson and McFetridge (1985) Hofstede (1983) Kobrin (1979) Ward (1973) Goodnow and Hansz (1972) Schooler (1971)
Interactive approach	Type 3 *Key question:* How does the interaction between firms from context A and firms from context B take shape? *Main sources of variation:* Firm-specific resources of home *and* host country firms *JIBS decade award winners:* Bresman et al. (1999) Lyles and Salk (1996) Madhok (1995) Kogut and Zander (1993) Parkhe (1991) Beamish and Banks (1987) Anderson and Gatignon (1986) Daniels (1970)	Type 4 *Key question:* How does country pair variation affect 'identical' firms? *Main sources of variation:* Country *pair* variation (Home-host distances) *JIBS decade award winners:* Kogut and Singh (1988)[a] Lecraw (1984) Bilkey and Ness (1982) Giddy and Dufey (1975)

Note: For further publication details of these JIBS decade award winning papers I refer to http://www.palgrave-journals.com/jibs/decade_award.html
[a]Kogut and Singh (1988) is included in cell 2 and cell 4 because the authors address both the country *pair* variation (which is their by now classic cultural distance index) and host country variation.

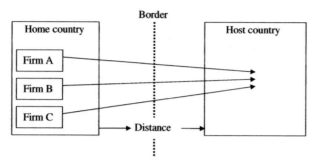

Fig. 1.   Comparative Analysis of Firms, No Contextual Variation.

conditions different firms are able to use their FSAs to internationalise successfully. The variation in LOF is not driven by the distance between home and host country (the country-level differences are constant for all firms), but because firms differ in the way they deal with the LOF. Typical *JIBS* decade award papers that follow such an approach are, for example, research on the export decision-making processes (Reid, 1981; Bilkey, 1978; Simpson, Jr., 1974), parent control systems (Geringer & Hebert, 1989) and also internationalisation process theory because of its focus on the individual involvement over time in a specific host country (Johanson & Vahlne, 1977). Other examples are Oviatt and McDougal (1994), Agarwal and Ramaswami (1992) and Rugman (1976). Research in this cell does not have its main focus on the role of contextual variation. For research explicitly looking into the role of contextual variation, we need to turn to the second cell in the matrix.

Type 2: Comparative Analysis of Context, No Variation in Firm Characteristics

This type of IB research aims to increase our understanding of context-specific differences and the way (similar) firms deal with them. The key issue here is that IB researchers are interested in the variation that is associated with different host country contexts. This is illustrated in Fig. 2 by the variation in distance from the home country to the three different host countries. The distance between the home country and host country 1 is smaller than between home and host country 2, respectively 3. LSAs and

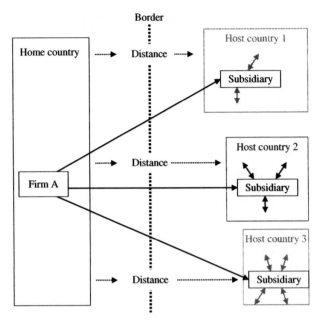

Fig. 2.   The Role of Contextual Variation.

disadvantages affect the specific choices a firm makes, and the question is how these country-level differences – graphically depicted as the number of arrows in the different host countries in Fig. 2 – affect the ability of similar firms to use their FSAs to overcome the distance associated with the decision to become operationally active in these different countries. Whereas the first type of research focuses on the potential variation between firms, this type of research focuses on variation in LSAs.

Research questions typically deal with the trade-off between adaptation to local circumstances or applying a universal approach. In many cases, cultural, institutional and economic differences lead to a need to adapt strategies, organisational structure or product. In fact, the adaptation paradigm (and the related contingency perspective) can be considered a corner stone in such IB research. Management practices should fit with the local environment, and such logic has been applied to a wide array of topics (for examples, see Beugelsdijk & Maseland, 2011). In most cases, IB scholars have interpreted the adaptation paradigm along cultural dimensions thereby relating to the second type of costs in Zaheer's definition of LOF. Aligning management practices to local cultures is typically argued to yield an improved fit between a firm's internal strategy and structure and its external cultural environment (Adler & Gundersen, 2008). MNEs aim to reduce the impact of cultural differences by adaptation, because multinational enterprises (MNEs) are rewarded for isomorphism with increased legitimacy, resources and survival capabilities in host countries, reducing the LOF (Kostova & Zaheer, 1999). Hence, many scholars agree on the importance of such a fit for MNEs to run their foreign operations successfully. This interest in (host) country variation is also reflected in *JIBS* decade award-winning papers, typically dealing with host country cultures (Ralston et al., 1997; Kogut & Singh, 1988; Hofstede, 1983), host country political restrictions and political risk (Gomes-Casseres, 1990; Kobrin, 1979) and host country differences in general (Davidson & McFetridge, 1985; Ward, 1973; Goodnow & Hansz, 1972; Schooler, 1971).

Type 3: Interactive Analysis of Firms, Contextual Variation is Constant

This third type of IB research deals with the *interaction* between firms coming from the home and host country. This is graphically illustrated in Fig. 3. Just like in the first type of research discussed (see Fig. 1), the focus is on firms and the contextual variation is limited to one host country. The difference with the first type is that the interaction with host country partners is the key issue

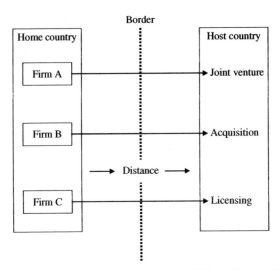

Fig. 3. The Interaction between Home and Host Country Firms.

here. Given the cultural, geographic, institutional and economic distance between home and host country, one important question is how to organise the way of entering the foreign country. The interaction between home country firms and host country partners affect the specific entry mode and the organisational and financial structure and human resource and marketing strategy. It is not uncommon to present such entry mode options as a continuum ranging from licensing, alliances and joint ventures to mergers and acquisitions. Each of these specific entry modes is associated with a certain intensity of interaction between partnering firms and a certain degree of commitment and risk related to such entry modes (Buckley & Casson, 1976; Hennart, 2009; Dunning & Lundan, 2008).

Local firms in the host country can both reduce and increase the LOF because they own assets that the internationalising firm wants to access. In his 'asset bundling theory', Hennart (2009) makes a strong case that this interactive aspect of the relationship between home country firms, the LOF they suffer from and LSAs in the host country has typically been ignored. He argues that none of the existing frameworks, including the OLI paradigm, explicitly considers the role of complementary local assets that are part of the overall LSAs a foreign firm wishes to access. On the basis of his earlier work (Hennart, 1988), he develops a view of IB activity in which the interaction (called bundling by Hennart) between the MNE and the local assets takes a prominent position. This bundling of home and host country-based assets is reflected in this third type of research included in my two-by-two matrix.

The *JIBS* decade award-winning articles in this cell deal with the transaction cost theory of the MNE, the explanation of entry mode choices made by firms and a further explanation of the determinants of joint ventures and strategic alliances. Given the focus on the interaction between home and host country firms (and their assets), this is not surprising. Articles are in the field of knowledge transfer and acquisition (Bresman et al., 1999; Lyles & Salk, 1996; Kogut & Zander, 1993), processual aspects of the interaction between firms, like the role of trust (Madhok, 1995) and inter-firm diversity in general (Parkhe, 1991; Beamish & Banks, 1987; Anderson & Gatignon, 1986; Daniels, 1970).

Type 4: Interactive Analysis of Context, No Variation in Firm Characteristics

The fourth cell of my two-by-two matrix deals with research concentrating on understanding bidirectional contextual variation or simply put country pair variation. In contrast with type 1 and type 3, the main focus is not on firms. The difference with type 2 is that it is not the variation between home or host countries, but the variation between home and host country *pairs*. LSAs and LOF do not play a role here as they do in the other three types of research in my two-by-two matrix, but they do shape the extent to which LSAs and LOF are relevant. They do not play a similar role here, because the main focus is on macro-level characteristics and the relation between two countries. This is graphically illustrated in Fig. 4. LSAs and LOF play an indirect role in this type of research. The reduction of contextual variation between countries at the macro level (or lack thereof leading to divergence) affects the extent to which there are differences in LSAs and thus in the LOF firms suffer from. Because of macro-level interaction between different locations, cultural, institutional and economic differences may change and the environment in which internationalising firms operate is affected. In this type of research, LSAs are not an input in understanding firm behaviour but an output of macro-level interaction processes.

It is typically sociologists, political scientists, cross-cultural psychologists and anthropologists who are interested in this type of research. IB scholars are however informed by the work of scholars from these parallel disciplines. The result of such research may then serve as an input in IB research. A typical example is the Kogut and Singh (1988) index of cultural distance that has extensively been used as a proxy for cultural differences between country pairs. Another example at the macro level is the role of trade agreements such as NAFTA, WTO, ASEAN and the EU, which contribute to the reduction of contextual differences by providing a (more) uniform context in which internationalising firms can operate. By reducing

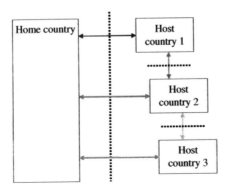

Fig. 4.   Differences between Country Pairs.

such barriers, the contextual distance is limited. This is an input in macro-level FDI and trade studies in which dummies for trade agreements and colonial ties are commonly included (e.g. Slangen & Beugelsdijk, 2010).

Because not many IB scholars have a specific interest in this type of research, and use it indirectly as an input in their analysis, the number of *JIBS* decade award-winning papers fitting this cell is smaller than in the three previously discussed types of research. I already mentioned the Kogut and Singh (1988) index of cultural distance between country pairs. Other examples are Lecraw (1984) focusing on the negotiation process with host countries, Bilkey and Ness (1982) explaining how products made in country X are evaluated by (inhabitants of) country Y, and Giddy and Dufey (1975) on exchange rate forecasting.

THREE CHALLENGES

After establishing the nature of IB research and developing a two-by-two matrix showing the 'pure', unadulterated research approaches that can be taken in IB, I turn to future research. I do so by focusing on three important aspects, which capture generic challenges to enrich the notion of both LSAs and LOF.

Challenge I: To Increase our Understanding of the Nature of Relative Advantage

In all four types of IB research discussed earlier, the notion of LSAs clearly refers to host country conditions relative to other host countries, and the relative attractiveness of a specific host country compared to the home country. LOF refers to the notion that firms need to overcome the distance between home and host, which requires FSAs. In doing so, the LOF literature positions internationalising firms relative to other firms in the host country. It is a comparison between (domestic) incumbents and the foreign entrant that creates the LOF. A quote by Dunning may serve to illustrate this.

In the 2008 edition of his book on the *Multinational Enterprise and the Global Economy*, Dunning writes (together with Lundan): 'At any given time, the more a country's enterprises – relative to those of another – possess desirable O advantages, [ ] the more they find it in their interest to access or exploit them in a foreign location, then the more they are likely to engage in outbound FDI. By the same token, a country is likely to attract inbound investment by foreign MNEs when the reverse conditions apply. [ ] Changes in the outward or inward direct investment position of a particular country can be explained in terms of changes in the O advantages of its enterprises relative to those of other nations, changes in its L assets relative to those of other countries [ ]' (Dunning & Lundan, 2008, p. 100). Dunning is even more explicit in his 2009 retrospective article, when he writes that the initial impetus for his research was his finding that in the 1950s, in the manufacturing industry the labour productivity of US firms in the United Kingdom was 2.5 times higher than that of UK firms in the United Kingdom (Dunning, 2009, p. 20).

Such a view of firms having a relative advantage compared to host country firms contrasts sharply with the view in IE. International economists have convincingly shown that those firms that go abroad are the most competitive ones of the overall population of firms in the home country (Bernard, Eaton, Bradford Jensen, & Kortum, 2003; Yeaple, 2009). Very often, this is measured in terms of productivity differences. The general finding is that a pecking order exists in which the most productive firms start producing abroad, the less-productive firms will serve host markets by exporting and the least productive firms focus on the domestic market. This fits the IB argument on FSAs because the most productive firms have 'something' that allows them to overcome the LOF confronted with in the host country. However, a crucial difference is the nature of the relative advantage.

In IB, the assumption is that internationalising firms need to be 'better' than other *host* country firms (to overcome the LOF), whereas in IE, the assumption is that those internationalising firms are 'better' than other *home* country firms. This raises an important question: relative advantage compared to whom? The combined insights from IB and IE would imply that MNEs belong to the right tail of the distribution of firm productivity in the overall population of firms (both at home and abroad). A further theoretical and empirical deepening of the nature of relative advantage is required. It may very well be that the comparison with other home country firms explains the decision to go abroad and that the comparison with host country firms explains the subsequent success of the decision to go abroad, but as far I know, this has not been addressed explicitly. To increase our understanding of LOF, we need to better understand the nature of the relative advantage.[7]

There is a second related dimension of the notion of relative advantage. Despite the emergence of strategic asset-seeking FDI, one of the main reasons why internationalising firms go abroad still is the opportunity to serve customers in foreign markets (Brainard, 1997; Beugelsdijk, Pedersen, & Petersen, 2009). And although the costs of going abroad are captured by the LOF concept, international marketing studies have argued that foreignness may also be beneficial to market-seeking firms (Ghauri & Cateora, 2006; Insch & Miller, 2005). Assuming that customers know a product's country of origin (Balabanis & Diamanopoulos, 2008), some studies have argued and found that local buyers evaluate products originating from culturally more distant countries more positively than those originating from culturally close countries (Chao, 1993; Insch & Miller, 2005). These studies suggest that the benefits of foreignness (BOF) associated with selling abroad may actually increase with distance, especially with cultural distance. This may especially hold true for western MNEs because the attitude of buyers in developing or emerging countries towards imported Western products tends to become more positive with cultural distance (Ghauri & Cateora, 2006; Insch & Miller, 2005).

This is however not a universal effect that holds for all modes of serving foreign markets (Slangen, Beugelsdijk, & Hennart, 2011). These BOF, which accrue to exports to culturally distant countries, are likely to be lower for goods sold by foreign affiliates in culturally distant countries. Goods sold by foreign affiliates of Western parents (local production) may be evaluated less positively by local customers than imports from the West (Johansson & Nebenzahl, 1986). For example, Heineken beer is considered a premium beer in the United States precisely because it is imported from the Netherlands rather than produced in the United States (Beugelsdijk, Slangen, & Van Herpen, 2002). Similarly, when Volkswagen announced that it would start to manufacture Rabbits in the United States for the US market, many of its American customers made efforts to buy Rabbits still made in Germany (Johansson & Nebenzahl, 1986).

Although these examples suggest that the BOF associated with exporting to certain countries are often higher than those associated with operating affiliates in such countries, the key issue is that there are not only liabilities of foreignness but also benefits. The legitimacy argument so often used in the LOF literature not just refers to a lack thereof, but can also be part of a firm's specific advantages. Exactly because they are foreign, some firms enjoy a benefit of foreignness they can use to overcome the distance associated with going abroad. When the home country provides such a BOF, it may contribute to the FSAs that are required to overcome the LOF associated with the host country. In those cases, it is the LOF and the BOF that jointly interact and determine the nature and success of the internationalisation process. Despite the fact that LSAs are usually presented as a country-level construct (Rugman, 2010), when a *home* country location advantage provides a BOF, this home country characteristic turns into a FSA. This complements Porter's (1991) argument that home country factors may push firms to internationalise, because it shows that 'just being a foreign firm' may be part of the pull factors as well. In other words, whereas a typical Porterian argument would, for example, be that firms internationalise to escape fierce competition at home, the BOF argument is that just because a firm is foreign it is able to be successful abroad.

　　Both the question on relative advantage and the BOF relate to the role of the home country and the way the characteristics of the home country feed into the extent to which firms suffer from a LOF. These types of questions directly relate to the first and third types of IB research discussed in my two-by-two matrix. By using the first typology, we can explain if it is indeed the most productive firms that go abroad and if this explains their subsequent success in a specific host country. With respect to the role of BOF, a setup of a research project as in type 1 may help explain which firms actually experience such a BOF. A research setup as in type 3 can subsequently help us to understand in what host country context such a BOF exists.

Challenge II: To Move from an Ergodic to a Non-ergodic World View

The need to move from an ergodic to a non-ergodic world view implies that we need to change our perspective from a static one to a more dynamic one to further increase our understanding the role of LSAs and LOF. Because IB is at least partly defined by its attention to cultural differences (Buckley, 2002), the discussion of a static versus a dynamic view of the world in IB has included the stability of culture.[8] Shenkar (2001) and more recently Tung and Verbeke (2010) critically discuss this assumption of stability of the cultural distance measure. Although their comments specifically relate to the measure of culture and cultural distance, this practice is actually widespread in IB and goes beyond the measurement aspects of culture and cultural differences. North (2005) uses the term 'ergodic world' to criticise such a static view in social sciences, and he makes a strong claim that we live in a non-ergodic world. The notion of a non-ergodic world means that the default assumption should not be a static one, but a dynamic one. And more important, this dynamic process is not random but also sensitive to initial conditions. In other words, path dependency matters. In IB, this means that the internationalisation process is not a random walk, but decisions of firms should be seen in the context of previous decisions these firms have made *and the changing context in which they operate.*

Many IB scholars have tried to incorporate dynamic elements in their research. The literature on investment development paths (Dunning & Lundan, 2008; Dunning & Narula, 1996), entry mode dynamics (Buckley & Casson, 1981; Rugman, 1981) and internationalisation process theory – most prominently the Uppsala model of internationalisation (Johanson & Vahlne, 1977, 2009) – come to mind. Learning processes, network relationships and the development of dynamic capabilities allow firms to internationalise more or less rapidly. The (implicit) assumption is that the LOF is reduced in such a process. Another more recent dynamic approach applied in IB is real option theory. The idea of real option theory in the context of IB is that internationalising firms decide for a specific entry mode (or investment mode in general) depending on the uncertainty associated with a specific market (Cuypers & Martin, 2010; Brouthers & Dikova, 2010; Li & Rugman, 2007). Changes in the host country conditions (LSAs), especially the uncertainty associated with market development, may lead firms to upgrade or downgrade their initial investment decisions. Real option theory links current strategic decisions with uncertainty about future outcomes (Cuypers & Martin, 2010, p. 50). Hence, real option theory predicts that firms make a certain investment decision at time 't' given the current and anticipated future level of uncertainty, and this investment decision can change at time '$t+1$' depending on the development of the level of uncertainty, a reasoning that is exactly in line with the non-ergodic view. The notion of (ir)reversibility is an important aspect of real option theory.

Despite the important steps taken so far, dynamics is often mostly included as the process of a MNE becoming more of an insider in a country thereby reducing the LOF over time (e.g. by experience). As Hennart (2009) rightfully argues, though, this is often driven by MNE-specific characteristics and tends to exclude the dynamics of local assets present in the host country. By presenting the internationalisation process as a stepwise increase in the level of commitment as done in the Uppsala model, path dependency is present, but only to the extent that it is MNE-specific and one-directional. Such a view is MNE centric and does not include the possibility that the underlying reason for the LOF (a 'strange' or 'hostile' foreign environment) may also change over time.

In a non-ergodic world, LSAs and LOF are not stable over time. Many IB scholars would subscribe to such a dynamic view of LOF and LSA. In fact,

Zaheer (2002) notes that LOF is 'inherently a dynamic concept' and has shown that changing environmental conditions affect the extent to which firms suffer from a LOF (Zaheer & Mosakowski, 1997). The reality is, however, that empirical studies like the one by Zaheer and Mosakowski (1997) taking such a dynamic perspective on LSAs and LOF are scarce. By using the typology developed before, it is easy to show how this can be included in future research though.

Following my two-by-two matrix, the first and third types of IB research focus on between firm variation and include only one host country. In the first type of research, the focus is on the firms from the home country, whereas in the third type of research, the interaction between home and host country partners is central. In both types of research, LSAs do not play a (major) role in an ergodic world. But in a non-ergodic world, LSAs change over time, leading some firms to revise their initial entry mode decision, nature of cooperation or the location decision in general. In line with Hennart's (2009) asset bundling theory referred to earlier, a non-ergodic world view implies that the interaction between home and host country assets changes over time (and not only because the MNE has learned). Despite the fact that there is only one host country in this type of research, dynamic variation in the LSAs leads to changes in the LOF and implies that firms may respond differently to these changes at time 't' and '$t+1$'. The real option approach fits nicely in such a research setup. With one host and one home country, the question can be answered how different firms deal with the different perceived levels of uncertainty in a specific host market and make different real option choices.[9]

In the second type of IB research with multiple host countries, the static variation in LSAs is what researchers are specifically interested in. Cultural distance between home and a set of host countries can be assumed to be stable (although this assumption is under heavy attack as mentioned before), but economic and institutional distances are by definition dynamic. Countries develop economically, and the type and quality of their institutional system changes over the years. Once allowing for a specific dynamic development path in each of the host countries, interesting research questions arise. For example, the static variation between emerging markets on the one hand and developed markets on the other hand has been on the agenda of IB scholars for a long time now. But emerging markets do not develop in similar ways. China, India, Russia and Brazil are all emerging markets that distinguish themselves from developed markets. The historical past of these countries differs and also shapes their future development paths. And although the static variation may be dominant at one point in time allowing us to treat these countries as one group, the differences between these countries become (more) important once they develop and, driven by their initial differences, may develop in different directions. In other words, LSAs change over time and firms can be expected to respond strategically to that.

Challenge III: To Incorporate Relevant Spatial Heterogeneity

As mentioned before, location is a key pillar of the OLI paradigm, recently re-emphasised by a decade award-winning paper in the *JIBS* (Dunning, 2009). Although the 'L' pillar is less of a 'neglected factor' (Dunning, 1998; Cantwell, 2009), in the current IB literature, the view of geographic space is relatively underdeveloped in IB (Beugelsdijk, McCann, & Mudambi, 2010; McCann & Mudambi, 2005). This arises from the fundamental building block of the discipline, namely the nation state and the associated role of national borders. As LSAs are interpreted as country-level constructs, the distance between home and host country is often used to proxy for the LOF that firms have to overcome. LOF is then operationalised along different distance dimensions. The IB literature tends to view space in terms of distance between countries, relying on measures such as cultural distance, institutional distance and distance between country centres, as discussed before. Because IB is concerned with firms crossing national borders, it is no surprise that spatial heterogeneity is conceptualised and measured at the country level. It can easily be argued, though, that the relevant spatial heterogeneity firms have to deal with can differ substantially from this country level.

Geographic distance is often measured by measuring the distance between capital cities, not taking into account the possibility that firms may be located close to the national border. The geographic distance can actually be larger within a country than between countries, depending on the exact location of firms. This is obviously a more serious problem for larger countries with multiple economic centres. Head and Mayer (2010) show that such existing measures of distance overestimate actual distances. Moreover, in large countries, it is not uncommon that different government policies exist regarding inward FDI. The example of export processing zones with preferential tax regimes in emerging markets such as China immediately comes to mind. Hence, both geographic and occasionally also institutional distance are incomplete proxies for the overall LOF when measured at the country level. A similar comment holds for economic distance. For example, when expanding abroad to developing countries, Starbucks specifically targets the big cities with wealthy consumers (Verbeke, 2009). A comparison of the average level of GDP per capita of these countries with the United States would suggest a large economic distance and LOF, whereas the reality is that Starbucks managed to reduce the economic distance (and LOF) by following a strategy of locating in big relatively wealthy cities.

As argued before, the measure of cultural distance is based on the assumption of homogenous cultures. Potential intra-country heterogeneity is not taken into account by using country-level measures. It is important to realise that the LOF argument and the often hypothesised negative effect of cultural distance between a home and host country on investment flows are contingent on this cultural homogeneity assumption. Once relaxing the homogeneity assumption, part of the LOF argument does not hold any longer and the question rises how the cultural distance argument is affected. Zaheer (1995) clearly defined the cultural unfamiliarity component of the LOF as firm's specific costs, and a national level measure of cultural differences assumes a generic effect for all firms (Shenkar, 2001). The concept of psychic distance – which is an individual-level construct (Dow & Karunaratna, 2006) – is an interesting alternative, but difficult to measure because of data collection constraints. It may be particularly relevant in type 1 and type 3, where national-level variation is absent (cultural distance is constant), but individual-level variation in psychic distance may still exist. Although the use of national-level scores in type 2 research may proxy for the underlying psychic distance at the individual level, such research suffers from an ecological fallacy.

This is not to say that spatial heterogeneity is not taken into account at all. There is a rich literature in IB on the MNE's local embeddedness (e.g. Andersson, Forsgren, & Holm, 2002), but its spatial aspects are often simply assumed; they have rarely been distinguished or explored in an explicit manner. Influential IB scholars have recently highlighted this lacuna (Dunning, 2009). IB analyses like the 'global factory' (Buckley & Ghauri, 2004; Buckley, 2009) and MNE strategy in the location of knowledge-intensive activities (Dunning, 2000) can be better understood by analysing the complex interplay between the MNE and its spatial environment (e.g. Cantwell & Janne, 1999; Lahiri, 2010). Moreover, the development of multilevel analyses in which the interaction between individual, firm- or country-level characteristics is explicitly modelled has recently taken off in IB (as reflected in the forthcoming special issue in the *JIBS*, Arregle, Makino, Martin, Peterson, & Swaminathan, forthcoming).

CONCLUSION

The core of IB concerns the notion of internationalising firms that wish to capitalise on LSA in a host country and need to overcome the LOF by exploiting and further exploring their FSA. This is however not so much a theory, but much more a phenomenon-driven – rather simple yet powerful – description of the nature of IB research. To increase our understanding of LOF and LSA, I have taken one step back to develop a general conceptual framework based on four key recurring terms in existing definitions and characterisations of IB research: firm, context, comparative and interactive. The resulting two-by-two matrix provides me with the tools to develop a 'pure', unadulterated typology of IB research. I subsequently describe four types of IB research, of which the fourth – which is based on macro-level interaction – serves much more as input in IB research and is not the core interest of many IB scholars. In line with the goal of this issue of *Advances in International Management* to 'further our knowledge of how the character-istics of foreign locations interact with entrant firm characteristics in shaping the costs and benefits that multinationals firms experience abroad', I have sketched three challenges we face.

The first relates to the need to increase our understanding of the nature of relative advantage. Exploring the nature of relative advantage does change our view on the relevant yardstick: are/should internationalising firms be more productive than other home country firms, or than host country firms? Or both? Or does it answer different questions? The tendency to exclude the home country (notwithstanding the 'Porterian' view) is also reflected in the sole focus on the LOF without the possibility that there may be BOF as well. The home country may lead to a BOF that contributes to the ability of internationalising firms to overcome the LOF. The question under what conditions such a BOF results is relevant in all three main types of IB research. Hence, whereas the call for papers of this issue of *Advances in International Management* refers to the interaction between *foreign* locations and firm characteristics, my suggestion would be to pay more attention to the interaction between firm characteristics and the *home* country.

Second, I argued that we need to take dynamics more seriously. In a non-ergodic world, LSAs and LOF are not stable over time. Hennart's (2009) asset bundling theory, real option theory and internationalisation theory are powerful approaches that fit the non-ergodic world view, under the condition that they conceptualise and measure true dynamics. That implies that we need to move from a cross-sectional analysis in which we observe firms making a certain investment decision at time 't' and relating this decision to a position on a universal (i.e. country generic) uncertainty ladder, to a truly dynamic approach in which we track firms' decisions over time within a specific country. Longitudinal analyses thus.

Third, I showed that we need to include the relevant spatial heterogeneity in our models instead of using country-level scores. This can be done in two ways, either by allowing for intra-country diversity or by making MNE-specific (or manager) adjustments in the way these national-level characteristics are (perceived to be) relevant. An example of the first would be to measure intra-country cultural diversity. An example of the latter would be to measure psychic distance of the manager. There is a trade-off. Whereas the MNE-specific constructs are probably the best, collecting these measures for a large sample of firms and host countries is difficult. On the contrary, measuring intra-cultural diversity may be easier given the existing culture databases presently used in IB research, but such research still suffers from an ecological fallacy attributing aggregate-level characteristics to individual-level phenomena.

These three challenges and my two-by-two matrix are by no means exhaustive (nor are they meant to be). One thing I did not discuss explicitly is the existence of cross-level effects that result when combining cells of my two-by-two matrix. For example, does the fact that some major MNEs are simultaneously present in a set of host countries (cell 2) influence the macro-level relationship between these countries (cell 4), which could in turn influence the decision space of these MNEs (cells 1 and 3)? And how is the relationship between firms from the same home country (cell 1) affected by their differential presence in a set of host countries (cell 2)? The framework and challenges presented in this chapter trigger a range of follow-up questions that go beyond the scope of this chapter. The goal of this chapter was to show how – while using the traditional concepts of LSAs, LOF and indirectly also FSAs – the IB research agenda can be extended and pushed. The phenomenon of IB requires an interdisciplinary approach that is unique in itself. The IB agenda is not out of steam (Buckley, 2002), but to progress, I do think we need to face the different challenges I described in this chapter.

NOTES

1. Acknowledging the obvious link between LOF, LSAs and FSAs, I refrain from an extensive analysis of the latter. I am aware that FSAs, and the important distinction between location bound, and non-location-bound FSAs are related, but I concentrate on LSAs and LOF in this chapter (for a discussion on FSAs, see Rugman, 1981, 1996; Rugman and Verbeke, 1990, 2002).

2. It goes beyond the scope of this chapter to present all interpretations of LOF. I follow the generally accepted definition originally introduced by Zaheer (1995) building on Hymer's (1976) work. For an overview of alternative interpretations, I refer to a special issue in the *Journal of International Management* edited by Luo and Mezias (2002).

3. The LOF literature is embedded in an older literature on the costs of doing business abroad, going back to the first-generation of IB scholars. Eden and Miller (2004) provide a historical analysis of the LOF and discuss the difference between LOF and the more economic interpretation of the costs of doing business abroad.

4. Because it goes beyond the scope of this chapter, I do not include the I (internalisation) dimension in my discussion of LOF and LSAs. Internalisation is obviously related to L and especially O. For a recent discussion on the relation between the O and the I dimensions, I refer to a special issue in the *Multinational Business Review* edited by Rugman (2010).

5. Three of the 32 decade award winning articles are written by John Dunning (1980, 1988, 1998). All three articles concern the OLI paradigm or extensions of it. Because of its eclectic nature focusing on both firm and context, and the interaction between them, these three Dunning articles are difficult to classify in the matrix. For that reason they are not included. For all the other award winning articles, the classification is based on the paper's main focus.

6. Porter's view implies that the home country may provide a push for firms to internationalise depending on the specific configuration of the five forces in Porter's diamond model, for example, because of home market saturation (see Verbeke, 2009, for a concise description).

7. That is not to say this issue has not been addressed at all. Parallel to Zaheer and Mosakowski (1997), a series of studies on the banking industry exists. DeYoung and Nolle (1996) have studied foreign-owned banks in the United States and showed that they were less profit-efficient than their US competitors. Li (2008) argues this liability of foreignness shapes the overall entry and exit rates and the nature of competition in the banking industry. Another insightful contribution is the study by Hennart, Roehl, and Zeng (2002), showing that a comparison of exit rates of foreign and domestic firms is an incomplete proxy for the measurement of LOF. Hennart et al. (2002) make a strong case for a further empirical analysis of the LOF. A similar comment has been made by Dunning and Lundan (2008, pp. 113–114).

8. IB scholars generally assume that cultures or at least cultural differences are stable (Yaprak, 2008). Doing so helps to reduce ambiguity and allows for a discussion of the fit between a certain culture and specific managerial and organisational practices, because it makes behavioral outcomes more predictable (Leung, Bhagat, Buchan, Erez, & Gibson, 2005). This allows us to include culture in our IB theories without running the risk of including a component that is partially random or one that changes over time. In doing so, many of us refer to Hofstede (2001) who himself claimed that mental programs of people around the world do not change rapidly but remain relatively constant over time. The discussion on cultural convergence versus that of divergence is still open, but the view of culture as a dynamic process has been gaining ground in social sciences (Beugelsdijk & Maseland, 2011).

9. The empirical application of real option theory in IB is however not always in line with such a non-ergodic view. Despite the dynamic nature of the theoretical arguments, many of these studies operationalise such an idea in a cross-sectional setting, thereby assuming that changes over time are reflected in different positions of countries on an universal uncertainty measure (but without observing the true changes over time). When doing so, within-country variation over time is redefined as between-country variation. Real option theory is an important first step towards presenting the internationalisation process in a non-ergodic way, but the next step would be to do a longitudinal analysis and measure the within-country variation over time.

ACKNOWLEDGMENTS

I thank Nicolai Foss, Arjen Slangen, Li-Janne Leusink, Sathyajit Gubbi and the conference participants of the Copenhagen Business School workshop for their useful comments and suggestions.

REFERENCES

Adler, N. J., & Gundersen, A. (2008). *International dimensions of organizational behavior* (5th ed.). Mason, OH: Thomson.

Andersson, U., Forsgren, M., & Holm, U. (2002). The strategic impact of external networks: Subsidiary performance and competence development in the multinational corporation. *Strategic Management Journal, 23*(11), 979–996.

Arregle, J. L., Makino, S., Martin, X., Peterson, M. F., & Swaminathan, A. (forthcoming). Multilevel empirical research in International Business. *Journal of International Business Studies*, special issue.

Balabanis, G., & Diamanopoulos, A. (2008). Brand origin identification by consumers: A classification perspective. *Journal of International Marketing, 16*(1), 39–71.

Barney, J. (1991). Firm resources and sustained competitive advantage. *Journal of Management, 17*(1), 99–120.

Bernard, A., Eaton, J., Jensen, J. B., & Kortum, S. (2003). Plants and productivity in international trade. *American Economic Review, 93*(4), 1268–1290.

Beugelsdijk, S. (2010). IB research: Homo ludens meets homo economicus. Inaugural Lecture University of Groningen.

Beugelsdijk, S., & Maseland, R. (2011). *Culture in economics: History, methodological reflections and contemporary applications*. Cambridge, UK: Cambridge University Press.

Beugelsdijk, S., McCann, P., & Mudambi, R. (2010). Place, space and organization; economic geography and the multinational enterprise. *Journal of Economic Geography, 10*(4), 485–493.

Beugelsdijk, S., Pedersen, T., & Petersen, B. (2009). Is there a trend towards global value chain specialization? An examination of cross border sales of US foreign affiliates. *Journal of International Management, 15*(2), 126–141.

Beugelsdijk, S., Slangen, A. H. L., & Van Herpen, M. (2002). Drivers and determinants of organizational change; the case of Heineken Inc. *Journal of Organizational Change Management, 15*(3), 311–326.

Brainard, S. L. (1997). An empirical assessment of the proximity-concentration trade-off between multinational sales and trade. *American Economic Review, 87*(4), 520–544.

Brouthers, K., & Dikova, D. (2010). Acquisitions and real options: The Greenfield alternative. *Journal of Management Studies, 47*(6), 1048–1071.

Buckley, P. J. (2002). Is the international business research agenda running out of steam? *Journal of International Business Studies, 33*(2), 365–373.

Buckley, P. J. (2009). The impact of the global factory on economic development. *Journal of World Business, 44*(2), 131–143.

Buckley, P., & Casson, M. (1976). *The future of the multinational enterprise.* London: MacMillan.

Buckley, P., & Casson, M. (1981). The optimal timing of foreign direct investment. *The Economic Journal, 91*, 75–87.

Buckley, P. J., & Ghauri, P. (2004). Globalisation, economic geography and the strategy of multinational enterprises. *Journal of International Business Studies, 35*(2), 81–98.

Cantwell, J. A. (2009). Location and the multinational enterprise. *Journal of International Business Studies, 40*(1), 35–41.

Cantwell, J., & Brannen, M. Y. (2011). Positioning JIBS as an interdisciplinary journal. *Journal of International Business Studies, 42*(1), 1–9.

Cantwell, J. A., & Janne, O. (1999). Technological globalisation and innovative centres: The role of corporate technological leadership and locational hierarchy. *Research Policy, 28*(2–3), 119–144.

Caves, R. (1998). Research on international business: Problems and prospects. *Journal of International Business Studies, 29*(1), 5–19.

Chao, P. (1993). Partitioning country of origin effects: Consumer evaluations of a hybrid product. *Journal of International Business Studies, 24*(2), 291–306.

Cuypers, I., & Martin, X. (2010). What makes and what does not make a real option? A study of equity shares in international joint ventures. *Journal of International Business Studies, 41*(1), 47–69.

DeYoung, R., & Nolle, D. E. (1996). Foreign owned banks in the US: Earning market share of buying it?. *Journal of Money, Credit, and Banking, 28*(4), 622–636.

Dow, D., & Karunaratna, A. (2006). Developing a multidimensional instrument to measure psychic distance stimuli. *Journal of International Business Studies, 37*(5), 578–602.

Dunning, J. H. (1998). Location and the multinational enterprise: A neglected factor? *Journal of International Business Studies, 29*(1), 45–66.

Dunning, J. H. (2000). *Regions, globalization and the knowledge-based economy.* Oxford: Oxford University Press.

Dunning, J. H. (2009). Location and the multinational enterprise: John Dunning's thoughts on receiving the Journal of International Business Studies 2008 Decade Award. *Journal of International Business Studies, 40*(1), 20–34.

Dunning, J. H., & Lundan, S. M. (2008). *Multinational enterprises and the global economy* (2nd ed.). Cheltenham, UK: Edward Elgar.

Dunning, J. H., & Narula, R. (1996). *Foreign direct investment and governments: Catalysts for economic restructuring.* London, New York: Routledge.

Eden, L., & Miller, S. R. (2004). Distance matters: Liability of foreignness, institutional distance and ownership strategy. In: M. Hitt & J. L. Cheng (Eds), *Advances in International Management* (Vol. 16, pp. 187–221). Bingley, UK: Emerald.

Ghauri, P., & Cateora, P. (2006). *International marketing* (2nd ed.). Maidenhead, UK: McGraw-Hill.

Ghemawat, P. (2001). Distance still matters, the hard reality of global expansion. *Harvard Business Review, 79*(8), 137–147.

Head, K., & Mayer, T. (2010). Illusory border effects: Distance mismeasurement inflates estimates of home bias in trade. In: P. Van Bergeijk & S. Brakman (Eds), *The gravity model in international trade.* Cambridge, UK: Cambridge University Press.

Hennart, J. F. (1988). A transaction costs theory of equity joint ventures. *Strategic Management Journal, 9*(4), 361–374.

Hennart, J. F. (2009). Down with MNE centric theories! Market entry and expansion as the bundling of MNE and local assets. *Journal of International Business Studies, 40*(9), 1432–1454.

Hennart, J. F., Roehl, T., & Zeng, M. (2002). Do exits proxy for a liability of foreignness? The case of Japanese exits from the United States. *Journal of International Management, 8*(3), 241–264.

Hymer, S. H. (1976). *The international operations of national firms: A study of foreign direct investment.* Cambridge, MA: MIT Press.

Insch, G. S., & Miller, S. (2005). Perception of foreignness: Benefit or liability? *Journal of Managerial Issues, 17*(4), 423–438.

Johanson, J., & Vahlne, J.-E. (1977). The internationalization process of the firm – A model of knowledge development and increasing foreign market commitments. *Journal of International Business Studies, 8*(1), 23–32.

Johanson, J., & Vahlne, J. E. (2009). The Uppsala internationalization process model revisited: From liability of foreignness to liability of outsidership. *Journal of International Business Studies, 40*(9), 1411–1431.

Johansson, J. K., & Nebenzahl, I. D. (1986). Multinational production: Effect on brand value. *Journal of International Business Studies, 17*(3), 101–126.

Kostova, T., & Zaheer, S. (1999). Organizational legitimacy under conditions of complexity: The case of the multinational enterprise. *Academy of Management Review, 24*(1), 64–81.

Lahiri, N. (2010). Geographic distribution of R&D activity: How does it affect innovation quality?. *Academy of Management Journal, 53*(5), 1194–1209.

Lenartowicz, T., Johnson, J., & White, C. (2003). The neglect of intra-country cultural variation in international management research: An Iberoamerican perspective. *Journal of Business Research, 56*(12), 999–1008.

Lenartowicz, T., & Roth, K. (2001). Does subculture within a country matter? A cross-cultural study of motivational domains and business performance in Brazil. *Journal of International Business Studies, 32*(2), 305–325.

Leung, K., Bhagat, R. S., Buchan, N. R., Erez, M., & Gibson, C. B. (2005). Culture and international business: Recent advances and their implications for future research. *Journal of International Business Studies, 36*(4), 357–378.

Li, J., & Rugman, A. (2007). Real options and the theory of foreign direct investment. *International Business Review, 16*(6), 687–712.

208   SJOERD BEUGELSDIJK

Luo, Y., & Mezias, J. M. (2002). Liabilities of foreignness: Concepts, constructs and consequences. *Journal of International Management, 8*(3), 217–221.
McCann, P., & Mudambi, R. (2005). Analytical differences in the economics of geography: The case of the multinational firm. *Environment and Planning A, 37*(10), 1857–1876.
Negandhi, A. R. (1983). Cross cultural management research: Trend and future directions. *Journal of International Business Studies, 14*(2), 17–28.
Nehrt, L. C., Truitt, J. F., & Wright, R. W. (1970). *International business research: Past, present and future*. Indiana University Graduate School of Business, Bloomington, IN.
North, D. (2005). *Understanding the process of economic change*. Princeton, NJ: Princeton University Press.
Porter, M. (1991). Towards a dynamic theory of strategy. *Strategic Management Journal, 12*(S2), 95–117.
Ricks, D. A. (1985). International business research: Past, present and future. *Journal of International Business Studies, 16*(2), 1–4.
Rugman, A. (1981). *Inside the multinationals*. London: Croom Helm.
Rugman, A. (1996). *The theory of multinational enterprises: Volume one of the selected scientific papers of Alan Rugman*. Cheltenham, UK: Edward Elgar.
Rugman, A. (2010). Reconciling internalization theory and the eclectic paradigm. *Multinational Business Review, 18*(2), 1–12.
Rugman, A., & Verbeke, A. (1990). *Global corporate strategy and trade policy*. London: Routledge.
Rugman, A., & Verbeke, A. (2008). Internalization theory and its impact on the field of international business. In: J. J. Boddewyn (Ed.), *International business scholarship: AIB fellows on the first 50 years and beyond (Research in Global Strategic Management)* (Vol. 14, pp. 155–174). Bingley, UK: Emerald Group Publishing Limited.
Seno-Alday, S. (2010). International business thought: A 50-year footprint. *Journal of International Management, 16*(1), 16–31.
Shenkar, O. (2001). Cultural distance revisited: Towards a more rigorous conceptualization and measurement of cultural differences. *Journal of International Business Studies, 32*(3), 519–535.
Slangen, A. H. L., & Beugelsdijk, S. (2010). The impact of institutional hazards on foreign multinational activity: A contingency perspective. *Journal of International Business Studies, 41*(6), 980–995.
Slangen, A. H. L., Beugelsdijk, S., & Hennart, J. F. (2011). The impact of cultural distance on bilateral arm's length exports; an IB perspective. *Management International Review 50 year anniversary issue* (forthcoming).
Tung, R. L., & Van Witteloostuijn, A. (Eds). (2008). From the editors: What makes a study sufficiently international? *Journal of International Business Studies, 39*(2), 180–183.
Tung, R. L., & Verbeke, A. (2010). Beyond Hofstede and GLOBE: Improving the quality of cross-cultural research. *Journal of International Business Studies, 41*(7), 1259–1274.
Verbeke, A. (2009). *International business strategy*. Cambridge, UK: Cambridge University Press.
Yaprak, A. (2008). Culture study in international marketing: A critical review and suggestions for future research. *International Marketing Review, 25*(2), 215–229.
Yeaple, S. (2009). Firm heterogeneity and the structure of US multinational activity. *Journal of International Economics, 78*(2), 206–215.

Zaheer, S. (1995). Overcoming the liability of foreignness. *Academy of Management Journal,* *38*(2), 341–363.
Zaheer, S. (2002). The liability of foreignness, Redux: A commentary. *Journal of International Management, 8*(3), 351–358.
Zaheer, S., & Mosakowski, E. (1997). The dynamics of the liability of foreignness: A global study of survival in financial services. *Strategic Management Journal, 18*(6), 439–464.

APPENDIX

Journal of International Business (*JIBS*) decade award-winning papers 1970–2000 (for further details see www.palgrave-journals.com/jibs/decade_award.html)

1. Dyer and Chu (2000): Comparison of supplier-automaker relationship in three countries
2. Bresman, Birkinshaw, and Nobel (1999): Knowledge transfer in international acquisitions by Swedish parent firms
3. Dunning (1998): The role of location in the OLI paradigm
4. Ralston et al (1997): The impact of ideology on work values of managers in four countries
5. Lyles and Salk (1996): Knowledge acquisition from parents in IJVs in one country.
6. Madhok (1995): Trust based approach towards (international) JVs
7. Oviatt and McDougall (1994): International new ventures
8. Kogut and Zander (1993): Knowledge transfer and firm boundaries
9. Agarwal and Ramaswami (1992): Entry mode preferences of US leasing firms in three countries (because main focus is on firm differences, and host country differences are limited to only three countries, it is included in cell 1 and not in cell 2)
10. Parkhe (1991): Inter-firm diversity in international strategic alliances
11. Gomes-Casseres (1990): Variation in host country restrictions on entry mode decisions
12. Geringer and Hebert (1989): Parent control of IJVs
13. Dunning (1988): The eclectic paradigm
14. Kogut and Singh (1988): Cultural differences and entry mode choice; both country pair variation (cell 4) and country variation in uncertainty avoidance (cell 2). The reason to include it in cell 4 as well is the fact that the Kogut and Singh measure of cultural distance between country pairs has become a standard in the field of IB

15. Beamish and Banks (1987): Joint venture success, specific focus on JVs in LDCs
16. Anderson and Gatignon (1986): Entry mode theory including characteristics of foreign agents and internationalising firms
17. Davidson and McFetridge (1985): Host country factors affecting choice between licencing or direct investment for technology transfer (including transaction specific characteristics)
18. Lecraw (1984): Relative bargaining power of MNEs and the host government (the focus is on interaction between home firm and host context; multiple home countries, multiple host countries. It could however also be included in cell 2, but the main focus is on the negotiation process, hence interactive approach)
19. Hofstede (1983): Summary of work related culture dimensions
20. Bilkey and Ness (1982): Conceptual discussion of country of origin effects: how are products made in country X evaluated in country Y?
21. Reid (1981): Role of decision-maker in export decision
22. Dunning (1980): Eclectic theory of international production
23. Kobrin (1979): Political risk in host countries
24. Bilkey (1978): Export decision models
25. Johanson and Vahlne (1977): Internationalisation process theory model, specific focus on increasing involvement over time in individual host country
26. Rugman (1976): Do US firms that sell more international have lower levels of variations in earnings?
27. Giddy and Dufey (1975): Exchange rate forecasting (although they only use the US as the home country, and a set of host countries, the analysis boils down to country pair variation)
28. Simpson, Jr. (1974): Export decision process
29. Ward (1973): To what extent do firms from different European home countries adapt their marketing strategies to enter the US?
30. Goodnow and Hansz (1972): Entry strategies of US firms in a large sample host countries, depending on host country factors
31. Schooler (1971): Empirical country of origin analysis (how are products for a set of countries evaluated in a US sample?)
32. Daniels (1970): Analysis of foreign firms in the US and the interaction with the US partners

LIABILITY OF FOREIGNNESS AND INTERNATIONALISATION OF EMERGING MARKET FIRMS

Ajai S. Gaur, Vikas Kumar and Ravi Sarathy

ABSTRACT

Liability of foreignness (LOF) is a well-known concept in international business domain. At the core of LOF is the insight that firms face social and economic costs when they operate in foreign markets. Extant literature acknowledges that the ability of firms to overcome LOF in host locations varies; however, it does not discuss the possibility that the LOF itself could vary for different firms at the same location. We extend this literature by examining how a firm's interaction with the host and the home country environments affect the LOF that it faces in foreign markets.

We argue that there are two sources of LOF – environmentally derived LOF and firm-based LOF. The environmentally derived LOF has its source in home and host country environments. Firm-based LOF, on the contrary, derives from firm-specific characteristics including ownership structure, firm-specific resources, learning and network-based linkages such as affiliation to a business group. Furthermore, we argue that both the environmentally derived and the firm-based LOF are different for emerging market (EM) firms as compared to developed market (DM) firms. We develop testable propositions about how environment-specific

Dynamics of Globalization: Location-Specific Advantages or Liabilities of Foreignness?
Advances in International Management, Volume 24, 211–233
ISSN: 1571-5027/doi:10.1108/S1571-5027(2011)0000024016

and firm-specific factors affect LOF and suggest directions for future research.

INTRODUCTION

Liability of foreignness (LOF) is a well-known concept in international business domain, initially conceptualised by Hymer (1960/1976) as costs of doing business abroad. At the core of LOF is the insight that firms face social and economic costs when they operate in foreign markets. Some of these costs, such as becoming familiar with the language and economic systems of the host country, can be overcome over time. However, there are other costs such as unfamiliarity and relational and discriminatory hazards, which persist longer and often put foreign firms in a disadvantageous position as compared to domestic firms (Eden & Miller, 2004). A review of the LOF literature shows that scholars often view LOF as an exogenous variable, primarily from the singular view of host locations (Barnard, 2010). Extant literature acknowledges that the ability of firms to overcome LOF in host locations varies; however, it does not discuss the possibility that the LOF itself could vary for different firms at the same location. Such an approach ignores the possibility that some components of LOF may be endogenous, arising from the interaction of a firm and its home and host country environments.

The firm-location interaction dynamic underpinning LOF is particularly important in the case of emerging market (EM) firms as may be inferred from the vastly different internationalisation trajectories that some of these firms have pursued (Luo & Tung, 2007; Ramamurti & Singh, 2009). For example, the born global phenomenon, or rapid internationalisation of EM firms, contradicts the traditional view of LOF, which suggests that firms internationalise gradually as they overcome LOF over time. A natural question, with potential to significantly impact future international business research, emerges – *How does a firm's interaction with the host and home country environments affect the LOF that it faces in foreign markets?*

To answer the above question, we take a more holistic perspective on LOF as it pertains to firms from developed markets (DMs) and EMs. We argue that there are two sources of LOF – *environmentally* derived LOF and *firm-based* LOF. The environmentally derived LOF has its source in home and host country environments. The home and the host country governments, institutions and cultures and the nature and structure of industry in the home and the host countries affect the intensity and magnitude of LOF that firms face (Nachum, 2003; Zaheer, 1995). Firm-based LOF, on the contrary, derives from firm-specific characteristics including ownership structure, firm-specific resources, learning and net-work-based linkages such as affiliation to a business group (Johanson & Vahlne, 2009; Petersen & Pedersen, 2002). Stated differently, the magnitude of LOF that different firms face in a given market will vary based on certain firm-specific characteristics. Furthermore, we argue that both the environmentally derived and the firm-based LOF are different for EM firms as compared to DM firms. For example, the importance of host government is more salient in the case of EM firms than for DM firms. Governments in EMs often provide overt and covert support to domestic firms in their internationalisation operations (*The Economist*, 2010). For example, the Taiwanese Government supported Taiwan's semiconductor industry, an effort that began in the 1960s, and resulted in the current global leadership position of Taiwan's semiconductor firms (Tung, 2001). Such government support allowed Taiwanese firms to upgrade from merely selling as suppliers in the industrial product markets to now selling branded products in both EMs and DMs. In the process, Taiwanese firms developed global brand image to overcome negative county-of-origin effects and detrimental terms of exchange.

Learning from Taiwan, China has implemented similar industrial policies, such as supporting its nascent solar energy industry, allowing Chinese firms to gain significant market shares globally (Bradsher, 2010). Such focused government support can diminish the intensity as well as magnitude of LOF that firms face. Likewise, affiliation to business groups, which is common to many EMs, may help firms collectively reduce the LOF that they would individually face in foreign markets.

We build on the above arguments to examine the endogenous nature of LOF, and how the interaction between a firm and its home and host environment affects LOF. We argue that not all firms entering a foreign market experience the same level of LOF as capacity to overcome newness varies based on firm-specific characteristics and its interaction with host and home location conditions. For the sake of easy conceptualisation, we divide the world markets into developed and emerging. Fig. 1 shows different directions in which firms can move between EMs and DMs and our conceptualisation of how LOF varies based on directionality of foreign investment. We build on this conceptualisation to suggest that LOF arises from environment-specific and firm-specific factors and develop propositions for both these sets of factors. The following four examples provide

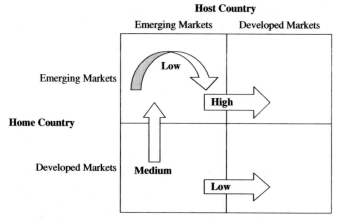

Fig. 1. Internationalisation Paths and Liability of Foreignness.

some insight into how the source and destination of international investments, broadly divided between EMs and DMs, can differentially influence
LOF.

1. *EM firm entering a DM*: Dr. Reddy's Laboratories (DRL), an Indian
   pharmaceutical company, acquired the German generic drug company
   Betapharm for around €500 million. DRL had to write off nearly half its
   value soon after acquisition, as German generic drug distribution
   regulations changed, reducing the value of Betapharm's salesforce, which
   called on German doctors and hospitals. As an outsider from an EM,
   DRL was perhaps unaware of regulatory information that may have
   alerted them to potentially value-destroying regulatory changes in the
   generic drug industry. As such, the LOF for DRL in the German market
   was arguably higher than that for DM firms who might have been better
   informed of the potential for such regulatory change.
2. *EM firm entering another EM*: Ranbaxy, India's leading generic pharmaceutical company, acquired a South African generic firm, Be-Tabs, for $70
   million, in 2007, to obtain local manufacturing capability and market
   presence in an effort to meet South Africa's need for quality medicines
   at affordable prices. Ranbaxy's years of experience in meeting similar needs
   in the Indian market helped it position itself for the South African market
   with similar characteristics in terms of disease incidence, affordability and
   local manufacturing needs. As such, the LOF faced by Ranbaxy in the

South African market was arguably lower than that for other firms, particularly those from DMs with less experience in mass manufacturing of generic drugs.

3. *DM firm entering an EM*: Royal Dutch Shell in Russia was forced to give up majority ownership of its Sakhalin LNG project to a Russian state-owned enterprise, Gazprom, at less than cost, in part because Shell on entry divided Sakhalin ownership between itself (with a majority position) and two Japanese firms, as permitted by the prevailing laws in 1995. This foreign majority and complete ownership was in contrast to the presence of Russian partners in every other large oil and gas project in Russia that were later implemented. This ownership problem was compounded by the increasing power of the Putin administration and growing doubts over Shell's legitimacy in Russia's oil and gas sector. However, Shell did not change its ownership over the next 10 years, until forced to cede majority ownership to Gazprom in 2006. As a DM firm in Russia, without the benefit of local partner advice and insight, Shell may have been unaware of the growing opposition to foreign majority ownership in the oil and gas sector in Russia. Shell's LOF in Russia was definitely higher than other EM firms.

4. *DM firm entering another DM*: European clothing retailers such as H&M (Hennes and Mauritz) and Zara (from Spain) first expanded across Europe before venturing into the US market. However, the experience gained from expanding across Europe helped both firms adapt more easily to US market conditions, emboldening them to increase their rate of expansion across the US market, with considerable success.

As these examples suggest, it may be useful to explore in depth the nature of LOF facing firms from different backgrounds as they internationalise into markets with varying degrees of competitiveness and development. Our arguments draw some parallels with the process model of internationalisation in the sense that experiential knowledge of foreign business environment, institutions and internationalisation is helpful in alleviating perceived internationalisation costs (Eriksson, Johanson, Majkgard, & Sharma, 1997). However, in our arguments, we incorporate the differential effect on inter-nationalisation cost as a result of the direction of international investment (from EM to DM and vice versa), thus augmenting the internationalisation process models. In the following section, we first review important studies to identify the theoretical arguments, constructs and variables used in analysing LOF. We then develop our arguments and propositions and put forth recommendations for future extension of literature in this domain.

WHAT IS LOF

The LOF concept has its origins in Stephen Hymer's (1960/1976) thesis on the disadvantages that foreign firms face as compared to domestic firms while operating in host markets. Hymer identified four types of disadvantages that foreign firms face. First, foreign firms have information disadvantage as compared to domestic firms. Foreign firms need to incur costs in the initial acquisition of this information, which domestic firms do not incur. Second, foreign firms face risks associated with foreign exchange currency fluctuations. Third, foreign firms may face discriminatory treatment at the hand of host governments, which adds to their costs of establishing operations. Finally, the home governments may put some restrictions on the firms' internationalisation. Hymer termed these foreign firm-specific disadvantages as costs of doing business abroad (CDBA).

Several scholars delved into Hymer's thesis to further analyse the sources and consequences of CDBA. For example, Buckley and Casson (1976) and Hennart (1982) referred to costs that firms incur when they set up their foreign operations as similar to those proposed by Hymer. Buckley and Casson (1976) suggested that the additional costs for foreign firms include communication costs, resource costs, host government discrimination costs and governance costs. Hennart's (1982) list included costs associated with communication, travel, foreign exchange and unfamiliarity with the cultural, legal and institutional aspects of doing business in a foreign country. Although these conceptualisations of CDBA were richer than that proposed by Hymer, scholarly attention shifted from analysing the costs to identifying the firm-specific advantages that were needed to overcome the costs (Buckley & Casson, 1976; Dunning, 1977; Hennart, 1982; Rugman, 1981).

The CDBA concept was further explored in the 1980s through the works of Doz and colleagues (Doz, 1980; Doz & Prahalad, 1984; Prahalad & Doz, 1987) and Bartlett and Ghoshal (1989) on the conflicting pressures of global integration and local responsiveness that multinational corporations (MNCs) face. Doz (1980) argued that given the additional costs that MNCs face, they are exposed to the twin pressures of reducing costs through global integration on the one hand, and minimising their disadvantages as compared to local firms on the other hand, by tailoring their offerings to local markets. Bartlett and Ghoshal (1989, 1990) further developed the global integration–local responsiveness framework and suggested that there are costs of meeting the conflicting demands of responsiveness to local environments and integration within the MNC network.

Following the above conceptual developments, several scholars conducted systematic empirical analyses to confirm the existence of differential costs for foreign firms in comparison to domestic firms (Mezias, 2002a, 2002b; Miller & Parkhe, 2002; Zaheer, 1995; Zaheer & Mosakowski, 1997). In one of the earliest empirical works, Zaheer (1995) examined the exit patterns of the trading rooms of US and Japanese banks in New York and Tokyo. Zaheer (1995) used the words CDBA and LOF interchangeably, referring to the differential costs arising from spatial distance, unfamiliarity with the host country environment, and home and host country restrictions. Zaheer (1995) suggested two ways in which firms can overcome the LOF, by using their ownership-specific advantages or by becoming isomorphic to local firms. Zaheer and Mosakowski (1997) further analysed the exit patterns of a larger sample of trading rooms over a 20-year period and found that the exit rates for foreign banks were similar to domestic banks during the first 2 years or after 16 years since establishment and higher in the 2-year to 16-year time period. On the basis of this, Zaheer and Mosakowski (1997) concluded that LOF diminishes as firms gain more host country-specific experience and even disappears after some time. This finding was an extension of Hymer's original thesis, which suggested that most components of CBDA were fixed, would decrease over time, but never become zero (Eden & Miller, 2004).

Further empirical and conceptual work on LOF assumed these costs to be dynamic in nature, but amenable to mitigation by various firm-specific and environment specific factors. In this line of work, scholars examined various factors that could reduce LOF such as strategic posture of a firm (Petersen & Pedersen, 2002), mode of entry (Eden & Miller, 2001), firm-specific advantages (Nachum, 2003) and firm-level offensive and defensive strategies to cope with LOF (Eden & Molot, 2002; Luo, Shenkar, & Nyaw, 2002). More recent scholarly work also attempted to differentiate between the CDBA and the LOF concepts. Zaheer (2002) argued that the difference between CDBA and LOF lay in the underlying theoretical approaches. Whereas CDBA has its origins in the economic explanations of MNCs, LOF has its origins in the institutional theory approach. The recent developments in the institutional perspective incorporate the sociological, economic and political explanations in onefold (Scott, 2001), blurring the differences between CDBA and LOF.

In this chapter, we follow the recent developments to suggest that LOF is a dynamic concept, which has its origins, not only in the home and the host country environments, but also in firm characteristics. Rather than debating the differences between CDBA and LOF, we consider them to be similar concepts that reflect the differential costs that firms have to incur while operating in foreign markets. We further argue that firms from developed and EM experience different levels of LOF, depending on their internationalisation patterns and use different strategies to overcome the LOF. In the following section, we discuss different sources of LOF and how internationalisation patterns affect the LOF that firms face.

SOURCES OF LOF

The dynamic view on LOF suggests that LOF decreases over time and may even become zero. We extend this view to argue that even at a given point in time, not all firms operating in a host country face the same level of LOF. The extent to which a firm faces LOF depends on the internationalisation pattern of the firm in terms of home and host countries. Fig. 1 presents a 2×2 matrix depicting different paths of international investment across the world and associated LOF. In the matrix, we categorise both the home and the host markets as emerging or developed. We argue that the extent to which firms face LOF is dependent on two sets of factors – environment- and firm-specific factors.

Environmental Factors

Environmentally derived LOF has its origins in the home country as well as the host country of a firm's international operations. Countries differ in the level of their institutional development and factor endowments, which has consequences for different aspects of business activities (North, 1990). With respect to institutional environment, there are three aspects of institutions that affect LOF – regulatory, normative and cognitive (Scott, 2001). The regulatory dimension refers to the formal rules and regulations that have a sanction from the state (North, 1990). The normative dimension refers to legitimate means sanctioned by society to pursue legitimate goals (Scott, 1995). The cognitive dimension refers to mental schema, values and beliefs held by people in the society (DiMaggio & Powell, 1983). The regulatory institutions are more formal in nature, whereas the normative and cognitive institutions are more informal in nature. The formal and informal dimensions of institutions affect the way business is conducted in a country.

Although the sociological approach to institutions does not classify them as more or less developed, institutional economists argue that some countries have more developed institutions than others (La Porta, Lopez-de-Silanes, Shleifer, & Vishny, 1999; North, 1990). Along these lines, Khanna and Palepu (2000) argued that many emerging economies lack the institutions needed for efficient, market-based economic transactions. The resulting institutional voids create several challenges for firms operating in these countries. Some of these challenges include difficulty in raising capital from external sources, hiring skilled employees and procuring raw material at competitive prices (Khanna & Palepu, 2000). EM firms develop skills and adopt organisational structures to successfully operate in environments with institutional voids. For example, firms organise themselves in the form of business groups in many EMs (Khanna & Rivkin, 2001). Business groups replace the institutional voids by creating internal markets for capital, labour and products (Leff, 1978). Holburn and Zelner (2010) suggest that firms develop political capabilities that help them protect their market position in country environments with weak institutional constraints and strong redistributive pressures. These capabilities of EM firms can be used in other similar environments with less-developed institutions. However, these capabilities may not be of much help when EM firms internationalise to DMs with well-developed institutions (Gaur & Kumar, 2010).

The institutional environment in a country, as discussed earlier, affects LOF in two ways. First, the absolute level of institutional development in a country affects the LOF faced by internationalising firms. Firms coming from well-developed institutional environments may face less LOF as compared to firms coming from less-developed institutional environments. The level of institutional development affects environmental munificence for undertaking new and riskier strategies. In a more munificent home country environment where different factors of production are readily available and institutions are well developed, firms find it easier to pursue riskier strategies such as product and international diversification and innovation. Firms from developed environments are likely to get quality advice from various trade experts and consultancy firms about the potential foreign markets, which reduces the uncertainty that firms face when they initiate internationalisation activities. The reduced level of uncertainty in turn negatively affects the LOF faced in foreign markets. In line with this, Wan and Hoskisson (2003) argued that international diversification has a positive effect on performance for firms that come from more munificent environments.

Second, in addition to the level of institutional development in the home country, the differences in institutional development between the home and the host countries also affect the LOF that firms face. As we discussed earlier, EM firms may have developed capabilities to operate in less-developed institutional environments. These firms are likely to face less LOF when they internationalise to other EMs than when they internationalise to other DMs. Likewise, DM firms are likely to face less LOF when they internationalise to other DMs than when they internationalise to EMs.

There is some recognition of the effect of institutional differences on the LOF firms experience in the institutional distance literature (Kostova, 1999; Kostova & Zaheer, 1999). Institutional distance refers to the extent of similarity or dissimilarity between the regulative, normative and cognitive aspects of institutions in two countries (Kostova, 1996). As the institutional distance between the home and the host countries increases, firms face a greater level of unfamiliarity, discrimination and relational hazards, resulting in increased LOF (Eden & Miller, 2004). Institutions create coercive, mimetic and normative pressures on firms to become isomorphic to each other (DiMaggio & Powell, 1983). Firms moving to countries with similar institutional environments are likely to have similar structures, and consequently face less isomorphic pressures. Firms must conform to local institutional norms in order to achieve legitimacy in a host country (Davis, Desai, & Francis, 2000). Kostova and Zaheer (1999) analysed the legitimacy of MNC subunits and suggested that subsidiaries that were isomorphic to local firms experienced less severe legitimacy challenges. Other scholars have suggested that firms operating in institutionally distant countries find it more difficult to transfer organisational routines and capabilities (Kostova, 1999; Kostova & Roth, 2002), and to adopt organisational structures that minimise the LOF (Gaur & Lu, 2007).

In addition to the institutional differences, the directionality of international investment also affects the LOF. Firms moving from a DM to an EM are likely to face less LOF as compared to firms moving from an EM to a DM, even though the absolute level of institutional distance will be the same in both the cases. DM firms have stronger brands and more visibility in EMs (Dawar & Frost, 1999), which reduces the uncertainty that DM firms face in EMs (Hoskisson, Eden, Lau, & Wright, 2000). There are several examples of such global brands from DMs that need relatively less investments to connect with the local customers, from Apple and Microsoft, to MTV, Nokia and McDonalds. EM firms, on the other hand, face greater legitimacy challenges when moving to DMs because customers often associate EM products with inferior quality. Firms such as Lenovo from China (acquired the IBM PC line of business with its well-regarded ThinkPad laptops) and Tata Motors from India (acquired the Jaguar and Land Rover automobile brands and businesses) faced similar liabilities and attempted to overcome these by acquiring well established brands from developed country firms. Consistent with these arguments, we propose that the directionality of international investments along with the differences in the level of institutional development between the home and the host countries affects the LOF.

Proposition 1. An internationalising firm will experience varying level of LOF, depending on the differences in institutional development in the home and the host countries.

Proposition 1a. An internationalising firm that moves to similar environments (developed to developed or emerging to emerging) will experience less LOF than a firm that moves to dissimilar environments.

Proposition 1b. An internationalising firm that moves from a developed market to an emerging market will experience less LOF than a firm that moves from an emerging market to a developed market.

The industry a firm belongs to constitutes the most proximate environmental condition, the specificities of which such as degree of competition, intensity of knowledge and capital versus labour intensity, global versus local scope and the like have an impact on firm strategy and performance. Consequently, we posit that the nature and characteristics of the industry will also have an impact on the LOF that firms will face while expanding internationally.

Porter (1980) suggests that the degree of competition in an industry largely determines firm strategy and performance. Although firms in more competitive industries are pressured to innovate and differentiate their offerings from their competitors, the average level of profitability remains low. New firms, particularly from foreign markets, that enter such industries are likely to face substantial costs as they not only have to deal with information and discrimination hazards of being a foreigner, but also have to adjust to the unfamiliar competitive dynamics of the industry. DMs typically have more competitive industries, populated by domestic as well as foreign firms. In EMs, on the contrary, there are relatively fewer industries that can match the level of competition present in similar industries in DMs. As such, the LOF of firms entering and operating in DMs is likely to be higher than those entering and operating in EMs. Moreover, if it is an EM firm that enters and operates in DM, the LOF is bound to be even higher as it is plausible that the EM firm has very limited experience of competing in competitive industries in its home country.

Besides the extent of competition, industries vary in terms of intensity of knowledge in their operations. Knowledge-intensive industries are those where the basis of operation and competition is primarily on knowledge-based assets. Knowledge-based assets consist of explicit knowledge such as patents, trademarks and trade secrets as well as tacit knowledge that reside in individual employees' minds or is embedded in organisational routines and processes (Zaheer, Hernandez, & Banerjee, 2010). In contrast, labour-intensive industries are those where the basis of competition centres on low costs, derived from abundant and easily accessible supply of both skilled and unskilled labour. A firm in a labour-intensive industry can expand into foreign markets that have a readily available workforce and start to compete with local domestic players with relative ease. They too endure LOF, but at a lower level when compared to firms in knowledge-intensive industries, where the basis of competitive advantage (knowledge-based assets) takes time to develop and may also be costly to acquire. In certain instances, where the knowledge is tacit, it becomes very difficult to correctly identify the major source of competitiveness in the industry. EM industries are typically more likely to be labour-intensive, whereas many DM industries are knowledge-intensive (at least in relation to their EM counterparts). The division reinforces our earlier assertion that EM firms, entering and operating in DMs, will carry a heavier baggage of LOF than when entering and operating in EMs. To succeed in knowledge-intensive industries, an EM firm will have to either acquire the knowledge-based asset or develop it in-house. Both of these will result in high cost in terms of capital as well as time delays. On the basis of the above arguments, we make the following propositions:

Proposition 2. An internationalising firm will experience varying level of LOF, depending on the industry it operates in.

Proposition 2a. Internationalising firms in knowledge-intensive industries will experience higher LOF as compared to firms in less knowledge-intensive industries.

We noted earlier in the chapter that Bartlett and Ghoshal's (1989) framework of global integration versus local responsiveness inspired many scholars to empirically examine the extent of LOF that foreign firms face. Here, we argue that the extent to which an industry is global, in terms of the level of standardisation of its products and processes, has an impact on the LOF that firms face. Firms operating in global industries where the nature of products demanded and organisational processes used are relatively standard are likely to face lower LOF than those operating in local industries where adapting products and processes is key to successful operations. Although it is difficult to clearly categorise industries in DMs and EMs on the basis of their global–local dimension, one can make some broad generalisations. Industries in DMs are more global in terms of the products and processes being used, whereas similar industries in EMs might require substantial localisation based on individual countries institutional and cultural requirements. Consequently, entering and operating in EMs will imply greater costs as a result of the required adaptations in products and processes and thus lead to higher LOF for all firms. On the contrary, internationalising into DMs, owing to the relative higher global dimension of industries, will lead to lower LOF for all firms in general.

Proposition 2c. Internationalising firms in local industries will experience higher LOF as compared to firms in global industries.

This attribute of the industry, we realise, runs counter to our preceding arguments. However, we posit that the overall effect on LOF will be determined by a *combination* of the specific industry attributes mentioned earlier as well as other influences discussed in preceding paragraphs.

Firm-Specific Factors

In the previous section, we discussed the exogenous nature of LOF and how environmental factors directly affect it. In this section, we argue that LOF is not a purely exogenous construct but is a result of interaction between a firm and its environment. The home and the host country environments in which firms operate shape the resources and capabilities that firms develop (Barnard, 2010). This in turn affects the organisational structure and strategic choices that firms pursue. All these factors that arise from the interaction of a firm with its environment have a bearing on the LOF that internationalising firms face.

Firm-Specific Resources and Capabilities

The traditional view on firm internationalisation suggests that foreign firms have ownership-specific advantages that help them overcome the LOF (Nachum, 2003; Zaheer, 1995). The advantages that foreign firms possess include financial and managerial resources, size and intangible assets (Nachum, 2003). In contrast, many firms coming from EMs often do not possess such resources. According to World Investment Report (2008), the average assets of the top 100 MNCs from EMs is about 15 percent of the average assets held by the top 100 MNCs from DMs. In such cases, the (inferred) resource gap that exists between foreign and local firms can itself contribute to LOF.

Many EM firms do not internationalise from a position of strength, but they do so to strengthen their long-term market and industry position (Gaur & Kumar, 2009; Makino, Lau, & Yeh, 2002). This is not to say that EM firms do not have any resources and capabilities. In fact, many EM firms derive resources and capabilities from their home country environment. These include cheaper access to labour in the home market, weaker intellectual property rights, which make it possible for firms to reengineer and imitate first-mover competitors, as well as capabilities that firms develop while operating in less-munificent environments. The pharmaceutical industry in India and several Internet-based firms in China (Youku, Toduo to name a few) are examples of firms benefiting from weaker intellectual property protection in their home markets. However, it is not obvious whether resources and capabilities that provide unique competitive advantages in one environment necessarily confer similar advantages in others. A lack of strategic fit between resources and the environment may reduce or enhance the competitive advantage conferred by the resource or capability. For example, political ties and political influence may be useful firm capabilities in countries with institutional voids, but may confer limited competitive advantage when the firm competes in markets characterised by free market environments and reduced returns to political rent-seeking.

The resource disparity makes it more difficult for EM firms to get equal treatment from customers and other stakeholders in foreign markets, contributing to the LOF. The resource gap is greater in the case of EM firms that are internationalising to DMs as compared to EM firms that are internationalising to other EMs. As a result, EM firms prefer to internationalise to other EMs or under-developed markets. For example, Cuervo-Cazurra and Genc (2008) showed that emerging multinationals did not face LOF in under-developed countries. Likewise, in an analysis of outward FDI from China, Morck, Yeung, and Zhao (2008) found that Asia, Latin America and Africa accounted for 63.9 percent, 26.3 percent and 3.4 percent of the FDI stock from China, respectively, with North America and Europe accounting for less than 3 percent each.

When internationalising into DMs, EM firms use tactics such as targeting the diaspora (Kapur & Ramamurti, 2001), acquiring local brands (Mathews, 2002, 2006) and partnering with DM firms in downstream activities (Ramamurti & Singh, 2009) to overcome the heightened LOF. The success of South African Breweries (SAB) illustrates this point well (Luo & Tung, 2007). SAB enjoyed a good reputation and success in many developing countries, based on the capabilities that it developed to operate in less-munificent environments. However, SAB recognised that it needed strong brand and marketing skills if it wanted to penetrate in the DMs and hence acquired US-based Miller, with significant market share in United States and other DMs. Although gaps in capabilities may generally lead to LOF, some resource gaps may lead to greater LOF than other resource gaps. For example, a firm may be able to acquire tangible assets from the market, but it may be more difficult to reduce the gap in intangible assets that are not traded in the market. Ranbaxy Laboratories, which became India's largest pharmaceutical firm in a protected domestic environment, faced difficulties in penetrating DMs, as its competences in developing (copycat) generic drugs were less useful in DMs that also needed new research-based patent-protected drugs. At the same time, the Japanese drug firm, Daiichi Sankyo, saw that the Japanese market, which had hitherto been relatively closed to generic drugs, was revising its drug market regulations to allow greater room for prescribing generic drugs. Hence, Daiichi Sankyo acquired Ranbaxy, to obtain know-how and market presence in the generic drug market in EMs, whereas Ranbaxy was able to gain access to routines and tacit knowledge underlying the development of new patent-protected drugs intended for DMs. This discussion leads to the following propositions about the role of firm resources in affecting LOF:

Proposition 3a. The resource gap between the internationalising firms and the local firms will affect the LOF – firms with resource strengths relative to their competition in the host country will experience diminished LOF as compared to firm with resource weaknesses.

Proposition 3b. The resource gap in assets that are more difficult to be acquired from markets will result in greater LOF than resource gap in assets that are less difficult to be acquired from markets.

Strategic Choices
The strategic choices that firms make with respect to motives, paths and process of internationalisation affect the LOF. Dunning (1993) identifies four motives for firms going abroad – natural resource-seeking, market-seeking, efficiency-seeking and capability-seeking. Although the same firm may enter different markets with different motives, and the motive within a host country may change over time, there are some common patterns in the internationalisation of EM and DM firms. The motives for EM firms include overcoming small scale in home markets, acquiring resources,

exploiting experience with labour-intensive technologies, risk diversification and serving the diaspora market among others (Deeds, Mang, & Frandsen, 2004; Gaur & Kumar, 2010; Miller, Thomas, Eden, & Hitt, 2008). On the contrary, the motives for DM firms include overcoming threats to existing markets, exploiting experience with high-technology production and exporting back to developed home markets (Gaur & Kumar, 2010). Thus, in Dunning's (1993) typology, the motives for EM firms include resource- and capability-seeking, whereas those for DM firms include market- and efficiency-seeking.

The motives set the path for internationalisation. With resource- and capability-seeking being the motive, EM firms initiate their foreign activities on a small scale, often starting with exports (Aulakh, Kotabe, & Teegan, 2000; Singh, 2009) and then moving to acquisition of small firms or becoming supply chain partners of big firms in DMs (Luo & Tung, 2007; Mathews, 2002, 2006). Although there are several examples of firms bypassing the incremental route and directly moving to FDI by acquiring foreign firms, in most cases, asset-seeking and asset augmenting has been the primary motive of EM firms' internationalisation (Makino et al., 2002). This approach of building foreign presence in an incremental manner, by acquiring host market firms, helps EM firms overcome LOF by gaining access to the assets and experience of the acquired firm. Industrial & Commercial Bank of China (ICBC), which is world's largest bank by market value, adopted this approach to enter the highly competitive and restrictive US market. ICBC acquired the US brokering unit Fortis Securities, which was previously controlled by France's BNP Paribas SA. This move is a foot-in-the-door approach for the Chinese bank to tap the international markets of financial services in America. Because the Fortis unit is not a deposit-taking institution, its acquisition by ICBC is not subject to strict US regulatory restrictions. On the basis of this discussion, we propose:

Proposition 4. EM firms that enter DMs with resource- and capability-seeking motive will experience less LOF than EM firms that enter DMs with market-seeking motive.

Governance Structure

In addition to resources and strategic choices, the governance structure of a firm also affects LOF. By governance structure, we refer to the ownership structure of a firm as well as the organisational form that a firm adopts. There are significant differences in the governance structures observed in different parts of the world (La Porta et al., 1999). For example, while firms in the United States, United Kingdom and several other DMs have a dispersed ownership structure, firms in many EMs follow a concentrated ownership structure and adopt a network form of organisation structure such as forming part of a business group. Affiliation to a business group, which is a common characteristic of firms in EMs (Khanna & Rivkin, 2001), helps in alleviating LOF in several ways. Even though group-affiliated firms are separate legal entities, they often take collective actions and help each other in strategic pursuits. For example, collective resources of a business group may help reduce the resource disparity between a group-affiliated firm and host market firms. Group-affiliated firms also provide avenues for other affiliated firms to enter foreign markets. In the case of Japanese Keiretsu networks, it has been observed that Japanese firms tend to replicate the relationship patterns that they have in domestic markets when they invest abroad (Gaur & Lu, 2007). In doing so, Japanese firms rely on each other to help overcome the LOF challenges in foreign markets arising due to high institutional distance. This leads to the following proposition:

Proposition 5. An internationalising firm that adopts a network form of organisation structure will experience less LOF as compared to other firms.

Another unique feature of governance structure of EM firms is government involvement. In the case of China, on an average, only one-third of the shares of listed companies are held by individual investors or private shareholders, with the rest being held by the state and legal entities (Chen, Firth, & Gao, 2002). There are two opposing consequences of high government involvement for the LOF that firms face. Government involvement means that firms can have preferential access to resources that are not available in the open market. Internationalising firms in EMs are often seen as championing the cause of the nation and are a matter of pride for governments. Hence, such firms may be given cheaper access to capital from government-owned financial institutions, tax breaks and benefit from active lobbying by political leaders in securing foreign contracts.

On the contrary, high government involvement makes foreign investors, governments and consumers nervous about the firm. A case in point is Huawei's attempt to establish itself in the US market. Huawei is a Chinese firm manufacturing telecommunication equipment, which had linkages with the Chinese military in the past. Because of the close linkages between Huawei and Chinese government, many US senators raised objection to a potential telecom equipment contract worth billions of dollars between

Huawei and Sprint-Nextel. Earlier, Huawei had to drop a bid for 3Com because of US government opposition. Under intense domestic scrutiny, Sprint-Nextel decided to exclude Huawei along with another Chinese firm, ZTE Limited, from the bidding process. Huawei has also been the subject of scrutiny by the Indian government over planned network equipment sales in India, with contracts held up for further Indian government study.

Similarly, solar cell manufacturers from China are facing difficulties in growing sales in Germany due to outcry over both Chinese government subsidies helping them lower domestic costs and German government solar energy subsidies designed to increase solar energy consumption benefiting foreign firms. Furthermore, government ownership may provide the state-owned firm with access to 'soft' funds, with budget shortfalls made up by additional government funding. Such soft funding may reduce the drive to efficiency in such state-owned firms, becoming a competitive disadvantage when competing in foreign markets, particularly DMs, where greater efficiency is likely to be the competitive norm.

Although the government involvement may indeed provide resources to counter LOF, government involvement simultaneously increases the LOF itself that EM firms face, particularly when they internationalise to other DMs. Accordingly, we propose:

Proposition 6a. EM firms with state ownership that internationalise to DMs will experience more LOF as compared to EM firms without state ownership.

Proposition 6b. EM firms with state ownership that internationalise to less-developed markets will experience less LOF as compared to EM firms without state ownership.

CONCLUSIONS

The central premise of our chapter is that LOF is determined by a combination of exogenous (environmentally derived) and endogenous (firm-specific) factors and the inherent interaction of the two. Extant literature has primarily focused on the environmentally derived exogenous factors affecting LOF, particularly in the context of DM-based firm internationalisation. We extend this notion by incorporating EM-based firm internationalisation, to include firm-specific endogenous factors as being an important determinant of LOF.

We posit that the internationalisation path or the directionality of investment can be a good predictor of the LOF that firms face in their international expansion. We contend EMs and DMs differ not only in terms of environmental conditions such as institutions and industry characteristics but also in terms of firm resources and capabilities, strategic choices and governance structures that firms adapt. These firm-specific and environment-specific factors interact with each other in unique ways to influence LOF. We develop six propositions, which broadly suggest that EM firms entering into DMs, on average, face higher LOF than other internationalisation paths (e.g. EM firms entering other EMs, DM firms entering EMs and DM firms entering other DMs). The extent of LOF is moderated by factors such as institutional distance, industry competitiveness and knowledge intensity, resource gap, internationalisation motive and governance structure.

There are several avenues to take our research forward. Empirical verification of all or some of the propositions we make in this chapter with data from DM and EM firms is the first potential avenue. This is quite feasible as several of our theoretical predictors such as institutional distance, industry competitiveness, resources, motives and organisational structure are well-established constructs, which have been amply used in international business research. Second, although we suggest that EM firms typically face higher level of LOF than DM firms in their internationalisation, we do not specify all the boundary conditions for this proposition. Depending on the specific industry, resource position, internationalisation motive, governance structure and the like, EM firms could actually experience low LOFs. Future studies may investigate the conditions under which LOF is lower for EM firms than DM firms.

Third, we argue (for Proposition 2) that differences in institutional development in home and host countries will affect LOF. Scholars interested in institutional theory and institution-based view may look into the specific components of institutions and investigate which ones play a more significant role in determining LOF. For example, if one adopts Scott's view on institutions and compartmentalise them into regulative, normative and cognitive dimensions, it is very likely that the difference in the regulatory dimension has different implications on LOF than differences in the normative and cognitive dimensions. Alternatively, if one adopts Khanna and Palepu's (2000) conceptualisation of institutional development in terms of capital, product and labour markets, one may observe different types of differences between EMs and DMs, which may affect the LOF firms face.

Practicing managers of internationalising firms can benefit by focusing on and capitalising from environmental- and firm-specific conditions that help alleviate the LOF. For example, managers of EM firms need not be unnecessarily wary of differences in institutional development when planning on entering into DMs; instead, they can focus on specific industry conditions, internationalisation motives and their organisational structure to better deal with the higher perceived LOF. Similarly, managers of DM firms need to be more careful when attempting to enter to EMs. Although they may be entering from a position of strength, the environmental complexity in terms of vast diversity in institutions and cultures even within an EM might result in very high LOF than what is typically perceived.

To conclude, we argue that LOF is not a constant for a given location. Firms with different resources and institutional experiences are faced with different magnitudes of LOF even for the same location. The extent of LOF that a firm faces in a host country is determined by environment-specific factors, firm-specific factors and the interaction between environment-specific and firm-specific factors.

REFERENCES

Aulakh, P. S., Kotabe, M., & Teegan, H. (2000). Export strategies and performance of firms from emerging economies: Evidence from Brazil, Chile, and Mexico. *Academy of Management Journal*, *43*(3), 342–361.

Barnard, H. (2010). Overcoming the liability of foreignness without strong firm capabilities: The value of market-based resources. *Journal of International Management*, *16*(2), 165–176.

Bartlett, C. A., & Ghoshal, S. (1989). *Managing across borders: The transnational solution.* Boston: Harvard Business School Press.

Bartlett, C. A., & Ghoshal, S. (1990). Matrix management: Not a structure, a frame of mind. *Harvard Business Review*, *68*(4), 138–145.

Bradsher, K. (2010). To conquer wind power, China writes the rules. *New York Times*, December 14.

Buckley, P., & Casson, M. (1976). *The future of the multinational enterprise.* London: Macmillan.

Chen, G., Firth, M., & Gao, N. (2002). The information content of concurrently announced earnings, cash dividends, and stock dividends: An investigation of the Chinese Stock Market. *Journal of International Financial Management and Accounting*, *13*(2), 101–124.

Cuervo-Cazurra, A., & Genc, M. (2008). Transforming disadvantages into advantages: Developing-country MNEs in the least developed countries. *Journal of International Business Studies*, *39*(6), 957–979.

Davis, P. S., Desai, A. B., & Francis, J. D. (2000). Mode of international entry: An isomorphism perspective. *Journal of International Business Studies*, *31*(2), 239–258.

Dawar, N., & Frost, T. (1999). Competing with giants: Survival strategies for local companies in emerging markets. *Harvard Business Review*, *77*(2), 119–129.

Deeds, D., Mang, P., & Frandsen, M. (2004). The influence of firms' and industries' legitimacy on the flow of capital into high-technology ventures. *Strategic Organization, 2*(1), 9–34.

DiMaggio, P. J., & Powell, W. (1983). The iron cage revisited: Institutional isomorphism and collective rationality on organization fields. *American Sociological Review, 48*(2), 147–160.

Doz, Y. (1980). Strategic management in multinational companies. *Sloan Management Review, 21*(2), 27–46.

Doz, Y., & Prahalad, C. K. (1984). Patterns of strategic control within multinational corporations. *Journal of International Business Studies, 15*(2), 55–72.

Dunning, J. (1977). The location of economic activity and the multinational enterprise: Search for an eclectic approach. In: B. Ohlin, P. Hesselborn & P. Wiskman (Eds), *The international allocation of economic activity* (pp. 395–418). London: Macmillan.

Dunning, J. H. (1993). *Multinational enterprises and the global economy*. Reading, MA: Addison-Wesley.

Eden, L., & Miller, S. R. (2001). *Opening the black box: The multinational enterprise and the costs of doing business abroad*. Best Paper Proceedings, Academy of Management.

Eden, L., & Miller, S. R. (2004). Distance matters: Liability of foreignness, institutional distance and ownership strategy. In: M. A. Hitt & J. L. C. Cheng (Eds), *Theories of the multinational enterprise: Diversity, complexity and relevance (Advances in International Management, Volume 16)* (pp. 187–221). Stamford, CT: JAI Press.

Eden, L., & Molot, M. A. (2002). Insiders, outsiders and host country bargains. *Journal of International Management, 8*, 359–388.

Eriksson, K., Johanson, J., Majkgard, A., & Sharma, D. D. (1997). Experiential knowledge and cost in the internationalization process. *Journal of International Business Studies, 28*(2), 337–360.

Gaur, A. S., & Kumar, V. (2009). International diversification, firm performance and business group affiliation: Empirical evidence from India. *British Journal of Management, 20*(2), 172–186.

Gaur, A. S., & Kumar, V. (2010). Internationalization of emerging market firms: A case for theoretical extension. In: T. M. Devinney, T. Pedersen & L. Tihanyi (Eds), *Advances in international management: The past, present and future of international business and management, Volume 23* (pp. 603–627). New York: Emerald.

Gaur, A. S., & Lu, J. (2007). Ownership strategies and subsidiary performance: Impacts of institutions and experience. *Journal of Management, 33*(1), 84–110.

Hennart, J. F. (1982). *A theory of multinational enterprise*. Ann Arbor, MI: University of Michigan Press.

Holburn, G. L. F., & Zelner, B. A. (2010). Political capabilities, policy risk, and international investment strategy: Evidence from the global electric power generation industry. *Strategic Management Journal, 31*(12), 1290–1315.

Hoskisson, R., Eden, L., Lau, C. M., & Wright, M. (2000). Strategy in emerging economies. *Academy of Management Journal, 43*(3), 249–267.

Hymer, S. (1960/1976). *The international operations of national firms: A study of direct foreign investment*. Cambridge, MA: MIT Press.

Johanson, J., & Vahlne, J. E. (2009). The Uppsala internationalization process model revisited: From liability of foreignness to liability of outsidership. *Journal of International Business Studies, 40*(9), 1411–1431.

Kapur, D., & Ramamurti, R. (2001). India's emerging competitive advantage in services. *Academy of Management Executive, 15*(2), 20–31.

Khanna, T., & Palepu, K. (2000). Is group membership profitable in emerging markets? An analysis of diversified Indian business groups. *Journal of Finance, 55*(2), 867–891.

Khanna, T., & Rivkin, J. W. (2001). Estimating the performance effects of business groups in emerging markets. *Strategic Management Journal, 22*(1), 45–74.

Kostova, T. (1996). *Success of the transnational transfer of organizational practices within multinational companies.* Unpublished doctoral dissertation, University of Minnesota, Minneapolis, MN.

Kostova, T. (1999). Transnational transfer of strategic organizational practices: A contextual perspective. *Academy of Management Review, 24*(2), 308–324.

Kostova, T., & Roth, K. (2002). Adoption of an organizational practice by subsidiaries of multinational corporations: Institutional and relational effects. *Academy of Management Journal, 43*(1), 215–233.

Kostova, T., & Zaheer, S. (1999). Organizational legitimacy under conditions of complexity: The case of the multinational enterprise. *Academy of Management Review, 24*(1), 64–81.

La Porta, R., Lopez-de-Silanes, F., Shleifer, A., & Vishny, R. (1999). The quality of government. *Journal of Law, Economics, and Organization, 15*(1), 222–279.

Leff, N. (1978). Industrial organization and entrepreneurship in the developing countries: The economic groups. *Economic Development and Cultural Change, 26*(4), 661–675.

Luo, Y., Shenkar, O., & Nyaw, M. (2002). Mitigating liabilities of foreignness: Defensive versus offensive approaches. *Journal of International Management, 8*(3), 283–300.

Luo, Y., & Tung, R. (2007). International expansion of emerging market enterprises: A springboard perspective. *Journal of International Business Studies, 38*(4), 481–498.

Makino, S., Lau, C. M., & Yeh, R. S. (2002). Asset-exploitation versus asset-seeking: Implications for location choice of foreign direct investment from newly industrialized economies. *Journal of International Business Studies, 33*(3), 403–421.

Mathews, J. A. (2002). Competitive advantage of the latecomer firm: A resource-based account of industrial catch-up strategies. *Asia Pacific Journal of Management, 19*(4), 467–488.

Mathews, J. A. (2006). Dragon multinationals: New players in 21st century of globalization. *Asia Pacific Journal of Management, 23*(1), 5–27.

Mezias, J. (2002a). How to identify liabilities of foreignness and assess their effects on multinational corporations. *Journal of International Management, 8*(3), 265–282.

Mezias, J. (2002b). Identifying liabilities of foreignness and strategies to minimize their effects: The case of labor lawsuit judgments in the United States. *Strategic Management Journal, 23*(3), 229–244.

Miller, S. R., & Parkhe, A. (2002). Is there a liability of foreignness in global banking? An empirical test of banks' efficiency. *Strategic Management Journal, 23*(1), 55–75.

Miller, S. R., Thomas, D. E., Eden, L., & Hitt, M. A. (2008). Knee deep in the big muddy: The survival of emerging market firms in developed markets. *Management International Review, 48*(6), 645–665.

Morck, R., Yeung, B., & Zhao, M. (2008). Perspectives on China's outward foreign direct investment. *Journal of International Business Studies, 39*(3), 337–350.

Nachum, L. (2003). Liability of foreignness in global competition? Financial service affiliates in the city of London. *Strategic Management Journal, 24*(12), 1187–1208.

North, D. (1990). *Institutions, institutional change, and economic performance.* Cambridge, UK: Cambridge University Press.

Petersen, B., & Pedersen, T. (2002). Coping with liability of foreignness: Different learning engagements of entrant firms. *Journal of International Management, 8*(3), 339–350.

Porter, M. E. (1980). *Competitive strategy*. New York: The Free Press.

Prahalad, C. K., & Doz, Y. (1987). *The multinational mission: Balancing local demands and global vision*. New York: The Free Press.

Ramamurti, R., & Singh, J. (2009). Indian multinationals: Generic internationalization strategies. In: R. Ramamurti & J. Singh (Eds), *Emerging Multinationals from Emerging Markets*. Cambridge, UK: Cambridge University Press.

Rugman, A. (1981). *Inside the multinationals: The economics of internal markets*. New York: Columbia University Press.

Scott, W. R. (1995). *Institutions and organizations*. Thousand Oaks, CA: Sage.

Scott, W. R. (2001). *Institutions and organizations* (2nd ed.). Thousand Oaks, CA: Sage.

Singh, D. A. (2009). Export performance of emerging market firms. *International Business Review, 18*(4), 321–330.

The Economist. (2010). The global revival of industrial policy. *The Economist*, August 7, pp. 68–70.

Tung, A. C. (2001). Taiwan's semi-conductor industry: What state did and did not. *Review of Development Economics, 5*(2), 266–288.

Wan, W. P., & Hoskisson, R. E. (2003). Home country environments, corporate diversification strategies, and firm performance. *Academy of Management Journal, 46*(1), 27–45.

World Investment Report. (2008). *Transnational corporations and the infrastructure challenge*. UNCTAD, New York and Geneva.

Zaheer, S. (1995). Overcoming the liability of foreignness. *Academy of Management Journal, 38*(2), 341–363.

Zaheer, S. (2002). The liability of foreignness, redux: A commentary. *Journal of International Management, 8*(3), 351–358.

Zaheer, A., Hernandez, E., & Banerjee, S. (2010). Prior alliances with targets and acquisition performance in knowledge intensive industries. *Organization Science, 21*(1), 1072–1091.

Zaheer, S., & Mosakowski, E. (1997). The dynamics of the liability of foreignness: A global study of survival in financial services. *Strategic Management Journal, 18*(6), 439–464.

EVOLUTION OF FIRM- AND COUNTRY-SPECIFIC ADVANTAGES AND DISADVANTAGES IN THE PROCESS OF CHINESE FIRM INTERNATIONALIZATION

Svetla Marinova, John Child and Marin Marinov

ABSTRACT

This chapter provides a logical extension to the understanding of firm-specific advantages and disadvantages and the enabling role of existing and emerging country-specific advantages relevant to the process of Chinese firm internationalization. Its longitudinal perspective considers the changing objectives and actions of firms that enable them to compensate for disadvantages and create new or strengthen existing competitive advantages. The case study evaluation reveals that the evolution of strategic resources is the key motivator behind the internationalization of Chinese firms. Decisively encouraged by the Chinese government firms with corporate entrepreneurship aspire to alter themselves from home market leaders and regional players into globally competing multi-nationals. This process is made possible via the development of firm-specific advantages and continuous compensation for firm-specific disadvantages. The aspiration for strategic asset acquisition from

Dynamics of Globalization: Location-Specific Advantages or Liabilities of Foreignness?
Advances in International Management, Volume 24, 235–269
ISSN: 1571-5027/doi:10.1108/S1571-5027(2011)0000024017

developed countries combined with cost leadership and independent customer-centred innovation brought about strong firm-specific advantages stimulating the internationalization process of firms. The chapter focuses on the interdependence of country- and firm-specific advantages and disadvantages, thus recognizing the significance of the home country institutional context in Chinese outward foreign direct investment. It has been identified that corporate entrepreneurship is a significant firm-specific advantage for firm internationalization being a major force in gaining, accumulating, utilizing and leveraging resources for transforming firm-specific disadvantages into advantages. We argue that if the relational framework between governmental institutions and firms is more developed, the impact of country-specific advantages on firm-specific advantages is more favourable. This assumes that the government espouses an ideology that is favourable to corporate entrepreneurship.

INTRODUCTION

For a long-time China has been attracting a huge volume of inward FDI, the stock of which has accumulated to US$758.9 billion by 2007 (CIA World Factbook, 2009). Recently outward FDI has grown steadily and in 2008 reached an annual figure of US$52.2 billion that was in sharp contrast with the global downturn in FDI flows (Davies, 2009).

The implementation of this policy is supported by a sizeable trade surplus, a positive saving-investment ratio and the attempt of the Chinese authorities to increase income from overseas ownership of fixed assets (Globerman & Shapiro, 2009). The accumulation of technological and marketing expertise by leading Chinese firms has accelerated the involvement of other Chinese enterprises in outward investment (Tong & Li, 2008).

Studies on Chinese outward FDI have addressed the motives, driving forces and trends of outward FDI from China (Liu & Li, 2002; Deng, 2004; Child & Rodrigues, 2005; Liu, Buck, & Shu, 2005; Buckley et al., 2007; Rui & Yip, 2008; Morck, Yeung, & Zhao, 2008).

As an attempt to account for the success or otherwise of Chinese internationalization, Rugman and Li (2007) have explored the importance of firm specific advantages (FSAs) and country-specific advantages (CSAs).

With the above in mind, this chapter examines FSDs and FSAs in a longitudinal perspective considering the changing objectives and actions that have relevance to the process of Chinese firm internationalization.

Unlike previous studies, the chapter takes account of country- and firm-specific disadvantages as well as advantages and grounds its analysis in six case studies. To meet its aim, the chapter proceeds as follows. First, the relevant theoretical background is analysed by summarizing mainstream views on firm internationalization simultaneously addressing the use of advantages and changes in competitive disadvantages. Issues pertaining to latecomer firms and their internationalization are also brought to light. Further on, case study data of internationalizing Chinese firms are examined. Drawing on the theoretical perspectives and case study analysis, the chapter offers propositions relating to the evolution of country- and firm-specific disadvantages and advantages in the process of firm internationalization. The closing discussion considers the implications of the study.

THEORETICAL PERSPECTIVES

Resource-Based View of the Firm

The resource-based view of the firm affirms that internationalization strategy depends on unique resources in the home country which give the firm a competitive advantage vis-à-vis other firms operating in a host country (Tan & Vertinsky, 1996; Teece, Pisano, & Shuen, 1997; Prien & Butler, 2001). Wernerfelt (1984) defines firm resources as tangible and intangible assets that belong to a firm over a specific period of time. Resources strengthen a firm's competitive advantage (Barney, 1991; Peteraf, 1993) depending on the specifics of the competitive environment (Tallman, 1992; Brush & Artz, 1999). The predominant view is that companies exploit their own competitive advantages to extend their operations into new markets (Dunning, 1991). However, this view overlooks the possibility that firms may also have resources that are disadvantageous and create firm-specific disadvantages (FSDs) when entering new markets.

Advantageous resources can provide a firm with a competitive edge in the long term if they are unique and difficult to replicate by a determined set of competitors (Barney, 1991; Amit & Schoemaker, 1993). Penrose (1959) suggests that key and enduring firm-specific assets form FSAs that might support firm internationalization. At a given point of time a firm may have greater strength with regard to some of these advantages compared to others and indeed it may possess some resources, which inhibit value creation and are disadvantageous for entering foreign markets (Leonard-Barton, 1992; Tallman, 1992; Hu, 1995; Rangan & Drummond, 2004).

Rugman (1981) suggested a CSA/FSA matrix, which was subsequently explored in relation to emerging market multi-nationals (Rugman, 2007; Rugman & Li, 2007). The FSAs are seen as proprietary to the firm, and they can be technology based, knowledge based or they can reflect managerial and/or marketing skills (Rugman & Verbeke, 2003). An important FSA can be entrepreneurship, which may be particularly significant in creating and mobilizing other FSAs into dynamic capabilities, as well as creating strategic opportunities for the firm partly through successful relationships or negotiations with external parties. CSAs stem from natural resource endowments, labour force characteristics, cultural and economic factors as well as in some cases an appealing country brand. Rugman (1981, 2007) argues that managers of multi-nationals employ policies that build on the interactions of CSAs and FSAs in order to create unique strategic possibilities.

The set of advantages and disadvantages can evolve over time due to the activities of the firm, the competitive pressure of the environment (Amit & Schoemaker, 1993), and the impact of institutional change (Child & Tse, 2001). Internationalization might be triggered by firm's aspirations to access and develop new FSAs, such as efficiency or knowledge, superior to those that the firm has in its host country (Dunning, 1993; Wesson, 2004). At the same time, Cuervo-Cazurra, Maloney, and Manrakhan (2007) have suggested that resources that are a source of advantages in the home market can become a disadvantage abroad. In short, firm internationalization should be viewed through an economic, social and political lens (Child & Rodrigues, 2005) considering the characteristics of the home and host context. Therefore an institutional view of internationalization, referring to social and political factors, is a complement to the more usual economic perspective.

Institution-Based View of the Internationalization of the Firm

The institution-based view argues that institutions, which are a set of formal and informal rules and their enforcement arrangements (Schmoller, 1900/1990) play the role of creating and enforcing formal and informal constraints on the activities of firms (North, 1990, 1993; Scott, 1995).

Institutions define, enable and constrain strategic choices made by firms (Peng & Delios, 2006) as they form the institutional embeddedness of business activities (North, 1990) in a specific country context. Peng (2003, 2006) has conceptualized the relationship of firm strategy with the interaction between FSAs, industry conditions and institutions. Institutional factors can constitute CSAs and CSDs. This has been recognized in research on institutional constraints in internationalization (Lu & Yao, 2006; Ma, Yao, & Xi, 2006; Lee, Peng, & Barney, 2007; Zhou, Tse, & Li, 2006; Meyer, Estrin, Bhaumik, & Peng, 2009).

Institutions define the rules and norms for functioning of firms and industries (Ring, Bigley, D'Aunno, & Khanna, 2005; Peng, Wang, & Jiang, 2008). In developed countries institutions are considered advantageous if they maintain conditions for the effective implementation of market mechanisms (Meyer et al., 2009). In emerging markets institutions are demoted as disadvantageous as they are less developed and not able to guarantee effective markets. Makino, Lau, and Yeh (2002) found that institutional differences in emerging markets are more salient and that both formal and informal institutions impact the development of business.

A combination of not particularly advantageous CSAs and FSAs has become to characterize the internationalization of latecomer firms, which have been seeking assets rather than exploiting existing assets.

Latecomer Firms

Latecomer firms from emerging markets arguably do not possess many strong competitive advantages when compared with global rivals (Rui & Yip, 2008). This is generally applicable to all firms from emerging markets at the beginning of their internationalization. Consequently, firms originating from such contexts exhibit serious disadvantages in terms of their international competitiveness. The latecomer perspective provides an interesting insight into how FSAs could be developed and how latecomers' internationalization could be used to compensate for initial competitive disadvantages (Matthews, 2002).

The most important latecomer advantages lie in labour intensive production, cost leadership, flexibility and speed of adaptation in terms of production processes and products (Makino et al., 2002). Some latecomer firms are embedded in a culture, such as Confucianism, that encourages continuous learning and self development vis-à-vis peers. Such disadvantages could range from lack of knowledge of the market dynamics to lack of technological or management knowhow. Innovations, knowhow, technology, production process, marketing and managerial expertise are readily available in developed country contexts where they could be accessed by latecomer firms. Thus, latecomer firms move into developed markets with the strategic intent to acquire assets with potential to create competitive advantage.

When latecomer firms move to other emerging market contexts, they seek markets and resources having some advantages vis-à-vis multinationals from developed countries. These, coupled with support by governments (Child & Rodrigues, 2005), enable them to compete against developed-country multi-nationals (Dawar & Frost, 1999) in contexts with under-developed institutional environment and market mechanisms (Khanna & Palepu, 1997, 2000).

The internationalization of latecomer firms, including those from China, presents a challenge to international business theory to focus on the potential relevance of domestic institutional factors in transitional contexts. It also presents an opportunity to explore the evolution of FSAs and CSAs in contexts where formal institutions appear immature from western perspective. Child and Rodrigues (2005, p. 404) have recognized the danger of 'understating the role of emerging economy governments in underwriting the process whereby their leading firms seek to achieve international competitiveness, not least when the foreign currency reserves for purchasing overseas assets are available'.

Research on latecomer firms highlights the constraints of an imperfect institutional context (Boisot & Child, 1996; Tsui, Schoonhoven, Meyer, Lau, & Milkovich, 2004). Evolving institutional change and transformation, as well as economic liberalization add to the greater dynamics and uncertainty in the institutional context of emerging economies. Therefore, government's strategic objectives, decisions and involvement have been seen as essential for the internationalization of Chinese firms (Deng, 2009).

Analytical Framework

The preceding review of theoretical perspectives suggests the framework shown in Fig. 1, which will guide our analysis of the case studies that are now to be considered.

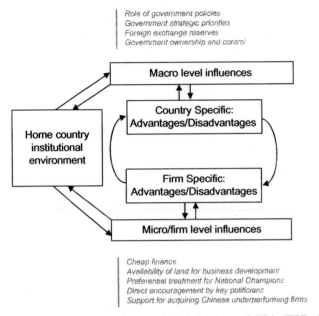

Fig. 1. A Framework of the Evolution of CSAs/CSDs and FSAs/FSDs Influenced by Home Country Institutional Environment.

CASE STUDIES

This study draws on secondary data in the form of descriptions, case studies, press releases, individual interviews, corporate and government publications. These have been used to formulate six case studies. The analysis followed the steps recommended by Yin (1994) and Eisenhardt (1989). The first step involved presenting and organizing the data in a case study format. The next step was to code the case data into categories according to the proposed theoretical model (Yin, 1994). Subsequently, each case was analysed separately and independently by the three researchers. All data were analysed simultaneously. The explanation building approach, as suggested by Yin (1994), was employed to increase the internal validity of the relationships. Discrepancies between case data and expectations called for extended data collection from previously unused sources and further theoretical evidence was intentionally sought. Finally cross-case patterns were identified and subsequently analysed.

The six case studies were selected to be in global mature manufacturing industries, i.e. white goods, telecommunications, computing and automotive. All firms strive to be National Champions. They have market leading positions in the home market, which have been used in their endeavours to compete globally.

Case Study 1 – Haier

The firm was founded in 1955 as a cooperative enterprise. It merged with a manufacturer of home appliances in 1979. The merged enterprise produced washing machines of poor quality which lacked market appeal. After 1984, the company's fortunes were turned round by its new director, Mr. Ruimin Zhang, a member of the Central Committee of the Chinese Communist Party. The indebted enterprise on the verge of financial collapse was transformed quickly into the domestic market leader. Starting outward internationalization as an OEM,[1] it eventually managed to create a worldwide presence with an internationally recognized brand name. By 2004, Haier had become the world's fourth largest white goods producer. A cumulative shift of objectives has led the firm through various stages of development. A summary of the evolution of Haier's FSAs and FSDs in a timeline since 1984 is presented in Table 1.

Case Study 2 – Galanz

The enterprise started its existence in 1978 as a small garment enterprise established by a visionary leader with local government support. In 1992, it began production of microwave ovens and was renamed the Galanz Enterprise Group. By the end of 1998, it became the biggest producer and the largest exporter of microwave ovens in the world. By that time it controlled almost three-quarters of the domestic market with its own brand. In foreign markets, Galanz used OEM that utilized its enormous production capacity and cost leadership. The firm formed partnerships requiring that partners' production of microwave ovens was shifted to China. In 2007, Galanz generated sales securing more than 50% of the world microwave oven market. Since 2008, the strategic focus shifted to independent global innovations targeting world markets via own brand production. OEM has been preserved on order only. The company has developed a global network of sales representative offices; established R&D centres in the United States,

Table 1. Timeline of the Evolution of FSDs and FSAs of Haier.

Timeline	Objective	FSDs	Actions	FSAs
In 1984		Lack of production and technological knowhow Lack of brand recognition Weak quality control systems Limited financial resources		(A) Entrepreneurial leader with strategic vision (B) Well developed institutional relationships ensuring government support (C) Low-cost production capability
From 1984 to 1991	Focus on knowledge and technology acquisition to develop home market and start internationalization	Limited knowledge of foreign markets OEM limits consumer awareness of product and brand Liability of foreignness	Build new production facilities Acquire foreign knowhow Introduce TQM Product development for domestic brand building Introduce new management practices	(A)–(C) reinforced (D) Economies of scale (E) Production and quality control capabilities (F) Fast market responsiveness and efficiency (G) Strong financial capabilities (H) Flexibility
From 1992 to 1998	Diversification to expand operations and strengthen home market position expand international activities	Insufficient knowledge of foreign markets Decreasing liability of foreignness Lack of internationally recognized brand	Related and unrelated diversification and integration of acquisitions in home market Product innovation and line extension Own brand development in home and host markets Export under own brand to developing and developed markets	(A)–(H) enhanced (I) Product innovation capabilities (J) Distribution system capabilities at home and abroad (K) Economies of scope (L) Development of market intelligence (M) International partnership development capabilities for entering and expansion in new markets

Table 1. (*Continued*)

Timeline	Objective	FSDs	Actions	FSAs
From 1999 to date	Achieve global market presence and international brand recognition	Gradual reduction of liability of foreignness Inconsistent global brand image	Expand international market presence via greenfield investment and acquisitions of strategic assets in developed and developing countries Create global network of own R&D centers Restructure organizational frameworks, processes and people Develop awareness of own global brand Initiate low-cost independent customer-oriented innovation	(A)–(M) further strengthened (N) Independent innovation capabilities (O) Customer driven market response and design (P) Preferential institutional support as National Champion (Q) Leveraged production and design capability across subsidiaries (R) Customer oriented competitiveness (S) Internationalization expertise (T) Consumer brand equity in developing countries (U) Value for money consumer brand equity for niche products in developed markets

South Korea and Japan developing forward and application technologies. Galanz has set up manufacturing facilities in Russia intending to extend production in other emerging markets. A summary of the evolution of the FSAs and FSDs of Galanz in a timeline is presented in Table 2.

Case Study 3 – Gree

Gree Electric Appliances is the world's largest residential air-conditioner manufacturer with 40,000 employees and annual production of 20 million air conditioner units. The company was formed in 1991 by the restructuring and merging of several inefficient state-owned enterprises. Although initially it imported Japanese technology from Toshiba, to date Gree has developed its own brand and advanced technology. Over 2,000 research engineers are involved in developing and enhancing the company's own world leading energy-saving technology using knowhow and customer-centred independent innovation.

Presently, the firm has production facilities in China, Brazil, Vietnam and Pakistan and a technology development partnership with Daikin of Japan. A summary of the evolution of Gree's FSAs and FSDs in a timeline is presented in Table 3.

Case Study 4 – Lenovo

Lenovo (initially named Legend) was set up in 1984 as a spin-off from the Institute for Computer Technology at the Chinese Academy of Sciences. The firm distributed and sold personal computers produced by foreign manufacturers gaining market intelligence, management skills and knowhow. To date, Lenovo is a multi-national IT firm with production sites in the United States, China and Singapore, and research centres in China and Japan. In 2005, Lenovo acquired the former IBM PC Division, and rights to the ThinkPad line trademark. The acquisition ensured knowhow transfer from IBM to Lenovo that provided worldwide access to a global customer base and increased Lenovo's bargaining power within the world PC industry. Presently, Lenovo is market leader in the Chinese PC market and the fourth largest personal computer firm in the world. A summary of the evolution of Lenovo's FSAs and FSDs in a timeline is presented in Table 4.

Table 2. Timeline of the Evolution of FSDs and FSAs of Galanz.

Timeline	Objective	FSDs	Actions	FSAs
In 1992	Start OEM	Lack of production and technological knowhow Lack of brand recognition Lack of production resources Lack of quality control system Limited financial resources	License technology and production knowhow from Toshiba	(A) Entrepreneurial leader with strategic vision (B) Good institutional relationships ensuring local government support (C) Low-cost production capability
From 1992 to 2003	Technology transfer to exploit cost leadership in microwave production and export	Strong liability of foreignness Limited knowledge of foreign markets OEM limits consumer awareness of product and brand	Create worldwide network of partnerships securing OEM Grow production facilities Lower costs Lead price wars to gain market leadership in domestic market	(A)–(C) reinforced (D) Economies of scale (E) Production and quality control capabilities (F) Partnership development capabilities for OEM (G) OEM exporting capabilities
From 2004 to 2007	Related diversification to expand operations and strengthen home market position Expand OEM	Strong liability of foreignness Limited knowledge of foreign markets OEM limits consumer awareness of product and brand	Apply cost leadership and high volume strategy for related products Increase market share in domestic rural market Start to export own brand	(A)–(G) reinforced

| From 2007 to date | Own brand development From "world's plant" to "global brand" | Strong liability of foreignness Limited knowledge of foreign markets OEM limits consumer awareness of product and brand | Focus on independent development and innovation of own brand as directed by the government Increase world market presence with own brand Establish R&D centers in developed markets Establish production sites and market development partnerships in emerging markets | (A)–(F) enhanced (H) Strengthened institutional relationship with central government (I) Economies of scope (J) Independent innovation capabilities (K) Consumer brand equity in developing countries |

Table 3. Timeline of the Evolution of FSDs and FSAs of Gree Electric Appliances.

Timeline	Objective	FSDs	Actions	FSAs
1991 initial position		Lack of production and technological knowhow Lack of brand recognition Weak quality control system Limited financial resources	Focus on air-conditioners	(A) Entrepreneurial leader with strategic vision (B) Good institutional relationships ensuring government support (C) Low-cost production capability
From 1992 to 2005	Focus on technology acquisition to develop home market	Strong liability of foreignness Lack of internationally recognized brand Limited experience in internationalization	Develop own brand Acquire foreign knowhow Introduce TQM	(A)–(C) reinforced (D) Economies of scale (E) Product quality and innovation (F) Market leader in air-conditioners in home market
From 2005 to 2007	Internationalization stage	Liability of foreignness Lack of internationally recognized brand Limited knowledge of foreign markets	Establish low cost production in Vietnam, Brazil and Pakistan Set up international distribution partnerships	(A)–(F) reinforced (G) Independent low-cost product innovation (H) Customer driven market response and design (I) International market intelligence (J) World leader in energy saving air-conditioning technology
From 2007 to date	Developing global brand	Decreasing liability of foreignness Limited brand recognition in developed markets outside Asia	Form technology development partnership with Daikin Corporation Penetrate emerging markets Develop brand in advanced markets	(A)–(J) enhanced (K) Brand awareness in emerging markets and developed markets of Asia-Pacific region (L) Customer-driven market response and design (M) Customer-oriented competitiveness

Table 4. Timeline of the Evolution of FSDs and FSAs of Lenovo.

Timeline	Objective	FSDs	Action	FSAs
In 1984	Distribute foreign PCs in China	Underdeveloped distribution network Lack of production and technological knowhow No brand recognition Strong liability of foreignness		(A) Entrepreneurial leader (B) Well developed institutional relationships ensuring government support (C) Research knowhow (D) Fast learning capabilities from competitors
From 1984 to 1998	Develop marketing expertise and enhance technological capability	Limited knowledge of foreign markets Lack of internationally strong customer brand equity Strong liability of foreignness	Distribute and sell PCs produced by foreign MNCs Form IJV for production with a Hong Kong firm Develop own brand in home market Start exporting of own brand to Asia-Pacific region	(A)–(D) reinforced (E) Domestic market intelligence (F) Domestic marketing capabilities (G) Regional market intelligence (H) Low-cost independent innovation
From 1998 to 2004	Enhance production capabilities in related products	Limited international customer brand equity Strong liability of foreignness outside the Asia-Pacific region	Related product diversification Domestic market development Continued product innovation Legend Group renamed Lenovo Enhance distribution and marketing competence	(A)–(H) enhanced

Table 4. (*Continued*)

Timeline	Objective	FSDs	Action	FSAs
From 2005 to date	Globalize via acquisition of strategic assets	Reduced liability of foreignness	Acquire the PC division of IBM Link the brand Lenovo to IBM Use trademark ThinkPad Move from a regional player to a global MNC Leverage distribution, production, management and marketing expertise worldwide	(A)–(H) enhanced (I) High bargaining power in the global PC industry (J) Worldwide customer reach (K) Leveraged worldwide market intelligence (L) Leveraged independent customer-driven innovation (M) Global brand recognition (N) Preferential institutional support as National Champion (O) Leveraged production and design capabilities

Case Study 5 – Huawei

Established in 1988 with a team of just seven persons, Huawei is currently a high-tech enterprise specializing in R&D, production and marketing of communications equipment and providing customized network solutions for telecommunications carriers. It has seven R&D centers in China, two in the United States, one each in Sweden, India, Ireland, Russia, Indonesia and the Netherlands. Internationalization has been the main intent since the early 1990s. The acquisition of Marconi was a means to obtain advanced technology and provide access to European markets with their local market intelligence and relationships with global giant communications companies. Huawei has formed numerous partnerships with leading multi-nationals such as ADI, Agere, Altera, HP, IBM, Intel, Microsoft and Motorola. These aim to improve corporate management knowhow, launch joint research activities and improve the time to market of products. A summary of the evolution of Huawei's FSAs and FSDs in a timeline is presented in Table 5.

Case Study 6 – Nanjing Automobile Group

Founded in 1947 as a repair service workshop in the East China Field Army, it produced light truck vehicles since 1958 to become market leader in the home market by 1979. Using related diversification via technology acquisition from global firms, it became a market leader in China's automotive market by 1982. In 2005, Nanjing purchased the remaining assets of the MG Rover group for £53million. In 2006, the Nanjing-MG project laid the foundations of the Nanjing Pukou New High Technology Industry Development Zone. In June 2006, the first batch of MG cars was exported to Europe. In December 2007, Nanjing Automobile and Shanghai Automotive Industry Corporation merged. A summary of the evolution of Nanjing's FSAs and FSDs in a timeline is presented in Table 6.

PROPOSITIONS

In this section propositions are discussed and formulated on the basis of the theoretical perspectives introduced in the literature review and the case study findings.

Table 5. Timeline of the Evolution of FSDs and FSAs of Huawei.

Timeline	Objectives	FSDs	Actions	FSAs
In 1988	Sell foreign communications equipment	Lack of production and technological knowhow Lack of brand recognition Underdeveloped distribution network Liability of foreignness		(A) Entrepreneurial leader with strategic vision (B) Good institutional relationships ensuring government support
From 1988 To 1996	Domestic market development	Limited production and technological knowhow Unknown brand name Underdeveloped distribution network Strong liability of foreignness	Develop and penetrate rural home market	(A) and (B) reinforced (C) Product imitation and low-cost innovation capabilities (D) Fast learning capabilities from competitors (E) Domestic market intelligence (F) Domestic marketing capabilities
From 1996 to 1999	Related diversification and internationalization	Lack of international customer brand equity Strong liability of foreignness	Penetrate urban home market Initiate internationalization under own brand Own brand development and leadership in home market	(A)–(F) enhanced (G) International market intelligence

| From 1999 to date | Globalization via partnerships and own brand | Reduced liability of foreignness | Worldwide distribution growth
Exporting
Develop and innovate products
Establish R&D centers overseas
Establish partnerships for product and technology development
Establish partnerships for market development and penetration | (A)–(G) enhanced
(H) Global brand recognition
(I) Preferential institutional support as National Champion
(J) Independent customer-driven innovation
(K) Global brand recognition |

Table 6. Timeline of the Evolution of FSDs and FSAs of Nanjing Automotive Works.

Timeline	Objectives	FSDs	Actions	FSAs
1947 founded 1958–1979		Limited technology Limited managerial knowhow	Focus on a single product category	(A) Entrepreneurial leadership (B) Good institutional relationships ensuring government support (C) Low-cost production capability
From 1979 to 1982	Serve home market	Lack of management knowhow Lack of quality control systems Limited technology No international experience and presence Strong liability of foreignness	Improve production processes Grow production capacity	(A) and (C) enhanced (D) Domestic market leadership in light trucks (E) Expertise in home market distribution (F) Production capabilities
From 1982 to 2005	Related diversification	Lack of international customer brand equity Limited international experience and presence Strong liability of foreignness	Form IJVs and licensing agreements for technological development with Isuzu, Fiat, Seat and Iveco	(A)–(F) reinforced (G) Market leader in home automotive market

From 2005 to 2007	Internationalization via acquisition of strategic assets	Limited independent innovation Reduced liability of foreignness	Acquire MG Rover assets and design capabilities International brand name acquisition (MG, Wolseley Austin, Morris, American Austin, Princess and Stirling) Acquire production knowhow and rights for engine manufacturing Create own low costs supply chain Gain distribution rights in 15 European countries, incl. Russia for the MG brand	(A)–(G) reinforced (H) Technological capability to produce a wider range of engines and vehicles (I) International market intelligence
From 2007 to date	Gain economies of scale and scope to target foreign markets as part of a larger group	Reduced liability of foreignness	Merger with SAIC Uniting the MG brand and engine production capabilities with the design for Rover 75, 25	(A)–(I) reinforced

Compensating for FSDs

Preparation for active international involvement may entail inward internationalization (Cavusgil & Naor, 1987; Korhonen, Luostarinen, & Welch, 1994; Child & Rodrigues, 2005), which allows for inward transfer of knowledge, technology, expertise and managerial knowhow that can subsequently become a basis for outward internationalization. At the same time, domestic acquisitions and mergers have also created economies of scale and scope that have prepared the ground for developing FSAs supporting outward internationalization. In some cases like Haier such acquisitions were supported by government, though in other cases government officials have tried to thwart this route to domestic consolidation (Meyer & Lu, 2005).

An approach to compensate for FSDs applied by companies from emerging markets is collaboration with overseas MNCs via international joint venture (IJV) formation and licensing (Lane, Salk, & Lyles, 2001). Similar to other developing economies (see e.g. Lyles & Salk, 1996) IJVs have been used as means for providing technology transfer at the time of the "Open door" policy in China. Extant research on IJVs has supplied some support for the transfer of valuable assets and knowledge such as production technology, managerial skills and marketing expertise from MNCs to their local partners (Luo, 2002; Matthews, 2002). Knowledge transfer presumably contributes to the compensation of FSDs of indigenous firms. IJVs via inward internationalization have limited the development of technological capabilities of Chinese firms due to the propensity for indigenous firms to become overdependent on joint ventures for innovative capabilities (Gao, 2004; Li & Zhou, 2008). Thus relying on compensation for FSDs via transfer from overseas partners can create the foundations for, but cannot ensure, endogenous and sustainable innovation in Chinese enterprises.

If an internationalizing firm from emerging markets has FSDs, it may attempt to acquire strategic resources such as technology, design and brands from companies in developed economies (Schüler-Zhou & Schüler, 2009). This is needed as the firm does not always have the capabilities or resources to turn FSDs into FSAs on its own or in partnership with foreign firms in its home country. The acquisitions may take a variety of forms such as direct knowledge acquisition, acquisition of production facilities or acquisition of human capital and knowhow when setting up R&D centres in host markets. According to Frost (2001) firms set up R&D centres overseas to overcome location disadvantages of the home base by tapping into location advantages overseas. Wang (2002) reports that 70% of Chinese research subsidiaries are based in developed economies. Many of those are R&D centres exploring opportunities for technological advancements, product and design innovation. Thus outward FDI is pulled towards unavailable, complementary and compatible resources, especially in the form of knowledge that can be used as a stepping stone to accelerate independent innovation. Compensating for FSDs has become key priority for the Chinese firms and government. The rapid internationalization of Chinese companies into developed economies attempts to reduce the gap by acquiring needed capabilities (Wesson, 2004) with the intention to use them for independent internal learning.

All firms from the case studies demonstrated initial FSDs in the form of a lack of production and technological knowhow. To compensate for this FSD Haier, Gree, Galanz and Nanjing Automotive Works licensed technology from world leading MNCs from developed countries. Later on, Galanz entered into IJVs to expand original equipment manufacturing (OEM) and become the world's biggest supplier of a single product category. Gree followed a route of internal learning and only when it developed core technology outperforming that of world leading producers, did the enterprise enter into a comprehensive strategic alliance for global strategic cooperation and form an IJV with Daiking from Japan. Haier started on the basis of OEM, but quickly developed its own technological advantage and formed IJVs for market access in developing countries. Following this, they used partnerships, greenfield investment and acquisition of production facilities in developed countries. Lenovo and Huawei compensated for their initial FSDs by distribution agreements and IJVs that enabled them to start production and supply of the Asia-Pacific market. Huawei later went into a number of partnerships and the acquisition of Marconi brought advanced technology and access to European markets and relationships with global communications carriers. Lenovo also used an acquisition of the PC Division of IBM for technology, management and market intelligence. Unlike Huawei, Lenovo also got access to the IBM-Lenovo brand for several years as well as the rights over the ThinkPad trademark.

Another initial FSD typical for all firms is the lack of brand recognition. The case companies dealt with this FSD in two ways. Haier, Gree and Huawei developed their own brand mostly through internal technology development based on technology transfer, innovation and independent learning. Consequently these enterprises aimed at developing their own brands with worldwide appeal. By contrast, Lenovo and Nanjing bought brand intangibles from companies with global brand recognition. Galanz is the only case among the six in which own brand development has been deterred by the strategy of OEM. The company has only recently embarked upon developing international consumer brand equity of their product category, encouraged by the Chinese authorities and the impact of the global economic crisis.

The initial FSD of liability of foreignness is compensated for most successfully by Haier via a global strategy securing their presence in most markets served. Galanz have lagged behind as they have not been able to develop their own standing in global markets, i.e. their presence has been hidden behind the brand names of other company and store brands due to their OEM strategic orientation. Huawei, Lenovo and Nanjing have managed to compensate for their liability of foreignness via targeted acquisitions and exploitation of world-known brands. Therefore:

P1. FSDs can be compensated for in the international arena via transfer (joint ventures, licensing, etc.), acquisition (e.g. technology, design, brand, etc.), and internal independent learning.

The Influence of Government on the Evolution of FSAs

Institutional theory suggests that formal institutions in emerging economies play a major role in supporting the international expansion of enterprises. Luo, Xue, and Han (2010) argue that government support for outward FDI helps compensate for the late-mover FSDs of emerging market MNCs such as a lack of unique capabilities and a liability of foreignness.

The role of government in a communist party driven political system is greater than that of governments in developed market-based societies. The Chinese government has defined the direction of development of Chinese enterprises from the 'Open door' policy initiated by Deng Xiaoping in the late 1970s to the policy of 'Going abroad' endorsed by Jiang Zemin in the early 2000s. Most recently, in his speech for the 60th anniversary of the People's Republic of China, the President Jintao Hu has announced a policy shift from 'made in China' to 'created in China' to lead the country to an innovation-driven economy. In 2004, the State Development and Reform Commission and the Export-Import Bank of China began to promote the formation of overseas R&D centres, and mergers and acquisitions to compensate for CSDs and enhance the FSAs of Chinese enterprises (WIR, 2006). The quality of outward FDI is encouraged and closely monitored by the government in terms of investment direction and performance, and its contribution to the national economy.

Child and Rodrigues (2005) and Deng (2004, 2007) have emphasized that the Chinese government uses state foreign exchange reserves in directing outward FDI to developed countries. Moreover, preferential credits have been offered by state banks to promote outward FDI. The Chinese government has also recognized the need for independent innovation that is based on acquired knowledge, which has been extended by intensive and persistent own R&D effort (Yuan, 2005). This objective is typical of the National Champions that government is said to transform into modern world-class corporations. This is also a process pursued by firms with different ownership structures, including SOEs, collective and private enterprises, which strive to gain government support in the form of tax rebates and low interest or interest-free loans (Luo et al., 2010).

All case study companies have received government support for the acquisition of tangible and intangible strategic assets over time. The support has been in line with government policies, which initially allowed firms to acquire technology and quality control systems or initiate production via purchase or partnerships in the form of strategic alliances and IJVs. Support has also been in the form of preferential loans, tax rebates, risk-safeguarding mechanisms, signing up of investment protection agreements with 115 countries (Luo et al., 2010), and direct governmental influence in shaping the investment expansion into developed and emerging economies, as well as providing a comprehensive business support and information system. Such government support and evolving policies have allowed firms to compensate for FSDs systematically and over time as changes in firm FSDs and FSAs have also informed government financial support and investment priorities. Therefore:

P2. FSDs can evolve into FSAs, assisted by government policies and financial support.

Impact of CSAs on the Development of FSAs

The evolution of CSDs into CSAs affects the home market business environment in which firms operate. When initial disadvantages are compensated for and turned into advantages, these assist domestic firms in using the CSAs to develop their FSAs. CSAs can be exploited by firms via direct transfer into FSAs. Thus by exploiting China's CSAs in cheap, unskilled and skilled labor, Chinese MNCs have internationalized. Formal institutions create conditions for the evolution of CSDs into CSAs that can improve the international standing of a country. Such CSAs, that are not necessarily business specific, may create opportunities for firms to develop unrelated FSAs. For example, China's greater bargaining power vis-à-vis foreign governments can negotiate favourable terms in a quest for knowledge transfer and technological upgrading via acquisition of western firms such as Rover, Volvo and the PC Division of IBM among others. Rugman and Verbeke (2003) suggest that FSAs and CSAs are critical parameters in describing and explaining the patterns of international expansion of multinational corporations. The emergence of FSAs is influenced by the home CSAs (Krishna, Sanjeev, & Kim, 1997) embedded in the interface of home country resource endowments, demand conditions, and industry characteristics (Porter, 1990). In addition, FSAs in emerging markets are strongly influenced by home institutional development and the government-business relational framework.

Initial CSAs included government policies to attract inward FDI on the basis of inward internationalization via licensing and IJVs that could potentially strengthen Chinese FSAs over time. CSDs that dealt with regulatory restrictions on firms going abroad in relation to approvals required and restrictions on foreign stock market listings; limited knowledge of foreign environments leading to strong liability of foreignness; and the unfavorable national image for being 'cheap and nasty' have evolved into CSAs over time. CSAs have gradually emerged by developing an institutional field supporting inward and subsequently outward FDI and by strategically informed target market selection driving purpose specific investment overseas. Thus the country has developed advantages in offering low cost funding for foreign expansion, willingness to relax regulatory restrictions on the build-up of relevant domestic strengths, reorientation of official ideology towards internationalization, assisting acquisition of supporting activities abroad (e.g. purchase of part-ownership of foreign banks) and negotiation with foreign governments of terms favourable to presence of Chinese firms in emerging regions such as Africa.

The evolution of CSDs into CSAs has created favourable conditions for FSAs that are associated with firm internationalization. This evolutionary process has supported inward internationalization through IJVs with OEMs; has made finance available for diversification in foreign markets; has encouraged firms to learn and adopt more effective modes of organization; has enhanced firm's ability to acquire foreign assets, giving access to international brands, technologies, markets and distribution systems and knowledge. Moreover CSAs emphasizing knowledge exploration and exploitation have set the pre-conditions for the growing ability of enterprises to innovate independently. Therefore:

P3. The evolution of CSDs into CSAs creates a favorable environment for the development of related and unrelated FSAs relevant to firm internationalization.

Importance of the Relational Framework between Governmental Institutions and Firms

Political economists have long recognized the important role of formal institutions in developed economies as regulators of the national economy and the competitive environment in which businesses operate (Rugman & Verbeke, 1992; Murtha & Lenway, 1994). On their part, businesses impact the institutional environment by their ability to support national development (Boddewyn & Brewer, 1994). Such an understanding of the role of businesses, formal institution and of governments in particular, has been justified by Moran (1985) and Boddewyn (1988) who have suggested that the interdependence of business and government creates a supportive environment for firm internationalization.

One of the characteristics of a highly institutionalized environment, such as China's, is that the intensive involvement in business affairs of government agencies and the Communist Party creates the conditions for strong 'relational frameworks' between institutions and organizations (Scott & Meyer, 1983). Paradoxically, strong relational frameworks do not just provide channels for officials to exert influence; they also provide potentially valuable access to the authorities through which enterprise leaders can hope to modify unfavourable CSAs. In the case of major enterprises such as the six enterprises featured here, the links that constituted relational frameworks included membership of key government committees, visits to the enterprises by key government figures and other regular meetings. They were supported ideologically by the favourable publicity accorded to the firms in the officially-controlled media. Their corporate entrepreneurship was celebrated so long as it did not threaten to become too autonomous from Party control. Although the dynamics of such enterprise–government relationships are highly confidential, there is little doubt that they assisted the development of CSAs and FSAs in a way that has supported internationalization. Notable examples include the relaxation of rules on domestic consolidation through acquisition in order to achieve economies of scale for internationally competitive low-cost production, as in Haier's case, and the provision of finance on favourable terms for the acquisition of major overseas assets, such as Lenovo's purchase of IBM's PC division. Therefore:

P4. The more developed the relational framework between governmental institutions and firms, the more favorable the impact of CSAs would be on FSAs.

The Role of Entrepreneurship

Entrepreneurship is 'concerned with the discoveries and exploitation of profitable opportunities' (Shane & Venkataraman, 2000, p. 217). Therefore, entrepreneurial management entails an understanding of the importance of being opportunistic, strategic and innovative. The actions of an entrepreneurial corporate leader can be one way in which institutional support is gained and developed. Baumol (1993) suggests that corporate entrepreneurship should be analysed by particularly focusing on the nature of the institutional arrangements that encourage the exercise of entrepreneurship and that provide incentives for it to take productive direction. Thus, to develop FSAs or compensate for FSDs, it is important for a firm to exploit the opportunities created by the interplay between the government and corporate entrepreneurship (Child & Rodrigues, 2005). Corporate entrepreneurial leadership promotes internationalization in close relationship with the government (Zhang & Van den Bulcke, 1996). Chinese corporate entrepreneurship is long-term oriented and represents a combination of opportunity ʼseeking and strategic behaviour (Hitt, Ireland, Kemp, & Sexton, 2001; Child & Rodrigues, 2005) that can secure advantages in firm internationalization. Child and Rodrigues (2005) have also argued that institutional entrepreneurship at government level is important in the case of Chinese firm internationalization. Institutional entrepreneurship is associated with the role of the government in identifying opportunities overseas and in providing funds for enterprise internationalization.

Four of the case study firms bring evidence about the important role of corporate entrepreneurship on firm level. Thus Haier and Gree have been led by visionary corporate entrepreneurs who have mobilized resources and developed firm strategies based on quality improvement, introduction of innovation, establishment of technological leadership, management innovation and own brand creation and development. The entrepreneurial leader of Galanz has managed to develop economies of scale that coupled with the innovative OEM formula have resulted in a world leadership position of the firm in the production of microwave ovens. Corporate entrepreneurship at Huawei has turned the company from a home market distributor to a world leading provider of telecommunication services. In all of these companies entrepreneurial leaders have been carefully monitored, listened to and encouraged by government officials. State leader visits to the production facilities have become synonymous with government appreciation of enterprise leadership and their contribution to the development of the Chinese economy. Such direct support is particularly evident at the time when the case companies had already become established national players. In the cases of Nanjing and Lenovo, institutional entrepreneurship coupled with corporate entrepreneurship has created conditions for technological upgrading, strategic asset acquisition and enhanced international market positions. Moreover, corporate entrepreneurship in all six cases has been helped by the political standing of firm managers who are members of the Chinese Communist Party. Such position of authority has provided additional support both at national and local institutional level. The firms' CEOs have been trusted advisors to the local and central government on business development issues that relate to the global reputation and competitiveness of China. Therefore:

P5. Corporate entrepreneurship is a significant FSA for internationalization so long as it is tolerated, encouraged and assisted by government.

DISCUSSION AND CONCLUSIONS

This study provides a logical extension to the understanding of FSDs into FSAs and the enabling role of existing and emerging CSAs that are relevant to the process of Chinese firm internationalization. It demonstrates the importance and impact of the institutional context in which firms are embedded. Specifically, the case study evaluation reveals the following findings. Supported by empirical evidence, we argue that the evolution of strategic resources is the key motivator behind the internationalization of Chinese firms. Decisively encouraged by the Chinese government firms with corporate entrepreneurship aspire to alter themselves from home market leaders and regional players into globally competing multinationals (Hennart, 2009). This process is made possible via the development of

FSAs and continuous compensation for FSDs. The aspiration for strategic asset acquisition from developed countries combined with cost leadership and independent customer-centred innovation brought about strong FSAs stimulating the internationalization process of firms. Successfully internationalizing enterprises such as Haier, Huawei, Gree and Lenovo, which have invested in developed countries with a particular intention to develop R&D centres, have based their FSAs on innovation and technological advancement. The research brings evidence that the six studied firms had well-developed institutional relationships with the government, economies of scale, product innovation capabilities, capacities to develop market intelligence and established leadership positions in the home market. These common FSAs have facilitated the internationalization process of the firms by creating preconditions for the development of other FSAs and compensating for existing FSDs. Firms that sought strategic assets wished to gain sustainable FSAs over time.

All case firms create advantages via accessing unavailable, complementary and compatible resources, especially in the form of knowledge that can be used as a stepping stone to accelerate home country independent innovation. Our findings are in line with Hennart (2009) who suggests that the increase in outward foreign direct investment flows by emerging-market firms is driven by their endeavour to acquire firms with technological advances that go together with their own firm-specific resources. FDI that has been used to compensate for initial disadvantages has been attracted by the country specific advantages in the form of a low-cost production base and large internal market. Subsequently, disadvantages have been compensated via outward FDI being pulled by strategic resources available overseas with a push by the corporate entrepreneurial management and state institutions. Such FDI has further enhanced the firm- and country-specific advantages.

We have discussed the advantages and disadvantages of internationalizing Chinese firms. The chapter makes the following contributions to the literature. First, we focus on the interdependence of CSAs and FSDs and FSAs, thus recognizing the significance of the home country institutional context in Chinese outward FDI. Further studies could explore the role played by both home and host country institutional environment as suggested by Cuervo-Cazurra and Genc (2008). We argue that the Chinese government has had a key role in defining the direction of development of Chinese enterprises. Thus an active involvement as a party of the relational framework with respective institutions has a positive contribution towards the evolution of FSAs. Second, the chapter recognizes that corporate entrepreneurship is a significant FSA for firm internationalization. Corporate entrepreneurship is a major force in gaining, accumulating, utilizing and leveraging resources (Floyd & Wooldridge, 1999) for transforming FSDs into FSAs. It ensures that firms develop new products, advanced technologies, strategies, management and marketing approaches that can provide firms with a sustainable position in the global competitive space. Further studies could explore the differences in institutional support and encouragement towards corporate entrepreneurship in firms with different ownership structure. Third, we argue that if the relational framework between governmental institutions and firms is more developed, the impact of CSAs on FSAs is more favourable. This assumes that the government in question espouses an ideology that is favourable to corporate entrepreneurship. In China's case, it took some 20 years since the start of the Economic Reform for this to come to full fruition with respect to internationalization. Although it is a considerable challenge to access relevant data, further study of how country (macro) and firm (micro) factors can constructively co-evolve in this way would provide valuable insights both for the agents of public policy and enterprise managers aiming to create strategic space for their firms.

NOTE

1. We use the term OEM in its original meaning of a company that produces hardware to be sold under another company's brand name.

REFERENCES

Amit, R., & Schoemaker, P. J. H. (1993). Strategic assets and organisational rents. *Strategic Management Journal, 14*(1), 33–46.

Barney, J. (1991). Firm resources and sustained competitive advantage. *Journal of Management, 17*(1), 99–120.

Baumol, W. (1993). *Entrepreneurship, management and the structure of pay-offs.* Cambridge, MA: MIT Press.

Boddewyn, J. (1988). Political aspects of MNE theory. *Journal of International Business Studies, 19*, 341–363.

Boddewyn, J., & Brewer, T. (1994). International business political behavior: New theoretical directions. *Academy of Management Review, 19*(1), 119–143.

Boisot, M., & Child, J. (1996). From fiefs to clans and network capitalism: Explaining China's emerging economic order. *Administrative Science Quarterly, 41*(4), 600–628.

Brush, T., & Artz, K. (1999). Toward a contingent resource-based theory: The impact of information asymmetry on the value of capabilities in veterinary medicine. *Strategic Management Journal, 20*(3), 223–250.

Buckley, P., Clegg, J., Cross, A., Liu, X., Voss, H., & Zheng, P. (2007). The determinants of Chinese outward foreign direct investment. *Journal of International Business Studies, 38*(4), 499–518.

Cavusgil, S. T., & Naor, J. (1987). Firm and management characteristics as discriminators of export marketing activity. *Journal of Business Research, 15*(3), 221–235.

Child, J., & Rodrigues, S. (2005). The internationalisation of Chinese firms: A case for theoretical expansion? *Management and Organization Review, 1*(3), 381–410.

Child, J., & Tse, D. K. (2001). China's transition and its implications for international business. *Journal of International Business Studies, 32*(1), 5–21.

CIA World Factbook. (2009). CIA World Factbook. Available at http://www.cia.gov/library/publications/the-world-factbook/rankorder/2078rank.html. Accessed on November 4.

Cuervo-Cazurra, A., & Genc, M. (2008). Transforming disadvantages into advantages: Developing country MNEs in the least developed countries. *Journal of International Business Studies, 39*(6), 957–979.

Cuervo-Cazurra, A., Maloney, M., & Manrakhan, S. (2007). Causes of the difficulties in internationalization. *Journal of International Business Studies, 38*(5), 709–725.

Davies, K. (2009). While global FDI falls, China's outward FDI doubles. *Colombia FDI Perspectives, 5*, May 26.

Dawar, N., & Frost, T. (1999). Competing with giants: Survival strategies for local companies in emerging markets. *Harvard Business Review, 77*(2), 119–129.

Deng, P. (2004). Outward investment by Chinese MNCs: Motivations and implications. *Business Horizons, 47*(3), 8–16.

Deng, P. (2007). Investing for strategic resources and its rationale: The case of outward FDI from Chinese companies. *Business Horizons, 50*(1), 71–81.

Deng, P. (2009). Why do Chinese firms tend to acquire strategic assets in international expansion?. *Journal of World Business, 44*(1), 74–84.

Dunning, J. (1991). The eclectic paradigm of international production: A personal perspective. In: C. Pitelis & R. Sugden (Eds), *The nature of the transnational firm* (pp. 117–136). London: Routledge.

Dunning, J. (1993). *Multinational enterprises and the global economy*. Addison Wesley: New York.

Eisenhardt, K. (1989). Building theories from case study research. *Academy of Management Review, 14*(4), 532–550.

Floyd, S., & Wooldridge, B. (1999). Knowledge creation and social networks in corporate entrepreneurship: The renewal of organizational capability. *Entrepreneurship Theory and Practice, 23*(3), 123–143.

Frost, T. (2001). The geographic sources of foreign subsidiaries' innovations. *Strategic Management Journal, 22*(2), 101–123.

Gao, P. (2004). Shaping the future of China's auto industry. *McKinsey Quarterly, 3*, 123–126.

Globerman, S., & Shapiro, D. (2009). Economic and strategic considerations surrounding Chinese FDI in the United States. *Asia Pacific Journal of Management, 26*(1), 163–183.

Hennart, J.-F. (2009). Down with MNE-centric theories! Market entry and expansion as the bundling of MNE and local assets. *Journal of International Business Studies, 40*(9), 1432–1454.

Hitt, M., Ireland, R., Kemp, S., & Sexton, D. (2001). Strategic entrepreneurship: Entrepreneurial strategies for wealth creation. *Strategic Management Journal, 22*(6), 479–491.

Hu, Y. (1995). The international transferability of the firm's advantages. *California Management Review, 37*(4), 73–88.

Khanna, T., & Palepu, K. (1997). Why focused strategies may be wrong for emerging markets? *Harvard Business Review, 75*(4), 41–51.

Khanna, T., & Palepu, K. (2000). The future of business groups in emerging markets: Long-run evidence from Chile. *Academy of Management Journal, 43*(3), 268–285.

Korhonen, H., Luostarinen, R., & Welch, L. S. (1994). Inward–outward internationalisation patterns and government policies for Finnish SMEs. Paper presented at the Annual Nordic Marketing Conference, University of Umea, November.

Krishna, E., Sanjeev, A., & Kim, S. (1997). Are firm-specific advantages location-specific too? *Journal of International Business Studies, 28*(4), 735–757.

Lane, P., Salk, J., & Lyles, M. (2001). Absorptive capacity, learning and performance in international joint ventures. *Strategic Management Journal, 22*, 1139–1162.

Lee, S.-H., Peng, M., & Barney, J. (2007). Bankruptcy law and entrepreneurship development: A real options perspective. *Academy of Management Review, 32*(1), 257–272.

Leonard-Barton, D. (1992). Core capabilities and core rigidities: A paradox in managing new product development. *Strategic Management Journal, 13*(S1), 111–126.

Li, J., & Zhou, C. (2008). Dual-edged tools of trade: How international joint ventures help and hinder capability building of Chinese firms. *Journal of World Business, 43*(4), 463–474.

Liu, H., & Li, K. (2002). Strategic implications of emerging Chinese multinationals: The Haier case study. *European Management Journal, 20*(6), 699–706.

Liu, X., Buck, T., & Shu, C. (2005). Chinese economic development, the next stage: Outward FDI? *International Business Review, 14*(1), 97–115.

Lu, Y., & Yao, J. (2006). Impact of state ownership and control mechanisms on the performance of group affiliated companies in China. *Asia Pacific Journal of Management, 23*(4), 485–503.

Luo, Y. (2002). Stimulating exchange in international joint ventures: An attachment-based view. *Journal of International Business Studies, 33*(1), 169–181.

Luo, Y., Xue, Q., & Han, B. (2010). How emerging market governments promote outward FDI: Experience from China. *Journal of World Business, 45*(1), 68–79.

Lyles, M., & Salk, J. (1996). Knowledge acquisition from foreign parents in international joint ventures: An empirical examination in the Hungarian contest. *Journal of International Business Studies, 27*(5), 877–903.

Ma, X., Yao, X., & Xi, Y. (2006). Business group affiliation and firm performance in a transition economy: A focus on ownership voids. *Asia Pacific Journal of Management, 23*(4), 467–483.

Makino, S., Lau, C., & Yeh, R. (2002). Asset-exploitation versus asset-seeking: Implications for location choice of foreign direct investment from newly industrialised economies. *Journal of International Business Studies, 33*(3), 403–421.

Matthews, J. (2002). Competitive advantages of the latecomer firm: A resource-based account of industrial catch-up strategies. *Asia Pacific Journal of Management, 19*(4), 467–488.

Meyer, K., Estrin, S., Bhaumik, S., & Peng, M. (2009). Institutions, resources and entry strategies in emerging economies. *Strategic Management Journal, 30*(1), 61–80.

Meyer, M., & Lu, X. (2005). Managing indefinite boundaries: The strategy and structure of a Chinese business firm. *Management and Organization Review*, *1*(1), 57–86.

Moran, T. (1985). *Multinational corporations: The political economy of foreign direct investment.* Lexington, MA: Lexington Books.

Morck, R., Yeung, B., & Zhao, M. (2008). Perspectives on China's outward foreign direct investment. *Journal of International Business Studies*, *39*(3), 337–350.

Murtha, T., & Lenway, S. (1994). Country capabilities and the strategic state: How national political institutions affect multinational corporations' strategies. *Strategic Management Journal*, *15*(S2), 113–129.

North, D. (1990). *Institutions, institutional change and economic performance.* Cambridge: Cambridge University Press.

North, D. (1993). Economic performance through time, Nobel Prize Lecture. Available at http://nobelprize.org/nobel_prizes/economics/laureates/1993/north-lecture.html. Accessed on November 7, 2009.

Peng, M. (2003). Institutional transitions and strategic choices. *Academy of Management Review*, *28*(2), 275–296.

Peng, M. (2006). *Global strategy.* Cincinnati: South-Western Thomson.

Peng, M., & Delios, A. (2006). What determines the scope of the firm over time and around the world? An Asia Pacific perspective. *Asia-Pacific Journal of Management*, *23*(4), 385–405.

Peng, M., Wang, D., & Jiang, Y. (2008). An institution-based view of international business strategy: A focus on emerging economies. *Journal of International Business Studies*, *39*(5), 920–936.

Penrose, E. (1959). *The theory of the growth of the firm.* Oxford: Oxford University Press.

Peteraf, M. (1993). The cornerstones of competitive advantage: A resource-based view. *Strategic Management Journal*, *14*(3), 179–191.

Porter, M. (1990). *The competitive advantage of nations.* New York: The Free Press.

Prien, R., & Butler, J. (2001). Is the resource based view a useful perspective for strategic management research? *Academy of Management Review*, *26*(1), 22–40.

Rangan, S., & Drummond, A. (2004). Explaining outcomes in competition among foreign multinationals in a focal host market. *Strategic Management Journal*, *25*(3), 285–293.

Ring, P., Bigley, G., D'Aunno, T., & Khanna, T. (2005). Perspectives on how governments matter. *Academy of Management Review*, *30*(2), 308–320.

Rugman, A. (1981). *Inside the multinationals: The economics of internal markets* ((Reissued in 2006 as *Inside the multinationals, 25th anniversary edition.* New York: Palgrave Macmillan).). New York: Columbia University Press.

Rugman, A. (2007). Multinational enterprises from emerging markets. Presented at the Berlin Roundtable meeting on the Role of the G8 in an Endangered Global Economic and Political Climate, Berlin, June 1–2.

Rugman, A., & Li, J. (2007). Will China's multinationals succeed globally or regionally? *European Management Journal*, *25*(5), 333–343.

Rugman, A., & Verbeke, A. (1992). A note on the transnational solution and the transaction cost theory of multinational strategic management. *Journal of International Business Studies*, *23*(4), 761–772.

Rugman, A., & Verbeke, A. (2003). Extending the theory of the multinational enterprise: Internalization and strategic management perspectives. *Journal of International Business Studies*, *34*(2), 125–137.

Rui, H., & Yip, G. (2008). Foreign acquisitions by Chinese firms: A strategic intent perspective. *Journal of World Business, 43*(2), 213–226.

Schmoller, G. (1900(1990). Simmels Philosophie des Geldes. In: P. U. Hein (Ed.), *Georg Simmel.* Frankfurt: Peter Lang.

Schüler-Zhou, Y., & Schüler, M. (2009). The internationalization of Chinese companies: What do official statistics tell us about Chinese outward foreign direct investment? *Chinese Management Studies, 3*(1), 25–42.

Scott, W. (1995). *Institutions and organizations.* Thousand Oaks, CA: Sage.

Scott, W., & Meyer, J. (1983). The organization of society sectors. In: J. W. Meyer & W. R. Scott (Eds), *Ritual and rationality* (pp. 129–154). Beverley Hills, CA: Sage.

Shane, S., & Venkataraman, S. (2000). The promise of entrepreneurship as a field of research. *Academy of Management Review, 25*(1), 217–226.

Tallman, S. (1992). A strategic management perspective on host country structure of multinational enterprises. *Journal of Management, 18*(3), 455–471.

Tan, B., & Vertinsky, I. (1996). Foreign direct investment by Japanese electronic firms in the United States and Canada: Modeling the timing of entry. *Journal of International Business Studies, 27*(4), 655–681.

Teece, D., Pisano, G., & Shuen, A. (1997). Dynamic capabilities and strategic management. *Strategic Management Journal, 18*(7), 509–533.

Tong, T., & Li, J. (2008). Real options and MNE strategies in Asia Pacific. *Asia Pacific Journal of Management, 25*(1), 153–169.

Tsui, A., Schoonhoven, C., Meyer, M., Lau, C., & Milkovich, C. (2004). Organization and management in the midst of societal transformation: The People's Republic of China. *Organization Science, 15*(2), 133–144.

Wang, M. (2002). The motivations behind China's government-initiated industrial investment overseas. *Pacific Affairs, 75*(2), 187–206.

Wernerfelt, B. (1984). A resource-based view of the firm. *Strategic Management Journal, 5*(2), 171–180.

Wesson, T. (2004). *Foreign direct investment and competitive advantage.* Cheltenham: Edward Elgar.

WIR. (2006). *FDI from developing and transition economies: Implications for development.* New York: UNCTD.

Yin, R. (1994). *Case study research: Design and methods* (2nd ed.). Newbury Park, CA: Sage Publications.

Yuan, W. (2005). China's government R&D institutes. *Science, Technology and Society, 10*(1), 11–29.

Zhang, H., & Van den Bulcke, D. (1996). International management strategies of Chinese multinational firms. In: J. Child & Y. Lu (Eds), *Management issues in China: International enterprises* (pp. 141–164). London: Routledge.

Zhou, K., Tse, D., & Li, J. (2006). Organizational changes in emerging economies: Drivers and consequences. *Journal of International Business Studies, 37*(2), 248–263.

FROM STAGES TO PHASES, A THEORY OF SMALL DEVELOPING COUNTRY INTERNATIONALIZATION

Nigel L. Williams, Tom Ridgman and Yongjiang S. Shi

ABSTRACT

Existing research in firm internationalization tends to adopt the perspective of relatively fixed country specific advantages and disadvantages. However, firms operating from small developing countries may experience rapidly shifting country-specific advantages due to industrial policy interventions. These changes influence the internal configuration and, ultimately, the internationalization paths of firms, a factor that is not captured by current theory. Using a combination of a country case study and nested multiple firm cases, data were collected on how organizations internationalized from Trinidad and Tobago, a small developing country. Unlike the relatively deterministic outward patterns predicted by existing theories, analysis revealed both evolutionary and co-evolutionary trajectories of development. These outcomes suggest that as a country moves to more open economic environment, network connections in the

Dynamics of Globalization: Location-Specific Advantages or Liabilities of Foreignness?
Advances in International Management, Volume 24, 271–298
Copyright © 2011 by Emerald Group Publishing Limited
ISSN: 1571-5027/doi:10.1108/S1571-5027(2011)0000024018

form of supplier and institutional relationships are of increased value for firms seeking to enter external markets.

INTRODUCTION: INTERNATIONALIZATION FROM A CHANGING DOMESTIC CONTEXT

Research in international business (IB) has focused on multinationals from developed countries, as they dominate international activity (Markusen, 1995; Rugman & Verbeke, 2005). With this perspective, small emerging economies have been viewed as 'peripheral' (Tavares, 2002) due to their lower level of MNE activity (Tavares, 2002; Hennart, 2009). Unlike their larger counterparts, firms in small developing countries (SDC) face changing country-specific advantages, a factor that has received little attention in current internationalization theory (Campa & Guillaon, 1999). Small economies have been previously defined as economic price takers, a definition that incorporates over 120 countries worldwide (Mellander, Vredin, & Warne, 1992). However, this grouping is relatively broad as it includes developed countries like Sweden, Denmark and the Netherlands (Belderbos, 1992), areas that have previously been extensively examined in internationalization research. A specific subset of these small economies, known as SDC small states (Henrikson, 1999) have received comparatively little attention.

SDC have been previously categorized by the Commonwealth and the World Bank based on origin, population and economic characteristics (Will, 1991). This chapter adopts the World Bank definition (WorldBank, 2007) that identifies countries as SDCs based on having a population of less than 1.5 million and specific economic characteristics. SDCs were initiated as a result of historical processes: decolonization and defederation (Henrikson, 1999). In decolonization, former colonial territories were given up by their former owners and became independent states. In defederation, clusters of geographically close territories were broken into individual countries. While countries such as Singapore also have a small population and similar origins, they do not share the economic characteristics of SDCs. SDCs are managed by (relatively) weak regulatory institutions and are funded by the export of a narrow range of commodities or services, generally through preferential trade agreements (Easterly & Kraay, 2000). Forty-five countries fit these criteria and exceptions regarding population are made for Botswana, Jamaica and Lesotho since they exhibit similar economic behaviour (Crowards, 2002). Owing to their limited institutional capacity and small size, SDCs have a reactive approach to policymaking, unlike successful developmental states in East Asia (Etzkowitz & Brisolla, 1999). In these countries, the effect of exogenous events such as changes in commodity prices or strategic decisions by multinational firms (Pantin, Sandiford, & Henry, 2002) are magnified (Downes, 2004), resulting in high volatility.

Current theory assumes relative stability in the home market and hence country-specific advantages as the firm moves outward (Mariotti & Piscitello, 2001). This assumption of low domestic volatility may reflect the country settings in which they were formulated: strong institutions, enforcement, diversified economies (North, 1990). Outside of these settings, higher levels of volatility may occur that can affect the development of domestic firms and, hence, internationalization.

Broadening the perspective of IB beyond its current vistas to more dynamic country settings like small states can deliver several benefits to a range of stakeholders. For researchers, it provides an opportunity to test or create theories in a new category of country environment. For policymakers in these states, lessons learned from this research can guide the development or selection of support mechanisms that are grounded in their particular country circumstances, possibly improving outcomes. Similarly, managers or owners of firms from these countries may benefit from guidance from these theories when crafting internationalization strategies. This research is an initial entry into what can emerge as a new category of IB theory. First, existing theoretical perspectives are reviewed and analysed, building a theoretical framework that models internationalization as a resource development process. Next, a nested case study approach is crafted to capture the effects of macro level change (environment) on micro-level (firm) evolution. The findings indicate that instead of distinct stages, outward development by indigenous firms from small states can be viewed movement through 'phases' in which several 'states' of internationalization can exist simultaneously.

RESEARCH SETTING

The most southern of the Caribbean Islands, Trinidad and Tobago (TT), has a population of 1.3 million and a GDP per capita of 14,000 USD. A former British colony, it began self-government in 1956 and since then has attempted industrial policy interventions to shift the local economy from export of primary resources to manufactured goods (Rodrik, 2000). The implications for domestic firms are significant because by pursuing a deliberate, policy led strategy of industrialization, political authority (Lenway & Murtha, 1994) superseded market forces, making TT a developmental state. The result has been mixed with the emergence of an energy industry dominated by foreign multinational firms (Jessen & Vignoles, 2004) and a smaller group of indigenous, export-oriented firms. However, the limited size of TT's oil and gas reserves make future growth based on the energy sector difficult and the local government has expressed a need to improve the performance of indigenous firms (Cook & Harrison, 2003). TT is also a member of a free trade group, CARICOM (Caribbean Community), comprised of former English, Spanish and Dutch colonies in the Caribbean Region (Benn & Hall, 2006).

EXISTING THEORETICAL PERSPECTIVES ON INTERNATIONALIZATION

There is some debate over the definition of the term 'internationalization' (Andersen, 1997). Some researchers have defined internationalization as outward activity only (Johanson & Mattson, 1988). Alternatively, it has been defined far more broadly as the process of increasing involvement in external activity (Welch & Luostarinen, 1988). This definition incorporates two directions of activity: outward internationalization, in which the firm extends marketing and production activities to serve international markets (Johanson & Vahlne, 1977) as well as inward internationalization, for example, the sourcing of items from foreign suppliers (Fletcher, 2001). Yet other scholars (Calof, 1994) define internationalization as adaptation, that is, the adjustment of organizational resources and coordination structures to the requirements of international markets. This chapter examines the patterns of outward internationalization by firms from SDC.

Over time, researchers have shifted the unit of analysis in internationalization research from country in international trade models (Ricardo, 1817), to firms (Hymer, 1976; Dunning, 1977), management teams (Johanson & Vahlne, 1977) and finally the individual (Jones & Coviello, 2005; Chandra, 2007). This diversity is summarized in Table 1 that shows the claims, underlying mechanisms and current criticisms of firm and management driven internationalization. Economic-based models describe

Table 1. Overview of Existing Paradigms in Firm Internationalization.

	Internalization (1976)	Eclectic (OLI) (1977)	Stage Models (1977, 1982)	Network Models (1988)	Born Globals/INV (1989)	U Model (1990)	Eclectic (Alliance Capital) (1993)	International Entrepreneurship (IE) (2000)	Institutional IE (2004)	LLL (2006)
Claim	MNE expansion based on type of resources owned by firm and host country characteristics	MNE expansion based on ownership advantages (assets and transactions), Locational advantages and internalization advantages	Incremental expansion following a pre-determined path	Relationship driven expansion of firms	Global environment lowers costs of and facilitates cross-border activity for new firms	Expansion based on increasing market knowledge/experience	MNE expansion based on need to enhance OLI by leveraging resources from partners and countries	Expansion based on pursuit of opportunities over international boundaries	Firms internationalize to exploit domestic resources	Rapid expansion to obtain resources unavailable in domestic market
Underlying mechanism	Firm resources, transaction costs at host location	Firm resources, country resource, country factors at host location (transaction costs)	Risk tolerance determines degree of international commitment	Firms' activities are performed in a business network comprising of suppliers, customers and competitors.	Combination of resources and networks existence of exploitable global niches, available international market knowledge from management/partners.	Market knowledge (Intangible resource) drives market commitment (resource commitment), resulting in international activity	Firm resources, country resources, country factors, relationships and networks	Combination of resources, networks and orientation. changing international conditions, entrepreneurial orientation and firm characteristics drive international behavior	Combination of resources, networks and orientation. entry into cross-national institution (ethnic or other network) enables exploitation of domestic resources externally	Combination of resources, networks and orientation. Firms adopt a global outlook to obtain resources and extend their presence through leveraging relationships
Empirical backing	Investment patterns by US	Investment patterns by US and Japanese firms	Expansion of European/US SMEs, e.g. Johanson and Vahlne (1977), Bilkey and Tesar (1977)	Expansion of Scandinavian SMES, e.g. Johanson and Mattson (1988)	Rapid expansion of high-technology SMEs, e.g. Bell (1995)	Expansion of European SMEs, e.g. Johanson and Vahlne (1977)	–	Development process of European/US SMEs, e.g. Andersson (2000)	Expansion of firms from Singapore and Hongkong	Expansion of firms from South America, India, China and Taiwan

Table 1. (*Continued*)

	Internalization (1976)	Eclectic (OLI) (1977)	Stage Models (1977, 1982)	Network Models (1988)	Born Globals/INV (1989)	U Model (1990)	Eclectic (Alliance Capital) (1993)	International Entrepreneurship (IE) (2000)	Institutional IE (2004)	LLL (2006)
Common criticisms	Does not explain how firms develop advantages	Static, conceptual framework for building theory	Context independent Unidirectional Deterministic Independent process	Does not describe content of international activity (Akhongas, 1998)	Little knowledge of development paths over time		Conceptual framework for building theory	Little knowledge of development paths over time	Little knowledge of development paths over time	Little knowledge of development paths over time
Research method	FDI statistics, case studies	FDI statistics	Case studies of European SMEs	Case studies of European SMEs	Case studies of European SMEs	Case studies of European SMEs	–	Case studies of European SMEs	Comparative interview	Case studies of Emerging market MNEs

the nature of a multinational firm's advantage over domestic rivals in a host market (Dunning, 1988) or the configuration a firm may choose when operating in external markets (Buckley & Casson, 1998). Examples of the former approach include the eclectic paradigm (Dunning, 2001), and more recently, the LLL model (Mathews, 2006) that examines the outward actions of emerging market multinationals. On the basis of transaction cost theory, internalization (Rugman & Verbeke, 2005) is the dominant paradigm of the latter approach.

Internationalization process models focus on the evolution of firms from domestic to international (Gabrielsson, Kirpalani, Dimitratos, Solberg, & Zucchella, 2008a, 2008b). Early work in this area employed behavioural research as their theoretical backing, indicating that a firm's outward expansion was determined by the risk tolerance of its management (Johanson & Vahlne, 1977). Later researchers have incorporated theoretical perspectives from entrepreneurship (Chandra, 2007), network (Hadley & Wilson, 2003) and institutional (Yeung, 2002) research.

While they rely on differing underlying mechanisms, current IB theory shares the implicit underlying assumption, which is that the home environment is fixed and domestic change does not affect internationalization activity (Makhija & Shenkar, 2004). While research in other management areas, notably, strategy acknowledge the possibility of changing home country advantages (Murtha & Lenway, 1994), the effects of these changes on firm internationalization has received little research attention (Bijmolt & Zwart, 1994).

Since these country environments have efficient markets, legal and regulatory systems (Narayanan & Fahey, 2005), an assumption of low volatility is valid. By contrast, SDC such as TT are dynamic environments with higher levels of uncertainty (Klinger, 2007) due to policy interventions.

Developing countries, with the possible exception of Hong Kong (Noland & Pack, 2002) have attempted to transform their economies using industrial policy. However, institutional constraints in SDCs result in a reactive approach to policymaking (Barclay, 2007). Governments tend to follow prescriptions and formulas for development based on international trends (Peres, 2006), with little understanding of the domestic context. As a result, over time, SDCs experience far higher volatility than their large counterparts and firms face difficulty in adapting to changing country specific advantages. The next section creates a theoretical framework that is applicable to the SDC environment for further investigation of this phenomenon.

THEORETICAL FRAMEWORK

Generally, small state environments are resource constrained, which limits their ability to build tradable, market-based capabilities (Wan, 2005). For example, risk financing such as venture capital is not widely available (Patro & Wald, 2005), and funding is raised internally or from private sources. Human resources are also limited as there is a high degree of net outward migration for skilled labour (Carrington & Detragiache, 1998). Organizations also face competition for skilled personnel from the multinational dominated primary sector (Pantin, 2007). Under these circumstances, firms that attempt to sustain or increase their level of activity are inherently entrepreneurial in their orientation (Garud & Karnøe, 2003) and engage in opportunity seeking behaviour for survival, not just growth. To engage in internationalization requires an even greater effort by organizations, as they are required to negotiate both domestic and export uncertainty, competing against firms without such handicaps (Baldacchino, 2005).

In country environments such as this, resource availability is a heavy influence on the actions of organizations (Pfeffer & Salancik, 2003). Firms may either attempt to seek resources to overcome constraints (Pollock, 2004) or attempt to avoid them by reducing the level of activity (Lee, Lim, & Tan, 1999). Generally, organizations from these countries require an inward internationalization step to access complementary foreign resources (Kumar, Kumar, & Persaud, 1999). While these fixed challenges are reflected in current theory, small states have the additional issue of high volatility with the effect of shifting country specific advantages and disadvantages.

Firm Resources

A resource-based perspective views individual firms as a collection of resources (Mahoney & Pandian, 1992) that are coordinated to generate rents or income (Penrose, 1959). Particular resource characteristics have been suggested by researchers in the resource-based view (RBV) from which competitive advantage can be derived (Barney, 1991): valuable, rare, inimitable (difficult to imitate) and non substitutable (VRIN). The RBV has been increasingly applied to explain the cross border activities of firms as it forms an adaptable framework for building theories (Kogut & Zander, 2003).

Rather than individual resources, organizations' distinctive performance may be enabled by particular resource combinations (Wang & Zajac, 2007). These combinations are composed of property and knowledge resources (Hennart, 1988). Discrete property-based resources (DPBR) (Miller & Shamsie, 1996) require the presence of a supporting legal framework to exhibit VRIN characteristics. Born Global and IE firms, for example, were first identified in high-technology sectors, in which they employ DPBR resources such as patents. Integration of DPBR resources such as a mineral lease with a processing facility can form an organizational systemic property-based resource (SPBR) that can support outward activity.

While skills such as product design are tacit and difficult to imitate (Barney, 1991), they can aid the firm in creating new products for foreign markets and become a source of competitive advantage (Rodriguez Cano, Carrillat, & Jaramillo, 2004). These resources can be classified as discrete knowledge-based resources (DKBR) and have been employed by stage (international experience) and the network (business relationships) models. Finally, individual DKBRs can be combined into systemic knowledge-based resources such as organization configuration and culture (Chetty & Holm, 2000) that support outward international activity by firms. They integrate individual skills or DKBRs to create a distinct resource in its own right considered SKB resources.

Firm Environment

Factors and institutions support transformational and transactional (network) activities (Wan, 2005) by firms. Factors include physical resources, human resources such as skilled people and intangible resources such as reputation (Wan, 2005). Institutions are social structures that determine the structure of economic activity in a given country (North, 1990). While a country's resource endowment and institutional structure are relatively fixed (Wan, 2005), selective government intervention in the form of industrial policies (Klak, 1995; Wint, 2003) can rapidly change. Domestic firms are required to adapt to conditions created by these policies, since they influence availability of domestic resources in the form of finance, skilled personnel and operating facilities. Selective trade barriers also control access to resources available through inward internationalization, such as equipment (Welch & Luostarinen, 1993).

These forces are summarized in Fig. 1. Outward internationalization is based on firm resources (S/DPBR and S/DKBR) that enable entry to

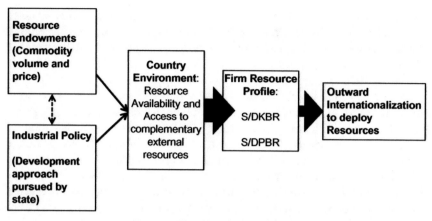

Fig. 1. Theoretical Framework.

external markets. These resources are formed in domestic markets from available country resources along with complementary resources accessible from foreign partners. The availability of the former and access to the latter is influenced by the country industrial policy. Changes in this macro-level context require firms to build or acquire new resources, influencing their position in international markets. The next section outlines the research method used to explore firm internationalization from a small state.

RESEARCH METHODOLOGY

Research into processes is highly complex as it requires the collection of data about how events, actions and decisions evolve over time (Langley, 1999). Understanding the context in which these processes evolve is a key component of this type of research as developments in the macro environment impact on the micro-level of firms. The analysis of this data is also a challenge as the researcher is required to integrate a heterogeneous group of data sources into an explanatory framework (Pettigrew, 1997). For processes like internationalization that occur over a long period of time, a historical perspective may be of value in theory building (Lawrence, 1984). History can provide an avenue for examining complex, evolving phenomena, determining underlying causal factors when current data are not available (Jones & Khanna, 2006). History-based research has been used to make essential contributions to management theory, highlighting the need to align organizational strategy and structure (Chandler, 1962). For this research, a historical perspective enabled the capture of an evolving firm level process (internationalization) within a changing country environment.

Data collection was conducted using case studies as they provide a framework for building theory in a given context (Voss, Tsikriktsis, & Frohlich, 2002). This study takes a nested approach to integrate two types of cases with complementary strengths: (1) a single case of the evolution of the TT resource environment and (2) multiple case studies of the evolution of individual exporters in TT.

1) Single case study: TT country environment

   Single cases enable the in depth exploration of a given setting (Voss et al., 2002) and was used in this research to examine domestic policies that influenced the TT resource environment. Initial sources of data on TT policy were identified in the archives of local research institutions. Documents were catalogued and the data compared within and across archives. A summary of the findings was then created, which formed the basis of discussions with state officials. On the basis of the feedback from policymakers, we identified additional sources and refined the policy review document. The summary was then analysed to provide insight into the changes in the TT policy environment as well as guide selection of participants for the organizational case studies.

2) Multiple case studies: TT exporters

   Multiple case studies are particularly useful for uncovering underlying causes and mechanisms as they enable comparison of findings. Results from a single case can be tested against subsequent cases and confirmed or discarded as necessary. In this way, a stronger or more useful theory can be built (Eisenhardt, 1989). A theoretical sampling method was used to select respondents with the specific criteria being the policy period in which firms were started.

For organizations, all publically available data from government and newspaper archives on these organizations was reviewed and compiled. On the basis of these data, an initial list of key incidents such as changes in manufacturing processes was formulated and used as an input to design data collection instruments. Interviews were then conducted with key personnel and after each interview, respondents were asked to suggest additional personnel for the study and provide documents for verification, where available. Narratives were created based on the data collected and discussed with the firms' management. Additional areas of inquiry were identified and data was collected and the narratives updated.

The findings from both the country and firm case studies were compared to identify patterns of resource development during internationalization by indigenous TT firms. These patterns were compared with extant theory to create a theoretical model of firm internationalization from a small state that incorporates the effect of home environmental change.

RESULTS: COUNTRY CASE STUDY

Since 1956, TT policymakers have employed four distinct approaches to industrial policy in an attempt to build a diversified, competitive export sector. Each of these policy frameworks was adopted to resolve particular historical circumstances: local and international economic conditions, social and political forces as described below.

State as Promoter (1956–1967)

TT like many other Caribbean counties at the time had high levels of unemployment and a low domestic income (Lewis, 1950). Inspired by the success of Puerto Rico, the state adopted a policy of industrialization by invitation (IBI). TT marketed itself as a multinational subsidiary location in an attempt to gain access to technology and foreign markets for domestic firms.

State as Entrepreneur (1967–1986)

IBI did not deliver the anticipated benefits and supported by increasing oil revenue, policymakers attempted industrial development through increasing state involvement. Foreign competition was restricted through import barriers and the state made a number of investments and acquisitions in domestic industry. The outcome was a rapidly growing manufacturing sector, from under 200 to over 1,400 firms. However, these firms were primarily domestic oriented, high cost and low quality.

State as Facilitator (1987–2000)

A fall in commodity prices led to a deep recession in TT. With the guidance of the IMF, TT began to open its economy, dismantling barriers to trade and foreign investments. Some state investments were divested and local firms were provided with support to encourage exports. As part of the CARICOM regional group, TT entered into a number of trade agreements to improve market access for exporters. These structural reforms proved successful, and firms moved rapidly into regional and extra regional markets.

State as Architect (2001 to Present)

Increases in energy prices brought improved revenue streams to the TT government. Outside of the energy sector, export growth stagnated due to a combination of increased low cost competition from East Asian firms and shortages of skilled labour. Mindful of the limited nature of their natural resources, the government embarked on an extensive transformation program to shift the economy from commodity to knowledge-intensive exports. An overall strategy, Vision2020 was crafted to facilitate this process, supported by investments in institutions to enable research development and commercialization.

These frameworks can be classified based on the approach to managing the domestic economy: closed economy and open economy. In the closed economy era (promoter and entrepreneur) vertical industrial policies were implemented, in a similar manner to other developing countries (Etzkowitz & Brisolla, 1999). For firms in this environment, the sole country-specific advantage was a secure pool of resources that was only accessible by government fiat (Brautigam, 1994). An economic crisis precipitated a change to more open economic policies (facilitator and architect) and the country-specific advantages available to firms shifted. Initially (1982–2001) policymakers implemented support mechanisms for exporters. Later, these incentives were removed, increasing the cost of international entry. In parallel to these developments, investment in education and accumulated experience in manufacturing increased the amount of skilled labour to firms. More recently, an increase in energy prices has also constrained skilled labour availability and recent policy initiatives to support science-based innovation have not yet benefited firms. Overall, since 2000, the

number of indigenous manufacturing firms and volume of export has fallen
(Mottley, 2008).

RESULTS: ORGANIZATIONAL CASE STUDIES

This section seeks to map the variations in exporter characteristics in the
face of environmental change. On the basis of the framework presented
previously, domestic conditions, specifically policy influence firm start up
and development. From the country case study, four main policy frameworks were attempted by the TT government that would have presented
varying challenges and opportunities to firms. Using a theoretical sampling
method, organizations were selected that entered international markets
during three policy periods: entrepreneur, facilitator and architect, and
continued operation until the present day (Table 2).

TT Electrical (TTE)

Located in Arima and Chaguanas, Trinidad, TTE is the largest Caribbean
manufacturer of electrical products, employing 200 persons and generating
70 million USD in sales. The organization produces and supplies electrical
enclosures, switchgear and cables.

Internationalization during Entrepreneur Period
TTE was started in 1969 as a joint venture (JV) between a UK and a local
conglomerate to produce electrical cables. The company quickly established
a presence in the local market and began regional exports to CARICOM,
winning a country export award in 1970. The company grew steadily,
diversifying from cable into switchgear, to meet the demands of the new
petrochemical sector. However, export sales during this period did not
experience similar growth and never contributed more than 10% of
company revenue. Sales fell when the TT construction market stagnated
in the 1980s and its owner made the strategic decision to exit manufacturing
investments.

Internationalization during Facilitator and Architect Periods
In 1995, TTE was offered to a competitor and the acquisition was completed
in 1997. Under new management, TTE expanded its export presence,
entering the non-English-speaking Caribbean in 2000 and Latin America in

Table 2. Case Study Selection.

Name	Product/Industry	Policy Period at First Export	Age	First Export	Size (No. of Employees)	Sales/ £Mil	Mode/Range	Export Intensity %
TT wire (TTW)	Electrical cables/ construction	Entrepreneur	40	1971	204	7	Direct export/extra regional	25
Office furnishings (OF)	Furniture	Facilitator	19	1991	200	4.0	Direct export/regional	33
Shipping containers (SC)	Cargo carrying units/transport	Architect	5	2005	30	2.5	Direct export/ manufacturing subsidiary (Brazil) marketing subsidiary (Venezuela)	30

2002. Partnerships were formed with established multinationals who entered into regional distribution and manufacturing arrangements for electrical products. The benefits sought were twofold; high-quality suppliers not only provided items for resale but were a source of manufacturing improvements. With additional knowledge, TTE also began modernizing its factory operation, improving its production facilities and marketing practices.

Owing to growth in energy revenues during the architect period, the local construction sector also expanded. TTE formed a project management division in 2004, acting as the main contractor and supplier on local construction projects. This section has grown rapidly and acts as a source of finance for the company's extra regional expansion.

TTE's Trajectory of Development
A closed domestic environment supported early growth by providing both protection from competition and a secure market. While the firm relied on foreign expertise to initiate operation, subsequent resource development was done internally. For example, the DKBR required to produce switchgear to meet local demand at the time. Acquisition by a competitor and opening of the TT environment during the facilitator era saw an increasing integration with international markets as the firm aggressively pursued foreign markets to meet its growth objectives. This integration was not only outward, but inward as the firm sought both products and process knowledge from supplier networks. These have been employed to upgrade the local facility, supporting investments in plant and management systems. TTE's international expansion pattern of a long period in domestic/regional operation followed by rapid international expansion is similar to 'born again' global firms (Bell, McNaughton, & Young, 2001).

Office Furniture

Operating out of several facilities in Trinidad, Office Furniture (OF) is the largest manufacturer and distributor of OF in the Caribbean. In addition to their own branded products, OF assembles and distributes furniture for a number of US and European suppliers.

Internationalization during Facilitator Era
OF was formed from the assets of several failed furniture firms by a group of investors. Using government support available for exporters, OF quickly moved into regional markets and established a presence in the English-speaking

Caribbean. In 1993, the firm began exporting to the US through a distributor and began exploring Latin America, with little success. Increasing competition from Asian firms forced OF to exit the US market in 1997 and focus its efforts on the CARICOM market. In 2001, OF began expansion of its capacity to serve the growing local market. While the company attempted to lobby for increased state support through forming an association of export manufacturers, this effort was ultimately unsuccessful. Instead, OF embarked on a diversification program capture TTs increasing wealth with the objective of doubling sales in five years. To reduce costs, the firm sought to leverage the newly liberalized trade environment and embrace outsourcing. Beginning with a few components, the company expanded the role of external suppliers to distribute production internationally: Designs are done in Trinidad and Mexico, metal bending (Tube) is done in Columbia and pre-cut flat designs are ordered from Taiwan and China.

OF's Trajectory of Development
Opening of the TT environment and targeted export support enabled rapid entry into regional markets and later, extra regional markets. However, the firm's presence in the latter was not sustained. Growing local demand has resulted in reversal of internationalization strategies. On the outward side, the firm has de-internationalized (Benito & Welch, 1997), exiting extra regional markets while simultaneously increasing the sophistication of inward internationalization.

Cargo Carrying Unit Manufacturer

Cargo Carrying Unit Manufacturer (CCUM) is a manufacturer and rental agency for certified cargo carrying units (CCUs), used in the local energy industry. Located on the Point Lisas Industrial estate, the company was formed in 2004 as an importer of products but has since expanded to manufacturing in Trinidad and Brazil.

Export during Architect Era
In 2004, CCUM formed a distribution JV with a Canadian firm to rent units locally. In 2005, they expanded internationally by winning a tender in Venezuela. Supported by the Canadian supplier, CCUM invested in a workshop to manufacture and repair units. CCUM also began lobbying the local safety bureau to implement international standards and were ultimately successful, which helped to reduce the level of competition from

uncertified units. The firm ended its JV in 2006, investing in resources to create designs and expand production. After achieving ISO 9000 certification in 2007, CCUM began examining ways to control rising production costs as skilled labour became scarce in the growing local economy. The company decided to focus on customized or rapid delivery items formed supply agreements with European firms for standard or long lead time items. CCUM has since expanded its presence in Venezuela and keeps a fleet dedicated to that market. The company has since invested in a manufacturing subsidiary in Brazil and intends to centralize production of units for the Latin American market there.

CCUM Trajectory of Development
CCUM has undergone extensive reconfigurations in a short period of time shifting its main activity from importer of items to manufacturer, exporter then international manufacturer. This process of rapid internationalization, like other born globals (Gabrielsson et al., 2008a, 2008b) was facilitated by DPBR resources such as design and DKBRs such as skills accessible from external sources. At the initial stage, their initial supplier guided construction of the local facility and specified the local fleet. This mode was continued as knowledge from suppliers was used to further improve manufacturing. Combined, these resources have facilitated entry to the Latin American market with the advanced step of establishing a production facility in Brazil.

CROSS CASE ANALYSIS: RESOURCE DEVELOPMENT PROCESSES DURING INTERNATIONALIZATION

Internationalization is a multidimensional, complex phenomenon involving the firm, domestic and external environments. Using an RBV framework, the inward and outward internationalization of TT manufacturing exporters, both outward and inward, was examined as an outcome of resource reconfigurations in a changing domestic context. Two resource development processes were identified in internationalizing firms as TT moved from a closed (promoter, entrepreneur) to open (facilitator, architect) domestic environment: (1) an evolutionary shift in resource profile composition, (2) a co-evolutionary change in resource development modes.

Evolutionary Resource Shift in Internationalizing Firms

Resource development has been conceptualized as an emergent process (March, 1991, p. 29) in which resources and relationships interact to create system-specific properties. Within a given industry cluster, similar capabilities can emerge as organizations not only manage their own resources but also imitate and counter the capabilities of competitors (Lampel & Shamsie, 2003). Over time, manufacturing exporters evolved from property resource led single site facilities to knowledge resource led dispersed production networks. For exporters that started in the first two eras (promoter and entrepreneur), firms required a license (DPBR) to begin operation due to the closed economy. Organizations then were able to acquire other property resources such as equipment or technology licenses through inward internationalization. Knowledge resources such as skills were then developed afterward within the firm.

However, more recently, accumulating country experience in manufacturing and increasingly accessible foreign suppliers have encouraged exporters to shift from property based to knowledge as the critical components of their initial resource profiles. SC and STE were based around local production expertise, with complementary resources being acquired afterward. Exporters currently acquire components from the Far East (OF, TTE), designs from Latin America (OF) or kits from Europe (CCU). These supplier relationships have enabled firms to lower costs by reducing the domestic labour content. In addition, they allow firms to focus on customization/localization demands of sustaining a presence in regional markets that require investments in marketing and product development. Finally, they enable access to technology resources that are not available locally, such as high end furniture designs.

Co-Evolutionary Changes in Resource Development Modes

While environmental change can affect the configuration of organizations or organizational evolution, organizations and environments may also adapt to each other or co-evolution (Rivkin & Siggelkow, 2003). While improvements in the country skill base through education and training helped reduce resource deficiencies, organizations also built experience and improved their understanding of the production requirements in the domestic environment (Sarasvathy, 2001).

TT's firms' development reflected this co-evolutionary process. In the early, closed economic era, firms utilized external resources at start-up, but subsequent development was internal. Later, as the environment opened, accumulated experience in production enabled more sophisticated use of externally available resources. Firms were able to utilize supplier knowledge to not only develop locally but also enter international markets. Past work with European SMEs identified four modes of resource development: firm driven internal, firm driven external, network driven internal and network driven external (Ahokangas, 1998). An additional mode was uncovered in this study, firm driven environmental resource development. Exporters attempted to use lobbying to either secure additional resources (OF) or shape the competitive landscape (CCUM). The latter was successful in introducing product standards that limited domestic competition in the early stages of their development. This change in local conditions spurred by a local organization can be seen as a co evolutionary development of the domestic environment.

Synthesis: Internationalization Model

Resource development processes are by their nature non-deterministic (Buchanan & Vanberg, 1991) and hence enable varied development paths. An analysis of TT exporters' internationalization paths reveals incidences of both incremental, life cycle like the U Model and teleological internationalization akin to Born Globals. Life cycle theories such as the U Model suggests a firm driven internal incremental resource development process as firms experiment with external markets, adjusting resource profiles after experience is accumulated, resulting in an incremental resource development path. Constrained by the closed environment, early expansion by TT firms was similarly incremental. After obtaining a license, firms acquired technology to build domestic manufacturing enterprises. Initial internationalization to CARICOM occurred to deploy excess capacity in regional markets (Path 1). Further expansion occurred after experimentation was proven to be successful. Opening of the TT environment and fluctuating oil prices introduced uncertainty (Knight, 1921) as competition from imports and demand variation increased.

An open economy along with export support in the facilitator and architect eras saw more diverse patterns of development. Rapid extra regional expansion (Path 2) was observed in TTW and CCUM. Alignment of resource profiles and market requirements also resulted in de-internationalization

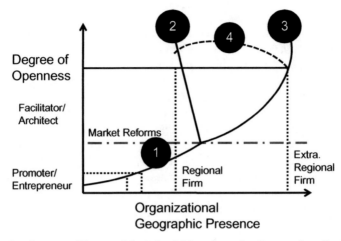

Fig. 2.   Stages to Phases of Sustained Manufacturing Internationalization.

(Path 3) in OF. For SMEs, the growth rate of domestic markets helps set benchmarks for firm growth and profitability (Bradburd & Caves, 1982). Research on exporters from New Zealand (Chetty & Holm, 2000) revealed that firms experienced a 'gusher' or a period of rapid growth when entering extra regional markets. OF encountered the opposite: a rapid increase in demand in markets closer to home, encouraging firms to change their strategies from export expansion to local exploitation (Elango, 1998). Overall, TT firm's development over time indicated that instead of a 'stage' process, small state internationalization can be viewed as a 'phase' process in which multiple 'states' of internationalization: forward, incremental, reverse, can exist simultaneously. This process is visualized in Fig. 2.

DISCUSSION AND CONCLUSION: SHIFTING COUNTRY-SPECIFIC ADVANTAGES AND INTERNATIONALIZATION

Past internationalization research has taken the environment as a fixed constraint and emphasis has been placed on identifying fixed country advantages or disadvantages and identifying strategies to overcome them (Zou & Stan, 1998). This chapter examined the internationalization process of firms from countries with shifting country-specific advantages. By modelling firms as heterogeneous resource combinations, the RBV was a useful way of opening the 'black box' of organizations (Sirmon, 2007), capturing internal changes over time. Overall, this approach enabled the reconceptualization of internationalization as an interactive process in which firm and environment act and are acted upon (Rivkin & Siggelkow, 2003).

The findings of this research contribute to the network theory of internationalization (Johanson & Vahlne, 2003). While the effect of country level network structures have been (Chetty & Holm, 2000) captured in previous research, the 'phase' model illustrates the effect of changing network access. As access to complementary resources increased, firms adopted network strategies involving suppliers or state agencies to both enter markets and improve internal operations. With accumulated experience, the latter strategy saw firms building customer and supplier networks around product standards to change the domestic environment. This research also suggests that initial commitment to internationalization is not a prerequisite for rapid growth (Oviatt & McDougall, 1994). Initially conceptualized as a domestic organization, CCUM entered markets within the time period specified for Born Globals (Moen & Servais, 2002) through supplier encouragement.

For owners or managers of these organizations in SDCs, this research can provide some useful guidance. Since learning from suppliers has played a critical role in the establishment and upgrading of TT exporters, organizations seeking to expand from SDCs can consider an extended period of inward internationalization with a high-end product. In this way, domestic operations through interaction with a high-quality supply network. For this process, opportunities for initiating relationships can be generated through attendance at international conferences or trade shows. Organizations should also not discount the possibility of proactively influencing the domestic environment as early adoption of technical standards may also aid resource development efforts. The relationships and resources created around adopting these standards can also support subsequent internationalization to other emerging markets.

REFERENCES

Ahokangas, P. (1998). Internationalization and resources: An analysis of processes in Nordic SMSs. Ph.D. thesis, *Management and Organization*, Universitas Wasaensis, Vaasa.

Andersen, O. (1997). Internationalisation and market entry mode: A review of theories and conceptual frameworks. *Management International Review, 2,* 27–42.

Baldacchino, G. (2005). Island entrepreneurs: Insights from exceptionally successful knowledge-driven SMEs from 5 European island territories. *Journal of Enterprising Cultures, 13*(2), 1–32.

Barclay, L. A. (2007). Can domestically owned manufacturing firms of small developing countries compete in a liberalized trading environment. In: G. Benito & R. Narula (Eds), *Multinationals on the periphery* (pp. 25–48). Houndsmills, Basingstoke: Palgrave MacMillan.

Barney, J. (1991). Firm resources and sustained competitive advantage. *Journal of Management, 17*(1), 99–121.

Belderbos, R. (1992). Large multinational enterprises based in a small economy: Effects on domestic investment. *Review of World Economics, 128*(3), 543–557.

Bell, J., McNaughton, R., & Young, S. (2001). 'Born-again global' firms: An extension to the 'born global' phenomenon. *Journal of International Management, 7*(3), 173–189.

Benito, G., & Welch, L. (1997). De-internationalization. *Management International Review, 37*(1), 7–25.

Benn, D., & Hall, K. (2006). *Production integration in Caricom.* Kingston: Ian Randle Publishers.

Bijmolt, T., & Zwart, P. (1994). Impact of internal factors on the export success of Dutch small and medium sized firms. *Journal of Small Business Management, 32*(2), 69–84.

Bilkey, W., & Tesar, G. (1977). The export behaviour of smaller Wisconsin manufacturing firms. *Journal of International Business Studies, 9*(Spring/Summer), 7.

Bradburd, R. M., & Caves, R. E. (1982). A closer look at the effect of market growth on industries' profits. *The Review of Economics and Statistics, 64*(4), 635–645.

Brautigam, D. A. (1994). What can Africa learn from Taiwan? Political economy, industrial policy, and adjustment. *The Journal of Modern African Studies, 32*(1), 111–138.

Buchanan, J. M., & Vanberg, V. J. (1991). The market as a creative process. *Economics and Philosophy, 7*(2), 167–186.

Buckley, P., & Casson, M. (1998). Analyzing foreign market entry strategies: Extending the internalization approach. *Journal of International Business Studies, 29*(3), 539–561.

Calof, J. C. (1994). The relationship between firm size and export behaviour revisited. *Journal of International Business Studies, 25*(2), 367–387.

Campa, J. M., & Guillaon, M. F. (1999). The internalization of exports: Firm- and location-specific factors in a middle-income country. *Management Science, 45*(11), 1463–1478.

Carrington, W. J., & Detragiache, E. (1998). *How big is the brain drain?* SSRN eLibrary, IMF Working Paper No. 98/102.

Chandler, A. D. (1962). *Strategy and structure: Chapters in the history of the American industrial enterprise.* Cambridge, MA: MIT Press.

Chandra, Y. (2007). Internationalization as an entrepreneurial process. Australian School of Business, University of New South Wales. PhD: 340.

Chetty, S., & Holm, D. B. (2000). Internationalisation of small to medium-sized manufacturing firms: A network approach. *International Business Review, 9*(1), 77–93.

Cook, I., & Harrison, M. (2003). Cross over food: Re-materializing postcolonial geographies. *Transactions of the Institute of British Geographers, 28*(3), 296–317.

Crowards, T. (2002). Defining the category of 'small' states. *Journal of International Development, 14*(2), 143–179.

Downes, A. S. (2004). Arthur Lewis and industrial development in the Caribbean: An assessment. The Lewis Model after 50 years: Assessing Sir Arthur Lewis' Contribution to Development Economics and Policy. University of Manchester, p. 32.

Dunning, J. (1977). Trade location of economic activity and the multinational enterprise: A search for an eclectic approach. In: B. Ohlin, P. Hesselborn & P. M. Wijkman (Eds), *The international allocation of economic activity: Proceedings of a Nobel symposium held at Stockholm.* London: Macmillan.

Dunning, J. (1988). The eclectic paradigm of international production: A restatement and some possible extensions. *Journal of International Business Studies, 19*(1), 1–31.

Dunning, J. (2001). Eclectic paradigm of international production, past, present and future. *International Journal of the Economics of Business, 8*(2), 173–190.

Easterly, W., & Kraay, A. (2000). Small states, small problems? Income, growth, and volatility in small states. *World Development, 28*(11), 2013–2027.

Eisenhardt, K. M. (1989). Building theories from case study research. *Academy of Management Review, 14*(4), 532–550.

Elango, B. (1998). An empirical examination of the influence of industry and firm drivers on the rate of internationalization by firms. *Journal of International Management, 4*(3), 201–221.

Etzkowitz, H., & Brisolla, S. N. (1999). Failure and success: The fate of industrial policy in Latin America and South East Asia. *Research Policy, 28*(4), 337–350.

Fletcher, R. (2001). A holistic approach to internationalisation. *International Business Review, 10*(1), 25–49.

Gabrielsson, M., Kirpalani, V. H. M., Dimitratos, P., Solberg, C. A., & Zucchella, A. (2008a). Born globals: Propositions to help advance the theory. *International Business Review, 17*(4), 385–402.

Gabrielsson, M., Kirpalani, V. H. M., Dimitratos, P., Solberg, C. A., & Zucchella, A. (2008b). Conceptualizations to advance born global definition: A research note. *Global Business Review, 9*(1), 45–51.

Garud, R., & Karnøe, P. (2003). Bricolage versus breakthrough: Distributed and embedded agency in technology entrepreneurship. *Research Policy, 32*(2), 277–300.

Hadley, R. D., & Wilson, H. I. M. (2003). The network model of internationalisation and experiential knowledge. *International Business Review, 12*(6), 697–717.

Hennart, J.-F. (1988). A transaction costs theory of equity joint ventures. *Strategic Management Journal, 9*(4), 361–374.

Hennart, J.-F. (2009). Down with MNE-centric theories! Market entry and expansion as the bundling of MNE and local assets. *Journal of International Business Studies, 40*(9), 1432–1454.

Henrikson, A. K. (1999). Small states in world politics conference on small states, St Lucia, February, p. 61.

Hymer, S. (1976). *The international operations of national firms.* Boston, MA: MIT Press.

Jessen, A., & Vignoles, C. (2004). Trinidad and Tobago: Trade performance and policy issues in an era of growing liberalization. Buenos Aires, IDB-INTAL, p. 77.

Johanson, J., & Mattson, L. G. (1988). Internationalisation in industrial systems: A network approach. In: N. Hood & J. Vahlne (Eds), *Strategies in global competition.* New York: Groom Helm.

Johanson, J., & Vahlne, J. E. (1977). The internationalization process of the firm – a model of knowledge development and increasing foreign market commitments. *Journal of International Business Studies, 8*(1), 23–32.

Johanson, J., & Vahlne, J. E. (2003). Business relationship learning and commitment in the internationalization process. *Journal of International Entrepreneurship, 1*(1), 83–101.

Jones, G., & Khanna, T. (2006). Bringing history (back) into international business. *Journal of International Business Studies, 37*(4), 453–468.

Jones, M. V., & Coviello, N. E. (2005). Internationalisation: Conceptualising an entrepreneurial process of behaviour in time. *Journal of International Business Studies, 36*(3), 284–303.

Klak, T. (1995). A framework for studying Caribbean industrial policy. *Economic Geography, 71*(3), 297–317.

Klinger, B. (2007). *Uncertainty in the search for new exports working paper*. Boston, Kennedy School of Government & Center for International Development Harvard University, p. 31.

Knight, F. H. (1921). *Risk, uncertainty and profit*. Boston, MA: Riverside Press.

Kogut, B., & Zander, U. (2003). Knowledge of the firm and the evolutionary theory of the multinational corporation. *Journal of Business Studies, 24*, 625–645.

Kumar, V., Kumar, U., & Persaud, A. (1999). Building technological capability through importing technology: The case of Indonesian manufacturing industry. *The Journal of Technology Transfer, 24*(1), 81–96.

Lampel, J., & Shamsie, J. (2003). Capabilities in motion: New organizational forms and the reshaping of the Hollywood movie industry. *Journal of Management Studies, 40*(2), 2189–2210.

Langley, A. (1999). Strategies for theorizing from process data. *Academy of Management Review, 24*(4), 19.

Lawrence, B. S. (1984). Historical perspective: Using the past to study the present. *Academy of Management Review, 9*(2), 307–312.

Lee, K. S., Lim, G. H., & Tan, S. J. (1999). Dealing with resource disadvantage: Generic strategies for SMEs. *Small Business Economics, 12*(4), 299–311.

Lenway, S. A., & Murtha, T. P. (1994). The state as strategist in international business research. *Journal of International Business Studies, 25*, 513–535.

Lewis, A. W. (1950). The industrialization of the British West Indies. *Caribbean Economic Review, 2*(May), 1–39.

Mahoney, J. T., & Pandian, J. R. (1992). The resource-based view within the conversation of strategic management. *Strategic Management Journal, 13*(5), 363–380.

Makhija, M., & Shenkar, O. (2004). National context and the metanational perspective in international strategy. In: T. Devinney, T. Pedersen & L. Tihanyi (Eds), *Advances in international management* (Vol. 16). Bingley, UK: Emerald.

March, J. G. (1991). Exploration and exploitation in organizational learning. *Organization Science, 2*(1), 71–87.

Mariotti, S., & Piscitello, L. (2001). Localized capabilities and the internationalization of manufacturing activities by SMEs. *Entrepreneurship and Regional Development, 13*(1), 65–80.

Markusen, J. R. (1995). The boundaries of multinational enterprises and the theory of international trade. *The Journal of Economic Perspectives, 9*(2), 169–189.

Mathews, J. (2006). Dragon multinationals: New players in 21st century globalization. *Asia Pacific Journal of Management, 23*(1), 5–27.

Mellander, E., Vredin, A., & Warne, A. (1992). Stochastic trends and economic fluctuations in a small open economy. *Journal of Applied Econometrics, 7*(4), 369–394.

Miller, D., & Shamsie, J. (1996). The resource-based view of the firm in two environments: The Hollywood Film Studios from 1936 to 1965. *The Academy of Management Journal, 39*(3), 519–543.

Moen, O., & Servais, P. (2002). Born global or gradual global? Examining the export behavior of small and medium-sized enterprises. *Journal of International Marketing*, *10*(3), 49–72.

Mottley, W. (2008). *Trinidad and Tobago Industrial Policy 1959–2008*. Kingston: Ian Randle Publications.

Murtha, T. P., & Lenway, S. A. (1994). Country capabilities and the strategic state: How national political institutions affect multinational corporations' strategies. *Strategic Management Journal*, *15*(S2), 113–129.

Narayanan, V. K., & Fahey, L. (2005). The relevance of the institutional underpinnings of Porter's five forces framework to emerging economies: An epistemological analysis. *Journal of Management Studies*, *42*(1), 207–225.

Noland, M., & Pack, H. (2002). Industrial policies and growth: Lessons from international experience. In: N. Loayza & R. Soto (Eds), *Economic growth: Sources, trends, and cycles* (p. 85). Santiago, Chile: Central Bank of Chile Papers.

North, D. C. (1990). *Institutions, institutional change, and economic performance*. Cambridge: Cambridge University Press.

Oviatt, B. M., & McDougall, P. P. (1994). Toward a theory of international new ventures. *Journal of International Business Studies*, *24*(1), 45–64.

Pantin, J. (2007). Labour shortage in Trinidad and Tobago. Trinidad and Tobago Manufacturers Association, pp. 1–28.

Pantin, D., Sandiford, W., & Henry, M. (2002). Cake, mama coca or? Alternatives facing the Caribbean banana industry. In: K. Nurse (Ed.), *Caribbean economies and global restructuring* (pp. 47–87). Kingston: Ian Randle Publications.

Patro, D. K., & Wald, J. K. (2005). Firm characteristics and the impact of emerging market liberalizations. *Journal of Banking and Finance*, *29*(7), 1671–1695.

Penrose, E. T. (1959). *The theory of the growth of the firm*. Oxford: Oxford University Press.

Peres, W. (2006). The slow comeback of industrial policies in Latin America and the Caribbean. *Cepal Review*, *88*(April), 67–83.

Pettigrew, A. M. (1997). What is a processual analysis?. *Scandinavian Journal of Management*, *13*(4), 337–348.

Pfeffer, J., & Salancik, G. R. (2003). *The external control of organizations – A resource dependence perspective*. Stanford: Stanford University Press.

Pollock, T. G. (2004). Constructing deal networks: Brokers as network "architects" in the US IPO market and other examples. *Academy of Management Review*, *29*(1), 50–72.

Ricardo, D. (1817). *On the principles of political economy and taxation*. London: John Murray.

Rivkin, J. W., & Siggelkow, N. (2003). Balancing search and stability: Interdependencies among elements organizational design. *Management Science*, *49*(3), 290–311.

Rodriguez Cano, C., Carrillat, F. A., & Jaramillo, F. (2004). A meta-analysis of the relationship between market orientation and business performance: Evidence from five continents. *International Journal of Research in Marketing*, *21*(2), 179–200.

Rodrik, D. (2000). Participatory politics, social cooperation, and economic stability. *The American Economic Review*, *90*(2), 140–144.

Rugman, A. M., & Verbeke, A. (2005). Towards a theory of regional multinationals: A transaction costs economics approach. *Management International Review*, *45*(1), 5–17.

Sarasvathy, S. D. (2001). Causation and effectuation: Toward a theoretical shift from economic inevitability to entrepreneurial contingency. *The Academy of Management Review*, *26*(2), 243–263.

Sirmon, D. G. (2007). Managing firm resources in dynamic environments to create value: Looking inside the black box. *Academy of Management Review, 32*(1), 273–292.

Tavares, A. T. (2002). Multinational subsidiary evolution and public policy: Two tales from the European periphery. *Journal of Industry, Competition and Trade, 2*(3), 195–213.

Voss, C., Tsikriktsis, N., & Frohlich, M. (2002). Case research in operations management. *International Journal of Operations & Production Management, 22*(2), 195–219.

Wan, P. W. (2005). Country resource environments, firm capabilities, and corporate diversification strategies. *Journal of Management Studies, 42*(1), 161–182.

Wang, L., & Zajac, E. J. (2007). Alliance or acquisition? A dyadic perspective on interfirm resource combinations. *Strategic Management Journal, 28*(13), 1291–1317.

Welch, L. S., & Luostarinen, R. (1988). Internationalization: Evolution of a concept. *Journal of General Management, 14*(2), 34–55.

Welch, L. S., & Luostarinen, R. (1993). Inward-outward connections in internationalization. *Journal of International Marketing, 9*(1), 44–57.

Will, W. M. (1991). A nation divided: The quest for Caribbean integration. *Latin American Research Review, 26*(2), 3–37.

Wint, A. G. (2003). *Competitiveness in small developing states: Insights from the Caribbean.* Kingston: University of the West Indies Press.

WorldBank. (2007). Defining a small economy. Available at http://go.worldbank.org/QLCDU7B8T0. Retrieved on February 2, 2011.

Yeung, H. W. (2002). *Entrepreneurship and internationalization of Asian firms: An institutional perspective.* Cheltenham, UK: Edward Elgar.

Zou, S. M., & Stan, S. (1998). The determinants of export performance: A review of the empirical literature between 1987 and 1997. *International Marketing Review, 15*(5), 333–356.

APPENDIX. MULTIPLE CASE STUDY DATA COLLECTION

Initial Interview

1. Key decision maker in the firm
   Name
   Function
   - Owners
   - Founders
   - Chief executive/managing director
   - Senior manager
2. Identify key events in company's history by policy period
   - Entrepreneur (1967–1986)
   - Facilitator (1987–2000)
   - Architect (2001 to present)

For each era
General:
1) Size of business
2) Industries served
3) Number of employees
4) International activity
5) Ratio of international sales
6) Number of international markets
7) Motives for seeking international activity
8) Type of international activity undertaken
9) Modes employed
Supporting documents for review
Brochures, products, photos, newspaper clippings, annual report

Second Interview

Resources identified in events in each period

- DPBR
- SPBR
- DKBR
- SKBR

Review with respondent:

1) Reason for resource acquisition(provide details)
   - Internal requirement?
   - Legal/statory requirement?
   - Local customer requirement?
   - Foreign customer requirement?
   - Which country?
2) Source of resource/mode of resource adjustment(internal/external)
   - Was it developed or acquired?
   - What was the involvement of other companies?
   - What was the involvement of state agencies or institutions?

WHAT LIES BENEATH THE INTERNATIONALIZATION OF FIRMS IN A REGIONAL INNOVATION SYSTEM?

Silvia R. Sedita, Fiorenza Belussi and Gianluca Fiscato

ABSTRACT

The aim of the chapter is to identify the internationalization models of SME industrial district firms within a very integrated and dynamic Regional Innovation System (RIS) of Italy. By doing so, we investigate which are the strategies of firms embedded in a RIS to access global suppliers and markets. Accordingly, this chapter explores the role of SMEs firms' dynamic capabilities, its linkage with the industry investments in ICT (information and communication technologies) and the impact of the utilization of regional knowledge intensive business services (KIBS) in shaping the degree of internationalization of local firms.

The analysis is based on a survey addressed during 2004 to entrepreneurs or managers of a sample of 125 SMEs firms operating in 7 industrial districts (biomedical, ceramics, shipbuilding, footwear, textile, plastics and packaging) of the Emilia Romagna.

Dynamics of Globalization: Location-Specific Advantages or Liabilities of Foreignness?
Advances in International Management, Volume 24, 299–326
ISSN: 1571-5027/doi:10.1108/S1571-5027(2011)0000024019

The results coming from a structural equation model revealed factors that impact on firms' degree of internationalization in the input (relocalization of foreign purchases through global value chains) and in the output dimension (export sales). Some interesting insights on what lies beneath the internationalization of firms in a very dynamic regional innovation system like that one of Emilia Romagna are provided.

INTRODUCTION

The aim of the chapter is to identify the most efficient internationalization strategies of SMEs firms belonging to various industrial districts localized in a particularly dynamic Regional Innovation System (RIS) like that one of the Emilia Romagna, one of the most affluent and industrialized regions of Italy. By doing so, we investigate which are the strategies adopted by SMEs industrial district firms to access global suppliers and to enter into foreign markets. Our analysis has selected three important elements that could be considered potentially ideal explanatory factors in influencing the degree of internationalization of local SMEs: the presence of firms' specific dynamic capabilities, the presence of a high (sectoral) level of investment in Information and Communication Technologies (ICT) and the recourse of district SMEs to external regionally based consultants, thus to regional Knowledge Intensive Business Service (KIBS).

Several recent studies tackled the importance for firms to be open, establishing global production or research networks. Internationalization strategies appear as positively associated with higher competitiveness, both related to cost reduction (through outsourcing of less strategic activities to low labor cost countries) and knowledge procurement strategies (through R&D agreements or research collaborations with advanced partners). The development of dense relationships with other actors (such as suppliers of intermediary goods, clients and customers, competitors, universities and research institutes) located in the proximity of the district or outside appears to be a key factor to manage the uncertainty generated by the innovative pressure and by the global competition. Traditionally, it is acknowledged that SMEs suffer for the liability of foreignness and they are constrained by resource poverty. However, the fact that SMEs do not work in isolation but they belong to highly connected industrial systems, like the Italian industrial districts, could in principle moderate the negative impact of the small size in preventing the path towards the internationalization. The same could be hypothesized as regards the positive impact of an existing dynamic regional innovation system. Although, traditionally, small firms do not find many innovation sources internally, or they lack the resources to invest in in-house innovation search, the existence of many knowledgeable local-regional technical knowledge suppliers in the region could facilitate the access and incorporation of new knowledge inputs into the SMEs production cycle. Accordingly, firms belonging to industrial districts operating into a dynamic RIS could overcome the economical barriers that prevent them to develop abroad, and to reach high degrees of internationalization. Few contributions shed light on the factors that are more likely to be linked with a high degree of internationalization both in the input (recourse to foreign suppliers) and in the output (exports) dimension. The chapter fills this gap exploring the strategies which are more likely to impact positively on internationalization. Considering the factors that we selected as being important in pushing forwards this process, we question if is it the firms' dynamic capabilities alone, is the industry ICT intensity, is the strong role of regional KIBS, or is a combination of them that more efficiently sustain the degree of internationalization?

The analysis is based on a survey addressed during 2004 to entrepreneurs or managers of a sample of 125 firms operating in 7 Emilia Romagna industrial districts (biomedical, ceramics, shipbuilding, footwear, textile, plastics and packaging). The results coming from a structural equation model confirmed the importance of the selected factors in having an impact on firms' internationalization.

The chapter proceeds as follows. Firstly, it illustrates the theoretical background, and puts forward three testable hypotheses. Secondly, it describes the methodology applied and the empirical evidences. Finally, some conclusive remarks are proposed.

THEORY AND HYPOTHESES

Dynamic Capabilities and Internationalization Strategies

In this section the role of firm specific dynamic capabilities in the determination of firms' internationalization performances is investigated. This approach captures the antecedent learning and knowledge building processes that precede internationalization (Uppsala model that explains how the internationalization process begins, Andersen, 1993). Scholars have examined the role of firm variables, such as international entrepreneurial

orientation and market knowledge, to conceptualize the firm internationalization process, with a specific focus on the global born firm phenomenon
(Oviatt & McDougall, 2005). In particular, the international entrepreneurial
orientation of the founders was not only considered important (Knight &
Cavusgil, 2004; Oviatt & McDougall, 1997) but also the entrepreneur-
manager's prior international experience (Zahra, Ireland, & Hitt, 2000;
Autio & Sapienza, 2000). The liability of foreigners (Zaheer, 1995) is
moderated by age, managerial experience and resource fungibility. Other
contributions have underlined the drivers beneath the success of the
firm internationalization strategies: availability of specific resources
(Cuervo-Cazurra, Maloney, & Manrakhan, 2007), ability to implement
firm diversification and concentration strategies (Saarenketo, Puumalainen,
Kyläheiko, & Kuivalainen, 2008), resources-base versatility, accumulated
expertise and network dependence (Tuppura, Saarenketo, Puumalainen,
Jantunen, & Kyläheiko, 2008). It has been suggested that prior business
experience leads to greater absorptive capacity in the firm (Cohen &
Levinthal, 1990) and thus, this brings additional knowledge that accelerates
market entry. However, both these perspectives are static. They fail to
capture the whole knowledge acquisition processes and changes in attitudes.
The incompleteness of these conceptualizations points to the need for a
stronger conceptualization that incorporates a more comprehensive understanding of knowledge, as provided by a dynamic capabilities framework
(Teece, Pisano, & Shuen, 1997; Zollo & Winter, 2002). We argue that
innovation needs to be centrally located in any comprehensive attempt to
model internationalization, regardless of the nature of the industry in which
the firm competes. For this reason we think that this approach may also be
applied in the case of the analysis of the internationalization process of
SMEs district firms.

The concept of capabilities is rooted on the evolutionary economics
approach, which emphasizes knowledge creation, variety and selection.
Nelson and Winter (1982) defined capabilities as 'the nature and sources of
continuity in the behavioural patterns of an individual organization' (p. 96),
in other words as 'routine' or 'program', which 'refer to a repetitive pattern of
activity in an entire organization' or to 'an individual skill'. In their
conceptualization routines are knowledge repertoire, a set of skills that a
particular member of the organization can use in order to perform a task
avoiding costly and time consuming decision processes. A crucial aspect is the
ability to choose the appropriate routine and when to perform it (Nelson,
1992, 1994). Blueprints are only a small part of what is needed to be stored in
the organizational memory of a firm, to reproduce and replicate a task

effectively. Innovation occurs in the Nelson and Winter framework, when the process of searching and exploring ends up with a change in routines (p. 128). 'Routine' is an ambiguous surrogate for capabilities because it is an executable program for repeated performance in some selected context learned by an organization in response to selective pressure, whereas the concept of capabilities refers to the organizational knowledge that lies behind the executed performance (Loasby, 1999). The concept of capabilities is strictly related to the firm strategic behaviour and to the entrepreneurial imagination (Augier & Teece, 2008; Witt, 1996). Capabilities have a cumulative nature and they are path-dependent. In other words, firms may be victims of their past history, become inertial, and experiment lock-in effects (a successful organization will tend to conserve its capability even if the context would require some adjustment or replacement – Fransman, 1994). In order to develop their capabilities, firms invest in knowledge and in the development of new technology through R&D and innovation search processing of exploration and exploitation (Cohen & Levinthal, 1990).

Dynamic capabilities (Teece et al., 1997) are the antecedent organisational and strategic routines by which managers alter their firms' resource base through acquiring, shedding, integrating and recombining resources to generate 'fresh value-creating strategies that cannot be easily duplicated by competing firms' (Eisenhardt & Martin, 2000, p. 1105). The dynamic capabilities view (Weerawardena, Sullivan Mort, Liesch, & Knight, 2007) has evolved from the static resource-based view (RBV) of competitive strategy. It provides a theoretical foundation to capture the evolution of these capabilities. The RBV suggests that firms in the same industry perform differently because they differ in their resources and capabilities (e.g. Wernerfelt, 1984). However, the dynamic capabilities view suggests distinguishing capabilities from resource. Competences and capabilities are assets that typically must be built by firms because they cannot be bought. Dynamic capabilities (Zollo & Winter, 2002) are also connected to organizational learning (Argyris & Schön, 1978; Levitt & March, 1988). Organizational learning is viewed as routine-based, history-dependent and target-oriented. Firms must learn from multiple sources, and that knowledge results from various learning processes. Organizational learning is therefore connected to investment in related complementarities (Teece, 1987, 1989). Researchers have argued that storing new knowledge and using stored knowledge are key components of organizational learning, and they have investigated the tools (or social mechanisms) used by firms as memory systems, like social networks, ICT intranet, electronic bulletins and knowledge centres (Olivera, 2000).

Dynamic capabilities also reflect the ability of firms to 'create, extend, or modify' their knowledge base in order to respond to changing technologies and markets. We build on the definition given by Zollo and Winter (2002), who identify dynamic capabilities as the organizational collective activity of generating and modifying operating routines through the exploitation of learning mechanisms. Accordingly, firm strategic decision making is the result of internal knowledge creation process (Eisenhardt & Martin, 2000).

Scattered contributions have explored the relationships between the firm-specific dynamic capabilities and the entry timing in new markets (Lee, 2008), both in terms of product innovation and internationalization. The relevance of dynamic capabilities as a determinant of internationalization strategies has been recently discussed by Petersen, Pedersen, and Sharma (2003) and Sapienza, Autio, George, and Zahra (2006), who have proved that an early internationalization strategy can be triggered by the prompt adjustment of the firm resources configuration to support the cross border activity. A co-evolution pattern between internationalization and dynamic capabilities has been discussed (Pajunen & Maunula, 2008).

Aligning with the finding of this brief theoretical review, the first hypothesis is put forward.

Hypothesis 1. The firm specific dynamic capabilities of acquiring, creating and transferring knowledge assets impact positively and significantly to the degree of internationalization of industrial districts SMEs.

Regional Innovation Systems (RIS) and Knowledge Intensive Business Services (KIBS): Their Influence on the Internationalization Strategies of SMEs

RIS is one of the most influential concepts developed in the context of regional science studies, which has grown rapidly since the middle of the 1990s (Asheim, Isaksen, Nauwelaers, & Tödtling, 2003; Braczyk, Cooke, & Heidenreich, 1998; De la Mothe & Paquet, 1998; Howells, 1999; Cooke, Uranga, & Etxebarria, 1997; Tödtling & Trippl, 2005). The notion of RIS lies on the crossroads of two main bodies of literature: evolutionary theories of economic and technical change, which conceptualize innovation as the result of complex, non-linear social processes, stimulated and nurtured by several actors and factors within and outside the firm (Freeman, 1995; Edquist, 1997), and theories of regionalization and clustering, which emphasize that economic growth and innovation do not take place in abstract spaces, but are locally rooted, in industrial districts (Becattini, Bellandi, & De Propis, 2009) or, more generally in clusters (Porter, 1998; Cooke, 2002), thanks to the advantages of spatial proximity, social embeddedness, interaction with local institutions and knowledge spillovers (Camagni, 1991; Maskell & Malmberg, 1999; Storper, 1997). As Asheim and Gertler (2005) pointed out: regional innovation systems are not sufficient on their own to remain competitive in a globalizing economy. Local firms have therefore some incentives to access also national and supra national innovation systems. This line of reasoning is followed to a point where the regional innovation system expands beyond its own boundaries through a process of economic integration and globalization. External linkages with customers and clients in international markets are crucial to the commercial success of innovative new products (Coenen, Moodysson, & Asheim, 2004; Asheim & Isaksen, 2002; Archibugi & Michie, 1997; Carlsson, 2006). Access to knowledge flows can occur around nodes of excellence interconnected by global networks (Feldman, 2004; Cooke, 2004). Doloreux (2004) investigated empirically the dimension of distant knowledge flows in a RIS, providing evidence that in the Ottawa and Beauce regions of Canada 'firms rely as much on external networks of customers and suppliers, as those based in their own region' (Doloreux, 2004, p. 491).

Autio (1998) illustrates RIS as composed by two interdependent sub-systems embedded in a common regional socioeconomic and cultural setting. The industry sub-system, which includes the companies, their clients, suppliers and competitors, and the institutional sub-system, which consists of various institutions that are engaged in the production and diffusion of knowledge and skills such as public research institutions, technology mediating organizations, universities and other educational institutions. Key actors of the institutional sub-system are KIBS. KIBS may be defined as 'consultancy' firms in a broad sense (Miles, 2005); more generally 'KIBS can be described as firms performing, mainly for other firms, services encompassing a high intellectual value-added' (Muller, 2001, p. 2). KIBS provide customized problem solving assistance to their clients, through tacit and codified knowledge exchange. Besides, KIBS play a two-fold role, acting as external knowledge source for their client firms and introducing internal innovations (Den Hertog, 2000; Miles, 2005; Toivonen, 2004; Muller & Zenker, 2001; Wood, 2005). It has been observed that the interactions between KIBS and local small firms stimulate the generation and diffusion of knowledge within a regional innovation system (Muller & Zenker, 2001). Considering the importance of long distance collaborations for the innovation process, we expect also to find that the more the firm relies on KIBS, the more it embarks in interactions with distant clients and suppliers. Wood (2006, p. 53) maintains, in fact, that the quality of KIBS depends on the access they offer to national and international sources of innovation. This is particularly true for SMEs, which often do not have the strength to face autonomously international business relationships. Interactions with KIBS are for them the best way to stay competitive through market internationalization and FDI. KIBS work as gatekeepers of knowledge which is further distributed within the regional system (Cheng & Yu, 2008).

Therefore we add on this debate by putting forward our second hypothesis.

Hypothesis 2. The use of KIBS for industrial district SMEs in a dynamic RIS impacts positively and significantly to the degree of internationalization.

Investments in Information and Communication Technology (ICT) Evaluated at Industry Level and Their Impact on Internationalization Strategies

Many authors (Gilmore & Pine, 2000; Weill & Vitale, 2001; Pilat, 2003) argue that ICTs have given to small firms new ways to communicate and coordinate over short and long distances. Accordingly, the use of web-based technologies are an opportunity to build and maintain an international competitive advantage (Eid, Trueman, & Ahmed, 2002; Hamill & Gregory, 1997; Poon & Jevons, 1997). Indeed, a positive correlation between Internet access and a firm's market potential is claimed by many authors (Samiee, 1998; Porter, 2001; Piscitello & Sgobbi, 2004; Loane, Bell, & Deans, 2007; OECD, 2004a; Hamill & Gregory, 1997; Bennett, 1997, 1998; Etemad & El Trash, 2003). The availability of low cost Internet access is particularly important for SMEs, which have now the opportunity to acquire and exchange information be competitive internationally at a rather low cost. These technologies, in fact, reduce the liabilities of foreignness, lowering marketing and communication costs. ICTs indeed allow the establishment of contacts with distant clients and suppliers (Huber, 1990; Coltman, Devinney, Latukefu, & Midgley, 1999), allowing SMEs to overcome the limitation of their small size, helping them to approach successfully new and larger markets, regardless of the industry they belong to (Austrade, 2002). Some detailed empirical studies offered uncontroversial evidence. Raymond,

Bergeron, and Blili (2005), in a survey on manufacturing SMEs in Canada, found that the use of e-business explains the 5% of their export performance. Lal (2002, 2004), studying the Indian textile industry, found a positive correlation between IT adoption and export performance. However, other research works have denied the existence of a close relationship between ICT adoption and export performance. For instance, some international studies have underlined (OECD, 2004a, 2004b; Schreyer, 1996; Sakai, 2002) that SMEs represent more than 50% of national GDP-and 60% of employment-but they contribute only between one quarter and one third of manufactured exports. In addition to that, as discussed by Mata, Fuerst and Barney (1995), the concept of IT as a powerful competitive weapon, despite the fact that it has been strongly emphasized in the literature, is still not well-explained. ICT investment can be very risky and the performance of ICT application might be at the beginning over-valued, ICT proprietary technologies can be copied from competitors, technical IT skills rapidly diffuse in the environment. Thus, for the authors only managerial ICT skills might perhaps be sources of sustained competitiveness in firms. All things considered, in order to shed light on this dozy issue we put forward our third hypothesis.

Hypothesis 3. The use and investments in ICT impact positively and significantly on the degree of internationalization of industrial district SMEs.

DATA AND METHODS

The Sample

During 2004 we conducted a survey on a set of small and medium industrial district final firms[1] in the Emilia Romagna region, operating in sectors characterized by diverse technology intensity and degree of competitiveness. According to Cooke and Morgan (1998), a strict reading of the literature would suggest that only three regions in the world can be considered true regional innovation systems: Silicon Valley, Emilia-Romagna and Baden-Württemberg. Moreover, other previous works provided empirical findings which allow us to treat this particular region as a regional innovation system (Belussi, Sammarra, & Sedita, 2008). Broadly speaking, we selected a significant pool of firms located in various Emilia Romagna industrial districts in order to illustrate the knowledge access strategy of firms in a context of internationalization. The firms, operating in diverse industries, belong to the following 7 districts: the biomedical district of Mirandola (18 firms), the ceramics district of Sassuolo (29 firms), the footwear district of San Mauro Pascoli (18 firms), the packaging district of Val d'Enza (13 firms), the plastics district of Correggio (10 firms), the shipbuilding district located along the High Adriatic coast (17 firms) and the textile district of Carpi (20 firms). We decided to exclude by the sample the larger leading firms, to focus our attention to the median firm of our sample, and thus to the more interesting cases of non-leading firms, which might manifest (or not) a large propensity towards internationalization.

The snowball sampling method was selected to draw our sample of firms. According to Atkinson and Flint (2001) snowball sampling can be applied as a formal methodology for making inferences about hidden and/or hard-to-reach populations. Snowball method begins considering a small amount of actors. The initial set of actors was chosen selecting for each cluster the top 10 firms, (in terms of size, age and turnover) excluding the few well-known local leaders. The choice was supported by suggestions provided by local policy makers and trade associations. The sample was then created by asking every respondent the name of one or more players who might be inserted in the study, because considered relevant to increase the understanding of the district dynamics. This process is based on the assumption that exist a link between the initial sample and the target population (Berg, 1988). The process stopped when the sample covered all the final firms of the district, the snowball method has problems of representativeness, due to selection process of initial set (Atkinson & Flint, 2001). The size of the sample for every cluster solves these problems.

Table 1 shows some descriptive statistics for our firms: they are mainly medium size (more than 69 employees) and mature (about 20 years old) firms. Furthermore, the analysis reveals differences between districts in

Table 1. Description of the Sample by Cluster.

	N	Size	Sales (Mln Euro)	Age
Biomedical cluster	18	25.94	1.71	13.00
Footwear cluster	18	58.61	9.44	17.94
Ceramic cluster	29	132.66	27.96	22.28
Shipbuilding cluster	17	23.53	7.98	16.71
Packaging cluster	13	33.08	7.98	23.77
Plastics cluster	10	210.50	31.90	34.10
Textile cluster	20	18.60	3.36	18.78

terms of size, sales and age of the firms. The average size ranges from 19 employees in the textile district of Carpi to 210 in the plastics cluster of Correggio. The oldest firms are located in the plastics district of Correggio (34 years old), whereas the youngest ones belong to the biomedical district of Mirandola (13 years old). In term of sales the best result, on average, comes from the plastics district of Correggio (27.96 mln euro) and the worst comes from the biomedical district (1.71 mln euro). Table 2 shows a grouping breakdown of the principle variables utilized in our analysis. We calculated the average value by district firm of the items referred to internationalization, presence of dynamic capabilities, use of ICT and utilization of technological intensive business services (KIBS), as presented in Appendix B.

All firms operating in the footwear and textile districts are low-tech. The great majority (more than 85%) of ceramics, plastics and shipbuilding district firms are medium-tech. In the biomedical and packaging districts it is possible to find both medium (70%) and low-tech (30%) firms.

Firms differ according to size, sales, age as well as industry belonging, giving rise to a heterogeneous sample where to test properly our hypotheses. Data were collected on the basis of a questionnaire, which was kept relatively short in order to obtain a high response rate. It was formed by two parts. The first part contained self-explicatory questions, and was sent by e-mail.[2] It was oriented to collect structural information, such as the contact details, the prevalent economic activities (ATECO codes), sales, age and size of the firm,[3] the level of industry competitiveness, the percentage of export

Table 2.   Average Variables' Value by District.

Variables	Biomedical	Ceramic	Shipbuilding	Packaging	Plastic	Textile	Footware	Total
ES	30,929	63,556	58,750	54,667	54,500	69,588	66,583	56,939
FP	23,571	33,778	78,750	26,833	55,000	66,647	47,500	47,440
DC1	2,643	2,889	1,875	2,750	2,250	1,941	2,417	2,395
DC2	2,571	2,148	1,750	2,000	2,000	1,353	2,000	1,975
DC3	2,000	2,556	1,125	2,083	2,000	1,412	1,500	1,811
ICT1	3,000	3,778	2,375	3,583	3,500	3,176	2,917	3,190
ICT2	3,143	3,815	2,375	2,583	3,750	3,294	3,750	3,244
ICT3	2,357	3,000	2,750	2,917	3,667	2,941	2,750	2,912
ICT4	2,357	3,692	2,500	2,833	3,750	3,118	2,667	2,988
TK1	2,286	3,269	3,714	3,100	3,750	2,941	2,778	3,120
TK2	2,286	4,148	2,750	3,250	3,000	2,824	2,364	2,946
TK3	2,000	2,500	2,000	2,889	2,333	2,412	2,583	2,388

sales and purchases by foreign suppliers. The second part, which contained more complex items, was delivered through face to face interviews to firms' entrepreneurs or managers. It was structured into three sub-parts: (1) Relevance and type of links with external actors of the Emilia Romagna the regional system, (2) Assessment of the ICT sectoral average utilization, (3) Assessment of firm's specificity in knowledge management procedures and in product development strategies. The items belonging to the second part were measured on a five-point Likert-type scale, ranging from 'absolutely non–important' to 'remarkably important'. Although the first draft of the questionnaire was based on existing literature, the final version derived by discussing each item with academics and practitioners operating in the field, and consequently testing it in a pilot study. During the snowball process we contacted by telephone 300 enterprises and sent by e-mail the first part of the questionnaire. A total number of 125 questionnaires were returned by the firms that were subsequently interviewed on the second part of the questionnaire.

Structural Equation Model

Structural equation modelling (SEM) grows out of and serves purposes similar to multiple regression, but in a more powerful way, which takes into account the modelling of interactions, nonlinearities, correlated independents, measurement error, correlated error terms, multiple latent independents each measured by multiple indicators and one or more latent dependents also each with multiple indicators. SEM allows for the simultaneous estimation of the 'cause and effect' relationships between the exogenous variables, and the various levels of the endogenous variables (Steensma & Lyles, 2000). In addition, it provides also more refined measures of latent constructs, which are measured with multiple observed variables.

The structural equation modelling process centres around two steps: validating a proposed measurement model developed on the basis of theory and fitting the structural model. In our work the former was accomplished through confirmatory factor analysis[4]: each variable in the model is conceptualized as a latent one, measured by multiple indicators. The objective of this first step is to establish how well the indicators measure the corresponding latent variables. Fig. 1 shows the structural theoretical model that we further estimated. The hypothesized model (Fig. 1) consisted of ten exogenous (independent) variables and two endogenous (dependent)

T-KIBS: Technological KIBS   ICT: Importance and use of ICT   DC: Dynamic Capabilities

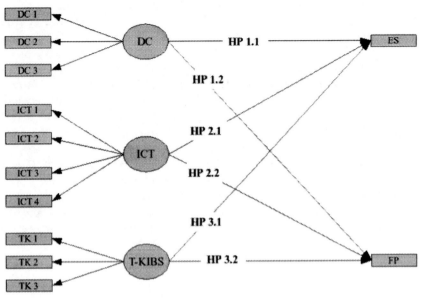

Fig. 1.   Proposed Model.

variables. Variables entered in the factor analysis are listed and described in Appendix C.

In order to test our hypotheses we estimated a path model using Measured Variable Path Analysis in LISREL 8.54 (Jöreskog & Sörbom, 2000), which allows for the estimation of the relative importance of alternative paths of influence, and also measures the direct and indirect effects that one variable has on another (Shook, Ketchen, Hult, & Kacmar, 2004). LISREL provides both an overall assessment of the fit of a hypothesized path model to the data and test of individual hypotheses.

Measures

In order to test the hypotheses, we developed a set of measures based on the items of the questionnaire (see Appendix A). The measures used are the following:

- *Dynamic capabilities.* Dynamic capabilities were measured with a three-item Lykert-type scale adapted from literature (Cohen & Levinthal, 1990).

The construct consists of four indicators: 'ability to manage the knowledge at firm level', 'importance of spontaneous learning at firm level' and 'importance of formal learning at firm level'.

- *Technological knowledge intensive business services.* Technological Knowledge Intensive Business Services was measured with a three-item Lykert-type scale adapted from literature (Miles, 2003, 2005). The construct consists of three indicators: 'availability and readiness to acquire technology process in the Region', 'availability and readiness to access to R&D facilities in the Region' and 'availability and readiness to access to IT related services in the Region'.
- *Use and investments in ICT.* The use and investments in ICT was measured with a four-item Lykert-type scale adapted from literature. The construct consists of four indicators: 'importance to use ICT technologies to connect with clients and suppliers at industry level', 'importance to invest in ICT for management purposes at industry level', 'importance to have developed an e-commerce strategy at industry level' and 'importance to invest in ICT to improve the network efficiency at industry level'.
- *Degree of internationalization.* It was captured by two indicators: export sales (measured as percentage of total sales) and foreign purchases (measured as percentage of total purchases). Both were rescaled as continuous variables ranging from 0 to 5.

Reliability Analysis

The prime consideration in selecting indicators is whether they are theoretically sound and reliably measured. Reliability indicates the extent to which different items, measures, or assessments are consistent with one another. Table 3 shows the Cronbach's alpha for all the variables. The alpha for the Dynamic Capabilities construct (DC1, DC2 and DC3) is only slightly lower than 0.60 the cut-off value suggested by Bagozzi and Yi (1988).[5] The alpha for ICT and T-KIBS constructs is above 0.60, which

Table 3. Reliability Analysis for Independent Variables.

	DC	ICT	TK
Cronbach's Alpha	0.592	0.770	0.629

indicates that the items form a scale with reasonable internal consistency reliability.

VALIDATION

Before discussing the tests of the specific hypotheses from the structural equation model, it is important to evaluate the overall fit of the theoretical model to the data. We assessed the overall fit of the model to the data using the Full Information Maximum Likelihood (FIML) method that is suitable for missing data and Root Mean Square Error of Approximation (RMSEA) (Jöreskog & Sörbom, 2000). The χ^2 statistic is oversensitive to sample size and it could suggest that a model does not adequately fit the data even when it fits. According to Kline (2005), in order to reduce the sensitivity of the χ^2 statistic to sample size, it is recommended to use the rule 'χ^2/df lower than 3' to decide the acceptability of the χ^2 value. The FIML χ^2 (47; $N = 125$) $= 63.10$ P $= 0.058$. FIML χ^2 divided by the degrees of freedom was 1.34, suggesting adequate fit of the model to the data. The RMSEA is 0.053 and the 90% confidence interval is from 0.0 to 0.084. The point estimate of RMSEA is slightly above 0.05 as well as the upper confidence limit is only slightly above the 0.08 value suggested by Browne and Cudeck (1993). These indexes suggest a reasonable fit of the model to the data. However, the objective of this study was not to achieve the 'better fitting' model, but rather to assess the relationships among the different latent variables.[6]

RESULTS

The means, standard deviations and correlations among all variables entered in the SEM model appear in Appendix C.

SEM results are presented in Fig. 2.

Let us start with some general comments. Our descriptive variables are presented in Table 2. The dependent variables included in the model ES and FP show that industrial districts SMEs of Emilia Romagna have reached a high degree of internationalization, both in terms of export flows (on average they export 56.9% of sales) and as propensity to interact with foreign suppliers and subcontractors (on average they declare a share of foreign purchases of 47.4% on total purchases). These positive results are largely spread in all district firms, with the minor exception of the

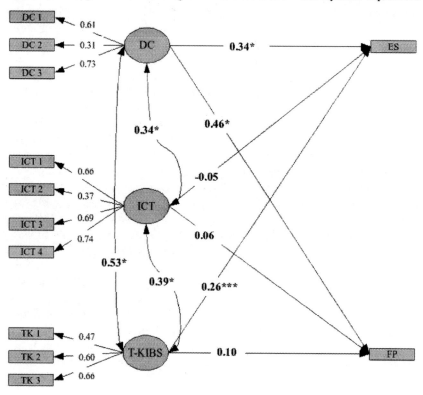

* p<0.01 ** p<0.05 *** p<0.1

Chi-Square=63,10 , df=47, P-value=0.05831, RMSEA=0.053

Fig. 2.   Path Coefficients for the Hypothesized Model.

biomedical district of Mirandola, where, however, the leading local firms (excluded by our sample), like Gambro, Baxter and Fresenius, are some of the largest global MNCs, and SMEs district firms deal with them interacting more at local level than on a global scale. The items referred to dynamic capabilities issues, on a 1–5 scale, score on average a not-too-high rank. However, improving the existing routines (2.4) appears higher than informal (2.0) or formal (1.8) learning. The recourse to dynamic capability appears to be lower in shipbuilding and in textile firms. The evaluation of firms about the spread of ICT among their competitors in their specific sectors is quite significant: it appears evident that we are witness, within the Italian districts, such as already emerged in others research works (Belussi, 2005), of an ample and intense process of technology diffusion, both to connect clients and suppliers (3.2), for management purposes (3.2), to improve network efficiency (3.0) and to deal with e-commerce (2.9). Also the use of technological KIBS emerges at the same time as widely diffused, both in terms of external technological acquisitions (3.1), access to R&D facilities (2.9), and access to ICT related services (2.4).

Let us turn to our structural equation model. Can we establish a theoretical link between the degree of internationalization and the independent variables above described? The advantage in using our LISREL methodology is related to the possibility of cluster our variables and to create some other latent aggregate variables, as proposed in Fig. 1. In addition to that we can also measure the interdependence among the latent variables as calculated in Fig. 2. In other words, we can try to disentangle the complex relationships between the use of ICT and the capabilities autonomously developed by the SMEs district firms. How exactly do the firm's (learning/dynamic) capabilities interact with the effect of ICT? Do firms with high capabilities gain higher benefits from ICT, or do high capabilities lead to high ICT?

Let us discuss Hypothesis 1. It predicts a positive impact of firm dynamic capabilities on the success of firm internationalization strategies. The results of SEM show that there is a significant positive correlation between the three factors we analyzed as determinants for internationalization strategies: firm dynamic capabilities, export and foreign purchases. Further-more, there is to note that the dynamic capabilities factor has the highest coefficient.

Hypothesis 2 predicts a positive correlation between the availability of regional technological KIBS and the success of internationalization strategies. Results show that regional technological KIBS impact signifi-cantly only on export performances and not on foreign purchases. Internationalization processes, in terms of ability to develop global supply chains or to acquire sophisticated technological inputs from suppliers are related to the building of firms –specific capabilities. They can not simply be acquired by intermediated service firms. KIBS, on the contrary, play a role in supporting export flows. Thus, more complex organizational forms of internationalizations require internal capabilities, while the capabilities to leverage export flows are more transactional, and can be bought on markets.

These results are in line with the findings of others contributions (Saarenketo et al., 2008).

Hypothesis 3 predicts a positive impact of ICT adoption on internationalization performance. The evidence reported in Fig. 2 point out that the tendency to invest on ICT does not significantly impact on the firm degree of internationalizations. This is probably because ICT investments are location-specific but not firm-specific, so they do not offer a distinguishable set of unique competitive advantages. This point of view supports the findings of Mata et al. (1995), while it is in slight contrast with the writing of Prashantham and Young, which seem to believe more on the unconditioned positive impact of ICT on firms' international performance (2004).

A striking result of our research is the evaluation of the combined effect of all tree factors/latent variables. In fact, a strong correlation between the three factors emerges in Fig. 2. Therefore, we can argue that dynamic capabilities appear a necessary condition for firms to lever on ICT intensity and to use productively the available knowledge and technology provided by KIBS in order to improve their internationalization performance.

In conclusion, among the three variables analyzed, the dynamic capabilities issue appears to be the most important factor, whereas regional T-KIBS and ICT adoption at industry level appear to play only a complementary, even if significant, role.

CONCLUSIONS

This study, empirically driven, has provided some interesting evidence on the role played by different factors in influencing the degree of internationalization of industrial district SMEs in a particularly dynamic regional innovation system. Internationalization processes were measured through two indicators: the propensity of firms to export and the use of foreign suppliers. Considering the small size of our firms we did not study the potential role of FDI. The empirical context chosen is the Emilia Romagna region of Italy, an appropriate empirical laboratory where to analyze the evolution of industrial district firms and they process of internationalization. Having chosen a significant sample, involving 125 final firms operating in 7 different low-tech and medium tech districts, we maintain that our results have a generalization power and they hold also for other Italian or European regions.

Our chapter offers an original contribution, based on the operationalization of the concept of dynamic capabilities (see Appendices A and B), together with the analysis of the location specific explanatory factors situated behind the internationalizations performance. Out of all factors examined, dynamic capabilities (linked to the existence of high levels of informal and formal learning and to the issue of the improvement of the existing routines) proved to be the most influential factor. ICT investments did not come out as a significant factor. However, when ICT investments are combined with a high level of internal dynamic capabilities, they create a synergic effect. The connections to technical KIBs located in the region appear positively linked with the degree of internationalization, but mainly they affect the export of firms (and less the extent of the use of foreign suppliers and subcontractors). However, regional technical KIBs in our investigation appear also a complementary asset for enhancing firm internal dynamic capabilities. Industrial district SMEs, which often do not possess enough internal resources to initiate a self-sustained pattern of competence building, can be supported in their development by external knowledgeable agents (external to the firm, internal to the regional innovation system), which activate positive externalities. Although our research attempted to make a significant contribution to the debate on the internationalization strategies of SMEs, there are some points in need of further investigation. First we acknowledge that our sample of firms limits our study only to one regional innovation system; a comparison between different RISs is desirable. Firms are clearly located within multi-level innovation systems, and for this reason it would be worth also addressing our analysis to national contexts. Moreover, our structural equation model investigates only some of the potential factors affecting the internationalization performance of industrial district SMEs. A larger sample of firms might allow exploring better the role of other factors. A final note is due to the collected information: our model relied on respondents' perceptions, and it is not based on objective quantitative measurements.

NOTES

1. A final district firm is a firm operating at the end of the industry value chain which sells finished products.

2. Firms were previously contacted by phone or mail in order to solicit their participations and to provide them with a background of the research project and a description of the questionnaire.

3. The structural data concerning sales, age, and size of the firm were controlled, where available (8 out of 125 firms) with the information obtained by the AIDA database; whereas difference were noticed, AIDA source was considered.

4. Factor analysis is a statistical method used to test whether a set of observed variables may be indicator of a smaller set of unobserved variables (called latent variables or factors). It is possible to distinguish between two categories of factor analysis: the Exploratory Factor Analysis (EFA), which is used to explore relational patterns in the data, and the Confirmatory Factor Analysis (CFA), which is used to test explicitly some stated hypotheses. Long (1983) suggested that EFA is most appropriate when there are none or few knowledge about data whereas CFA is a powerful tool when a model, or at least some relations between the variables have already been well established in the literature. As already observed in previous sections, many relations have been hypothesised and enunciated in the literature, therefore CFA better applies.

5. The reliability analysis gives better result for Dynamic Capabilities measure whether calculate excluding from the sample the firm with missing data and equally meaningful for the other measures. The Cronbach's Alpha scores: 0.61 for DC; 0.737 for ICT and 0.652.

6. The assessment of the overall fit of the model to the data using excluding from the sample the firm with missing data gives a better fitting. Furthermore, the RMSEA is 0.05 and the CFI is 0.95 (Hu & Bentler, 1999). Another indication that the model fits well is that the ECVI for the model (1.51) is less than the ECVI for the saturated model (2.0). In fact, the confidence interval for ECVI is from 1.40 to 1.81. We conclude that the model fits well and represents a reasonably close approximation in the population (Browne & Cudeck, 1993).

7. Where it is not specified differently these items were linked to a five point Likert-type scale.

REFERENCES

Andersen, O. (1993). On the internationalization of process of firms: A critical analysis. *Journal of International Business Studies, 24*(2), 209–231.

Archibugi, D., & Michie, J. (1997). Technological globalisation or national systems of innovation? *Futures, 29*, 121–137.

Argyris, C., & Schön, D. (1978). *Organisational learning.* Reading, MA: Addison-Wesley.

Asheim, B. T., & Gertler, M. (2005). Regional innovation systems and the geographical foundations of innovation. In: J. Fagerberg, D. Mowery & R. R. Nelson (Eds), *The Oxford handbook of innovation* (pp. 291–317). Oxford: Oxford University Press.

Asheim, B. T., & Isaksen, A. (2002). Regional innovation systems: The integration of local 'Sticky' and Global 'Ubiquitous' knowledge. *Journal of Technology Transfer, 27*, 77–86.

Asheim, B. T., Isaksen, A., Nauwelaers, C., & Tödtling, F. (2003). *Regional innovation policy for small-medium enterprises.* Cheltenham, UK: Edward Elgar.

Atkinson, R., & Flint, J. (2001). Accessing hidden and hard-to-reach populations: Snowball research strategies. *Social Research Update, 33*, 33–41.

Augier, M., & Teece, D. (2008). Strategy as evolution with design: The foundations of dynamic capabilities and the role of managers in the economic system. *Organization Studies, 29*(8/9), 1187–1208.

Austrade (Australian Trade Commission). (2002). *Knowing and Growing the Exporter Community*. Austrade.

Autio, E. (1998). Evaluation of RTD in regional systems of innovation. *European Planning Studies, 6*, 131–140.

Autio, E., & Sapienza, H. J. (2000). Comparing process and born global perspectives in the international growth of technology-based new firms. In: *Frontiers of entrepreneurship research* (pp. 413–424). Babson Park, MA: Center for Entrepreneurial Studies, Babson College.

Bagozzi, R. P., & Yi, Y. (1988). On the evaluation of structural equation models. *Journal of the Academy of Marketing Science, 16*(1), 74–94.

Becattini, G., Bellandi, M., & De Propis, L. (2009). *Handbook of industrial districts* (pp. 457–470.). Cheltenham, UK: Edward Elgar.

Belussi, F. (2005). Are industrial districts formed by networks without technologies? The diffusion of Internet applications in three Italian clusters, July. *European Urban and Regional Studies, 12*(3), 247–268.

Belussi, F., Sammarra, A., & Sedita, S. R. (2008). Managing long distance and localized learning in the Emilia Romagna Life Science Cluster. *European Planning Studies, 16*(5), 665–692.

Bennett, R. (1997). Export marketing and the Internet. *International Marketing Review, 14*, 324–344.

Bennett, R. (1998). Using the World Wide Web for international marketing: Internet use and perceptions of export barriers among German and British businesses. *Journal of Marketing Communications, 4*, 27–43.

Berg, S. (1988). Snowball sampling. In: S. Kotz & N. L. Johnson (Eds), *Encyclopedia of statistical sciences* (pp. 528–532). New York: Wiley.

Braczyk, H., Cooke, P., & Heidenreich, M. (1998). *Regional innovation systems*. London: UCL Press.

Browne, M. W., & Cudeck, R. (1993). Alternative ways of assessing model fit. In: K. A. Bollen & J. S. Long (Eds), *Testing structural equation models* (pp. 136–162). Beverly Hills, CA: Sage.

Camagni, R. (1991). Local milieu, uncertainty and innovation networks: Towards a new dynamic theory of economic space. In: R. Camagni (Ed.), *Innovation networks: Spatial perspectives* (pp. 121–144). London, UK: Belhaven Press.

Carlsson, B. (2006). Internationalization of innovation systems: A survey of the literature. *Research Policy, 35*(1), 56–67.

Cheng, H. L., & Yu, C. M. J. (2008). Institutional pressures and initiation of internationalization: Evidence from Taiwanese small- and medium-sized enterprises. *International Business Review, 17*(3), 331–348.

Coenen, L., Moodysson, J., & Asheim, B. T. (2004). Nodes, networks and proximities: On the knowledge dynamics of the Medicon Valley biotech cluster. *European Planning Studies, 12*, 1003–1018.

Cohen, W. M., & Levinthal, D. A. (1990). Absorptive capacity: A new perspective on learning and innovation. *Administrative Science Quarterly, 35*(1), 128–152.

Coltman, T. T., Devinney, M., Latukefu, A., & Midgley, D. F. (1999). E-business: Revolution, evolution or hype? Centre for Corporate Change, Australian Graduate School of Management.

Cooke, P. (2002). *Knowledge economies: Clusters, learning and cooperative advantage*. London, UK: Routledge.

Cooke, P. (2004). Regional knowledge capabilities, embeddedness of firms and industry organisations: Bioscience, metacentres and economic geography. *European Planning Studies, 12*, 625–642.

Cooke, P., & Morgan, K. (1998). *The associational economy: Firms, regions, and innovation.* Oxford: Oxford University Press.

Cooke, P., Uranga, M. G., & Etxebarria, G. (1997). Regional innovation systems: Institutional and organisational dimensions. *Research Policy, 26*(4), 475–491.

Cuervo-Cazurra, A., Maloney, M. M., & Manrakhan, S. (2007). Causes of the difficulties in Internationalization. *Journal of International Business Studies, 38*(5), 709–725.

De la Mothe, J., & Paquet, G. (1998). *Local and regional systems of innovation.* Amsterdam, NL: Kluwer Academic Publishers.

Den Hertog, P. (2000). Knowledge-intensive business services as co-producers of innovation. *International Journal of Innovation Management, 4*, 491–528.

Doloreux, D. (2004). Regional innovation systems in Canada: A comparative study. *Regional Studies, 38*, 479–492.

Edquist, C. (1997). *Systems of innovation: Technologies, institutions and organizations.* London, UK: Routledge.

Eid, R., Trueman, M., & Ahmed, A. M. (2002). A cross-industry review of B2B critical success factors. *Internet Research: Electronic Networking Applications and Policy, 12*, 110–123.

Eisenhardt, K., & Martin, J. (2000). Dynamic capabilities: What are they?. *Strategic Management Journal, 21*, 1105–1121.

Etemad, H., & El Trash, S. E. (2003). E-commerce as a mechanism of SMEs internationalization. *McGill International Entrepreneurship Conference*, Northern Ireland, Londonderry.

Feldman, M. S. (2004). Resources in emerging structures and processes of change. *Organization Science, 15*(3), 295–309.

Fransman, M. (1994). Information, knowledge, vision and theories of the firm. *Industrial and Corporate Change, 3*(3), 713–757.

Freeman, C. (1995). The 'National System of Innovation' in historical perspective. *Cambridge Journal of Economics, 19*(1), 5–24.

Gilmore, J. H., & Pine, B. J. (2000). *Markets of one: Creating customer-unique value through mass customization.* Boston, MA: Harvard Business School Press.

Hamill, J., & Gregory, K. (1997). Internet marketing in the internationalisation of UK SMEs. *Journal of Marketing Management, 13*(1-3), 9–28.

Howells, J. (1999). Regional systems of innovation?. In: J. Howells, D. Archibugi & J. Michie (Eds), *Innovation policy in a global economy* (pp. 69–73). Cambridge, UK: Cambridge University Press.

Hu, L., & Bentler, P. M. (1999). Cutoff criteria for fit indexes in covariance structure analysis: Conventional criteria versus new alternatives. *Structural Equation Modeling, 6*(1), 1–55.

Huber, G. P. (1990). A theory of the effects of advanced information technologies on organizational design, intelligence, and decision making. *Academy of Management Review, 15*, 47–71.

Jöreskog, K. G., & Sörbom, D. (2000). *LISREL 8.5: User's reference guide.* Chicago, IL: Scientific Software International.

Kline, R. B. (2005). *Principles and practice of structural equation modeling.* New York: The Guilford Press.

Knight, G. A., & Cavusgil, S. T. (2004). Innovation, organizational capabilities, and the born-global firm. *Journal of International Business Studies, 35*(4), 124–141.

Lal, K. (2002). E-business and manufacturing sector: A study of small and medium-sized enterprises in India. *Research Policy, 31*, 1199–1211.

Lal, K. (2004). E-Business and export behavior: Evidence from Indian firms. *World Development, 32*, 505–517.

Lee, G. (2008). Relevance of organizational capabilities and its dynamics: What to learn from entrants' product portfolios about the determinants of entry timing. *Strategic Management Journal, 29*, 1257–1280.

Levitt, B., & March, J. G. (1988). Organisational learning. *Annual Review of Sociology, 14*, 319–340.

Loane, S., Bell, J., & Deans, K. R. (2007). Internet adoption by rapidly internationalising SMEs: A further challenge to staged e-adoption models. *International Journal of Entrepreneurship and Small Business, 4*, 277–290.

Loasby, B. (1999). *Knowledge, institutions, and evolution in economics.* London, UK: Routledge.

Maskell, P., & Malmberg, A. (1999). Localised learning and industrial competitiveness. *Cambridge Journal of Economics, 23*, 167–185.

Mata, F. J., Fuerst, W. L., & Barney, J. B. (1995). Information technology and sustained competitive advantage: A resource-based analysis. *MIS Quarterly, 19*(4), 487–505.

Miles, I. (2003). Services innovation: Coming of age in the knowledge-based economy. In: B. Dankbaar (Ed.), *Innovation management in the knowledge economy* (pp. 59–82). London, UK: Imperial College Press.

Miles, I. (2005). Knowledge intensive business services: Prospects and policies. *Foresight: The Journal of Future Studies, Strategic Thinking and Policy, 7*(6), 39–63.

Muller, E. (2001). *Innovation interactions between knowledge-intensive business services and small- and medium-sized enterprises – analysis in terms of evolution, knowledge and territories.* Heidelberg: Physica.

Muller, E., & Zenker, A. (2001). Business services as actors of knowledge transformation: The role of KIBS in regional and national innovation systems. *Research Policy, 30*, 1501–1516.

Nelson, R. R. (1992). The roles of firms in technical advance: A perspective from evolutionary theory. In: G. Dosi, R. Giannetti & P. Toninelli (Eds), *Technology and enterprise in a historical perspective* (pp. 164–184). Oxford: Oxford University Press.

Nelson, R. R. (1994). Innovation and the firm. In: R. England (Ed.), *The Elgar companion to institutional and evolutionary economics* (pp. 139–156). Ann Arbor: The University of Michigan Press.

Nelson, R. R., & Winter, G. S. (1982). *An evolutionary theory of economic change.* Cambridge, UK: Belknap Press and Harvard University Press.

OECD. (2004a). *Facilitating SMEs access to international markets.* Paris, FR: OECD.

OECD. (2004b). ICT, E-Business and SMEs. In: *2nd OECD Conference of Ministers Responsible for Small and Medium-Sized Enterprises (SMEs)*, OECD, Paris, FR.

Olivera, F. (2000). Memory systems in organizations: An empirical investigation of mechanisms for knowledge collection, storage and access. *Journal of Management Studies, 37*(6), 811–832.

Oviatt, B. M., & McDougall, P. P. (1997). Challenges for internationalization process theory: The case of international new ventures. *Management International Review, 37*(2), 85–99.

Oviatt, B. M., & McDougall, P. P. (2005). Defining international entrepreneurship and modeling the speed of internationalization. *Entrepreneurship Theory & Practice, 29*(5), 537–553.

Pajunen, K., & Maunula, M. (2008). Internationalisation: A coevolutionary perspective. *Scandinavian Journal Management, 24,* 247–258.

Petersen, B., Pedersen, T., & Sharma, D. D. (2003). The role of knowledge in firms' internationalisation process: Wherefrom and whereto? In: A. Blomstermo & D. D. Sharma (Eds), *Learning in the internationalisation process of firms* (pp. 36–55). Cheltenham, UK: Edward Elgar.

Pilat, D. (2003). *Seizing the benefits from ICT – An international comparison of the impacts of ICT on economic performance.* Paris, FR: OECD DSTI/IND/ICCP.

Piscitello, L., & Sgobbi, F. (2004). Globalisation, E-Business and SMEs: Evidence from the Italian District of Prato. *Small Business Economics, 22*(5), 333–347.

Poon, S., & Jevons, C. (1997). Internet-enabled international marketing: A small business network perspective. *Journal of Marketing Management, 13,* 29–41.

Porter, M. E. (1998). *On competition.* Boston, MA: Harvard Business School Press.

Porter, M. E. (2001). Strategy and the Internet. *Harvard Business Review, 79,* 62–79.

Prashantham, S., & Young, S. (2004). The internet and the internationalisation of small knowledge-intensive firms: Promises, problems and prospects. *International Journal of Entrepreneurship and Small Business, 1*(1), 153–175.

Raymond, L., Bergeron, F., & Blili, S. (2005). The assimilation of E-business in manufacturing SMEs: Determinants and effects on growth and internationalization. *Electronic Markets, 15*(2), 106–118.

Saarenketo, S., Puumalainen, K., Kyläheiko, K., & Kuivalainen, O. (2008). Linking knowledge and internationalization in small and medium-sized enterprises in the ICT sector. *Technovation, 8*(9), 591–601.

Sakai, K. (2002). *Global industrial restructuring: Implications for small firms.* STI Working Paper. Paris.

Samiee, S. (1998). Exporting and the Internet: A conceptual perspective. *International Marketing Review, 15,* 413–426.

Sapienza, H. J., Autio, E., George, G., & Zahra, A. A. (2006). A capabilities perspective on the effects of early internationalization on firm survival and growth. *Academy of Management Review, 31*(4), 914–933.

Schreyer, P. (1996). *SMEs and Employment Creation: Overview of selective qualitative studies in OECD member countries.* STI Working Paper. Paris.

Shook, C. L., Ketchen, D. J., Hult, G. T. M., & Kacmar, K. M. (2004). Research notes and commentaries: An assessment of the use of structural equation modeling in strategic management research. *Strategic Management Journal, 25,* 397–404.

Steensma, H. K., & Lyles, M. A. (2000). Explaining IJV survival in a transitional economy through social exchange and knowledge-based perspectives. *Strategic Management Journal, 21,* 831–851.

Storper, M. (1997). *The regional world territorial development in a global economy.* New York: Guilford Press.

Teece, D. (1987). Profiting from technological innovation: Implication for integration, collaboration, licensing, and public policy. *Research Policy, 15,* 285–305.

Teece, D. (1989). Inter-organisational requirements of the innovation process. *Managerial and Decision Economics, 10*(Special Issue), 35–42.

Teece, D., Pisano, G., & Shuen, A. (1997). Dynamic capabilities and strategic management. *Strategic Management Journal, 41*(1), 204–217.

Tödtling, F., & Trippl, M. (2005). One size fits all? Towards a differentiated regional innovation policy approach. *Research Policy, 34,* 1203–1219.

Toivonen, M. (2004). Expertise as business: Long-term development and future prospects of knowledge-intensive business services (KIBS). Doctoral Dissertation, Helsinki University of Technology.

Tuppura, A., Saarenketo, A., Puumalainen, K., Jantunen, A., & Kyläheiko, K. (2008). Linking knowledge, entry timing and internationalization strategy. *International Business Review, 17*(4), 473–487.

Weerawardena, J., Sullivan Mort, G., Liesch, P. W., & Knight, G. (2007). Conceptualizing accelerated internationalization in the born global firm: A dynamic capabilities perspective. *Journal of World Business, 42*(3), 294–306.

Weill, P., & Vitale, M. R. (2001). *Place to space: Migrating to e-business models.* Cambridge, MA: Harvard Business School Press.

Wernerfelt, B. (1984). A resource-based view of the firm. *Strategic Management Journal, 5*(2), 171–180.

Witt, U. (1996). *Imagination and leadership – The neglected dimension of the (evolutionary) theory of the firm.* Max Plank Institute Working Papers, 5.

Wood, P. (2005). A service-informed approach to regional innovation – or adaptation?. *The Service Industries Journal, 25,* 429–445.

Wood, P. (2006). Regional significance of knowledge-intensive services in Europe. *Innovation, 19,* 51–66.

Zaheer, S. (1995). Overcoming the liability of foreignness. *Academy of Management Journal, 38*(2), 341–363.

Zahra, S., Ireland, R. D., & Hitt, M. (2000). International expansion by new venture firms: International diversity, mode of market entry, technological learning, and performance. *Academy of Management Journal, 43*(5), 925–950.

Zollo, M., & Winter, S. (2002). Deliberate learning and the evolution of dynamic capabilities. *Organisation Science, 13,* 339–351.

APPENDIX A. SCALE ITEMS

Dynamic capabilities:

- Which tool of knowledge management is used by the firm? From 1 (every one is responsible of his learning and knowledge is not shared between employees) to 5 (there is a continuous process revision and improvement of routines related to externalization, codification, sharing and storing of the knowledge).
- How many of these spontaneous learning activities are implemented?
  - On-the-job training;
  - On-the-job training with the supervision of experts;
  - Clients/Supplier Interaction;
  - Use of consultants and
  - Imitation of strategies and product of competitors.
- How many of these formal learning activities are implemented?
  - Internal training;
  - External training;
  - Benchmarking activities;
  - Participation to institutional project and initiatives promoted by local and/or industry association and
  - Visit to 'best practice' companies.

Technological Knowledge Intensive Business Services (T-KIBS):

- Availability and readiness to acquire technology process in the region from 1 (= completely unsatisfied) to 5 (= completely satisfied);
- Availability and readiness to access to R&D facilities in the region from 1 (= completely unsatisfied) to 5 (= completely satisfied) and
- Availability and readiness to access to IT related services in the region from 1 (= completely unsatisfied) to 5 (= completely satisfied).

Use and investments in ICT:

- How important is at industry level use ICT technologies to connect with clients and suppliers?
- How important is at industry level invest in ICT for management purposes?
- How important is at industry level have developed an e-commerce strategy?
- How important is at industry level invest in ICT to improve the network efficiency?

Firm Internationalization Performance:

- Which is the percentage of export sales?
- Which is the percentage of foreign purchase?

APPENDIX B. VARIABLES DESCRIPTION – VARIABLE AND LABEL[7]

1. Firm Items – Dynamic Capabilities
   DC 1: Ability to manage and improve the knowledge at firm level improving the existing routines.
   DC 2: Importance of spontaneous learning at firm level (number of spontaneous learning activities that are doing at firm level).
   DC 3: Importance of formal learning at firm level (number of formal learning activities that are doing at firm level like R&D investment).
2. Regional Items – Technological Knowledge Intensive Business Services (T-KIBS)
   TK 1: Availability and readiness to acquire external technology process.
   TK 2: Availability and readiness to access to external R&D facilities.
   TK 3: Availability and readiness to access to external ICT related services.
3. Industry Items – Use and investments in ICT
   ICT 1: Importance in the sector to use ICT technologies to connect with clients and suppliers.
   ICT 2: Importance in the sector to invest in ICT for management purposes.
   ICT 3: Importance in the sector to have developed an e-commerce strategy.
   ICT 4: Importance in the sector to invest in ICT to improve the network efficiency.
4. Dependent Variables – Firm degree of Internationalization
   ES: Export sales (percentage total sales rescaled as continuous variable from 0 to 5).
   FP: Foreign purchases (percentage of total purchases rescaled as continuous variable from 0 to 5).

APPENDIX C. MEANS, STANDARD DEVIATIONS AND CORRELATIONS BETWEEN VARIABLES

	DC1	DC2	DC3	TK1	TK2	TK3	ICT1	ICT2	ICT3	ICT4	ES	FP
DC1	1.00											
DC2	0.25**	1.00										
DC3	0.42**	0.29**	1.00									
TK1	0.29**	0.00	0.214*	1.00								
TK2	0.20*	0.01	0.29**	0.40**	1.00							
TK3	0.01	−0.11	0.00	0.43**	0.398**	1.00						
ICT1	0.01	−0.09	0.01	0.48**	0.40**	0.56**	1.00					
ICT2	0.00	0.01	0.01	0.00	0.10	0.08	0.26**	1.00				
ICT3	0.00	0.01	0.31**	0.24*	0.12	0.08	0.25**	0.33**	1.00			
ICT4	0.25*	−0.01	0.35**	0.198*	0.091	0.01	0.10	0.38**	0.36**	1.00		
ES	0.34**	0.01	0.317**	0.198*	0.11	0.07	0.056	0.08	0.35**	0.29**	1.00	
FP	0.33**	0.025	0.41**	0.12	0.11	0.22*	0.10	0.09	0.09	0.33**	0.33**	1.00
Mean	2.52	2.09	1.90	3.19	3.28	2.86	2.99	3.13	3.12	2.47	1.65	0.71
SD	1.01	0.97	1.10	0.91	0.98	1.17	1.15	1.06	1.29	1.10	1.57	1.08

*Correlation is significant at the 0.05 level (2-tailed).
**Correlation is significant at the 0.01 level (2-tailed).

LOCATION DETERMINANTS OF FDI IN SUB-SAHARAN AFRICA: AN EMPIRICAL ANALYSIS

Satwinder Singh, Kirandeep Dhillon, Florian Kaulich and Weifeng Chen

ABSTRACT

The chapter adopts the international production typology offered by the OLI paradigm whereby firms are classified principally as market seekers, efficiency seekers, natural resource seekers or partner seekers. These motives to reach overseas are tested against 26 location factors, categorised under 'business climate', 'market conditions', 'local resources' and 'incentive packages', and three sets of control variables: industry, age and entry mode. The empirical analysis based on firm-level data from 15 sub-Saharan countries shows that, for all types of firm, the presence of local markets, regional markets and key clients are the positive determining location factors, followed by business climate factors, such as labour costs, the availability of skilled labour, raw materials and local suppliers. For market-seeking MNEs, the political and economic stability, infrastructure, country's legal framework and the transparency of investment all rate high. Importantly, the implication for host-nation promotion agencies is that once the motive to enter their economies is clear, they can – and should – play a skilful negotiation game with MNEs

Dynamics of Globalization: Location-Specific Advantages or Liabilities of Foreignness?
Advances in International Management, Volume 24, 327–356
Copyright © 2011 by Emerald Group Publishing Limited
All rights of reproduction in any form reserved
ISSN: 1571-5027/doi:10.1108/S1571-5027(2011)0000024020

at the entry point itself. Based on the empirical analysis, a conceptual two-step approach to understanding FDI decisions, intimately linked to the liability of foreignness concept, is suggested.

INTRODUCTION

Africa is a mini-puzzle in terms of attracting foreign direct investment (FDI). The continent is abundant in minerals and human power, but still attracts only a small percentage of FDI flowing into the developing world. In 2009, for example, the FDI flows to developing countries amounted to $478.35 billion, in which the share of whole of Africa was a mere $58.57 billion (12.2%). For the same year, the stock of FDI in the developing world was placed at $4.89 trillion, of which the African continent share was $514.76 billion (10.5%) (UNCTAD, WIR 2010). Essentially, the lack of infrastructure, institutional policies and political instability are often readily cited, common causes hindering the flow of foreign investment into the continent vis-à-vis other developing economies. Furthermore, several general and Africa-specific studies have found this to be true (see Kinda, 2010; Deichmann, Socrates, & Sayek, 2003; Globerman & Shapiro, 2002; Asiedu, 2002; Morrisset, 2000; Cheng & Kwan, 2000). Notably, it is alleged that most of the recent FDI in the African continent is largely owing to Chinese investment in the natural resource industries. The OLI paradigm of FDI classifies international production into four broad categories: natural resource seeking, market seeking, efficiency seeking and strategic asset or capability seeking. The purpose of this chapter is to examine empirically the extent to which these various types of international production modes are influenced by different location factors in the case of sub-Saharan African countries. The study is important for several reasons. Firstly, the majority of applied academic studies use aggregate data, such as market size, labour costs, GDP, trade, tax and exchange rate regimes in order to arrive at the attractiveness of a foreign location for FDI (see Pistoresi, 2000; Wheeler & Mody, 1992; Blonigen & Feenstra, 1996; Tsai, 1994; Blonigen, 1997; Billington, 1999). The analysis in this chapter is based on firm-level response data from multinational enterprises (MNEs) in relation to 26 location factors. Secondly, there are only a handful of studies of this nature – even at the macro level – in the context of Africa (Asiedu, 2002, 2006; Bende-Nabende, 2002; Bartels, Eicher, Bachtrog, & Rezonja, 2009) and only a scant few in the context of sub-Saharan Africa (SSA). With this in mind, this chapter therefore makes a contribution to the literature on FDI in the context of SSA. Thirdly, the results in the study should prove useful for policy makers who can devote attention to significant variables known to influence the choice of location. Finally, we hope that, following the empirical results, a conceptual model of FDI decision – as outlined in the discussion section – will prove useful in future empirical research.

The rest of the chapter is organised as follows: second section summarises the key theoretical and empirical literature on the theories of FDI; third section lists the predictions and hypotheses drawn from these two sets of literature; fourth section describes the research methods; and the analysis and results take fifth section, with the discussion finally provided in sixth section.

THEORY DEVELOPMENT

An Overview of Theoretical Explanations of FDI

Theories of FDI explain a country's propensity and ability to investment. The FDI process, as undertaken by MNEs, has reached a fertile area in terms of research, with excellent summaries of research now available (see Rugman, 2009; Dunning & Lundan, 2010) and, as a result, the purpose of this section will be to provide an overview to serve as a backdrop for discussion in the remaining sections of the chapter.

Notably, more space will be devoted to the location as a choice factor for MNEs. In this regard, we take the cut-off point with Hymer (1960), who postulated his explanation on investment occurring as a result of market imperfections and the MNE's possession of monopolistic advantage. This initiated variations in foreign investment motives as an oligopolistic defence strategy (Knickerbocker, 1973) through the product lifecycle (Vernon, 1966), or otherwise owing to capital market imperfections (Aliber, 1971). The internationalisation model of FDI is an extension of the behavioural (Cyert & March, 1963) and growth (Penrose, 1959) theory of the firm, and posits the internationalisation of a firm through a stages approach. Johanson and Wiedersheim-Paul (1975) theorise an evolutionary and sequential build-up of foreign commitments over time. The stages of international expansion are illustrated by the dynamic establishment chain, where initial investments occur from physical and psychic proximity, thereby leading to a slow and gradual move towards deeper commitment and more diversified cross-border activities. The main assumption of the theory is that knowledge can only be gained through lengthy 'learning by doing' experience in a location, providing the capacity to recognise risk and opportunity factors, which ultimately encourage future resource commitment (Eriksson, Johanson, Majkgard, & Sharma, 1997). In the final stage, the sophistication of local market knowledge over time reduces psychic distance, uncertainty and information costs, accordingly increasing the propensity to FDI. Alternatively, an entrepreneurial-based explanation elucidates that the decision to internationalise and the location chosen are considered to be a part – or as a consequence of – similar economic conditions to the host and the company's strategy, whereby internalisation spurs from entrepreneurial action (Luostarinen & Welch, 1988). Coviello and Munro (1997) theorise that the formation of network relationships and links between firms and industries influence the foreign market selection and the mode of entry. Each internationalisation conceptualisation is based on the concepts of market commitment and incremental attainment of market knowledge. Notably, the internalisation approach, as initiated by Coase (1937), explains the existence and growth of MNEs in terms the costs and benefits from transactions and resource allocation occurring through internal hierarchies relative to the market. The theory posits that the costs arising from resource allocation through the market via the price mechanism occur owing to transactional market failure, known as transaction costs. Transaction costs develop from information asymmetries, bargaining and administration techniques. Buckley and Casson (1976) have transformed internalisation into a full theory of international business and multinational activity by including dynamicity and industry level determinants into a previously country-specific and static conception. They assume that firms aim to maximise profits in an imperfect world market, thereby creating incentives to bypass costs through internal markets connected by common ownership. This explains why MNEs undertake FDI rather than simply exporting goods.

By applying the internalisation theory to the location choice of investment, an MNE may be motivated to locate activities where there is the potential to achieve increasing returns to scale on production, and also where knowledge-intensive locations exist for high-value activities. Therefore, the optimal investment location cannot be based on regional factor analysis, as explained by traditional location models; rather, knowledge of market failures in investment locations allows transaction costs to be evaluated, and therefore determines the location choice. An alternative approach from Zander and Kogut (1995) abandons the market failure approach, and instead proposes that accumulation and the transfer of tacit

knowledge explains internalisation. Subsequently, Dunning (1993) introduced a holistic framework in his eclectic paradigm which seeks to explain
the level and pattern of international production. He recognises the
importance of structural and transaction cost imperfections in terms of
ownership, location and internalisation advantages, and later categorised
FDI motivations into market seeking, resource seeking, efficiency seeking
and strategic asset seeking.

Moreover, Dunning (1998) further highlights that the initial emphasis in
academic research on the firm-specific determinants is now complemented
with renewed interest in the spatial dimensions of FDI, as location factors
can ultimately affect the global competitiveness of firms, and thereby
determine their chances of future survival. Markedly, theory states that the
location decisions of MNEs are determined by the relative location
advantages of particular countries for certain activities. Implicit in these
formulations is the assumption that particular location advantages have the
same value for all MNEs; however, the differences in the investment motives
of individual MNEs mean that they will place varying degrees of importance
on location factors. For example, market size is often considered to be a
major location advantage, enabling firms to benefit market share and scale
advantages (Dunning, 1993). Whilst this characteristic of markets is a highly
valuable advantage for large firms, benefiting from standardisation, it may
have limited value for small, specialised firms, the core competitive
advantage of which lies in a highly specialised technology (Nachum &
Wymbs, 2007). This clarifies that location factors should not be analysed in
isolation from the MNE investment motive, thereby forming the basis of
this research. It has been proposed that, in SSA, transaction costs from
location factors arise from imperfect information concerning the market,
unstable bargaining, volatile political and economic systems and a lack of
transparency. It can be further argued that this has occurred because, in
SSA, markets emerged before institutions were created (Meyer, 2001).

Empirical Studies on the Location of FDI

As is the case with the theoretical explanations on the existence of FDI, a
large number of studies on the factors impacting the attraction of FDI have
also been undertaken. With this in mind, this discussion shall be divided
under three broad headings: factors relating to business climate, market
conditions and local resources. This typology follows the UNIDO survey
questionnaire which was used to collect data on foreign direct investor

perceptions in sub-Saharan region; this data is also used for empirical analysis in this chapter. Specific empirical studies on the FDI activities of MNEs in SSA are scant. Where appropriate, the findings from these studies have been incorporated in the following sections.

Business Climate Factors
Business climate, as a generic term, can be defined to include factors ranging from, or emanating from, the institutional set-up of a country's political, economic, technical, legal and social environment. In a broader definition, it can also be defined to include the state of the infrastructure. Amongst these, the role of institutions is perhaps the most important factor. The role of institutions can be characterised as bodies which formulate arrangements between people facilitating cooperative activity (Nelson & Sampat, 2001), creating the 'rules of the game'. This affects the predictability and uncertainty in the local environment, thereby influencing foreign investment behaviours. For example, Globerman and Shapiro (2003) used economic analysis on US FDI flows to 145 countries with the objective to illustrate the importance of 'good' governance infrastructure in affecting the amount of FDI a country receives. This is depicted by factors such as the promotion of open markets and the quality of political institutions. Moreover, numerous improvements in governance infrastructure are known to result in diminishing returns, which is relevant specifically for developing and transition countries, which ultimately have the most to gain (in terms of greater FDI inflows) relative to developed countries. This inverse relationship has also been evidenced in many other studies (Schneider & Frey, 1985; Loree & Guisinger, 1995).

More specifically, the study of Henisz and Delios (2001) indicates that poor host government credibility and attitude towards inward investment may discourage investment. For the MNE in question, differences in host institution characteristics represent immobile factors in the global market space in which instability can raise uncertainty and therefore potential costs, subsequently affecting the attractiveness for FDI. This is further supported by the work of Dunning (1998) on the revival of the importance of location, giving institution variances a larger weighting than other location factors. This may mean that the importance of determinants is changing owing to globalisation, although this has not received much focus in the literature. Furthermore, Dow and Karunaratna (2006) emphasise that there are great differences in political systems between the host and home country, which will also hinder the business–government relationship and therefore the overall effectiveness of MNE foreign activity. This is evident by global FDI trends which are focused on developed nations. Moreover, political instability and institutional variances can potentially explain the level of inward FDI flows into SSA. Reinhart and Rogoff (2002), for example, used susceptibility to war indices for the period of 1960–2001, subsequently establishing that war was most likely to occur in Africa than in any other regions presenting a volatile and risky business environment unlikely to attract FDI. It has also been argued, however, that political risk is just one of many business risks associated with international investment, and therefore should not be overemphasised (Agarwal, 1980).

Amongst the economic environment, macroeconomic stability via the exchange rate mechanism has been cited repeatedly as a determinant of FDI. This is consistent with the 'currency area' hypothesis, whereby it is considered that the weaker the currency, the less likely foreign investors will be attracted. The assumption of there being a bias in the capital market means that an income flow is capitalised at a higher rate by the market when it is owned by a weaker currency firm, therefore affecting MNEs' profit potential (Aliber, 1971). However, empirical studies show mixed results: Tumar and Emmert's (1999) study in Latin America finds an insignificant relationship between inward FDI and real exchange rate fluctuations, whereas Blonigen (1997) states that there is a strong correlation between a weaker dollar and higher levels of Japanese FDI in the United States. For the SSA region, macroeconomic stability in the form of currency crashes and high inflation has been related to determining levels of FDI (Onyeiwu & Shrestha, 2004). Host trade liberalisation policies are also identified as impacting the level and motives for FDI. Buckley and Casson (1981) explain that in order to overcome bureaucratic trade barriers and high transportation costs through exportation, MNEs consider horizontal FDI as a substitute for trade. This supports the 'tariff jumping' hypothesis. Initially, fixed costs from this method would be high; however, if the host market is large enough, scale economies would settle in. An alternative perspective is that FDI complements trade; this relates to vertical FDI where the production process is divided and located within the most favourable location attributes, so that intermediate products are exported between nations whereby trade openness is significant. Prominently, however, there is mixed empirical evidence concerning the significance of trade barriers as a FDI determinant. Singh and Jun (1995), for example, conducted a study of 39 countries over 23 years, and accordingly stated that export-orientated location advantages provide one of the strongest FDI determinants in developing countries. In addition, the panel data research carried out by Morrisset (2000) on a sample of 29 African countries controlled for resource availability focused specifically on business climate factors. The results show that, generally, government policies and reforms yield FDI interest, and the GDP growth rate and trade openness are correlated positively with inward investment. However, political risk factors are concluded as insignificant.

Increased competition between institutional bodies – particularly in developing countries – has resulted in offers of special programmes and incentives to attract potential investors. Aggarwal and Agmon (1990) highlight how government support in the form of financial and non-financial incentives can offset any ownership and location disadvantages overseas; this illustrates the occurrence of inward FDI as a function of the relative bargaining power of host governments and firms (Vernon, 1971), and that, in the case of developing countries, there is concern that increasing competition to attract foreign investors may be a zero-sum game. The empirical evidence demonstrating a positive relationship with FDI is, at best, inconclusive. For instance, the regression analysis carried out by Gastanaga, Nugent, and Pashamiova (1998) shows that corporate tax rates exert a significant, negative effect on FDI in 49 developing countries. Moreover, the study of Rolfe, David, Pointer, and McCarthy (1993) in LDCs of the Caribbean region evaluated the attractiveness of 20 host country incentives, subsequently stating that the effectiveness of incentives was extremely context-specific to the firm, and depended on the type and size of investment and geographic location etc. Conversely, Wheeler and Mody (1992) state that incentives have had no significant effects on US FDI in developing countries; therefore, it can be conceded that, in general, investment incentives cannot be a substitute for the other location factors determining FDI inflows, but conceptually create an opportunity to differentiate location attractiveness from competitors.

An inadequate and inefficient infrastructure system can increase transaction costs and interrupt network formation between businesses and customers, ultimately hindering productivity and profitability. Wheeler and Mody's (1992) study using aggregate data shows that infrastructure development can be significant when explaining US FDI to developing countries in the 1980s. This has been corroborated by recent studies proving that 'good' infrastructure has a significantly positive effect on the probability of foreign investment in developing countries (Cheng & Kwan, 2000; Deichmann et al., 2003). However, such studies do not determine whether or not infrastructure was the most important location factor relative to others or in accordance to the investment motives. Importantly, the study of Asiedu (2002) on SSA states that investment and better infrastructure have positive impacts on inward FDI into non-SSA African countries, but not into SSA countries; on the other hand, trade liberalisation had the expected result. One explanation for this result could be the heterogeneity of MNEs in terms of their investment motive and therefore the value placed on different location factors not mentioned in the study. The author, however, did recognise the need to test the model with a broader range of variables.

Market Conditions and Efficiency Seeking
Demand-side variables, such as the size and potential growth of the host market, are arguably the most tested and common factors in influencing the choice of location (Billington, 1999). It is suggested that opportunities for enhancing international competitiveness are created through securing market share, exploiting resources and scale possibilities. Early studies focus on Western economies – mainly US FDI flows, and used regression techniques – subsequently concluding mixed results concerning the relation-ship between market size and FDI. For example, Scaperlanda and Mauer (1969) used data over a 13-year time horizon to investigate US inflows into Western Europe; they found the significance of market size varied over time, and proceeded to explain that FDI reacts positively with market size once it is large enough to allow production efficiencies. More recent empirical studies using GDP as a market variable highlight the importance of market factors (Agarwal, 1980; Wheeler & Mody, 1992; Billington, 1999; De Mello, 1997); however, these particular researches focus on cross-country comparisons on developed economies, leaving a gap for analysis and comparisons with imminent developing countries. As such, the question is posed: Does the trend identified in developed economies transcend into the developing? One analysis provides contradictory results, which is that of Lim (1983), who investigated 27 developing countries – mostly in Asia – and determined that the prosperity of the economic environment was more significant in the long run than traditional market factors. Furthermore, the panel data analysis of Carstensen and Toubal (2004) on Central European countries over a 6-year duration extends previous research and highlights the greater significance of regional market factors. One explanation for this could be geographic and cultural proximity between neighbouring economies. On balance, studies do seem to support the importance of market factors in attracting foreign investment.

   Foreign investment is said to be efficiency seeking when the firm can gain from cost advantages in the form of economies of scale, specialisation and learning experiences through the common governance of geographically dispersed activities. This is also consistent with internalisation theory

(Buckley & Casson, 1976) whereby the existence of transactional market imperfections results in cross-border activities of intermediate products to be internalised rather than determined by market forces. Unlike forms of horizontal FDI, vertical FDI aims to benefit from low costs where an MNE can delineate its production activities into locations according to variations in factor costs and resource availability. The determinants of horizontal and vertical FDI therefore differ, and the effects of identical location factors would, in turn, affect the MNE differently in accordance with its motives. For example, efficiency-seeking investment is attracted to lower wage rates, as shown in the research of Love and Lage-Hidalgo (2000), which considers US inflows to Mexico, and which places greater importance on labour cost location factors. Similarly, the quality of supporting industries, character-istics of local competition and macro-policies will also affect the attractiveness of a location for this type of investment.

Resource Seeking Including Labour Costs
According to factor-endowment hypothesis, asymmetry in natural endow-ments and variations in factor costs amongst countries go some way to explaining the geographical pattern of inward FDI – particularly in developing countries (Buckley, Devinney, & Louviere, 2007). According to Shatz and Venables (2000), international differences in raw material prices, labour costs and refinements in production technology tend to encourage vertical FDI, whereby the production process is distributed to the optimum location. This type of FDI is associated with the relatively long-term commitment of capital, and also with relatively tolerant investors who aim to secure input supply (Maxfield, 1998). This form of defensive FDI occurs in response to intense global cost pressures and sustain competitive stance against rivals in an oligopolistic market structure. In conjunction with market-seeking investment, this is analogous to Knickerbocker's (1973) explanation, whereby MNEs exhibit a bandwagon effect, subsequently resulting in the bunching-up of MNEs in certain industries and countries. Therefore, owing to the immobile and location-bound nature of these resources, it can be inferred that MNEs, with resource-seeking motives, will place greater importance on the cost and availability of raw materials and the macro-stability of the host country to exploit the resources, as well as the trade regimes and availability of joint venture partnerships (Dunning & Narula, 2000).

Traditionally, total production costs have mainly comprised labour costs. In an increasingly competitive market, the globalisation process has permitted MNEs to relocate in developing countries of low-cost labour locations; this is consistent with empirical studies where labour costs have been found to have a negative effect on FDI (Lankes & Venables, 1996). However, the importance of labour costs may be offset by the importance of labour skills. Theoretically, the ability of developing countries to attract inward FDI is consistent with aspects of the 'dependency' hypotheses; this elucidates the international division of labour, where the high-skill and high-wage jobs stay with the home country whilst the remainder low skill and low pay remain in the host. However, in the SSA region, Onyeiwu and Shrestha's (2004) panel data estimation for 29 African countries over 29 years recognises infrastructure and labour costs to be unimportant for FDI flows to Africa, whilst placing greater importance on economic development and stability. The importance of labour costs may potentially vary with industry and investment type: for example, Wheeler and Mody's (1992) panel data analysis on 42 developed and developing countries highlights its importance for manufacturing industries, export-orientated and vertical forms of FDI. One explanation is that such types of investments are driven by different investment motives, therefore exaggerating the importance of certain location factors, such as labour costs. Conversely, other researches have shown a positive relationship between higher wages and FDI, which suggests that, in the long-term, labour costs are less relevant (Aggarwal, 1997). An alternative explanation could be that foreign investors are influenced relatively more by market factors according to their investment motive, and place less weight on short-term labour costs.

PREDICTIONS AND HYPOTHESES SUGGESTED IN THE THEORETICAL AND EMPIRICAL STUDIES

This section lists the predictions and hypotheses suggested in the theoretical and empirical studies as reviewed above.

H_1. Host country political and economic stability positively impacts on *all types of FDI*.

H_2. Institutional factors positively impact on *all types of FDI*. In this study, institutional factors studied are 'government agency support', 'country legal framework', 'transparency of investment', 'investment promotion agency' and 'incentive factors'.

H_3. Quality of infrastructure impacts positively on *all types of FDI*.

H_4. 'Local markets' and 'regional markets' will positively impact on 'market-seeking' *FDI*.

H_5. 'Local resources' (labour costs, availability of skilled labour, raw materials and local suppliers) will positively impact on *efficiency-seeking FDI*.

In fifth section, these hypotheses are put to test with the assistance of firm-level data from 15 SSA countries. Before we examine the results, the research methods used to arrive at the results are presented.

RESEARCH METHODS

Data Sources

Data for this study comes from a UNIDO survey on 'foreign direct investor perceptions in sub-Saharan Africa (SSA)'. SSA is defined as the region of Africa that lies to the south of the Sahara desert. The survey by UNIDO covers 15 countries: Burkina Faso, Cameroon, Cote d'Ivoire, Ethiopia, Ghana, Guinea, Kenya, Madagascar, Malawi, Mali, Mozambique, Nigeria, Senegal, Tanzania and Uganda. The survey, inter alia, is aimed towards improving the 'support services provided by local agencies, especially national investment promotion agencies, to existing and potential foreign investors and to provide empirical evidence to national policy makers on the potential impact of satisfied foreign investors on the national economy' (UNIDO, FDI Survey, 2005, p. 1). The questionnaire was sent in 15 SSA countries to 3,484 foreign investors, from whom 1,216 valid responses were received by the agency (UNIDO, 2005,p. 10). The questionnaire had eight sections: profile of the company and its operations, section for exporters, workforce profile, profile of the foreign investor, profile of the local partner (if JV), impact on the local economy, investment and operating experience and closing questions. The countries surveyed are rich in natural resources, have large untapped markets and are steadily liberalising their investment frameworks by removing trade restrictions and promoting investment incentives. However, it seems that although the improvements have been made with the help of institutional bodies and external funding, there still remain problems – and consequently risk – for foreign investors relative to the rest of the world. As a result, the survey – which is periodically conducted – is aimed at fact-finding, and assists investment promotion agencies in their efforts to attract FDI.

Measures of Constructs

Motivation for the Foreign Investor to Invest in Host Country
We measure this with four choices that the survey instrument posed to the investors: (1) to access new markets, (2) to lower production costs, (3) to access natural resources/inputs and (4) to join a specific partner. These were converted into binary-dependent variables. It needs to be reiterated that the choices are ex post; that is, the firms have already made the decision to enter the market based on one of these four dominant factors. Therefore, in this sense, the construct is robust in that the choice has already been exercised, and is not in the process of consideration.

Choice of Location Factors
Twenty-six (26) location factors are classified under four headings: 'business climate conditions', 'market conditions', 'local resources' and 'other location factors'. Under each one of these headings are listed, respectively, 12, 5, 4 and 5 location-specific factors (Table 1). Responding firms were asked to rate the importance of these location factors on a five-point Likert scale, with 5 being the crucially important factor in the choice of the location for the firm. These 26 independent variables are hypothesised to influence, in varying degrees, the choice of location factors.

Control Variables
In testing our hypotheses, the age of the firm, the business activity and the mode of entry were controlled. The age of the firm is a dummy, taking the value 1 for firms established on or after 1990, and 0 if earlier. Business activity has three binary-converted variables: (i) production and manufacturing; (ii) distribution, sales and marketing and (iii) financial services. Three modes of entries are accounted: entry by way of Greenfield operation, entry by way of acquisition of existing assets from private owners and entry by way of acquisition of existing state owned assets through a privatisation programme.

Table 1. Reliability and Validity (CFA) Test Results.

Items	Confirmatory Factor Analysis			Reliability
	Standardized loading factor		Components extracted	Cronbach's α
Business climate	BC1	BC2	2	
1. Political stability	0.654			0.837
2. Economic stability	0.763			
3. Quality of infrastructure	0.718			
4. Government agency support	0.478			
5. Country legal framework	0.632			
6. Transparency of investment	0.633			
7. Quality of life	0.588			
8. Physical security	0.685			
9. Existing foreign investor		0.605		0.758
10. Double taxation treaties		0.729		
11. Bilateral trade agreements		0.811		
12. Availability of export processing zones		0.780		
Market conditions	MC	MC1 (deducted)	1	
13. Market factors	0.843			0.590
14. Regional market	0.520			
15. Presence of key clients	0.784			
16. African growth & opp. Act (AGOA)		0.932		
17. Everything but arms (EBA)		0.934		
Local resources	LR		1	
18. Labour costs	0.760			0.747
19. Availability of skilled labour	0.766			
20. Availability of raw materials	0.739			
21. Local suppliers	0.790			
Other location factors	OR		1	
22. Incentive factors (other)	0.682			0.781
23. Investment Promotion Agency (IPA)	0.721			
24. Acquisition of existing assets	0.719			
25. Presence of JV partner	0.725			
26. Specific investment proposal	0.801			

Assessing the Reliability and Validity of Measures

The methodology adopted to analyse data is the factor analysis and the Multinomial Logit Regression (MLR) model. Given a large number of independent variables, Confirmatory Factor Analysis (CFA) (with Varimax rotation) was applied in order to test the validity and reliability of the measures. The results of this exercise are shown in Table 1.

All the items loaded significantly on the expected constructs, therefore indicating convergent and discriminatory measure validity. For the 'Business Climate' group of variables, two factors (BC1 and BC2) were extracted. Two factors were extracted for 'Market Condition' variables, of which only one was retained (MC). For 'Local Resources' and for variables under the 'Other Reasons category' one factor each (LR and OR, respectively) was retained.

Multinomial Logit Regressions

Once the reliability and validity of measures were established, these were ready to test in terms of their influence on the choice of the entry mode selected by the investing firm. As stated earlier, four entry modes to enter a market were chosen; these were entry owing primarily to access new markets, or to lower production costs or to access natural resources/inputs, and finally to join a specific partner. Owing to the choices involved being multiple, MLR was employed.

In multinomial logistic regression, one category of the dependent variable is chosen as the comparison category. Separate odd ratios are determined for all independent variables for each category of the independent variable, with the exception of the comparison category of the dependent variable, which is omitted from the analysis. The model can be expressed as follows:

$$\Pr(y_i = j) = \frac{\exp(X_i\beta_i)}{1 + \sum_{j=1}^{J} \exp(X_i\beta_i)} \quad \text{and} \quad \Pr(y_i = 0) = \frac{1}{1 + \sum_{j=1}^{J} \exp(X_i\beta_i)}$$

where y_i is the observed outcome and X_i is a vector of explanatory variables. The parameters β_j are estimated by maximum likelihood method. The solution is found using iterative procedure.

RESULTS

Table 2 reports the results of MLR which identify which set of location variables, if any, affects the probability of perusing one of four investment motives, and in what way. The model estimates the log odds of the dependent variable in accordance with each independent variable. The model fitting statistics reported at the bottom of the table show that the model is a good fit to the data. The large chi-square values and the small p-values show that there is no significant difference between the actual and observed probabilities. For the sake of convenience, the discussion will follow the set of hypotheses predicted by the theoretical and empirical studies, as listed in third section. In this section, we shall present the results with the discussion carried out in the next section.

The first three of these five hypotheses state that we expect the political and economic stability, institutional factors and quality of infrastructure to be a positive function of *all types of motives of FDI*. These variables are embedded within 'business conditions' (Group 1 in Table 2) and 'other location factors' (Table 2). The results show that the coefficient sign for this group of variables is positive (barring in one instance) for all types of FDI; however, it is significant only in the case of FDI which is undertaken by MNEs to access new markets.

H_4 states that 'local markets' and 'regional markets' will positively impact on *market-seeking FDI*. The coefficient results for this hypothesis come out as expected – positive and highly significant – not only in the case of *market-seeking* FDI but also in the case of those intending to *join partners*.

In H_5, we expected the set of local resources (labour costs, availability of skilled labour, raw materials and local suppliers) to be a positive function of *efficiency-seeking FDI*. The coefficient for this set of variables embedded in factor 'Local Resources' comes out to be significant not only for *efficiency-seeking* FDI but for *market-seeking* and *partner-seeking* FDI as well. The significant negative coefficient tells us that different type of investors will be inclined to undertake FDI so long the labour costs are low, and skilled labour, raw materials, and local suppliers are available in plenty. Notably, the first of these three are essential inputs to a production process, whilst the fourth one is an essential link to complete the supply chain. Recall that our reference category is 'to access natural resources/inputs'. What this means is that, with the increase in the importance of local resources, the likelihood of motivation to invest 'to access natural resources/inputs' increases. The result therefore indicates that local resources attract resource-seeking firms.[1] Furthermore, controls for entry modes, industry and age had also been

Table 2. Model Results.

Motivation to Invest in a Host Country: Dependent Variable	Independent Variables	Coefficient-β	Significance	Exp(β)	95% Confidence Interval Exp(β)	
					Lower bound	Upper bound
(1)	(2)	(3)	(4)	(5)	(6)	(7)
Motivation – To access new markets	Intercept	0.314	0.903	–	–	–
	Firm age	0.015	0.607	1.015	0.960	1.072
	Business conditions Group-1	0.910	0.120^	2.484	0.789	7.823
	Business conditions Group-2	−0.549	0.176	0.577	0.260	1.280
	Market conditions	1.737	0.000***	5.682	2.542	12.702
	Local resource	−1.491	0.007**	0.225	0.077	0.663
	Other location factors	−0.250	0.512	0.779	0.369	1.644
	Industry-1: Production/manufacturing	−0.426	0.634	0.653	0.113	3.771
	Industry-2: Distribution/sales marketing	9.000	0.945	8100.013	7.187E-107	9.129E113
	Industry-3: Financial services	9.407	0.954	12172.700	5.157E-136	2.873E143
	Entry-1: Greenfield	1.922	0.054**	6.836	0.966	48.380
	Entry-2: Via acquisition	0.766	0.485	2.151	0.250	18.495
Motivation – Efficiency seeking	Intercept	−1.269	0.694	–	–	–
	Firm age	−0.014	0.693	0.986	0.918	1.059
	Business conditions Group-1	0.809	0.254	2.246	0.559	9.033
	Business conditions Group-2	−0.022	0.965	0.978	0.373	2.568
	Market conditions	0.453	0.337	1.572	0.625	3.958
	Local resource	−1.447	0.027**	0.235	0.065	0.850
	Other location factors	0.132	0.784	1.141	0.445	2.928
	Industry-1: Production/manufacturing	1.207	0.375	3.343	0.232	48.181
	Industry-2: Distribution/sales marketing	−0.289	0.999	0.749	1.097E-168	5.119E167
	Industry-3: Financial services	10.598	0.948	40060.285	1.678E-135	9.561E143
	Entry-1: Greenfield	1.746	0.220	5.729	0.353	93.068
	Entry-2: Via acquisition	0.581	0.718	1.788	0.077	41.732
Motivation – To join a specific partner	Intercept	−4.169	0.293	–	–	–
	Firm age	−0.059	0.338	0.942	0.835	1.064
	Business conditions Group-1	1.100	0.255	3.006	0.452	19.990
	Business conditions Group-2	−0.566	0.357	0.568	0.170	1.893
	Market conditions	1.860	0.006*	6.425	1.694	24.367
	Local resource	−1.397	0.086*	0.247	0.050	1.221
	Other location factors	0.048	0.935	1.049	0.331	3.331
	Industry-1: Production/manufacturing	−0.170	0.894	0.844	0.069	10.250
	Industry-2: Distribution/sales marketing	8.825	0.946	6802.167	5.961E-107	7.762E113
	Industry-3: Financial services	−1.637	na	na	na	na
	Entry-1: Greenfield	1.729	0.239	5.637	0.316	100.456
	Entry-2: Via acquisition	0.714	0.690	2.042	0.061	68.381

$\chi^2 = 78.556$, df = 33, $N = 264$, $p < .001$; −2 Log likelihood = 303.621; Cox & Snell $R^2 = 0.257$; Nagelkerke $R^2 = 0.377$. $n = 264$.
Reference category for motivations is 'to access natural resources/inputs'; Reference category for industry is 'other services'; Reference category for entry mode is 'to access natural resources/inputs'; na is not applicable owing to small n. ***significant at .01; **significant at .05; *significant at .10; ^significant at .15.

introduced. Of these, Greenfield entry motive turns out to be a positive and significant function of *market-seeking FDI*.

DISCUSSION

Summary

Together with the liberalisation of investment barriers and global competitive pressures, FDI activity is showing a shift from being previously concentrated in developed nations and instead moving to relatively untapped and developing markets location. This has led to the revival in the interest of literature on location determinants, which have focused traditionally on developed nations. This chapter has sought to extend the theory of location determinants of MNEs by incorporating the main investment motivation of the MNE – ultimately affecting the value of a specific host-location advantage and hence the investment location choice. By explicitly acknowledging the heterogeneity between MNEs, we move away from the traditional approaches of explaining location decisions, which tend to ignore this. The chapter focuses on the context of the SSA region, which has attracted only a small proportion of FDI going into the developing world. Although the recent trends (UNCTAD, WIR 2009, 2010) are encouraging, the region nevertheless remains an enigma. Furthermore, which factors make a location attractive for investment is still a rewarding area of research which, hitherto, has not been explored in the context of SSA.

Following on from our review of theoretical and empirical literature, five testable hypotheses were listed for the empirical work. What comes out to be a factor of supreme importance for *all types of FDI* is the 'market condition variables' and the importance of 'local resources'. Factor analysis conducted led us to include three variables in 'market conditions' – presence of local markets, presence of regional markets and presence of key clients – as well as four variables in 'local resources' – labour costs, availability of skilled labour, raw materials and local suppliers. In second place, came the group of eight business condition variables in the case of *market-seeking MNEs*: political stability, economic stability, infrastructure, country's legal framework, support, and transparency of investment, quality of life and physical security. Entry by way of Greenfield ventures was also found to impact positively on market-seeking MNEs. The study accordingly points to several implications, as discussed below.

Implications

The study has the strength that it helps to see the wood amidst the trees. Out of several commonly argued conjectural and empirical study-based variables, those related to market conditions, local resources and (to a lesser extent) those related to business conditions come to be of supreme importance as reasons for undertaking FDI in SSA. These are informative results. What they tell us is that if the local and regional markets are present and can absorb the goods and services produced in the region, MNEs would undertake investment. Within a growing economy, the purchasing power of the masses rises pari passu. Therefore, even if the markets were growing slowly, an early mover could then establish considerable advantage over late-movers.

Importantly, a breakdown of entry dates shows that 42% of MNEs ($n = 1,173$) entered SSA between 1991 and 2000, whilst 25% entered during 2001 or later. Thus, almost two-thirds of entries have taken place since the 1990s. With this in mind, it is possible that rival firms have followed each other, move for move, as so often happens – particularly in oligopolistic markets. The results that market condition variables impact positively and significantly on *market*-seeking and *partner*-seeking FDI support the literature that highlights the importance of local markets in creating market opportunities, from relatively untapped markets and economies of scale. Does this mean that 'market factors' are causing MNE's to 'market seek' in the SSA? An examination of FDI data shows that, in general, those countries with relatively higher GDP per capita (Fig. 1) are also attractive

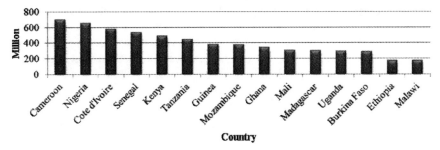

Fig. 1. Real Per Capita GDP (Using U.S. Dollars, at 2000 Prices), of SSA Sample in 2008. *Source*: Authors construction based on IMF (2008), World economic and financial surveys.

investment countries in SSA; however, there are some exceptions, such as Ghana.

The results show that firms value the stability of business climate conditions, including factors such as political and economic stability, institution support and transparency of investment. What is very clear, however, is that investing firms have a clear motive of lure of expanding markets, which makes them undertake investment. The implication of this result is that, no matter what the investment promotion agencies may have in mind, investing MNEs are very clear as to what *their* motive is to come into a host country. The investment promotion agencies should take note of this if they do not wish to end up with a losing game. Moreover, particularly during negotiation stages, they would do well to unearth the true motive behind investment; on the basis of which then, the suitable incentive package can be worked out. At the same time, the host nations would do well to pay attention to business climate factors, including the transparency of climate, which, in an earlier exercise, was also established as a highly important factor.[2] This result was somewhat expected from previous literature, as transparency enables a level playing field for young foreign investors relative to experienced or indigenous competitors, and also reduces uncertainty, information asymmetry and consequently additional costs. This is related to the bargaining power theory (Wint & Densil, 2002), where investment decisions are affected by the shift of power from the deciding MNE to the host policy makers, which would be more concerning in a bureaucratic location.

Given the volatile political environment in several SSA countries, some comments on the physical security aspect are in order. Historically, the SSA region is associated with corruption, political upheaval and a risk of expropriation. Through a local joint venture, such problems can be scaled down, thereby allowing the transfer of local business and cultural knowledge, and reducing the fear of the loss of business. We calculated (Fig. 2) that the 'no violence/risk' rating estimate of our sample of 15 countries and, although the overall conflict levels in SSA have declined since the 1990s, more recently, there have been various challenges to consolidate peace and hold free presidential election in Cote d'Ivoire; similarly, the emergence of post-election violence in Kenya has impacted on growth. It can thus be expected that countries with the lowest 'physical security' and risk rating in SSA have more joint venture investment.

For our sample data, we also calculated that Nigeria (11) and Cameroon (8) have the highest number of joint ventures, which is consistent with their high score as depicted in the figure. Accordingly, the question then arises: Does this

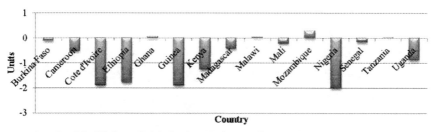

Fig. 2. No Violence/Risk Rating Estimates for the SSA Sample in 2008.
Source: Authors construction using World Bank (2010), African development indicators.

also mean that countries with low 'physical security' have relatively lower levels of inward FDI? Notably, however, this does not seem to be the case as the most attractive countries for the FDI are also Nigeria, Ghana, Cote d'Ivoire and Kenya, which, excluding Ghana, have the lowest levels of 'physical security'. This supports the proposition that some location factors are only relevant with a particular type of investment motives – in our case, 'physical security' with 'joint venture' investment, which assumes the availability of local firms.

Some comments on the oft-cited quality of infrastructure as a motivator of FDI are also in order. For our sample of SSA countries, we calculated 'Telephones/1000 people' is a commonly used indicator of infrastructure development (Fig. 3). Overall, the four most attractive FDI host countries (Nigeria, Ghana, Cote d'Ivoire and Kenya) have the highest number of phone connections. Infrastructure links with market investment, as it represents the development of local markets, differentiating large markets with low income and purchasing power from those more developed. This factor saw significant relationship with 'efficiency-seeking' investment in our sample.

These results also illustrate the importance of 'local resources' having an impact on all types of FDI. A large aspect of business activity is concentrated in the production and manufacturing sector in SSA, which is dominantly labour intensive. An examination of raw data shows the importance of 'availability of skilled labour': the low levels of literacy and education restrict the capacity of future learning, and therefore goes some way to explaining the overall low level of 'efficiency-seeking' investment in the sample. This is typical of low-income SSA countries which invest the

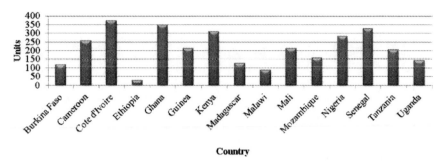

Fig. 3. Telephone Subscribers/1,000 People in Sample of SSA in 2008.
Source: Authors using World Bank (2010), African development indicators.

smallest proportion of GNP in education, of which there are 12 in this
sample. In 2006, on average, they collectively spent less than 4% of total
GNP on education (UNESCO, 2009). It can be argued that the lack of
labour skill could be an inhibiting factor for all types of FDI.

The strong impact of 'availability of raw materials', as well as 'labour
costs' with the propensity to investment, is supported by previous literature
(Asiedu, 2004), which explains SSA's dependence on resource-seeking
investment with countries such as Uganda and Nigeria being endowed with
oil and minerals, and consequently receiving higher levels of inward FDI.
Some comments on the 'unimportance' of group of variables in 'other
resources' is in order. National and regional agencies in SSA use marketing
strategies and incentives to attract foreign investors. Importantly, a previous
study (Dupasquier & Osakwe, 2006) shows that foreign investors attracted
to this service are those that require information concerning business
conditions (e.g. tariffs, regulation and taxation), the costs of doing business
and information relating to customers and markets. Therefore, this
acquisition of knowledge and local information may act as a substitute
against a joint venture entry mode. Furthermore, MNEs are able to
internalise and maintain ownership advantages, as well as to minimise
transaction costs through better information on local conditions. The
insignificant result (negative in the case of market-seeking FDI) highlights
the ineffectual nature of these agencies. This demands careful attention from
the state-supporting agencies promoting the work of inward investment.
With this in mind, why such agencies are not successful in what they are
doing should be examined in detail; these agencies have the potential to

improve investor confidence and alter the historically fixed bad perceptions of the SSA region.

A Conceptual Two-Step Approach to Explanations of FDI

In the final analysis, it seems that the relatively low levels of FDI in SSA have occurred due to risk overweighting the advantages, whereas those that do invest are more willing to accept a combination of host location factors – whether owing to historical or cultural ties, or otherwise as part of the overall business strategy. With this in mind, initial investment can be seen a two-step decision where, once investment has been made, the strength of general location factors, such as those of the business climate, has greater weighting. With this insight in view, an attempt can be made to develop a model of a two-step decision theory of FDI. The suggested model for this could be on the following lines.

Potential MNEs consider a list of variables before entering an overseas market. This list is categorised into three parts: the first part consists of crucial entry conditions which can loosely termed as 'pre-requisites', which have to be met; the second part comprises entry conditions which are important but which 'can be taken care of later', that is, once the entry has occurred, the firm has come to understand the institutional system better and learnt to wade through the bureaucracy; and the third and final part includes factors which are 'long-term issues' and which affect all firms in equal proportion, and over which no firm has any control or advantage. These factors can only be sorted with the help of macroeconomic policies in the long run.

As an example – and based on the analysis in this chapter – the 'pre-requisite' factors could be the existing of domestic and regional markets; 'second-level' factors could be the political and economic stability, quality of infrastructure, transparency of investment; and the 'third level' (long-term) factors could be the availability of skilled labour and local suppliers and a stable financial system. The decision process to enter or not to enter an overseas market would depend on what a firm's view is in relation to such factors. For instance, if the firm holds the belief that, once the entry has taken place it can deal with the second-level factors, it will enter the market. The decision to enter or not to enter is purely a strategic one, which is taken under conditions of uncertainty and on the assessment of degree of liability of foreignness (LOF) that the investing firm perceives it would face once it has entered the host nation. The LOF comprises internal environment factors specific to a country; these may range from variety of languages spoken within the country through to bureaucratic eccentricities of state and national-level institutions. The decision to enter or not to enter will depend crucially on the firm's confidence in handling of the LOF variables once it has entered the host nation. The entering firm would, in all probability, attempt to reduce the degree of uncertainty by gathering and synthesising as much information as it can with regard to LOF variables prior to using it in its decision-making process.

The aforementioned approach of overseas FDI has resonance with Johanson and Wiedersheim-Paul (1975) and Eriksson (Eriksson et al., 1997) evolutionary and sequential build-up of foreign commitments over time. The difference lies in the fact that the evolutionary and sequential approach is ex post: entry in some form – either by way of exports or minority commitment, or in some other nature – has already occurred, and the investor is then on the learning curve. Once the learning index has reached a critical minimum, the decision to commit or not to commit further is then taken. In our suggested model, the decision to enter or not to enter is taken ex ante; that is, before the firm has established any foothold in the host country. This decision is based on the collection and synthesis of information critical to entry, and is done before entry of any nature has taken place. The suggested model can be tested without difficulty in a survey-based approach on entry decisions by asking questions of the kind related to three entry-level conditions.

Limitations and Avenues for Future Research

The limitation of the study arises from the nature of predominant entry motives examined in the chapter. In the survey, firms were asked to select one dominant reason for entering the host market. With this in mind, it is quite possible that some firms have various motives for entering. Secondly, the analysis has been carried out at the aggregate level. Future studies can classify the countries in groups based on some common characteristics or regions in order to determine if inter-regional differences exist. Notably, we could not conduct this as our sample size shrunk to a complete but smaller data set required to do the statistical exercise. The factors that make a location tick for an investing firm include a fertile area of research which can be examined with the help of available models in the IB field. In the final section, we suggested a simple two-step model of FDI decision, which is easy to test empirically. The authors very much hope that this will be put to test.

NOTES

1. We are grateful to Christian Asmussen and Torben Pedersen for pointing this to us.

2. In an earlier version of this chapter, we ran four individual logistic regressions for four types of motives, and found that transparency of climate was a highly significant coefficient.

ACKNOWLEDGMENTS

The authors wish to record their gratitude to participants of 'Dynamics of Globalization: Location-Specific Advantages or Liabilities of Foreignness?' conference held at Copenhagen Business School 17–18 January 2011 for helpful comments and feedback. In particular, we are grateful to Christian Asmussen and Torben Pedersen who went through our several drafts so patiently providing precious comments and feedback. We also record our thanks to Srilata Zaheer, Aks Zaheer, and Alan Rugman for their valuable suggestions at the conference. All shortcomings are ours.

Authors are grateful to UNIDO for providing the data used in this study. The views expressed are those of the authors and do not in any way represent UNIDO.

REFERENCES

Agarwal, J. P. (1980). Determinants of foreign direct investment: A survey. *Weltwirschaftliches Archive, 116*(4), 737–768.

Aggarwal, R. (1997). Labour policies, employment and worker's earnings and international experience. *Indian Journal of Labour Economics, 40*(4), 631–653.

Aggarwal, R., & Agmon, T. (1990). The international success of developing country firms: Role of government-directed comparative advantage. *Management International Review, 30*(2), 163–180.

Aliber, R. Z. (1971). The multinational enterprise in a multiple currency world. In: J.H. Dunning (Ed.), (pp. 49–60). London: Allen and Unwin.

Asiedu, E. (2002). On the determinants of foreign direct investment to developing countries: Is Africa different? *World Development, 30*(1), 107–119.

Asiedu, E. (2004). Policy reform and foreign direct investment in Africa: Absolute progress but relative decline. *Development Policy Review, 22*(1), 41–48.

Asiedu, E. (2006). Foreign direct investment in Africa: The role of natural resources, market size, government policy, institutions and political stability. *World Economy, 29*(1), 63–77.

Bartels, F., Eicher, M., Bachtrog, C., & Rezonja, G. (2009). Foreign direct investment in sub-Saharan Africa: Changing location-specific advantages as signals of competitiveness. *The Developing Economies, 47*(3), 244–278.

Bende-Nabende, A. (2002). Foreign direct investment determinants in sub-Saharan Africa: A co-integration analysis. *Economic Bulletin, 6*(4), 1–19.

Billington, N. (1999). The location of foreign direct investment: An empirical analysis. *Applied Economics, 31*(1), 65–76.

Blonigen, B. A. (1997). Firm specific assets and the link between exchange rates and foreign direct investment. *The American Economic Review, 87*(3), 447–465.

Blonigen, B. A., & Feenstra, R. C. (1996). *Effects of U.S. trade protection and promotion policies.* Working Paper no. 5285. Natural Bureau of Economic Research, Cambridge, MA.

Buckley, P. J., & Casson, M. C. (1976). *The future of the multinational enterprise.* London: MacMillan.

Buckley, P. J., & Casson, M. C. (1981). The optimal timing of a foreign direct investment. *Economic Journal, 91*(361), 75–87.

Buckley, P. J., Devinney, T. M., & Louviere, J. J. (2007). Do managers behave the way theory suggests? A choice theoretic examination of foreign direct investment location decision making. *Journal of International Business, 38,* 1069–1094.

Carstensen, K., & Toubal, F. (2004). Foreign direct investment in Central and Eastern European countries: A dynamic panel analysis. *Journal of Comparative Economics, 32*(1), 3–22.

Cheng, L. K., & Kwan, Y. K. (2000). What are the determinants of the location of foreign direct investment? The Chinese experience. *Journal of International Economics, 51*(2), 379–400.

Coase, R. (1937). The nature of the firm. *Economica, 4*(16), 386–405.

Coviello, N. J., & Munro, H. J. (1997). Network relationships and the internationalization process of the small software firm. *International Business Review, 6*(4), 361–386.

Cyert, R. M., & March, J. G. (1963). *A behavioral theory of the firm* (2nd ed.). Blackwell Publishers Limited.

Deichmann, J., Socrates, K., & Sayek, S. (2003). Foreign direct investment in Turkey: Regional determinants. *Applied Economics, 35*(16), 1767–1778.

De Mello, L. R. (1997). Foreign direct investment in developing countries and growth: A selective survey. *Journal of Development Studies, 34*(1), 1–34.

Dow, D., & Karunaratna, A. (2006). Developing a multidimensional instrument to measure psychic distance stimuli. *Journal of International Business Studies, 37*(5), 578–602.

Dunning, J. H. (1993). *Multinational enterprises and the global economy* (140). Wokingham, Berkshire: Addison-Wesley.

Dunning, J. H. (1998). Location and the multinational enterprise: A neglected factor? *Journal of International Business Studies, 29*(1), 45–66.

Dunning, J. H., & Lundan, S. M. (2010). *Multinational enterprises and the global economy* (2nd ed.). Cheltenham, UK: Edward Elgar.

Dunning, J. H., & Narula, R. (2000). Industrial development, globalisation and multinational enterprises: New realities for developing countries. *Oxford Development Studies, 28*(2), 141–167.

Dupasquier, C., & Osakwe, P. (2006). Foreign direct investment in Africa: Performance, challenges, and responsibilities. *Journal of Asian Economics, 17*(2), 241–260.

Eriksson, K., Johanson, J., Majkgard, A., & Sharma, D. (1997). Experiential knowledge and cost in the internationalization process. *Journal of International Business Studies, 28*(2), 337–360.

Gastanaga, V., Nugent, J., & Pashamiova, B. (1998). Host country reforms and FDI inflows: How much difference do they make? *World Development, 26*(7), 1299–1314.

Globerman, S., & Shapiro, D. (2002). The impact of government policies on foreign direct investment: The Canadian experience. *Journal of International Business Studies, 30*(3), 513–532.

Globerman, S., & Shapiro, D. (2003). Governance infrastructure and U.S. foreign direct investment. *Journal of International Business Studies, 34*(1), 19–39.

Henisz, W. J., & Delios, A. (2001). Uncertainty, imitation, and plant location: Japanese multinational corporations, 1990–1996. *Administrative Science Quarterly, 46*(3), 443–475.

Hymer, S. H. (1960). *The international operations of national firms: A study of direct foreign investment*. Ph.D. dissertation, MIT Press, Cambridge, MA (published 1976).

Johanson, J., & Wiedersheim-Paul, F. (1975). The internationalization of the firm: Four Swedish cases. *Journal of Management Studies, 12*(3), 305–322.

Kinda, T. (2010). Investment climate and FDI in developing countries: Firm-level evidence. *World Development, 38*(4), 498–513.

Knickerbocker, F. T. (1973). *Oligopolistic reaction and the multinational enterprise*. Harvard, MA: Harvard University Press.

Lankes, P., & Venables, A. (1996). Foreign direct investment in economic transition: The changing pattern of investments. *Economics of Transition, 4*(2), 331–347.

Lim, D. (1983). Fiscal incentive and direct foreign investment in less developed countries. *The Journal of Development Studies, 19*, 207–212.

Loree, D. W., & Guisinger, S. (1995). Policy and non-policy determinants of U.S. equity foreign direct investment. *Journal of Business Studies, 26*(2), 281–299.

Love, J. H., & Lage-Hidalgo, F. (2000). Analysing the determinants of US direct investment in Mexico. *Applied Economics, 32*(10), 1259–1267.

Luostarinen, R., & Welch, L. (1988). Internationalization: Evolution of a concept. *Journal of General Management, 14*(2), 34–55.

Maxfield, S. (1998). Understanding the political implications of financial internationalization in emerging market countries. *World Development, 26*(7), 1201–1219.

Meyer, K. E. (2001). Institutions, transaction costs and entry mode choice. *Journal of International Business Studies, 31*(2), 357–368.

Morrisset, P. (2000). Foreign direct investment to Africa: Policies also matter. *Transnational Corporation, 9*(2), 107–125.

Nachum, L., & Wymbs, C. (2007). The location and performance of foreign affiliates in global cities: Regional aspects of multinationality and performance. In: A. Rugman (Ed.), *Research in global strategic management* (Vol. 13, pp. 221–259). Bingley, UK: Emerald Group Publishing Ltd.

Nelson, R. R., & Sampat, B. N. (2001). Making sense of institutions as a factor shaping economic performance. *Journal of Economic Behavior & Organization, 44*(1), 31–54.

Onyeiwu, S., & Shrestha, H. (2004). Determinants of foreign direct investment in Africa. *Journal of Developing Societies, 20*(1–2), 89–106.

Penrose, E. T. (1959). *The theory of the growth of the firm*. New York: Oxford University Press.

Pistoresi, B. (2000). Investimenti diretti esteri e fattori di localizzazione: LAmerica Latina e il Sud Est asiatico, Rivista di Politica. *Economica, 90*, 27–44.

Reinhart, C. M., & Rogoff, K. S. (2002). FDI to Africa: The role of price stability and currency instability. Paper presented at the Annual World Bank Conference on Development Economics, Washington, DC, 29–30 April. (cited in Musila, J. W., & Sigue, S. P. (2006), Accelerating foreign direct investment flow to Africa: From policy statements to successful strategies, *Managerial Finance, 32*(7), 577–593).

Rolfe, R. J., David, A. R., Pointer, M. M., & McCarthy, M. (1993). Determinants of FDI incentive preferences of MNEs. *Journal of International Business Studies, 24*(2), 335–355.

Rugman, A. A. (Ed.) (2009). *The Oxford handbook of international business.* Oxford: Oxford University Press.

Scaperlanda, A. E., & Mauer, L. S. (1969). The determinants of U.S. direct investment in the EEC. *American Economic Review, 59*, 558–568.

Schneider, F., & Frey, B. (1985). Economic and political determinants of foreign direct investment. *World Development, 13*(2), 161–175.

Shatz, J. H., & Venables, A. J. (2000). *The geography of international investment.* Centre for Economic Policy Research (CEPR), World Bank Policy Research Working Paper no. 2338. Available at http://papers.ssrn.com/sol3/papers.cfm?abstract_id=630710. Retrieved on 22 August 2010.

Singh, H., & Jun, K. W. (1995). *Some new evidence on determinants of foreign direct investment.* Working Bank Policy Research, World Bank Working Paper no. 1531, World Bank. Available at http://econpapers.repec.org/paper/wbkwbrwps/1531.htm. Retrieved on 22 July 2010.

Tsai, P. L. (1994). Determinants of direct foreign investment and its impact on economic growth. *Journal of Economic Development, 19*, 137–163.

Tumar, J. P., & Emmert, C. F. (1999). Explaining Japanese foreign direct investment in Latin America, 1979–1992. *Social Science Quarterly, 80*(3), 539–555.

UNCTAD. (2009). World investment report 2009: Transnational corporations. Agricultural production and development. Available at http://unctad.org/en/docs/wir2009_en.pdf. Retrieved on 2 May 2010.

UNCTAD. (2010). World investment report 2010: Investing in a low carbon economy. Available at http://unctad.org/en/docs/wir2010_en.pdf. Retrieved on 15 October 2010.

UNESCO. (2009). Overcoming inequality: Why governance matters. Available at http://www.unesco.org/education/gmr2009/press/Factsheet_SSA.pdf. Retrieved on 16 August 2010.

UNIDO. Africa Foreign Investor Survey. (2005). Vienna: UNIDO. Available at: http://www.unido.org/index.php?id=o53658

Vernon, R. (1966). International investment and international trade in the product cycle. *Quarterly Journal of Economics, 80*(2), 190–207.

Vernon, R. (1971). *Sovereignty at bay: The multinational spread of US enterprises.* New York: Basic Books.

Wheeler, D., & Mody, A. (1992). International investment location decisions. *Journal of International Economics, 33*(1–2), 57–76.

Wint, A. G., & Densil, A. W. (2002). Attracting FDI to developing countries: A changing role for government? *The Journal of Public Sector Management, 15*(5), 361–374.

Zander, U., & Kogut, B. (1995). Knowledge and the speed of the transfer and imitation of organizational capabilities: An empirical test. *Organization Science, 6*(1), 76–92.

APPENDIX

Table A1. Likelihood Ratio Tests.

Effect	Model Fitting Criteria	Likelihood Ratio Tests		
	−2 Log likelihood of reduced model	Chi-square	df	Sig.
Intercept	225.065	0.000	0	
Age	230.406	5.341	3	0.148
BC1	227.681	2.616	3	0.455
BC2	228.481	3.416	3	0.332
Market condition	258.071	33.006	3	0.000
Local resource	234.473	9.408	3	0.024
Other	226.649	1.584	3	0.663
Industry	234.443	9.378	9	0.403
Entry mode	229.394	4.329	6	0.632

Table A2. Case Processing Summary.

	Case Processing Summary	N	Marginal Percentage (%)
Motivation variables	To access new markets	225	85.2
	To lower production costs	16	6.1
	To access natural resources/inputs	15	5.7
	To join a specific partner	8	3.0
Main business activity	Production and manufacturing	146	55.3
	Distribution/sales and marketing	39	14.8
	Financial services	18	6.8
	Other services	61	23.1
Mode of entry if wholly owned	Establishment of a new operation (Greenfield)	204	77.3
	Acquisition of existing assets from private owners	40	15.2
	Acquisition of existing state-owned assets through a privatisation programme	20	7.6
Valid		264	100.0
Missing		952	
Total		1216	
Sub-population		264[a]	

[a]The dependent variable has only one value observed in 264 (100.0%) sub-populations.

Table A3. Classification: Observed and Predicted.

Observed	Predicted				
	To access new markets	To lower production costs	To access natural resources/inputs	To join a specific partner	Percent correct (%)
To access new markets	223	0	2	0	99.1
To lower production costs	14	0	2	0	0.0
To access natural resources/inputs	9	0	6	0	40.0
To join a specific partner	8	0	0	0	0.0
Overall percentage (%)	96.2	0.0	3.8	0.0	86.7

INTERNATIONAL ENTREPRENEURSHIP AT THE FOREIGN MARKET LEVEL: TOWARDS A NETWORK PERSPECTIVE

Sara Melén, Emilia Rovira Nordman, Daniel Tolstoy and D. Deo Sharma

ABSTRACT

The purpose of this chapter is to contribute to research in the field of international entrepreneurship by complementing existing levels of analysis with a network perspective that captures how the pursuit of international opportunities at the foreign market level unfolds through processes ingrained in the network structures that firms are embedded in. By performing a multilevel review of 50 studies within the international entrepreneurship research field, the chapter contributes with an analysis of the evolvement of the international entrepreneurship field between the years 1994 and 2010, a discussion of the field's current status and where it is going from here. The results of the review show that whereas early work in the field of international entrepreneurship is primarily concentrated on individual entrepreneurs or individual firms, network-level-focused studies dominate

Dynamics of Globalization: Location-Specific Advantages or Liabilities of Foreignness?
Advances in International Management, Volume 24, 357–387
ISSN: 1571-5027/doi:10.1108/S1571-5027(2011)0000024021

among the later publications. Studies that adopt explicit network approaches have the potential to contribute to international entrepreneurship research by being able to shed light on the actual mechanisms and processes by which foreign market opportunities are exploited.

INTRODUCTION

International entrepreneurship has emerged as a valuable perspective in international business studies to capture the subversive elements of internationalisation, that is, the proactive pursuit of business opportunities in foreign markets. Whereas many studies in the field have highlighted issues such as the age, speed, and scope of internationalisation (e.g. Oviatt & McDougall, 1994; Knight & Cavusgil, 1996; Madsen & Servais, 1997; Andersson & Wictor, 2003), few studies have concentrated on the actual mechanisms by which business actually is created in the international marketplace. Hence, in contrast to studies on early internationalisation (e.g. born globals and international new ventures), which have outlined the overall *patterns* of internationalisation, this study focuses on the *processes* by which discrete international opportunities are pursued (e.g. acts of new business creation). This standpoint corresponds to the argument by Zahra (2005) who claimed that international entrepreneurship has more to do with how firms exploit opportunities once they have entered a foreign market than it has to with how they get there in the first place. Hence, based on classic entrepreneurship theory, international entrepreneurship is here understood as a cognitive process (cf. Kirzner, 1985, 1997), which underlies the creation of competitive advantages in foreign market locations.

To be able to unravel these processes, we need to be able pinpoint who the international entrepreneur actually is in a given situation. Several different views have been presented on this topic. One strand of research in the field has emphasised the individual level, portraying single founders and leaders as entrepreneurs that make the key decisions for the internationalisation of their businesses (e.g. Freeman & Cavusgil, 2007). The other strand of research has focused on the firm level, describing, for example, born globals (e.g. Melén & Nordman, 2009) and international new ventures (Lianxi, Barnes, & Yuan, 2010) as bold and groundbreaking by nature, and therefore, the units in which exploitation of foreign market opportunities are studied. Hence, there exists an ambiguity about the level of analysis, blurring the underpinnings of theoretical conceptualisations (e.g. the entrepreneur) as well as about the operationalisations of key constructs (e.g. entrepreneurial cognition, exploration and exploitation). In this chapter, we argue that it is important for scholars to clearly distinguish between the levels of analysis applied in empirical studies and also explain for what reasons a certain perspective is favoured in a particular investigation. Such an approach would open up for fine-grained models allowing researchers to, with greater accuracy, describe entrepreneurial processes at the foreign market level. In this vein, we claim that there is yet another valid approach for analysing international entrepreneurial activity. We have noticed that there are surprisingly few examples of studies that have taken on a broad perspective on international entrepreneurship, that is, by claiming that foreign market opportunities emerge in networks that include actors outside the boundaries of the firm. Empirical evidence on especially smaller firms and high-tech firms show that business creation may arise in shared cognitive frameworks that span numerous cross-border network relationships (e.g. Fernhaber, Gilbert, & McDougall, 2008; Tolstoy, 2010). This is similar to Weick's (1979) notion that business opportunities are not *out there*, but rather conceived in interplay between the firm and its environment. Hence, network models contextualise acts of international entrepreneurship and enable researchers to analyse entrepreneurship from a specific foreign market location perspective. This enables us to investigate how firms create advantages by combining their resources with resources residing at the foreign market level. Furthermore, a network model can offer an all-encompassing unit of analysis, capturing the individual dimension, the organisational dimension and the structural dimension. The structural dimension, which is unique to the network perspective, is essential to be able to unravel the inter-organisational and interpersonal resource configurations that in essence constitute foreign market ventures.

Smaller firms are known to scale up their activities by leveraging the resources of other firms, organisations and individuals. Many of these firms have been observed to operate in industries with short innovation cycles and therefore tend to seek novel knowledge from partners to transform or extend their own competences fast (Nordman & Melén, 2008). These observations are empirically substantiated by the growth of, for example, industrial clusters, incubators and global communities. We here argue that foreign market opportunities are born in constellations of firms and individuals. It may, in some instances, even be more accurate to discuss entrepreneurial networks than entrepreneurial firms. Shepherd (2011), for example, advocates a multilevel perspective in entrepreneurship research while acknowledging that decisions are determined by the entrepreneurial context. The specific characteristics of the network can confer unique advantages (or disadvantages) shaping the entrepreneurial behaviour at the foreign market level. Building on this idea, the purpose of this chapter is to contribute to research in the field of international entrepreneurship by complementing existing levels of analysis with a network perspective that captures how the pursuit of international opportunities at the foreign market level unfolds through processes ingrained in the network structures that firms are embedded in.

METHODOLOGY

To answer the purpose of this chapter, we take on a comparative theory by reviewing a selection of influential articles in the field and from this review reveal some basic theoretical and methodological implications from using the individual, firm or network levels of analysis. These findings are then used as a point of departure to further elucidate a network-based view that explains international entrepreneurial activity. Our review focuses on influential scientific publications in the field of international entrepreneurship. In 1994, the seminal article 'Toward a theory of international new ventures' by Oviatt and McDougall was published in *Journal of International Business Studies*. This article made important contributions to the field of international entrepreneurship and has also inspired much research in the field during the past decade. Hence, 1994 mark the starting year for the review and 2010 mark the end. By investigating studies published within this time period, we seek to capture contemporary scientific contributions in the field of international entrepreneurship. This can also help us to identify some evolution in the analytical frameworks used within international entrepreneurship research.

To identify the studies for this review, we used the Social Sciences Citation Index (SSCI), a citation index that covers about 5,700 journals that represent most disciplines in the social sciences. The SSCI database is particularly useful to locate articles and authors who have conducted research on a specific topic. It also enables the researcher to develop a chronological list of references that documents the historical evolution of an idea (Creswell, 2003).

The studies that we chose to include in the review had to be closely related to the research field of international entrepreneurship. To ensure this, we chose to include only publications that contained one of the following topics when searching the database: 'born global', 'global start-up', 'international entrepreneurship' and 'international new venture'. A search for these keywords in the selected database revealed that there are a multitude of interesting studies to choose from in conducting a review about international entrepreneurship.[1] To further narrow down the number of studies to be included in our review, we used two additional criteria. The candidate published work should (1) belong to the most influential scientific studies in the research field of international entrepreneurship; (2) be drawn from core, leading publications within the international research discipline. To ensure that criterion 1 was followed, we used the SSCI to identify which publications have been cited most frequently. Because publications that have been published more recently (i.e. during the last three years) have not yet had sufficient time to impact current research in the same manner as older studies, we used the following formula to calculate publication impact:

$$\frac{\text{Number of citations}}{\text{Current year (2011)} - \text{Publication year}} = \text{Publication impact}$$

After calculating the publication impact of the different studies, we decided to include all studies with a publication impact number of ≥ 2 in our review and this gave us a sample of 50 studies (see appendix). After going through the 50 studies that were included, we also could ensure that criterion 2 was met as all of these studies have appeared in core, leading publications within the international research discipline such as *Academy of Management Journal, Entrepreneurship Theory and Practice, International Business Review, International Marketing Review, Journal of Business Venturing, Journal of International Business Studies, Journal of International Marketing, Journal of Management, Journal of World Business, Progress in Human Geography, Regional Studies, Strategic Management Journal* and *Technovation*. These journals have all contributed to the development of the international entrepreneurship field, by publishing leading studies discussing questions related to international entrepreneurship.

The next step in performing our literature review was to go through the selected studies to see which ones had a mainly theoretical focus (i.e. that focused on building theory based on previous studies, for example, review studies and conceptual studies) and which studies were based on empirical data. By studies based on empirical data, we mean studies where the author or authors pose a question or hypothesis, collect data and try to answer the question or support the hypothesis (Creswell, 2003). This analysis revealed that 29 of the selected publications were based on empirical data (Table 1). In our continued analysis, we decided to focus on these studies; because they could offer a larger breadth and capture more dimensions (particularly from a methodological point of view) when further investigating the development of the international entrepreneurship research field.

To be able to add analytical depth to the patterns found when investigating these 29 studies, we also decided to analyse a little more than half of the studies (16 out of 29) in a more in-depth manner than the rest. We chose which studies to analyse in-depth based on the way that they

Table 1. The Empirical Articles Included in the Review.

Nr	Authors (Year)	Focus of Article	Level of Analysis
1	**McDougall et al. (1994)**	**Empirical**	**Individual-level**
2	**Burgel and Murray (2000)**	**Empirical**	**Firm-level**
3	**Thomas and Mueller (2000)**	**Empirical**	**Individual-level**
4	Yeoh (2000)	Empirical	Firm-level
5	Kotha, Rindova, and Rothaermel (2001)	Empirical	Firm-level
6	Kuemmerle (2002)	Empirical	Firm-level
7	Moen (2002)	Empirical	Firm-level
8	**Moen and Servais (2002)**	**Empirical**	**Firm-level**
9	Carpenter, Pollock, and Leary (2003)	Empirical	Individual-level
10	**Chetty and Campbell-Hunt (2004)**	**Empirical**	**Firm-level**
11	**Knight and Cavusgil (2004)**	**Empirical**	**Firm-level**
12	Knight, Madsen, and Servais (2004)	Empirical	Firm-level
13	Crick and Spence (2005)	Empirical	Firm-level
14	George, Wiklund, and Zahra (2005)	Empirical	Firm-level
15	**Coviello (2006)**	**Empirical**	**Network-level**
16	Freeman, Edwards, and Schroder (2006)	Empirical	Network-level
17	**Loane and Bell (2006)**	**Empirical**	**Network-level**
18	Mort and Weerawardena (2006)	Empirical	Network-level
19	**Acedo González and Jones (2007)**	**Empirical**	**Individual-level**
20	**Fan and Phan (2007)**	**Empirical**	**Firm-level**
21	**Freeman and Cavusgil (2007)**	**Empirical**	**Individual-level**
22	**Gassmann and Keupp (2007)**	**Empirical**	**Firm-level**
23	Kuivalainen, Sundqvist, and Servais (2007)	Empirical	Firm-level
24	Presutti, Boari, and Fratocchi (2007)	Empirical	Firm-level
25	**Zhou, Wu, and Lou (2007)**	**Empirical**	**Network-level**
26	**Fernhaber et al. (2008)**	**Empirical**	**Network-level**
27	Gabrielsson, Kirpalani, Dimitratos, Solberg, and Zucchella (2008)	Empirical	Network-level
28	**Khavul et al. (2010)**	**Empirical**	**Firm-level**
29	**Tolstoy and Agndal (2010)**	**Empirical**	**Network-level**

Note: The 16 articles included in the in-depth analysis are marked in bold.

could serve as typical or representative for the larger group of studies. The studies that we chose provided a good representation of the group of 29 studies and could not be considered extreme (e.g. in terms of methodological foundations or their use of individual, firm or network levels of analysis). Thus, these 16 studies are chosen based on irregular intervals (e.g. we have not chosen studies solely based on publication year), and some are published in the same year as each other.[2] When choosing which studies to include in the in-depth analysis, we also wanted to include studies that offered a spread in perspective. Hence, when we came upon more than one study (among the larger sample of 29 studies) that had been written by the same team of authors, we chose to include only one of these publications in our in-depth review of 16 studies.

In sum, it is important to note that this review does not attempt to identify the entire population of work related to international entrepreneurship during the time period of 1994–2010. Because the reviewed studies are published in journals that belong to the forefront of discourse about international business, international marketing, international management and international entrepreneurship, we, however, argue that our review includes a significant number of academic works that contribute to the evolution of academic research in the field of international entrepreneurship. Hence, by investigating these studies, we can reveal some basic results concerning how the study of international entrepreneurship has changed over the years and where it is going from here.

ANALYSES OF THE REVIEW

We started our analysis of the 29 reviewed studies by examining the level of analysis used in each study (see Table 1). We also analysed what methodology (i.e. qualitative or quantitative) the 29 studies used. We then continued with a more in-depth analysis of 16 of the 29 articles. Each of the 16 articles was content-analysed by the authors to identify the following issues: (1) research focus and conclusions; (2) methodology (including data collection method and sample) and (3) theoretical foundations used for analysis. We chose to focus on these issues in our in-depth analysis because they can provide us with a basic understanding and point of departure to further elucidate a network-based perspective.

Analysis of Research Focus and Conclusions

Table 1 presents the 29 empirical studies that have been reviewed, in particular, which level of analysis is used by these studies. As is shown here, five studies adopt an individual-level analysis. The in-depth analysis presented in Table 3, moreover, shows that a common focus in these studies is their aim to understand the entrepreneurs in the firm, that is, often the owners/managers and these individuals' abilities to recognise entrepreneurial opportunities. More specifically, these studies are focused on identifying and describing the competences (McDougall, Shane, & Oviatt, 1994), characteristics (Thomas & Mueller, 2000) and mindsets (Acedo González & Jones, 2007; Freeman & Cavusgil, 2007) of the individual entrepreneurs, and how these relate to the search for opportunities. McDougall et al. (1994) conclude that the individual entrepreneurs in International New Ventures (INVs) see opportunities that others do not see because of the competencies that are unique to them. The authors also conclude that to explain the formation process of INVs, it is necessary to focus on the individual and small group level of analysis. Similar line of arguments are found in the article by Acedo González and Jones (2007), who emphasise the need for the field of international entrepreneurship to focus more on the individual. The authors specifically emphasise the need for researchers to shift perspectives towards 'the conditions that foster opportunity recognition, and in particular, the mindsets and orientations held by managers that might influence that process' (Acedo González & Jones, 2007, p. 238).

Table 1 also shows that 16 of the 29 studies in our review adopt a firm-level of analysis. The in-depth analysis of the firm-level-focused studies highlights that these are focused on understanding how firm-level variables influence the pattern of entry, performance and the speed of internationalisation of the firm. Therefore, as shown in Table 3, the focus of these studies is the internationalisation behaviour and strategies of born global firms, INVs and start-ups. Knight and Cavusgil (2004), for example, examine how the innovativeness and development of particular types of knowledge in rapidly internationalising firms influenced their international performance. Gassmann and Keupp (2007) also focus on the intra-firm resources and capabilities that enable the firms' internationalisation processes. The authors put forward strong arguments towards the need to focus on the firm-level of analyses to explain early and rapidly internationalising small and medium-sized enterprises (SMEs). They specifically emphasise that 'The lack of studies that focus on organisational characteristics is apparent' (Gassmann & Keupp, 2007, p. 352). According to Gassmann and Keupp (2007), this lack of studies is due to the fact that the literature in the field almost exclusively has looked at personal, cognitive and behavioural traits of entrepreneurs and owners.

Table 1, moreover, shows that eight studies in our review adopt a network-level analysis. The in-depth analysis of this group of studies highlights that a common research focus among these studies is to understand and explain the impact, nature and dynamics of networks within born globals, INVs and new ventures. Coviello (2006) positions her study by arguing that 'Our focus is on INV networks rather than the INV per se, and the network is positioned as the "dependent variable"' (Coviello, 2006, p. 714). Loane and Bell (2006) position their study in a similar way and put forward that they focus on the networking dimensions of rapid internationalisation. As is indicated in Table 3, several of the studies adopting a network level of analysis include both personal networks of individual entrepreneurs and the business network at the level of the firm in their analyses. In addition, some of the studies specifically encourage a more multilevel analytical approach. Loane and Bell (2006), as for example, conclude that 'there was clear evidence that where relevant networks existed actors within the firms were actively leveraging them at many levels. These included exploiting intrafirm networks, personal networks and social network to gain an entrée to decision-makers in target firms, gather knowledge and resources ...' (Loane & Bell, 2006, p. 479).

On the basis of our in-depth analysis of the 16 reviewed articles, there appear to be an ambiguity within the field of international entrepreneurship regarding what unit of analysis that shall guide future research in the field. The arguments put forward by McDougall et al. (1994) as well as Acedo González and Jones (2007) concerning the need for an individual level of analysis clearly differs from the arguments presented by Gassmann and Keupp (2007). Hence, there exist conflicting arguments concerning the question of the level of analysis preferred. To shed further light on this issue, it is interesting to reflect upon how the field has developed in terms of level of analysis used. Table 1 notes that between the years 1994 and 2006, the individual-level- and firm-level-focused studies clearly dominates. Eleven of the sixteen firm-level studies in our review are actually published before 2006. The network-level-focused studies are, however, not represented among the early publications (before 2006 in our review). These studies instead dominate among the later publications between the years 2006 and 2010.

Following the differences in research focus among the three levels of analyses, the in-depth analysis also revile some differences among the reviewed studies in terms of research scope. Those studies adopting an individual-level analyses are more focused towards understanding the formation of entrepreneurial firms (McDougall et al., 1994; Thomas & Mueller, 2000) or the early internationalisation processes of these firms (Acedo González & Jones, 2007). Among the studies adopting a firm level of analysis, some studies use a more process-oriented perspective in their analysis of the born global phenomenon (Moen & Servais, 2002; Chetty & Campbell-Hunt, 2004). Others are limited to a more static-oriented perspective, as their analyses only capture decisions and behaviours at one specific situation of time, such as the firms' initial decision to internationalise (Fan & Phan, 2007; Gassmann & Keupp, 2007; Khavul, Perez-Nordtvedt, & Wood, 2010). The network-level studies differ from the other reviewed studies in that a majority of the studies have a process-oriented perspective. Coviello (2006), for example, argues that to understand how networks change, there is a need to investigate networks in a manner that is sensitive to time.

On the basis of the findings presented about the research focus and scope, it is interesting to note that studies from all three levels of analysis identify a gap in international entrepreneurship research in terms of process-oriented studies. Acedo González and Jones (2007) acknowledge that the field has focused particularly on the early phases of a firm's internationalisation process and the distinct characteristics of rapidly internationalising firms. In light of these arguments, Coviello (2006) highlights the need for process-oriented research, and Fan and Phan (2007) call for research that uses a long-term perspective to explain how INVs internationalise. Thus, there seems to be a gap in the field in terms of research that captures and understands the dynamics of international entrepreneurship.

Analysis of Methods Used

To obtain an overview of the methods used in the 29 reviewed studies, we started to analyse whether qualitative or quantitative methods were used. Inspired by the review of Rialp, Rialp, and Knight (2005), Fig. 1 was designed to present an overview of the methods used in the reviewed studies. The horizontal axis in Fig. 1 differentiates between the three levels of analysis: individual level, firm level and network level of analysis. The vertical axis differentiates between qualitative and quantitative methods. On the basis of the analytical findings of the review, we have also added a diagonal arrow to Fig. 1. The arrow illustrates the evolution in the field and

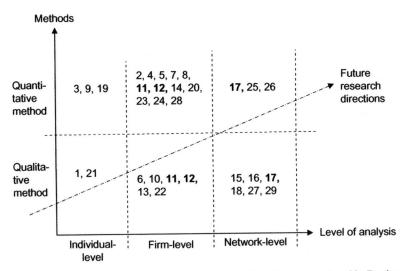

Fig. 1. Qualitative and Quantitative Methods Used among the 29 Reviewed Articles. *Note:* Numbers marked in bold are based on both qualitative and quantitative methods.

what we believe to be the direction for future research in the field of international entrepreneurship, in terms of level of analysis and methods used.

The results presented in Fig. 1 indicate that 11 studies have used a qualitative approach as their main research method and 15 studies have used a quantitative approach as their main research method. Three studies have, moreover, used both qualitative and quantitative methods (Knight & Cavusgil, 2004; Knight et al., 2004; Loane & Bell, 2006), and these studies are marked in bold in Fig. 1. It is clearly demonstrated in Fig. 1 that most firm-level-focused studies have used a quantitative method in analysing how firm-level variables influence the behaviour and strategies of internationalising firms. To understand and explain the nature, impact and dynamics of networks in international entrepreneurial firms, most of the network-focused studies have adopted a qualitative method. Looking specifically at studies using individual-level analysis, quantitative methods slightly dominate in analysing the competences, characteristics and mindsets of individual entrepreneurs. The in-depth analysis based on 16 studies, moreover, shows that among the qualitative-based studies, case studies dominate and the main data collection method is to conduct in-depth interviews with key individuals in the firms, such as founders, managers and CEOs. Among the quantitative-based studies, the main research method is to collect survey data.

The in-depth analysis also gives an indication of what geographical regions are studied. Even though several regions of the world are represented within the reviewed studies, most studies have examined firms from European countries. Empirical studies also encompass firms from the United States, Australia and New Zealand. We can, moreover, see that among the recently published articles, there are studies that have examined firms from China (Khavul et al., 2010; Zhou et al., 2007), India and South Africa (Khavul et al., 2010). Khavul et al. (2010) also acknowledge that the pace of internationalisation from emerging markets is increasing. The authors, however, also point out that 'yet the nexus of international entrepreneurship and emerging markets research remains sparsely addressed' (Khavul et al., 2010, p. 105).

On the basis of the analytical findings regarding the methodologies used among the three levels of analysis, Fig. 1 can help us identify a number of areas within international entrepreneurship that still are relatively unexplored. First, early publications in the field (i.e. publications published between the years 1994 and 2006 in our review) have concentrated on the individual or the firm levels of analyses, with a heavy focus on the firm level of analysis. The network level of analyses is still relatively unexplored. We believe future research should direct more attention to the network level of analyses. This direction for future research is important because such research has the potential to contribute to the understanding of the dynamics of international entrepreneurship. Second, several studies in our review also acknowledge that limited amount of research within the field have adopted a longitudinal research design. Acedo González and Jones (2007) state 'There is still a great need for longitudinal studies ...' (p. 248) and Khavul et al. (2010) argue 'Clearly, future research should seek to study the phenomenon in a longitudinal setting, ideally using time-series data' (p. 116). It is important to give attention to this gap in the field because longitudinal research designs have the potential to capture the dynamics of international entrepreneurship. Third, looking specifically at the network-level-focused studies, Fig. 1 shows that studies so far have generated knowledge based on qualitative studies. Knowledge based on quantitative research designs is still limited when it comes to analysis at the network level. Future research should therefore, as a next step, work towards developing network-based measures that can be used for quantitative studies. Fourth, our review also suggests that studying international entrepreneurship from emerging markets could potentially contribute new insights into the field. This is especially relevant as Rialp et al. (2005) in their review pointed out that international entrepreneurship studies published before 2003 had not examined the emergence of international entrepreneurial firms in less-developed countries.

Analysis of the Theoretical Foundations

In their article about the formation of *International New Ventures*, McDougall et al. (1994) discuss why the five generally accepted theories of international business cannot explain the formation of INVs. The five theories of international business that are discussed are monopolistic advantage theory (Caves, 1982), product lifecycle theory (Vernon, 1966), internationalisation process theory (Johanson & Vahlne, 1977) oligopolistic reaction theory (Knickerbocker, 1973) and internalisation theory (Hennart, 1982). According to McDougall et al. (1994), these theories fail to explain the formation process of INVs because 'they all focus on firm-level analysis of large, mature firms, rather than on individual and small group analysis of the entrepreneur and his or her social network of business alliances' (McDougall et al., 1994, p. 471). The authors instead suggest that there is a need to use and integrate concepts from entrepreneurship literature, the resource-based view and strategic management literature.

In light of the statements made by McDougall et al. (1994), our in-depth analysis shows interesting patterns in terms of the main theoretical foundations that are used. Table 2 sums up the main theoretical foundations that are used in 16 of the 29 reviewed articles. From Table 2, it is noted that internationalisation process theory (IP theory) still serves as the main theoretical foundation in 6 of the 16 reviewed studies. The traditional IP theory, which describes how firms gradually intensify their activities in foreign markets, is usually divided into the so-called Uppsala internationalisation model (Johanson & Vahlne, 1977) and the innovation-related internationalisation models (Bilkey & Tesar, 1977; Cavusgil, 1980). We find evidence of both models in the theoretical foundations among the 16 in-depth analysed studies (we thus include both models when referring to IP theory). The use of IP theory is particularly evident in studies using a firm level of analysis, but this theory is also applied in studies adopting an individual-level analysis. Moreover, in several of the studies, IP theory is the

Table 2.   The Main Identified Theoretical Foundations Used by the 16
In-Depth Analysed Articles.

	Individual-Level	Firm-Level	Network-Level
International process theory (IP theory)	19, 21	2, 8, 10, 20	
Business network theory	21		15, 17, 29
Social network theory	21	22	15, 17, 25, 29
Resource-based view (RBV)	1, 21	11	17, 29
Austrian economics	1, 3		
Transaction cost theory[a]		2	
Organisational learning theory		2, 11, 22	17
Ecological theory[b]			26
Entrainment theory[c]		28	

Note: The numbers that appear are those that are used in Table 1.

[a]Transaction cost theory has given focus to the choice of governance or entry mode and the minimisation of the costs of carrying out particular transactions. The theory is concerned with comparing different institutional arrangements for carrying out economic activity (Williamson, 1985).

[b]Ecological theory focuses on the role of the local environment in providing access to key resources (Fernhaber et al., 2008). The theory fosters an understanding of how the availability of and competition for resources shape the ultimate outcome of affected firms (Hannan & Freeman, 1977).

[c]Entrainment theory focuses on the process by which activity cycles of one system synchronize to those of another, more dominant system (see Khavul et al., 2010).

main theory used in building up the analytical frameworks (Moen & Servais, 2002; Chetty & Campbell-Hunt, 2004; Fan & Phan, 2007).

Among the individual-level-focused studies, Table 2 indicates that apart from IP theory, the RBV and Austrian economics have had a significant influence on analysis of the individual entrepreneur and his/her recognition of opportunities. The RBV as a theory focuses on a firm's ability to utilise, combine and develop resources. Hence, the differential endowment of resources is an important determinant of organisational capabilities and performance in the RBV (Barney, 1991). Those two individual-focused studies that have adopted the RBV (McDougall et al., 1994; Freeman & Cavusgil, 2007) have used it to analyse the value and combination of unique assets and capabilities within these firms. The two studies that have used Austrian economics as a theoretical foundation (McDougall et al., 1994; Thomas & Mueller, 2000) have focused on traditional (e.g. Schumpeter, 1965) and more contemporary views within the Austrian school (e.g. Kirzner, 1973), which explains the function of individuals who perceives and pursues economic opportunities in the face of uncertainty.

Table 2 in particular notes that IP theory has had a significant influence on studies focusing on the firm-level and analyses of the behaviour and strategies of internationalising firms. Among these studies, Table 2 also marks the frequent use of organisational learning theory to understand the firm's knowledge resources and how these relate to the firm's internationalisation behaviour, strategies and performance. In this review, we use the term organisational learning theory to include views from both the knowledge-based view (e.g. Grant, 1991) and the more traditional organisational learning literature (e.g. Cohen & Levinthal, 1990).

Finally, Table 2 highlights that network theories are foremost used by studies adopting a network unit of analysis. Several of these studies also use both business network and social network theories in their analytical frameworks. The business network approach focuses on the multiple interlinked business relationships that reside within a business network (Johanson & Mattsson, 1987, 1988). These relationships typically consist of customers, suppliers, distributors or even competitors (Blomstermo, Eriksson, Lindstrand, & Sharma, 2004). The social network approach (e.g. Granovetter, 1973; Burt, 1992) on the contrary focuses on the social structures made up by individuals (within organisations), which are tied by different interdependencies such as friendship and kinship.

On the basis of the findings of Tables 1, 2 and 3, it becomes clear that network theories have entered into the analytical framework of international entrepreneurship studies rather recently. In our review, it is not until 2006 that network theories actually are used as main theoretical foundations. It is here interesting to note that the importance of networks for the internationalisation of born globals/INVs often is highlighted in the earlier publications of our review (e.g. McDougall et al., 1994; Moen & Servais, 2002; Chetty & Campbell-Hunt, 2004). However, the theoretical linkage between networks and entrepreneurship remains weak in these studies. This observation is supported by Coviello (2006), who acknowledges that networks have been widely recognised as influential in INV studies, but relatively, few studies have focused on assessing INV networks per se. Therefore, surprisingly, few of the reviewed articles have actually integrated theories of entrepreneurship with network theories. Fernhaber et al. (2008), however, move towards the notion of integrating the concepts of networks and entrepreneurship by suggesting that to more accurately understand new venture internationalisation, the firm's resources and the resources of its embedded network should be jointly rather than separately considered.

Table 3. The 16 Reviewed Articles that Have Been Analysed In-Depth.

Number (as Given in Table 1)	Author (Date)	Level of Analysis	Methodology	Main Theoretical Foundation	Research Focus and Conclusions
1.	McDougall et al. (1994)	Individual-level	Qualitative method: 24 case studies of INVs from Brazil, Czechoslovakia, France, Germany, Israel, New Zealand, Singapore, Switzerland, the United Kingdom and the United States	Austrian economics, RBV	The study addresses the formation process of INVs and highlights the question: Who are the founders of INVs? The results show that the founders of INVs already from inception see opportunities for business across national borders because of the competences that are unique to them
2.	Burgel and Murray (2000)	Firm-level	Quantitative method: Based on a questionnaire survey of 246 technology-based start-ups with international activities based in the United Kingdom	IP theory, Transaction cost theory, Organisational learning theory	The study addresses the lack of empirical analysis of foreign market entry forms. The findings show that entry mode decisions are a trade-off between resources available and the support requirements of customers. The authors argue that an organisational capability perspective offers a better explanation of their entry decisions than either transaction cost or stage theory
3.	Thomas and Mueller (2000)	Individual-level	Quantitative method: Approximately 1,800 responses to a survey of third and fourth year students at universities in United States, Canada, Ireland, Germany,	Austrian economics	The study examines the relationship between culture and four personality characteristics commonly associated with entrepreneurial motivation. The study demonstrates systematic variation in entrepreneurial characteristics across

			Belgium, China, Singapore, Croatia and Slovenia		cultures, which raises questions about the boundaries of international entrepreneurship research
8.	Moen and Servais (2002)	Firm-level	Quantitative method: A questionnaire survey where hypotheses are tested on a sample of 677 exporting SMEs in Denmark, France and Norway	IP theory	The study addresses the identification of manifestations of a gradual development among exporting SMEs. The results suggest that export intensity, distribution, market selection and global orientation are not influenced by the firms' year of establishment or first year of exporting activity
10.	Chetty and Campbell-Hunt (2004)	Firm-level	Qualitative method: 16 in-depth historiographic case studies in New Zealand based on the use of semi-structured interview data	IP theory	The study investigates the internationalisation process of the firm. The results show that many of the phenomena believed to distinguish born global internationalisation path are also characteristic of firms that began their internationalisation in the traditional way
11.	Knight and Cavusgil (2004)	Firm-level	Qualitative and quantitative method: 24 case studies of early internationalising firms and a questionnaire survey where hypotheses are tested on a sample of 203 manufacturing firms across the United States	Organisational learning theory RBV	The study addresses the orientation and strategies of born global firms. The results show that the innovative nature of born global firms supports the development of particular types of knowledge, which drives the development of organisational capabilities that support these firms' superior performances in international markets
15.	Coviello (2006)	Network-level	Qualitative method: Interview data from managers in three small international new ventures in New Zealand	Business network theory Social network theory	The study addresses the question of how networks are associated with INV formation. The results show that the evolution of networks is intertwined with the formation of INVs

Table 3. (*Continued*)

Number (as Given in Table 1)	Author (Date)	Level of Analysis	Methodology	Main Theoretical Foundation	Research Focus and Conclusions
17.	Loane and Bell (2006)	Network-level	Quantitative and qualitative method: Email survey of 143 firms in Australia, New Zealand, Canada and Ireland Interviews were conducted with CEOs in 53 of these firms	Business network theory Social network theory RBV Organisational learning theory	The study investigates the role of networks in the acquisition of knowledge and resources among small entrepreneurial firms. In studying the networking behavior of rapidly internationalising entrepreneurial firms, the results show that while a high proportion access existing networks to develop their international capabilities, an even higher number have to build new networks to do so
19.	Acedo González and Jones (2007)	Individual-level	Quantitative method: Interviews by using questionnaires with the top managers in 216 Spanish SMEs	IP theory	The study investigates how selected aspects of managerial cognition, that is, elements of the owner/manager's mindset, relate to the speed of internationalisation. The results show that international orientation leads to higher levels of proactivity and lower perceptions of risk
20.	Fan and Phan (2007)	Firm-level	Quantitative method: A survey of new ventures in the European airline industry. Hypotheses are tested on a sample of 135 new ventures (whereof 67 are born globals)	IP theory	The study examines INV's patterns of entry into international markets. The results show that the decision for a new venture (absent a specific technological advantage) to internationalise at inception is influenced by the size of the home market, its inaugural production capacity as well as by cultural and economic forces (e.g. level of competition)

No.	Author (year)	Level	Method	Theory	Description
21.	Freeman and Cavusgil (2007)	Individual-level	Qualitative method: Multicase study research based on in-depth interviews with executives in 12 smaller born global firms in Australia	IP theory Business network theory Social network theory RBV	The study investigates the attitudinal orientations of senior management in smaller born global firms. Four entrepreneurial attitudinal states for accelerated internationalisation are identified. The states can be characterised as the strategic mindset of senior managers for accelerated internationalisation of smaller born globals
22.	Gassmann and Keupp (2007)	Firm-level	Qualitative method: 6 case studies of internationally active biotechnology SMEs from Switzerland, Germany and Australia. Interviews and secondary sources were used	Organisational learning Social network theory	The study focuses on the competitive advantage of early and rapidly internationalising SMEs in the biotechnology industry. The results suggest that the 'liability of smallness' of born globals has been overstated. They use many innovative measures to overcome the problem of limited tangible resources
25.	Zhou et al. (2007)	Network-level	Quantitative method: Interview-based questionnaire surveys with top managers in 129 Chinese born global SMEs	Social network theory	The study addresses that internationalisation orientation influence firm performance through home-based social networks. The results suggest that social networks are efficient in helping born globals to go abroad rapidly and profitably
26.	Fernhaber et al. (2008)	Network-level	Quantitative method: Sample of 156 publicly held US-based new ventures. The data used about these firms were sourced from the Compustat	Ecological theory	The study investigates how new ventures gain access to the resources that enable them to internationalise. The results show that location influences new venture internationalisation

Table 3. (*Continued*)

Number (as Given in Table 1)	Author (Date)	Level of Analysis	Methodology	Main Theoretical Foundation	Research Focus and Conclusions
28.	Khavul et al. (2010)	Firm-level	database, individual IPO prospectuses and the Cluster mapping project Quantitative method: A survey of INVs in China, India and South Africa. Hypotheses are tested on a sample of 166 INVs	Entrainment theory	The study focuses on the temporal fit in the activity cycles between exchange partners. The results suggest that when INVs attain temporal fit with their most important international customers, they can implement their strategic goals in international markets more effectively. The study also highlights the relevance of internationalisation to INVs coming from emerging economies
29.	Tolstoy and Agndal (2010)	Network-level	Qualitative method: The study comprises six case studies of new business ventures in foreign markets of Swedish biotech firms (distinguishing between product ventures and market ventures)	RBV Business network theory Social network theory	By investigating new international market ventures and new international product ventures, the study looks at how internationalising biotech firms commercialise innovations by combining resources in networks. The authors find that new international product ventures, in particular, demand a broad scope of network resources as well as a high degree of interaction between network partners to meet the multifaceted challenges of redefining the product and redefining the market

CONCLUDING DISCUSSION – TOWARDS A NETWORK PERSPECTIVE ON INTERNATIONAL ENTREPRENEURSHIP

Our literature review reveals that early work in the field of international entrepreneurship is primarily concentrated on individual entrepreneurs or individual firms. In some instances, this focus can be explained by the specific empirical content of the studies, for example, observations of strikingly resourceful founders that by themselves bring their firms into international markets (McDougall et al., 1994). Though, in many cases, the preference of choosing the individual level and the firm level of analysis appear to have been set almost by default with no obvious motivation. A plausible explanation may be the massive theoretical heritage stemming from paradigms listed in the literature review: for example, the Austrian entrepreneurship school of thought (individual focused (cf. Kirzner 1985, 1997)), the resource-based view (organisation focused) and IP theory (organisation focused). These theoretical frameworks have undoubtedly had a serious impact on the multidisciplinary field of international entrepreneurship although they have not been able to fully cover the complexities imposed by network factors such as shared cognitive frameworks, resource combinations across organisational boundaries and opportunities ingrained in network relationships.

At this point in the discussion, it is important to recognise that seminal studies in international entrepreneurship indeed have acknowledged the phenomenon of networks and their merits in providing resources and serving as sources of foreign market knowledge. Furthermore, research in international entrepreneurship has traditionally favoured smaller firms in their empirical investigations. These firms typically lack internal resources in terms of, for example, capital, know-how and technology. As a logical consequence, researchers have deduced a link between firms' shortages of internal resources with their aspirations to leverage external resources in network relationships. Despite the documented outward orientation of firms, there are, until recently, few examples of studies the field of international entrepreneurship that have applied networks as units of analysis. Nor have researchers devised explicit network models for understanding entrepreneurial activity in foreign markets. Multilevel approaches have previously been advocated to discern between the psychosocial characteristics of individuals and the information/knowledge systems of organisations (e.g. Staw, Sandelands, & Dutton, 1981). Network models naturally comprise these characteristics and can also unravel structural aspects such as shared cognitive frameworks, resource configurations and coordination of work flows.

However, judging by our literature review, there is an increasing stream of research that (potentially) demarks the beginning of a new approach to international entrepreneurship. In these studies, scholars have made networks an integral part in discussions of how firms discover and exploit opportunities in foreign markets. In contrast to early work in the field, these studies are rooted in the idea that entrepreneurial cognition and action can take place in constellations of firms rather than in single entities. We believe that studies that adopt explicit network approaches have the potential to greatly contribute to international entrepreneurship research by being able to probe deeper into the actual mechanisms by which foreign market opportunities are exploited. Such studies could also enable us to better understand the particular business dynamics at the foreign market level by offering insights into how change in the local networks in which firms are embedded may affect the development of entrepreneurial opportunities. Hence, similar to Weick's (1979) idea, international entrepreneurship develops in interplay between the firm and its environment. Entrepreneurial behaviour can, thus, be understood as a phenomenon that, in many situations, largely is conceived outside the boundaries of firms.

Implications for Future Research

To date, international entrepreneurship research has been primarily focused on the *patterns* of internationalisation. On the basis of previous network studies in the field, we believe that the network perspective provides a viable framework for analysing the *processes* of how opportunities are discovered and exploited at the foreign market level, ultimately enhancing international growth. As indicated by, for example, Coviello (2006), using the network as a level of analysis gives us means to determine where and how processes of entrepreneurship take place. That is, by treating the international venture as synonymous to the network in which firms are embedded, we can see how the business unfolds as consequence of the actions of a number of interconnected actors. The network perspective thus confers a broader contextualisation of the concept international entrepreneurship, which previously been primarily substantiated by behavioural parameters referring to single entities. This view implies that the significance of speed and age at internationalisation as determinants of entrepreneurship are relaxed.

Arguably, international entrepreneurship can be understood as a concept less concerned about the overall trajectory of internationalisation and more about specific events of business creation in foreign markets. From a network point of view, it is argued that entrepreneurship may involve shared cognitive frameworks and coordinated actions that span numerous network relationships that drive the entrepreneurial exploitation of international ventures. Hence, network dynamics imply that entrepreneurial behaviour can be triggered at any time when the cognitive frameworks and resource bases of different entities cross paths. We recommend that researchers should probe deeper into these processes and also investigate how they are affected by, for example, country of origin, cultural, geographical and institutional influences at the foreign market level and industrial structures (e.g. presence of global networks).

On the basis of this reasoning, firms have to be both proactive and reactive because actions in networks tend to have ramifications that firms need to deal with. International ventures are woven into networks where the extent of international opportunities unfolds little by little as firms intensify their foreign market operations. Although firms can indeed influence networks by proactive strategies, they are at the same time influenced by networks, which, in turn, calls for reactive strategies. For example, the launch of a new product at the foreign market level (proactive) may trigger a demand for complementary products, perhaps to be developed in collaboration with suppliers in another market (reactive). Apart from spin-offs, it is also conceivable that opportunities are transformed entirely when different types of network knowledge are combined. For example, new technology that is developed in collaboration with suppliers may turn out to be completely different from what was first anticipated, thus forcing firms to find new application areas and new customer segments. It is here claimed that the capabilities of many firms are, to a large extent, embedded in network relationships and develop in tandem with changes in the overall network structure. Opportunities for new business thus exist only at certain points in time and space and may quickly disappear and reappear as a result of network dynamics (e.g. changing customer requirements, increased competition or new supplier technology). Hence, internationalisation may unfold as an ongoing entrepreneurial activity of creating new business in ever-evolving network contexts. Method-wise, this implies a need to complement studies based on cross-sectional data with data sets that can capture the processes by which networks evolve (i.e. based on longitudinal data). One must, of course, recognise that such data sets require considerable resources and effort to create. Data may need to be collected at several points in time if reliable historical data is not available, which is time-consuming. Furthermore, it is a widely recognised problem that it is hard to draw the boundaries around a specific network, which open up for arbitrary delimitations. Finally, it is difficult to get reliable data about all network actors in the venture, which may favour the stories of a few and thus bias the findings.

The literature review indicates that the field of international entrepreneurship has been studied through both explorative qualitative methods and confirmatory quantitative methods. Consequently, the field has reached a relatively mature stage where researcher have both generated and tested theory, especially at the individual and the firm levels. In line with the principal arguments of this study, however, we believe that the time has come to develop and test network models to better account for the inter-organisational and interpersonal dynamics of international entrepreneurship. However, to this date, we have seen few quantitative studies that have actually operationalised network effects, possibly because of the many difficulties such a conduct entails. Regardless, we believe that such studies would be extremely valuable to open up the black box of business creation in foreign markets. Thus, we strongly support scholars to develop such measures, preferably based on data collected at different points.

In short, the network perspective implies a 'boundary-less' view of firms, given that the resources to cope with (or provoke) entrepreneurial behaviour to a large extent are conceived, modified and transformed in constellations of entities. If firms were detached from critical network relationships, their entrepreneurial capabilities could very well be compromised (in the same way that they could be reinforced if the firms were connected with compatible partners). Managers should recognise that the image of the independent entrepreneurial hero is often a false idol. It is likely that entrepreneurial networks have greater potential than individuals to stimulate business creation, primarily by producing heterogeneous knowledge that can serve as a hotbed for innovation. Networks also provide the opportunity to experiment with new business solutions because investments and risks are shared by multiple network partners. By interacting in a variety of network relationships, firms are inevitably scrutinised from the multiple perspectives of different international partners. Partners can contest existing ways of doing business, which prevents firms from becoming hampered by 'taken-for-granted' mentalities. They can also kindle new ideas and provide connections to key actors and new markets. Networks can both induce and alleviate liability of foreignness. Dense networks may be difficult to enter, but once firms find a way in, they can use the network to acquire resources and knowledge needed on that particular market. In contrast to previous research that has conceptualised the liability of foreignness basically as a mindset (e.g. psychic distance), we propose that one should adopt a structural view on this issue (i.e. measuring the degree to which the firm is embedded in the foreign market network).

Finally to clarify our posture, it is important to note that we do not push for making the network perspective an exclusive frame of reference for studying international entrepreneurship phenomena. Rather, we advocate a multilevel approach as starting point based, where the specific level of analysis is selected based on how well it corresponds to the empirical content. Entrepreneurial ventures may indeed be undertaken with little external influence by, for example, venture capitalists or by individual initiative. Nonetheless, we firmly advocate that the worldwide developments we are witnessing comprising global industries, global markets and social network tools are strengthening the validity of a network perspective as a valuable complement, and sometimes substitute, to extant views.

NOTES

1. A search in the SSCI revealed the following number of hits for the selected topics: 'born global' (73 hits), 'global start-up' (3 hits), 'international entrepreneurship' (109 hits) and 'international new venture' (11 hits).
2. The distribution of publication year for the 16 studies are 1994 (1 study), 2000 (2 studies), 2002 (1 study), 2004 (2 studies), 2006 (2 studies), 2007 (5 studies), 2008 (1 study) and 2010 (2 studies).

REFERENCES

Acedo González, F. J., & Jones, M. V. (2007). Speed of internationalization and entrepreneurial cognition: Insights and a comparison between international new ventures, exporters and domestic firms. *Journal of World Business, 42*(3), 236–252.

Andersson, S., & Wictor, I. (2003). Innovative internationalisation in new firms: Born Globals – the Swedish case. *Journal of International Entrepreneurship, 1*(3), 249–276.

Autio, E. (2005). Creative tension: The significance of Ben Oviatt's & Patricia McDougall's article 'toward a theory of international new ventures'. *Journal of International Business Studies, 36*(1), 9–19.

Baker, T., Gedajlovic, E., & Lubatkin, M. (2005). A framework for comparing entrepreneurship processes across nations. *Journal of International Business Studies, 36*(5), 492–504.

Barney, J. B. (1991). Firm resources and sustained competitive advantage. *Journal of Management, 17*(1), 99–120.

Bilkey, W. J., & Tesar, G. (1977). The export behavior of smaller-sized Wisconsin manufacturing firms. *Journal of International Business Studies, 8*, 93–98.

Blomstermo, A., Eriksson, K., Lindstrand, A., & Sharma, D. D. (2004). The perceived usefulness of network experiential knowledge in the internationalizing firm. *Journal of International Management, 10*(3), 355–373.

Burgel, O., & Murray, G. C. (2000). The international market entry choices of start-up companies in high-technology industries. *Journal of International Marketing, 8*(2), 33–62.

Burt, R. S. (1992). *Structural holes: The social structure of competition.* Cambridge, MA: Harvard University Press.

Carpenter, M. A., Pollock, T. G., & Leary, M. M. (2003). Testing a theory of reasoned risk-taking: Governance, the experience of principals and agents, and global strategy in high-technology IPO firms. *Strategic Management Journal, 24*(9), 803–820.

Caves, R. E. (1982). *Multinational enterprise and economic analysis.* Cambrigde, MA: Cambridge University Press.

Cavusgil, S. T. (1980). On the internationalization process of firms. *European Research, 8*(6), 273–281.

Chetty, S., & Campbell-Hunt, C. (2004). A strategic approach to internationalization: A traditional versus a born-global approach. *Journal of International Marketing, 12*(1), 57–81.

Cohen, W., & Levinthal, D. (1990). Absorptive capacity: A new perspective on learning and innovation. *Administrative Science Quarterly, 35*(1), 128–152.

Coviello, N. E. (2006). The network dynamics of international new ventures. *Journal of International Business Studies, 37*(5), 713–731.

Coviello, N. E., & Jones, M. V. (2004). Methodological issues in international entrepreneurship research. *Journal of Business Venturing, 19*(4), 485–508.

Creswell, J. W. (2003). *Research design: Qualitative, quantitative and mixed methods approaches* (2nd ed.). Thousand Oaks, CA: Sage.

Crick, D., & Spence, M. (2005). The internationalisation of 'high performing' UK high-tech SMEs: A study of planned and unplanned strategies. *International Business Review, 14*(2), 167–185.

Dimitratos, P., & Jones, M. V. (2005). Future directions for international entrepreneurship research. *International Business Review, 14*(2), 119–128.

Drori, I., Honig, B., & Wright, M. (2009). Transnational entrepreneurship: An emergent field of study. *Entrepreneurship Theory and Practice, 33*(5), 1001–1022.

Fan, T., & Phan, P. (2007). International new ventures: Revisiting the influences behind the 'born-global' firm. *Journal of International Business Studies, 38*(7), 1113–1131.

Fernhaber, S. A., Gilbert, B. A., & McDougall, P. P. (2008). International entrepreneurship and geographic location: An empirical examination of new venture internationalization. *Journal of International Business Studies, 39*(2), 267–290.

Freeman, S., & Cavusgil, T. (2007). Toward a typology of commitment states among managers of born-global firms: A study of accelerated internationalization. *Journal of International Marketing, 15*(4), 1–40.

Freeman, S., Edwards, R., & Schroder, B. (2006). How smaller born-global firms use networks and alliances to overcome constraints to rapid internationalization. *Journal of International Marketing, 14*(3), 33–63.

Gabrielsson, M., Kirpalani, V. H. M., Dimitratos, P., Solberg, C. A., & Zucchella, A. (2008). Born globals: Propositions to help advance the theory. *International Business Review, 17*(4), 385–401.

Gassmann, O., & Keupp, M. M. (2007). The competitive advantage of early and rapidly internationalizing SMEs in the biotechnology industry: A knowledge-based view. *Journal of World Business*, *42*(3), 350–366.

George, G., Wiklund, J., & Zahra, S. A. (2005). Ownership and the internationalization of small firms. *Journal of Management*, *31*(2), 210–233.

Granovetter, M. (1973). The strength of weak ties. *American Journal of Sociology*, *78*(6), 481–510.

Grant, R. M. (1991). The resource-based theory of competitive advantage: Implications for strategy formulation. *California Management Review*, *33*(3), 114–135.

Hannan, M. T., & Freeman, J. (1977). The population ecology of organizations. *The American Journal of Sociology*, *82*(5), 929–964.

Hennart, J. F. (1982). *A theory of the multinational enterprise*. Ann Arbor, MI: The University of Mitchigan Press.

Johanson, J., & Mattsson, L.-G. (1987). Interorganizational relations in industrial systems: A network approach compared with the transaction-cost approach. *International Studies of Management and Organization*, *17*(1), 34–48.

Johanson, J., & Mattsson, L.-G. (1988). Internationalisation in industrial systems – A network approach. In: N. Hood & J.-E. Vahlne (Eds), *Strategies in global competition* (pp. 287–314). New York: Croom Helm.

Johanson, J., & Vahlne, J.-E. (1977). The internationalization process of the firm – A model of knowledge development and increasing foreign market commitments. *Journal of International Business Studies*, *8*(1), 23–32.

Jones, M. V., & Coviello, N. E. (2005). Internationalisation: Conceptualising an entrepreneurial process of behavior in time. *Journal of International Business Studies*, *36*(3), 284–303.

Keupp, M. M., & Gassmann, O. (2009). The past and the future of international entrepreneurship: A review and suggestions for developing the field. *Journal of Management*, *35*(3), 600–633.

Khavul, S., Perez-Nordtvedt, L., & Wood, E. (2010). Organizational entrainment and international new ventures from emerging markets. *Journal of Business Venturing*, *25*(1), 104–119.

Kirzner, I. M. (1985). *Discovery and the capitalist process*. Chicago, IL: University of Chicago Press.

Kirzner, I. M. (1973). *Competition and Entrepreneurship*. Chicago, IL: University of Chicago Press.

Kirzner, I. M. (1997). Entrepreneurial discovery and the competitive market process: An Austrian approach. *Journal of Economic Literature*, *35*(1), 60–85.

Knickerbocker, F. T. (1973). *Oligopolistic reaction and the multinational enterprise*. Cambridge, MA: Harvard University Press.

Knight, G. A., & Cavusgil, S. T. (1996). The born global firm: A challenge to traditional internationalization theory. *Advances in International Marketing*, *8*, 11–26.

Knight, G. A., & Cavusgil, S. T. (2004). Innovation, organizational capabilities, and the born-global firm. *Journal of International Business Studies*, *35*(2), 124–141.

Knight, G. A., Madsen, T. K., & Servais, P. (2004). An inquiry into born-global firms in Europe and the USA. *International Marketing Review*, *21*(6), 645–665.

Kotha, S., Rindova, V. P., & Rothaermel, F. T. (2001). Assets and actions: Firma specific factors in the internationalization of US Internet firms. *Journal of International Business Studies*, *32*(4), 769–791.

Kuemmerle, W. (2002). Home base and knowledge management in international ventures. *Journal of Business Venturing, 17*(2), 99–122.

Kuivalainen, O., Sundqvist, S., & Servais, P. (2007). Firms' degree of born-globalness, international entrepreneurial orientation and export performance. *Journal of World Business, 42*(3), 253–267.

Lianxi, Z., Barnes, B., & Yuan, L. (2010). Entrepreneurial proclivity, capability upgrading and performance advantage of newness among international new ventures. *Journal of International Business Studies, 41*(5), 882–905.

Loane, S., & Bell, J. (2006). Rapid internationalisation among entrepreneurial firms in Australia, Canada, Ireland and New Zealand – An extension to the network approach. *International Marketing Review, 23*(5), 467–485.

Madsen, K. T., & Servais, P. (1997). The internationalization of born globals: An evolutionary process. *International Business Review, 6*(6), 561–583.

Mathews, J. A., & Zander, I. (2007). The international entrepreneurial dynamics of accelerated internationalization. *Journal of International Business Studies, 38*(3), 387–403.

McDougall, P. P., & Oviatt, B. M. (2000). International entrepreneurship: The intersection of two research paths. *Academy of Management Journal, 43*(5), 902–908.

McDougall, P. P., Shane, S., & Oviatt, B. M. (1994). Explaining the formation of international new ventures: The limits of theories from international business research. *Journal of Business Venturing, 9*(6), 469–487.

Melén, S., & Nordman, E. R. (2009). The internationalisation of born globals: A longitudinal study. *European Management Journal, 27*(4), 243–254.

Moen, Ø. (2002). The born globals – A new generation of small European exporters. *International Marketing Review, 19*(2–3), 156–175.

Moen, Ø., & Servais, P. (2002). Born global or gradual global? Examining the export behavior of small and medium-sized enterprises. *Journal of International Marketing, 10*(3), 49–72.

Mort, G. S., & Weerawardena, J. (2006). Networking capability and international entrepreneurship – How networks function in Australian born global firms. *International Marketing Review, 23*(5), 549–572.

Nordman, E. R., & Melén, S. (2008). The impact of different kinds of knowledge for the internationalization process of born globals in the biotech business. *Journal of World Business, 43*(2), 171–185.

Oviatt, B. M., & McDougall, P. P. (1994). Toward a theory of international new ventures. *Journal of International Business Studies, 25*(1), 45–64.

Oviatt, B. M., & McDougall, P. P. (2005a). Defining international entrepreneurship and modeling the speed of internationalization. *Entrepreneurship Theory and Practice, 29*(5), 537–553.

Oviatt, B. M., & McDougall, P. P. (2005b). The internationalization of entrepreneurship. *Journal of International Business Studies, 36*(1), 2–8.

Peng, M. W. (2001). The resource-based view and international business. *Journal of Management, 27*(6), 803–829.

Presutti, M., Boari, C., & Fratocchi, L. (2007). Knowledge acquisition and the foreign development of high-tech start-ups: A social capital approach. *International Business Review, 16*(1), 23–46.

Rialp, A., Rialp, J., & Knight, G. A. (2005). The phenomenon of early internationalizing firms: What do we know after a decade (1993–2003) of scientific inquiry? *International Business Review, 14*(2), 147–166.

Schumpeter, J. A. (1965). Economic theory and entrepreneurial history. In: H. G. J. Aitken (Ed.), *Explorations in enterprise*. Cambridge, MA: Harvard University Press.

Shepherd, D. A. (2011). Multilevel entrepreneurship research: Opportunities for studying entrepreneurial decision making. *Journal of Management, 37*(2), 412–420.

Staw, B. M., Sandelands, L. E., & Dutton, J. E. (1981). Threat-rigidity effects in organizational behavior: A multilevel analysis. *Administrative Science Quarterly, 26*(4), 501–525.

Thomas, A. S., & Mueller, S. L. (2000). A case for comparative entrepreneurship: Assessing the relevance of culture. *Journal of International Business Studies, 31*(2), 287–301.

Tolstoy, D. (2010). Network development and knowledge creation within the foreign market. *Entrepreneurship & Regional Development, 22*(5), 379–402.

Tolstoy, D., & Agndal, H. (2010). Network resource combinations in the international venturing of small biotech firms. *Technovation, 30*(1), 24–36.

Vernon, R. (1966). International investment and international trade in the product cycle. *Quarterly Journal of Economics, 80*(2), 190–207.

Weerawardena, J., Mort, G. S., Liesch, P. W., & Knight, G. A. (2007). Conceptualizing accelerated internationalization in the born global firm: A dynamic capabilities perspective. *Journal of World Business, 42*(3), 294–306.

Weick, K. E. (1979). *The social psychology of organizing*. Reading, PA: Addison-Wesley.

Williamson, O. E. (1985). *The economic institutions of capitalism*. New York: The Free Press.

Wright, R. W., & Ricks, D. A. (1994). Trends in international-business research 25 years later. *Journal of International Business Studies, 25*(4), 687–701.

Wright, M., Westhead, P., & Ucbasaran, D. (2007). Internationalization of small and medium-sized enterprises (SMEs) and international entrepreneurship: A critique and policy implications. *Regional Studies, 41*(7), 1013–1029.

Yamakawa, Y., Peng, M. W., & Deeds, D. L. (2008). What drives new ventures to internationalize from emerging to developed economies? *Entrepreneurship Theory and Practice, 32*(1), 59–82.

Yeoh, P. L. (2000). Information acquisition activities: A study of global start-up exporting companies. *Journal of International Marketing, 8*(3), 36–60.

Yeung, H. W. C. (2009). Transnationalizing entrepreneurship: A critical agenda for economic geography. *Progress in Human Geography, 33*(2), 210–235.

Zahra, S. A. (2005). A theory of international new ventures: A decade of research. *Journal of International Business Studies, 36*(1), 20–28.

Zahra, S. A., Korri, J. S., & Yu, J. F. (2005). Cognition and international entrepreneurship: Implications for research on international opportunity recognition and exploitation. *International Business Review, 14*(2), 129–146.

Zhou, L., Wu, W., & Luo, X. (2007). Internationalization and the performance of born-global SMEs: The mediating role of social networks. *Journal of International Business Studies, 38*(4), 673–690.

APPENDIX. LIST OF THE INCLUDED ARTICLES

Nr	Authors (Year)	Focus of article
1	Oviatt and McDougall (1994)	Theoretical
2	McDougall et al. (1994)	Empirical
3	Wright and Ricks (1994)	Theoretical
4	Burgel and Murray (2000)	Empirical
5	McDougall and Oviatt (2000)	Theoretical
6	Thomas and Mueller (2000)	Empirical
7	Yeoh (2000)	Empirical
8	Kotha et al. (2001)	Empirical
9	Peng (2001)	Theoretical
10	Kuemmerle (2002)	Empirical
11	Moen (2002)	Empirical
12	Moen and Servais (2002)	Empirical
13	Carpenter et al. (2003)	Empirical
14	Chetty and Campbell-Hunt (2004)	Empirical
15	Coviello and Jones (2004)	Theoretical
16	Knight and Cavusgil (2004)	Empirical
17	Knight et al. (2004)	Empirical
18	Autio (2005)	Theoretical
19	Baker, Gedajlovic, and Lubatkin (2005)	Theoretical
20	Crick and Spence (2005)	Empirical
21	Dimitratos and Jones (2005)	Theoretical
22	George et al. (2005)	Empirical
23	Jones and Coviello (2005)	Theoretical
24	Oviatt and McDougall (2005a, p. 1)	Theoretical
25	Oviatt and McDougall (2005b, p. 2)	Theoretical
26	Rialp et al. (2005)	Theoretical
27	Zahra (2005)	Theoretical
28	Zahra, Korri, and Yu (2005)	Theoretical
29	Coviello (2006)	Empirical
30	Freeman et al. (2006)	Empirical
31	Loane and Bell (2006)	Empirical
32	Mort and Weerawardena (2006)	Empirical
33	Acedo González and Jones (2007)	Empirical
34	Fan and Phan (2007)	Empirical
35	Freeman and Cavusgil (2007)	Empirical

Nr	Authors (Year)	Focus of article
36	Gassmann and Keupp (2007)	Empirical
37	Kuivalainen et al. (2007)	Empirical
38	Mathews and Zander (2007)	Theoretical
39	Presutti et al. (2007)	Empirical
40	Weerawardena, Mort, Liesch, and Knight (2007)	Theoretical
41	Wright, Westhead, and Ucbasaran (2007)	Theoretical
42	Zhou et al. (2007)	Empirical
43	Fernhaber et al. (2008)	Empirical
44	Gabrielsson et al. (2008)	Empirical
45	Yamakawa, Peng, and Deeds (2008)	Theoretical
46	Drori, Honig, and Wright (2009)	Theoretical
47	Keupp and Gassmann (2009)	Theoretical
48	Yeung (2009)	Theoretical
49	Khavul et al. (2010)	Empirical
50	Tolstoy and Agndal (2010)	Empirical

THE IMPORTANCE OF INTERNAL AND EXTERNAL KNOWLEDGE SOURCING AND FIRM PERFORMANCE: A LATENT CLASS ESTIMATION

Torben Pedersen, Christine Soo and Timothy M. Devinney

ABSTRACT

This research examines the differential impact of the importance of internally and externally sourced information and knowledge and their relationship to absorptive capacity and firm performance. In addition, this analysis deals directly with the unobservable heterogeneity amongst firms that is generally viewed as the raison d'être for a unique resource-based perspective of organizational performance. Latent class, finite mixture regression models are used that show that a single model relating knowledge sourcing, absorptive capacity and firm performance is inadequate in explaining even a minor portion of the variation which is seen between firms.

Dynamics of Globalization: Location-Specific Advantages or Liabilities of Foreignness?
Advances in International Management, Volume 24, 389–423
Copyright © 2011 by Emerald Group Publishing Limited
ISSN: 1571-5027/doi:10.1108/S1571-5027(2011)0000024022

INTRODUCTION

The notion that knowledge is a source of competitive advantage has been advocated extensively in the management literature (i.e. Winter, 1987; Quinn, 1992; Nonaka & Takeuchi, 1995) and remains one of the most complex yet compelling areas of discussion among strategy scholars and practitioners. There are numerous theoretical and empirical studies examining the relationship between knowledge and firm performance. The essence of these studies is that the higher the level of knowledge acquired or accumulated, the greater the level of firm performance. For example, both Stuart (2000) and Steensma and Lyles (2000) found that a major contributing factor to the growth, innovation rate and survival of interorganizational alliances was the resources and knowledge flowing from the alliance partners. Similarly, Lane, Salk, and Lyles (2001) showed that knowledge acquired by an international joint venture from its parent company contributed to its performance. In related work, McEvily and Chakravarthy (2002) established that the complexity and tacitness of a firm's technological knowledge contributed to shielding its product innovation from imitation, hence reinforcing the importance of knowledge-based advantage as a source of sustained firm performance.

A close examination of the literature finds two gaps that the current paper attempts to address. The first of these is the distinction between acquisition of knowledge that is internal to the firm and that which is external to the firm. Although something of a gross oversimplification, most studies either deal with direct transfers of information and knowledge between individuals in an organization (von Hippel, 1994; Szulanski, 1996; Leonard & Sensiper, 1998; Tsai, 2001) or transfers and spillovers between organizational entities (Mowery, Oxley, & Silverman, 1996; Lane & Lubatkin, 1998; Lorenzoni & Lipparini, 1999; Lane et al., 2001), such as between consultants and firms or alliance partners. In the current work we attempt to examine (1) the marginal importance of internal versus external sourcing of knowledge and (2) the differential role being played by absorptive capacity (Cohen & Levinthal, 1990) with respect to these diffcrent types of sources. This is relevant since it is argued that firms invariably rely on a combination of internal and external knowledge and it is unlikely that the management and impact of this differential knowledge will be identical. As we will discuss in later sections, few studies have dealt with this and we will have something to say about the extent to which this might be true.

A second area where the literature has been inadequate, and wholly so, is in dealing with the heterogeneity of firms with respect to knowledge sourcing. The underlying assumption of all the quantitative modelling used in strategy to date is that (1) what matters are the observed differences between firms and (2) unexplained error variance is nothing more than random. Although these may be correct assumptions, their validation is ultimately an empirical, and not a theoretical, question. To address this issue we utilize latent class, finite mixture regression to evaluate the existence of relevant but unobserved heterogeneity amongst firms – that is, that heterogeneity exists for substantive reasons but may not be explained directly with the observable measures available. Latent class mixture regression models 'search' for the correct number of models underlying the data while estimating the posterior probability that any specific model is relevant for any specific firm. This technique allows us to determine whether or not the different models apply to different groups of firms and to do so simultaneously with the estimation of the models themselves. Although extensively used in marketing and other fields, mixture modelling has had almost no exposure in the organization and strategy literature (the one exception being DeSarbo, Jedidi, and Sinha (2001), and this is arguably a marketing application).

The combination of these two issues – the importance of internal/external knowledge sourcing and heterogeneity between firms – allows us to deal with a key component of modern resource-based thinking: that the origins of competitive advantage reside in unique firm-specific attributes. By utilizing latent class mixture regression, we apply techniques that are more in line with the theoretical assumptions underlying the resource-based theory (RBT) of the firm. While focussing on both internal and external knowledge sourcing, we deal with the combinative ability of the organization to add external knowledge to the pool of internal knowledge circulating throughout the firm.

In the following sections, we develop the paper's hypotheses through an examination of the existing literature on two fronts – first, the area of knowledge sourcing and its impact on firm performance and, second, the role of the firm's absorptive capacity as a moderating variable in the relationship between knowledge sourcing and firm performance. We then move on to a general discussion and our methodology. We show that mixtures of firms do exist that are receiving differential gains from different knowledge sources and their application of absorptive capacity. In addition, we show that standard linear modelling techniques (ordinary least squares,

OLS) that do not account for firm heterogeneity are inadequate at discovering this complex set of relationships.

A MODEL OF KNOWLEDGE SOURCING AND FIRM PERFORMANCE

Many studies have investigated the nature of knowledge sourcing and the impact on firm performance. The basic premise of these studies is that a firm needs to constantly source or acquire new knowledge in order to renew capabilities, innovate and guard against technological obsolescence and competitive imitation. It is very much the essence of Teece, Pisano, and Shuen's (1997, p. 516) notion of dynamic capabilities – that is, the firm's ability to 'integrate, build and reconfigure internal and external competences to address rapidly changing environments'.

External Knowledge Sourcing and Firm Performance

The importance of knowledge sourcing is present in earlier studies on boundary-spanning activities in innovative environments. Various studies on R&D management (Tushman & Katz, 1980; Ebadi & Utterback, 1984) have indicated that in a dynamic technology-intensive research environment, the ability to span organizational boundaries is extremely important. Dollinger's (1984) study on small business entrepreneurs revealed a strong relationship between boundary-spanning activity and organizational performance. In the biotechnology industry, 'research breakthroughs demand a range of intellectual and scientific skills that far exceed the capabilities of any single organization' (Powell, Koput, & Smith–Doerr, 1996, p. 118). In the area of pharmaceutical research, Henderson and Cockburn (1994, p. 67) have shown that the ability to 'encourage and maintain an extensive flow of information across the boundaries of the firm' is important to the productivity of drug discovery.

Similarly, the area of interorganizational relationships contains a significant amount of work on knowledge sourcing and firm performance. Early attention was focused on exchange and reciprocity as the main drivers of interorganizational linkages (Levine & White, 1961), while the resource-dependent view (Pfeffer & Salancik, 1978) focused on issues of power and control over scarce resources. More recent studies in this area have looked at the role of interorganizational links as a source of innovation and firm performance. In a series of longitudinal studies, Mitchell and Singh (1996), Miner, Amburgey, and Stearns (1990) and Stearns, Hoffman, and Heide (1987) concluded that interorganizational linkages played a significant role in buffering firms against adverse environmental impact (and hence increasing their chances of survival). Bresman, Birkinshaw, and Nobel (1999) found evidence of knowledge transfer in international acquisitions in the form of communication and visits. In addition, their case study research revealed that later stage transfer involved 'high levels of collaboration, sharing of resources, and transfers of individuals between units ... the knowledge in such cases was more tacit than in early-stage transfers' (Bresman et al., 1999, p. 456). Stuart, Hoang, and Hybels's (1999) study on biotechnology firms revealed that firms with prominent alliance partners enjoyed greater valuations at the initial public offering than firms lacking such connections. In a later study on interorganizational alliances, Stuart (2000) concluded that firms exhibited higher growth rates when in partnerships with large and innovative alliance partners. Andersson, Forsgren, and Holm's (2002) study on multinational corporations (MNCs) found that new product and process development conducted in conjunction with external customers and suppliers was positively related to expected market performance.

The area of organizational networks contains a substantial number of studies investigating the issues of knowledge sourcing, innovation and performance. The major premise of this body of work is that 'a firm's networks allow it to access key resources from its environment, such as information, access, capital, goods, services and so on that have the potential to maintain or enhance a firm's competitive advantage' (Gulati, Nohria, & Zaheer, 2000). Studies (e.g. Dyer, 1996; Almeida & Kogut, 1999) have found evidence to support the role of networks as a source of knowledge and innovation, which contributes to the performance of firms. More recently, Baum, Calabrese, and Silverman's (2000) study on biotechnology start-up firms found that initial performance increased with the size of the start-up's alliance network. Dyer and Nobeoka (2000, p. 365) investigated the knowledge-sharing routines developed within Toyota's production network and concluded that 'if the network can create a strong identity and effective coordinating rules, then it may be superior to a firm as an organizational form at creating and recombining knowledge owing to the greater diversity of knowledge that resides within a network'.

The importance of social capital as a source of knowledge is becoming increasingly prevalent in the literature. Network scholars (e.g. Blau, 1977; Burt, 1992; Liebeskind, Oliver, Zucker, & Brewer, 1996) emphasize the significance of social relationships as a firm resource, acknowledging that 'beneath most formal ties ... lies a sea of informal relations ... that carries benefits beyond the particular exchange designated in a formal agreement' (Powell et al., 1996, p. 120). Social capital scholars emphasize the benefits embedded in social relationships, such as the development of intellectual capital (Nahapiet & Ghoshal, 1998), resource exchange and product innovation (Tsai & Ghoshal, 1998) and knowledge acquisition (Yli-Renko, Autio, & Sapienza, 2001).

Internal Knowledge Sourcing and Firm Performance

Discussion so far has focused on the importance of interorganizational relationships and networks as sources of resources, knowledge and sustained performance for firms. However, the internal network is potentially an equally important resource for knowledge as personal networks within the firm are often the first point of contact for employees. Soo, Devinney, Midgley, and Deering's (2002) case studies on professional services organizations revealed that employees depended heavily on their personal networks for information and knowledge. Freeman (1991, p. 501) argues that 'both empirical and theoretical research has long demonstrated the importance for successful innovation of both external and internal networks of information and collaboration'.

There exists a broad range of research examining the role of internal knowledge sharing and transfer as a source of competitive advantage. Grant (1996, p. 113) argues the importance of understanding 'the organizational processes through which firms access and utilize the knowledge possessed by their members'. Argote and Ingram (2000, p. 150) propose that 'by embedding knowledge in interactions involving people, organizations can both effect knowledge transfer internally and impede knowledge transfer externally'. This certainly followed consistently from Brown and Duguid's (1991) notion of 'communities-of-practice', which acknowledges that people often work, learn and innovate within informal communities that are usually not recognized in formal organizational designs or job descriptions. This is further reinforced by Paulus and Yang's (2000) experiment suggesting that idea generation and sharing conducted in a group environment resulted in enhanced creativity and performance, as opposed to individual idea generation.

The importance of effective knowledge sharing and transfer within the firm is an area that has received considerable attention in the literature – for example, Szulanski (1996) examined the factors impacting the transfer of best practices within the firm; O'Dell and Grayson (1998) emphasized issues such as reward systems, technological support and leadership to ease the difficulties inherent in the transfer of internal best practices; and Hansen's (2002) study on knowledge networks revealed that the possession of related knowledge and short network paths increased the likelihood of knowledge sharing among business units. Foss and Pedersen (2002) studied the determinants of knowledge transfer from subsidiaries to other MNC-units and found that the levels of both internally and externally sourced knowledge were important determinants of the knowledge sharing.

The Need for Both Internal and External Knowledge Sourcing

The issue of whether the firm engages in internal or external knowledge sourcing and the impact of the different acquisition behaviours on firm performance have interesting implications. Both types of sourcing beha- viours are important for the firm as they are generally viewed as mutually interdependent and complementary learning processes (Bierly & Chakrabarti, 1996).

Several studies have investigated the different knowledge-sourcing patterns undertaken by firms and concluded that both internal and external sources of knowledge are equally important. In their study on pharmaceutical firms, Bierly and Chakrabarti (1996) uncovered four generic knowledge-strategy groups – that is, 'explorers', 'exploiters', 'loners' and 'innovators' – and found that firms with a good balance of both internal and external learning and with a tendency towards more radical learning (i.e. 'innovators' and 'explorers') exhibited consistently higher levels of profitability. In a similar study of the optical disk industry, Rosenkopf and Nerkar (2001) found that explorations that span both organizational and technological boundaries had the highest impact on technological developments. Iansiti and Clark's (1994) case studies on the automobile and mainframe computer industries revealed that consistently high performing firms engaged in active internal and external integration – that is, the ability to tap into external sources of information and knowledge, as well as the ability to coordinate and communicate across organizational subunits. Nobel and Birkinshaw (1998) examined the nature of communication and control in international R&D operations and ascertained that international creators (with more responsibilities to innovate rather than to improve and adapt) maintain strong internal and external networks of relationships. Rulke, Zaheer, and Anderson (2000) revealed that store managers in the retail food industry relied on both internal and external sources of information for organizational self-knowledge (i.e. managers' knowledge of their units' capabilities and shortcomings). Nagarajan and Mitchell (1998) looked at the lithotripsy industry and concluded that different types of technological changes were associated with the methods of knowledge acquisition – that is, firms relied on interorganizational relationships for encompassing and complementary changes and internal R&D for incremental changes.

From this discussion we can make three related hypotheses:

Hypothesis 1A. Firms relying on high levels of internal knowledge sourcing exhibit higher levels of performance than firms relying on low levels of internal knowledge sourcing.

Hypothesis 1B. Firms relying on high levels of external knowledge sourcing exhibit higher levels of performance than firms relying on low levels of external knowledge sourcing.

Hypothesis 1C. Firms relying on higher levels of both internal and external knowledge sourcing exhibit higher levels of performance than firms relying on only internal or only external sources of knowledge.

Hypotheses 1A and 1B relate to estimating the direct effects of knowledge sourcing and Hypothesis 1C addresses the interaction of the two sources together.

THE ROLE OF ABSORPTIVE CAPACITY

Although numerous studies have shown that both the external and internal environments of the firm constitute valuable resources for knowledge and learning, there exists another important element, the firm's own capabilities to recognize, absorb and apply the knowledge. Cohen and Levinthal's (1990) concept of absorptive capacity has been widely studied in relation to its impact on organizational knowledge sourcing, learning and performance.

A plethora of work has found evidence to support the notion that absorptive capacity plays an important role in the firm's ability to acquire knowledge and learn from various sources. In their study of strategic alliances, Mowery et al. (1996) examined the role of absorptive capacity in a firm's ability to acquire its partner's capabilities and found that experience in an area related to the alliance partner's increased the chances of inter-firm knowledge transfer. Similarly, Veugelers (1997, p. 314) revealed that when a firm engages in R&D cooperation, the impact on its own R&D was shown to be significant only when absorptive capacity (i.e. full-time, staffed R&D department) was present, hence supporting 'the idea that indeed absorptive capacity is necessary to be able to capitalize on the complementarities between internal and external know-how'.

ABSORPTIVE CAPACITY AND FIRM PERFORMANCE

Cohen and Levinthal's (1990) definition of the concept includes the ability to recognize and assimilate new knowledge and apply it to commercial ends, thus suggesting the need for knowledge absorption as well as knowledge utilization. Unfortunately, the predominant measure of absorptive capacity – either R&D expenditure or some measure of R&D employment – is confounded with innovative investment and is only an instrumental reflection of an organization's underlying practices.

In their reconceptualization of the concept, Zahra and George (2002, p. 185) identified two subsets of absorptive capacity: (1) *'potential capacity* compris[ing] knowledge acquisition and assimilation capabilities'; and (2) *'realized capacity* center[ing] on knowledge transformation and exploitation'. The authors propose that although potential absorptive capacity (PACAP) allows firms greater flexibility in reconfiguring their resource base, it is realized absorptive capacity (RACAP) that converts knowledge into performance. Consistent with Zahra and George's (2002) position is evidence that the interaction of network centrality and absorptive capacity contributed significantly to business unit innovation and performance (Tsai, 2001). This finding suggests that although an organization has access to knowledge sources through its network links, its ability to absorb and exploit such knowledge depends on its level of absorptive capacity – that is, 'high absorptive capacity is associated with a better chance to successfully apply new knowledge toward commercial ends, producing more innovations and better business performance' (Tsai, 2001, p. 1003).

Building on the work of Zahra and George (2002) and Tsai (2001), we acknowledge the importance of RACAP in allowing firms to absorb, apply and exploit knowledge towards commercial ends. Although Cohen and Levinthal's (1990) conceptualization pertains to the ability to absorb and apply external knowledge, we extend this to the absorption and application of internal knowledge as well, following Szulanski's (1996) finding that absorptive capacity plays a crucial role in the effectiveness of internal knowledge transfer. Hence, we argue that it is not only important for firms to actively source knowledge (both internally and externally) but also that the application of that knowledge for commercial ends depends on the firm's level of absorptive capacity. We are also cognizant of the distinction between practices that make knowledge acquisition relevant (PACAP) and the ability to make those practices work (RACAP). To test this, we formulate the following hypotheses:

Hypothesis 2A. The relationship between internal knowledge sourcing and firm performance is moderated by organizational incentives to absorb and apply that knowledge (absorptive capacity).

Hypothesis 2B. The relationship between external knowledge sourcing and firm performance is moderated by organizational incentives to absorb and apply that knowledge (absorptive capacity).

The basic underlying model structure we posit is shown in Fig. 1 with the relevant hypotheses highlighted.

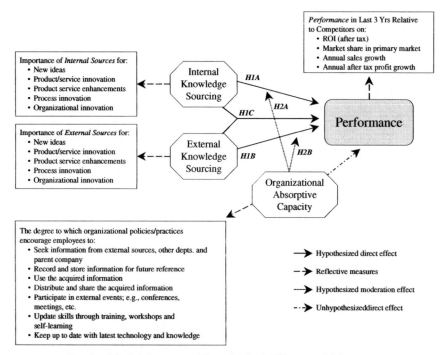

Fig. 1.   Model Structure, Hypothesized Effects and Measures.

FIRM HETEROGENEITY

According to the RBT of the firm, it is the unique, externally non-replicable, durable, path-dependent, causally ambiguous assets of the firm that allow it to accrue rents and to sustain its position to do so vis-à-vis its competitors (Wernerfelt, 1984; Barney, 1986; Peteraf, 1993). If this is indeed the case, it is unlikely that firms will be influenced identically even by similar environments or that their reactions to those environments will, or even should, be the same. In addition, it seems equally unlikely that the factors that would determine latent similarity between firms would necessarily be found by examining observable characteristics, such as the normal controls found in the literature – size, employee numbers, industry and so on.

A number of recent studies have attempted to come to grips with both the characterization and empirical modelling of firm heterogeneity. Noda and Collis (2001) take a process approach in asking how intra-industry heterogeneity can arise and, once having arisen, be sustained in a competitive environment. They concentrate on the mixture of converging and diverging forces at the industry and firm level. McEvily and Zaheer (1999) use a network model to understand how geographic clusters maintain their unique set of competences. From our standpoint, the important point of this work is that these authors, amongst others, show the sustainability of heterogeneity and that heterogeneity is not random. Accordingly, we propose the following hypothesis:

Hypothesis 3. A single model is inappropriate in understanding the relationship between the type of knowledge sourcing, absorptive capacity and performance.

Although firm heterogeneity is considered one of the pinnacles of modern strategic thinking and the distinctive characteristic that separates much of this work from a purely industrial organization (IO) perspective, much of this work has been beset by methodological issues that make it difficult to distinguish random effects from true heterogeneity. In addition, the empirical work that has been done relating to heterogeneity deals mainly with intra-industry homogeneity and heterogeneity – that is, either relating to strategic groups or how firms in the same industry differ. An equally important question from a research methodology perspective is the mixture of similarities and differences across firms in different industries. Traditional industry-level IO analysis mistakenly assumes homogeneity (with some random differences) amongst firms within the same industry and substantial differences between industries. The RBT makes no such constraining assumption but fails to explain why firms across industries might be driven by similar structural models but differ significantly from firms within their own industry. Furthermore, empirical RBT studies to date use methods that account only for observed differences between firms through the use of control variables, and even then account mainly for observed heterogeneity associated with the dependent variable. This may increase the predictive validity associated with the dependent variable but does nothing to determine the nature of heterogeneity associated with the entire model.

METHODOLOGY

We applied two sets of empirical analyses to survey data collected from key informants from 317 firms with the intent of determining the validity of the model presented in Fig. 1 and to understand the degree of firm heterogeneity with respect to knowledge sourcing and performance. The first analysis was a simple OLS regression to determine whether or not the model proposed operates in the aggregate. The second analysis applies finite mixture-modelling techniques (assuming mixtures of normal distributions) to determine whether different forms of the model apply to different groups within the sample. A description of the sample and constructs used is followed by a general overview of mixture models and their relevance to the current research. The individual measures are described in Fig. 1.

Construct Measures

All the constructs utilized – internal and external knowledge sourcing, absorptive capacity and firm performance – are measured by multiple item reflective scales. Each is discussed in detail in the sections below. All survey questions (except those pertaining to firm and industry demographics) use a seven-point Likert scale.

Internal and External Knowledge Sourcing

This study is unique in looking at a broad cross-section of existing firms and questioning the marginal value of the source of knowledge acquired by the firm. Given that no measures were available we created six items that we used to reflect the degree to which the firm relies on internal sources versus external sources of knowledge. Respondents were asked to indicate the importance of internal staff – colleagues within the business unit and firm – and external parties – customers, suppliers, competitors and consultants[1] – as 'sources of information and/or know-how' for the following activities: (1) the generation of new ideas, (2) product/service innovation, (3) product/service enhancements, (4) process improvements and (5) organizational innovations and improvements. The Cronbach alpha for these measures was 0.84 for the case of internal knowledge sourcing and 0.82 for external knowledge sourcing.

To check further the validity of this measure, we collected information on the overall frequency (from a 'very small extent' to a 'very large extent') to which these sources were used. The correlations (all significant at the 0.05 level) between the aggregate external knowledge measure used here and these frequency measures are given in Appendix A. If these measures were indeed capturing activities relating to internal and external knowledge sourcing, we would expect strong correlations between the measures used here and the independently collected frequency information. This is indeed the case. The use of the aggregate measures was deemed better than the pure frequency measures because the aggregate measures focus not just on the frequency of use but also on the importance of use for specific valued outcomes.

Absorptive Capacity
To measure the concept of absorptive capacity, we go beyond Cohen and Levinthal's (1990) emphasis on R&D investment, recognizing that this may not be applicable across industries, particularly when related to services. Hence, in order to develop generalizable measures as well as adhering tightly to the authors' conceptual definitions, we use measures that capture the essence of Zahra and George's (2002) notions of PACAP and RACAP. First, we account for *active information-sharing behaviours* (effectively a proxy for RACAP) by measuring the degree to which respondents actively seek external information, record it for future reference, use the acquired information in their work and distribute the information to fellow colleagues. Second, we recognize that the development of absorptive capacity is essentially path dependent; that is, it is a function of both past and on-going *investments in knowledge accumulation* (effectively a proxy for PACAP). To measure this, we investigated the degree to which respondents participate in academic/industry conferences, update their skills through training and self-learning and keep abreast with the latest technology and knowledge related to their organization's business. Our measures are organizational – that is, they deal with the extent to which the firm has policies and procedures that encourage employees to seek external information and invest in knowledge accumulation. Again Fig. 1 presents the wording of these measures.

It is important to emphasize that our operationalization of absorptive capacity is both broader and more direct than previous empirical work where the emphasis is on the *proxies* of absorptive capacity. For example, Pennings and Harianto (1992) measured past accumulated technological experience as a proxy for absorptive capacity. Lane and Lubatkin (1998) hypothesized that absorptive capacity is a function of the similarity between the student and teacher firms' compensation practices and organizational structures. In contrast, we employ a more direct approach by examining the extent to which a range of *actions* are taken to recognize, absorb and assimilate new external information and knowledge into the organization. The Cronbach alpha for this measure is 0.89.

Firm Performance

Firm performance is measured as a perceptual measure using both market measures – market share and annual sales growth – and financial measures – after-tax return on investment and growth in total after-tax profits for the firm in the last 3 years, *relative to competitors*. These are commonly used in the strategy and marketing literatures (e.g. Banbury & Mitchell, 1995) and reflect the multidimensional pressures managers face on a day-to-day basis. These measures were treated as reflective indicators of an existing latent 'performance' construct. The Cronbach alpha for this measure was 0.83.

Sample

Our survey instrument was extensively pre-tested through interviews and a pilot sampling trial. Soo, Devinney, and Midgley (2001) outline the nature of the tests used to validate the survey and ensure convergent and discriminant validity.

The survey was mailed to 2,137 organizations (all with more than 20 employees) randomly selected from 17 manufacturing and service industries (based on two-digit SIC codes). The objectives of this procedure were to ensure generalizability of results across industries and to target industries where issues of knowledge acquisition and innovation are *important and relevant*. Specifically, we targeted industries facing dynamic and competitive environments – hence the need for continuous knowledge acquisition and learning. The issue of relevance is also crucial to obtaining a reasonable response rate and high-quality responses (questions are more easily understood if they are important and relevant).

The questionnaire was addressed to the CEO or managing director of each organization. To minimize the limitations of using single-informant methodology, we took precautions to ensure informant competency. First, the key objectives of the study and its central themes were outlined in a cover letter. If the CEO was unable to complete the survey, they were asked to give it to a middle/senior-level manager with sufficient knowledge of the study's objectives. Second, we included criteria for assessing informant competency, such as tenure in the organization, industry and current position.

The number of responses totalled 343 (yielding a 16 per cent response rate). After eliminating surveys due to large proportions of missing data, the final 289 responses used in the analysis were seen to be fairly evenly distributed across manufacturing (44 per cent) and service (56 per cent) sectors as well as across the 17 industries. Firm size was also well distributed, with 40 per cent small firms (100 or less employees), 30 per cent medium-sized firms (100–800 employees) and 30 per cent large firms (more than 800 employees). The average and median sizes of these firms were 2,024 and 175 employees, respectively. Tests of the distribution of returned surveys indicate that no industry or size bias existed in the responses received (Table 1).

Analysis of respondent characteristics indicated that respondents had sufficient knowledge of the key issues of the study – all respondents occupied middle–senior management roles, and the average tenures at the organization, industry and current position were 12, 17 and 5 years, respectively. Following the procedures of Armstrong and Overton (1977), we also tested for non-response bias by examining the construct means of early versus late respondents, and found no significant differences.

With surveys such as this there is always a concern about single-respondent bias. In a related study, our survey was used in conjunction with six case studies (Soo et al., 2002) and an identical model was estimated for each company. In this situation, as many as 120 responses were received from a single firm; hence we had both repeated measures of firm variables and estimates of the variance of individual measures. Although the models differed in the magnitude of various effects (as one would expect), the general form of the model and key conclusions remained valid. To test for common-method bias, we applied Harmann's ex-post one-factor test (Podsakoff & Organ, 1986) across the entire survey, which includes the measures used here. Nineteen distinct factors were needed to explain the 80 per cent of the variance in the measures used, with the largest factor only accounting for 17 per cent of the variance. Hence, there was no 'general factor' in the data that would represent a common-method bias.

Table 1. Response Rates and Sample Characteristics.

Industries Included in the Study	Per Cent of Total Responses	Per Cent Response Within Industry
Metal mining	5	13
Oil and gas extraction	1	9
Petroleum refining	2	16
Chemicals and allied products	11	10
Primary metal industries	4	8
Machinery, except electrical	11	10
Electrical and electronic machinery	5	8
Transportation equipment	3	8
Measuring instruments	2	6
Banking	3	10
Credit agencies	3	8
Security and commodity brokers	2	5
Insurance	6	14
Business services	20	13
Health services	4	9
Legal services	5	10
Miscellaneous services	13	12
Total (per cent)	100	

Method of Estimation

Mixture models are useful in estimating the likelihood that a specific firm fits into a class of firms for which a particular model applies (see Wedel and Kamakura (2000) for a general explanation). More specifically, mixture models assume that we are interested in decomposing a population of firms (indexed by k), for which we have a set of n observations $\mathbf{y}_n = (y_{nk})$, that we believe is a mixture of S segments in proportions $\pi_1, \dots, \pi_S$ (note: all indicators in bold are vectors). A priori we have no idea from which segment each particular firm comes but we do know that the likelihood of the firm coming from each of the segments is constrained to be 1; that is, $\sum_{s=1}^{S} \pi_s = 1$. Given that the observations y_{nk} come from segment s, the conditional distribution function of $\mathbf{y}_n$ can be represented as $f_s(\mathbf{y}_n|\mathbf{\theta}_s)$, where $\mathbf{\theta}_s$ is the vector of unknown parameters associated with the specific density function chosen; for example, normal, Poisson, multinomial, Dirichlet, exponential gamma or inverse Gaussian. Mixture models are estimated using maximum likelihood, where the vector $\mathbf{\phi} = (\pi, \mathbf{\theta})$ is estimated based on the likelihood of $\mathbf{\phi}$ being $L(\mathbf{f}; \mathbf{y}) = \prod_{n=1}^{N} f(\mathbf{y}_n|\phi)$, where $f(\mathbf{y}_n|\phi) = \sum_{s=1}^{S}$

$\pi_s f(\mathbf{y}_n | \boldsymbol{\phi}_s)$ represents the unconditional probability of $\mathbf{y}_n$ given $\boldsymbol{\phi}$. Once an estimate of $\boldsymbol{\phi}$ is obtained, it is a simple task of using Bayes' theorem to calculate the posterior probability that any firm n with $\mathbf{y}_n$ comes from any segment s, $p_{ns} = \pi_s f(\mathbf{y}_n | \theta_s) / \sum_{s=1}^{S} \pi_s f(\mathbf{y}_n | \theta_s)$.

Mixture regression models, the procedure used here, are estimated identically to mixture models except that we are interested in predicting the means of the observations in each segment by using a set of explanatory variables (Wedel & DeSarbo, 1995). We can therefore identify for each segment s, a linear predictor, η_{nsk}, that is the product of a set of P explanatory variables, $\mathbf{X}_p = (\mathbf{X}_{nkp})$, and parameters, $\boldsymbol{\beta}_s = (\beta_{sp})$, such that $\eta_{nsk} = \sum_{p=1}^{P} \mathbf{X}_{nkp} \beta_{sp} . \eta_{nsk}$ is related to the mean of the distribution, μ_{sk}, through a link function $g(\bullet)$ that varies with the distribution chosen.[2] In the mixture regression case, the parameters being estimated are once more $\boldsymbol{\phi}_s = (\pi_s, \boldsymbol{\theta}_s)$, with $\boldsymbol{\theta}_s = (\boldsymbol{\beta}_s, \lambda_s)$, where λ_s is a measure of dispersion in the distribution of segment s (in the case of the normal distribution, λ_s would be the variance of the observations in the segment).

Like any clustering technique, the appropriateness of mixture models is determined first by theory and second by the ability to find meaningful and significant differences in the population at hand. There is no single criterion for the choice of the number of segments. One such set of criteria, known as information criteria, is based on assessing the degree of improvement in explanatory power adjusted for the number of degrees of freedom taken up by the estimation of additional parameters (essentially adjusting for over-parameterization): $C = -2\ln(L) + Pd$, where L is the likelihood, P is a penalty equal to the number of parameters estimated and d is a constant. The most common information criteria are the Akaike (1974) information criteria (AIC), which arise when $d = 2$, and the consistent Akaike information criterion (CAIC), where $d = \ln(N+1)$ and N is the number of firms.[3] The CAIC is more conservative and is skewed to models with fewer segments as it imposes an additional sample-size penalty. In addition to dealing with over-parameterization as the number of segments increase, one needs to be assured that the segments are sufficiently distinctive. To do this, one needs to compare the estimated posterior probabilities of segment membership. Celeux and Soromenho (1996) propose a normed entropy criterion $-\text{NEC}(S) = E_S / [\ln L(S) - \ln L(1)]$, where E_S is an entropy measure[4] accounting for the separation in the estimated posterior probabilities and $[\ln L(S) - \ln L(1)]$ adjusts for over-parameterization relative to a single segment model. E_S is measured as $1 - \sum_{n=1}^{N} \sum_{s=1}^{S} -p_{ns} \ln(p_{ns}) / N$, where p_{ns} is the posterior probability of firm n being in segment s.[5]

The problem ultimately comes down to the fact that no single criterion appears able to determine the 'correct' number of segments, and one must rely on these criteria as well as the structure of the models arising and how they relate to the theory being tested.

RESULTS

The results of the full OLS and mixture regressions are presented in Table 3, with effect size estimates presented in Table 4. The effect size estimates are determined by computing the value of the estimated coefficient times the mean of the independent variable. This provides a more accurate picture of the contribution of that variable to the dependent variable and allows for aggregation so that direct, moderated and total effects can be distinguished more clearly.

Several things should be noted about this analysis and where it differs from more standard approaches. The first important point is that there is no attempt to control for industry or firm-level influences with respect to either the dependent or independent variables. The approach is to apply first the pure model from Fig. 1 and then to seek to understand what determines segment membership at the second stage. This should be clear shortly.

Second, the choice of a three-segment solution is based on the improvement in the fit as measured by R^2 and NEC(S) even though the information criteria (CAIC and AIC) imply slightly less parsimony. Table 2 provides these statistics. The three-segment solution provides the clearest set

Table 2. Measures of Model Fit and Parsimony by Segment.

	Number of Segments				
	1	2	3	4	5
Likelihood	−421.6	−407.6	−400.2	−372.92	−371.11
AIC	859.2	849.3	852.5	**815.86**	831.42
CAIC	**896.5**	928.6	939.51	979.18	1036.74
Entropy	−	0.6515	**0.7805**	0.7456	0.6902
NEC(S)	−	0.0465	**0.1055**	0.0153	0.0136
R^2	0.06	0.53	0.83	0.91	0.92
Degrees of freedom	8	15	23	31	39

Note: Bold items indicate either minimum (AIC, CAIC, MAIC, NEC(S)) or maximum (entropy) measures.

of between-segment distinctions, although a two-segment solution might be viewed as also being a reasonable representation of the data, except for the fact that it does not provide sufficient distinction between the segments (lowest entropy measure). Ultimately, the choice of the three-segment solution was based on NEC(S), the entropy measure and the theoretical meaning of the results. Clearly larger segment solutions are neither parsimonious nor theoretically compelling when one looks at the segment sizes (some of which are small) and the structure of the models (which do not show greater distinctiveness in the added segments). Hence, the choice becomes one of three or fewer segments. Therefore, we will discuss the one-, two- and three-segment solutions in the first instance.

The most obvious piece of information in coming from the above analysis is that based on OLS estimation there is only weak evidence that knowledge sourced from anywhere or absorptive capacity has a strong influence on performance. Although each of the individual measures, except for externally sourced knowledge, is correlated with performance (see Appendix B for a correlation matrix), the fit of the OLS model is quite poor – implying a 'relationship' but one subject to huge inter-firm variance. The R^2 is low at 6 per cent and all of this is driven by the intercept (see Tables 3 and 4).

The OLS model is not improved upon when we attempt to examine separate parts of the model and deal with the issue of co-linearity in the data; again, Appendix B shows that the variables in the model are strongly co-linear but also shows that the fit is very poor (this is seen in the R^2 computed for each bivariate correlation). Table 5 breaks down the OLS analysis in finer detail and, although we can generate some significance for some of the independent variables, two things need to be noted. First, and most critically, the R^2 can never improve and the fit of the model is not great. This combination of variables, considered so important by the literature, explains little, if anything, about performance according to this analysis. Second, there is no clear pattern as to what might be the most appropriate model. At best, we can say that internal sourcing appears somewhat more important in determining marginal performance but we cannot say this with much confidence. In the end, we would conclude from this analysis that it was possible only to accept Hypotheses 1A, 1C, 2A and 2B based on direct comparisons of the correlations with performance. However, when we apply mixture regressions we see a startlingly different pattern of results.

The two-segment solution leads to an increase in R^2 to 53 per cent and also to the lowest AIC. Based on this solution, we find that external sourcing and absorptive capacity explain performance well; it is just the combination

Table 3.   Model Estimates.

	OLS	Two-Segment Solution		Three-Segment Solution		
		Segment 1	Segment 2	Segment 1	Segment 2	Segment 3
Intercept	2.80*	3.31***	3.93**	1.61	5.77***	4.70***
	(−1.63)	(−1.36)	(−2)	(−1.28)	(−1.88)	(−1.51)
Internal sources	0.28	0.33	−0.02	0.83***	−0.44	−0.61***
	(−0.29)	(−0.24)	(−0.37)	(−0.23)	(−0.35)	(−0.26)
External sources	−0.49	−0.60***	−0.67*	−0.12	−0.76***	−0.89***
	(−0.3)	(−0.24)	(−0.39)	(−0.23)	(−0.36)	(−0.28)
Organizational absorptive capacity	0.15	0.09	−0.12	−0.23	−0.48	1.09***
	(−0.37)	(−0.3)	(−0.46)	(−0.31)	(−0.42)	(−0.31)
External × absorptive capacity	0.06	0.08***	0.11*	0.13***	0.12*	−0.14***
	(−0.05)	(−0.04)	(−0.07)	(−0.03)	(−0.05)	(−0.04)
Internal × absorptive capacity	−0.07	−0.07	−0.07	−0.09*	0.01	−0.03
	(−0.06)	(−0.05)	(−0.07)	(−0.05)	(−0.06)	(−0.05)
Internal × External sources	0.04	0.04	0.06	−0.04	0.06	0.20***
	(−0.05)	(−0.04)	(−0.07)	(−0.04)	(−0.06)	(−0.05)
Class size of segment	1	0.74	0.26	0.42	0.18	0.4
Number of observations	289	72	217	118	49	122
Log likelihood	−421.6	−407.6		−400.2		
AIC	859.2	849.3		852.5		
CAIC	896.5	928.6		939.5		
R^2	0.06	0.53		0.83		

Note: $^*p<0.10$, $^{**}p<0.05$, $^{***}p<0.01$.

that is different between the groups. Based on this information alone, we would be forced to reject Hypotheses 1A and 1C relating to internal knowledge sourcing and its interaction with external knowledge sourcing, as well as Hypothesis 3 dealing with whether or not a single model is appropriate. What the two-segment solution suggests is that a single model is probably correct (the significant variables imply this) but that the magnitudes of the coefficients in that model are subject to some differences. In other words, performance is related to external sourcing and absorptive capacity with minor variation in the extent of the influence across firms. The comparatively low entropy measure (0.6515) and small value for NEC(S) (0.0465) indicate weak distinction between the groups as would be expected given the parameter estimates.

Table 4. Effect Sizes Associated with Model Estimates.

	One Segment Solution	Two-Segment Solution		Three-Segment Solution		
		Segment 1	Segment 2	Segment 1	Segment 2	Segment 3
Direct effects						
Intercept	**2.80**	**3.31**	**3.93**	1.61	**5.77**	**4.70**
Internal sources	1.60	1.83	-0.12	**4.65**	-2.46	**-3.41**
External sources	-2.32	**-2.82**	**-3.16**	-0.57	**-3.48**	**-4.19**
Organizational absorptive capacity	0.66	0.41	-0.55	-1.00	-2.25	**4.96**
Moderating effects						
External × absorptive capacity	1.32	**1.78**	**2.41**	**2.82**	**2.60**	**-3.03**
Internal × absorptive capacity	-1.70	-1.69	-1.81	**-2.21**	0.25	-0.76
Internal × external sources	1.09	1.09	1.48	-0.94	1.52	**5.44**
Total effects[a]						
Internal sources	0.99	1.23	-0.45	1.41	-0.69	1.14
External sources	0.09	0.05	0.73	1.20	0.60	-1.88
Organizational absorptive capacity	0.28	0.51	0.05	-0.46	0.59	0.97

Note: For direct and moderating effects, estimates based on significant coefficients from Table 3 are shown in bold.
[a]Includes all interaction effects, so some double counting will occur across sources and absorptive capacity.

The most compelling picture comes from the three-segment solution where a more complex picture arises. There is an increase in R^2 to 83 per cent although our information criteria indicate this model may be less parsimonious (both AIC and CAIC increase). Examination of the entropy measure (0.7805) signifies greater distinctiveness between the segments and the NEC(S) (0.1055) increases dramatically, indicating that the increase in discrimination between groups accounting for the reduced parsimony is best in this case. Segment 1 relies heavily on internal knowledge with some influence of external knowledge in conjunction with absorptive capacity. It has the highest overall performance (Performance = 4.45 – see Table 6). Segment 2 relies almost exclusively on external knowledge, both directly and in conjunction with absorptive capacity. It is the poorest performing group (Performance = 1.80). Segment 3 is the most complex group with an intricate

Table 5.   OLS Estimates of Variations in Basic Model.

	Full Model	Internal Sourcing		External Sourcing		Internal and External		
		Model 1	Model 2	Model 1	Model 2	Model 1	Model 2	Model 3
Intercept	2.80*	2.08***	1.33	2.89***	4.34***	2.17***	3.39***	2.09***
	(1.63)	(0.34)	(1.35)	(0.31)	(0.89)	(0.39)	(1.26)	(0.39)
Internal sources	0.28	0.21***	0.43	–	–	0.22***	0.01	0.21***
	(0.29)	(0.06)	(0.24)			(0.06)	(0.22)	(0.08)
External sources	−0.49	–	–	0.02	−0.30	0.01	0.05	0.00
	(0.30)			(0.06)	(0.19)	(0.05)	(0.05)	(0.01)
Organizational absorptive capacity	0.15	0.05	0.23	0.11*	−0.24	–	–	0.05
	(0.37)	(0.06)	(0.32)	(0.06)	(0.21)			(0.06)
External × absorptive capacity	0.06	–	–	–	0.08*	–	–	–
	(0.05)				(0.04)			
Internal × absorptive capacity	−0.07	–	−0.03	–	–	–	–	–
	(0.06)		(0.06)					
Internal × External sources	0.04	–	–	–	–	–	−0.26	–
	(0.05)						(0.27)	
R^2	0.06	0.04	0.04	0.01	0.02	0.04	0.04	0.04

Note: *$p < 0.10$, ***$p < 0.01$.

mixture of internal and external sources plus absorptive capacity driving performance. It is an intermediate performing group (Performance = 3.17). It should be pointed out that with this group the direct effects of knowledge sourcing are less relevant than the impact of absorptive capacity and internal and external sourcing in combination.

What we see from an analysis of these results is that all the hypotheses are supported when treated conditionally on the fact that they all need not apply to all firms.

Those unfamiliar with finite mixture regression might, at this point, argue that all we have done is estimated additional parameters in a complex way and hence generated more fit. This undervalues the insights that are revealed from the data and the fact that unobserved heterogeneity is *by definition* imperceptible ex ante. Therefore, we must engage in ex-post determination as to what is structurally correlated with segment membership. In other words, we want to know what it is about the difference between the estimated segments that is relevant but cannot do this until we have seen

Table 6. Group Differences and Similarities.

	Segment 1	Segment 2	Segment 3	*F*-Value
Variables in the model				
Performance[a]	4.45 (A)	1.80 (C)	3.17 (B)	424.90**
Internal sources[a]	5.52 (B)	5.82 (A)	5.58 (A,B)	1.45
External sources[a]	4.60 (B)	4.95 (A)	4.78 (A,B)	1.62
Absorptive capacity[a]	4.46 (B)	4.86 (A)	4.35 (B)	3.42**
Structural variables				
Multinationals (per cent of sample)	57 (A)	41 (B)	60 (A)	2.51*
Employees in business unit	445 (A)	333 (A)	416 (A)	0.21
Employees in organization	3,181 (A)	1,287 (A)	3,225 (A)	0.60
Service firms (per cent of sample)	62 (A)	52 (A)	52 (A)	1.32
Percentage staff devoted to the following activities[b]				
Basic research	2.14 (A,B)	2.80 (A)	1.41 (B)	2.25*
Product development	7.37 (A)	4.53 (A)	7.44 (A)	0.89
Manufacturing	19.06 (B)	28.59 (A)	24.09 (A,B)	1.67
Service delivery	40.13 (A)	34.05 (A)	37.72 (A)	0.58
Management	7.40 (B)	9.14 (A)	7.39 (B)	1.70
Marketing and sales	13.27 (A)	7.90 (B)	11.85 (A,B)	1.87
General administration	9.65 (B)	12.87 (A)	11.40 (A,B)	2.83*
Innovation measures				
Overall innovation index[a]	1.45 (A)	1.34 (B)	1.33 (B)	3.92**
New product prototypes	4.54 (A)	4.20 (A,B)	3.86 (B)	5.79***
New products – new to market	4.32 (A)	4.10 (A)	3.50 (B)	9.08***
New products – new to the firm	4.50 (A)	4.51 (A)	4.32 (A)	0.62
Significant modifications of products	4.76 (A)	4.27 (B)	4.40 (A,B)	2.23
Manufacturing techniques	4.16 (A)	4.46 (A)	4.14 (A)	0.62
Patents	4.57 (B)	4.57 (B)	4.39 (A)	2.97*
Research and development	8.03 (A)	6.39 (A)	8.23 (A)	0.32
Characteristics of knowledge environment				
Codifiability	4.94 (A)	4.98 (A)	4.86 (A)	0.13
Teachability	4.15 (A)	4.36 (A)	4.19 (A)	0.65
Complexity	5.22 (B)	5.51 (A)	5.14 (B)	2.13
System dependence	4.93 (A)	5.19 (A)	5.14 (A)	1.86
Observability	3.70 (A)	3.80 (A)	3.80 (A)	0.12

Table 6. (*Continued*)

	Segment 1	Segment 2	Segment 3	F-Value
Individual performance (measured relative to competitors)				
Return on investment	4.41 (A)	2.00 (C)	3.13 (B)	110.73*
Market share	4.65 (A)	1.98 (C)	3.43 (B)	116.51*
Increase in sales	4.40 (A)	1.70 (C)	3.21 (B)	162.30*
Increase in profits	4.30 (A)	1.49 (C)	2.92 (B)	176.18*

Note: The letters in parentheses indicate which means are significantly different. For each variable those not different are indicated by the same letter – for example, (A) in the case of codifiability. Those where a difference exists are indicated by a different letter – for example, in the case of ROI all three groups are different and significant since three different letters are used. In situations where two letters are shown, it indicates that this segment is not different from two other segments – for example, in the case of internal sources of knowledge, segment 3 is not different from segments 1 and 2 but segments 1 and 2 are different from one another.
*$p < 0.10$, **$p < 0.05$, ***$p < 0.01$.
[a]Denotes an aggregate measure.
[b]Percentages do not add up to 100 per cent due to overlap. For example, not all manufacturing firms would provide high levels of service and service firms high levels of manufacturing.

what the differences are that emerge from the data given the model structure we have proposed.

Hence, to obtain a more complete picture of these different segments we attempt to determine whether or not there are observable factors related to the likelihood of segment membership. Table 6 uses the three-segment solution and presents the means by group for a selected number of observable characteristics. Table 7 outlines multinomial logit (MNL) estimates relating to group membership. Segment membership was determined by the posterior probability of a firm being in that segment, and each firm was assigned to that segment for which it had the maximum probability of being in.

Our first set of comparisons is based on a casual comparison of the means of the different segments (Table 6). As noted before, segment 2 is the worst performer and this is true even though it has the highest level of internal and external knowledge sourcing and absorptive capacity, although the two knowledge sources are not significantly different across the groups. This segment also has the fewest numbers of multinationals and the smallest number of employees. It is least likely to be involved in product development (in terms of the percentage of employees devoted to this) but

Table 7. Multinomial Logistic Regressions on Segment Membership (Base = Segment 3).

	Analysis 1		Analysis 2		Analysis 3	
	Segment 1	Segment 2	Segment 1	Segment 2	Segment 1	Segment 2
Structural variables:						
Multinationals (per cent of sample)	0.150	−0.836**	0.186	−0.837**	0.132	−0.799**
	(0.289)	(0.402)	(0.291)	(0.398)	(0.277)	(0.374)
Staff distribution by activity						
Product development	−0.006	−0.035				
	(0.013)	(0.023)				
Service delivery	0.001	−0.008				
	(0.006)	(0.008)				
Marketing and sales	−0.001	−0.026	−0.005	−0.021		
	(0.011)	(0.019)	(0.009)	(0.017)		
Innovation: Overall innovation index			−0.962**	−0.807	−1.085***	−0.866*
			(0.409)	(0.555)	(0.350)	(0.515)
Knowledge environment						
Complexity	−0.159	0.329	−0.152	0.252		
	(0.146)	(0.215)	(0.137)	(0.198)		
System dependence	0.311**	0.215	0.371**	0.297	0.318**	0.377**
	(0.154)	(0.202)	(0.155)	(0.200)	(0.145)	(0.196)
Industry dummies						
Natural resources	1.455*	1.824**	1.357*	2.067**	1.326***	2.230***
	(0.823)	(0.917)	(0.802)	(0.877)	(0.800)	(0.848)
Business services	−0.193	−0.604				
	(0.422)	(0.710)				
Legal, health and other services	−0.363	−0.443				
	(0.379)	(0.534)				
Log Likelihood	−251.22		−253.18		−273.08	
McFadden's Pseudo R^2	0.067		0.066		0.051	
Per cent correctly classified	53.20		50.60		52.00	

Note: *$p < 0.10$, **$p < 0.05$, ***$p < 0.01$.

more likely to be involved in research and manufacturing based on percentage of employees. It has the lowest level of marketing and sales intensity of any group. Segment 1, the best performer, is equal to segment 3 in terms of the number of multinationals and firm size. It is the second highest in research and development measured in dollar terms and equally high in research and product development (measured in number of employees). Both of these facts are related to this group's significantly higher innovation numbers, which also shows up in its higher numbers in terms of marketing, sales and services. Segment 3 is the second best performer and closer to segment 1 than segment 2 in terms of the number of multinationals, firm size, product development and marketing and sales focus. It is the least likely to be involved in research and development in terms of employees but most heavily involved in product development.

Table 7 contains MNL estimates for the best subset of deterministic variables to predict segment membership. This best subset was determined by winnowing down the variables in Table 6, excluding those included in the finite mixture regression. In all cases, the comparison in the MNL is against segment 3, the middle-performing group of firms.

Analysis 3 (in Table 7) is the most parsimonious model with the largest absolute log likelihood (546.16) and best segment prediction (52 per cent). The three analyses show that the distribution of staff is less relevant when we include an innovation measure. What is most amazing about this analysis is that it shows that groups 1 and 2 differ from group 3 based on their greater likelihood of being a natural resources company, with less innovation and greater system dependence. The impact of complexity disappears (although it is slightly correlated with system dependence). However, what distinguishes group 2 from groups 1 and 3 is that they tend to be local rather than multinational organizations! If we look at where the misclassifications occur this evidence is reinforced. Segment 1 firms that are misclassified are misclassified wholly (100 per cent) as segment 3 firms. Segment 3 firms when misclassified are almost wholly (98 per cent) misclassified as segment 1 firms. When misclassifications of segment 2 firms occur, in 61 per cent of the cases they are placed in segment 1.

DISCUSSION AND CONCLUSION

We began this analysis with the simple task of asking whether internal and external knowledge sourcing had the same marginal impact on performance. In setting this agenda, we wanted to go beyond simply stating the obvious that both internal and external knowledge are important to firm performance or that absorptive capacity matters. Without accounting for unobserved firm heterogeneity, it would have been impossible to discern the relative value of these two important sources of knowledge since they are so obviously related, and standard empirical techniques in use in the literature would have been overwhelmed by this correlation. What we have shown is that the picture of knowledge sourcing and absorptive capacity is complex and needs sophisticated empirical techniques to get at even a simple understanding of what is going on. As we have revealed, there is enormous power in using latent class, finite mixture regression as a way of understanding not just firm differences but also in discerning the different models that might apply. All too often we look for confirmation of our hypotheses – for example, absorptive capacity is important, all knowledge sourcing is valuable – without paying attention to the fact that our models do not explain most of the variance in our data. As is shown here, there are patterns in the results which compel us to come up with more robust and parsimonious explanations of the phenomena we are investigating.

These techniques do not, however, determine for us the theoretical value of what we have uncovered; nor do they necessarily provide immediate insight into why the results are the way they are. For example, we still cannot establish without more information why segment 2, with its high level of sourcing, is the weakest performing group. Perhaps this group represents failed attempts at change. For example, our measure of performance is a 3-year average, but our measure of sourcing and absorptive capacity is contemporaneous. If these firms have performed poorly and are only now instituting knowledge programs that might explain the relationship. The fact that they are affected most by external sourcing is consistent with this logic; that is, if they were performing poorly, they might have less confidence in what they have available within the firm. It is also telling that the effect of this external sourcing is moderated by absorptive capacity but not by enough to counter the negative direct effect. Alternatively, maybe these are the firms that have reached the point of significant diminishing marginal returns on what they know, leading to greater reliance on outside sources. What is very clear is that this group is not performing poorly because of the structural characteristics of their industry makeup or because the group is lower on the variables of interest, the importance of the knowledge sources and absorptive capacity. The MNL analysis shows that segment 2 differs from segment 1, a significantly better performing group of firms, only on its level of multinationality. What we do know is that their poor performance is due to something more systemic.

We can also say that there may be less to our understanding of the relationship between knowledge-intensive firms and performance than we would like to acknowledge. It has become something of a truism in the literature, as stated in our introduction, to assert that knowledge is one of the last remaining sources of sustainable competitive advantage. Yet we can show that there are groups of firms in the market (in our case approximately 17 per cent) for whom this is clearly not the case at all. These firms deserve more in-depth study, as they may be critical to our understanding of the circumstances where access to certain types of knowledge pays. Again as evidenced from the MNL, one would have great difficulty in picking these firms out ex ante relying on public information only. A real value of latent class regression analysis is that it can identify who these firms are so that more in-depth analysis can address why they might not fit the 'norm'.

In examining segments 1 and 3, we find that internal sources of knowledge appear extremely important to performance. Both groups are evidence of this. Where they differ is in how they capitalize external knowledge. In the case of segment 1, external knowledge sourcing interacts with absorptive capacity. In the case of segment 3, external knowledge interacts with internal knowledge. Hence, while they are the two groups that are driving the overall relationship between the importance of internal knowledge sourcing and performance, they do so in very different ways. Again, assuming a single model for all firms would have masked this effect.

The result shows that external knowledge in itself is rarely determining performance. If anything, the direct effect of external knowledge is negative (true for all three segments). However, when moderated by either absorptive capacity (in segment 1) or internal knowledge (in segment 3) the value of external knowledge becomes positive. This indicates that external knowledge needs to be transformed and internalized, which happens when combined with existing knowledge (absorptive capacity) or new internally generated knowledge in order to realize the full potential of the external knowledge.

This research is not without its limitations. There is the problem of co-linearity in our constructs that may be simply part and parcel of the problem we are studying. Unless we purposely sample firms with internal and external sourcing characteristics that allow for better distinctions between these groups, we may never be able to understand the true distinction between knowledge sourced from inside the firm and that sourced outside. This is true of absorptive capacity as well. To attempt to account for this issue, we also estimated some simpler models. Two models were used with the following independent variables: (1) the importance of internal knowledge, absorptive capacity and the interaction between these two and (2) the importance of external knowledge, absorptive capacity and the interaction between these two. These models under-performed our proposed specification in terms of fit and parsimony, but confirmed the basic conclusions: the general negative effect of external sources and the existence of three segments. To account for the fact that we may have mis-specified the interaction between the importance of internal and external knowledge sources, we estimated a model using a ratio of internal and external sourcing rather than a straight interaction. This implies that the balance of internal and external sourcing is important. This model also under-performed the one reported here.

From a methodological perspective, we need to remember that segment solutions in finite mixture regressions are conditional upon the model structure being chosen. Hence, the hypotheses are joint tests of the appropriateness of the segment structure *given* the model structure. We have attempted to deal with this, but it is possible that more complex structures may exist that we have not proposed and may imply different segment structures.

Finally, we should note that our results show that the poor performance of the OLS is not due either to co-linearity in the constructs or erroneous definitions of the constructs. Some might question our definition of absorptive capacity or the importance of internal and external knowledge sourcing. However, the finite mixture regressions do show that these measures explain a vast majority of the variance in the data and have consistent and compelling implications, albeit ones that do not match immediately to extant theory in an easy and simple way.

We have shown that firm heterogeneity not only exists but also can be categorized without reliance on ex-ante speculation as to what determines heterogeneity. In doing so, we show that a singular view of the importance of different knowledge sources is not as clear as simple theory might imply. For example, simply because a firm has high levels of absorptive capacity or access to knowledge sources does not necessarily imply that they will realize the value of that knowledge (Zahra & George, 2002). As Soo et al. (2002) show in a series of case studies, many attempts to develop and utilize knowledge fail to meet expectations. What we have done is provide some insight into how we can model this complexity while still taking advantage of large-scale, generalizable, empirical survey research. However, to take this further we need a deeper understanding of the processes that lead to these differences and we need to integrate this into the analysis so that we can determine the process by which such heterogeneity arises. For example, our analysis does indicate that contemporaneous industry and environmental factors are not the only determinants of segment member-ship. What needs to be the subject of future work is formulating the dynamic structural antecedents to firm heterogeneity as well as the role that managerial decisions play in determining 'consistently' heterogeneous outcomes.

NOTES

1. The list of external sources included not just these four but also other businesses, sales/distribution agents, universities, research institutes, government or quasi-government agencies and advertising agencies. These groups accounted for a very small proportion of the sourcing activity of the firms surveyed.

2. For example, in the case of the normal distribution the link function would be simply, $\eta_{nsk} = \mu_{sk}$.

3. All these criteria have limitations and there are numerous others that have been proposed. The general rule is that those based on a variant of the likelihood ratio test, such as AIC or CAIC, are to be used in conjunction with more sophisticated approaches (Deb & Trivedi, 1997).

4. The entropy measure is bounded between 0 and 1 with lower values indicating smaller separation between the segment identities as measured by the posterior probabilities.

5. NEC(S) is shown to perform in a similar manner to Bozdogan's (1994) information theoretical measure – a measure that is more robust than CAIC or AIC since it is based on the properties of the information matrix – for mixtures of normal distributions. Hence, although NEC(S) is not a general measure it is applicable here since we are using mixtures of normal distributions.

REFERENCES

Akaike, H. (1974). A new look at the statistical model identification. *IEEE Transactions on Automatic Control, 19*(1), 67–75.

Almeida, P., & Kogut, B. (1999). Localization of knowledge and the mobility of engineers in regional networks. *Management Science, 45*(7), 905–917.

Andersson, U., Forsgren, M., & Holm, U. (2002). The strategic impact of external networks: Subsidiary performance and competence development in the multinational corporation. *Strategic Management Journal, 23*(11), 979–996.

Argote, L., & Ingram, P. (2000). Knowledge transfer: A basis for competitive advantage in firms. *Organizational Behavior and Human Decision Processes, 82*(1), 150–169.

Armstrong, J. S., & Overton, T. (1977). Estimating nonresponse bias in mail surveys. *Journal of Marketing Research, 14*, 396–402.

Banbury, C. M., & Mitchell, W. (1995). The effect of introducing important incremental innovations on market share and business survival. *Strategic Management Journal, 16*(S1), 161–182.

Barney, J. (1986). Strategic factor markets: Expectations, luck and business strategy. *Management Science, 32*(10), 1231–1241.

Baum, J. A. C., Calabrese, T., & Silverman, B. S. (2000). Don't go it alone: Alliance network composition and startups' performance in Canadian biotechnology. *Strategic Management Journal, 21*(3), 267–294.

Bierly, P., & Chakrabarti, A. (1996). Generic knowledge strategies in the U.S. pharmaceutical industry. *Strategic Management Journal, 17,* 123–135.

Blau, P. M. (1977). A macrosociological theory of social structure. *American Journal of Sociology, 83*(1), 26–54.

Bozdogan, H. (1994). Mixture-model cluster analysis using model selection criteria and a new informational measure of complexity. In: H. Bozdogan (Ed.), *Multivariate statistical modeling, volume 2, Proceedings of first US/Japan Conference on the Frontiers of Statistical Modeling: An Informational Approach* (pp. 69–113). Dordrecht, the Netherlands: Kluwer Academic Publishers.

Bresman, H., Birkinshaw, J., & Nobel, R. (1999). Knowledge transfer in international acquisitions. *Journal of International Business Studies, 30*(3), 439–462.

Brown, J. S., & Duguid, P. (1991). Organizational learning and communities-of-practice: Toward a unified view of working, learning, and innovation. *Organization Science, 2*(1), 40–57.

Burt, R. S. (1992). *Structural holes: The social structure of competition.* Cambridge, MA: Harvard University Press.

Celeux, G., & Soromenho, G. (1996). An entropy based criterion for assessing the number of clusters in a mixture model. *Journal of Classification, 13*(2), 195–212.

Cohen, W. M., & Levinthal, D. A. (1990). Absorptive capacity: A new perspective on learning and innovation. *Administrative Science Quarterly, 35*(1), 128–152.

Deb, P., & Trivedi, P. K. (1997). The demand for medical care by the elderly: A finite mixture approach. *Journal of Applied Econometrics, 12*(3), 313–336.

DeSarbo, W. S., Jedidi, K., & Sinha, I. (2001). Customer value analysis in a heterogeneous market. *Strategic Management Journal, 27*(5), 845–858.

Dollinger, M. (1984). Environmental boundary spanning and information processing effects on organizational performance. *Academy of Management Journal, 27*(2), 351–368.

Dyer, J. H. (1996). Specialized supplier networks as a source of competitive advantage: Evidence from the auto industry. *Strategic Management Journal, 17,* 271–291.

Dyer, J. H., & Nobeoka, K. (2000). Creating and managing a high-performance knowledge-sharing network: The Toyota case. *Strategic Management Journal, 21*(3), 345–367.

Ebadi, Y. M., & Utterback, J. M. (1984). The effects of communication on technological innovation. *Management Science, 30*(5), 572–585.

Foss, N. J., & Pedersen, T. (2002). Transferring knowledge in MNCs: The role of sources of subsidiary knowledge and organizational context. *Journal of International Management, 8*(1), 49–67.

Freeman, C. (1991). Networks of innovators: A synthesis of research issues. *Research Policy, 20*(5), 499–514.

Grant, R. M. (1996). Toward a knowledge-based theory of the firm. *Strategic Management Journal, 17,* 109–122.

Gulati, R., Nohria, N., & Zaheer, A. (2000). Strategic networks. *Strategic Management Journal, 21*(3), 203–216.

Hansen, M. T. (2002). Knowledge networks: Explaining effective knowledge sharing in multiunit companies. *Organization Science, 13*(3), 232–248.

Henderson, R., & Cockburn, I. (1994). Measuring competence? Exploring firm effects in pharmaceutical research. *Strategic Management Journal, 15,* 63–84.

Iansiti, M., & Clark, K. B. (1994). Integration and dynamic capability: Evidence from product development in automobiles and mainframe computers. *Industrial and Corporate Change, 3*(3), 557–605.

Lane, P. J., & Lubatkin, M. (1998). Relative absorptive capacity and interorganizational learning. *Strategic Management Journal, 19,* 461–477.

Lane, P. J., Salk, J. E., & Lyles, M. A. (2001). Absorptive capacity, learning, and performance in international joint ventures. *Strategic Management Journal, 22*(12), 1139–1162.

Leonard, D., & Sensiper, S. (1998). The role of tacit knowledge in group innovation. *California Management Review, 40*(3), 112–132.

Levine, S., & White, P. (1961). Exchange as a conceptual framework for the study of interorganizational relationships. *Administrative Science Quarterly, 5*(4), 583–601.

Liebeskind, J. P., Oliver, A. L., Zucker, L., & Brewer, M. (1996). Social networks, learning, and flexibility: Sourcing scientific knowledge in new biotechnology firms. *Organization Science, 7*(4), 428–443.

Lorenzoni, G., & Lipparini, A. (1999). The leveraging of interfirm relationships as a distinctive organizational capability: A longitudinal study. *Strategic Management Journal, 20*(4), 317–338.

McEvily, B., & Zaheer, A. (1999). Bridging ties: A source of firm heterogeneity in competitive capabilities. *Strategic Management Journal, 20*(12), 1133–1156.

McEvily, S. K., & Chakravarthy, B. (2002). The persistence of knowledge-based advantage: An empirical test for product performance and technological knowledge. *Strategic Management Journal, 23*(4), 285–305.

Miner, A. S., Amburgey, T. L., & Stearns, T. M. (1990). Interorganizational linkages and population dynamics: Buffering and transformation shields. *Administrative Science Quarterly, 35*(4), 689–713.

Mitchell, W., & Singh, K. (1996). Precarious collaboration: Business survival after partners shut down or form new partnerships. *Strategic Management Journal, 17*(S1), 99–115.

Mowery, D. C., Oxley, J. E., & Silverman, B. S. (1996). Strategic alliances and interfirm knowledge transfer. *Strategic Management Journal, 17,* 77–91.

Nagarajan, A., & Mitchell, W. (1998). Evolutionary diffusion: Internal and external methods used to acquire encompassing, complementary, and incremental technological changes in the lithotripsy industry. *Strategic Management Journal, 19*(11), 1063–1077.

Nahapiet, J., & Ghoshal, S. (1998). Social capital, intellectual capital, and the organizational advantages. *Academy of Management Review, 23*(2), 242–266.

Nobel, R., & Birkinshaw, J. (1998). Innovation in multinational corporations: Control and communication patterns in international R&D operations. *Strategic Management Journal, 19,* 479–496.

Noda, T., & Collis, D. J. (2001). The evolution of intraindustry firm heterogeneity: Insights from a process study. *Academy of Management Journal, 44*(4), 897–925.

Nonaka, I., & Takeuchi, H. (1995). *The knowledge-creating company.* New York: Oxford.

O'Dell, C., & Grayson, C. J. (1998). If only we knew what we know: Identification and transfer of internal best practices. *California Management Review, 40*(3), 154–174.

Paulus, P. B., & Yang, H. (2000). Idea generation in groups: A basis for creativity in organizations. *Organizational Behavior and Human Decision Processes, 82*(1), 76–87.

Pennings, J. M., & Harianto, F. (1992). The diffusion of technological innovation in the commercial banking industry. *Strategic Management Journal, 13,* 29–46.

Peteraf, M. A. (1993). The cornerstone of competitive advantage: A resource based view. *Strategic Management Journal, 14,* 179–192.

Pfeffer, J., & Salancik, G. R. (1978). *The external control of organizations: A resource dependence perspective.* New York: Harper & Row.

Podsakoff, P., & Organ, D. (1986). Self reports in organizational research: Problems and prospects. *Journal of Management, 12*(4), 531–544.

Powell, W., Koput, K., & Smith–Doerr, L. (1996). Interorganizational collaboration and the locus of innovation: Networks of learning in biotechnology. *Administrative Science Quarterly, 41*(1), 116–145.

Quinn, J. B. (1992). *Intelligent enterprise: A knowledge and service based paradigm for industry.* New York: Free Press.

Rosenkopf, L., & Nerkar, A. (2001). Beyond local search: Boundary-spanning, exploration, and impact in the optical disc industry. *Strategic Management Journal, 22*(4), 287–306.

Rulke, D. L., Zaheer, S., & Anderson, M. H. (2000). Sources of managers' knowledge of organizational capabilities. *Organizational Behavior and Human Decision Processes, 82*(1), 134–149.

Soo, C. W., Devinney, T. M., & Midgley, D. F. (2001). *The process of knowledge creation in organizations.* Unpublished manuscript.

Soo, C. W., Devinney, T. M., Midgley, D. F., & Deering, A. (2002). Knowledge management: Philosophy, pitfalls and processes. *California Management Review, 44*(4), 129–150.

Stearns, T. M., Hoffman, A. N., & Heide, J. B. (1987). Performance of commercial television stations as an outcome of interorganizational linkages and environmental conditions. *Academy of Management Journal, 30*(1), 71–90.

Steensma, H. K., & Lyles, M. A. (2000). Explaining IJV survival in a transitional economy through social exchange and knowledge-based perspectives. *Strategic Management Journal, 21*(8), 831–851.

Stuart, T. E. (2000). Interorganizational alliances and the performance of firms: A study of growth and innovation rates in a high technology industry. *Strategic Management Journal, 21*(8), 791–811.

Stuart, T. E., Hoang, H., & Hybels, R. C. (1999). Interorganizational endorsements and the performance of entrepreneurial ventures. *Administrative Science Quarterly, 44*(2), 315–349.

Szulanski, G. (1996). Exploring internal stickiness: Impediments to the transfer of best practice within the firm. *Strategic Management Journal, 17,* 27–43.

Teece, D., Pisano, G., & Shuen, A. (1997). Dynamic capabilities and strategic management. *Strategic Management Journal, 18,* 509–533.

Tsai, W. (2001). Knowledge transfer in intraorganizational networks: Effects of network position and absorptive capacity on business unit innovation and performance. *Academy of Management Journal, 44*(5), 996–1004.

Tsai, W., & Ghoshal, S. (1998). Social capital and value creation: The role of intrafirm networks. *Academy of Management Journal, 41*(4), 464–476.

Tushman, M. L., & Katz, R. (1980). External communication and project performance: An investigation into the role of gatekeepers. *Management Science, 26*(11), 1071–1084.

Veugelers, R. (1997). Internal R&D expenditures and external technology sourcing. *Research Policy, 26*(3), 303–315.

von Hippel, E. (1994). Sticky information and the locus of problem solving: Implications for innovation. *Management Science, 40*(4), 429–439.

Wedel, M., & DeSarbo, W. S. (1995). A mixture likelihood approach for generalized linear models. *Journal of Classification, 12*(1), 1–35.

Wedel, M., & Kamakura, W. A. (2000). *Market segmentation: Conceptual and methodological foundations*. London: Kluwer.

Wernerfelt, B. (1984). A resource-based view of the firm. *Strategic Management Journal, 5*(2), 171–180.

Winter, S. (1987). Knowledge and competence as strategic assets. In: D. Teece (Ed.), *The competitive challenge: Strategies for industrial innovation and renewal*. Cambridge, MA: Ballinger.

Yli-Renko, H., Autio, E., & Sapienza, H. J. (2001). Social capital, knowledge acquisition, and knowledge exploitation in young technology-based firms. *Strategic Management Journal, 22*(6–7), 587–614.

Zahra, S. A., & George, G. (2002). Absorptive capacity: A review, reconceptualization, and extention. *Academy of Management Review, 27*(2), 185–203.

APPENDIX A. RELATIONSHIP BETWEEN THE AGGREGATE KNOWLEDGE-SOURCING MEASURES AND FREQUENCY OF SOURCING FROM SELECTED GROUPS

Frequency of Acquiring Knowledge from Selected Sources	Internal Knowledge	External Knowledge
Customers	0.234***	0.112*
Suppliers	0.304***	0.117*
Competitors	0.225***	0.019
Consultants	0.231***	0.118*
Colleagues from the same or other business units	0.125*	0.441***
R^2	0.16	0.21

Note: The R^2 for external sources includes only customers, suppliers, competitors and consultants and that for internal sources, colleagues, parent company (conditional on being a multinational) and other business units.
*$p<0.10$, ***$p<0.01$.

APPENDIX B. CORRELATION MATRIX OF
CONSTRUCTS IN THE MODEL

	Performance	Internal Sources	External Sources
Internal sources	0.212*** (0.042)	1.000	
External sources	0.057 (0.003)	0.243*** (0.059)	1.000
Organizational AC	0.121** (0.015)	0.359*** (0.129)	0.336*** (0.113)

Note: Number in parentheses is the R^2 from a simple one-variable regression.
**$p < 0.05$, ***$p < 0.01$.

A KNOWLEDGE SYSTEM APPROACH TO THE MULTINATIONAL COMPANY: CONCEPTUAL GROUNDING AND IMPLICATIONS FOR RESEARCH

Nicolai J. Foss and José F. P. dos (Joe) Santos

ABSTRACT

The role of knowledge, organizational learning and innovation as levers of competitive advantage is now a commonly acknowledged insight in research in international management, specifically in the emerging 'knowledge-based view'. However, this view has not yet developed into a unifying framework and there are significant holes in the understanding of how knowledge may be turned into a source of competitive advantage for MNCs. In order to advance the knowledge-based view of the MNC – and particularly of the metanational company – we develop the notion of the MNC as a global knowledge system that links local knowledge structures and combines local knowledge elements that are complementary in order to achieve strategic advantage. These ideas are used to frame the changing environments, strategic intents and learning stances that characterize MNCs, and to derive a set of research challenges for MNC research.

Dynamics of Globalization: Location-Specific Advantages or Liabilities of Foreignness?
Advances in International Management, Volume 24, 425–453
Copyright © 2011 by Emerald Group Publishing Limited
All rights of reproduction in any form reserved
ISSN: 1571-5027/doi:10.1108/S1571-5027(2011)0000024023

INTRODUCTION: THE KNOWLEDGE CHALLENGES TO INTERNATIONAL MANAGEMENT RESEARCH

Knowledge as a factor influencing the growth and competitiveness of the multinational company (MNC) has been apparent in theories of foreign direct investment (e.g. Hymer, 1976) and theories of the firm (Penrose, 1956, 1959) from the start of international management as a research field (Buckley & Casson, 1976). However, the shift of conceptual lens from internationalization theories towards a knowledge-based view of the MNC has only taken place within the last ten to fifteen years (Tallman, 2003). In this chapter, we argue that this shift still has to coalesce into an organizing, coherent framework, but also identify key dimensions of such a framework as well as the research challenges that it implies.

The international management literature contains impressive work on, for example, MNC knowledge flows and how administrative apparatus can be deployed to influence such flows, and the MNC is now conventionally conceptualized as a network that accesses, produces, transfers and combines knowledge (e.g. Gupta & Govindarajan, 1991, 1994, 2000; Hedlund, 1986; Kogut & Zander, 1993, 1995; Minbaeva, Pedersen, Björkman, Fey, & Park, 2003), a literature that is sometimes conceptualized as the 'differentiated MNC' literature (Foss & Pedersen, 2004; Forsgren, Holm, & Johanson, 2005). However, this is more of a label that usefully organizes some convergent insights than a new organizing framework. Moreover, the basic framework informing this literature (even the sophisticated evolutionary contributions of Kogut and Zander, 1993, 1995) is still one in which the network of subsidiaries and headquarters is the primary unit of analysis.

Two decades ago, Buckley (1990, p. 663) argued that what is required in the core theory of international management research is ' … careful redefinition of the relationship between key explanatory variables so that new developments grow organically from the theory rather than being added in a piecemeal and arbitrary fashion'. We attempt to constructively meet Buckley's statement by proposing a view of the MNC as a system of knowledge – a view that synthesizes important strands in existing research – and offer a number of suggestions for research in the MNC that aim at bringing us closer towards such a framework. An important starting point is the clarification of the challenge of obtaining and turning knowledge into a source of strategic advantage for MNCs. Traditionally, MNCs relied on home-based knowledge leadership, both in market development and in technology (Vernon, 1966; Johanson & Vahlne, 1977). To access foreign markets, companies often applied a standard formula.

Thus, they projected to foreign markets a bundle of carefully packaged knowledge, often in the form of 'best practises' and usually created, tested and honed at home. However, in many industries, national efforts to promote local science and innovation, the diffusion of technology triggered by MNCs' manufacturing and outsourcing overseas, the emergence of local skills from the combination of imported techniques and local customs and even the local spillover effects from military and other local government-led activities have implied increasing knowledge dispersion worldwide (e.g. Dunning, 2002).

This has led managers of global firms to seek knowledge whenever and wherever it is to be found (Cantwell, 1989; Dunning, 1996, 2002). Companies that are able to access distributed pockets of local knowledge, and combine and meld such knowledge from global sources into innovative products and new business concepts gain an advantage over those that remain dependent on home-based knowledge. Such companies engage in knowledge sensing worldwide and seek to capitalize not only on distributed intra-firm (MNC) knowledge (Ghoshal & Bartlett, 1990; Nohria & Ghoshal, 1997) but also on distributed inter-firm knowledge through alliances and partnerships, namely with customers, suppliers and competitors (Badaracco, 1991; Doz & Hamel, 1998), and distributed knowledge from other organizations (namely local universities and research institutes). In so doing each firm may develop a unique knowledge network worldwide that its competitors find it hard to match, especially when they still rely mainly on knowledge emanating from their home bases. Such firms have been dubbed 'metanational MNCs' (Doz, Santos, & Williamson, 2001).

In this chapter, we seek to address some of the fundamental issues in the development of a knowledge-based conceptualization of the MNC. Specifically, we develop a view of the MNC as a geographically distributed system of local knowledge structures, a view that is particularly consistent with the metanational MNC. This view is based on earlier contributions to the knowledge system view of firms (Loasby, 1976; Lyles & Schwenk, 1992; Hedlund, 1994; Doz et al., 2001; Yayavaram & Ahuja, 2008) and to the part of complex systems theory that has taken its cues from Herbert Simon's work (1962, 1973) and from evolutionary biology (Wright, 1930; Kauffman, 1993).[1] Combining these perspectives makes it possible to understand the existence, scope and performance of MNCs by conceptualizing MNCs as searching for local knowledge structures, and connecting these into systems that map into peaks in some performance landscape (Levinthal, 1997; Fleming, 2001; Ethiraj & Levinthal, 2004; Nickerson & Zenger, 2004; Foss & Ishikawa, 2007; Yayavaram & Ahuja, 2008).

In this perspective, recent MNC evolution may be understood in terms of an expanding knowledge search space: the change from 'projecting' knowledge-based artefacts (from a product to a business strategy and its respective activity-system) developed in an national base (Vernon, 1966), to improving such home-based artefacts through transnational innovation (Bartlett & Ghoshal, 1989), to creating new artefacts through 'learning from the World' and metanational innovation (Doz et al., 2001) is one that involves addressing a much expanded set of possible knowledge sources and combinations (Denrell, Fang, & Winter, 2003). While this represents many new opportunities, it also raises considerable problems for MNC organization and management, as search behaviour, absorptive capacity and learning are challenged by the heavily expanding set of knowledge structures and of the explosion in the possible combinations of knowledge elements across these structures. The firms that succeed in the emerging global competition are those that best match their search and learning strategies to the changing landscape of knowledge sources and combinations.

THE MULTINATIONAL COMPANY AS A KNOWLEDGE SYSTEM: CONCEPTUALIZATION

Stocks and Flows in the Knowledge-Based View of the MNC

A very large part of the recent knowledge-based MNC literature focuses on knowledge transfers between subsidiaries (Kogut & Zander, 1993, 1995; Foss & Pedersen, 2002, 2004; Forsgren et al., 2005), often with a focus on obstacles to such flows, and sometimes with an explicit consideration of the role organizational structures and systems plays in the process of knowledge transfer (e.g. Hedlund, 1986; Bartlett & Ghoshal, 1986, 1989; Birkinshaw, 1996; Gupta & Govindarajan, 1991, 1994, 2000; Holm & Pedersen, 2000). This almost paradigmatic research has only been partly embedded in an overall, coherent conceptualization of the MNC as a knowledge-based entity. Kogut and Zander (1993, 1995) is perhaps the most systematic attempt to construct an organizing framework (although the main thrust of their work remains on knowledge transfer). Specifically, they propose an evolutionary view of the MNC in which new knowledge is created in the headquarters or home base; then transferred to foreign subsidiaries; re-combined there with local knowledge and, eventually, that new knowledge (a 'variation') is (somehow) transferred to the network of national subsidiaries and even the headquarters. In contrast to this flow-based view, our view of the MNC as a knowledge system is about the structure (or stock) that allows for combinations and re-combinations to occur in the MNC.

It is recognized in the knowledge view of the MNC literature that flows emerge *from* some knowledge stock, such as particular technological or marketing competencies controlled by MNC headquarters. However, little attention has been devoted to systematically addressing how MNC knowledge flows emerge from the distribution of knowledge in the different locations where the units (or 'sites') of the MNC reside across the world. In fact, there is a separate treatment of knowledge stocks and flows in the literature. Thus, in his eclectic framework and OLI model, Dunning (1988) emphasizes stocks by acknowledging the importance of national subsidiaries and their knowledge creation and repository role with the notion of location-specific advantages (cf., Rugman & Verbeke, 2001). Ghoshal (1987), Bartlett and Ghoshal (1989) and Hedlund (1994) furthermore consider the importance of worldwide learning and intra-MNC knowledge sharing (e.g. of 'best practises'), and therefore put the main emphasis on flows. However, flows emerge from stocks, and they change other stocks. Which flows emerge is partly dependent on the composition of the knowledge stock – that is, the set of local knowledge structures – just as the outputs that emerge from the overall stock of capital in society are dependent on the composition of that stock (Lachmann, 1956). But, in turn, knowledge flows within the MNC change the local knowledge structures and the MNC's ability to exploit them (Yayavaram & Ahuja, 2008). Therefore, a time-dimensioned, knowledge-based understanding of the MNC *requires* that analytical attention be paid to both flows and the composition and geographic distribution of the knowledge stocks.

The MNC as a Knowledge System: Terminology

To integrate stocks and flows of knowledge, we define a *knowledge system* in terms of (geographically defined) local knowledge structures and the relationships between them. The MNC knowledge system is not given, but malleable and changing, as firms absorb new knowledge elements into local knowledge structures, augmenting their knowledge stocks, and link existing knowledge structures in novel ways, creating innovations from enhanced knowledge flows. We can thus conceive the MNC as a system with knowledge *links* connecting local knowledge structures.

To describe the MNC more formally, let K_{ij} refer to knowledge element i in geographic location j. We define the quality of K_{ij} as its (maximum) value creation potential. Therefore, if the quality of K_{ih} is superior to K_{it}, then the performance of a firm in h is potentially superior to that of a similar firm in t. A 'location' is not just a geographic point in space, but also a shorthand for a set of contextual features (such as a national culture that reflects the identity and history of a particular people) that make local knowledge both different and hard to transfer. 'Location' is thus a point in space (geography) *and* time (history and the evolution of a culture). The set of knowledge elements that exist in a location constitute the substantive part of the local knowledge structure. A local knowledge structure is expressed as a set of local knowledge elements that are readily connected by the pre-existing links among the knowledge holders.

A very simple firm would be constituted by the combination of two knowledge elements, K_1 and K_2. Suppose further that both K_1 and K_2 exist in location h (home) and location t (host). If $K_{ih} \equiv K_{it}$ for $i = 1$, 2, the knowledge at the two locations is identical and there is no reason for a MNC to exist on the basis of combining these two knowledge elements. However, if K_2 does not exist in t, an indigenous firm cannot exist there either. If the firm in h is able to transfer (internally) K_2 from h to t, and combine K_1 and K_2 there, it becomes an MNC. Per implication it will realize a superior performance over any indigenous firm (i.e. the motive for becoming an MNC). With the knowledge transfer direction set from the location with superior knowledge to that of inferior knowledge, the theory of the MNC in this case is also a theory of strategic advantage. In general, we assume that an MNC will attempt to combine the relevant K_{ij} $(i = 1, \dots, n)$ by choosing j $(j = 1, \dots, m)$ in order to maximize its performance.

Note that there is no need to assume that, say, K_2 moves from h to t to be combined there; indeed, the combination mode could involve a 'virtual team', with members holding K_2 in h and members holding K_1 in t and producing an innovation that would originate from the MNC, without each local sub-team learning the knowledge of the other local sub-team. Put differently, knowledge elements can be combined without being transferred or shared across locations. By providing relatively similar internal contexts to knowledge held in h and t, contrary to independent entities or alliance partners whose organizational contexts would likely be deeply different, the MNC is a common ground which facilitates the combination of knowledge without having to attempt to share or even transfer such knowledge across locations. The continuity and reliability in the provision of combined knowledge that a single ownership and common administrative structure encourages, may be the constitutive characteristics of the MNC form, rather than its superior ability to transfer knowledge.

In fact, the MNC does not necessarily have to transfer knowledge, but only to represent knowledge from various locations effectively enough to allow the development of new products or processes that rely on knowledge from various locations, thus allowing one to transcend the location-specificity of knowledge. Some economists (e.g. Stiglitz, 2003) argue that knowledge is a global public good, equating knowledge to information. However, a key tenet in a number of literatures, such as international management, strategic management, organizational studies and economic geography, is exactly that much knowledge that is commercially relevant to MNCs is context-dependent and rooted in local circumstances. A knowledge-based theory of the MNC must take this fundamental stylized fact into account.

The MNC as a Hierarchical Knowledge System

The definition that we have articulated conceptualizes the MNC as a global knowledge *system* linking local knowledge *structures* and combining local knowledge *elements* that are complementary to confer strategic advantage. We use the word structures at the local level to denote that the knowledge elements available in any particular location constitute a set that while characterized by possibly ambiguous interaction between the elements is characterized by enduring interaction. At the global level, we use the word system to denote the fact that the configuration of linkages between locations within an MNC can evolve more rapidly, but through a set of complex systemic interactions many of which are purposefully built. We now develop the three constructs in greater detail.

Knowledge Elements

The basic unit in the knowledge structure conceptualization of the local MNC unit is the knowledge element. Examples of knowledge elements are a particular expertise embodied in individuals, personalized client relationships, a technological capability (typically at the level of a department or a plant) etc. As these examples suggest, knowledge elements may exist on different levels in an organization. They may be personal knowledge (as in the case of tacit knowledge) (Polanyi, 1962) or they may belong to the realm of objective knowledge (Popper, 1972). However, knowledge elements are discrete in the sense that they have boundaries, although such boundaries are not always apparent.[2] Extant literature (e.g. Winter, 1987; Kogut & Zander, 1993) suggests that knowledge elements possess a number of different attributes. The attributes that are of the essence here are those that bind a knowledge element with a location: for example, the extent to which a knowledge element is tacit or the extent to which a knowledge element is collective (i.e. embodied in a co-located team rather than in an individual).

Of particular importance is the location-specificity of a knowledge element, that is, the extent to which its quality depends on other, complementary knowledge elements in the same location, especially those elements that are tacit and collective (e.g. components of the local culture). For example, the skills in design for manufacturability of printers in Vancouver, USA, in Singapore and in Barcelona, Spain (three sites of Hewlett-Packard) are differentiated knowledge elements. The reason for such difference lies in the contextual nature of knowledge (Doz & Santos, 1997; Brannen, Liker, & Fruin, 1999). Knowledge, contrary to information, is location-specific, embedded in a particular context (physical and social) that characterizes one location (city, district, country, depending on the relevant unit of geography) at a particular moment of time. However, scientific knowledge, deemed universal, is not bound by location (K_{ij} is the same for all j). Arts and craft knowledge, on the other extreme, can be highly differentiated across locations ($K_{ij} \neq K_{im}$ for $m \neq j$).

Knowledge elements are the basic building blocks of knowledge structures. The structure's property primarily emerges from the knowledge elements' co-location. The knowledge structure provides itself a crucial part of the context in which each one of its knowledge elements becomes meaningful.

Knowledge Structures

A knowledge structure is defined as a set of knowledge elements available in a given location, and the interaction among them. Local units of an MNC (i.e. the MNC 'sites' in the location), as well as local (indigenous) firms, constitute knowledge structures. A knowledge structure is bound to its location insofar as some or all of its interconnected knowledge elements are embedded in the local context. If this were not the case – that is, if all knowledge elements were non-excludable in geography – there would be no special case for the MNC. If all knowledge elements would exist everywhere, the knowledge structure of a 'local' company and of a 'global' company could be the same.

A location can be understood as a set of (local) knowledge structures. For example, Badaracco (1991, p. 95) refers to 'knowledge and capabilities [residing] in geographic regions – in the interstices of social, financial, technological, and managerial relationships that can link *nearby* organizations' (italics added). So does Saxenian (1994), looking at Silicon Valley and Route 128. The location-dependency of knowledge lies on the observation that knowledge elements and knowledge structures that are meaningful, useful and valid (i.e. high quality) in a particular location may be meaningless, dysfunctional and not valid (i.e. low quality) in other locations. Szulanski (1996), studying the intra-firm transfer of best practises, found that the eventfulness of best practise transfer was induced by the very 'stickiness' of knowledge. Tyre and von Hippel (1997) present evidence of 'situated' knowledge, knowledge that depends on the physical elements of context. For instance, organizational routines are 'executable capabilities for repeated performance in *some context* that have been learned by an organization in response to selective pressures' (Cohen & Levinthal, 1990, p. 683; italics added). The dimension of location-dependency considered here exhibits an embeddedness that extends beyond social embeddedness (Granovetter, 1985).

A local knowledge structure (K_j) can be characterized in two dimensions:

- *scope* (or breadth), defined as the number n of different types of knowledge in the structure (K_{ij}, $i = 1 \ldots n$)
- *density*, defined as the number of linkages or interactions between the different knowledge elements (as a ratio to the total possible number of such linkages).

The knowledge interactions (or relations) that form the structure of knowledge elements give meaning to a K_{ij} by indicating which other knowledge elements are complementary to K_{ij} – that it would be comprehended in a full rendition of K_{ij}. We call these linkages *explanatory* relations.

Knowledge System

Our view of the MNC is a hierarchical one. However, it differs from the extant knowledge-based view in the MNC literature by emphasizing the hierarchical dimensions of the MNC knowledge structure. According to Simon (1962), 'hierarchies' are systems composed of interrelated (complementary) subsystems where each of the subsystems (e.g. a knowledge structure) is hierarchical in nature, until some elementary subsystem is reached at the lowest level (e.g. the knowledge element). 'In hierarchic systems', Simon explains, '... we can distinguish between the interactions *among* subsystems on the one hand, and the interactions *within* subsystems – i.e., among the parts of those subsystems – on the other' (1962, p. 473). In decomposable systems the interactions among the subsystems are negligible; in non-decomposable systems the interactions among the subsystems are substantial; and in nearly decomposable systems the interactions among the subsystems are weak (or weaker than within-subsystem interaction), but not negligible (1962, p. 129). This categorization can be seen to mirror classic classifications of MNCs as multi-domestic or global, respectively, with transnational or heterarchic MNCs corresponding to partly decomposable and recomposable systems, where the level of systemic integration may vary.

The knowledge interactions that exist in an MNC are of two types:

- *explanatory* relations, in part firm-specific (i.e. non-existent in the local knowledge structures and forming knowledge sets that exist only inside the MNC) and in part location-specific (i.e. acquired with sets of K_{ij} from local knowledge structures);
- *combinatory* relations, also specific to the MNC, that allow for new combinations of knowledge (innovations) by the MNC.

Dimensions of the MNC Knowledge System

If the MNC is conceived of as a knowledge system, how can the knowledge system itself be dimensionalized? Answering this is important to the extent that (as we believe to be the case) there are systematic relationships between dimensions of the knowledge system and MNC corporate strategy, organization and performance. Because the interest in developing a knowledge-based conceptualization of the MNC ultimately lies in putting forward better answers to questions concerning MNC strategy, organization and performance, the relevant dimensions are those that are likely to impact these aspects of the MNC.

One important dimension is the degree of *knowledge specialization*; for example, how many different knowledge elements or sets (e.g. technological disciplines) are required for optimal performance of the MNC and how different these are (cf. Brusoni, Prencipe, & Pavitt, 2001). The higher a degree of knowledge specialization within an MNC, the higher the degree of knowledge asymmetry across the sites of the MNC and the knowledge structures they are part of. A second dimension is the degree of *location specialization*, the inverse of the number of locations where it is possible to find all the knowledge elements that compose an MNC. In the case of a location specialization of one, a particular location contains all the knowledge that the MNC needs: the MNC can start as an indigenous firm in that location and then expand internationally from its home base – and most MNCs have done. If location specialization is very low (close to zero), MNCs can only exist if they are metanational (or 'homeless').

A third dimension is the *complexity* of the knowledge system. Knowledge systems that lie near the non-decomposable end of the spectrum are characterized by a high degree of 'complexity', where 'by complexity we mean the degree to which cognitive units are interrelated, creating a complex internal structure' (Lyles & Schwenk, 1992, p. 164). Simon (1962, p. 161) defines a complex system as one that is ' ... made up of a large number of parts that interact in a non-simple way ... . In such systems ... given the properties of the parts and the laws of their interaction, it is not a trivial matter to infer the properties of the whole'. Complex knowledge systems have high levels of structural uncertainty, as they exhibit large number of potential combinations of knowledge elements and unpredictable performance implications of such combinations (Ethiraj & Levinthal, 2004, p. 161). Structural uncertainty increases the sustainability of a firm's strategy and has been associated with dispersed knowledge (Minkler, 1993). As Lyles and Schwenk (1992, p. 167) suggest, the performance outcomes of search and learning efforts are dependent on the complexity of the knowledge system: 'The complexity of the knowledge structure influences the ability of organizational members to retrieve [knowledge] elements'.[3] They furthermore suggest that the complexity of the firm's knowledge system will influence its 'ability to adjust to change and be flexible' (p. 167).

THE MULTINATIONAL COMPANY AS A KNOWLEDGE SYSTEM: SEARCH AND LEARNING BEHAVIOUR

Work on search in complex systems (Levinthal, 1997; Fleming, 2001) demonstrates how the overall performance of the search effort is highly dependent on the characteristics of the system, notably whether it is decomposable, non-decomposable, or nearly decomposable. In particular, search in systems that lie close to the non-decomposable end of the spectrum is a tough undertaking, even more so when the search methods are primitive (e.g. gradient search) because in such systems the 'landscape' of knowledge combinations from multiple structures will have multiple peaks (in extreme cases, this may produce a 'complexity catastrophe', Kauffman, 1993).[4] In strongly decomposed systems, the landscape may be single-peaked, so that even simple learning modes may quickly reach the peak. In more concrete terms, what knowledge is needed for a particular innovation will be easily located and the relevant combination established.

Knowledge Combination

Knowledge elements are combined to solve problems of any kind, from mundane daily operations to ambitious innovation projects (Nickerson & Zenger, 2004). Solutions to problems may become embodied in routines and capabilities (Nelson & Winter, 1982) spanning knowledge structures and applied to recurrent problems. Or, knowledge elements may be combined for the purpose of solving a one-shot problem. Intermediate cases exist. In all cases, however, knowledge elements are complementary. The notion of complementarity between knowledge elements here simply refers to whether potential gains exist from combining knowledge elements (Thompson, 1967; Buckley & Carter, 1999). For example, knowledge elements pertaining to marketing controlled by one subsidiary or site (or the MNC headquarters) may be a useful addition to existing marketing knowledge in another subsidiary, so that the relevant knowledge elements are *additive* (Buckley & Carter, 1999). Alternatively, subsidiary knowledge may be an input prior to the building of knowledge in another part of the MNC, as when knowledge of local tastes is transferred to centralized R&D functions, so that the relation of complementarity is *sequential* (*ibid.*; Thompson, 1967). Finally, dependencies may go both ways (Milgrom & Roberts, 1990). For example, knowledge gained from combined marketing knowledge in a number of subsidiaries may be transferred back to these as best practise knowledge. Thompson's (1967) notions of pooling, sequential and parallel coordination mirror, organizationally, the three types of relationships between knowledge elements.

Combinations of knowledge elements map into a performance landscape. Strategically, firms search for combinations that are high in appropriable value. Among the determinants of the net value from combining complementary knowledge elements are the characteristics of the relevant knowledge elements (e.g. what kind of complementarity is involved and tacitness); the governance costs implied by these characteristics, that is, the costs of motivating organization members to transfer and absorb knowledge and the direct costs of transferring knowledge. Many of these factors have been extensively discussed in the MNC literature (e.g. Kogut & Zander, 1993; Szulanski, 1996; Buckley & Carter, 2004). However, what is usually not considered is that a new knowledge combination may have to be fitted into existing knowledge structures and span across them, and that this may give rise to additional costs and benefits (a further exemplification of the point above on stocks and flows).

Optimizing the MNC Knowledge System

An MNC seeks to optimize its knowledge system in the sense that it wishes to maximize the appropriable value stemming from this system over some time horizon. It does so in three ways; first, by modifying the set of knowledge structures that it may link (i.e. searching for added locations); second, by modifying the linkages between knowledge elements that reside in different knowledge structures (i.e. searching for new combinations) and, third, by drawing on the evolving knowledge structures (i.e. learning new knowledge elements). All of these may be seen as entrepreneurial acts in the sense that judgment is applied in the search over highly rugged landscapes of knowledge combinations (Foss & Ishikawa, 2007). Following Knight (1921), 'judgment' is the cognitive faculty that is applied in to those situations where there is no obviously correct decision rule or indeed any decision rule at all.

Searching for Added Locations
Any location that the MNC will add to its existing set of knowledge structures has to bring either knowledge elements that are new to the MNC or knowledge elements of a superior quality (i.e. higher value creation potential) relative to those that the MNC has already. What determines such search is the way companies make a trade-off between the benefits of added diversity of knowledge elements and the cost of combining such knowledge elements from an expanded set of knowledge structures. Adding locations increases the landscape of new combinations. The optimal choice of new locations implies maximizing the diversity of knowledge structures, subject to physical and contextual distances not exceeding the levels dictated by the knowledge transfer costs and overall MNC routines and capabilities.

Searching for New Combinations
MNC value creation stems from new combinations of knowledge elements from multiple structures. Such combinations map into a performance landscape; for example, some new knowledge elements (like the proverbial 'missing piece of the puzzle') create enormous value, and some combinations of existing knowledge elements may be very high in appropriable value,

some may be small and some may be negative. However, search is necessary to identify the relevant knowledge elements (Lyles & Schwenk, 1992) and to ascertain their relations (Yayavaram & Ahuja, 2008). As Lachmann (1956, p. 3) noted in his discussion of the theory of capital, '[t]he 'best' mode of complementarity is ... not a "datum". It is in no way "given" to the entrepreneur who, on the contrary, as a rule has to spend a good deal of time and effort in finding out what it is'. In that sense, the entrepreneurial dynamics in the MNC (i.e. individual managers and teams of managers) becomes essential in our framework.

Search efforts give rise to certain outcomes in terms of finding solutions to problems (Nickerson & Zenger, 2004). Problem-solving activity can be local or global. In local search, managers of specific sites (i.e. in given local knowledge structures) look for complementary knowledge elements within the local structure's stock. In global search, managers of multi-site activities (say a global product development project or a corporate officer) look for knowledge elements in the set of locations susceptible to provide missing elements. How to access and appropriate such new knowledge elements is a subsequent decision (e.g. between acquisition or an alliance with a local entity that controls the relevant knowledge element).

Learning New Knowledge Elements
The knowledge structures from which an MNC can draw knowledge change over time, albeit relatively slowly as they typically co-evolve with a complex local context that itself changes only slowly.

The knowledge structure of an MNC at each location will be augmented through its normal business activities. There are four possibilities for such normal development: new knowledge elements can be created internally in the MNC local site (e.g. a local R&D project); new knowledge elements can be created jointly with other firms locally (e.g. in a learning alliance); new (to the MNC) knowledge elements can be acquired externally from other local knowledge structures (e.g. from a lead customer or a supplier (von Hippel, 1988)); and new knowledge elements can be acquired externally from new knowledge elements created in other knowledge local structures (e.g. a local university). Doz et al. (2001, chap. 6) provide an analysis and empirical evidence of such 'sensing' activities.

A local knowledge structure is also changed over time though learning-by-doing in the local context. Such improvement (i.e. higher value creation potential) in existing knowledge elements (e.g. the skills of design for manufacturability) – which may have been initially transferred (internally) by the MNC from another location – will be different in different local contexts and will add to the diversity of knowledge elements in the MNC system. The contextual differences that will create such diversity over time may be internal to the MNC units (e.g. different product lines in different sites) or external (e.g. different education and training systems in each location).

Antecedents to Search

The antecedents to search outcomes include the mode of search (Levinthal, 1997), for example, whether search takes place through incremental, trial-and-error search ('gradient search') or whether it takes place based on explicit theories of causes and effects ('heuristic search') (Gavetti & Levinthal, 2000). Firms may have different dominant logics for their search efforts (Lyles & Schwenk, 1992) and this will influence paths of knowledge stock augmentation.

Another antecedent of local search is the knowledge structure itself. Thus, Vayavaram and Ahuja argue that a firm's (a site's, in the terminology proposed here) knowledge structure influences which interdependencies between knowledge elements are searched for recognized and established. In other words, it influences the process of search for new valuable combinations of knowledge elements. Knowledge is thus embodied not just in the knowledge elements but also in ties between these (Lyles & Schwenk, 1992; Langlois, 2002; Baldwin & Clark, 1999). For example, marketing knowledge may have to be closely coordinated with R&D (von Hippel, 1988; Dierickx & Cool, 1989); the ties between two such knowledge elements are also part of the site's knowledge structure. The site's knowledge structure influences search and learning for at least two reasons. First, the knowledge structure is an antecedent of absorptive capacity: If sites do not already control knowledge elements that are in some dimensions related to the knowledge they seek to absorb, or if they do not understand how external knowledge elements may complement internal elements, they will likely not succeed in the absorption task. Second, knowledge elements that are discovered through search efforts may simply not fit into the site's knowledge structure.

The Nature of the MNC Knowledge System and Its Optimization

With time, the MNC can expand its knowledge system (add locations with new or improved knowledge elements) or search for new knowledge elements in the locations where it is – and establish new relationships between the new elements and the existing ones. Here, the complexity of the knowledge system is determinant. If the system is decomposable, then learning can occur sequentially or in a pooling mode.

If the system is not decomposable, then learning is problematic: each new knowledge element in a knowledge structure may change the outcome of existing relations with knowledge elements in other knowledge structures. This implies that in a non-decomposable structure, learning itself needs to be guided, either by entrepreneurial insight (Knight, 1921) or by an organizational artefact ('magnet') such as a global lead customer or a product platform which 'calls for' certain knowledge elements available only in specific sites (Doz et al., 2001). Similarly, innovation arising from new knowledge combinations between distinct structures needs to be guided, except perhaps in early stages where random encounters between hitherto separate knowledge elements can lead to creative discoveries (Nonaka & Takeuchi, 1995).

While establishing new complementarities may bring local innovation, it also brings complexity (Doz, Angelmar, & Prahalad, 1985). The reason lies in the interdependent nature of the overall knowledge structure itself. Thus, a new complementarity likely impacts other ones. In highly integrated knowledge systems, this can mean that overall performance becomes very difficult to predict and control (Baldwin & Clark, 1999). Small changes in the knowledge system can result in structure-wide perturbations that ' ... inhibit the ability of a system to systematically improve and exploit the intelligence of prior learning efforts' (Ethiraj & Levinthal, 2004, p. 160). The performance landscape underlying such knowledge structures is highly rugged.

Consistent with complexity theory and knowledge structure theory we can therefore characterize knowledge systems in terms of complexity, this being a composite measure of the number of knowledge elements and their relations. Thus, in a strongly decomposed (modular) knowledge system, learning (search) is more likely to take place within individual structures (i.e. specific sites) than as recombinant search over knowledge elements from different structures. The landscape that decision makers confront is flat. Simple (gradient) search often suffices to find the optimum.

As knowledge systems become less decomposed, multiple peaks of varying heights emerge and finding the optimal combination of knowledge elements becomes more complicated. A search in a 'simple search mode' makes no a priori assumptions about which knowledge elements are in the search space, how they may be connected and what are the value implications of this begins at an essentially arbitrary place and proceeds by means of trial and error. Search and innovation become increasingly sophisticated as decision makers make explicit assumptions about which elements are relevant and how elements connect. The insight that finding the optimal (highest) peak is far from trivial is consistent with the findings that firms often find it difficult to comprehend 'architectural' knowledge, that is, knowledge of the multiple links between product components (Henderson & Clark, 1990) and that technological innovation with many interdependencies among knowledge elements are particularly hard to implement for MNC firms (Doz et al., 1985; Santos, Doz, & Williamson, 2004). Such assumptions are usefully summarized in, for example, the distinction between MNCs as 'global teachers' and MNCs as 'global learners'. In terms of the knowledge structure view, the former firms define the landscape of knowledge combinations that they can search over more narrowly than the latter firms.

From the standpoint of MNC management research, we can suggest that MNCs are particularly relevant governance forms for knowledge combinations at intermediate levels of knowledge systems' decomposability. If the knowledge system required for an innovation is both novel and non-decomposable, a single knowledge structure holding all the relevant knowledge elements may well be a condition for the innovation to emerge, and will in any case outperform an MNC knowledge system.[5] If the knowledge system is decomposable, then a less onerous form of governance than an MNC is feasible.[6]

CHALLENGES AND IMPLICATIONS

In the preceding sections, we have developed a knowledge-based conceptualization of the MNC, and we have discussed the possible theoretical support for such a conceptualization. In the following, we suggest how these ideas can be turned into researchable themes in MNC research.

The Search for Knowledge Structures

Three advantages derive from MNCs accessing multiple knowledge structures: (1) the drastic increase in the number of potential unique knowledge combination opportunities available to an MNC; (2) the increasing diversity of the knowledge elements it accesses and (3) the ability to exploit contextually dependent knowledge. However, these advantages need to be created by the MNC, beginning with searching for knowledge. In this regard, MNCs' search behaviour, that is, their search rules, constraints and search optimization, and how such search is constrained by the MNC knowledge system, need more research. There is also a need to look into the essentially entrepreneurial decisions relating which search rules shall be applied, in what directions search shall take place etc.

Ideally, accessing wide knowledge structures optimizes the MNC's knowledge system. A full complement of knowledge elements can be found, while limiting the number of knowledge structures to be added. Furthermore, serendipitous knowledge creation may take place more easily in wide knowledge structures, taking advantage of co-location. Yet such knowledge structures may not exist in an emerging industry or in a new field, or be so much sought after to be hard to access effectively (due to some crowding out effect, providing access only perhaps for a few leading firms), or so widely accessed as to hardly provide any advantage. Existing literature suggests that the search for added locations is mostly driven by search rules determined by a focus on specific knowledge elements (Almeida, Song, & Grant, 2002; Asakawa & Lehrer, 2003). There seems to be little search by MNCs conducted with the intent of accessing wider or superior quality knowledge structures. Regulatory barriers in sensitive areas (e.g. nuclear energy) and concerns with under-defined or un-enforced regulatory regimes provide added constraints to search, externally- or self-imposed.

The above means that the optimal deployment or concentration of knowledge structures, for a given MNC, and the heuristics that should guide the search for an optimal configuration deserve more research. Marginal cost and value frameworks (e.g. Santos et al., 2004) need further development and empirical investigation. We need to investigate how managers represent local knowledge structures (beyond the notion of 'right location' or 'right cluster' for some activity or business).

Moreover, it is unclear how global firms mobilize their functions, such as human resources, to seek and obtain knowledge from multiple locations. Access to locally differentiated knowledge by MNCs is contingent upon knowledge entrepreneurship at the local subsidiary level, unless it is a distinct CEO-driven corporate process (but such a separate process may not allow access to context-dependent knowledge which requires the legitimacy and co-practise opportunity of an operational local presence).

Put differently, subsidiary managers are expected to develop an original, differentiated, valuable set of knowledge that can make contributions from their local environment to the global network (Birkinshaw, 1997). In fact, ironically, inter-unit knowledge transfer, or system-wide organizational learning in an MNC becomes self-defeating, insofar as they homogenize the knowledge bases across locations within the MNC. Differences in local knowledge structures within the MNC knowledge systems are key. Ultimately, the value of an organization lies in the fact that the members do not have to hold the same knowledge in order to produce something together.[7] Only insofar as new externally driven local knowledge creation, or learning, takes place to enrich and augment local knowledge structures does the value of knowledge transfers between such structures endure. For an MNC, learning means getting access to a K_i that it did not have, that is, augmenting its knowledge structures. The members of the MNC have, on average, an increased knowledge asymmetry as the MNC local units learn more (in different and/or more locations). New elements may be added to existing structures or new structures added to the system, for example, via acquisitions.

Alliances are also a means to search and acquire elements of knowledge that exist in a location and which are not public (they exist inside a local company or a local unit of another MNC). The very existence of alliances has been equated with knowledge links between firms (Badaracco, 1991). Learning alliances may constitute a privileged conduit for linking knowledge structures around specific projects, or capabilities to be acquired, provided partners put in place appropriate mechanisms, and their learning intents are mutually acceptable or sufficiently surreptitious to go undetected (Hamel, Doz, & Prahalad, 1989; Hamel, 1991).

Another area that begs for understanding is what prompts knowledge search. Do firms seek for new knowledge structures (say, by establishing a new site in a particular location) because the optimal performance in a business forces them to do so or because they want to explore the feasibility of some new combination of knowledge elements (innovation) that may optimize the firm's performance? These different perspectives, external determinism and internal strategic choice, may even be present in the same MNC under some circumstances. For example, the rationale that drives IBM towards India may be of a very different nature that has driven the location of an IBM centre in Finland: matching lower costs and high quality of emerging global competitors from India, such as Infosys or Wipro versus discovering new business creation opportunities around aging and wellness in an intensely connected society willing to engage in social experiments. Even in the same country the same MNC can follow very different logic, Hewlett-Packard in India, for instance, follows both the usual cost reduction quality enhancement approach and also attempts to discover, via a separate HP Labs investment, new business models for low income, low literacy mass markets in education or public transportation.

Unit of Analysis

The focus on 'national subsidiaries' in the MNC and especially in international business research may be detrimental to the search for knowledge structures, or for access. The focus needs to shift from countries to sites, and thus local knowledge structures, such as clusters or knowledge hubs. Research also needs to identify how firms seek and obtain new knowledge, how local access spans boundaries between the firm's local unit(s) and the external knowledge, who is likely to take on the role of 'knowledge activist', or knowledge entrepreneur and how the reporting, communication processes and modes of interaction (Dhanaraj, Lyles, Steensma, & Tihanyi, 2004) of dispersed locations influence these processes. The social embeddedness of managers, in the local context and in the global NMC knowledge system, may influence how knowledge is obtained, and then made available to the MNC.

One national subsidiary may be composed of a number of sites. Instead of having a local subsidiary as the unit of analysis, we should have the local 'site' as the relevant unit.[8] The better we understand the rules of site location by MNCs, the more we will realize how present the search for different knowledge structures in location decisions by MNCs is. We need to improve our understanding of the relationship between a particular location and its characteristics and the knowledge structure in it. How do attributes of a location, such as 'tolerance' (cf. Florida, 2002, 2005), shape the local knowledge structure? How do they facilitate or impede awareness and access by an MNC to the local knowledge elements? For example, are MNCs myopic in that they do not seek for new knowledge structures but rather for specific knowledge elements, or is it that such structures are invisible from a distance?

Understanding the Local Knowledge Context

Current academic research is slow in addressing these challenges when applied to complex context-dependent knowledge. Most research addresses more stable conditions and simple tasks when relying mainly on explicit knowledge is possible such as in software development projects. Yet the more difficult, and often the more relevant, areas involve complicated learning processes as well as tacit knowledge identification and mobilization. In this vein, there is a need to develop a deeper understanding of the context-specificity of knowledge (Doz & Santos, 1997; Brannen, Doz, & Santos, 2007). While few will dispute the simple proposition that 'context matters', how it matters, and how to define and characterize the context of knowledge most effectively still remains an unsolved issue.

Learning about new locations and new knowledge combinations in the context of MNCs is a relatively under-researched area in the IB literature, except incidentally through the narrow and potentially distorting lens of the foreign market entry literature (Hill, Hwang, & Kim, 1990), and the also limiting lens of learning through strategic alliances, in which cross-border cross-context knowledge access and learning is subclass of research issues, but seldom centre-stage (Hamel et al., 1989; Hamel, 1991). We submit, however, that the widening knowledge landscape that MNCs can draw from necessitates a sustained research effort in the search and learning behaviour that MNCs can undertake in this wider knowledge landscape.

A different way in which learning may be seen to be dependent on a knowledge context is that successful learning also requires unlearning, in particular to reframe past success programs to fit with changing environments and contexts (Nystrom & Starbuck, 1984; Lyles, 1988). Mistakes, failures, organizational and personal discontinuities and performance crises may trigger unlearning. Unlearning may also stem from challenges that originate from the periphery of the organization, and help trigger a shift from an existing frame of lower level learning. Thus, global learners may have a greater ability to use challenges from the periphery to adapt dominant frames.

Improving the Understanding of Knowledge Transfer

The relative inattention to knowledge structures and the absence of a knowledge system conceptualization in the extant MNC literature imply certain shortcomings. First, an important shortcoming has to do with understanding the costs and benefits of knowledge transfer. The determinants of costs and benefits of knowledge transfer are hard to frame in the absence of an explicit theory of MNC knowledge structures. This is because the motive for combining knowledge elements in a new way, the need for actual knowledge transfer rather than mere juxtaposition and the difficulties of knowledge transfer are all related to the specific characteristics of the knowledge and contexts of both the sending and receiving organizational units (Brannen et al., 2007). Thus, the relationship between the transferred knowledge elements, the MNC 'home' and 'host' knowledge structures, and the overall knowledge system has implications for costs and benefits of knowledge transfer.

Improving the Understanding of the Quality of a Knowledge Element

We defined the quality of a knowledge element (K_i) as its value creation potential. This potential arises from the element's intrinsic quality, its validity as knowledge, its truthfulness or effectiveness in action. However, the superior intrinsic quality of a knowledge element is not sufficient to determine its superior quality. If an MNC finds the 'same' knowledge element in two or more locations, how can it predict the quality of K_i in each location? For example, if two locations h and t have a common knowledge element K_i (e.g. a particular skill) such that K_{ih} and K_{it} are equally effective in action but the cost of acquiring K_{ih} is lower than that of K_{it} than the quality of K_{ih} is superior to that of K_{it}. Therefore, two elements of the same knowledge are identical – that is, have the same quality – if and only if they are both equal in validity and cost.

Connecting Knowledge Structures

The crucial value of the MNC as an organization is its capability to combine knowledge elements that exist in separated knowledge structures. In this respect, the evidence that MNCs tend to squelch the entrepreneurial behaviour of distant subsidiaries (Birkinshaw, 1997) is far from the idea of heterarchy (Hedlund, 1986). We need to understand much better under what conditions managers of an MNC choose to create purposeful links between distant knowledge elements. Is this challenge of a political nature (and different knowledge structures seen as a threat to the power of the centre unit) or is it just an expression of uncertainty avoidance? Or could it be simply that managers may not see the possible connections?

If the connection of knowledge structures would be there just to allow for the transfer of internal knowledge in an MNC (such as the findings of Gupta and Govindarajan (2000) seem to indicate), it is not clear how the MNC can benefit from the external knowledge it encounters in a particular location. But it may also be that if an MNC is in a particular location for reasons other than local knowledge (say, lower wages or access to a local raw material), the coordination and control across units would justify the findings highlighting the flows of internal knowledge.

How is knowledge combined or melded at a distance? What is the role of the interactions between the individuals of a virtual team across sites in an MNC? Is there always a need for some object that acts as a magnet of dispersed knowledge (Doz et al., 2001)? What is the nature of the shared context that minimizes the cost of knowledge integration at a distance?

CONCLUDING REMARKS

Research on the multinational firm is in need of a change of mindsets. Both corporate executives and academic researchers have been trained in an age of knowledge projection, where the United States and a few Western European countries, and later Japan, accounted for a totally disproportionate share of knowledge (and wealth) creation. The new challenges for managers in MNCs and researchers in international management have to do with an increasing knowledge dispersion globally, and an accompanying need to source knowledge from many more and more heterogeneous sites, and combine, integrate and utilize this knowledge subsequently.

Although knowledge flows between MNC units have surely been central in international management research over the last two decades, this focus has not been anchored in an overall knowledge-based conceptualization of the MNC, one that links together knowledge stocks and knowledge flows, and explains how stocks are structured and how this impacts flows. The contribution of this work has been to, first, develop a knowledge-based conceptualization of the MNC, and, second, and relatedly, to suggest a research agenda for knowledge-based research in the MNC that corresponds to the changed realities. Both our conceptualization exercise and the definition of the research agenda begin from noting that many of the right components are 'there'. Thus, the search for strategic knowledge assets, the attempts to build distributed innovation networks and engaging in strategic alliances and networks for the purpose of sourcing knowledge are now key ideas in the (recent) MNC literature. Authors such as Prahalad and Doz (Doz & Prahalad, 1981; Prahalad & Doz, 1981), Gupta and Govindarajan (2000), Almeida et al.(2002), Zhou and Frost (2005), Nohria and Ghoshal (1997) and others have addressed this shifting of the learning field and how MNC strategies change to reflect this.

However, what is missing in the knowledge-based view is an overall organizing perspective. Such a perspective can be found in work on complex systems (Simon, 1962; Kauffman, 1993), and can be aligned with a conceptualization of MNCs as knowledge systems, that is, patterns of connections between dispersed knowledge structures. In addition to the subsidiaries of the firm, knowledge structures can include local third parties and be accessed through various types of alliances and collaborative arrangements.[9] The knowledge combination performance landscape may be rugged, with many peaks and valleys, or it may be more flat with few peaks. Success in identifying combinations of knowledge elements that are high in appropriable value is influenced not only by the characteristics of the landscape but also by the search mode of the firm.

In a 'flat world', the combination of external determinism, efficiency-seeking and very low transaction costs would eradicate the MNC as an organizational form and governance mode in business. Paradoxically, in a global world where we can be anywhere, anytime, international trade would replace the international firm. Economies of scale would exist in local firms (in certain locations) serving distant local firms elsewhere. New combinations of local knowledge would be exploited by local firms elsewhere, the risk of distance addressed by a combination of licensing and partnerships. In such circumstances, the place for the MNC seems reduced to that of connecting distant and different knowledge structures. The MNC will remain as an organization specifically fit to align the views and interests of distant peoples between which markets fail. Above all, the MNC will be a knowledge system fit for innovation, while operations may increasingly rely on networks of local firms.

NOTES

1. Recent applications to business administration include Levinthal (1997), Gavetti and Levinthal (2000), Fleming (2001), Ethiraj and Levinthal (2004), Nickerson and Zenger (2004) and Yayavaram and Ahuja (2008).

2. Of course, how 'discrete' is a matter of degree. For example, a patent may look highly discrete, but often builds on several other patents.

3. Since Lyles and Schwenk do not explicitly refer to multi-site companies, one can infer that by knowledge structure they mean knowledge system if in a multi-site corporation.

4. The height of peaks may here be taken as a measure of the strategic advantage implications of a certain combination of knowledge elements.

5. Note, though that this does not necessarily disqualify an MNC as the innovator, but only provided it does not act as one in crucial phases of the

innovation. IBM, for instance, when it developed the IBM 360 series, integrating knowledge from dispersed and differentiated structures, assembled its core development task force in a single location, to establish the architecture of the computer product family and of its development process, making the knowledge system of the project decomposable, and allowing subsequent development work to take place at different sites (annals of computing).

6. A local firm in the location where all the relevant knowledge elements exist.

7. See, for example, Conner and Prahalad (1996) and also Alchian and Demsetz (1972) and Demsetz (1993).

8. The emergence of the knowledge-based view of business activities has already induced a number of studies on multi-site R&D.

9. This is a significant distinction between the transnational (e.g. Bartlett & Ghoshal, 1989) and the metanational approach (Doz et al., 2001).

ACKNOWLEDGEMENTS

A great debt is owed to Yves Doz for numerous valuable discussions that had a significant bearing on the writing of this manuscript. Thanks to Maurizio Zollo for comments on an earlier version of this chapter.

REFERENCES

Alchian, A. A., & Demsetz, H. (1972). Production, information costs, and economic organization. *American Economic Review, 62*(5), 772–795.

Almeida, P., Song, J., & Grant, R. M. (2002). Are firms superior to alliances and markets? An empirical test of cross-border knowledge building. *Organization Science, 13*(2), 147–161.

Asakawa, K., & Lehrer, M. (2003). Managing local knowledge assets globally: The role of regional innovation relays. *Journal of World Business, 38*(1), 31–42.

Badaracco, J. L. (1991). *The knowledge link: How firms compete through strategic alliances.* Boston: Harvard Business School Press.

Baldwin, C. Y., & Clark, K. B. (1999). *Design rules.* Cambridge, MA: MIT Press.

Bartlett, C. A., & Ghoshal, S. (1986). Tap your subsidiaries for global reach. *Harvard Business Review, 64*(6), 87–94.

Bartlett, C. A., & Ghoshal, S. (1989). *Managing across borders.* Boston: Harvard Business School Press.

Birkinshaw, J. M. (1996). How multinational subsidiary mandates are gained and lost. *Journal of International Business Studies, 27*(3), 467–495.

Birkinshaw, J. M. (1997). Entrepreneurship in multinational corporations: The characteristics of subsidiary initiatives. *Strategic Management Journal, 18*(3), 207–229.

Brannen, M. Y., Liker, J. K., & Fruin, W. M. (1999). Recontextualization and factory-to-factory knowledge transfer from Japan to the United States: The case of NSK. In: J. K. Liker, W. M. Fruin & P. S. Adler (Eds), *Remade in America: Transplanting and transforming Japanese management systems.* New York: Oxford University Press.

Brannen, M. Y., Doz, Y., & Santos, J. (2007). *Unpacking absorptive capacity: Understanding the nature and contexts of knowledge.* Working Paper.

Brusoni, S., Prencipe, A., & Pavitt, K. (2001). Knowledge specialization, organizational coupling, and the boundaries of the firm: Why do firms know more than they make? *Administrative Science Quarterly, 46*(4), 597–621.

Buckley, P. J. (1990). Problems and developments in the core theory of international business. *Journal of International Business Studies, 21*(4), 657–665.

Buckley, P. J., & Carter, M. (1999). Managing cross-border complementary knowledge. *International Studies of Management and Organization, 29*(1), 80–104.

Buckley, P. J., & Carter, M. J. (2004). A formal analysis of knowledge combination in multinational enterprises. *Journal of International Business Studies, 35*(5), 371–384.

Buckley, P. J., & Casson, M. (1976). *The future of the multinational enterprise.* London: Macmillan.

Cantwell, J. A. (1989). *Technological innovation and multinational corporations.* Oxford: Basil Blackwell.

Cohen, W. M., & Levinthal, D. A. (1990). Absorptive capacity: A new perspective on learning and innovation. *Administrative Science Quarterly, 35*(1), 128–152.

Conner, K. R., & Prahalad, C. K. (1996). A resource-based theory of the firm: Knowledge versus opportunism. *Organization Science, 7*(5), 477–501.

Demsetz, H. (1993). The nature of the firm revisited. In: O. E. Williamson & S. G. Winter (Eds), *The nature of the firm: Origins, evolution, and development.* Oxford: Oxford University Press.

Denrell, J., Fang, C., & Winter, S. G. (2003). The economics of strategic opportunity. *Strategic Management Journal, 24,* 977–990.

Dhanaraj, C., Lyles, M., Steensma, K., & Tihanyi, L. (2004). The dynamics of relational embeddedness: Tacit and explicit learning in international joint ventures. *Journal of International Business Studies, 35*(5), 428–443.

Dierickx, I., & Cool, K. (1989). Asset stock accumulation and the sustainability of competitive advantage. *Management Science, 35*(12), 1504–1511.

Doz, Y., Angelmar, R., & Prahalad, C. K. (1985). Technological innovation and interdependence: A challenge for the large, complex firm. *Technology in Society, 7*(2–3), 105–125.

Doz, Y., & Hamel, G. (1998). *Alliance advantage: The art of creating value through partnering.* Boston: Harvard Business School Press.

Doz, Y., & Prahalad, C. K. (1981). Headquarters influence and strategic control in MNCs. *Sloan Management Review, 23*(1), 15–29.

Doz, Y., & Santos, J. (1997). On the management of knowledge: From the transparency of collocation and co-setting to the quandary of dispersion and differentiation. INSEAD Working Paper no. 97/119/SM. INSEAD, France.

Doz, Y., Santos, J., & Williamson, P. (2001). *From global to metanational: How companies win in the knowledge economy.* Boston: Harvard Business School Press.

Dunning, J. H. (1988). *Explaining international production.* Boston: Allen & Unwin.

Dunning, J. H. (1996). The geographical sources of the competitiveness of firms: Some results of a new survey. *Transnational Corporations, 5*(3), 1–29.

Dunning, J. H. (2002). *Regions, globalization, and the knowledge-based economy.* New York: Oxford University Press.

Ethiraj, S. K., & Levinthal, D. (2004). Modularity and innovation in complex systems. *Management Science, 50*(2), 159–173.

Fleming, L. (2001). Recombinant uncertainty in technological search. *Management Science*, *47*(1), 117–132.

Florida, R. (2002). *The rise of the creative class*. New York: Basic Books.

Florida, R. (2005). *Cities and the creative class*. New York: Routledge.

Forsgren, M., Holm, U., & Johanson, J. (2005). *Managing the embedded network: A business network view*. Cheltenham, UK: Edward Elgar.

Foss, N. J., & Ishikawa, I. (2007). Towards a dynamic resource-based view. *Organization Studies*, *28*(5), 749–772.

Foss, N. J., & Pedersen, T. (2002). Transferring knowledge in MNCs: The role of sources of subsidiary knowledge and organizational context. *Journal of International Management*, *8*(1), 49–67.

Foss, N. J., & Pedersen, T. (2004). Organizing knowledge processes in the multinational corporation. *Journal of International Business Studies*, *35*(5), 340–349.

Gavetti, G., & Levinthal, D. (2000). Looking forward and looking backward: Cognitive and experiential search. *Administrative Science Quarterly*, *45*(1), 113–147.

Ghoshal, S. (1987). Global strategy: An organizing framework. *Strategic Management Journal*, *8*(5), 425–440.

Ghoshal, S., & Bartlett, C. A. (1990). The multinational corporation as an interorganizational network. *Academy of Management Review*, *15*(4), 603–625.

Granovetter, M. (1985). Economic action and social structure: The problem of embeddedness. *American Journal of Sociology*, *91*(3), 485–510.

Gupta, A. K., & Govindarajan, V. (1991). Knowledge flows and the structure of control within multinational corporations. *Academy of Management Review*, *16*(4), 768–792.

Gupta, A. K., & Govindarajan, V. (1994). Organizing for knowledge flows within MNCs. *International Business Review*, *3*(4), 443–457.

Gupta, A. K., & Govindarajan, V. (2000). Knowledge flows within multinational corporations. *Strategic Management Journal*, *21*(4), 473–496.

Hamel, G. (1991). Competition for competence and inter-partner learning within international strategic alliances. *Strategic Management Journal*, *12*(Summer Special Issue), 83–103.

Hamel, G., Doz, Y., & Prahalad, C. K. (1989). Collaborate with your competitors and win. *Harvard Business Review*, *67*(1), 133–139.

Hedlund, G. (1986). The hypermodern MNC – A heterarchy? *Human Resource Management*, *25*(1), 9–35.

Hedlund, G. (1994). A model of knowledge management and the N-form corporation. *Strategic Management Journal*, *15*, 73–90.

Henderson, R. M., & Clark, K. B. (1990). Architectural innovation: The reconfiguration of existing product technologies and the failure of established firms. *Administrative Science Quarterly*, *35*, 9–30.

Hill, C., Hwang, P., & Kim, W. C. (1990). An eclectic theory of the choice of international entry mode. *Strategic Management Journal*, *11*, 117–128.

Holm, U., & Pedersen, T. (2000). *The emergence and impact of MNC centres of excellence*. Basingstoke, UK: MacMillan Press.

Hymer, S. H. (1976). *The international operations of national firms: A study of direct foreign investment*. Cambridge, MA: MIT Press.

Johanson, J., & Vahlne, J.-E. (1977). The internationalization process of the firm: A model of knowledge development and increasing foreign market commitment. *Journal of International Business Studies*, *8*(1), 23–32.

Kauffman, S. A. (1993). *The origins of order: Self-Organization and selection in evolution*. New York: Oxford University Press.

Kogut, B., & Zander, U. (1993). Knowledge of the firm and the evolutionary theory of the multinational corporation. *Journal of International Business Studies, 24*(4), 625–645.

Kogut, B., & Zander, U. (1995). Knowledge and the speed of the transfer and imitation of organizational capabilities: An empirical test. *Organization Science, 6*(1), 76–91.

Knight, F. H. (1921). *Risk, uncertainty, and profit*. New York: Augusts M. Kelley (reprint 1965).

Lachmann, L. M. (1956). *Capital and its structure*. Kansas City: Sheed Andrews and McNeel (reprint 1978).

Langlois, R. N. (2002). A modularity theory of the firm. In: N. J. Foss & P. G. Klein (Eds), *Entrepreneurship and the firm: Austrian approaches to economic organization*. Aldershot, UK: Edward Elgar.

Levinthal, D. A. (1997). Adaptation on rugged landscapes. *Management Science, 43*(7), 934–950.

Loasby, B. J. (1976). *Choice, complexity, and ignorance*. Cambridge: Cambridge University Press.

Lyles, M. A. (1988). Learning among joint-ventures sophisticated firms. *Management International Review, 28*(4), 85–98.

Lyles, M. A., & Schwenk, C. R. (1992). Top management, strategy, and organizational knowledge structures. *Journal of Management Studies, 29*(2), 155–174.

Milgrom, P., & Roberts, J. (1990). The economics of modern manufacturing: Technology, strategy and organization. *American Economic Review, 80*(3), 511–528.

Minbaeva, D., Pedersen, T., Björkman, I., Fey, C. F., & Park, H. J. (2003). MNC knowledge transfer, subsidiary absorptive capacity, and HRM. *Journal of International Business Studies, 34*, 586–599.

Minkler, A. P. (1993). The problem with dispersed knowledge: Firms in theory and practice. *Kyklos, 46*(4), 569–587.

Nelson, R. R., & Winter, S. G. (1982). *An evolutionary theory of economic change*. Cambridge: Belknap Press.

Nickerson, J., & Zenger, T. (2004). A knowledge-based theory of the firm: The problem-solving perspective. *Organization Science, 15*(6), 617–632.

Nohria, N., & Ghoshal, S. (1997). *The differentiated network: Organizing multinational corporations for value creation*. San Francisco: Jossey-Bass.

Nonaka, I., & Takeuchi, H. (1995). *The knowledge-creating company*. New York: Oxford University Press.

Nystrom, P. C., & Starbuck, W. (1984). To avoid organizational crises, unlearn. *Organizational Dynamics, 12*(4), 53–65.

Penrose, E. T. (1956). Foreign investment and the growth of the firm. *Economic Journal, 66*, 220–235.

Penrose, E. T. (1959). *The theory of the growth of the firm*. Oxford: Blackwell.

Polanyi, M. (1962). Tacit knowing: Its bearing on some problems of philosophy. *Reviews of Modern Physics, 34*(4), 601–616.

Popper, K. R. (1972). *Objective knowledge*. Oxford: Oxford University Press.

Prahalad, C. K., & Doz, Y. L. (1981). An approach to strategic control in MNEs. *Sloan Management Review, 22*(4), 5–14.

Rugman, A., & Verbeke, A. (2001). Subsidiary-specific advantages in multinational enterprises. *Strategic Management Journal, 22*(3), 237–250.

Santos, J., Doz, Y., & Williamson, P. (2004). Is your innovation process global? *Sloan Management Review, 45*(4), 31–37.

Saxenian, A. (1994). *Regional advantage: Culture and competition in silicon valley and route 128.* Boston: Harvard University Press.

Simon, H. A. (1962). The architecture of complexity. *Proceedings of the American Philosophical Society, 106*(6), 467–482.

Simon, H. A. (1973). The structure of ill-structured problems. *Artificial Intelligence, 4*, 181–201.

Stiglitz, J. E. (2003). *Globalization and its discontents.* New York: W.W Norton and Company.

Szulanski, G. (1996). Exploring internal stickiness: Impediments to the transfer of best practice within the firm. *Strategic Management Journal, 17*(Winter Special Issue), 27–43.

Tallman, S. (2003). The significance of Bruce Kogut's and Udo Zander's article, 'knowledge of the firm and the evolutionary theory of the multinational corporation'. *Journal of International Business Studies, 34*(6), 495–497.

Thompson, J. D. (1967). *Organizations in action.* McGraw Hill: New York.

Tyre, M., & von Hippel, E. (1997). The situated nature of adaptive learning in organizations. *Organization Science, 8*(1), 71–83.

Vernon, R. (1966). International investment and international trade in the product cycle. *Quarterly Journal of Economics, 80*(2), 190–207.

von Hippel, E. (1988). *The sources of innovation.* Cambridge: Cambridge University Press.

Winter, S. G. (1987). Knowledge and competence as strategic assets. In: D. J. Teece (Ed.), *The competitive challenge: Strategies for industrial innovation and renewal.* Cambridge, MA: Ballinger.

Wright, S. (1930). The genetical theory of natural selection: A review. *Journal of Heredity, 21*(8), 349–356.

Yayavaram, S., & Ahuja, G. (2008). Decomposability in knowledge structures and its impact on the usefulness of inventions and knowledge-base malleability. *Administrative Science Quarterly, 53*(2), 333–362.

Zhou, C., & Frost, T. S. (2005). *Subsidiary's inflow and outflow of knowledge within MNCs.* Academy of International Business Best Paper, Quebec City, Canada.

AUTHOR BIOGRAPHIES

Ruth V. Aguilera is an associate professor and a Fellow at the Center for Professional Responsibility for Business and Society at the College of Business at the University of Illinois at Urbana-Champaign. She also holds courtesy appointments at the School of Labor and Employment Relations, the College of Law and the Department of Sociology at Illinois. She received MA and PhD degrees in Sociology from Harvard University. Her research interests fall at the intersection of economic sociology and international business, specifically in the fields of comparative corporate governance, foreign location choices and corporate social responsibility. She has published in the leading journals in International Business and Management. Dr. Aguilera currently serves as a member of an associate editor of Corporate Governance: International Review and is a member of the Editorial Boards of the following peer reviewed top tier journals: *Academy of Management Perspectives, Global Strategy Journal, Journal of International Business Studies, Journal of Management Studies, Management International Review, Organization Studies* and *Strategic Management Journal.* She also serves in the board of IMDEA Social Sciences (Madrid) and CSR IMPACT Project (Brussels).

Björn Ambos is professor of International Management and director of the MSc in International Management/CEMS at WU Vienna. He holds a MA in Business Administration and a PhD in International Management from the University of Hamburg. His research interests revolve around innovation, strategy and management of technology driven multinational firms. His works have appeared in *International Business Review, International Journal of Technology Management, Journal of International Management, Journal of World Business, Strategic Management Journal, Long Range Planning, Management International Review* and *Research Policy.* He currently serves on editorial boards of the *Strategic Management Journal, Journal of International Management, Management International Review* and *Global Strategy Journal.* He teaches strategy and international management to MSc/ PhD and executives.

Christian G. Asmussen is an assistant professor of strategic management and international business at the Department of Strategic Management and

Globalization, Copenhagen Business School. Christian received his Ph.D. from Copenhagen Business School in 2007. His research revolves around globalization and the international expansion trajectories of multinational corporations. Drawing on a background in formal economics but applying a multidisciplinary approach to his research, he has focused in particular on the interaction between competitive advantage and geographic scope.

Fiorenza Belussi obtained her PhD in 1993, from Science Policy Research Unit (University of Sussex, United Kingdom). Since 1993 she has been associate professor at the Department of Economics 'Marco Fanno' at the Faculty of Science Policy, University of Padua (Italy) and obtained recently the title of Professor in 'Economics and Management of Firms'. Her areas of interest include: (a) Management of innovation and creativity, creative industries, theoretical models on innovation diffusion through gatekeepers; knowledge management and ICT applications in firm networks, studies of open innovation and innovation sources; (b) International business and the impact of globalization on local economies, small-born district multi-nationals, analysis of the processes of delocalization, onshore and offshore outsourcing; (c) Analysis of firm dynamics in low-tech and high-tech sectors, industrial demography: entry and exit of firms, evolution of local systems and Italian industrial districts, policies for the evolution of local systems, policies for the transfer of knowledge and innovation between university and firms. She has published more than 160 articles and book chapters. Among others, she has published in: *International Journal of Technology Management, Futures, European Planning Studies, Research Policy, Cambridge Journal of Economics, Urban Studies* and numerous other Italian Journals.

Gabriel R.G. Benito (PhD, Norwegian School of Economics and Business Administration) is a professor and director of Center for International Strategy at BI Norwegian School of Management, where he currently also serves as Dean of Doctoral Studies. He is a consulting editor of *Journal of International Business Studies* and member of the Editorial Boards of *Global Strategy Journal, International Business Review* and *Management International Review*. Recent books include *Foreign Operation Methods* (with L.S. Welch and B. Petersen, 2007, Edward Elgar), and *Multinationals on the Periphery* (with R. Narula, 2007, Palgrave). His research agenda currently concentrates on strategies and structures of multinational enterprises. His research has appeared in many books and journals, including *Journal of International Business Studies, Journal of Management Studies, Journal of Economic Geography, Applied Economics, Managerial and Decision*

Economics, Management International Review, Journal of Business Research and *International Business Review*.

Sjoerd Beugelsdijk is a full professor of International Business at the University of Groningen, The Netherlands. He received his PhD from Tilburg University. His research interests include comparative economic organization theory, comparative institutional analysis and economic geography. He has published in a wide range of journals including the *Journal of International Business Studies, Organization Studies, Journal of International Management* and *Journal of Economic Geography*. He is the author of the monograph "Culture in economics; history, methodological reflections and contemporary applications" published by Cambridge University Press. He is currently the academic director of the International Business program at the University of Groningen, and serves as a department head.

Weifeng Chen holds B.Eng., M.Sc. in Mathematics and Computing, and Ph.D. in Management Studies from Brunel University, UK. He is presently working as lecturer in Brunel University Business School in the United Kingdom and is allied with the Centre for International Business and Strategy in Emerging Markets (CIBSEM) within the School. His research interests include R&D management, international business strategies of MNEs from emerging economies. Weifeng also consults for Sino-UK businesses.

John Child is a professor Emeritus of Commerce at the Birmingham Business School, University of Birmingham. He received his PhD from the University of Cambridge. He is a Fellow of the Academy of Management, the Academy of International Business and the British Academy of Management. In 2006, he was elected a Fellow of the British Academy [FBA]. His recent books include Organization (Wiley-Blackwell 2005), and Corporate Co-evolution (with Suzana Rodrigues, Wiley 2008). This last book won the Academy of Management Terry Award in 2009. He is a past editor-in-chief of Organization Studies and is currently senior editor for Management and Organization Review. His main current interest is the problem of hierarchy.

Kim Clark is a doctoral candidate at The University of Texas – San Antonio. She received her MBA from the University of Nevada Las Vegas. Her research focuses on institutional environments of multinational enterprises, international strategic human resource management and entrepreneurship. She has presented papers at the Academy of Management and Academy of International Business annual meetings.

Timothy M. Devinney is a professor of Strategy at the University of Technology, Sydney. He has published 7 books and more than 80 articles in leading journals. In 2008 he was the first recipient in management of an Alexander von Humboldt Research Award and was Rockefeller Foundation Bellagio Fellow. He is a Fellow of the Academy of International Business, an International Fellow under the auspices of the AIM Initiative in the United Kingdom and a Fellow of ANZAM (Australia New Zealand Academy of Management). He served as Chair of the International Management Division of the Academy of Management. He is an associate editor and incoming co-editor of *Academy of Management Perspectives* and the head of the International Business & Management Network of SSRN. He is on the editorial board of more than 10 of the leading international journals.

Kirandeep Dhillon is a recent postgraduate from Brunel University, with her study focusing on facets of International Business. Before that, she completed her BSc from King's College London where she read Mathematics with Management with particular enthusiasm in topics of Applied Probability and Stochastic Modelling. Her prime research interests include investigation into the challenges in international management, the role and significance of institutional variation and the determinants of Foreign Direct Investment (FDI) with application to the African region. Kirandeep is looking forward to expand her research activities while pursuing a career in international management consultancy.

Jonathan P. Doh is the Herbert G. Rammrath Endowed Chair in International Business, founding Director of the *Center for Global Leadership*, and professor of Management and Operations at the Villanova School of Business. His research on strategy for emerging markets, ofshoring of services, and global corporate corporate responsibility has been published in the top management and international business journals, and in numerous books, the most recent of which is *NGOs and Corporations: Conflict and Collaboration* (Cambridge University Press, 2009). He is the recipients of numerous awards and honors, and was recently ranked among the top 20 most prolific international business scholars. He received his PhD from the George Washington University.

Gianluca Fiscato is an external consultant of the 'Marco Fanno' Department of Economics and Management, at the University of Padua, Italy. He received his PhD from IULM University of Milan. Gianluca Fiscato spent two years at the University of Newcastle upon Tyne at the Center of Urban and Regional Development Studies as visiting PhD Researcher. His current research interests include internationalization, knowledge sharing and industrial policies.

Nicolai J. Foss is a professor of Strategy and Organization at the Copenhagen Business School and a professor of Knowledge-based Organization at the Norwegian School of Economics and Business Administration. He is also the Svenska Handelsbanken visiting professor at the University of Lund and Visiting Professor at LUISS, Roma. Foss' research interests include the resource-based view, knowledge governance and the economics of the firm. He serves on the boards of numerous journals, including *Strategic Management Journal* and *Organization Science*. Foss' work has been published in journals such as *the Academy of Management Review, Academy of Management Journal* and *Journal of Business Studies*.

Jörg Freiling (PhD, Ruhr University of Bochum, Germany) is a professor at the University of Bremen, Faculty for Business Studies and Economics. He holds the Chair in Small Business & Entrepreneurship and is currently Dean of Study Affairs in the faculty. His research interests include internationalization processes of SMEs, governance modes of firms in international business, international entrepreneurship, start-up management, management of intellectual properties as well as management of knowledge & competences. He has published in academic journals such as *Organization Studies, International Journal of Technology Intelligence and Planning, Management Revue, International Journal of Entrepreneurship Education* and *Advances in Applied Business Strategy*.

Ajai S. Gaur is an assistant professor at the Rutgers University from 2009. Before that, he was an assistant professor at the Old Dominion University, Norfolk, VA during 2007–2009. He received a PhD in Business Policy and Strategy from National University of Singapore in 2007. Ajai's research interests lie at the intersection of strategy and international business. His work has appeared in outlets such as *Journal of Management, Journal of Management Studies, Management International Review, Corporate Governance: An International Review*, and *British Journal of Management* among several others. Ajai is the recipient of *AIB Best Dissertation Proposal Award* and *Richard N Farmer Best Dissertation Award* at the Academy of International Business annual meetings in 2006 and 2008, respectively. He is on the editorial board of *Journal of Management Studies, Corporate Governance: An International Review* and *Canadian Journal of Administrative Sciences*.

Florian Kaulich holds an M.Sc. in Economics and an M.A. in Development Studies from the University of Vienna, Austria, where he is currently pursuing Ph.D. in Economics. His research interests include the determinants of international trade specialization patterns, the impact of FDI on host countries, and the relationship between FDI and exports. Since 2008, he is working as research consultant with the United Nations Industrial Development Organization (UNIDO) at their Headquarters in Vienna. His current work for UNIDO includes data collection and analysis for Africa Investor Surveys to investigate the economic impact of FDI and designing evidence-based investment policies.

Stephen J. Kobrin is William Wurster Professor of Multinational Management at The Wharton School of the University of Pennsylvania. He received a PhD from the University of Michigan and an MBA from Wharton. His research interests include globalization and its impact on the multinational firm, global governance and multinational firms and human rights. His is a past president of the Academy of International Business and a past Chair of the International Management Division of the Academy of Management. He has published in journals such as *Business Ethics Quarterly*, *JIBS*, *International Organization*, *International Studies Quarterly* and the *Strategic Management Journal*.

Vikas Kumar is senior lecturer in the Discipline of International Business at the University of Sydney Business School. From 2004 to 2009 he was assistant professor of International Business and Strategy in the Department of Management at Bocconi University in Milan, Italy. He was a visiting scholar at the Collaboratory for Research on Global Projects at Stanford University from 2008 to 2009. He received his PhD in International Business in 2004 from the Boeing Institute of International Business at Saint Louis University. His research has been published in premier international business/management journals such as *Management International Review (MIR)*, *Coprorate Governance: An International Review*, *Journal of World Business*, *British Journal of Management* and *Thunderbird International Business Review (TIBR)*. He is on the Editorial Review Board of MIR and TIBR and is co-guest editor of the special issue on 'Offshoring and Outsourcing' in the *Journal of Management Studies*.

Sven M. Laudien is an assistant professor at the University of Bremen, faculty for Business Studies and Economics, Chair for Small Business & Entrepreneurship. He received his PhD from the University of Bremen, Germany and his Diploma in Business Administration from the Christian-Albrechts-University Kiel, Germany. His research focuses on formal and informal coordination of transnational business activities. Furthermore, he deals with issues of international entrepreneurship, entrepreneurial failure, management of knowledge and competences and service innovation.

Randi Lunnan is a professor of Strategy at the Norwegian School of Management where she also serves as associate dean of Doctoral Studies in Strategy. She is currently a visiting professor at Temple University. Research interests include strategic alliances as well as the structuring of multinational enterprises. She is a board member of the *International Journal of Strategic Business Alliances*. Her research has appeared in several books and journals including *Strategic Management Journal, Journal of Management, Journal of Management Studies, Journal of World Business* and *International Journal of Strategic Business Alliances*.

Marin Marinov is a professor of International Business and Management at the Business School of the University of Gloucestershire. He received his PhD from the Technical University in Sofia, Bulgaria. He consults for companies, national governments and academic bodies on strategic development in emerging markets. Among his recent publications are Marketing in the Emerging Markets of Latin America (2005) and Marketing in the Emerging Markets of Islamic Countries (2007), both published by Palgrave Macmillan. He is on the editorial board of several academic journals, such as *Advances in International Marketing* and *Journal of Islamic Marketing*. His major research interest is internationalization theory.

Svetla Marinova is an associate professor of International Business at the University of Aalborg in Denmark. She received her PhD from Copenhagen Business School in Denmark and her MBA from the University of Warwick in the United Kingdom. She has published in the *European Journal of Marketing, International Marketing Review* and *Thunderbird International Business Review* among others. She has co-authored the book Foreign Direct Investment in Central and Eastern Europe and the first European edition of a textbook on International Business. Her research interest is in the role of governments and firms from emerging economies in building and sustaining competitive advantages.

Derrick McIver is a PhD candidate in organization and management studies at the University of Texas at San Antonio. His main research interests include processes of global knowledge and innovation management. He has presented papers at the Academy of Management and Academy of International Business annual meetings.

Sara Melén received her PhD in international marketing after presenting her thesis *New Insights on the Internationalisation Process of SMEs* in April 2009 at the Stockholm School of Economics. Sara Melén conducts research on the international expansion of small and medium sized enterprises (SMEs) and is currently a research fellow at the Department of Marketing and Strategy at the Stockholm School of Economics. Sara has published her research amongst others in *the Journal of World Business, the International Business Review* and *the European Management Journal.*

Stewart R. Miller is an associate professor of Management at The University of Texas – San Antonio. He received his PhD in strategic management from the Kelley School of Business at Indiana University. His research focuses on multinational enterprises, in particular, liability of foreignness (foreign subsidiary performance), international joint ventures, and internationalization. Also, his works examines emerging markets. His studies appear or are forthcoming in *Journal of International Business Studies, Advances in International Management, Academic of Management Journal, Strategic Management Journal, Organization Science, Long-Range Planning* and *Management International Review,* among others. Stewart is a member of the editorial review board of the *Journal of International Business Studies.* He is a Local Arrangements Co-Chair for the 2011 Academy of Management annual meeting in San Antonio.

Lilach Nachum is a professor of International Business and Management, Baruch College, City University New York. Professor Nachum's major professional interests and expertise are the theory of the MNE and the distinctiveness of these firms as an organizational form, technology and value creation across distance, and location decisions and firms' strategy. Her research in these areas is summarized in two books and a large number of articles, published in journals such as *Management Science, Strategic Management Journal* and the *Journal of International Business Studies,* among others. Professor Nachum is a consulting editor and a Board Member of the *Journal of International Business Studies* and a Board Member of the *Global Strategy Journal, Management International Review,* the *Journal of International Management* and the *Journal of Management Studies.* Before joining Baruch College in 2002, Professor Nachum was a Senior Research Fellow at Cambridge University, UK. Earlier, she held a Senior Member position in the Research Division on Foreign Investment and Transnational Corporations at the United Nations in Geneva, Switzerland. In conjunction with these positions, she has been acting as consultant to a number of national and international organizations, including the United Nations, the World Bank, the European Union, London's Westminster City Council. Professor Nachum has also been holding visiting research and teaching positions at universities in Austria, China, Hong-Kong, Israel, Italy, Poland, Singapore, Sweden, Switzerland, Taiwan and the United Kingdom.

Phillip C. Nell is an assistant professor at Copenhagen Business School. He received his PhD from WU Wien (Vienna University of Economics and Business). His main research interests include headquarter–subsidiary relationships in multinational corporations with a specific emphasis on headquarter roles and activities, as well as interorganizational relationships. He has published in *Research Policy*, *Management International Review* and *Journal of World Business*.

Torben Pedersen is professor of international business at the Copenhagen Business School's Department of Strategic Management and Globalization. He has published over 100 articles and books concerning the managerial and strategic aspects of globalization. His research has appeared in prominent journals such as *Academy of Management Journal, Strategic Management Journal, Organization Science, Journal of International Business Studies, Journal of Management Studies* and *Journal of Corporate Finance*. His research interests are located at the interface between strategy, institutional economics and international business and with a strong interest in areas like knowledge management, offshoring/outsourcing and reconfiguration of the value chain, subsidiary entrepreneurship and management of the differentiated MNC. He is co-editor of Global Strategy Journal and serves on numerous editorial boards.

Indu Ramachandran is a doctoral candidate at The University of Texas – San Antonio. She received her MBA from Texas Tech University. Her research focuses on organizational learning and knowledge management in multinational enterprises, international joint ventures and entrepreneurship. Her work also examines the institutional environment in emerging markets. She has presented papers as the *Academy of Management* and Academy of International Business annual meetings. Her research has been published in the 2010 Academy of Management best paper proceedings.

Tom Ridgman is a director of External Education at the Institute for Manufacturing which part of the engineering division of the University of Cambridge. He teaches manufacturing management on the Industrial Systems Manufacture and Management Masters course and has just completed setting up a masters in Industrial innovation entrepreneurship and Management for the University of Trinidad and Tobago. His research interests span industrial development for emerging economies, industrial sustainability and education for manufacturing industry. Before coming to Cambridge in 1995 he spent two years at Warwick University running a research programme examining ways of reducing industrial leadtime. In his earlier career he spent 20 years in the automotive industry in a number of engineering and senior management roles.

Emilia Rovira Nordman is a research fellow at the Department of Marketing and Strategy at the Stockholm School of Economics where she also received her PhD in International Marketing in December 2009. Her fields of specialization include the effects of personal interaction on the internationalization of SMEs and the internationalization of born globals in the biotech field. Emilia has published her research amongst others in *the Journal of World Business, the International Business Review* and *the European Management Journal.*

José F. P. dos (Joe) Santos is a professor of Practice in Global Management (Affiliated) at INSEAD, senior lecturer in Global Economics and Management at MIT Sloan School of Management, and 'Professor Catedrático Convidado' (Guest Professor) at the Universidade Católica Portuguesa. He holds an MSc in Management Science by the University of London at London Business School, and 20 years experience as an executive. He returned to the academic world in 1995 by joining INSEAD after ten years as MD of an Italian multinational company. His research and teaching focuses on the management of the multinational enterprise, particularly on the management of global integration, global innovation and on metanational advantage. The book 'From Global to Metanational: How Companies Win in the Knowledge Economy', co-authored with colleagues Yves Doz and Peter Williamson, was published by Harvard Business School Press.

Ravi Sarathy is a professor of Strategy & International Business in the College of Business, Northeastern University. He received his PhD from the University of Michigan in International Business, a post-graduate degree from the Indian Institute of Management, Ahmedabad, and an MS from Northwestern University. His current research focuses on emerging market firms, and he has published numerous academic articles in journals such as the *Journal of International Business Studies, Journal of Management Studies, Management International Review, California Management Review, Transportation Journal, Small Business Economics, Long Range Planning, International Marketing Review, Business Horizons* and *Journal of Business Ethics.*

Bodo B. Schlegelmilch is a dean of the WU Executive Academy and Chair of the Institute for International Marketing Management at WU Vienna University of Economics and Business. He studied at Cologne University of Applied Sciences and holds an MSc and two doctorates (PhD and DLitt) from Manchester Business School. He has also been awarded a Distinguished Fellowship by the

Academy of Marketing Science and a Fellowship of the Chartered Institute of Marketing. Before joining WU Vienna, he held tenured professorships in the United States (Thunderbird) and the United Kingdom (University of Wales, Swansea) and worked as a lecturer at the University of Edinburgh. He also held visiting professorships at Berkeley, Miami, Thammasat and Leeds University, and worked for Deutsche Bank and Procter & Gamble. Bodo has won various teaching and research awards and conducted seminars and board-level workshops for major multinationals on six continents.

Silvia R. Sedita, PhD in economics and management of small firms and local systems at the University of Florence, is currently an assistant professor of economics and management at the Faculty of Political Science of the University of Padua. Her main research interests include the analysis of inter-organizational learning mechanisms in industrial districts and clusters, and the management of creativity and innovation networks. She has visiting scholar at CBS (Copenhagen Business School), DK, and at the University of Tokio, JP. She published articles in various international journals, among others: *Research Policy*, *European Planning Studies*, *Urban Studies* and *Industry and Innovations*.

D. Deo Sharma is a professor of International Marketing at the Department of Marketing and Strategy at the Stockholm School of Economics. He received his PhD from Uppsala University. His research interest include marketing, including buyer-seller network and co-operation, loyalty and trust in buyer-seller exchange, key account management, strategic alliances, changes in market structure and government-firm interaction and relationships. He has served on the editorial board of several academic journals including *International Business Review, Journal of International Entrepreneurship, Journal of Euro-Marketing and International Journal of Business, Management and Economics*. He has published his research in international journals such as *Journal of International Business Studies, Journal of Business Research, Journal of Business and Industrial Marketing, Journal of Business-to-Business Marketing, Journal of International Studies of Management and Organization, Scandinavian International Business Review, International Business Review, Journal of International Management, Management International Review, International Marketing Review, Journal of Service Marketing, Scandinavian Journal of Management, Thunderbird International Business Review*, etc.

Yongjiang S. Shi is the University Lecture of Industrial Systems in Engineering Department, and research director of the Centre for International Manufacturing in the Institute for Manufacturing, Cambridge

University. He has been studying management of international manufacturing network and supply chain for over 15 years. His recent research interests have covered global manufacturing strategy, network system design, technology transfer in the contexts of intra-company coordination and inter-company collaboration, and emerging Chinese manufacturing companies including the Shangzhai Phenomenon, indigenous innovation, industrial upgrading and Chinese outward FDI. He is working on several research projects – Global manufacturing virtual network (GMVN) to develop new manufacturing architecture for collaborative manufacturing network between companies; and Post Mergers and Acquisitions (M&As) Integration to help company achieve synergy; emerging nations' multinational corporations development; and different countries' culture characteristics and their impacts on global supply network development.

Satwinder Singh holds an M.A. (Econ.) from Jawaharlal Nehru University and a Ph.D. degree in Economics from the University of Pune, India. He is presently working as lecturer in Brunel University Business School in the United Kingdom and is allied with the CIBSEM within the School. He has previously worked as Senior Research Fellow at University of Reading, Department of Economics. He has also consulted for private and public organisations and was based in Geneva as a full time consultant with UNCTAD in 2003–2004. Dr. Singh has published over 40 papers and chapters in edited volumes on International Business. His specific areas of research interests are multinational enterprises (MNEs), human resource management in uninational and MNEs, strategic behaviour of firms, and entrepreneurship.

Christine Soo is an assistant professor of Management at the University of Western Australia Business School. She received her PhD from the University of New South Wales. Her research interests include organizational learning processes, knowledge and innovation management and developing dynamic capabilities in organizations. Her research has been published in *California Management Review, Organizational Dynamics* and *International Journal of Technology Management*. She currently serves on the editorial board of Organization Studies.

Laszlo Tihanyi is the B. Marie Oth Associate Professor in Business Administration in the Mays Business School at Texas A&M University, USA. He received a Ph.D. in strategic management from Indiana University and a doctorate in business economics from Corvinus University of Budapest in his native Hungary. He is also a honorary professor at

Corvinus University. His main research areas are internationalization, corporate governance in multinational firms, and organizational adaptation in emerging economies. His current research interests include the involvement of board of directors in FDI, the institutional environment of internationalization decisions, and the effects of social movements on multinational firms.

Daniel Tolstoy received his PhD in August 2010. He is currently a research fellow at the Department of Marketing and Strategy at the Stockholm School of Economics. His research interests span a wide range of topics within the field of international business. Daniel is currently involved in projects that focus on international entrepreneurship in networks, international retailing and global sourcing. He has published his research among others in *Journal of Small Business Management, Technovation, and Entrepreneurship & Regional Development*.

Sverre Tomassen (PhD, BI Norwegian School of Management) is an associate professor in international strategy at BI Norwegian School of Management. His current research interests include international management, and strategies and structures of multinational enterprises. His research has appeared in several books and journals, including *Journal of Management Studies, Scandinavian Journal of Management* and *International Business Review*.

Nigel L. Williams is a senior lecturer in Project Management in the Business Systems Department at the University of Bedfordshire. Nigel completed PhD in 2010 at the Institute for Manufacturing, University of Cambridge examining the international evolution of Small Manufacturing firms from Trinidad and Tobago. His current research interests include SME Production Systems, Organizational Project Management and Festival Internationalization. Before joining the University, Nigel worked for 15 years as an Engineer, Project Manager and Business Consultant for organizations in the Caribbean Region. A member of the Project Management Institute, he holds the Project Management Professional certification along with the Prince 2 qualification.